Augmenting Empathetic Leadership Through Agentic AI

Nitin Simha Vihari
Middlesex University, Dubai, UAE

IGI Global
Scientific Publishing
Publishing Tomorrow's Research Today

Vice President of Editorial Melissa Wagner
Director of Acquisitions Mikaela Felty
Director of Book Development Jocelynn Hessler
Production Manager Mike Brehm
Cover Design Jose Rosado

Published in the United States of America by
IGI Global Scientific Publishing
701 East Chocolate Avenue
Hershey, PA, 17033, USA
Tel: 717-533-8845 | Fax: 717-533-7115
Website: https://www.igi-global.com E-mail: cust@igi-global.com

Library of Congress Cataloging-in-Publication Data

LCCN: 2025043715 (CIP Data Pending)
ISBN13: 9798337366500
Isbn13Softcover: 9798337366517
EISBN13: 9798337366524

British Cataloguing in Publication Data
A Cataloguing in Publication record for this book is available from the British Library.

Table of Contents

Preface xvi

Section 1
Conceptual Foundations of empathetic Leadership and Agentic AI

Chapter 1
Augmenting Empathetic Leadership Through Agentic AI: AI-Mediated Team Leadership In Hybrid and Remote Environments 1
Gülizar Gülcan Şeremet, Çankırı Karatekin University, Turkey

Chapter 2
Augmenting Empathetic Leadership Through Agentic AI: Redefining Human–AI Collaboration in the Workplace 31
Ramadevi Vitthal Salunkhe, G.H. Raisoni College of Engineering, Nagpur, India
Smita Dattatray Salunkhe, KES Society Rajarambapu Institute of Technology, India
Jyotsna S. Gawai, K.D.K. College of Engineering, Nagpur, India
Yogeshri Dayaram Choudhari, K.D.K. College of Engineering, Nagpur, India
Sanket Ashok Joshi, St. Vincent Pallotti College of Engineering and Technology, Nagpur, India
Roshan Ramesh Kolte, K.D.K. College of Engineering, Nagpur, India
Pradnya Sumit Moon, St. Vincent Pallotti College of Engineering and Technology, Nagpur, India
Manisha Dyneshwar Raut, G.H. Raisoni College of Engineering, Nagpur, India

Chapter 3
Designing the Human-AI Partnership in Leadership: Towards Building Safe, Transparent, and Empathetic Work Environments 69
Tanusree Chakraborty, Administrative Staff College of India, India
Rituparna Basak, Muralidhar Girls' College, India
Koushik Vedula, Administrative Staff College of India, India
S. K. Pooja, Administrative Staff College of India, India

Chapter 4
Human-AI Collaboration in Leadership and Decision Making 103
Pardeep Kumar, Lovely Professional University, India
Sanjeev Kumar, Lovely Professional University, India

Chapter 5
Leadership Capability Building for Digital and Agentic Intelligence: An Integrated Competency Framework 131
Nitin Simha Vihari, Middlesex University, Dubai, UAE

Section 2
AI-Enabled Leadership Practice, Communication, and Teaming

Chapter 6
How Conversational AI Is Transforming Leadership Communication and Trust 163
Karan Gupta, Christ University, India
Babita Jha, Christ University, India

Chapter 7
AI at the Leadership Table: Coaching, Mentoring, and Empowering Human Potential 191
Gurpreet pal Kaur, Lovely Professional University, India
Mushtaq Ahmed Shah, Lovely Professional University, India

Chapter 8
AI as an Enabler of Inclusive and Equitable Leadership: Integrating Ethical Governance, Cultural Contexts, and Organizational Outcomes 219
Richa Kapoor Mehra, O.P. Jindal Global University, India
Iva Rani Das, Daffodil Institute of IT, Bangladesh

Section 3
Well Being, Resilience, and Ethical Leadership in the Digital Age

Chapter 9
Predictive Care: Using AI to Foresee Burnout and Identify Needs Proactively 249
Mohit Yadav, JGBS, O.P. Jindal Global University, India
Ali Najeeb, Qasim Ibrahim School of Business, Villa College, Maldives

Chapter 10
Employee Digital Well-Being in the Age of Agentic AI: HR Leaders as Gatekeepers of Ethical Governance 265
Nitin Simha Vihari, Middlesex University, Dubai, UAE

Chapter 11
Digital Taylorism and AI Impact on Psychological Well-Being and Innovation in HR Within the Energy and Marine Industries 295
Navya Puttaraju, Middlesex University, Dubai, UAE

Section 4
Developing Empathy, Emotional Intelligence, and Reflective Leadership Through AI

Chapter 12
Agentic AI as an Empathy Scaffolding Tool: Enhancing Emotional Intelligence in Leadership Development 333
Divya Dubey, Jindal Institute of Behavioural Sciences, O.P. Jindal Global University, Sonipat, India

Chapter 13
Designing Leadership Development Tools With AI Empathy Scaffolds 371
Tushar, United College of Engineering and Research, Prayagraj, India
Pooja Jaiswal, University of Allahabad, Prayagraj, India
Manish Kumar, P.K. University, Shivpuri, India

Chapter 14
The Bias Interceptor: How AI Can Mitigate Unconscious Leadership Blind Spots.. 399
Mohit Yadav, JGBS, O.P. Jindal Global University, India
Ali Najeeb, Villa College, Maldives
Narayanage Jayantha Dewasiri, Sabaragamuwa University of Sri Lanka, Belihuloya, Sri Lanka & Qasim Ibrahim School of Business, Villa College, Maldives

Chapter 15
Impact of Emotional Intelligence on Leadership Development: A Thematic Review... 413
Sonal Juyal, Sardar Bhagwan Singh University, Dehradun, India
Vibhuti Jain, Graphic Era (Deemed to be) University, Dehradun, India
Komal Patwal, Graphic Era (Deemed to be) University, Dehradun, India
Nakate Susan, Graphic Era (Deemed to be) University, Dehradun, India
Abhishek Danu, H.N.B. Garhwal University, Srinagar, India
Kamlesh kohli, H.N.B. Garhwal University, Srinagar, India
Rajesh Tiwari, Graphic Era (Deemed to be) University, Dehradun, India

Section 5
Applied and Sectoral Perspectives on AI-Augmented Leadership

Chapter 16
Digital Leadership and Agentic AI in Higher Education 447
Rosemol Pappachan, BITS Pilani, Dubai, UAE
Shazi Shah Jabeen, BITS Pilani, Dubai, UAE

Compilation of References 471

About the Contributors 553

Index 563

Detailed Table of Contents

Preface xvi

Section 1
Conceptual Foundations of empathetic Leadership and Agentic AI

Chapter 1
Augmenting Empathetic Leadership Through Agentic AI: AI-Mediated Team Leadership In Hybrid and Remote Environments 1
Gülizar Gülcan Şeremet, Çankırı Karatekin University, Turkey

This chapter examines the expanding influence of artificial intelligence on contemporary leadership, especially in hybrid and remote work settings where human–AI interaction shapes organizational dynamics. Advances in AI enhance leaders' ability to process complex information, coordinate distributed teams, and support data-driven decisions. Yet AI integration also brings subtle challenges. AI-based performance metrics may reinforce visibility bias by privileging more observable employees, while AI-mediated empathy remains limited due to its inability to reflect diverse human experiences. These dynamics reveal both the transformative potential and the constraints of AI in leadership. The chapter argues that although AI can strengthen decision-making, communication, and coordination, its use requires caution to avoid unintended inequities and to maintain the relational foundations essential for effective leadership.

Chapter 2
Augmenting Empathetic Leadership Through Agentic AI: Redefining Human–AI Collaboration in the Workplace 31
Ramadevi Vitthal Salunkhe, G.H. Raisoni College of Engineering, Nagpur, India
Smita Dattatray Salunkhe, KES Society Rajarambapu Institute of Technology, India
Jyotsna S. Gawai, K.D.K. College of Engineering, Nagpur, India
Yogeshri Dayaram Choudhari, K.D.K. College of Engineering, Nagpur, India
Sanket Ashok Joshi, St. Vincent Pallotti College of Engineering and Technology, Nagpur, India
Roshan Ramesh Kolte, K.D.K. College of Engineering, Nagpur, India
Pradnya Sumit Moon, St. Vincent Pallotti College of Engineering and Technology, Nagpur, India
Manisha Dyneshwar Raut, G.H. Raisoni College of Engineering, Nagpur, India

This chapter examines how intelligent digital systems can support empathetic and ethically grounded leadership in contemporary organizations. As artificial intelligence becomes embedded in managerial decision-making, leadership practices risk emphasizing efficiency over human well-being. Drawing on emotional intelligence, ethical leadership, and relational leadership theories, this chapter per the authors presents a human-centered framework in which intelligent systems act as context-aware support tools that enhance leaders' ethical reflection and inclusive decision-making while preserving human authority through human-in-the-loop governance.

Chapter 3
Designing the Human-AI Partnership in Leadership: Towards Building Safe, Transparent, and Empathetic Work Environments 69
Tanusree Chakraborty, Administrative Staff College of India, India
Rituparna Basak, Muralidhar Girls' College, India
Koushik Vedula, Administrative Staff College of India, India
S. K. Pooja, Administrative Staff College of India, India

The chapter discusses the opportunities of human-AI collaboration that has the potential to transform leadership by incorporating trust, transparency, psychological safety, and empathy to AI-powered workplaces. With AI becoming more and more involved in making decisions, developing and supporting staff, as well as running business activities, leaders need to make sure that technology will not replace human control and interaction. The chapter looks into explainable and ethical AI systems, AI-based processes that bolster psychological safety and introductions of empathy scaffolds that facilitate leader development. It also examines organizational preparedness, governance needs as well as hybrid leadership models that compromise human intuition and algorithmic insight. The chapter is practical as it provides useful guidelines that can be used to create the safe, transparent and empathetic environments of AI-enabled leadership by introducing a holistic, human-centered framework.

Chapter 4
Human-AI Collaboration in Leadership and Decision Making 103
Pardeep Kumar, Lovely Professional University, India
Sanjeev Kumar, Lovely Professional University, India

The course of organizational strategies, modes of management and governance across industries and sectors are shifting as a consequence of human and artificial intelligence instituting leadership and decision-making. Leaders can make better, timely, and objective decisions as they use artificial intelligence (AI) to analyze the data, generate new scenario prediction models, and simulate the situations. Such collaboration is a boost to problem-solving because of the natural human ability to neurologize, moralize, and contextualize the problem alongside the computing ability, pattern-recognition ability, and scale of AI. To achieve proper integration, trust in AI systems must be developed, transparency must be given to the algorithms, and some form of human control must be maintained to help address the risks associated with forms of bias, responsibility, and ethical issues. Also, team structures promote adaptive leadership, which allows organizations to deal dynamically with complex-challenging environments in a rapidly changing environment.

Chapter 5
Leadership Capability Building for Digital and Agentic Intelligence: An Integrated Competency Framework.. 131
Nitin Simha Vihari, Middlesex University, Dubai, UAE

The rapid advancement of agentic artificial intelligence is reshaping how leadership is enacted in contemporary organisations. Unlike earlier digital technologies that functioned primarily as supportive tools, agentic AI systems can plan, act, and adapt autonomously, introducing non-human actors into core organisational decision-making processes. Drawing on strategic leadership theory, digital leadership scholarship, and emerging research on agentic AI, this chapter develops an integrated leadership competency framework to support effective human-machine collaboration. The framework conceptualises leadership as the orchestration of shared agency rather than the exercise of direct control and identifies four interconnected capability domains supported by a foundational leadership mindset al. By bridging previously parallel literatures and addressing the realities of distributed authority, this chapter contributes to leadership theory and offers actionable guidance for practitioners and educators seeking to prepare leaders for the complexities of agentic transformation.

Section 2
AI-Enabled Leadership Practice, Communication, and Teaming

Chapter 6
How Conversational AI Is Transforming Leadership Communication and Trust 163
Karan Gupta, Christ University, India
Babita Jha, Christ University, India

In this chapter, the author will discuss conversational artificial intelligence (AI) that is changing the face of leadership by altering communication, development of trust, and moral judgement in the digital organizational context. It describes how conversational AI is used as an intermediary that promotes responsiveness, facilitates information processing, and promotes relational communication and accounts for its deficiency to decode real emotional intelligence. Through four theoretical perspectives, the chapter includes the process of developing, maintaining, or breaking trust in AI-enabled leadership. The positive effects made by empirical evidence include better psychological safety and efficiency in communication, and adverse effects like bias, surveillance issues, and decayed human interaction. This chapter ends with the strategic advice on how to adopt AI in a responsible manner so that technological efficiency could be used to add to ethical and empathetic leadership.

Chapter 7
AI at the Leadership Table: Coaching, Mentoring, and Empowering Human Potential 191
Gurpreet pal Kaur, Lovely Professional University, India
Mushtaq Ahmed Shah, Lovely Professional University, India

The chapter examines how AI augments human leadership. Although 88% of organisations use AI, fewer than one-third succeed, signalling the need for leaders who blend emotional intelligence with technological fluency. It draws on socio-technical systems theory, transformational and empathetic leadership, adult learning theory, and human-AI collaboration to propose a four-layer framework: AI Intelligence, Human Leadership, Interaction, and Outcome. The model shows that agentic AI can enhance behavioural insight, emotional sensitivity, and personalised growth when paired with empathy, relational judgement, and ethical awareness. Human-AI coaching ecosystems can democratise learning, strengthen inclusivity, and improve decision-making, yet raise issues of privacy, fairness, and power imbalance. The chapter concludes with future research directions, including validation studies, cross-cultural insights, longitudinal assessment, co-leadership models, and new competency frameworks for ethical and effective AI-enabled leadership.

Chapter 8
AI as an Enabler of Inclusive and Equitable Leadership: Integrating Ethical Governance, Cultural Contexts, and Organizational Outcomes 219
Richa Kapoor Mehra, O.P. Jindal Global University, India
Iva Rani Das, Daffodil Institute of IT, Bangladesh

The chapter shows that AI can be used to minimize bias, increase accessibility and guide mindful decision-making under the impact of ethical and human-oriented leadership because of the systematic consideration of organizational practices, legal environments, and real-life case studies. A conceptual model is shown between AI tools and leadership mediation and governance mechanisms and organizational outcomes. The chapter ends by providing practical implications on leaders on matters that can be applied to ensure that AI incorporation into organizational operations ethically enhances inclusion, equity, and organizational performance.

Section 3
Well Being, Resilience, and Ethical Leadership in the Digital Age

Chapter 9
Predictive Care: Using AI to Foresee Burnout and Identify Needs Proactively 249
Mohit Yadav, JGBS, O.P. Jindal Global University, India
Ali Najeeb, Qasim Ibrahim School of Business, Villa College, Maldives

This chapter explores the transformative potential of artificial intelligence (AI) in predicting and proactively managing workplace burnout. By analyzing diverse datasets—from digital communication patterns and workload metrics to physiological signals—AI enables early detection of burnout risk, facilitating timely, personalized interventions. Traditional burnout detection methods, often reactive and limited by self-report biases, are increasingly supplanted by machine learning models such as decision trees, support vector machines, and neural networks that provide dynamic risk assessments. Wearable technologies augment these insights by providing continuous physiological data. AI-driven early warning systems deliver personalized real-time recommendations, promoting healthier work habits and mitigating burnout progression. However, ethical challenges around privacy, consent, and algorithmic bias necessitate transparent governance frameworks. Emerging trends, including augmented intelligence and federated learning, promise to enhance accuracy and privacy.

Chapter 10
Employee Digital Well-Being in the Age of Agentic AI: HR Leaders as Gatekeepers of Ethical Governance 265
Nitin Simha Vihari, Middlesex University, Dubai, UAE

This chapter examines the emergence of agentic AI and its profound implications for employee digital well-being within contemporary organisations. It moves beyond the era of traditional human resource information systems, which were largely oriented toward administrative efficiency, and instead explores a shift toward augmented intelligence, in which autonomous systems and human actors jointly shape strategic and operational decisions. Drawing on a socio-technical systems perspective, employee digital well-being is conceptualised as the responsible and holistic management of human flourishing through the dynamic interaction between people, tasks, and digital systems. The chapter introduces the Sense-Predict-Reconfigure framework as a continuous learning loop that enables organisations to operationalise workforce resilience in AI-enabled environments. By combining analytical foresight with human empathy, HR leaders can ensure that advances in agentic AI strengthen employee digital well-being and contribute to more sustainable and humane forms of work rather than undermining them.

Chapter 11
Digital Taylorism and AI Impact on Psychological Well-Being and Innovation in HR Within the Energy and Marine Industries 295
Navya Puttaraju, Middlesex University, Dubai, UAE

The Fourth Industrial Revolution is transforming HRM through advanced technologies, especially Artificial Intelligence (AI). AI's integration with Big Data, IoT, and robotics is reshaping work dynamics and daily life. This qualitative study in a leading marine and energy company examines AI's impact on HR, focusing on psychological well-being and innovation. Rather than just technical advances, it highlights how AI changes employees' emotions and behaviour. Findings stress to avoid a "one-size-fits-all" approach and adopting best-fit solutions that respect cultural nuances for sustainable organisational success. Automation allows HR to focus on strategic, creative tasks, boosting job satisfaction. Successful AI adoption depends on continuous leadership support and aligning AI capabilities with employee expectations to avoid cognitive dissonance. Maintaining a balance between technology and the human element is vital for a fair, inclusive, and innovative workplace. Ultimately, continuous learning, ethical approach ensures to reduce bias, find purpose and drive innovation in an AI environment. After all, there is no algorithm for being human.

Section 4
Developing Empathy, Emotional Intelligence, and Reflective Leadership Through AI

Chapter 12
Agentic AI as an Empathy Scaffolding Tool: Enhancing Emotional Intelligence in Leadership Development 333
Divya Dubey, Jindal Institute of Behavioural Sciences, O.P. Jindal Global University, Sonipat, India

This chapter examines how agentic artificial intelligence can function as an empathy scaffold to support emotionally intelligent and relationally grounded leadership in digitally mediated organizations. Drawing on emotional intelligence theory, empathetic leadership research, and sociocognitive models of scaffolding, it explains how AI-enabled tools—such as real-time emotional feedback, conversational coaching, and adaptive learning systems—can enhance leaders' emotional awareness, reflective capacity, and ethical judgment. Organizational applications, including Microsoft Viva, Workday Peakon, BetterUp, and Zoom IQ, illustrate how agentic AI is being used to surface emotional patterns and support leadership development in practice. At the same time, the chapter critically examines concerns related to authenticity, cultural interpretation, algorithmic bias, privacy, and the risk of emotional surveillance. It concludes by proposing principles for the ethical and transparent design of AI systems that augment human empathy and judgment rather than attempting to replace them.

Chapter 13
Designing Leadership Development Tools With AI Empathy Scaffolds 371
Tushar, United College of Engineering and Research, Prayagraj, India
Pooja Jaiswal, University of Allahabad, Prayagraj, India
Manish Kumar, P.K. University, Shivpuri, India

Agile dynamics surrounding modern workplaces globalization, remote work and increasingly everything centered on psychological safety have also helped empathy evolve from a soft skill into a leadership job requirement. Leaders with high levels of empathy experience better team cohesion, engagement, retention and problem-solving. While empathy comes easy to some people, it is at heart a learnable skill. We refer to these temporary intelligent support systems inspired by educational psychology as AI Empathy Scaffolds, designed to allow leaders to learn empathy with the help of temporally-continuous realistic simulations and real-time behaviour feedback. AI works to facilitate reflection, analyse emotional and cognitive reactions as well as provide personalised learning paths and in so doing acts a coach and mirror rather than a substitute for human interaction. This chapter includes an examination of future direction and ethical implications in forging genuinely human-centred, technology-enabled leadership.

Chapter 14
The Bias Interceptor: How AI Can Mitigate Unconscious Leadership Blind Spots 399
Mohit Yadav, JGBS, O.P. Jindal Global University, India
Ali Najeeb, Villa College, Maldives
Narayanage Jayantha Dewasiri, Sabaragamuwa University of Sri Lanka, Belihuloya, Sri Lanka & Qasim Ibrahim School of Business, Villa College, Maldives

Unconscious biases remain among the most persistent challenges undermining leadership effectiveness and organizational equity. These cognitive blind spots—ranging from affinity bias to confirmation bias—often distort decision-making in recruitment, promotions, and resource allocation, limiting diversity and trust. Advances in artificial intelligence (AI) offer novel mechanisms to detect, surface, and mitigate such hidden biases by providing data-driven diagnostics, predictive insights, and interpretive feedback that leaders alone may overlook. This chapter conceptualizes AI as a "Bias Interceptor," outlining its potential to augment reflective leadership, strengthen evidence-based decision-making, and improve fairness across organizational systems. It also addresses ethical dilemmas, including algorithmic bias, privacy risks, and overreliance on automation. Drawing on psychological theory, empirical studies, and applied practices, the chapter proposes a roadmap for leveraging AI responsibly to reduce leadership blind spots and foster more inclusive organizational cultures.

Chapter 15
Impact of Emotional Intelligence on Leadership Development: A Thematic Review 413
Sonal Juyal, Sardar Bhagwan Singh University, Dehradun, India
Vibhuti Jain, Graphic Era (Deemed to be) University, Dehradun, India
Komal Patwal, Graphic Era (Deemed to be) University, Dehradun, India
Nakate Susan, Graphic Era (Deemed to be) University, Dehradun, India
Abhishek Danu, H.N.B. Garhwal University, Srinagar, India
Kamlesh kohli, H.N.B. Garhwal University, Srinagar, India
Rajesh Tiwari, Graphic Era (Deemed to be) University, Dehradun, India

Emotional intelligence has a strong correlation with leadership. EI affects a person both positively and negatively, but being aware of one's emotions is the best way to manage them, which can also help one control them. People's emotions can be influenced by the environment they are surrounded in. Everything is based on EI as one has to control their feelings and emotions, and also know how to handle others in the workplace. Our current research aims to gather all studies conducted between 2000 and 2024 on Emotional Intelligence and Leadership Development. The VOS viewer software is used in this bibliometric study. A database comprising 423 articles from 2000 to 2024 is created for this purpose using the Scopus database. A comprehensive examination of publication trends, productive writers, journals, and international collaboration is carried out. This study provides a simple information source that encompasses all of the research in the subject for academics interested in investigating leadership development and emotional intelligence.

Section 5
Applied and Sectoral Perspectives on AI-Augmented Leadership

Chapter 16
Digital Leadership and Agentic AI in Higher Education 447
Rosemol Pappachan, BITS Pilani, Dubai, UAE
Shazi Shah Jabeen, BITS Pilani, Dubai, UAE

The rapidly advancing digital transformation of higher education requires skilled digital leadership to manage complex technological and organisational changes. This advancement is presently being facilitated by the emergence of Agentic Artificial Intelligence (AI). These advanced agents provide innovative educational opportunities by serving as proactive tutors, metacognitive coaches, and collaborative teaching assistants, capable of tailored learning experiences and reducing administrative responsibilities for educators. The incorporation of these highly autonomous AI presents significant pedagogical and ethical issues. This chapter incorporates these converging dynamics, suggesting that academic leaders must proactively coordinate balanced human-AI collaborations to enhance educational achievement while strictly preserving human agency, equity, and academic integrity.

Compilation of References 471

About the Contributors 553

Index 563

Preface

AN OVERVIEW OF THE SUBJECT MATTER

The development of artificial intelligence has advanced well beyond automation, prediction, and efficiency. We are now entering a phase in which AI demonstrates increasing autonomy, initiative, and contextual awareness that begin to resemble agency within organisational settings. The renewed urgency of a longstanding question in leadership studies, as systems become smarter, defines what remains distinctly human in effective leadership. This volume argues that the answer lies not just in control, strategy, or decision speed, but in empathy, ethical judgment, relational intelligence, and the ability to build trust in increasingly complex work environments.

Augmenting Empathetic Leadership Through Agentic AI has been conceived at a time when organisations across sectors are being reshaped by digital transformation, platform work, hybrid collaboration, real-time analytics, and machine-supported decision making. In such contexts, leaders no longer respond solely to human expectations. They are also expected to understand data systems, algorithmic processes, and AI-enabled workflows that influence how people communicate, perform, learn, and experience work. As these systems become more advanced, it becomes increasingly clear that technology alone cannot sustain engagement, belonging, fairness, or well-being. These are leadership responsibilities, and they remain fundamentally human.

The central idea of this book is that agentic AI should be seen not only as a technical development but also as a leadership challenge and an opportunity. Agentic AI can coordinate communication, support reflection, recognise patterns, personalise learning, detect early signs of burnout, and expand access to information and developmental support. At the same time, it may reinforce bias, diminish human discretion, increase surveillance, or erode trust if used without ethical clarity and empathetic leadership. This dual potential makes the current volume both relevant and essential.

A Description Of Where Your Topic Fits In The World Today

Across industries such as business, education, hospitality, and health, as well as wider organisational settings, leaders are being asked not only to adopt AI tools but also to build human-centred systems around them. This involves deciding how AI should be utilised, determining when human judgment should override machine suggestions, assessing fairness, fostering inclusion, and safeguarding employee dignity in environments where intelligence is increasingly shared between people and digital systems. The chapters in this book explore these issues from various perspectives. Collectively, they represent a growing and important area of study that links leadership, human resource management, employee well-being, ethics, trust, digital skills, and organisational design.

The concept of empathetic leadership is particularly important in the current situation. Empathy in leadership is often mistaken for a gentle or secondary trait. In fact, it is vital for leaders to create psychological safety, handle conflict, support resilience, respond to uncertainty, and make decisions that are not only effective but also fair and compassionate. In digitally connected workplaces, empathetic leadership is even more crucial because leaders often need to influence people remotely, through screens, across different time zones, and increasingly through systems that manage or shape communication. Agentic AI may assist leaders in providing support and insights on a scale, but it cannot replace moral responsibility, emotional presence, or the building of trust on its own. Therefore, this book does not praise AI without critique. Instead, it examines how AI can be designed and utilised to reinforce the human foundations of leadership rather than undermine them.

A Description Of The Target Audience

This volume is designed for a wide yet interconnected audience. It will be beneficial for scholars in leadership studies, human resource management, organisational behaviour, higher education, business ethics, digital transformation, and management learning. It is equally relevant to practitioners, including HR leaders, organisational development professionals, consultants, learning designers, technology strategists, and senior managers who are currently managing AI enabled workplace change. The book also targets postgraduate students and early career researchers seeking a modern understanding of how leadership theory and practice are evolving in response to intelligent systems. The chapters feature conceptual discussions, applied frameworks, thematic reviews, and context-based analyses, making the book both academically significant and practically accessible.

One of the strengths of this collection is that it does not perceive agentic AI as a single, uniform phenomenon. Instead, the contributors examine multiple expressions of AI enabled leadership support, including conversational systems, predictive tools, empathy scaffolds, decision-support mechanisms, inclusive design approaches, metrics of emotional understanding, and educational innovation. This range reflects the reality of the field. Agentic AI is already entering organisations in diverse and uneven ways. Its impact depends not only on technical sophistication but also on context, culture, governance, leadership maturity, and organisational intent. For this reason, the chapters in this volume are complementary rather than repetitive. Each offers a different pathway into the broader question of what empathetic leadership might look like when intelligence is shared between humans and machines.

The chapter contributions also highlight a significant shift in the broader literature. Much of the earlier debate around AI and work concentrated on substitution, job losses, efficiency, or digital disruption. While these issues remain important, there is now an increasing need to explore the quality of human experience within AI-mediated systems. Some of the pertinent questions from the AI driven leadership literature are as follows:

- How do leaders maintain meaning, fairness, and trust when machine intelligence influences daily work?
- How should leadership development adapt when emotional and social skills become more, rather than less, vital in digital environments?
- How can organisations ensure that technological progress does not outpace ethical reflection?

These questions are no longer peripheral as they are central to the future of responsible management and institutional legitimacy. What follows in this volume is therefore not just a collection of chapters but also an ongoing dialogue. It is a dialogue about augmentation rather than replacement, responsibility rather than technological enthusiasm, and leadership as a relational practice that must stay attentive to human needs even as work becomes smarter and more automated. The chapters collectively suggest that the future of leadership will rely on the ability to combine analytical power with empathy, digital intelligence with moral clarity, and innovation with care.

THE IMPORTANCE OF EACH CHAPTER IS OUTLINED BELOW.

Chapter 1: Augmenting Empathetic Leadership Through Agentic AI: AI Mediated Team Leadership in Hybrid and Remote Environments

This chapter addresses one of the most visible realities of contemporary work, namely, the persistence of hybrid and remote teams and the leadership challenges that arise within them. Its importance lies in showing how AI can support coordination, communication, and responsiveness in distributed contexts where traditional cues of presence and engagement are often reduced. The chapter contributes to the book by demonstrating that empathetic leadership must now function through digitally mediated interactions rather than solely through physical proximity. It is particularly useful for leaders managing dispersed teams who need to balance efficiency with human connection. The discussion helps position AI as a support mechanism for relational leadership in environments where fragmentation and distance can otherwise weaken trust.

Chapter 2: Augmenting Empathetic Leadership Through Agentic AI: Redefining Human AI Collaboration in the Workplace

This chapter is important because it moves beyond the idea of AI as a tool and examines it as a collaborative presence within organizational workflows. It invites readers to consider how leadership itself changes when decision processes, information flows, and task execution are increasingly shaped by intelligent systems. The strength of the chapter lies in its effort to rethink collaboration not only between people but also between human and machine actors. This gives the volume a strong conceptual foundation and helps frame many of the chapters that follow. It is especially relevant to organizations seeking to design more thoughtful and responsible forms of AI integration.

Chapter 3: Designing the Human AI Partnership in Leadership: Towards Building Safe, Transparent, and Empathetic Work Environments

This chapter makes an important design-oriented contribution by asking how organisations can intentionally build safer and more transparent relationships between people and intelligent systems. Rather than examining whether partnerships emerge naturally, it examines the conditions under which such partnerships can be trusted and sustained. Its emphasis on safety, transparency, and empathy aligns closely with the volume's core identity. The chapter is valuable because it connects leadership theory with organizational architecture and governance practice. It is likely to resonate strongly with readers interested in responsible innovation and the design of humane digital workplaces.

Chapter 4: Human AI Collaboration in Leadership and Decision Making

Decision-making remains one of the defining functions of leadership, and this chapter addresses how it is being reshaped through collaboration with AI systems. Its importance lies in examining the opportunities and tensions that arise when leaders rely on machine-generated insights, recommendations, or patterns in making judgments that affect people and organisations. The chapter helps readers move beyond simplistic assumptions that more data always leads to better decisions. It foregrounds the continuing need for discretion, accountability, and contextual understanding. In this way, it strengthens the book's argument that collaboration with AI must enhance rather than displace responsible human leadership.

Chapter 5: Leadership Capability Building for Digital and Agentic Intelligence: An Integrated Competency Framework

This chapter is particularly important for both academics and practitioners because it offers a structured approach to leadership development in a rapidly evolving digital environment. Instead of viewing future readiness as an abstract concept, it presents an integrated competency perspective that can guide curriculum design, executive development, and organizational capability planning. Its strength lies in translating broad debates about AI and leadership into a practical developmental framework. The chapter provides guidance for those needing to identify what leaders should know, understand, and be able to do in AI-influenced settings. It enhances the volume's practical value and is likely to serve as a helpful reference for programme design and leadership training.

Chapter 6: How Conversational AI is Transforming Leadership Communication and Trust

Communication is at the heart of leadership, and this chapter examines how conversational AI is beginning to mediate that relationship in new and significant ways. Its contribution is important because communication technologies do more than transmit messages; they shape tone, accessibility, speed, and the quality of interaction. The chapter explores how trust may be supported or undermined when conversational systems participate in leadership communication. This is particularly relevant in organizations where chat-based systems, AI assistants, and automated responses are becoming normal. The chapter strengthens the volume by highlighting that trust is built not only through intent but also through the design of communicative environments.

Chapter 7: AI at the Leadership Table: Coaching, Mentoring, and Empowering Human Potential

This chapter makes a valuable contribution by examining AI in relation to coaching and mentoring, two areas that have traditionally depended on trust, dialogue, and developmental sensitivity. Its importance lies in asking whether and how AI can support growth-oriented leadership processes without flattening their relational depth. The chapter opens with useful questions about access, scale, personalisation, and the boundaries of machine-supported development. It is especially relevant to leadership educators, executive coaches, and talent development professionals. Within the volume, it helps position AI as a possible enabler of human growth when used with discernment.

Chapter 8: AI as an Enabler of Inclusive and Equitable Leadership Integrating Ethical Governance, Cultural Contexts, and Organizational Outcomes

This chapter is particularly important because it addresses inclusion and equity in a field where technological solutions are often presented as neutral, even when they reproduce social bias. Its contribution lies in connecting ethical governance to cultural context and organizational outcomes, thereby refusing to separate technical design from social consequence. The chapter reminds readers that empathetic leadership must also be inclusive leadership. It deepens the volume by bringing fairness and cultural sensitivity into the conversation around AI enabled leadership. This makes it especially useful to global organizations and institutions operating across diverse workforce contexts.

Chapter 9: Predictive Care: Using AI to Foresee Burnout and Identify Needs Proactively

This is one of the timeliest chapters in the volume because employee burnout, fatigue, and emotional strain have become defining challenges across sectors. The chapter is important for its proactive approach, demonstrating how AI can be used not only to address visible issues but also to identify early signals and support preventative measures. It promotes a more humane vision of AI by connecting predictive capability with leadership responsibility and employee well-being. The practical implications are significant for HR leaders, managers, and organisational designers. It also reinforces the volume's broader argument that technological insight must be guided by empathy and ethical care.

Chapter 10: Employee Digital Well Being in the Age of Agentic AI: HR Leaders as Gatekeepers of Ethical Governance

This chapter is central to the book's concern with ethics and responsible organizational design. It places HR leaders in a pivotal role, not just as administrators of systems but as guardians of employee wellbeing and ethical boundaries. The importance of the chapter lies in its recognition that digital well-being is now a leadership and governance issue rather than a personal coping issue alone. It encourages readers to think carefully about workload, surveillance, digital overload, and algorithmic fairness. In doing so, it gives the volume a strong people-management perspective and offers practical relevance to the future of HR leadership.

Chapter 11: Digital Taylorism and AI Impact on Psychological Well Being and Innovation in HR within the Energy and Marine Industries

This chapter is particularly important because it introduces a critical perspective that prevents the volume from becoming overly celebratory about AI. Engaging with digital Taylorism highlights the risks of control, standardisation, and intensified monitoring in technologically managed workplaces. Its industry focus gives the discussion practical depth and shows how AI can have uneven consequences depending on sectoral conditions. The chapter contributes much-needed balance to the book by emphasising that innovation and well-being do not automatically progress together. It is likely to be especially valuable for HR professionals and scholars interested in the labour process implications of AI.

Chapter 12: Agentic AI as an Empathy Scaffolding Tool: Enhancing Emotional Intelligence in Leadership Development

This chapter deepens the book's developmental theme by linking agentic AI directly to emotional intelligence and leadership growth. Its importance lies in challenging the assumption that AI and emotional capability belong to separate domains. Instead, it argues that AI may support emotional learning when designed as a scaffold rather than an authority. The chapter contributes a thoughtful bridge between technological innovation and leadership pedagogy. It will be especially useful for those designing leadership interventions that must remain relevant in digitally transformed contexts while still preserving a strong focus on human capability.

Chapter 13: Designing Leadership Development Tools with AI Empathy Scaffolds

Leadership development is a major concern in the age of AI, and this chapter offers an innovative perspective on how developmental tools can be designed to support empathy rather than simply technical competence. Its importance lies in the idea of scaffolding, which suggests that AI can support reflection, perspective taking, and emotional awareness when embedded thoughtfully in leadership learning. The chapter contributes practical and pedagogic value to the volume. It is likely to be relevant for educators, executive coaches, learning designers, and organizational development professionals. Focusing on design rather than abstract aspiration gives readers concrete ways to think about future leadership development.

Chapter 14: The Bias Interceptor: How AI Can Mitigate Unconscious Leadership Blind Spots

This chapter addresses a critical concern in leadership practice, namely the persistence of unconscious bias in judgment, evaluation, and opportunity allocation. Its importance lies in showing that AI, when designed responsibly, may help reveal patterns that human leaders overlook or normalize. At the same time, the chapter cautions that bias mitigation requires thoughtful design and governance rather than blind faith in technical neutrality. It contributes strongly to the book's ethical and inclusive orientation. For practitioners, it offers an especially relevant entry point into using AI to improve fairness in leadership practice.

Chapter 15: Impact of Emotional Intelligence on Leadership Development: A Thematic Review

This chapter provides an important foundation for the volume, as emotional intelligence remains one of the most established ways to understand the affective side of leadership. Through a thematic review, it brings together the wider literature and provides conceptual grounding for many of the arguments developed across the book. Its importance lies in reminding readers that while AI introduces new possibilities, the human capacities that support effective leadership remain deeply significant. The chapter serves as a useful bridge between established leadership scholarship and emerging AI related discussions. It will help readers situate the volume within a broader intellectual tradition.

Chapter 16: Digital Leadership and Agentic AI in Higher Education

The final chapter is important because higher education is both a site of knowledge production and a sector undergoing rapid digital transformation. By focusing on digital leadership in this context, the chapter extends the volume's relevance to universities, educators, administrators, and policy actors. Its contribution lies in showing how agentic AI may reshape teaching, learning, governance, and academic leadership. It also demonstrates that leadership challenges around trust, ethics, inclusion, and capability are not confined to business organizations. Ending the volume with higher education is fitting because it points toward the future formation of leaders who will themselves work with and govern AI enabled systems.

CONCLUSION

Taken together, these chapters demonstrate that the conversation around agentic AI and leadership is not narrow, technical, or limited to a single discipline. It is broad, urgent, and deeply connected to the future of work, learning, well-being, and institutional responsibility. The volume shows that empathetic leadership is not made less relevant by AI. On the contrary, it becomes more necessary. As systems become more capable of analysis and action, leaders are challenged to become more capable of judgment, care, fairness, and relational understanding.

This book, therefore, contributes to the field in several ways. First, it brings together a diverse and contemporary set of perspectives on AI's role in shaping leadership thought and practice. Second, it moves the discussion beyond efficiency and automation by placing empathy, psychological safety, trust, inclusion, and well-being at the centre of analysis. Third, it offers both conceptual depth and applied relevance, making it useful across academic and practitioner audiences. Finally, it encourages a more balanced and responsible narrative about AI, one that neither rejects technological possibility nor accepts it uncritically.

As editor, I view this collection as an invitation to think more carefully about what leadership should become in the age of agentic systems. The future will not be shaped by technology alone. It will be shaped by the values, judgments, and relationships through which technology is interpreted and applied. In that sense, the most meaningful question is not whether AI can lead, but how leaders can ensure that intelligent systems are used in ways that deepen humanity rather than diminish it. It is my hope that this volume will support that conversation and offer a useful foundation for further scholarship, practice, and reflection in this emerging field.

Section 1

Conceptual Foundations of empathetic Leadership and Agentic AI

Chapter 1
Augmenting Empathetic Leadership Through Agentic AI:
AI-Mediated Team Leadership In Hybrid and Remote Environments

Gülizar Gülcan Şeremet
http://orcid.org/0000-0002-5790-2780
Çankırı Karatekin University, Turkey

ABSTRACT

This chapter examines the expanding influence of artificial intelligence on contemporary leadership, especially in hybrid and remote work settings where human–AI interaction shapes organizational dynamics. Advances in AI enhance leaders' ability to process complex information, coordinate distributed teams, and support data-driven decisions. Yet AI integration also brings subtle challenges. AI-based performance metrics may reinforce visibility bias by privileging more observable employees, while AI-mediated empathy remains limited due to its inability to reflect diverse human experiences. These dynamics reveal both the transformative potential and the constraints of AI in leadership. The chapter argues that although AI can strengthen decision-making, communication, and coordination, its use requires caution to avoid unintended inequities and to maintain the relational foundations essential for effective leadership.

DOI: 10.4018/979-8-3373-6650-0.ch001

INTRODUCTION

The global shift towards hybrid and remote working models has significantly changed organisational structures and leadership practices. While technological advances and globalisation had already made flexible work possible, the COVID-19 pandemic greatly accelerated its widespread adoption. As a result, hybrid work has become a standard organisational model rather than a temporary solution. As organisations moved beyond emergency remote work, they began to develop more sustainable hybrid arrangements. This transition has transformed work environments from traditional, physically co-located offices into digitally connected and geographically dispersed organisational systems (Newman et al., 2017; Athanasiadou & Therious, 2021; Bizilj et al., 2021; Gifford, 2022; Carrasco-Garrido et al., 2023).

Hybrid and remote working models have introduced new organisational challenges. Increased physical distance between leaders and employees can weaken communication, limit informal interactions, and deepen inequalities in access to information and resources (Zhang et al., 2020). During the COVID-19 pandemic, remote work expanded rapidly across many countries. OECD (2021) data indicate that the share of employees working remotely reached 47% in France and the United Kingdom and more than doubled in Brazil. As hybrid work became a permanent organisational practice, it also began to reshape workplace culture. These models have supported greater flexibility and creativity, while at the same time reducing environmental impact and operational costs (Fayard et al., 2021; Kaushik & Guleria, 2020).

These changes require new forms of leadership suited to distributed work environments. Although traditional leadership skills remain important, they are no longer sufficient in settings marked by geographical distance, cultural diversity and digital communication. Leaders must balance team cohesion with individual autonomy, manage increased digital demands, and support psychological safety without regular face-to-face interaction. Leadership in hybrid contexts therefore extends beyond individual traits or behaviours. It can be understood as a socio-technical practice that combines relational judgement with the effective use of digital tools (Froese et al., 2025; Gupta, 2024).

Artificial intelligence (AI) has become a key technology in shaping contemporary leadership. By analysing large and complex sets of organisational data, AI can help leaders better understand employee needs, track performance trends and identify potential problems at an early stage (Çeri & Doğan, 2025; Li et al., 2024). While AI cannot replace human capacities such as empathy, intuition or moral judgement, it can provide valuable insights into emotional dynamics, communication patterns and workload distribution through advanced analytics. In this sense, AI operates as a complementary cognitive support system rather than a substitute for leadership. It strengthens leaders' ability to make timely, inclusive and ethically informed decisions, particularly in hybrid and geographically dispersed work environments (Sevinç, 2025; Yıldız, 2025; Nalbantoğlu, 2023; Asıl, 2025; Roshanaei et al., 2025).

Practical applications of AI in leadership are already becoming more widespread. Sentiment analysis tools can identify early signs of burnout or disengagement among employees (Yurdasever, 2024; Gerçek & Özveren, 2023). In addition, LLM-based communication assistants can examine team interaction patterns and offer data-informed suggestions on how to initiate or structure interpersonal conversations (Bastola et al., 2023; Almutairi et al., 2025).

AI is also increasingly used in leadership development. Programmes that incorporate simulations, analytical dashboards and conversational agents provide ongoing feedback and support leaders' self-reflection and learning processes (Weidmann et al., 2025; Sevinç, 2025; Kandasamy, 2024).

However, the increasing use of AI in leadership also brings important ethical, psychological and organisational challenges. Algorithmic systems can reinforce existing biases, misinterpret emotional signals in culturally diverse settings, or threaten employee privacy (Floridi & Cowls, 2022). In addition, AI-generated expressions of empathy may be perceived as artificial, which can weaken trust between leaders and employees. As AI takes on a more active role in organisational processes—shifting from a supportive tool to a real-time analytical partner or even a "devil's advocate" in decision-making—leaders face new responsibilities. They must ensure that efficiency gains do not come at the expense of ethical integrity, transparency or human judgement (Ma et al., 2024; Abositta et al., 2024; Joshi, 2025a).

The spread of hybrid work has increased the need for leadership skills that combine technical, relational and strategic elements. Digitalisation is reshaping how people communicate, collaborate and experience organisational culture. As a result, effective leadership increasingly depends on managing interactions between humans and AI systems.

As organisations adopt AI-driven practices, leaders are expected to work not only with human employees but also alongside non-human agents (Kollmann et al., 2023). Organisational efficiency and effectiveness are therefore strengthened not by treating leadership and AI as separate forces, but by aligning their complementary capabilities.

Given these developments, existing research remains fragmented. Many studies examine isolated aspects of AI—such as performance tracking or virtual coaching—without integrating the broader social, technological and organisational factors shaping AI-mediated leadership. This gap underscores the need for comprehensive frameworks capturing how leaders, employees and AI systems interact within distributed work ecosystems.

This chapter addresses these gaps by examining:

(1) Leadership Dynamics in Hybrid and Remote Work;
(2) The Role of AI Technologies in Leadership;
(3) Challenges of Leading Hybrid and Remote Teams Through AI and
(4) Future Research Directions and Strategies

Taken together, these insights frame leadership as a socio-technical process shaped not solely by human capabilities but by dynamic interactions between humans and AI. The chapter concludes by highlighting strategic principles for implementing AI-mediated leadership practices that balance technological sophistication with human-centred values.

LEADERSHIP DYNAMICS IN HYBRID AND REMOTE WORK

The acceleration of digitalization has fundamentally diminished the salience of physical space, consequently redefining the nature of leader–employee relationships and the characteristics of organizational communication. Communication networks have been structurally reconstituted, particularly within hybrid and remote work models, with information sharing and interaction modalities migrating to digital platforms (Wu et al., 2023). This transformation necessitates not only an evolution in work practices but also the integration of advanced technological tools, specifically Artificial Intelligence (AI)-based communication and knowledge management systems, into leadership praxis.

AI technologies—including robotic systems, autonomous vehicles, facial recognition tools, natural language processing, and virtual agents—are now utilized to tackle diverse and complex challenges (Berente et al., 2021) and have become central drivers of societal digitalization (Cooper, 2023). AI has instigated profound shifts across sectors, from business and healthcare to education and manufacturing, yielding significant transformations in the realm of leadership and management (Teng et al., 2022).These technological advances mandate a critical re-evaluation of traditional management approaches and compel leaders to cultivate new competencies (Singh, 2023). As contemporary organizations transition toward digital work environments, digital leadership has become paramount for ensuring successful digital transformation (Arham et al., 2022; Ghavifekr & Pei, 2023). Digital leadership functions as an umbrella term in the literature, encompassing various interchangeable styles such as Leadership 4.0, virtual leadership, technology leadership, e-leadership, and (Karakose & Tülübaş., 2023).

Conversely, the non-verbal cues, social proximity, and interaction density afforded by face-to-face engagement are diminished in virtual settings. This circumstance rigorously demands that leaders exhibit an elevated degree of clarity, transparency, and consistency in their communication (Bravo-Duarte, et al., 2025; Newman and Ford, 2021). Consequently, leadership practices must not be solely task-oriented but must also assume an inclusive and supportive character that is attentive to the psychological needs of employees (Caniëls, 2023). In environments marked by uncertainty, flexibility emerges as one of the most definitive competencies for leadership within the context of remote work (Çelik & Taşkıran, 2023).

Sustaining trust, commitment, and motivation in remote and hybrid teams constitutes one of the most intricate leadership dynamics. Organizational behavior literature consistently emphasizes that trust serves as a fundamental determinant of performance and cooperation, particularly in virtual teams (Badrinarayanan, 2024; Kloepfer & Carbon, 2025). Nevertheless, under conditions where physical contact and spontaneous interaction are limited, trust is predominantly constructed through the leader's consistent conduct, transparency, accountability, and equitable practices (Yeşil, 2011; Jerab, 2025). Remote and hybrid work environments have confronted leaders with new imperatives, including establishing effective digital communication, ensuring employee motivation, maintaining collaboration, and enhancing organizational productivity (Al, 2024). According to Frey and Osborne (2017), the fear of job displacement can contribute to negative employee attitudes toward AI, as the technology's potential to substitute human labor introduces uncertainties that foster negative perceptions. However, transformational leaders are positioned to mitigate these perceptions by enabling employees to comprehend the value proposition AI offers to organizational processes; this leadership style can play a significant role in overcoming resistance to AI adoption (Pabuçcu & İşcan, 2025).

The effectiveness of hybrid and remote working is contingent upon various factors, including leadership competencies, management practices, organizational support, and the broader socio-technical environment. Onnis (2016) emphasizes the pivotal role of management practices in translating HRM policies into sustainable remote working practices, focusing particularly on occupational commitment and motivation. Building on this, recent research suggests that supportive leadership behaviors, clear communication structures, and the strategic use of digital technologies are essential for maintaining employee engagement and ensuring the long-term effectiveness of flexible work arrangements. Avlani and Charalampous (2024) argue that effective remote leadership requires trust-building, proficient digital communication and technological literacy, as well as problem-solving capabilities and situational awareness. Furthermore, Arunprasad et al. (2022) propose a conceptual framework linking technology orientation, leadership practices, HRM strategies, organizational culture and external organizational processes. They highlight that alignment across these domains is critical for achieving engagement, collaboration, and organizational agility in hybrid contexts.

Operational disruptions, communication delays, and coordination issues arising from different time zones or working hours necessitate a proactive approach from leaders. In this context, agile and digital leadership styles are critically important for sustaining performance, leveraging skills such as rapid decision-making and integrating scenario development and risk analysis with digital systems (Menteşe & Menteşe, 2023; Karaman, 2024; Al, 2024). While traditional leadership competencies retain their validity, they must become functional in the specific conditions demanded by virtual and hybrid settings. Core leadership skills such as effective communication, vision creation, empathy, conflict management, and decision-making must be implemented in a more conscious, structured, and strategic manner during online interactions, and must be supported by data-driven feedback and AI-supported tools (Sevinç, 2025; Yıldız, 2025; Roshanaei et al., 2025).

In conclusion, leadership in the contemporary environment, characterized by the permanence of hybrid and remote work models, represents a complex managerial domain where not only spatial separation is managed, but organizational structures, cultural norms, communication processes, and employee expectations are simultaneously redefined (Khan, 2024; Al, 2024). Therefore, leadership must be conceived as a multi-dimensional process that is capable of adapting to changing organizational realities, is empowered by digital competencies, and possesses a high relational dimension (Al, 2024; Zhou et al., 2022; Bai & Vahedian, 2023). Effective leadership necessitates the deliberate integration of technical, relational, and strategic competencies.

THE ROLE OF AI TECHNOLOGIES IN LEADERSHIP

Artificial intelligence (AI) is fundamentally reshaping leadership by transforming the foundations of decision-making processes (Medlama et al., 2025; Joshi, 2025b). As noted by Huang and Rust (2018), although business analytics programs have expanded rapidly in the era of big data, AI is expected to surpass humans in analytical tasks within a relatively short time frame. Accordingly, future education and leadership development systems must increasingly delegate analytical operations to AI while prioritizing the cultivation of distinctly human capabilities such as intuition, empathy, and ethical judgment. This transformation indicates that the most enduring human advantage in service-oriented fields will reside in so-called "soft skills." In this context, Daugherty and Wilson (2018) argue that AI is redefining leadership roles and giving rise to a new management paradigm referred to as Human–Machine Collaboration.

AI extends leaders' data-driven decision-making (DDDM) capabilities beyond inherent human cognitive limitations (Provost & Fawcett, 2013). Its strategic value materializes across three analytical tiers. The first tier, Diagnostic Analytics ("Why did it happen?"), uncovers the root causes of past events, enabling leaders to focus on underlying problems rather than surface-level symptoms (Davenport et al., 2010; Popovič et al., 2018; Chiang & Storey, 2012). For instance, platforms such as IBM Watson Discovery can rapidly synthesize customer complaints, sales data, and social media feedback to reveal that a decline in product sales stems not from pricing errors but from disruptions in the distribution network (Stewart et al., 2011; Gandomi & Haider, 2015).

The second tier, Predictive Analytics ("What will happen?"), analyzes historical patterns to generate forecasts about future events, thereby enabling leaders to adopt proactive strategies (Davenport et al., 2010; Popovič et al., 2018). AI-based financial risk models estimate the probability of credit default and provide early warning signals for institutions. Similarly, human resource platforms such as Workday analyze behavioral and survey data to identify employees at risk of turnover, allowing leaders to implement preventive interventions such as mentoring or incentive programs (Tursunbayeva et al., 2022).

The most advanced tier, Prescriptive Analytics ("What should we do?"), goes beyond prediction by generating optimal decision scenarios under existing constraints. At this stage, leaders must integrate AI's mathematically optimized recommendations with ethical, cultural, and human considerations before making final judgments (Davenport et al., 2010; Popovič et al., 2018). In supply chain management, for example, advanced AI systems simultaneously analyze demand forecasts, inventory levels, and geographical conditions to recommend the fastest and most cost-effective logistics routes (Dash et al., 2019; Waller & Fawcett, 2013).

Taken together, these analytical layers enable leaders to make faster, more comprehensive, and strategically robust decisions, representing a paradigmatic shift in contemporary leadership (Quaquebeke & Gerpott, 2023).

Human resource management (HRM) is undergoing substantial transformation as a result of AI's increasing integration. AI-driven applications accelerate and optimize HR functions ranging from recruitment to performance evaluation, thereby improving efficiency and decision quality (Sreelakshmy et al., 2023; Baruah et al., 2024). By analyzing employee behavior, AI enables the development of personalized training and development programs, strengthening the strategic foundations of HR decisions (Baruah et al., 2024). Real-time analytics and predictive modeling further enhance organizational responsiveness to environmental change (Ransbotham et al., 2017).

Supported by advances in machine learning, natural language processing, computer vision, and robotics, AI technologies have become critical drivers of organizational transformation and competitive advantage (Kordon, 2020). These technologies underpin a wide range of applications, including chatbots, virtual assistants, customer service systems, and quality control mechanisms (Pollak, 2021; Kotkar & Potdar,

2024; Zhou et al., 2022). AI also enhances risk management, inventory optimization, and recruitment processes by enabling more accurate, consistent, and timely decisions (Teng et al., 2022; Niranjan et al., 2021; Tewari & Pant, 2020).

By continuously scanning global markets, competitors' digital footprints, and macroeconomic indicators, AI allows leaders to detect weak signals that may escape human analysts, thereby increasing organizational agility (Bustos et al., 2025; Reza et al., 2025; Sullivan & Wamba, 2024). In crisis contexts—particularly cybersecurity incidents—AI systems detect threats within seconds and activate automated response protocols, significantly reducing leaders' information-gathering burden during critical early stages (Farzaan et al., 2024; Mohamed, 2025). In operational crises, digital twin technologies enable leaders to simulate production lines or supply chains in virtual environments, facilitating scenario testing without real-world losses.

The diffusion of AI has also introduced a new leadership paradigm commonly referred to as algorithmic management. Widely adopted in call centers, delivery services, and software development teams, these systems automate micro-management functions such as performance monitoring, task allocation, and workflow optimization. Consequently, leaders increasingly shift from directly managing employees to overseeing whether algorithmic systems operate ethically, fairly, and in alignment with organizational objectives (Wu et al., 2023; Parent-Rocheleau & Parker, 2022; Woodcock, 2022). Leaders must therefore strategically determine which tasks should be fully automated, which require human–AI collaboration, and which—due to creativity or ethical considerations—must remain strictly human. Given AI's potential for error, ultimate legal and ethical accountability must remain with human leaders, who are responsible for managing and intervening in the consequences of AI-driven actions (Batool & Zowghi, 2023).

Leaders are increasingly using artificial intelligence, with tangible applications in team performance and decision-making processes. Microsoft 365 Copilot is creating tangible and transformative effects on productivity, creativity, and time management in the workplace. According to research, 70% of users report being more productive, and 68% report improved work quality. Using Copilot enables tasks such as searching, writing, and summarizing information to be completed 29% faster overall, while summarizing missed meetings is approximately four times faster. From a time management perspective, users save an average of 1.2 hours per week. This tool, which reduces email processing time by 64% and speeds up file searching by 75%, is considered indispensable by 77% of users (Microsoft, 2023).

Although AI cannot itself possess emotional intelligence (EQ), it has become a powerful tool for enhancing leaders' emotional awareness, empathic sensitivity, and capacity to foster psychological safety (Dwivedi, 2025). Meeting and interaction analysis technologies examine variables such as speaking time, tone, and interaction patterns to detect early indicators of employee withdrawal, declining motivation, or emerging conflict (Alhussein et al., 2025; Shenoy & Sardana, 2020). These insights enable leaders to intervene in a more timely, sensitive, and trust-building manner. Nevertheless, translating AI-generated insights into genuine empathy, relationship-building, and appropriate human action remains an indispensable leadership responsibility (Von et al., 2019).

In conclusion, AI strengthens leadership by supporting knowledge management, real-time performance monitoring, and emotional insight, thereby enabling more coordinated and informed decision-making processes (Haefner et al., 2021; Huang & Rust, 2018). When combined with targeted training and continuous learning initiatives, AI enhances digital literacy and fosters a collaborative organizational culture, particularly in geographically dispersed teams (Jarrahi, 2018; Mikalef & Gupta, 2021). However, evidence from large-scale disruptions such as the COVID-19 pandemic demonstrates that traditional leadership approaches often struggle to respond with sufficient speed and flexibility, especially in resource-constrained environments (Javed et al., 2019). The effectiveness of AI-enabled leadership ultimately depends on leadership styles and employees' technological perceptions, which shape trust, engagement, and the overall success of AI-mediated organizational processes (Hu et al., 2025).

CHALLENGES OF LEADING HYBRID AND REMOTE TEAMS THROUGH AI

The acceleration of digitalization has transformed organizational work structures, making hybrid and remote work models a new institutional norm. As geographically dispersed teams rely increasingly on digital systems for coordination, leadership practices have shifted from traditional face-to-face interactions toward technology-mediated, multidimensional, and more complex processes (Al, 2024; Aydogan, 2025). At the center of this transformation lies Artificial Intelligence (AI), which provides leaders with advanced tools for monitoring performance, allocating tasks, and optimizing decision-making. Yet these capabilities simultaneously introduce profound ethical, cultural, psychological, and operational challenges that leaders must navigate carefully (Jain & Kanwar, 2024; Jia et al., 2025; García-Madurga et al., 2024). Consequently, the leadership of hybrid and remote teams increasingly requires sophisticated socio-technical judgment that balances efficiency with responsibility.

Within remote work contexts, leaders frequently rely on AI-enabled monitoring systems to assess whether employees are fulfilling their responsibilities effectively (Yılmaz, 2023). Algorithmic management—characterized by continuous tracking of performance indicators, workflow patterns, and micro-behaviors such as typing frequency, screen time, or email traffic—has thus become a widespread managerial mechanism (Kinowska & Sienkiewicz, 2023). However, electronic performance monitoring (EPM) has been shown to heighten privacy concerns, reduce employees' sense of autonomy, and increase disengagement, especially among remote workers. Studies further demonstrate that privacy-related anxiety engendered by EPM is associated with negative attitudes toward monitoring and reduced job satisfaction (Andrade et al., 2025). Nevertheless, existing research provides limited clarity on the conditions under which these effects intensify, leaving an important gap regarding how monitoring quality and transparency shape psychological safety in telework. Addressing this gap, recent work examines how organizational openness about monitoring practices and employee access to collected data influence learning, voice behavior, and knowledge sharing (Brinson et al., 2024; Li & Wang, 2024).

Many organizations employ software that captures screenshots or logs application use to determine employee "activity levels" outside the office (Andrade et al., 2025). Although the managerial intent is often to increase productivity, this approach raises tensions between legitimate performance oversight and employees' right to privacy (Al-Rjoub et al., 2008). While employers may have operational reasons for a certain degree of surveillance, excessive or opaque monitoring risks deteriorating trust and psychological well-being. Research notes that electronic surveillance can harm not only employees (Ball & Margulis, 2011; Cascio & Montealegre, 2016; Ravid et al., 2019; Stanton et al., 2000; Yost et al., 2018) but also supervisors and organizational functioning more broadly (Reilly, 2010; Yost et al., 2018). Conversely, when implemented developmentally rather than punitively, EPM has the potential to enhance satisfaction, performance, and well-being (Ravid et al., 2019; Wells et al., 2007). These divergent findings underscore the importance of context and leadership intent in determining the organizational consequences of AI-supported monitoring.

AI-driven decision systems also pose serious risks in talent management. When historical data include demographic or cultural biases, algorithms inevitably learn and reproduce them (Raghavan et al., 2020; Binns, 2018). Consequently, AI-based recruitment tools may classify qualified applicants from underrepresented groups as "low potential," thereby undermining diversity and inclusion efforts and reinforcing cognitive homogeneity. Leaders may falsely assume that AI guarantees objectivity, while in practice the technology can perpetuate structural inequities (Cowgill, 2019; Barocas et al., 2023). In hybrid teams, AI may further associate in-office visibility with higher performance, producing a "visibility bias" that disproportionately disadvantages remote employees. Because AI systems typically fail to capture face-to-face interactions, remote workers risk being inaccurately evaluated relative to their on-site peers (Ball, 2010; Sewell & Taskin, 2015; Bloom et al., 2015). Thus, algorithmic outcomes can distort leaders' judgments unless interpreted critically and supplemented with contextual understanding.

Furthermore, when leaders cannot explain AI-generated outputs, employees often perceive resulting decisions as arbitrary or erroneous, weakening interpersonal and organizational trust (Glikson & Woolley, 2020; Citron & Pasquale, 2014). Leaders bear responsibility for validating AI-derived information, and any errors that propagate through remote teams can escalate rapidly due to accelerated digital communication flows (Park & Nan, 2025). These concerns are compounded by automation bias, the tendency to overtrust AI recommendations even when incorrect. In domains such as clinical decision support, high perceived accuracy has been shown to increase user compliance with erroneous machine suggestions, illustrating how "false agreement" can emerge subtly yet dangerously (Kücking et al., 2024). Complementarily, automation complacency reduces attentiveness and vigilance, particularly in time-pressured or cognitively demanding contexts, thus compromising leaders' judgment (Parasuraman & Manzey, 2010). Together, these phenomena highlight the risk that AI systems can diminish human oversight, especially within hybrid team environments that depend heavily on digital intermediaries.

Research on human–AI collaboration further indicates that overreliance on AI weakens human decision-makers' perceived responsibility and can be interpreted by others as a form of "responsibility ambiguity" (Van Der Waa et al., 2021). This issue becomes particularly salient in leadership, where both outcomes and the decision-making process itself are scrutinized. Empirical findings show that employees trust leaders more when they exhibit transparency and human reasoning, rather than uncritically deferring to AI recommendations (Dietvorst & Bharti, 2020). Consequently, leaders who adopt AI tools without maintaining strong analytical and relational competencies risk damaging their credibility and influence. This dynamic is amplified in hybrid teams, where digital mediation can already obscure interpersonal cues and reduce opportunities for trust-building.

At the organizational level, leaders increasingly face a pronounced "leadership capability gap" in understanding how AI tools work and how their limitations shape decision-making (Schwarzmüller et al., 2018). Insufficient AI literacy not only hampers effective tool utilization but also elevates institutional risk, as leaders may overlook algorithmic constraints, data flaws, or systemic biases (Batarseh & Freeman, 2022). Similarly, AI-enabled business model transformation requires advanced technological and strategic competence among both senior executives and mid-level managers; however, many organizations continue to exhibit deficiencies in these areas (Huang & Rust, 2021). These findings demonstrate that AI-driven transformation is not merely a technical shift but a profound leadership challenge requiring deep cognitive, analytical, and strategic adaptation.

Traditional leadership approaches have shown limitations in responding to large-scale disruptions under resource constraints, such as those encountered during the COVID-19 pandemic (Javed et al., 2019). Virtual teams, in particular, impose demands that exceed those of co-located teams, as leaders must devote additional time and effort to building trust and relational cohesion through digital channels (Hoch & Dulebohn, 2017; Iorio & Taylor, 2015; Johnston & Rosin, 2011). Establishing context-rich communication, sustaining shared understanding, and mitigating interpersonal distance also become more challenging (Eubanks et al., 2016). Hybrid and remote leadership must integrate not only technological proficiency but also advanced interpersonal sensitivity, emotional intelligence, and communication agility.

Organizational responses to AI adoption are further shaped by employee attitudes. Some employees may resist AI because they prefer collaborating with human colleagues, while others express positive attitudes when they perceive clear personal benefits (Lichtenthaler, 2020). These contrasting reactions produce a paradox in which the same individual may exhibit both positive and negative attitudes toward AI depending on situational cues. The complexity of this attitude spectrum underscores the need for leaders to manage expectations, provide support, and communicate transparently during AI-driven transitions. Adding to this complexity, Singh's (2023) and Dwivedi and collegaus (2021) findings indicate that AI integration increases skill gaps and training needs, further complicating remote leadership.

Beyond organizational dynamics, the integration of AI also intersects with broader sociological concerns. Questions regarding transparency, algorithmic accountability, data ownership, and the reproduction of power structures illustrate how AI reshapes social relations and norms (Law & McCall, 2024). Excessive reliance on digital systems can generate feelings of isolation, alienation, or emotional detachment, weakening interpersonal bonds (Howirtz et al., 2023). Remote work itself may exacerbate challenges such as limited colleague interaction, insufficient health and safety assurance, digital inequality, and overly autonomous task structures (Allen et al., 2015). From a structural perspective, organizations also grapple with the erosion of cultural foundations and the practical limitation that not all tasks can be performed remotely (Silva & Coelho, 2022; Boeri et al., 2020; Dingel & Neiman, 2020).

Empathy represents another domain in which AI reshapes leadership dynamics. Although AI cannot genuinely "feel," it can provide analyses that help leaders interpret emotional signals within teams (Endsley, 2023; Jiang et al., 2023). Tools such as "AI on My Shoulder" have demonstrated potential in supporting stress management and emotional resilience among employees (Das Swain et al., 2025). Yet algorithmic biases, cultural insensitivity in emotion recognition, and privacy risks may undermine employees' trust if empathetic AI feedback feels inauthentic or intrusive (Floridi & Cowls, 2022). Moreover, coaching research emphasizes that human judgment and emotional intelligence remain indispensable for navigating nuanced and complex interpersonal dynamics (Passmore & Tee, 2023; Terblanche & Cilliers, 2020).

This broader evolution requires leaders to develop not only technical competencies but also the social and psychological skills needed to support distributed teams. As Yozi and Mbokota (2024) note, hybrid work environments heighten the importance of relational sensitivity and emotional awareness. Ferreira et al., (2023) similarly find that communication, collaboration, problem solving, and time management have become critical in remote work arrangements. Finally, Bell, McAlpine, and Hill (2023) argue that leadership effectiveness in hybrid teams depends on integrating technology with an intentional effort to sustain social cohesion and interpersonal connection. Together, these findings underscore that AI-mediated leadership must balance technological capability with deep human-centered competence.

FUTURE RESEARCH DIRECTIONS AND STRATEGIES

Recent advances in artificial intelligence (AI) have substantially expanded the technical capacities that shape contemporary leadership practice, particularly in the domains of perception, prediction, and content generation. These developments have enabled leaders to access richer information, anticipate emerging conditions, and support decision-making with unprecedented speed and precision (Song et al., 2024). Nevertheless, although AI performance in task-focused competencies has progressed rapidly, reasoning remains a capability that often operates implicitly beneath task execution and still trails behind other performance dimensions (Song et al., 2024). This uneven development raises important questions about how leadership must evolve in response to the growing presence of intelligent systems in organizational life.

As the pace of technological progress accelerates, the limitations of traditional leadership models—models historically grounded in interpersonal influence and human-to-human interaction—become increasingly apparent. The integration of autonomous and semi-autonomous systems disrupts assumptions about how influence, responsibility, and judgment are exercised within organizations. Consequently, leadership must be reconceptualized to include human–machine collaboration and to reposition attention, ethical judgment, and responsibility within a broader socio-technical context (Uğurlu, 2025). In this emerging landscape, leadership is no longer solely about guiding people; it is also about orchestrating collaboration among humans and intelligent systems in ways that sustain trust, transparency, and accountability.

Within this context, research on cognitive transformation in decision-making has gained particular momentum. Scholars have demonstrated that different levels of automation—from decision-support tools to fully autonomous agents—produce distinct patterns of cognitive bias and influence how humans interpret and act upon

AI-generated outputs (Van Rooy, 2024). While human–machine collaboration offers substantial benefits, it simultaneously introduces new vulnerabilities, especially in relation to bias amplification and opaque reasoning processes. Effective governance therefore requires a deliberate balancing of human and machine strengths, coupled with explicit mechanisms for mitigating their respective weaknesses. Only by achieving this kind of balance can organizations develop governance structures that are technologically sophisticated yet cognitively coherent, enabling more thoughtful and accountable decision-making. (Van Rooy, 2024).

Although considerable progress has been made in developing AI systems capable of supporting interaction-focused competencies—such as situational awareness (Endsley, 2023), and shared awareness (Jiang et al., 2023)—these capabilities still lag behind progress in task execution (Song et al., 2021). This gap reveals key opportunities for future research: scholars must continue developing operational strategies for implementing emerging AI–leadership frameworks, while also integrating constructs or perspectives that existing models may have overlooked. Understanding how improvements in interactive capacities can meaningfully augment leadership effectiveness is particularly critical in an era characterized by digitalization, distributed teams, and rapidly shifting work conditions.

At the same time, AI holds strong potential for supporting more empathetic, collaborative, and knowledge-driven leadership. By improving access to organizational knowledge and enabling timely, well-informed decision-making, AI can help leaders coordinate dispersed teams and sustain collaboration even under conditions of uncertainty (Haefner et al., 2021; Huang & Rust, 2018). When AI adoption is paired with targeted training and continuous learning initiatives, participation in knowledge-sharing behaviors can increase as employees develop both competence and confidence in using these systems (Jarrahi, 2018; Mikalef & Gupta, 2021).

Despite these promising developments, significant limitations persist—particularly in the domain of empathy. Empathy is rooted in deeply diverse human experiences shaped by culture, identity, and context, making it extremely difficult to design AI interactions that generalize reliably across social boundaries (Shao, 2023). When empathetic design fails to generalize, unintended negative effects may occur, reminding researchers and practitioners alike that both ethical and technical caution must accompany the development of AI-mediated empathic systems.

Taken together, the convergence of AI and leadership competencies creates new opportunities for building adaptive and effective hybrid teams. Leaders who integrate AI can improve decision-making and enhance employee well-being, yet AI must complement—not replace—human judgment. Embedding AI in leadership development can therefore promote more evidence-driven, ethical, and empathetic leadership.

In essence, the future of leadership depends on understanding how human and artificial capabilities can jointly shape effective guidance in increasingly complex organizational contexts.

CONCLUSION

This book chapter examines the increasing impact of Artificial Intelligence on organizational leadership from a comprehensive perspective and reveals how AI transforms leadership practices, decision-making processes, and the structural nature of working relationships. In today's hybrid and remote working environments, AI-supported leadership stands out as a rapidly developing field shaped at the intersection of technology, organizational behavior, and human psychology (Zárate-Torres et al., 2025; Chowdhury et al., 2022). Successful leaders use AI as a support tool that enriches communication, accelerates information flow, and strengthens empathic interaction (Li et al., 2024), while also paying attention to the ethical dimensions of technology and the preservation of human values.

This approach requires leaders to correctly grasp the possibilities and limitations of AI, to interpret the data provided by AI, and to reflect these appropriately in their decision-making processes. It is important that future research focuses on how a balanced interaction can be established between human contribution and AI support, on the long-term effects of AI-supported leadership on employee well-being, and on how potential risks can be managed. When used consciously in a complementary manner with human empathy and judgment, AI can contribute to organizations forming hybrid or remote teams with high adaptability, resilience, and strong commitment.

REFERENCES

Abositta, A., Adedokun, M. W., & Berberoğlu, A. (2024). Influence of artificial intelligence on engineering management decision-making with mediating role of transformational leadership. *Systems*, *12*(12), 570. DOI: 10.3390/systems12120570

Al, B. (2024). Uzaktan ve hibrit çalışma modellerinde liderliğin dönüşümü: Dijital liderlik ve sanal ekip yönetimi üzerine bibliyometrik bir analiz. *Sosyal Bilimler Metinleri*, *2024*(2), 121–140. DOI: 10.56337/sbm.1561098

Al-Rjoub, H., Zabian, A., & Qawasmeh, S. (2008). Electronic monitoring: The employees point of view. *Journal of Social Sciences (New York, N. Y.)*, *4*(3), 189–195. DOI: 10.3844/jssp.2008.189.195

Alhussein, G., Ziogas, I., Saleem, S., & Hadjileontiadis, L. J. (2025). Speech emotion recognition in conversations using artificial intelligence: A systematic review and meta-analysis. *Artificial Intelligence Review*, *58*(7), 198. DOI: 10.1007/s10462-025-11197-8

Allen, T. D., Golden, T. D., & Shockley, K. M. (2015). How effective is telecommuting? Assessing the status of our scientific findings. *Psychological Science in the Public Interest : A Journal of the American Psychological Society*, *16*(2), 40–68. DOI: 10.1177/1529100615593273 PMID: 26403188

Almutairi, M., Chiang, C., Bai, Y., & Gomez-Zara, D. (2025, June). tAIfa: Enhancing team effectiveness and cohesion with AI-generated automated feedback. In *Proceedings of the 4th Annual Symposium on Human-Computer Interaction for Work* (pp. 1–25). ACM. DOI: 10.1145/3729176.3729197

Andrade, M. D., Martínez-Córcoles, M., Fialho, P., & Guimaraes, M. (2025). The effects of being under watch: The impact of electronic monitoring on remote workers' psychological safety. *Journal of Management & Organization*, •••, 1–18. DOI: 10.1017/jmo.2025.10039

Arham, A. F., Norizan, N. S., Arham, A. F., Hasbullah, N. N., Malan, I. N. B., & Alwi, S. (2022, March). Digital leadership in education: A meta-analysis review. In *International Conference on Business and Technology* (pp. 849–857). Cham: Springer International Publishing.

Arunprasad, P., Dey, C., Jebli, F., Manimuthu, A., & El Hathat, Z. (2022). Exploring the remote work challenges in the era of COVID-19 pandemic: Review and application model. *Benchmarking*, *29*(10), 3333–3355. DOI: 10.1108/BIJ-07-2021-0421

Asıl, S. (2025). *Yapay zekâ etiği: Temel ilkeler, sorunlar ve disiplinlerarası yaklaşımlar. İnönü Üniversitesi İletişim Fakültesi Elektronik Dergisi (İNİF E-Dergi), 10*(1), 152–175.

Athanasiadou, C., & Theriou, G. (2021). Telework: Systematic literature review and future research agenda. *Heliyon, 7*(10), e08165. Advance online publication. DOI: 10.1016/j.heliyon.2021.e08165 PMID: 34703928

Avlani, A., & Charalampous, M. (2024). Exploring the significance of remote leadership competencies in the virtual workplace: A systematic literature review. *Authorea Preprints.*

Aydogan, S. (2025). Impact of AI-augmented digital leadership on remote team performance: An exploratory study of Turkish SMEs. *Access Journal, 6*(3), 615–633. DOI: 10.46656/access.2025.6.3(9)

Badrinarayanan, V. (2024). Trust building strategies for virtual leaders in the post pandemic era. *Project Leadership and Society, 5*, 100126. DOI: 10.1016/j.plas.2024.100126

Bai, A., & Vahedian, M. (2023). *Beyond the screen: Safeguarding mental health in the digital workplace through organizational commitment and ethical environment.* arXiv preprint arXiv:2311.02422.

Ball, K. (2010). Workplace surveillance: An overview. *Labor History, 51*(1), 87–106. DOI: 10.1080/00236561003654776

Ball, K. S., & Margulis, S. T. (2011). Electronic monitoring and surveillance in call centres: A framework for investigation. *New Technology, Work and Employment, 26*(2), 113–126. DOI: 10.1111/j.1468-005X.2011.00263.x

Barocas, S., Hardt, M., & Narayanan, A. (2023). *Fairness and machine learning: Limitations and opportunities.* MIT Press.

Baruah, A., Shaikh, M., Kumar, R. M., Shaikh, I. A. K., Thomas, S. N., & Natrayan, L. (2024, April). Artificial Intelligence influence on leadership styles in human resource management for employee engagement. In *2024 Ninth International Conference on Science Technology Engineering and Mathematics (ICONSTEM)* (pp. 1–5). IEEE. DOI: 10.1109/ICONSTEM60960.2024.10568819

Bastola, A., Wang, H., Hembree, J., Yadav, P., Gong, Z., Dixon, E., . . . McNeese, N. (2023). *LLM-based smart reply (LSR): Enhancing collaborative performance with ChatGPT-mediated smart reply system.* arXiv preprint arXiv:2306.11980

Batarseh, F. A., & Freeman, L. (Eds.). (2022). *AI assurance: Towards trustworthy, explainable, safe, and ethical AI.* Academic Press.

Batool, A., Zowghi, D., & Bano, M. (2023). *Responsible AI governance: A systematic literature review.* arXiv preprint arXiv:2401.10896.

Bell, B. S., McAlpine, K. L., & Hill, N. S. (2023). Leading virtually. *Annual Review of Organizational Psychology and Organizational Behavior*, *10*(1), 339–362. DOI: 10.1146/annurev-orgpsych-120920-050115

Berente, N., Gu, B., Recker, J., & Santhanam, R. (2021). Managing artificial intelligence. *Management Information Systems Quarterly*, *45*(3), 1433–1450. DOI: 10.25300/MISQ/2021/16274

Binns, R. (2018). Fairness in machine learning: Lessons from political philosophy. In *Conference on Fairness, Accountability and Transparency* (pp. 149–159). PMLR.

Bizilj, S., Boštjančič, E., & Sočan, G. (2021). Perceived efficacy of virtual leadership in the crisis of the COVID-19 pandemic. *Changing Societies & Personalities*, *5*(3), 389–404. DOI: 10.15826/csp.2021.5.3.141

Bloom, N., Liang, J., Roberts, J., & Ying, Z. J. (2015). Does working from home work? Evidence from a Chinese experiment. *The Quarterly Journal of Economics*, *130*(1), 165–218. DOI: 10.1093/qje/qju032

Boeri, T., Caiumi, A., & Paccagnella, M. (2020). Mitigating the work-safety trade-off. *ovid Economics, 2(8), 60-66.*

Bravo-Duarte, F., Tordera, N., & Rodríguez, I. (2025). Overcoming virtual distance: A systematic review of leadership competencies for managing performance in telework. *Frontiers in Organizational Psychology*, *2*, 1499248. DOI: 10.3389/forgp.2024.1499248

Brinson, N., Amini, B., Lemon, L., & Bawole, C. (2024). Electronic performance monitoring: The role of reactance, trust, and privacy concerns in predicting job satisfaction in the post-pandemic workplace. *Cyberpsychology (Brno)*, *18*(5), 10. Advance online publication. DOI: 10.5817/CP2024-5-10

Bustos, O., Pomares-Quimbaya, A., & Stellian, R. (2025). Machine learning, stock market forecasting, and market efficiency: A comparative study. *International Journal of Data Science and Analytics*, *20*(7), 6815–6839. DOI: 10.1007/s41060-025-00854-4

Caniëls, M. C. (2023). How remote working increases the importance of positive leadership for employee vigor. *Frontiers in Psychology*, *14*, 1089557. DOI: 10.3389/fpsyg.2023.1089557 PMID: 36743246

Carrasco-Garrido, C., De-Pablos-Heredero, C., & Rodríguez-Sánchez, J. L. (2023). Exploring hybrid telework: A bibliometric analysis. *Heliyon, 9*(12), e23119. DOI: 10.1016/j.heliyon.2023.e22472 PMID: 38076145

Cascio, W. F., & Montealegre, R. (2016). How technology is changing work and organizations. *Annual Review of Organizational Psychology and Organizational Behavior, 3*(1), 349–375. DOI: 10.1146/annurev-orgpsych-041015-062352

Çelik, E., & Taşkıran, E. (2023). Dijital liderlik. In *Örgütsel Davranış* (s. 81–102).

Çeri, M., & Doğan, A. (2025). Yapay zekâ destekli insan kaynakları yönetimi: Çalışan deneyiminin dönüşümü. *İzmir Yönetim Dergisi, 6*(1), 122–141.

Chiang, R. H. L., & Storey, V. C. (2012).. . *Management Information Systems Quarterly, 36*(4), 1165–1188. DOI: 10.2307/41703503

Chowdhury, S., Budhwar, P., Dey, P. K., Joel-Edgar, S., & Abadie, A. (2022). AI–employee collaboration and business performance: Integrating knowledge-based view, socio-technical systems and organisational socialisation framework. *Journal of Business Research, 144*, 31–49. DOI: 10.1016/j.jbusres.2022.01.069

Citron, D. K., & Pasquale, F. (2014). The scored society: Due process for automated predictions. *Washington Law Review (Seattle, Wash.), 89*, 1–34.

Cooper, G. (2023). Examining science education in ChatGPT: An exploratory study of generative artificial intelligence. *Journal of Science Education and Technology, 32*(3), 444–452. DOI: 10.1007/s10956-023-10039-y

Cowgill, B. (2019). *Bias and productivity in humans and algorithms* (Columbia Business School Research Paper No. 19-54)

Das Swain, V., Zhong, Q. J., Parekh, J. R., Jeon, Y., Zimmermann, R., Czerwinski, M. P., & Hernandez, J. (2025, April). AI on my shoulder: Supporting emotional labor in front-office roles with an LLM-based empathetic coworker. In *Proceedings of the 2025 CHI Conference on Human Factors in Computing Systems* (pp. 1–29). ACM DOI: 10.1145/3706598.3713705

Dash, R., McMurtrey, M., Rebman, C., & Kar, U. K. (2019). Application of artificial intelligence in automation of supply chain management. *Journal of Strategic Innovation and Sustainability, 14*(3), 43–53. DOI: 10.33423/jsis.v14i3.2105

Davenport, T. H., Harris, J. G., & Morison, R. (2010). *Analytics at work: Smarter decisions, better results*. Harvard Business Press.

Dietvorst, B. J., & Bharti, S. (2020). People reject algorithms in uncertain decision domains because they have diminishing sensitivity to forecasting error. *Psychological Science, 31*(10), 1302–1314. DOI: 10.1177/0956797620948841 PMID: 32916083

Dingel, J. I., & Neiman, B. (2020). How many jobs can be done at home? *Journal of Public Economics, 189*, 104235. Advance online publication. DOI: 10.1016/j.jpubeco.2020.104235 PMID: 32834177

Dwivedi, D. (2025). Emotional intelligence and artificial intelligence integration strategies for leadership excellence. *Advances in Research, 26*(1), 84–94. DOI: 10.9734/air/2025/v26i11235

Dwivedi, Y. K., Hughes, L., Ismagilova, E., Aarts, G., Coombs, C., Crick, T., Duan, Y., Dwivedi, R., Edwards, J., Eirug, A., Galanos, V., Ilavarasan, P. V., Janssen, M., Jones, P., Kar, A. K., Kizgin, H., Kronemann, B., Lal, B., Lucini, B., & Williams, M. D. (2021). Artificial intelligence (AI): Multidisciplinary perspectives on emerging challenges, opportunities, and agenda for research, practice and policy. *International Journal of Information Management, 57*, 101994. DOI: 10.1016/j.ijinfomgt.2019.08.002

Endsley, M. R. (2023). Supporting human-AI teams: Transparency, explainability, and situation awareness. *Computers in Human Behavior, 140*, 107574. DOI: 10.1016/j.chb.2022.107574

Eubanks, D. L., Palanski, M., Olabisi, J., Joinson, A., & Dove, J. (2016). Team dynamics in virtual, partially distributed teams: Optimal role fulfillment. *Computers in Human Behavior, 61*, 556–568. DOI: 10.1016/j.chb.2016.03.035

Farzaan, M. A. M., Ghanem, M. C., El-Hajjar, A., & Ratnayake, D. N. (2024). AI-enabled system for efficient and effective cyber incident detection and response in cloud environments. *arXiv Preprint* arXiv:2404.05602.

Fayard, A.-L., Weeks, J., & Khan, M. (2021). Designing the hybrid office. *Harvard Business Review*, 1–11.

Ferreira, C., Robertson, J., & Pitt, L. (2023). Business (un)usual: Critical skills for the next normal. *Thunderbird International Business Review, 65*(1), 39–47. DOI: 10.1002/tie.22276

Floridi, L., & Cowls, J. (2022). A unified framework of five principles for AI in society. In *Machine Learning and the City: Applications in Architecture and Urban Design* (pp. 535–545). Springer.

Frey, C. B., & Osborne, M. A. (2017). The future of employment: How susceptible are jobs to computerisation? *Technological Forecasting and Social Change, 114*, 254–280. DOI: 10.1016/j.techfore.2016.08.019

Froese, F. J., Blay, T., Gibson, C. B., Shaffer, M. A., & Benitez, J. (2025). Global virtual work: A review, integrative framework, and future research opportunities. *Journal of International Business Studies, 56*(6), 1–29. DOI: 10.1057/s41267-025-00775-1

Gandomi, A., & Haider, M. (2015). Beyond the hype: Big data concepts, methods, and analytics. *International Journal of Information Management, 35*(2), 137–144. DOI: 10.1016/j.ijinfomgt.2014.10.007

García-Madurga, M. Á., Gil-Lacruz, A. I., Saz-Gil, I., & Gil-Lacruz, M. (2024). The role of artificial intelligence in improving workplace well-being: A systematic review. *Businesses, 4*(3), 389–410. DOI: 10.3390/businesses4030024

Gerçek, M., & Özveren, C. G. (2023). Yapay zeka araçları İKY için nasıl değer yaratabilir? Çalışan duygu analizinin uygulama alanlarının incelenmesi. *Yönetim Bilimleri Dergisi, 21*(50), 1048–1076. DOI: 10.35408/comuybd.1285706

Ghavifekr, S., & Pei, X. (2023). Leading global digitalization in higher education. In *Global Perspectives on the Internationalization of Higher Education* (pp. 1–15). IGI Global. DOI: 10.4018/978-1-6684-5929-4.ch001

Gifford, J. (2022). Remote working: Unprecedented increase and a developing research agenda. *Human Resource Development International, 25*(1), 105–113. DOI: 10.1080/13678868.2022.2049108

Glikson, E., & Woolley, A. W. (2020). Human trust in artificial intelligence: Review of empirical research. *The Academy of Management Annals, 14*(2), 627–660. DOI: 10.5465/annals.2018.0057

Gupta, M. (2024). AI-powered conflict resolution: Transforming virtual team dynamics in real time. *Proceedings of the International Journal for Multidisciplinary Research, 6*(6), 31182–31195. DOI: 10.36948/ijfmr.2024.v06i06.31182

Haefner, N., Wincent, J., Parida, V., & Gassmann, O. (2021). Artificial intelligence and innovation management: A review, framework, and research agenda. *Technological Forecasting and Social Change, 162*, 120392. DOI: 10.1016/j.techfore.2020.120392

Hoch, J. E., & Dulebohn, J. H. (2017). Team personality composition, emergent leadership and shared leadership in virtual teams: A theoretical framework. *Human Resource Management Review, 27*(4), 678–693. DOI: 10.1016/j.hrmr.2016.12.012

Howirtz, M., Milosavljevic, M., & Van den Bulck, H. (2023). The use of artificial intelligence by public service media: Between advantages and threats. In El Morr, C. (Ed.), *AI and society: Tensions and opportunities* (pp. 127–140). CRC Press.

Hu, X., Gao, H., Agafari, T., Zhang, M. Q., & Cong, R. (2025). How and when artificial intelligence adoption promotes employee knowledge sharing? The role of paradoxical leadership and technophilia. *Frontiers in Psychology*, *16*, 1573587. DOI: 10.3389/fpsyg.2025.1573587 PMID: 40470012

Huang, M. H., & Rust, R. T. (2018). Artificial intelligence in service. *Journal of Service Research*, *21*(2), 155–172. DOI: 10.1177/1094670517752459

Huang, M. H., & Rust, R. T. (2021). Engaged to a robot? The role of AI in service. *Journal of Service Research*, *24*(1), 30–41. DOI: 10.1177/1094670520902266

Iorio, J., & Taylor, J. E. (2015). Precursors to engaged leaders in virtual project teams. *International Journal of Project Management*, *33*(2), 395–405. DOI: 10.1016/j.ijproman.2014.06.007

Jain, C., & Kanwar, M. J. (2024). *The AI-driven workplace: How automation is reshaping flexible work arrangements.*

Jarrahi, M. H. (2018). Artificial intelligence and the future of work: Human-AI symbiosis in organizational decision making. *Business Horizons*, *61*(4), 577–586. DOI: 10.1016/j.bushor.2018.03.007

Javed, B., Naqvi, S. M. M. R., Khan, A. K., Arjoon, S., & Tayyeb, H. H. (2019). Impact of inclusive leadership on innovative work behavior: The role of psychological safety. *Journal of Management & Organization*, *25*(1), 117–136. DOI: 10.1017/jmo.2017.3

Jerab, D. (2025, January 10). *Effective leadership strategies for virtual and remote teams. SSRN.* https://doi.org/DOI: 10.2139/ssrn.5092307

Jia, J., Ning, X., & Liu, W. (2025). The consequences and theoretical explanation of workplace AI on employees: A systematic literature review. *Journal of Digital Management*, *1*(1), 14. DOI: 10.1007/s44362-025-00016-3

Jiang, J., Karran, A. J., Coursaris, C. K., Léger, P. M., & Beringer, J. (2023). A situation awareness perspective on human-AI interaction: Tensions and opportunities. *International Journal of Human-Computer Interaction*, *39*(9), 1789–1806. DOI: 10.1080/10447318.2022.2093863

Johnston, K. A., & Rosin, K. (2011, May). *Global virtual teams: How to manage them.* In *2011 International Conference on Computer and Management (CAMAN)* (pp. 1–4). IEEE. DOI: 10.1109/CAMAN.2011.5778849

Joshi, S. (2025a). *Review of artificial intelligence in management, leadership, decision-making and collaboration.*

Joshi, S. (2025b). *Artificial intelligence in leadership and management: Current trends and future directions.*

Kandasamy, U. C. (2024). *Ethical leadership in the age of AI: Challenges, opportunities and framework for ethical leadership* (arXiv:2410.18095). arXiv. https://arxiv.org/abs/2410.18095

Karakose, T., & Tülübaş, T. (2023). Digital leadership and sustainable school improvement: A conceptual analysis and implications for future research. *Educational Process: International Journal, 12*(1), 7–18. DOI: 10.22521/edupij.2023.121.1

Karaman, F. (2024). Sivil havacılık sektöründe çevik ve dijital liderlik tarzlarının örgütsel çeviklik ve çalışan performansları ile ilişkisi. *JOEEP: Journal of Emerging Economies and Policy*, *9*(2), 129–147.

Kaushik, M., & Guleria, N. (2020). The impact of pandemic COVID-19 in workplace. *European Journal of Business and Management, 12*(15), 9–18. DOI: 10.7176/EJBM/12-15-02

Khan, M. A. (2024). *Examining the influence of organizational structure and leadership on innovation in hybrid work settings: The mediating role of organizational culture in enhancing team collaboration and innovation outcomes.*

Kinowska, H., & Sienkiewicz, Ł. J. (2023). Influence of algorithmic management practices on workplace well-being: Evidence from European organisations. *Information Technology & People*, *36*(8), 21–42. DOI: 10.1108/ITP-02-2022-0079

Kloepfer, S., & Carbon, C.-C. (2025). Leadership and trust in virtual teams. *Human Systems Management*, *44*(5), 890–900. DOI: 10.1177/01672533251331488

Kollmann, T., Kollmann, K., & Kollmann, N. (2023). Artificial leadership: Digital transformation as a leadership task between the chief digital officer and artificial intelligence. *International Journal of Business Science and Applied Management*, *18*(1), 76–95. DOI: 10.69864/ijbsam.18-1.172

Kordon, A. (2020, August). Applied artificial intelligence-based systems as competitive advantage. In *2020 IEEE 10th International Conference on Intelligent Systems (IS)* (pp. 6–18). IEEE. https://doi.org/DOI: 10.1109/IS48319.2020.9200097

Kotkar, R. V., & Potdar, S. M. (2024). Investigating the development and uses of natural language processing in educational settings. *IBMRD's. Journal of Management Research, 13*(1), 77–85. DOI: 10.17697/ibmrd/2024/v13i1/173526

Kücking, F., Hübner, U., Przysucha, M., Hannemann, N., Kutza, J. O., Moelleken, M., Erfurt-Berge, C., Dissemond, J., Babitsch, B., & Busch, D. (2024). Automation bias in AI-decision support: Results from an empirical study. *Studies in Health Technology and Informatics, 317*, 298–304. DOI: 10.3233/SHTI240871 PMID: 39234734

Law, T., & McCall, L. (2024). Artificial intelligence policymaking: An agenda for sociological research. *Socius: Sociological Research for a Dynamic World, 10*, 1–13. DOI: 10.1177/23780231241261596

Li, N., Zhou, H., & Mikel-Hong, K. (2024). *Generative AI enhances team performance and reduces need for traditional teams* (arXiv:2405.17924). arXiv.

Li, S., & Wang, Y. (2024). A study on the positive and negative effects of different supervisor monitoring in remote workplaces. *Frontiers in Psychology, 15*, 1383207. DOI: 10.3389/fpsyg.2024.1383207 PMID: 38699578

Lichtenthaler, U. (2020). Extremes of acceptance: Employee attitudes toward artificial intelligence. *The Journal of Business Strategy, 41*(5), 39–45. DOI: 10.1108/JBS-12-2018-0204

Ma, S., Zhang, C., Wang, X., Ma, X., & Yin, M. (2024). *Beyond recommender: An exploratory study of the effects of different AI roles in AI-assisted decision making* (arXiv:2403.01791). arXiv.

Medlama, M., Vianney, L., Piring, R., Ilham, S., & Annamalah, S. (2025). The impact of artificial intelligence on leadership decision-making: Opportunities and challenges. *Communications on Applied Nonlinear Analysis, 32*(9s), 1878–1885. DOI: 10.52783/cana.v32.4359

Menteşe, S., & Menteşe, C. D. (2023). Dijitalleşen dünyada yöneticilerin değişen karar mekanizmaları. *Munzur Üniversitesi Sosyal Bilimler Dergisi, 12*(2), 153–173. DOI: 10.61337/tusbd.1362971

Microsoft. (2023, 15 November). *What can Copilot's earliest users teach us about generative AI at work?* Retrived from: https://www.microsoft.com/en-us/worklab/work-trend-index/copilots-earliest-users-teach-us-about-generative-ai-at-work/

Mikalef, P., & Gupta, M. (2021). Artificial intelligence capability: Conceptualization, measurement calibration, and empirical study on its impact on organizational creativity and firm performance. *Information & Management, 58*(3), 103434. DOI: 10.1016/j.im.2021.103434

Mohamed, N. (2025). Artificial intelligence and machine learning in cybersecurity: A deep dive into state-of-the-art techniques and future paradigms. *Knowledge and Information Systems, 67*(8), 1–87. DOI: 10.1007/s10115-025-02429-y

Nalbantoğlu, C. B. (2023). Yapay zeka ve uygulamalarının örgüt kültürü üzerine etkisi. *İzlek Akademik Dergi, 7*(2), 1–10.

Newman, A., Donohue, R., & Eva, N. (2017). Psychological safety: A systematic review of the literature. *Human Resource Management Review, 27*(3), 521–535. DOI: 10.1016/j.hrmr.2017.01.001

Newman, S. A., & Ford, R. C. (2021). Five steps to leading your team in the virtual COVID-19 workplace. *Organizational Dynamics, 50*(1), 100802. DOI: 10.1016/j.orgdyn.2020.100802 PMID: 36536689

Niranjan, K., Narayana, K. S., & Rao, M. N. (2021, January). Role of artificial intelligence in logistics and supply chain. In *2021 International Conference on Computer Communication and Informatics (ICCCI)* (pp. 1–3). IEEE. DOI: 10.1109/ICCCI50826.2021.9402625

OECD. (2021). *Measuring telework in the COVID-19 pandemic*. OECD Digital Economy Papers.

Onnis, L. L. (2016). What is a sustainable remote health workforce? People, practice and place. *Rural and Remote Health, 16*(3), 1–13. DOI: 10.22605/RRH3806

Pabuçcu, R., & İşcan, Ö. F. (2025). Yapay zekâ ve liderlik: Dönüştürücü liderlik tarzının çalışan tutumlarına etkisi. *Uluslararası Ekonomi, İşletme ve Politika Dergisi, 9*(1), 195–210. DOI: 10.29216/ueip.1607837

Parasuraman, R., & Manzey, D. H. (2010). Complacency and bias in human use of automation: An attentional integration. *Human Factors, 52*(3), 381–410. DOI: 10.1177/0018720810376055 PMID: 21077562

Parent-Rocheleau, X., & Parker, S. K. (2022). Algorithms as work designers: How algorithmic management influences the design of jobs. *Human Resource Management Review, 32*(3), 100838. DOI: 10.1016/j.hrmr.2021.100838

Park, S., & Nan, X. (2025). Generative AI and misinformation: A scoping review of the role of generative AI in the generation, detection, mitigation, and impact of misinformation. *AI & Society, 41(2), 1501-1515.*

Passmore, J., & Tee, D. (2023). Can chatbots like GPT-4 replace human coaches? Issues and dilemmas for the coaching profession, coaching clients and for organisations. *The Coaching Psychologist, 19*(1), 47–54. DOI: 10.53841/bpstcp.2023.19.1.47

Pollak, Z. (2021). Predicting customer lifetime values—Ecommerce use case. *arXiv Preprint*, arXiv:2102.05771.

Popovič, A., Hackney, R., Tassabehji, R., & Castelli, M. (2018). The impact of big data analytics on firms' high value business performance. *Information Systems Frontiers*, *20*(2), 209–222. DOI: 10.1007/s10796-016-9720-4

Provost, F., & Fawcett, T. (2013). *Data science for business: What you need to know about data mining and data-analytic thinking*. O'Reilly Media.

Quaquebeke, N. V., & Gerpott, F. H. (2023). The now, new, and next of digital leadership: How artificial intelligence (AI) will take over and change leadership as we know it. *Journal of Leadership & Organizational Studies*, *30*(3), 265–275. DOI: 10.1177/15480518231181731

Raghavan, M., Barocas, S., Kleinberg, J., & Levy, K. (2020). Mitigating bias in algorithmic hiring: Evaluating claims and practices. In *Proceedings of the 2020 Conference on Fairness, Accountability, and Transparency* (pp. 469–481). DOI: 10.1145/3351095.3372828

Ransbotham, S., Kiron, D., Gerbert, P., & Reeves, M. (2017). Reshaping business with artificial intelligence: Closing the gap between ambition and action. *MIT Sloan Management Review*, *59*(1).

Ravid, D. M., Tomczak, D. L., White, J. C., & Behrend, T. S. (2019). EPM 20/20: A review, framework, and research agenda for electronic performance monitoring. *Journal of Management*, *46*(1), 100–126. DOI: 10.1177/0149206319869435

Reilly, S. M. (2010). *The use of electronic surveillance and performance measures in the workplace: A qualitative investigation* (Doctoral dissertation, Durham University)

Reza, S. A., Rahman, M. K., Rahman, M. D., Sharmin, S., Mithu, M. F. H., Hasnain, K. N., . . . Kabir, R. (2025). Machine learning enabled early warning system for financial distress using real-time digital signals. *arXiv Preprint*, arXiv:2510.22287.

Roshanaei, M., Rezapour, R., & Seif El-Nasr, M. (2025). Talk, listen, connect: How humans and AI evaluate empathy in responses to emotionally charged narratives. *AI & Society*, 1–17.

Schwarzmüller, T., Brosi, P., Duman, D., & Welpe, I. M. (2018). How does the digital transformation affect organizations? Key themes of change in work design and leadership. *Management Review*, *29*(2), 114–138.

Sevinç, H. G. (2025). Yönetimin değişen paradigması: Yapay zekâ liderliği. *Liberal Düşünce Dergisi*, *118*(118), 89–116. DOI: 10.36484/liberal.1542213

Sewell, G., & Taskin, L. (2015). Out of sight, out of mind in a new world of work? Autonomy, control, and spatiotemporal scaling in telework. *Organization Studies*, *36*(11), 1507–1529. DOI: 10.1177/0170840615593587

Shao, R. (2023, April). An empathetic AI for mental health intervention: Conceptualizing and examining artificial empathy. In *Proceedings of the 2nd Empathy-Centric Design Workshop* (pp. 1–6). DOI: 10.1145/3588967.3588971

Shenoy, A., & Sardana, A. (2020). Multilogue-net: A context-aware RNN for multimodal emotion detection and sentiment analysis in conversation. *arXiv Preprint*, arXiv:2002.08267. DOI: 10.18653/v1/2020.challengehml-1.3

Silva, A., & Coelho, N. (2022). The moderating role of organizational culture on the relationship between workers' attitudes towards telework and happiness. *Kybernetes*. Advance online publication. DOI: 10.1108/K-02-2022-0231

Singh, S. (2023). Leadership challenges and strategies in the era of AI transformation. In *2023 International Conference on Computational Science and Computational Intelligence (CSCI)* (pp. 119–124). https://doi.org/DOI: 10.1109/CSCI62032.2023.00025

Song, B., Soria Zurita, N. F., Nolte, H., Singh, H., Cagan, J., & McComb, C. (2021). Addressing challenges to problem complexity: Effectiveness of AI assistance during the design process. In *IDETC-CIE 2021: International Design Engineering Technical Conferences and Computers and Information in Engineering Conference.*

Song, B., Zhu, Q., & Luo, J. (2024). Human–AI collaboration by design. *Proceedings of the Design Society*, *4*, 2247–2256. DOI: 10.1017/pds.2024.227

Sreelakshmy, R., Kumar, A. K., Titus, A., Hemajothi, S., Venkatesh, J., & Lavanya, A. (2023). Design and development of an AI-based intelligent door for home security system. In *2023 International Conference on Advances in Computing, Communication and Applied Informatics (ACCAI)* (pp. 1–8). IEEE. DOI: 10.1109/ACCAI58221.2023.10200307

Stanton, J. M., & Weiss, E. M. (2000). Electronic monitoring in their own words: An exploratory study of employees' experiences with new types of surveillance. *Computers in Human Behavior*, *16*(4), 423–440. DOI: 10.1016/S0747-5632(00)00018-2

Stewart, J. M., Tittel, E., & Chapple, M. (2011). *CISSP: Certified information systems security professional study guide*. John Wiley & Sons.

Sullivan, Y., & Wamba, S. F. (2024). Artificial intelligence and adaptive response to market changes: A strategy to enhance firm performance and innovation. *Journal of Business Research*, *174*, 114500. DOI: 10.1016/j.jbusres.2024.114500

Teng, Z., Cai, Y., Gao, Y., Zhang, X., & Li, X. (2022). Factors affecting learners' adoption of an educational metaverse platform: An empirical study based on an extended UTAUT model. *Mobile Information Systems*, *2022*(1), 5479215. DOI: 10.1155/2022/5479215

Terblanche, N., & Cilliers, D. (2020). Factors that influence users' adoption of being coached by an artificial intelligence coach. *Philosophy of Coaching*, *5*(1), 61–70. DOI: 10.22316/poc/05.1.06

Tewari, I., & Pant, M. (2020). Artificial intelligence reshaping human resource management: A review. In *2020 IEEE International Conference on Advent Trends in Multidisciplinary Research and Innovation (ICATMRI)* (pp. 1–4). IEEE. DOI: 10.1109/ICATMRI51801.2020.9398420

Tursunbayeva, A., Pagliari, C., Di Lauro, S., & Antonelli, G. (2022). The ethics of people analytics: Risks, opportunities and recommendations. *Personnel Review*, *51*(3), 900–921. DOI: 10.1108/PR-12-2019-0680

Uğurlu, F. (2025). Yöneticilerin yapay zekaya yönelik algılarının liderlik stilleri üzerindeki etkileri. *Bucak İşletme Fakültesi Dergisi*, *8*(2), 117–127. DOI: 10.38057/bifd.1780438

Van der Waa, J., Verdult, S., van den Bosch, K., van Diggelen, J., Haije, T., van der Stigchel, B., & Cocu, I. (2021). Moral decision making in human-agent teams: Human control and the role of explanations. *Frontiers in Robotics and AI*, *8*, 640647. DOI: 10.3389/frobt.2021.640647 PMID: 34124173

Van Rooy, D. (2024). Human–machine collaboration for enhanced decision-making in governance. *Data & Policy*, *6*, e60. DOI: 10.1017/dap.2024.72

Waller, M. A., & Fawcett, S. E. (2013). Data science, predictive analytics, and big data: A revolution that will transform supply chain design and management. *Journal of Business Logistics*, *34*(2), 77–84. DOI: 10.1111/jbl.12010

Weidmann, B., Xu, Y., & Deming, D. J. (2025). Measuring human leadership skills with artificially intelligent agents. *arXiv preprint arXiv:2508.02966.*

Wells, D. L., Moorman, R. H., & Werner, J. M. (2007). The impact of the perceived purpose of electronic performance monitoring on an array of attitudinal variables. *Human Resource Development Quarterly*, *18*(1), 121–138. DOI: 10.1002/hrdq.1194

Wilson, H. J., & Daugherty, P. R. (2018). *Human + machine: Reimagining work in the age of AI.*

Woodcock, J. (2022). Artificial intelligence at work: The problem of managerial control from call centers to transport platforms. *Frontiers in Artificial Intelligence, 5*, 888817. DOI: 10.3389/frai.2022.888817 PMID: 36092976

Wu, X., Liu, Q., Qu, H., & Wang, J. (2023). The effect of algorithmic management and workers' coping behavior: An exploratory qualitative research of Chinese food-delivery platform. *Tourism Management, 96*, 104716. DOI: 10.1016/j.tourman.2022.104716

Wu, Y. J., Antone, B., DeChurch, L., & Contractor, N. (2023). Information sharing in a hybrid workplace: Understanding the role of ease-of-use perceptions of communication technologies in advice-seeking relationship maintenance. *Journal of Computer-Mediated Communication, 28*(4), zmad025. DOI: 10.1093/jcmc/zmad025

Yeşil, S. (2011). Sanal takımlar: Kritik başarı faktörleri üzerine derinlemesine bir bakış ve bir değerlendirme. *Journal of Graduate School of Social Sciences, 15*(1).

Yıldız, F. Z. (2025). İnsan kaynakları yönetiminde yapay zeka: Uygulamalar ve gelecek yönelimleri üzerine kapsamlı bir çalışma. *Yönetim Bilimleri Dergisi, 23*(57), 1569–1594. DOI: 10.35408/comuybd.1569970

Yılmaz, C. (2023). Uzaktan çalışma kabusu: İnsan kaynakları yöneticilerinin uzaktan çalışmada kullandıkları uzaktan denetim mekanizmaları. *Journal of Mehmet Akif Ersoy University Economics and Administrative Sciences Faculty, 10*(3), 1956–1975.

Yost, A. B., Behrend, T. S., Howardson, G., Darrow, J. B., & Jensen, J. M. (2018). Reactance to electronic surveillance: A test of antecedents and outcomes. *Journal of Business and Psychology, 34*(1), 71–86. DOI: 10.1007/s10869-018-9532-2

Yozi, K., & Mbokota, S. (2024). Leadership for the future: Empowering virtual teams with emotional intelligence. *Journal of Leadership & Organizational Development, 43*(2), 189–204.

Yurdasever, E. (2024). İşletmelerde çalışanlara yönelik duygu analizinin uygulanması: Potansiyel faydalar ve zorluklar. *Ömer Halisdemir Üniversitesi İktisadi ve İdari Bilimler Fakültesi Dergisi, 17*(3), 462–488.

Zárate-Torres, R., Rey-Sarmiento, C. F., Acosta-Prado, J. C., Gómez-Cruz, N. A., Rodríguez Castro, D. Y., & Camargo, J. (2025). Influence of leadership on human–artificial intelligence collaboration. *Behavioral Sciences (Basel, Switzerland), 15*(7), 873. DOI: 10.3390/bs15070873 PMID: 40723657

Zhang, X., Qian, J., Wang, B., & Chen, M. (2020). The role of reward omission in empowering leadership and employee outcomes: A moderated mediation model. *Human Resource Management Journal*, *30*(2), 226–243. DOI: 10.1111/1748-8583.12260

Zhou, L., Zhang, L., & Konz, N. (2022). Computer vision techniques in manufacturing. *IEEE Transactions on Systems, Man, and Cybernetics. Systems*, *53*(1), 105–117. DOI: 10.1109/TSMC.2022.3166397

KEY TERMS AND DEFINITIONS

AI-Driven Decision Support: Analytical processes in which AI systems provide predictions that inform managerial choices while relying on human oversight.

Algorithmic Management: The use of AI-driven systems to monitor, evaluate, and coordinate employee tasks and behaviors.

Artificial Intelligence–Augmented Leadership: Leaders' use of AI systems to enhance decision-making, communication, and coordination processes while maintaining human responsibility and judgment.

Electronic Performance Monitoring (EPM): Technology-based tracking of employee activities used to assess performance but often associated with privacy concerns and reduced psychological safety.

Empathy Constraints in AI: The limitations of AI systems in interpreting and responding to complex human emotions, due to their reliance on generalized patterns rather than lived human experience.

Human–AI Interaction Competence: The leader's ability to interpret, coordinate, and evaluate AI-generated information while aligning technological outputs with organizational values and team needs.

Visibility Bias: A systematic distortion that occurs when employee performance is judged based on physical presence rather than actual contribution, disadvantaging remote or less visible workers.

Chapter 2
Augmenting Empathetic Leadership Through Agentic AI:
Redefining Human-AI Collaboration in the Workplace

Ramadevi Vitthal Salunkhe
http://orcid.org/0009-0005-0247-0115
G.H. Raisoni College of Engineering, Nagpur, India

Smita Dattatray Salunkhe
http://orcid.org/0009-0006-3625-9868
KES Society Rajarambapu Institute of Technology, India

Jyotsna S. Gawai
K.D.K. College of Engineering, Nagpur, India

Yogeshri Dayaram Choudhari
K.D.K. College of Engineering, Nagpur, India

Sanket Ashok Joshi
http://orcid.org/0009-0003-0699-7569
St. Vincent Pallotti College of Engineering and Technology, Nagpur, India

Roshan Ramesh Kolte
http://orcid.org/0009-0005-1861-8399
K.D.K. College of Engineering, Nagpur, India

Pradnya Sumit Moon
St. Vincent Pallotti College of Engineering and Technology, Nagpur, India

Manisha Dyneshwar Raut
http://orcid.org/0009-0008-0645-9134
G.H. Raisoni College of Engineering, Nagpur, India

DOI: 10.4018/979-8-3373-6650-0.ch002

ABSTRACT

This chapter examines how intelligent digital systems can support empathetic and ethically grounded leadership in contemporary organizations. As artificial intelligence becomes embedded in managerial decision-making, leadership practices risk emphasizing efficiency over human well-being. Drawing on emotional intelligence, ethical leadership, and relational leadership theories, this chapter per the authors presents a human-centered framework in which intelligent systems act as context-aware support tools that enhance leaders' ethical reflection and inclusive decision-making while preserving human authority through human-in-the-loop governance.

1. INTRODUCTION

The contemporary workplace is undergoing a profound transformation driven by rapid technological advancement, increasing workforce diversity, and heightened expectations for ethical and human-centered leadership. In this evolving organizational landscape, leaders are no longer evaluated solely on their ability to achieve performance targets or manage operational complexity. Instead, growing emphasis is placed on leaders' capacity to demonstrate empathy, ethical sensitivity, and responsiveness to the emotional and psychological needs of employees. This shift has positioned empathetic leadership as a critical competency for sustaining trust, engagement, and long-term organizational effectiveness, particularly in complex and digitally mediated organizational contexts (Ashkanasy & Daus, 2005; Brown & Treviño, 2006; Greer et al., 2018).

AI-driven systems are increasingly deployed to support recruitment, performance evaluation, service delivery, and strategic decision-making, offering benefits such as efficiency, scalability, and consistency (Faraj et al., 2018; Jarrahi, 2018). Despite these advantages, scholars have raised significant concerns regarding AI's implications for human agency, ethical accountability, and the quality of leader–employee relationships. In particular, algorithmic decision-making in managerial contexts risks depersonalizing leadership processes by prioritizing efficiency and optimization over emotional, relational, and moral considerations that are essential for human-centered leadership (Hancock et al., 2011; Raisch & Krakowski, 2021).

Most organizational AI applications to date have been designed as decision-support or automation tools, focusing on prediction, classification, and optimization. These systems typically operate reactively on predefined inputs and historical data, with limited capacity to interpret social context, emotional nuance, or ethical complexity. As a result, conventional AI tools are poorly suited to supporting leadership functions that require empathy, ethical judgment, and sensitivity to individual and cultural differences (Miller, 2019; Bryson, 2018). This limitation has contributed to a growing scholarly consensus that leadership contexts require new forms of AI designed to augment rather than constrain human leadership capabilities.

Recent advances in agentic AI offer a promising alternative. Agentic AI refers to intelligent systems capable of autonomous, goal-directed behaviour, contextual reasoning, and adaptive learning while operating within human-defined ethical and organizational constraints (Frankish & Ramsey, 2014; Dignum, 2019). Unlike conventional AI tools, agentic AI systems can proactively identify emerging patterns, anticipate risks, and engage in ongoing interaction with human users. These characteristics position agentic AI as a collaborative partner in leadership processes, capable of supporting leaders in sense-making, ethical reflection, and informed decision-making without displacing human authority or accountability.

To illustrate this conceptual shift, Figure 1 provides an overview of the evolution from traditional AI-supported management to agentic AI–augmented empathetic leadership. The figure highlights the chapter's central argument: rather than functioning as a decision-making substitute, agentic AI operates as an augmentation layer that enhances leaders' awareness of emotional, ethical, and relational dynamics while preserving human judgment, responsibility, and oversight.

Figure 1. Evolution from Traditional AI-Supported Management to Agentic AI–Augmented Empathetic Leadership

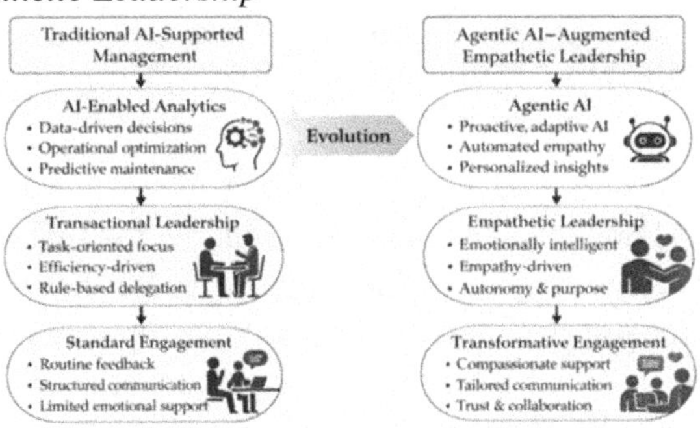

Empathetic leadership is grounded in established leadership theories, including emotional intelligence, ethical leadership, authentic leadership, and servant leadership, all of which emphasize attentiveness to human experience, moral responsibility, and relational engagement (Avolio & Gardner, 2005; Greenleaf, 2002; Mayer et al., 2008). However, sustaining empathy becomes increasingly challenging in digitally mediated and hybrid work environments, where leaders rely on indirect and fragmented cues to assess employee well-being and engagement. These challenges are further amplified in large and geographically distributed organizations, where leaders manage diverse teams across cultural, temporal, and organizational boundaries.

To clarify how AI adoption reshapes leadership practice, Table 1 summarizes the key differences between conventional AI-supported leadership and agentic AI–augmented empathetic leadership across dimensions relevant to managerial decision-making. The comparison demonstrates a shift from efficiency-driven, reactive decision support toward leadership practices that balance performance with human well-being, ethical sensitivity, and trust-building.

Table 1. Leadership Characteristics in Conventional AI-Supported and Agentic AI–Augmented Contexts

Aspect	Conventional AI-Supported Leadership	Agentic AI–Augmented Empathetic Leadership
Leadership Focus	Efficiency and performance optimization	Human well-being and ethical performance balance
AI Role	Reactive decision-support tool	Proactive, context-aware collaborator
Emotional Sensitivity	Minimal consideration of emotions	Emotion- and sentiment-aware insights
Decision Style	Predominantly data-driven	Data-informed with human empathy
Context Awareness	Limited situational understanding	Adaptive to social and organizational context
Human Control	Potential over-reliance on automation	Human-in-the-loop authority preserved
Ethical Integration	External compliance-based ethics	Embedded ethical and transparency mechanisms
Employee Trust	Risk of depersonalization	Trust-enhancing and inclusive leadership

While agentic AI presents significant opportunities to enhance empathetic leadership, it also introduces important ethical considerations. Scholars caution against risks such as emotional surveillance, algorithmic bias, opacity, and over-reliance on automated recommendations if AI systems are not governed responsibly (Bryson, 2018; Floridi et al., 2018; Dignum, 2019). These concerns underscore the necessity of embedding ethical principles, transparency, and human-in-the-loop governance mechanisms into AI-enabled leadership systems.

Against this backdrop, this chapter examines how agentic AI can be leveraged to augment empathetic leadership in organizational settings. Rather than framing AI as a substitute for human leaders, the chapter conceptualizes agentic AI as an intelligent partner that enhances leaders' capacity for emotional awareness, ethical reflection, and inclusive decision-making. By integrating insights from leadership theory, organizational research, and responsible AI scholarship, the chapter advances a structured, human-centered perspective on redefining human–AI collaboration in the workplace.

Novel Contribution of the Chapter.

This chapter contributes to the literature by:

i. Conceptualizing agentic AI as an empathy-augmenting leadership collaborator rather than a decision substitute;
ii. Integrating leadership theory with human–AI collaboration and responsible AI governance; and
iii. Proposing a human-centered framework that guides the ethical and effective deployment of agentic AI in organizational leadership contexts.

2. THEORETICAL FOUNDATIONS OF EMPATHETIC LEADERSHIP

Empathetic leadership is grounded in a well-established body of organizational and leadership theory that emphasizes emotional awareness, ethical responsibility, and relational engagement. Rather than representing a departure from classical leadership models, empathetic leadership synthesizes insights from emotional intelligence theory, ethical leadership, servant leadership, and relational perspectives. These theoretical foundations explain why empathy is central to effective leadership and why it must be preserved as organizations increasingly integrate data-driven and AI-enabled decision-making into managerial practice (Ashkanasy & Daus, 2005; Brown & Treviño, 2006; Avolio & Gardner, 2005).

2.1 Emotional Intelligence and Empathy in Leadership

Emotional intelligence (EI) theory constitutes a foundational pillar of empathetic leadership and leadership effectiveness (Goleman, 1998). EI refers to the ability to perceive, understand, regulate, and appropriately respond to emotions in oneself and others (Ashkanasy & Daus, 2005; Mayer et al., 2008). Extensive empirical research demonstrates that leaders with high emotional intelligence are better equipped to recognize emotional cues, manage interpersonal conflict, and foster psychologically safe environments that support engagement and well-being (Greer et al., 2018).

Empathy represents the relational application of emotional intelligence in leadership practice. While EI provides the cognitive capacity to interpret emotions, empathetic leadership involves translating emotional awareness into considerate action, such as supportive communication, fair decision-making, and responsiveness to employee concerns. Empirical studies consistently link emotionally intelligent and empathetic leadership with higher levels of trust, ethical conduct, and organizational commitment (Ashkanasy & Daus, 2005; Brown & Treviño, 2006).

In digitally mediated and data-intensive work environments, leaders increasingly rely on indirect indicators—such as communication patterns, engagement metrics, and performance signals—to infer employee emotions. This shift increases the cognitive demands placed on leaders and creates conditions where AI-based systems may support emotional sense-making, provided that human judgment remains central (Miller, 2019; Raisch & Krakowski, 2021).

2.2 Transformational, Authentic, and Servant Leadership Perspectives

Empathetic leadership is closely aligned with transformational leadership theory, which emphasizes individualized consideration and attention to followers' unique needs, values, and aspirations (Avolio & Gardner, 2005). Transformational leaders must understand employees' perspectives to motivate, inspire, and develop them effectively, making empathy a core leadership capability rather than an auxiliary skill.

Authentic leadership further reinforces empathy through its emphasis on self-awareness, relational transparency, and values-based action. Authentic leaders build trust by aligning internal values with external behavior and engaging openly with diverse viewpoints, particularly during periods of organizational uncertainty and change (Avolio & Gardner, 2005). Empathy enables such leaders to recognize emotional undercurrents and respond in ways that enhance legitimacy and credibility.

Similarly, servant leadership theory places empathy at the ethical core of leadership practice. Servant leaders prioritize the growth, well-being, and dignity of followers, viewing leadership as a moral responsibility rather than a position of authority (Greenleaf, 2002; Liden et al., 2008). This perspective positions empathy as both a relational mechanism and a normative obligation that guides leadership behavior.

To synthesize these perspectives, Table 2 summarizes the major leadership theories that underpin empathetic leadership, highlighting their core emphases and relevance for empathy-driven leadership practice.

Table 2. Leadership Theories Underpinning Empathetic Leadership

Leadership Theory	Core Emphasis	Relevance to Empathetic Leadership
Emotional Intelligence Theory	Perception and regulation of emotions	Forms the cognitive and emotional basis for empathy and emotional awareness.
Transformational Leadership	Individualized consideration and inspiration	Encourages understanding of individual needs and personalized leadership support.
Authentic Leadership	Self-awareness and relational transparency	Reinforces trust, openness, and empathy-driven leader–follower relationships.
Servant Leadership	Service, care, and follower well-being	Positions empathy as a moral and ethical leadership responsibility.
Ethical Leadership	Fairness, integrity, and accountability	Integrates empathy into ethical decision-making and stakeholder sensitivity.
Relational Leadership	Leadership as a social process	Highlights empathy as essential for interaction, collaboration, and shared meaning.
Social Exchange Theory	Reciprocity and trust	Explains how empathetic behaviour strengthens leader–member relationships.

2.3 Ethical Leadership and Moral Foundations

Ethical leadership theory provides a critical normative foundation for empathetic leadership. Ethical leaders are characterized by fairness, integrity, accountability, and concern for stakeholder well-being, and they actively consider the human consequences of organizational decisions (Brown & Treviño, 2006). Empathy strengthens ethical leadership by enabling leaders to anticipate how decisions affect individuals and groups, particularly those with limited power or voice.

From an ethical standpoint, empathy supports moral reasoning by facilitating perspective-taking and sensitivity to contextual factors. Scholars caution that leadership decisions driven purely by efficiency or algorithmic optimization risk ethical blindness if emotional and social considerations are ignored (Bryson, 2018; Floridi et al., 2018). This concern becomes especially salient in AI-augmented leadership contexts, where decision-making processes may become opaque or overly technical.

2.4 Relational and Social Exchange Perspectives

Relational leadership theories conceptualize leadership as a dynamic process that emerges through ongoing social interaction rather than formal authority alone. Within this framework, empathy functions as a mechanism for building shared understanding, managing power asymmetries, and sustaining cooperative relationships (Uhl-Bien, 2006).

Social exchange theory further explains how empathetic leadership strengthens leader–member relationships through reciprocity. When leaders demonstrate empathy, fairness, and concern, employees are more likely to respond with trust, commitment, and discretionary effort, reinforcing positive relational cycles that enhance team effectiveness and organizational cohesion (Greer et al., 2018).

In technology-mediated leadership environments, these relational dynamics can be weakened if decision-making becomes overly automated or impersonal. This highlights the importance of designing AI-supported leadership systems that reinforce, rather than erode, relational engagement.

2.5 Empathetic Leadership in Digitally Mediated Work Environments

The rise of digital communication platforms, remote work, and algorithmic systems has fundamentally altered how leaders perceive and respond to employee emotions. In digitally mediated environments, leaders often rely on indirect signals—such as communication frequency, engagement metrics, or performance indicators—to infer employee well-being (Hancock et al., 2011; Jarrahi, 2018). This shift increases the cognitive and emotional demands placed on leaders and complicates the enactment of empathy at scale.

Figure 2 illustrates how emotional intelligence, ethical reasoning, and relational leadership jointly form the theoretical foundation of empathetic leadership in digitally mediated organizations. The figure emphasizes that empathy remains a human capability, even as technological systems shape leadership contexts.

Figure 2. Theoretical Foundations of Empathetic Leadership in Digitally Mediated Organizations

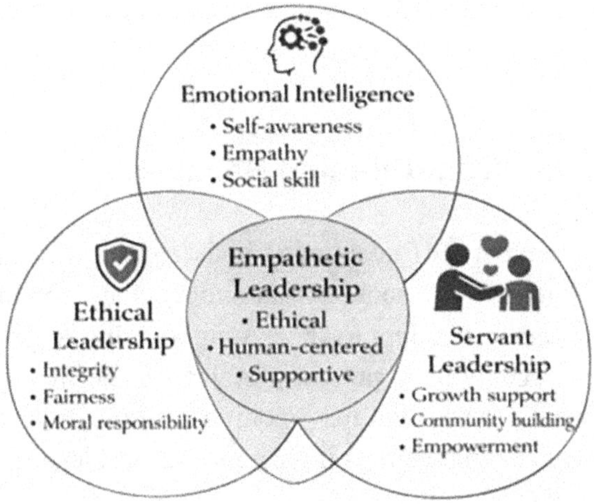

While these theories remain highly relevant, their application in technology-intensive workplaces reveals practical limitations. Leaders may struggle to consistently interpret emotional cues or balance competing demands across large and diverse teams. This theoretical and practical gap provides a clear justification for exploring how agentic AI systems can support leaders in sustaining empathy without diminishing human judgment, ethical responsibility, or relational accountability.

3. AGENTIC AI: CAPABILITIES AND DISTINGUISHING CHARACTERISTICS

The rapid advancement of artificial intelligence has produced a diverse ecosystem of intelligent systems ranging from rule-based automation to advanced machine learning models. While conventional AI systems have been successfully deployed for predictive analytics and process optimization, their applicability to leadership contexts remains limited. Leadership—particularly empathetic leadership—requires sensitivity to context, relational dynamics, and ethical nuance, dimensions that traditional AI systems are not inherently designed to address (Miller, 2019; Raisch & Krakowski, 2021). In response to these limitations, agentic AI has emerged as a distinct paradigm emphasizing autonomy, contextual reasoning, and adaptive interaction with human users.

Agentic AI refers to intelligent systems capable of pursuing delegated goals through proactive and goal-directed behaviour while operating within human-defined ethical and operational constraints (Frankish & Ramsey, 2014; Dignum, 2019). Unlike conventional AI tools that rely on predefined inputs and static models, agentic AI systems continuously interact with their environment, interpret multidimensional data, and adapt their behaviour over time. These capabilities make agentic AI particularly relevant for leadership augmentation, where dynamic sense-making and contextual awareness are essential.

3.1 Autonomy and Goal-Directed Behaviour

A defining characteristic of agentic AI is its capacity for autonomous, goal-directed action. In leadership contexts, autonomy does not imply independent decision authority; rather, it refers to the system's ability to proactively generate insights and recommendations in pursuit of objectives defined by human leaders. For example, an agentic AI system may monitor patterns in communication flow, workload distribution, or engagement indicators and alert leaders to emerging risks such as burnout or disengagement.

Goal-directed behaviour enables agentic AI systems to balance multiple objectives simultaneously, including productivity, employee well-being, and ethical considerations. By surfacing trade-offs among competing goals, agentic AI supports reflective leadership judgment rather than purely efficiency-driven decision-making. Importantly, the prioritization and interpretation of these trade-offs remain under human control.

Similar distinctions between predictive automation and adaptive, context-aware AI systems have been observed in applied domains such as intelligent automation and data-driven system design (Dhawas et al., 2024a; Dhawas et al., 2024b).

3.2 Contextual and Emotional Awareness

Contextual awareness is another distinguishing capability of agentic AI. Leadership decisions are embedded within complex social, organizational, and temporal contexts, including team dynamics, organizational culture, and situational constraints. Agentic AI systems are designed to interpret data within such contexts, enabling more situationally appropriate and timely insights.

In leadership applications, contextual awareness often extends to emotional and behavioural indicators. Although agentic AI does not possess emotions, it can analyze patterns in language use, interaction frequency, and behavioural signals to infer shifts in workforce sentiment (Miller, 2019). When interpreted by human leaders, such insights can support timely and empathetic interventions without replacing human emotional judgment.

Figure 3 illustrates the layered intelligence architecture of agentic AI systems, highlighting how data processing, contextual interpretation, and adaptive reasoning interact to support leadership sense-making.

Figure 3. Layered Capabilities of Agentic AI for Leadership Augmentation

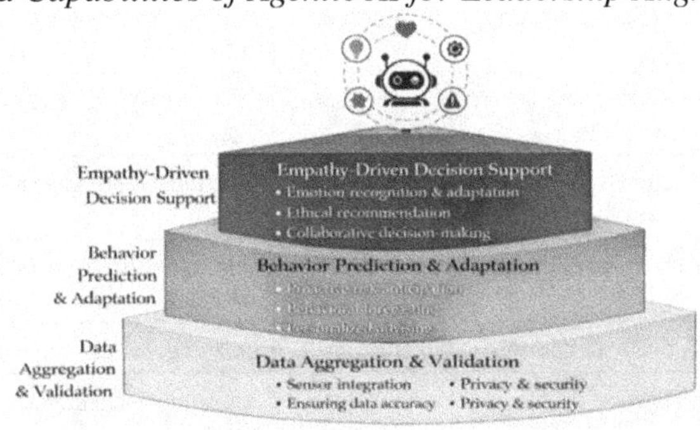

3.3 Adaptive Learning and Human Feedback

Agentic AI systems are further distinguished by their capacity for adaptive learning through ongoing interaction with human users and organizational environments. Unlike static models trained exclusively on historical data, agentic AI systems refine their behaviour based on feedback, observed outcomes, and evolving contextual conditions. This adaptive capability allows the system to align more closely with organizational values and leadership priorities over time.

Human-in-the-loop mechanisms play a central role in governing adaptive learning. By enabling leaders to validate, modify, or reject AI-generated insights, organizations can preserve human accountability while benefiting from AI-supported reflection and sense-making (Dignum, 2019; IEEE, 2019). Such collaborative learning processes mitigate risks associated with over-automation and bias reinforcement.

3.4 Distinguishing Agentic AI from Conventional AI Systems

To clarify the unique contribution of agentic AI in leadership contexts, Table 3 compares conventional AI systems with agentic AI across dimensions relevant to empathetic leadership. The comparison highlights differences in autonomy, contextual awareness, learning capability, and interaction style, illustrating why agentic AI is more suitable for leadership augmentation than traditional decision-support tools.

Table 3. Distinguishing Characteristics of Conventional AI and Agentic AI in Leadership Contexts

Dimension	Conventional AI Systems	Agentic AI Systems
Primary Purpose	Prediction, classification, and process automation	Goal-directed leadership support and sense-making
Autonomy Level	Operates only upon explicit user input	Proactively initiates actions within defined constraints
Context Awareness	Limited situational and organizational understanding	Interprets social, temporal, and organizational context
Emotional Sensitivity	Minimal consideration of emotional dynamics	Integrates sentiment and behavioral indicators
Learning Capability	Static or periodically updated models	Continuously adapts through interaction and feedback
Interaction Style	One-way or query-based interaction	Ongoing, collaborative human–AI interaction
Role in Leadership	Efficiency-focused decision-support tool	Empathy-aware leadership augmentation partner
Human Agency	Risk of over-reliance on automation	Human-in-the-loop authority explicitly preserved
Ethical Integration	Ethics managed externally through policy	Ethics embedded via transparency and governance mechanisms

This comparison underscores that, whereas conventional AI prioritizes efficiency and prediction, agentic AI emphasizes collaboration, adaptability, and contextual understanding—qualities that align with human-centered leadership paradigms.

3.5 Implications for Empathetic Leadership

The capabilities of agentic AI position it as a potential enabler of empathetic leadership in digitally mediated workplaces. By supporting leaders in recognizing emerging emotional patterns, anticipating ethical risks, and reflecting on decision consequences, agentic AI can enhance leadership effectiveness without undermining human agency. However, realizing this potential requires deliberate system design, transparent governance, and a clear delineation of human and machine roles.

This section establishes the technological foundation for understanding how agentic AI can complement empathetic leadership. The following section builds on this foundation by examining models of human–AI collaboration that ensure AI remains a supportive partner rather than an autonomous authority in leadership decision-making.

4. HUMAN–AI COLLABORATION IN LEADERSHIP CONTEXTS

As artificial intelligence becomes increasingly embedded in organizational decision-making, the nature of leadership is shifting from solitary judgment toward collaborative intelligence, where human leaders and intelligent systems jointly contribute to sense-making and action. In leadership contexts, this collaboration is particularly consequential because decisions often involve ethical trade-offs, emotional implications, and long-term relational consequences. Empathetic leadership, therefore, requires a human–AI collaboration model that enhances insight without diluting human agency or moral responsibility.

4.1 From Automation to Augmentation

Early organizational uses of AI focused primarily on automation—reducing human involvement in repetitive or data-intensive tasks. While automation delivers efficiency gains, scholars have argued that leadership functions are ill-suited to full automation due to their reliance on judgment, values, and empathy (Jarrahi, 2018; Raisch & Krakowski, 2021). As a result, a shift toward augmentation has gained prominence, wherein AI systems support rather than replace human decision-makers.

In augmentation-oriented models, AI provides analytical depth, pattern recognition, and scenario simulation, while human leaders retain responsibility for interpretation, ethical reasoning, and final decision-making. This division of labor is especially important for empathetic leadership, where understanding emotional nuance and contextual meaning cannot be fully delegated to algorithms.

4.2 Collaborative Sense-Making and Decision Support

Human–AI collaboration in leadership can be understood as a process of collaborative sense-making, where AI systems help surface insights that inform human reflection. Agentic AI systems can analyze large volumes of organizational data—such as communication patterns, engagement indicators, or service interactions—and identify trends that may signal stress, disengagement, or inequity. These insights can prompt leaders to engage more attentively with employees and consider empathetic interventions.

However, the value of such insights depends on how they are presented and interpreted. Research on trust in automation emphasizes that leaders must understand AI system limitations to avoid blind reliance or inappropriate skepticism (Hancock et al., 2011; Lee & See, 2004). Transparent explanations and interpretable outputs are therefore essential for effective collaboration (Miller, 2019).

Figure 4 illustrates a human–AI collaborative leadership loop, highlighting continuous interaction, feedback, and reflection between leaders and agentic AI systems.

Figure 4. Human–AI Collaborative Leadership Loop for Empathetic Decision-Making

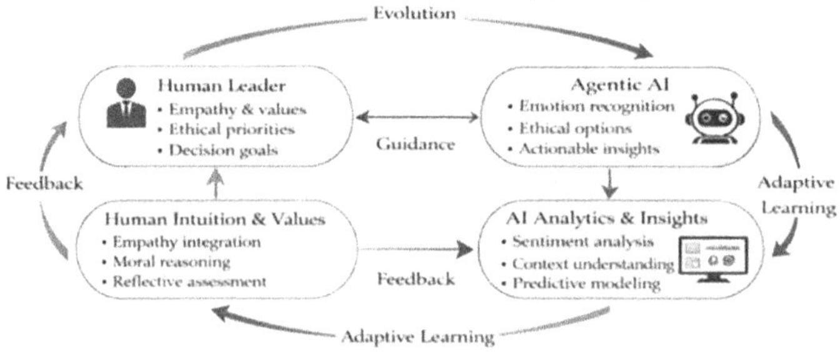

4.3 Human-in-the-Loop Governance

A central principle of responsible human–AI collaboration is human-in-the-loop governance, which ensures that humans remain actively involved in monitoring, validating, and guiding AI-supported decisions. Effective human–AI collaboration also depends on leaders' AI literacy and institutional readiness to interpret, question, and govern intelligent systems responsibly (Salunkhe et al., 2026).

In leadership contexts, this principle safeguards ethical accountability and preserves leaders' authority over decisions that affect people's livelihoods and well-being (Dignum, 2019; IEEE, 2019).

Human-in-the-loop mechanisms enable leaders to:

- Review AI-generated insights and recommendations
- Question assumptions or data sources
- Override or modify AI suggestions
- Provide feedback that shapes future system behaviour

Such mechanisms are particularly important when AI systems incorporate emotional or behavioral data, as misinterpretation can lead to unintended harm or perceptions of surveillance (Bryson, 2018; Floridi et al., 2018).

4.4 Trust Calibration and Role Clarity

Effective human–AI collaboration depends on appropriate trust calibration—neither excessive reliance on AI outputs nor undue dismissal of algorithmic insights.

Research suggests that trust in intelligent systems is shaped by perceived competence, transparency, and alignment with human values (Hancock et al., 2011). In leadership contexts, trust calibration is facilitated when the roles of humans and AI are clearly defined.

Agentic AI systems should be positioned as advisory partners that enhance leaders' awareness rather than authoritative decision-makers. Clear role boundaries help ensure that empathy remains a human responsibility, supported—but not substituted—by AI-generated insights.

Table 4 summarizes key elements of effective human–AI collaboration for empathetic leadership.

Table 4. Elements of Effective Human–AI Collaboration in Empathetic Leadership

Collaboration Element	Description	Relevance to Empathetic Leadership
Human-in-the-Loop Control	Human leaders review, validate, and override AI recommendations.	Preserves moral responsibility and empathetic judgment.
Role Clarity	Clear distinction between AI advisory role and human decision authority.	Prevents erosion of leadership accountability and trust.
Transparency and Explainability	AI systems provide interpretable and understandable outputs.	Enables leaders to reflect on emotional and ethical implications.
Trust Calibration	Balanced reliance on AI based on system reliability and context.	Avoids over-automation and supports informed empathy.
Context-Aware Insights	AI recommendations account for organizational and social context.	Enhances situational empathy and fairness.
Feedback and Adaptation	Leaders provide feedback that shapes AI behavior over time.	Aligns AI support with organizational values and culture.
Ethical Safeguards	Embedded governance, bias monitoring, and data protection.	Protects employee dignity and prevents misuse of emotional data.

4.5 Implications for Empathetic Leadership Practice

Human–AI collaboration offers a pathway to scaling empathetic leadership in complex, data-rich organizational environments. By supporting leaders in recognizing emotional patterns, reflecting on ethical implications, and anticipating relational consequences, agentic AI can enhance leadership effectiveness without undermining human judgment. At the same time, collaboration models must be carefully designed to prevent over-automation, preserve trust, and respect employee dignity.

This section underscores that empathetic leadership in the age of AI is not a matter of choosing between human or machine intelligence, but of designing collaboration that amplifies human values. The next section builds on this collaborative foundation by presenting a structured framework for augmenting empathetic leadership using agentic AI.

5. FRAMEWORK FOR AUGMENTING EMPATHETIC LEADERSHIP USING AGENTIC AI

While empathetic leadership is grounded in well-established leadership theories, its consistent application in complex, data-intensive, and digitally mediated organizations presents significant challenges. Leaders must balance performance pressures with ethical responsibility while attending to the emotional needs of increasingly diverse and distributed workforces. To address these challenges, this section proposes a structured framework that integrates agentic AI as a supportive mechanism for enhancing empathetic leadership without displacing human judgment or moral accountability.

5.1 Rationale for a Human-Centered Framework

The adoption of AI in leadership contexts necessitates a shift from tool-centric to human-centered system design. Research on responsible AI emphasizes that intelligent systems should be aligned with human values, social norms, and ethical principles rather than optimized solely for efficiency (Dignum, 2019; Floridi et al., 2018). In leadership applications, this alignment is particularly critical, as decisions influence employee well-being, trust, and organizational culture.

The proposed framework positions agentic AI as an augmentation layer that enhances leaders' situational awareness, emotional insight, and reflective capacity. Rather than automating leadership decisions, the framework emphasizes collaboration, transparency, and continuous human oversight.

5.2 Framework Components

The framework comprises five interrelated layers, each designed to support empathetic leadership while maintaining clear boundaries between human and machine roles.

(1) Human Leadership Values and Intent

At the foundation of the framework are the values, ethical commitments, and strategic intentions articulated by human leaders. These values guide the objectives assigned to agentic AI systems and define acceptable boundaries for AI-supported analysis and recommendation.

(2) Emotional and Organizational Data Inputs

Agentic AI systems draw on diverse data sources, including organizational metrics, communication patterns, and engagement indicators. Importantly, data collection is governed by ethical safeguards to ensure transparency, consent, and privacy protection (Bryson, 2018; IEEE, 2019).

(3) Agentic AI Reasoning and Adaptation Layer

In this layer, agentic AI integrates data with contextual and temporal information to identify patterns, anticipate risks, and generate insights. Adaptive learning mechanisms allow the system to refine its recommendations based on human feedback and evolving organizational contexts.

(4) Empathy-Aware Recommendations

Rather than producing prescriptive decisions, the AI generates empathy-aware recommendations that highlight potential emotional, ethical, and relational implications. These recommendations are designed to prompt reflection and dialogue rather than dictate action.

(5) Human Reflection and Ethical Judgment

The final layer centres on human leaders, who interpret AI-supported insights through the lens of empathy, ethical reasoning, and situational understanding. Leaders retain full authority over decisions and are accountable for outcomes.

Figure 5 illustrates the proposed framework for augmenting empathetic leadership using agentic AI.

Figure 5. Human-Centered Framework for Agentic AI–Augmented Empathetic Leadership

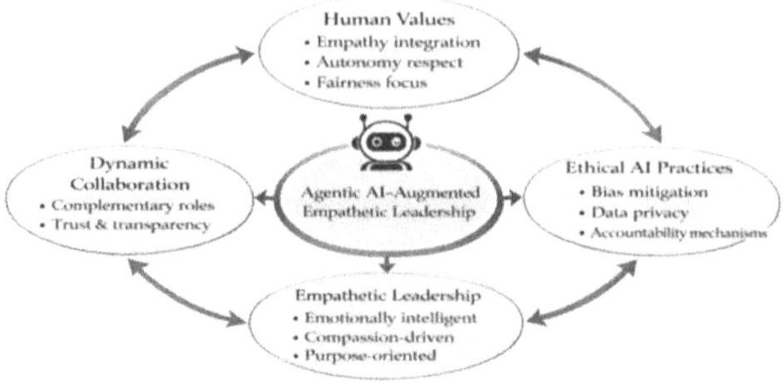

5.3 Operationalization of the Framework

For the framework to be effective in practice, organizations must integrate it into existing leadership processes and governance structures. This includes establishing clear policies for data use, defining accountability mechanisms, and providing leaders with training to interpret AI-generated insights responsibly. Human-in-the-loop governance ensures that AI systems remain aligned with organizational values and do not drift toward purely efficiency-driven objectives (Raisch & Krakowski, 2021).

Table 5 maps the framework components to leadership objectives and AI functions.

Table 5. Alignment of Framework Components with Leadership Objectives

Framework Component	Leadership Objective	Role of Agentic AI
Human Leadership Values and Intent	Ensure value-driven and ethical leadership direction	Align AI goals with human-defined values and constraints
Emotional and Organizational Data Inputs	Enhance awareness of employee well-being and dynamics	Aggregate and analyze ethically sourced organizational data
Agentic AI Reasoning Layer	Support informed and balanced decision-making	Integrate context, patterns, and feedback to generate insights
Empathy-Aware Recommendations	Promote emotionally and ethically sensitive leadership actions	Highlight potential human and relational implications
Human Reflection and Ethical Judgment	Preserve accountability and moral responsibility	Enable leaders to accept, modify, or reject AI suggestions
Feedback and Governance Mechanisms	Maintain trust and continuous alignment	Adapt system behavior based on human input and oversight

5.4 Illustrative Application of the Framework

To demonstrate how the proposed framework operates in practice, this subsection presents a brief illustrative example of agentic AI–augmented empathetic leadership in an organizational setting.

Consider a mid-sized technology organization operating in a hybrid work environment, where teams are distributed across multiple locations. A senior manager overseeing a cross-functional team observes declining participation in virtual meetings and an increase in project delays. Conventional performance dashboards indicate reduced productivity but do not reveal the underlying causes of these patterns.

Applying the proposed framework, the leader engages with an agentic AI system configured to support leadership sense-making rather than automated decision-making. Guided by human-defined leadership values and ethical constraints (Layer 1), the agentic AI analyzes ethically sourced organizational data such as communication patterns, workload distribution, and engagement indicators (Layer 2). Through contextual reasoning and adaptive learning (Layer 3), the system identifies a pattern of uneven workload allocation and emerging signs of burnout among specific team members.

Rather than prescribing actions, the agentic AI generates empathy-aware recommendations (Layer 4), prompting the leader to reflect on potential emotional and relational implications of continued workload imbalance. The system also highlights ethical considerations related to data sensitivity and the need for human validation, reinforcing the leader's accountability.

In the final stage (Layer 5), the leader interprets these insights through direct dialogue with team members. One-to-one conversations reveal increased role ambiguity and sustained workload pressure following recent organizational changes. In response, the leader redistributes tasks, clarifies role expectations, and introduces flexible deadlines. These actions are accompanied by transparent communication and support mechanisms aimed at restoring trust and psychological safety.

Throughout this process, the agentic AI system adapts based on leader feedback and evolving team dynamics, refining its future insights while remaining subordinate to human judgment. Final decisions regarding communication, workload redistribution, and employee support remain firmly human-led.

This illustrative example demonstrates how the proposed framework enables agentic AI to function as an empathetic leadership augmentation mechanism, supporting awareness, reflection, and ethical consideration without displacing human authority or responsibility.

5.5 Benefits and Safeguards

The proposed framework offers several benefits for empathetic leadership, including enhanced situational awareness, improved ethical sensitivity, and scalable support across large organizations. At the same time, it incorporates safeguards to mitigate risks related to bias, surveillance, and over-automation. By embedding transparency, feedback, and ethical oversight into the framework, organizations can leverage agentic AI to strengthen—not erode—human-centered leadership.

This framework provides a practical and conceptual foundation for deploying agentic AI in leadership contexts. The next section builds on this foundation by examining organizational applications and use cases, illustrating how the framework can be applied across different leadership scenarios.

6. ORGANIZATIONAL APPLICATIONS AND USE CASES OF AGENTIC AI–AUGMENTED EMPATHETIC LEADERSHIP

The practical value of agentic AI in leadership contexts lies in its ability to translate conceptual principles into actionable organizational practices. Empathetic leadership, while widely endorsed in theory, is often difficult to sustain consistently across large, diverse, and digitally mediated organizations. Agentic AI offers a means to support leaders in addressing this challenge by enhancing situational awareness, ethical sensitivity, and relational responsiveness across multiple leadership domains.

6.1 Employee Well-Being and Engagement Monitoring

One of the most immediate applications of agentic AI–augmented empathetic leadership is in monitoring employee well-being and engagement. Contemporary organizations generate extensive digital traces through communication platforms, collaboration tools, and workflow systems. When analyzed responsibly, these data can reveal patterns related to workload imbalance, disengagement, or emotional strain, reflecting broader shifts toward AI-enabled, human-centered service augmentation in organizational contexts (Faraj et al., 2018; Huang & Rust, 2018).

Agentic AI systems can proactively detect early signals of burnout or declining morale and alert leaders to potential concerns. Importantly, such systems do not replace direct human interaction; instead, they serve as an early-warning mechanism that prompts empathetic dialogue and timely intervention. By highlighting trends rather than individual surveillance, agentic AI supports leaders in adopting preventive and compassionate leadership practices while respecting employee dignity (Bryson, 2018; Dignum, 2019). Concerns related to surveillance, monitoring, and ethical oversight in AI-enabled organizational systems have been widely discussed in emerging research on intelligent surveillance and governance frameworks (Bhagat et al., 2025).

Similar uses of AI for continuous performance assessment and data-driven organizational oversight have been widely documented in professional domains such as accounting and auditing, underscoring the importance of transparency, responsibility, and ethical governance when deploying such systems in leadership contexts (Hasan, 2022).

6.2 Illustrative Scenario: Agentic AI–Supported Leadership in a Hybrid Workplace

Consider a mid-sized knowledge-intensive organization operating in a hybrid work environment, where employees alternate between remote and on-site work. The leadership team deploys an agentic AI system integrated with collaboration platforms, workflow management tools, and employee feedback channels. The system is designed to analyze aggregated and anonymized interaction patterns, such as meeting frequency, after-hours communication, response delays, and task completion rhythms, while adhering to strict privacy and ethical governance guidelines.

Over several weeks, the agentic AI system detects emerging patterns indicative of potential burnout within a cross-functional project team. These signals include increased workload concentration on specific individuals, prolonged online activity beyond regular working hours, and a gradual decline in collaborative engagement. Rather than issuing prescriptive recommendations or initiating automated interventions, the system generates a high-level alert for the team leader, accompanied by interpretable insights that explain the observed trends.

In response, the leader initiates empathetic engagement by scheduling individual check-ins and facilitating an open team discussion focused on workload balance and well-being. Based on these conversations, the leader redistributes responsibilities, introduces flexible deadlines, and encourages collective norms around availability and recovery time. The agentic AI system continues to monitor subsequent interaction patterns, providing feedback on whether the implemented changes contribute to improved engagement and reduced strain.

This scenario illustrates how agentic AI functions as an early-warning and decision-support mechanism rather than a substitute for human judgment. Empathy, moral reasoning, and contextual understanding remain firmly within the leader's domain, while AI augments situational awareness and supports timely, compassionate intervention. By maintaining human-in-the-loop oversight and emphasizing transparency and trust, agentic AI enables leadership practices that are both data-informed and deeply human-centered.

6.3 Inclusive and Fair Decision-Making

Empathetic leadership also involves ensuring fairness and inclusivity in organizational decisions. Bias—whether conscious or unconscious—can undermine trust and exacerbate inequality, particularly in high-stakes areas such as performance evaluation, promotion, and task allocation. Research has shown that AI systems, if poorly designed, can amplify existing biases; however, when governed responsibly, they can also help surface inequities that may otherwise go unnoticed (Jobin et al., 2019; Floridi et al., 2018).

Agentic AI can support empathetic leadership by identifying patterns of uneven workload distribution, differential performance feedback, or exclusion from opportunities across demographic or functional groups. These insights enable leaders to reflect on systemic issues and implement corrective actions grounded in empathy and ethical responsibility rather than reactive compliance.

6.4 Leadership Support in Hybrid and Remote Work Environments

The expansion of hybrid and remote work has significantly altered how leaders engage with employees. Physical distance reduces access to informal cues such as body language and spontaneous conversation, making it more difficult to assess emotional states and team dynamics. In such contexts, agentic AI can help leaders reconstruct situational awareness by synthesizing communication patterns, collaboration frequency, and engagement indicators.

Figure 6 illustrates how agentic AI supports empathetic leadership in hybrid and remote work environments by acting as a contextual awareness layer between digital interaction data and human leadership judgment.

Figure 6. Agentic AI Support for Empathetic Leadership in Hybrid Work Environments

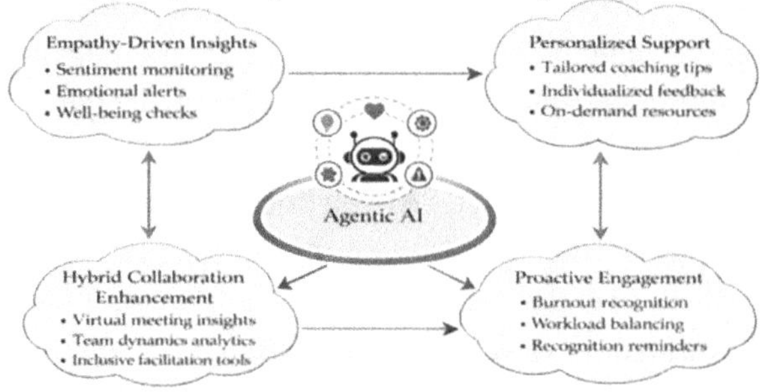

By providing context-aware insights rather than prescriptive decisions, agentic AI enables leaders to remain attentive and responsive despite reduced physical proximity.

6.5 Ethical Risk Anticipation and Leadership Reflection

Leadership decisions often involve ethical trade-offs with long-term consequences for organizational culture and employee trust. Agentic AI systems can support ethical leadership by simulating potential outcomes of alternative decisions and highlighting associated ethical risks. This reflective function aligns with ethical leadership principles, which emphasize foresight, accountability, and stakeholder consideration (Brown & Treviño, 2006).

For example, before implementing cost-reduction measures or restructuring initiatives, agentic AI can assist leaders in anticipating impacts on employee morale, trust, and psychological safety. Such anticipatory insight encourages leaders to engage in empathetic deliberation rather than purely cost-driven decision-making.

6.6 Summary of Organizational Use Cases

The diverse applications of agentic AI demonstrate its potential to support empathetic leadership across multiple organizational domains. However, the effectiveness of these applications depends on responsible design, transparent governance, and clear role boundaries between human leaders and AI systems.

Table 6 provides a summary of key organizational use cases, leadership objectives, and the role of agentic AI in supporting empathetic leadership.

Table 6. Organizational Applications of Agentic AI for Empathetic Leadership

Organizational Application	Leadership Objective	Role of Agentic AI
Employee Well-Being Monitoring	Identify early signs of stress and disengagement	Detect patterns and alert leaders for empathetic intervention
Inclusive Decision-Making	Promote fairness and equity in leadership actions	Highlight bias patterns and uneven opportunity distribution
Hybrid and Remote Team Leadership	Maintain emotional awareness across distributed teams	Synthesize digital interaction and engagement indicators
Ethical Risk Anticipation	Anticipate human and ethical consequences of decisions	Simulate scenarios and surface ethical trade-offs
Leadership Reflection and Development	Enhance self-awareness and empathetic capability	Provide feedback-supported insights for reflective learning
Organizational Culture Assessment	Sustain trust and psychological safety	Identify cultural trends affecting employee experience

7. ETHICAL CHALLENGES AND GOVERNANCE CONSIDERATIONS

The integration of agentic AI into leadership contexts presents significant ethical challenges that extend beyond technical performance and efficiency. While agentic AI offers opportunities to augment empathetic leadership, its deployment also introduces risks related to bias, transparency, accountability, and employee autonomy. Addressing these challenges requires robust governance mechanisms that ensure AI systems reinforce, rather than undermine, ethical and human-centered leadership practices.

7.1 Bias, Fairness, and Representation

One of the most widely recognized ethical concerns associated with AI systems is the risk of bias. AI models trained on historical organizational data may inadvertently reflect and amplify existing inequalities related to gender, race, seniority, or role visibility. In leadership contexts, such biases can have profound implications, particularly when AI-generated insights influence evaluations, promotions, or workload distribution (Jobin et al., 2019).

From the perspective of empathetic leadership, biased AI outputs not only undermine fairness but also erode trust and psychological safety. Leaders must therefore treat AI-generated insights as indicators for reflection rather than objective truths. Continuous auditing, diverse data representation, and human validation are essential to mitigate bias and preserve ethical integrity (Floridi et al., 2018; Dignum, 2019).

7.2 Transparency and Explainability

Transparency is a foundational requirement for ethical human–AI collaboration. Leaders must be able to understand how AI systems generate insights and recommendations in order to assess their relevance and limitations. Explainable AI principles emphasize the importance of interpretable outputs that allow users to trace the reasoning behind algorithmic suggestions (Arrieta et al., 2020; Miller, 2019).

In leadership settings, explainability supports empathetic decision-making by enabling leaders to contextualize AI insights within broader emotional, social, and ethical considerations. Lack of transparency, by contrast, risks promoting uncritical reliance on algorithmic outputs or skepticism that undermines potential benefits.

Figure 7 illustrates the relationship between transparency, trust, and ethical leadership outcomes in AI-augmented environments.

Figure 7. Transparency–Trust–Ethics Relationship in AI-Augmented Leadership

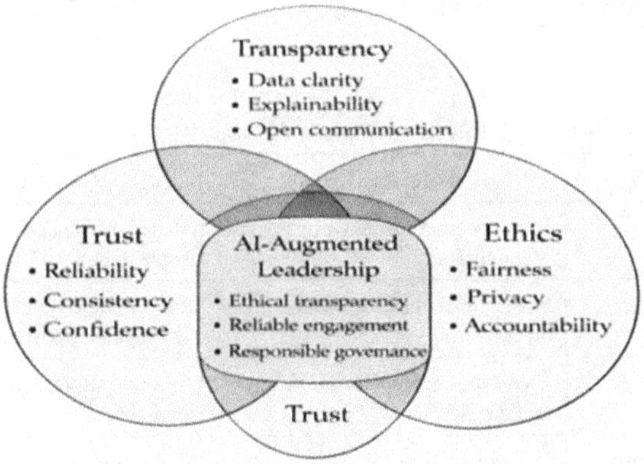

7.3 Privacy, Surveillance, and Employee Dignity

Agentic AI systems often rely on behavioral and interaction data to infer organizational patterns. While such data can support empathetic leadership, they also raise concerns about privacy, surveillance, and consent. Excessive or opaque data collection may lead employees to perceive AI-supported leadership as intrusive or controlling, thereby undermining trust and autonomy (Bryson, 2018).

Ethical governance frameworks emphasize the importance of data minimization, informed consent, and purpose limitation when deploying AI systems that analyze human behavior (IEEE, 2019). Leaders must ensure that AI-supported insights are used to support well-being and fairness rather than monitoring or disciplining employees.

7.4 Accountability and Human Oversight

Maintaining accountability in AI-augmented leadership is critical to ethical governance. While agentic AI systems may generate recommendations or highlight risks, responsibility for decisions must remain with human leaders. Delegating accountability to algorithms risks moral disengagement and weakens ethical leadership (Brown & Treviño, 2006).

Human-in-the-loop governance mechanisms ensure that leaders remain actively involved in reviewing, interpreting, and acting upon AI-supported insights. Such mechanisms reinforce the principle that AI systems are advisory tools rather than autonomous decision-makers.

Table 7 summarizes key ethical challenges associated with agentic AI in leadership and corresponding governance responses.

Table 7. Ethical Challenges and Governance Responses in AI-Augmented Leadership

Ethical Challenge	Potential Risk	Governance Response
Algorithmic Bias	Reinforcement of existing inequalities	Regular bias audits and diverse data representation
Lack of Transparency	Reduced trust and blind reliance on AI outputs	Explainable models and interpretable decision support
Privacy and Surveillance	Erosion of employee autonomy and dignity	Data minimization, informed consent, and access controls
Accountability Ambiguity	Diffusion of moral responsibility	Clear human-in-the-loop oversight and role definitions
Over-Automation	Reduced empathetic judgment and reflection	AI positioned as advisory, not decision-making authority
Misinterpretation of Emotional Data	Inaccurate or harmful leadership responses	Contextual validation and human review of AI insights
Ethical Drift Over Time	Misalignment with organizational values	Continuous governance reviews and feedback mechanisms

7.5 Establishing Responsible AI Governance Structures

Effective governance of agentic AI requires formal structures that integrate ethical principles into system design, deployment, and evaluation. Responsible AI governance includes multidisciplinary oversight committees, regular impact assessments, and ongoing stakeholder engagement (Floridi et al., 2018; IEEE, 2019).

By embedding governance mechanisms into organizational processes, leaders can ensure that agentic AI supports empathetic leadership while respecting human dignity, fairness, and accountability. Such governance structures are not merely compliance mechanisms; they are integral to sustaining trust and legitimacy in AI-augmented leadership environments. Similar governance challenges have been identified in advanced AI-driven scientific and technological systems, where adaptive learning and automation necessitate continuous human oversight and ethical validation (Salunkhe et al., 2026).

8. CHALLENGES, LIMITATIONS, AND FUTURE RESEARCH DIRECTIONS

While agentic AI presents promising opportunities to augment empathetic leadership, its application in organizational contexts is accompanied by several conceptual, technical, ethical, and governance-related challenges. Recognizing these limitations is essential to avoid technological determinism and to ensure that AI-supported leadership remains ethically grounded, human-centered, and contextually appropriate. This section critically examines the boundaries of agentic AI in leadership, including theoretical constraints, risks of over-automation, and concerns related to transparency and accountability, and uses these insights to outline key directions for future research and responsible design.

8.1 Conceptual and Theoretical Limitations

One of the primary conceptual challenges lies in the inherent distinction between human empathy and algorithmic approximation of emotional states. Empathy involves subjective experience, moral imagination, and situational judgment—capabilities that remain uniquely human. Although agentic AI systems can identify patterns in emotional and behavioral data, they do not possess genuine emotional understanding. Overstating AI's empathetic capability risks conflating emotional inference with moral sensitivity, potentially leading to misguided leadership practices and reinforcing the need to critically examine AI behavior as a distinct socio-technical phenomenon (Mayer et al., 2008; Bryson, 2018; Rahwan et al., 2019).

Furthermore, leadership theories emphasize that empathy is relational and context-dependent. Translating these nuanced theoretical constructs into computational representations may oversimplify complex human experiences. Future theoretical work must therefore clarify the boundaries between empathy augmentation and empathy substitution, ensuring that AI is framed as a supportive mechanism rather than an emotional surrogate.

8.2 Technical and Data-Related Constraints

From a technical perspective, agentic AI systems rely heavily on the quality, representativeness, and interpretation of organizational data. Incomplete or biased datasets may result in misleading insights that adversely affect leadership decisions (Jobin et al., 2019). Emotional and behavioral signals are particularly vulnerable to misinterpretation, as they are shaped by cultural norms, communication styles, and situational factors.

Additionally, adaptive learning systems may exhibit model drift over time, where changes in organizational behaviour reduce the accuracy or relevance of AI-generated insights. Continuous monitoring, validation, and recalibration are therefore necessary to maintain alignment between AI outputs and organizational realities (Floridi et al., 2018).

8.3 Organizational and Cultural Barriers

Organizational readiness represents another significant limitation. Leaders and employees may differ in their acceptance of AI-supported leadership, influenced by prior experiences, trust in technology, and perceptions of surveillance. Resistance may emerge if AI systems are perceived as intrusive, opaque, or misaligned with organizational values (Hancock et al., 2011).

Cultural variability further complicates the deployment of empathetic AI-supported leadership. Expressions of emotion, leadership expectations, and ethical norms vary across cultural contexts, limiting the generalizability of AI models trained within specific organizational or regional settings. This variability underscores the importance of localized adaptation and culturally sensitive governance structures.

8.4 Ethical and Governance Challenges

Despite the presence of governance frameworks, ethical challenges remain persistent and evolving. The dynamic nature of agentic AI systems necessitates ongoing ethical oversight rather than one-time compliance checks. Leaders must remain vigilant against subtle forms of ethical drift, where efficiency pressures gradually overshadow empathetic and ethical considerations (Raisch & Krakowski, 2021).

Moreover, maintaining clear accountability in hybrid human–AI decision-making processes continues to be a challenge. As AI systems become more sophisticated, distinguishing between human judgment and algorithmic influence may become increasingly difficult, reinforcing the need for explicit responsibility attribution and transparent decision documentation (Dignum, 2019; IEEE, 2019).

8.5 Directions for Future Research

Future research should prioritize empirical validation of agentic AI–augmented empathetic leadership models using primary data. Longitudinal studies examining leadership outcomes, employee trust, and well-being over time would provide valuable insights into the sustained impact of AI-supported empathy.

Cross-cultural research is also essential to understand how empathetic leadership augmentation operates across diverse organizational and cultural contexts. Additionally, experimental and mixed-methods studies could explore employee perceptions of AI-supported leadership and identify conditions under which such systems enhance or undermine trust.

Finally, future research should investigate leadership development implications, examining how interaction with agentic AI systems influences leaders' self-awareness, ethical reflection, and emotional competence. Such inquiry would contribute to a deeper understanding of how human and artificial intelligence can co-evolve in ethically responsible ways.

9. IMPLICATIONS OF AGENTIC AI–AUGMENTED EMPATHETIC LEADERSHIP

The integration of agentic AI into leadership practices carries important implications for managers, organizations, policymakers, and society at large. By positioning agentic AI as an augmentation mechanism rather than a replacement for human judgment, this chapter highlights how technology can be leveraged to enhance empathetic leadership while preserving ethical responsibility and human agency.

9.1 Managerial and Practical Implications

For organizational leaders, the findings of this chapter underscore the importance of adopting agentic AI as a decision-support and sense-making partner rather than an automated authority. Leaders should use agentic AI systems to enhance awareness of emotional, relational, and ethical dynamics within teams, particularly in digitally mediated and hybrid work environments where direct cues are limited.

Managers can leverage agentic AI to:

- identify early signals of employee stress, disengagement, or workload imbalance;
- support reflective decision-making by surfacing trade-offs between performance, well-being, and ethical considerations; and
- enable more inclusive leadership by drawing attention to perspectives or groups that may otherwise remain underrepresented.

However, effective use of agentic AI requires leaders to maintain active involvement in interpretation and action. Organizations should therefore invest in leadership development programs that strengthen emotional intelligence, ethical reasoning, and digital literacy, ensuring that leaders are equipped to critically engage with AI-generated insights rather than relying on them unreflectively.

9.2 Organizational and Governance Implications

At the organizational level, the adoption of agentic AI necessitates robust governance structures that clearly delineate the roles and responsibilities of human leaders and intelligent systems. Human-in-the-loop mechanisms must be institutionalized to preserve accountability, transparency, and trust in leadership decision-making processes.

Organizations should establish:

- clear policies defining the scope and limits of agentic AI autonomy;
- mechanisms for monitoring bias, unintended consequences, and system drift; and
- transparent documentation of how AI-supported insights are generated and used in leadership decisions.

Embedding ethical principles directly into the design and deployment of agentic AI systems can further support responsible leadership practices. Such governance approaches not only mitigate risk but also enhance employee trust by signaling that technology is used to support, rather than surveil or control, the workforce.

9.3 Policy and Regulatory Implications

From a policy perspective, the growing use of agentic AI in leadership contexts raises important questions regarding accountability, transparency, and worker protection. Regulators and policymakers should recognize that leadership-related AI applications differ fundamentally from purely operational or technical systems, as they influence human relationships, well-being, and organizational culture.

Policy frameworks should therefore:

- require transparency and explainability for AI systems used in managerial and evaluative contexts;
- mandate human oversight in leadership and people-management applications of AI; and
- promote standards that safeguard employee dignity, privacy, and autonomy.

Such policies can help ensure that advances in agentic AI contribute to more humane and ethical workplaces rather than reinforcing existing power asymmetries or biases.

9.4 Social and Ethical Implications

Beyond organizations, the use of agentic AI in leadership carries broader social implications. When deployed responsibly, agentic AI has the potential to support more empathetic, inclusive, and psychologically safe work environments. By enhancing leaders' awareness of employee experiences, AI-augmented leadership may contribute to improved well-being, reduced burnout, and more equitable organizational practices. Human-centered AI design principles have also been explored in applied smart systems that balance personalization, sustainability, and user well-being, reinforcing the importance of designing AI that supports human flourishing rather than efficiency alone (Salunkhe et al., 2026).

At the same time, ethical risks such as emotional surveillance, excessive monitoring, and erosion of human judgment must be carefully managed. Ensuring that agentic AI systems respect individual privacy and are used to empower rather than control employees is critical for maintaining social legitimacy and trust.

10. CONCLUSION

The accelerating integration of artificial intelligence into organizational decision-making has fundamentally reshaped leadership practices, creating both opportunities and challenges for human-centered management. This chapter has argued that, rather than diminishing the role of empathy in leadership, emerging forms of agentic AI can be strategically designed to augment empathetic leadership when embedded within responsible governance structures and human-in-the-loop frameworks. Empathetic leadership remains an inherently human capability, grounded in emotional intelligence, ethical reasoning, and relational engagement (Ashkanasy & Daus, 2005; Brown & Treviño, 2006).

By synthesizing leadership theory with advances in AI research, the chapter demonstrated that agentic AI differs significantly from conventional AI systems in its capacity for contextual reasoning, adaptive learning, and proactive support. These characteristics position agentic AI as a collaborative partner capable of enhancing leaders' situational awareness, ethical sensitivity, and reflective judgment without displacing human authority or moral accountability (Frankish & Ramsey, 2014; Raisch & Krakowski, 2021).

The proposed framework for agentic AI–augmented empathetic leadership underscores the importance of aligning technological capabilities with human values and organizational culture. Rather than automating leadership decisions, the framework emphasizes augmentation—where AI systems provide empathy-aware insights that inform, rather than dictate, leadership action. Such an approach addresses longstanding concerns related to algorithmic bias, transparency, and over-reliance on automated systems by preserving the central role of human judgment and responsibility (Dignum, 2019; Floridi et al., 2018).

Organizational applications discussed in this chapter illustrate that agentic AI can support empathetic leadership across diverse domains, including employee well-being, inclusive decision-making, hybrid work management, and ethical risk anticipation. However, these benefits are contingent upon responsible data practices, transparent system design, and continuous ethical oversight. Without such safeguards, AI-supported leadership risks reinforcing inequities, eroding trust, and undermining employee dignity (Bryson, 2018; Jobin et al., 2019).

In conclusion, empathetic leadership in the age of AI is not a question of human versus machine intelligence, but of how human and artificial intelligence can be integrated responsibly. Agentic AI offers a pathway to scaling empathy and ethical awareness in complex organizational environments, provided it is deployed as a supportive collaborator rather than an autonomous authority. By centering human values, accountability, and ethical reflection, organizations can leverage agentic AI to strengthen—not replace—the human foundations of leadership.

Future Research Directions

Future research should advance this agenda by:

- conducting longitudinal studies to examine how agentic AI–supported leadership influences empathy, trust, and employee well-being over time;
- exploring privacy-preserving approaches, such as federated or decentralized learning, to enable leadership analytics while safeguarding employee autonomy and data protection;
- developing regulatory and governance frameworks that clarify accountability, transparency, and ethical responsibility in agentic AI–augmented leadership systems.

Together, these directions can support the evolution of agentic AI that is not only technologically robust but also socially legitimate, ethically grounded, and aligned with human-centered leadership principles.

REFERENCES

Arrieta, A. B., Díaz-Rodríguez, N., Del Ser, J., Bennetot, A., Tabik, S., Barbado, A., Garcia, S., Gil-López, S., Molina, D., Benjamins, R., Chatila, R., & Herrera, F. (2020). Explainable artificial intelligence (XAI): Concepts, taxonomies, opportunities and challenges toward responsible AI. *Information Fusion*, *58*, 82–115. DOI: 10.1016/j.inffus.2019.12.012

Ashkanasy, N. M., & Daus, C. S. (2005). Rumors of the death of emotional intelligence in organizational behavior are vastly exaggerated. *Journal of Organizational Behavior*, *26*(4), 441–452. DOI: 10.1002/job.320

Avolio, B. J., & Gardner, W. L. (2005). Authentic leadership development: Getting to the root of positive forms of leadership. *The Leadership Quarterly*, *16*(3), 315–338. DOI: 10.1016/j.leaqua.2005.03.001

Bhagat, D., Hanwate, A., Salunkhe, R. V., Jagyasi, T., Sardare, P., & Sahu, M. (2025). *Future perspectives on surveillance systems*. IGI Global., DOI: 10.4018/979-8-3693-6996-8.ch014

Brown, M. E., & Treviño, L. K. (2006). Ethical leadership: A review and future directions. *The Leadership Quarterly*, *17*(6), 595–616. DOI: 10.1016/j.leaqua.2006.10.004

Bryson, J. J. (2018). Patiency is not a virtue: The design of intelligent systems and systems of ethics. *Ethics and Information Technology*, *20*(1), 15–26. DOI: 10.1007/s10676-018-9448-6

Dhawas, P., Bondade, A., Patil, S., Khandare, K. S., & Salunkhe, R. V. (2024 b). *Intelligent automation in marketing*. IGI Global., DOI: 10.4018/979-8-3693-3354-9.ch003

Dhawas, P., Ramteke, M. A., Thakur, A., Polshetwar, P. V., Salunkhe, R. V., & Bhagat, D. (2024 a). *Big data analysis techniques: Data preprocessing techniques, data mining techniques, machine learning algorithm, visualization*. IGI Global., DOI: 10.4018/979-8-3693-0413-6.ch007

Dignum, V. (2019). *Responsible artificial intelligence: How to develop and use AI in a responsible way* (1st ed.). Springer., DOI: 10.1007/978-3-030-30371-6

Faraj, S., Pachidi, S., & Sayegh, K. (2018). Working and organizing in the age of the learning algorithm. *Information and Organization*, *28*(1), 62–70. DOI: 10.1016/j.infoandorg.2018.02.005

Floridi, L., Cowls, J., Beltrametti, M., Chatila, R., Chazerand, P., Dignum, V., Luetge, C., Madelin, R., Pagallo, U., Rossi, F., Schafer, B., & Vayena, E. (2018). AI4People—An ethical framework for a good AI society: Opportunities, risks, principles, and recommendations. *Minds and Machines*, *28*(4), 689–707. DOI: 10.1007/s11023-018-9482-5 PMID: 30930541

Frankish, K., & Ramsey, W. M. (Eds.). (2014). *The Cambridge handbook of artificial intelligence*. Cambridge University Press. DOI: 10.1017/CBO9781139046855

Goleman, D. (1998). What makes a leader? *Harvard Business Review*, *76*(6), 93–102. PMID: 10187249

Greenleaf, R. K. (2002). *Servant leadership: A journey into the nature of legitimate power and greatness* (L. C. Spears, Ed.; illustrated & annotated ed.). Paulist Press.

Greer, L. L., de Jong, B. A., Schouten, M. E., & Dannals, J. E. (2018). Why and when hierarchy impacts team effectiveness: A meta-analytic integration. *The Journal of Applied Psychology*, *103*(6), 591–613. DOI: 10.1037/apl0000291 PMID: 29369654

Hancock, P. A., Billings, D. R., Schaefer, K. E., Chen, J. Y. C., de Visser, E. J., & Parasuraman, R. (2011). A meta-analysis of factors affecting trust in human–robot interaction. *Human Factors*, *53*(5), 517–527. DOI: 10.1177/0018720811417254 PMID: 22046724

Hasan, A. (2022). Artificial intelligence (AI) in accounting and auditing: A literature review. *Open Journal of Business and Management*, *10*(1), 440–465. DOI: 10.4236/ojbm.2022.101026

Huang, M.-H., & Rust, R. T. (2018). Artificial intelligence in service. *Journal of Service Research*, *21*(2), 155–172. DOI: 10.1177/1094670517752459

Jarrahi, M. H. (2018). Artificial intelligence and the future of work: Human–AI symbiosis in organizational decision making. *Business Horizons*, *61*(4), 577–586. DOI: 10.1016/j.bushor.2018.03.007

Jobin, A., Ienca, M., & Vayena, E. (2019). The global landscape of AI ethics guidelines. *Nature Machine Intelligence*, *1*(9), 389–399. DOI: 10.1038/s42256-019-0088-2

Lee, J. D., & See, K. A. (2004). Trust in automation: Designing for appropriate reliance. *Human Factors*, *46*(1), 50–80. DOI: 10.1518/hfes.46.1.50.30392 PMID: 15151155

Liden, R. C., Wayne, S. J., Zhao, H., & Henderson, D. (2008). Servant leadership: Development of a multidimensional measure and multi-level assessment. *The Leadership Quarterly*, *19*(2), 161–177. DOI: 10.1016/j.leaqua.2008.01.006

Mayer, J. D., Salovey, P., & Caruso, D. R. (2008). Emotional intelligence: New ability or eclectic traits? *The American Psychologist*, *63*(6), 503–517. DOI: 10.1037/0003-066X.63.6.503 PMID: 18793038

Miller, T. (2019). Explanation in artificial intelligence: Insights from the social sciences. *Artificial Intelligence*, *267*, 1–38. DOI: 10.1016/j.artint.2018.07.007

Rahwan, I., Cebrian, M., Obradovich, N., Bongard, J., Bonnefon, J.-F., Breazeal, C., Crandall, J. W., Christakis, N. A., Couzin, I. D., Jackson, M. O., Jennings, N. R., Kamar, E., Kloumann, I. M., Larochelle, H., Lazer, D., McElreath, R., Mislove, A., Parkes, D. C., Pentland, A. S., & Wellman, M. (2019). Machine behaviour. *Nature*, *568*(7753), 477–486. DOI: 10.1038/s41586-019-1138-y PMID: 31019318

Raisch, S., & Krakowski, S. (2021). Artificial intelligence and management: The automation–augmentation paradox. *Academy of Management Review*, *46*(1), 192–210. DOI: 10.5465/amr.2018.0072

Salunkhe, R. V., Joshi, S. A., Mane, P. D., Irkhede, T., Deosarkar, K. S., & Nausheen, I. (2026). *AI-powered personalization in smart kitchens: Adaptive cooking systems for health, taste, and sustainability*. IGI Global., DOI: 10.4018/979-8-3373-4042-5.ch009

Salunkhe, R. V., Raut, C. A., Chimote, G., Sarwate, S., Kolte, R. R., Ingole, P. K., & Kuthe, A. (2026). *Scaling faculty AI literacy: Strategic models for institutional transformation and sustainable adoption*. IGI Global., DOI: 10.4018/979-8-3373-4129-3.ch012

Salunkhe, R. V., Sathe, T. R., Shete, R. M., Wagh, P., Kolte, R., & Raut, R. (2026). *Nanomaterials discovery using AI-based technology accelerators: Innovation through predictive modeling and intelligent experimentation*. IGI Global., DOI: 10.4018/979-8-3373-2883-6.ch005

Uhl-Bien, M. (2006). Relational leadership theory: Exploring the social processes of leadership and organizing. *The Leadership Quarterly*, *17*(6), 654–676. DOI: 10.1016/j.leaqua.2006.10.007

KEY TERMS AND DEFINITIONS

Agentic AI: A class of artificial intelligence systems capable of autonomous, goal-directed, and proactive behaviour, with the ability to reason contextually, adapt through learning, and operate within human-defined ethical and operational constraints.

AI-Augmented Leadership: A leadership model in which AI systems support, enhance, and inform human decision-making without replacing human judgment, accountability, or ethical responsibility.

Automation–Augmentation Paradox: The tension between using AI to automate tasks for efficiency and using AI to augment human capabilities without diminishing human agency, judgment, or empathy.

Context-Aware Intelligence: The capability of AI systems to interpret data within social, organizational, temporal, and cultural contexts rather than relying solely on isolated quantitative indicators.

Conventional AI: Traditional AI systems primarily designed for prediction, classification, optimization, and automation, typically operating reactively on pre-defined inputs and historical data.

Digital or Hybrid Work Environment: Organizational settings characterized by remote, virtual, or technology-mediated interactions that reduce access to direct emotional cues and increase reliance on digital signals.

Emotion- and Sentiment-Aware Insights: AI-generated analyses that infer patterns related to workforce emotions or sentiment using behavioral, linguistic, or interaction data, intended to support empathetic reflection rather than automated judgment.

Emotional Intelligence (EI): The ability of individuals, particularly leaders, to perceive, understand, regulate, and appropriately respond to their own emotions and the emotions of others in organizational contexts.

Empathetic Leadership: A leadership approach that emphasizes understanding, sensitivity, and responsiveness to employees' emotional, psychological, and social needs while balancing ethical responsibility and organizational performance.

Empathy: The relational application of emotional intelligence that involves perspective-taking, emotional awareness, and compassionate action toward others' experiences and concerns.

Empathy-Aware Recommendations: AI-generated suggestions that explicitly highlight potential emotional, ethical, and relational consequences of leadership decisions rather than prescribing specific actions.

Ethical Governance: Organizational structures, policies, and oversight mechanisms that guide the ethical design, deployment, monitoring, and evaluation of AI systems in leadership contexts.

Ethical Leadership: A leadership framework characterized by fairness, integrity, accountability, and concern for stakeholder well-being, integrating moral reasoning into organizational decision-making.

Ethical Risk Anticipation: The use of analytical tools, including agentic AI, to forecast potential ethical, emotional, and relational consequences of leadership decisions before they are implemented.

Explainable AI (XAI): AI systems designed to provide interpretable and understandable explanations for their outputs, enabling users to assess reliability, limitations, and ethical implications.

Human–AI Collaboration: A cooperative interaction model in which human leaders and AI systems jointly contribute to sense-making, reflection, and decision support, with clearly defined roles and authority boundaries.

Human-in-the-Loop: A governance principle ensuring that human leaders remain actively involved in reviewing, validating, and making final decisions based on AI-generated insights or recommendations.

Relational Leadership: A leadership perspective that views leadership as a socially constructed process emerging through interaction, relationships, and shared meaning rather than formal authority alone.

Responsible AI: An approach to AI design and deployment that prioritizes transparency, fairness, accountability, privacy protection, and alignment with human values and societal norms.

Social Exchange Theory: A theoretical framework explaining leader–member relationships as reciprocal exchanges, where empathetic behaviour fosters trust, commitment, and cooperative effort.

Chapter 3 Designing the Human–AI Partnership in Leadership: Towards Building Safe, Transparent, and Empathetic Work Environments

Tanusree Chakraborty
http://orcid.org/0000-0003-0322-3990
Administrative Staff College of India, India

Rituparna Basak
http://orcid.org/0000-0003-4483-7841
Muralidhar Girls' College, India

Koushik Vedula
http://orcid.org/0009-0003-7836-6096
Administrative Staff College of India, India

S. K. Pooja
http://orcid.org/0009-0005-2012-841X
Administrative Staff College of India, India

ABSTRACT

The chapter discusses the opportunities of human-AI collaboration that has the potential to transform leadership by incorporating trust, transparency, psychological safety, and empathy to AI-powered workplaces. With AI becoming more and more involved in making decisions, developing and supporting staff, as well as running

DOI: 10.4018/979-8-3373-6650-0.ch003

business activities, leaders need to make sure that technology will not replace human control and interaction. The chapter looks into explainable and ethical AI systems, AI-based processes that bolster psychological safety and introductions of empathy scaffolds that facilitate leader development. It also examines organizational preparedness, governance needs as well as hybrid leadership models that compromise human intuition and algorithmic insight. The chapter is practical as it provides useful guidelines that can be used to create the safe, transparent and empathetic environments of AI-enabled leadership by introducing a holistic, human-centered framework.

1. INTRODUCTION

Organizational life is fast changing under the onrush of AI paradigms. While AI offers predictive insights, decision-support, and developmental tools, its role in human-centered leadership raises critical questions of trust, transparency, and empathy (Mann, 2024). Leadership today is no longer just about vision and direction—it is about co-creating environments where people feel valued and protected in the sense that algorithms can be just parts of certain decisions (Pandey, 2025) not all. Yet, the promise of AI-enabled leadership can only be realized if the design of human-AI collaboration is maintained. That is to say, trust should be placed in AI only when it can explain itself and is bound by *ethical guidelines*, *psychological safety* implying that that employees should not be relegated or laid in alienation with AI interventions; and *empathy*, which has at least until now been able to be unleashed only by humans, should also be engineered into AI-based leadership development tools to help make them more approachable and inclusive (Ryan, 2020).

In the case of leadership development, AI opens up new opportunities never seen before (Sposato, 2024). Adaptive learning systems, AI-based coaching, sentiment analysis and emotionally intelligent agents are able to simulate challenging interpersonal situations, individualize developmental paths, and recognize behavioral patterns that humans can ignore (Annapareddy et al., 2025). The innovations can make leadership development more democratic, offering scalable, data-driven, and emotionally sensitive learning experiences. However, they also bring up the issues of over-reliance, authenticity, and the moral application of psycho-behavioral information. The leaders should thus learn the ways in making use of these tools together in critical, responsible and empathetic ways. It becomes important to develop an empathetic AI mindset where technology serves to enhance human bonding, expand self-understanding, and build on what leadership values and feels important.

AI Empathy Scaffolds are guided artificial intelligence-based support tools, which can be used to help leaders to build and practise empathetic behaviours using structured feedback, personal emotional analytics, and through simulated interpersonal interactions. These systems do not substitute the role of human empathy, instead, they are considered as developmental tools, with the help of which the leaders can understand the signs of emotion, contemplate the communication trends, and enhance the responsiveness of relations under the complicated organizational conditions. Based on the notion of scaffolding in the learning theory, AI empathy scaffolds are transient cognitive and behavioral support systems based on the AI coaching agents, sentiment analysis system, and adaptive learning platform. The tools assist the leaders in being more conscious of emotional interactions within teams and engage in empathetic reactions within psychologically safe settings. Nevertheless, the creation of emotional meaning, sense of morality and genuine human bonding rests in the hands of those in leadership.

In order to be able to use AI empathy scaffolds responsibly in terms of their application in leadership development, one should define the scope between technological support and the innate human abilities. Although AI systems can assist the leaders in analysing behavioural patterns, creating insights and offering structured learning environments, they are not able to mimic real human empathy or moral judgment. AI thus can serve as an augmentative tool that enhances emotional awareness but not relational intelligence in human beings. The development of effective leadership could not happen without a balanced model where AI helps in learning and reflection and human leaders continue to be in charge of understanding emotions, make ethical choices, and create trust in teams. The AI systems are especially handy when it comes to recognising the behavioural patterns and delivering the data-based outcomes that could otherwise not be observed in the intricate organizational context. Yet empathy invariably depends on contextual awareness, rational judgment, and authentic emotion—capacities unique to humans. Hence, the adoption of AI within leadership development should be based on the concept of human-in-the-loop where AI enables guidance and feedback, and there is judgment, compassion, and relational sensitivity among the leaders.

Although the literature on AI in management has studied separately trust (Omrani et al., 2022; Afroogh et al., 2024), psychological safety (Shen et al., 2025) and empathy (Rubin et al., 2024) as design principles within AI-assisted leadership development, there has been scant attention on integrating them together. Most research looks at efficiency and performance, neglecting these softer human-related concerns upon which resting long-term organizational health may be constructed. This chapter, in filling this gap, conceptualizes empathetic AI integration as a leadership imperative giving a framework for industries to responsibly embed AI into leadership practices.

The literature does not include holistic frameworks that will explain (a) how leaders can work with AI systems, (b) how organisations can culture and emotion-prepared towards AI introduction, and (c) how AI empathy-centred tools can be ethically conducive to leadership change. More crucially, AI governance alongside human-based leadership has been understudied, particularly in terms of explainability, emotional intelligence, and well-being of an organization. The current chapter observes this essential deficiency by bringing together these dimensions into a single conceptual outlook.

At the root of this research gap is an increasing awareness of the fact that the social effects of AI cannot be disaggregated with its technical effects (Hammerschmidt et al., 2025). There are decisions in careers, performance reviews, workers in good health, inclusion, and psychological safety that are influenced by AI. As a result, organizations need to invest in models that bring explainability, bias blocking, emotional intelligence modelling and responsible governance into the very structure of AI. What comes out is a new world order in leadership- a leadership where leaders are required to bridge the gap between algorithmic logic and human experience whereby AI is used to support and not to override fairness, equity and trust. That is why the collaboration between humans and AI is not only a technological initiative, but also a moral and a relationship one (Chakraborty et al., 2024).

The chapter will attempt to comprehensively probe into how human-AI collaboration in leadership would be structured to enhance trust, transparency, psychological safety, and empathy in contemporary organizations. The fundamental idea of the chapter is to comprehend the possibility of developing and implementing AI systems in a way that is explainable, fair and ethically responsible enough to make employees trust the new technology and regard it as a trustworthy partner, instead of an inoperative, or even dangerous solution. It also analyses ways that AI may proactively contribute to psychological safety through the provision of impartial feedback, burnout identification, and secure employee representational avenues. Another aim is to develop and conceptualize the concept of AI empathy frameworks - emotionally intelligent, adaptive learning and coaching systems, which can help leaders develop greater levels of self-awareness, responsiveness, and relational competence. Along with it, the chapter also explores the actual concept of organizational preparedness concerning the empathetic use of AI, acknowledging that digital maturity, emotional preparedness, ethical governance, and change-management skill are all the necessary conditions to successfully integrate AI in the organization. Lastly, this chapter will work to convert these theoretical understandings into the context of practical industry implications and provide leaders in all industries with an idea of how AI-enabled efficiency can be balanced with human connection so that AI can supplement the leadership practice without undermining dignity, trust, or organizational culture.

2. METHODOLOGY

The chapter is based on the systematic literature review of 60 peer-reviewed works on the areas of human-AI collaboration, leadership research, AI ethics, and organizational psychology. The literature search drew on major academic databases, including Scopus, Web of Science, Google Scholar, and IEEE Xplore. Relevant keywords like the human-AI partnership, leadership, explainable AI, psychological safety, empathy scaffolds, AI governance, organizational readiness, and ethical decision-making were applied in various combinations to be able to cover a large number of relevant research. The review focused on studies published since 2021 to highlight the latest innovations in AI-influenced leadership practices. The literature review was done in a three-step screening process. The first step involved the analysis of titles and abstracts to find the studies that would involve the adoption of AI in the organizational or leadership setting. Second, specific inclusion criteria were applied to review full-text articles: (1) the study involved AI-mediated leadership behaviour, leadership development; (2) it involved trust, transparency, or explainable AI; (3) the study involved psychological safety, employee well-being, or workplace climate; (4) the study involved empathy modelling, AI-based coaching, or emotionally intelligent systems; (5) the study involved AI governance, organizational readiness, or ethical decision-making. Research that did not imply any organizational or leadership were excluded from the analysis.

The identified articles were analyzed using a thematic analysis approach after the final set of studies was selected. Similar concepts, arguments, and patterns were identified repeatedly throughout the literature and coded and sorted into conceptual clusters. By comparing and synthesizing these clusters in an iterative way, five dominant themes were identified that were the most regularly discussed when it comes to human-AI leadership dynamics. These are: (1) the theme of trust and transparency in AI-driven leadership, (2) the theme of psychological safety in AI-enabled workplaces, (3) the theme of AI empathy scaffolds in leadership development, (4) the theme of organizational readiness to adopt empathetic AI and (5) the theme of governance and ethical safeguards.

The themes were ranked according to three criteria, including their prevalence in the reviewed literature, their applicability in the leadership choices in the context of AI-mediated settings, and their role in the human-centred organizational performance in terms of trust, well-being, and ethical responsibility. Together, these themes suggestthat a humanistic conceptual framework can be used to explain how AI can assist leadership practices without compromising the empathy, transparency, and psychological safety within the organizations. This multidisciplinary literature made it possible to have a balanced appreciation of both the opportunities and threats in the human-AI collaboration in the ecosystem of leadership.

3. RESULTS AND DISCUSSION

The Results and Discussion section provides the highlights obtained as a result of researching sixty scientific articles revealing how AI changes leadership by introducing new requirements on the levels of trust, transparency, psychological safety, empathy, and ethical governance. Instead of presenting findings separately, this section connects findings together to demonstrate how the values of human-centered leadership should change with the adoption of AI. In order to be as point-by-point as possible, the discussion will be chronologicalized throughout the broader areas of interest, which recurred regular throughout the literature; (1) trust, transparency, and explainable AI; (2) psychological safety in AI-enabled workplaces; (3) AI empathy as a scaffold of leadership development; (4) organizational readiness to be empathetic to the adoption of AI; (5) balancing AI capabilities and human connection; (6) governance and ethical safeguarding. The combination of these themes can be used to define how AI can supplement leadership when carefully conceived and morally controlled as the conceptual foundation of the contributions of this chapter.

3.1 Trust, Transparency, And Explainability in AI Leadership

The introduction of artificial intelligence into the organizational leadership structures has significantly transformed the decision-making process in terms of decision making, perception, and judgment. The more AI is incorporated into strategic, operation-related, and people-management operations, the stronger the pressure on the leaders to create systems that employees are confident and knowledgeable about. The trust towards AI-assisted leadership does not come naturally, but rather is created with the help of transparency, explainability, fairness auditing, and well-defined accountability mechanisms (Ahmed et al., 2024; Hosseini et al., 2025). In modern studies, it is reiterated that it is no longer possible to implement AI within organizations as black boxes. Rather, leaders need to use so-called Explainable AI (XAI) frameworks which explain how models arrive at them, detect bias, and align ethically with organizational values (Muthusubramanian et al., 2024; Bhatia et al., 2024). Open and intelligible systems increase trust because the stakeholders are able to comprehend the rationale that dictates the choice of algorithms. It is especially important in those industries where AI-driven judgment may be of high stakes and ethical consequences, including the field of finance and healthcare. As an example, in financial risk assessment, explainable algorithms assure that credit rating or investment advice is not perpetuating subsurface prejudice or is producing discriminative results (Patidar et al., 2024). Transparency enhances the confidence of every clinician, as diagnosis choices become understandable in healthcare, and human specialists can verify, organize, or refute the output of machine intelligence

(Visave, 2025). The following examples exemplify how ethically responsible leadership can be reinforced through explainability since AI as a tool of efficiency but also a collaborative entity, is held responsible in decisions.

Leadership is decisive in nurturing the element of trust through instilling views of fairness and interpretability at the governance structures. According to Abbu et al. (2022), leaders should engage in defining the boundaries of ethics, create review committees, and introduce the norms of responsible AI use. This will involve the promotion of a culture in which AI decisions are regularly documented, audited and conveyed to the concerned stakeholders in a clear manner. By making AI transparency a norm that leaders normalize, the employees will feel that technology is enhancing, as opposed to being a danger. Recent studies conducted by Barnes and Hutson (2024) emphasize that the less people are aware of how AI makes its conclusions, the more are likely to express their acceptance, less resistance, and belief in the system.

To facilitate psychological safety at AI-argues workplaces, explainability is another factor. When the systems exhibit consistency in reasoning and equality among employees, then there is a high likelihood of them utilizing automated tools. According to Balasubramaniam et al. (2023), the explainability requirement should be reflected in design specifications, which need to reflect that transparency is not an accidental attribute, but a design principle. In the same vein, models like the responsible AI model by Abbu et al. (2025) present the ability of leadership to come up with ethics, data control, and talent development frameworks to build trustful AI ecosystems. The transparency linked to regulatory processes in the industry, including the GDPR and new worldwide AI Acts, further support the fact that such transparency has become not only an ethical suggestion but a mandatory part of compliance (Thalpage, 2023; Muthusubramanian et al., 2024). This regulatory momentum continues to push leaders to consider explainable and auditable AI processes whereby organizational practices are guided by the expectations of fairness, accountability, and inclusiveness in the society. The future of reliable AI is, according to Uddin (2025), tied to further cross-disciplinary collaboration among the technology developers, policymakers and business executives. Table 1 below explains core pillars of trust, transparency, and explainability in AI-driven leadership.

Table 1. Core Pillars of Trust, Transparency, and Explainability in AI-Driven Leadership

Pillar	What It Means	Leadership Implications	Employee Impact
Explainability (XAI)	Ability of AI to justify decisions in understandable terms	Leaders can communicate AI rationale, reduce ambiguity	Employees feel fairness, reduced fear of AI
Transparency	Visibility into how data is used and how AI systems operate	Builds ethical legitimacy	Higher trust, lower resistance
Fairness & Bias Control	Ensuring non-discrimination in AI outcomes	Leaders must mandate bias audits	Employees perceive justice in decisions
Accountability	Clear ownership of AI decisions	Leaders remain responsible, not machines	Protects employees from algorithmic harm
Data Governance	Privacy, consent, and security standards	Leaders set policies and oversight	Workers feel protected and respected

Source: Compiled by authors

Additionally, the explainable tools, including feature attribution, counterfactual explainability, and interpretable architectures of models can show a leader where the model action originated and clean up any latent biases that might negatively impact the trust in the workforce (Nikiforidis et al., 2025). AI systems are more believable when employees are able to picture why some decisions were made as well as the possibility of alternative decisions made. This degree of interpretability enhances a feeling of fairness, as it facilitates workers to appeal to the output of algorithms in a well-organized system, and not to view her as something unquestionable. Ethical identity is also enhanced in the face of transparency in leadership. Coming out to discuss the abilities, limitations, and dangers of artificial intelligence fosters trust by making leaders vulnerable and real. They are responsible and prove that any advanced systems still need monitoring, adjustment, and judgment (Von Eschenbach, 2021). Therefore, the trust in AI is created not only by technical integrity but also by the honesty and transparency of the leaders who have introduced such systems.

Overall, to become the trusted engineers with AI leadership systems, there should be a balanced solution between technological explainability, ethical governance, sustained bias auditing, and human-oriented accountability. All these factors combined will guarantee that AI-driven decisions will make workforce members even more confident and not break their confidence. Given the way that AI is coming to govern the future of organization leadership, the most relied leaders will be those that uphold transparency, defend fairness, and demystify the black box that makes AI look like an element of uncertainty, rather than one that provides impetus to responsible and empowered decision-making.

3.2 Psychological Safety in AI-Enabled Work Environments

The changing nexus of artificial intelligence (AI) and organizational well-being has reinstated psychological safety as a technological and human construct, *Psychological safety*. This implies the collective understanding of the fact that a person is not afraid to share ideas, concerns, and errors with retribution is a necessity of AI-enhanced workplaces. Recent research evidence shows that AI can greatly contribute to psychological safety in three major ways, namely, the provision of unbiased feedback, early signs of stress or burnout, and the establishment of safe and inclusive spaces of employee voice (Fiegler-Rudol et al., 2025; Chromčáková and Kriesel, 2025; Arboh et al., 2025).

Even though trust and psychological safety are related constructs in organizational behavior, they represent distinct dimensions of workplace dynamics. The main concept of trust can be considered to be the confidence of the employees in the reliability, honesty, and motives of the leaders and the organizational systems, including those that use AI to make decisions. There is hope that technological solutions and leadership practices will operate transparently and ethically. Conversely, psychological safety is the mutual belief that people can share ideas, issues or errors without fear of punishment or retaliation. Whereas trust is concerned with having confidence in systems and integrity of the leaders, psychological safety is concerned with liberty to express self and engage in discussions. Trust in AI-enabled workplaces makes sure that the employees will be convinced that AI systems are just and responsible, and psychological safety makes sure that the employees can be comfortable about challenging AI output, voicing concerns, or offering alternative views. Such a distinction helps guide organizations in developing AI-assisted environments that are both trustworthy and psychologically safe.

3.2.1 Unbiased Feedback and Fair Evaluation

Human resource management (HRM) systems, which have been driven by AI, are being hyped to reduce evaluation bias and facilitate fair performance feedback. In a study by Alwali and Alwali (2025), it has been found that AI-based HRM systems can decrease the use of subjective judgments when they are supported by the frameworks of emotional intelligence; data-driven feedback on observable behavior and outcomes with the help of the aforementioned framework. This impartiality also encourages psychological security by making employees believe that there is fairness and transparency in the evaluations. Meanwhile, Rhodes (2025) found that the organizations that adopted AI-based evaluation tools have reported higher trust in the management decisions as long as ethical use of data was upheld. Nevertheless, the availability of underlying algorithms is crucial; otherwise, the staff can develop a feeling of additional surveillance anxiety and psychological safety will be compromised, thereof. A good example of bias mitigation by use of AI-enabled performance monitoring is in the aviation industry. Given that airlines utilize AI-powered cockpit data analytics, pilots will receive objective feedback regarding procedural compliance and decision-making patterns that could be used to learn and improve as opposed to blaming (Fiegler-Rudol et al., 2025). The reflection culture is supported by data, which can improve psychological safety by strengthening the accountability oriented to learning.

3.2.2 Early Detection of Stress and Burnout

Psychological safety is also achieved with the help of AI-enabled analytics that can detect stress and burnout in employees at an early stage. According to Jetha et al. (2023), AI can assist companies in tracking the state of psychosocial and ergonomic metrics and preventing the threat to the health of workers regardless of whether it intensifies or not. As an example, speech tone, typing scale, or biometric devices on a watch can be used to identify fatigue and emotional tension through the analysis of machine learning models. Within the medical field, AI-based wellness apps are being implemented to scan nurse work schedules and emotional moods in electronic communications to predict burnout (Fiegler-Rudol et al., 2025; Arboh et al., 2025). On the same note, Nasaj et al. (2025) observe that collective anxiety in AI can be recognized and adaptive feedback systems implemented to detect stress in teams to enable organizations to develop timely coping interventions. High-performance industries such as aviation or IT where performance pressure is also high, AI-controlled well-being dashboards can help leaders during workload congestion adjustment priorities to emotional resiliency strategies to enhance the organizational psychological safety climates.

3.2.4 Safe Spaces for Employee Voice and Empowerment

AI is also transforming the systems in which employees can speak up or communicate novel ideas. According to Gandia, de Lucas Ancillo and colleagues (2025), AI communication tools formulate so-called digital voice channels that allow employees to speak out without any fear of punishment or propose ways to improve the process. These platforms also use natural language processing to identify emotional tone and raise concerning issues in AI-integrated IT service environments and make managerial interventions in psychologically supportive styles (Chromčáková et al., 2025). Arboh et al. (2025) choose the Job Demands - Resources (JD-R) model to expand on this point, demonstrating that the AI awareness and the participatory dialogue mechanisms improve the employee well-being and empowerment. Engagement, as well as psychological safety, can be enhanced when workers view AI as a helpful partner, but not a support system. Employees utilising AI-powered feedback systems in both healthcare and corporate contexts have been found to have increased confidence in their role to offer professional answers especially on patient care matters or ethical cases (Fiegler-Rudol et al., 2025; Rhodes, 2025). Table 2 below explains AI mechanisms that enhance psychological safety.

Table 2. AI Mechanisms That Enhance Psychological Safety

AI Feature	Function	Benefit to Employees	Risk if Misused	Leadership Role
Unbiased Evaluation Tools	Data-driven assessment	Fairness in performance reviews	Surveillance anxiety	Communicate purpose, ensure transparency
Burnout Detection Analytics	Identifies emotional strain from patterns	Early support and intervention	Emotional monitoring perceived as intrusive	Use with consent and empathy
Digital Voice Platforms	Anonymous input channels	Safe space for speaking up	Misinterpretation of sentiment	Ensure human follow-up
Sentiment Analysis	Tracks tone in communication	Signals distress early	Over-reliance without context	Combine insights with human judgment
Wellness Dashboards	Track workload-health balance	Helps teams self-regulate	Data privacy concerns	Protect confidentiality and intent clarity

Source: Compiled by authors

3.2.5 Case Applications and Implications

AI is also transforming the systems in which employees can speak up or communicate novel ideas. According to Gandia, de Lucas Ancillo and colleagues (2025), AI communication tools formulate so-called digital voice channels that allow employees to speak out without any fear of punishment or propose ways to improve the process. These platforms also use natural language processing to identify emotional tone and raise concerning issues in AI-integrated IT service environments and make managerial interventions in psychologically supportive styles (Chromčáková et al., 2025). Arboh et al. (2025) choose the Job Demands - Resources (JD-R) model to expand on this point, demonstrating that the AI awareness and the participatory dialogue mechanisms improve the employee well-being and empowerment. Engagement, as well as psychological safety, can be enhanced when workers view AI as a helpful partner, but not a support system. Employees utilising AI-powered feedback systems in both healthcare and corporate contexts have been found to have increased confidence in their role to offer professional answers especially on patient care matters or ethical cases (Fiegler-Rudol et al., 2025; Rhodes, 2025).

3.3 AI Empathy Scaffolds in Leadership Development

The idea of AI empathy scaffold in leadership development would be a radical shift in organizational approaches to developing emotionally intelligent and people-focused leaders. With the progress in artificial intelligence within workplace learning environments, the nature of leadership development has changed to be less instructional (traditional) and more adaptive, emotionally responsive, and data-driven. These inventions are signs of a greater realization that quality leadership is not merely cognitive and strategic but behavioral, based on compassion and moral judgment and a view of human emotions (Sposato, 2024). AI-guided empathy models thus serve as scaffolds, which are systematic aids that improve the ability of the leader to listen, discern emotional expressions, and react in a sympathetic manner within tricky organizational setups.

One of the most commonly used empathy scaffolds in modern-day leadership development is AI-driven coaching systems. The tools are based on the principles of natural language processing (NLP), sentiment analysis and behavioral analytics to simulate emotionally intelligent responses to stay sensitive to the leaders who can consider their patterns of communication and need to improve (Bhusan and Jain, 2024). AI coaching agents store leaders to a better level of self-awareness and emotional self-regulation through personalized feedback loops, which imitates the nature of empathic conversation partners. According to Gurulakshmi and Gayathri (2025), the models of human-AI partnership prompt leadership through the integration of machine-induced emotional understanding and human intuition, which at the end of the day would assist human leaders to boost empathy-based decisions. The adaptive learning platforms also complement this developmental position by making content relevant to personal emotional and cognitive requirements. These communication systems respond to the actions of users (such as their engagement, the tone of language, hesitation, and choice of responses) to both adaptively modify learning paths. Using adaptable platforms that combine AI empathy models, leaders are able to practice conflict management, inclusivity, and supportive communication on their own time, because the adaptable platforms provide psychologically safe learning environments. Nykyporets (2025) observes that AI tools do not only have visible progress in soft skills like empathy and ethical persuasion in higher and technical institutions but the same scaffolding can be applied to the business context with great effectiveness in corporate leadership.

Another important aspect of AI empathy scaffolding is sentiment analysis. Through studying impossible-to-fraid emotional cues of conversations or emails among teams and between staff and management in virtual environments, the AI systems assist in identifying early signs of burnout, disengagement, or interpersonal stress (Joshi, 2025). The knowledge can enable managers to be more sensitive to intervene and create the resilience and psychological safety in the team. This type of emotional diagnostics can help leaders to be more proactive in empathy by responding to expressed issues and also addressing sub-surface emotional undertones in the workforce. Empathy, as Zivkovic (2024) notes, is a core aspect of human-centric leadership and the instruments that boost emotional cognition can enable a leader to improve inclusion and trust in his or her organizations. MNCs are currently undertaking more experiments with AI models that replicate emotional intelligence characteristics. These systems are commonly used in leadership development games, and are able to read facial expressions, tone of voice, and language mood to generate a role-play environment. The leaders will therefore be trained to engage in challenging dialogues, including performance reviews, conflict resolution, or diversity-sensitive conversations, and get the AI-generated feedback on how empathetic their conversations are, whether their tones are appropriate or not, and what emotional responses they are likely to elicit. According to Bock and von der Oelsnitz (2025), with the continuous evolution of leadership competencies in the context of the integration of AI, empathy-increased abilities will be of primary importance in the area of collaborative, networked, and hybrid workplaces.

The AI systems have also changed the way mentorship and collaborative learning is organized. Huang et al. (2025) reveal that AI-supported entrepreneurial coach settings help increase the collaboration between mentors and novices regarding the cognition of emotional conditions and timely guidance at critical instances. This type of active scaffolding offers extra benefits as the quality of relationships is enhanced and more valuable leadership engagements emerge. On the same note, the adaptive scaffolding models in emerging markets can explain how AI systems that rely on empathy can be utilized in providing responsible and sustainable leadership education (Adiningrum et al., 2026). These instances point to AI as an accelerating factor in defining the practice of emotionally-founded leadership in various cultural backgrounds.

Though AI empathy scaffolds have huge potential, their use is ultimately limited by how willing the leaders are to interact with them in a natural manner. AI is not an antidote to emotional labor, but it increases the ability of leaders to know human beings and people better. The model of the human-AI partnership is built on the idea that empathy is inherently human but the AI can offer assistance, which is structured and consistent, as well as scaleable, to help it grow (Sposato, 2024). Implementing AI empathy models into the leadership process by organizations enhances not only the interpersonal competencies but also expands the organizational culture to be more inclusive, resilient, and supportive.

Altogether, AI empathy, scaffold tracks a significant change in the digital era of emotionally intelligent leadership. With the help of adaptive learning, AI-based coaching, sentiment analysis, and simulation of emotional reactions, the organizations can train leaders, who have a supportive possibility to communicate, foster trust and build meaningful human relations even in the most digitalized environment. With the world workforce becoming more multicultural and complicated, the combination of AI functions and human empathy will become a crucial part of creating future-proof leadership.

3.4 Organizational Readiness for Empathetic AI Integration

With the changing digital economy, the adoption of Artificial Intelligence (AI) in the organizational context has necessitated a re-consideration of leadership practice, preparedness models, and cultural synchronization strategies. Recent sources offer multi-dimensional methods of evaluating organizational readiness based on such factors as digital maturity, workforce readiness and change management where each factor defines the likelihood of AI adoption grow or diminish the effectiveness of leadership.

The basis of AI preparedness measurements is digital maturity. Johnk, Weissert, and Wyrtki (2021) note that the willingness of the firm to utilize AI greatly depends on its IT infrastructure and digital modularity. Flexible, modular systems allow quick AI deployment and limit technological bottlenecks as well as allow integration with existing enterprise platforms. They contend that this preparedness is a continuation of previous online transformation maturity, in which receptive infrastructures and information policy systems support scalable adoption of AI. In a similar manner, Koen (2022) extends the idea and offers a tri-dimensional model of the AI Readiness Prism, where technological preparedness, ethical alignment, and organizational culture are combined with one another. The model holds the view that readiness goes beyond technology to also cover governance, transparency, and accountability set-up that determines the long-term viability of AI adoption.

On the organizational front, leadership entails two aspects of organizational readiness, at both human and emotional levels. According to Francos (2022), empathy, trust, and worker involvement are important success factors in AI programs. The leaders have to be able to exercise emotional intelligence to overcome change resistance, which is also reflected by Ivchyk (2025) in her examination of the management systems that plan to adopt AI. Ivchyk notes that the fear and uncertainty among the employees are often based on the misconceptions about the fact that AI is taking human judgment. As a result, the uncertainty can be changed into cooperative willingness through compassionate leadership and open communication.

In addition, the adoption of AI depends on workforce acceptance as a determinant. Ubellacker (2025) shows that organizational trust and adoption rates depend on the perception of employees about AI limitations, specifically regarding the area of emotional intelligence. In cases where AI does not threaten workers by replacing their job, but enhancing it, they become more acceptive. In line, Asemota and Owoeye (2025) discuss the role of introducing human-centric AI into corporate learning to achieve a balance between automation and being human-centered in technological innovation to keep pace with human development. They conclude that it important that organizations should design AI systems that not only improve but also preserve psychological safety and inclusivity by directing interpersonal relationships.

Another major aspect of readiness relates to how organisations will manage change effectively through its Leaders' Change Management Process Framework developed by Urbani Ferreira and Lam (2024). This framework allows Leaders to evaluate their organisation's capability to accept technological change in a more integrated manner with their existing socio-technical issues associated with role redefinitions and knowledge diffusion. This aligns with Kumar et al. (2025), who provide empirical evidence that an organisation's ability to adopt generative AI will be determined not only by availability of technological enablers but also by the organisation's culture, commitment from leadership, and its view on the external environment.

Practical examples of how the readiness assessment occurs can be found in several companies that utilise technology within their Human Resource department to analyse talent using AI, which is utilising AI within their recruitment process. Often, the HR team within these companies employs digital maturity assessments to help assess scalable infrastructure and determine if the quality of the companies' data, as well as the degree of alignment across departments, was sufficient to move forward with the development and/or implementation of AI-driven recruitment solutions (Jöhnk et al., 2021). Alternately, companies that are deploying generative AI-based models or solutions typically use phased frameworks for assessing the ethical implications and/or change-management capabilities of a given company before moving forward to both develop and implement it into their enterprise-wide processes (Kumar et al., 2025). These approaches allow for the greatest level of usability when adopting new technology while preserving the Leaders' credibility by demonstrating foresight and accountability in the eyes of their Employees and/or Customers.

Randriamiary (2024) ultimately offers a new perspective on how to think about leadership in the context of the changes associated with AI. He argues that "AI preparedness" should be viewed as an ongoing developmental journey rather than a fixed point in time. In order to achieve success with AI, our leaders must find a way to balance technological ambition with human-centered behaviours such as empathy. By doing so, they can foster the development of resilience and adaptability throughout their organisations. This balance between digital and emotional intelligence, when incorporated into the culture of an organisation, enables AI to help, not hinder, the effectiveness of leadership. In conclusion, the emerging leaders' AI readiness assessment frameworks cluster around three distinct dimensions: technological maturity, workforce receptivity, and change management agility, and together, these dimensions allow for the integration of AI in such a way that they support and enhance the effectiveness of leaders in their ability to align innovation with human values, empathy, and resilience.

3.5 Balancing AI Integration with Human Connection

One of the most critical leadership issues in the modern workplace, where the world is evolving extremely fast, is the connection between AI integration and human connection. The leaders should use the power of AI to improve the quality of decisions, work performance, and innovation without compromising the real relationship and emotional aspect of the work relationships and motivational skills that foster trust, motivation, and collaboration. This part describes the mechanisms to prevent overdependence on AI, discusses hybrid forms of leadership when human intuition is combined with the insights of AI, and looks at collaborative platforms and multinational corporate practices, as examples of effective human-AI integration of leadership.

3.5.1 Mechanisms to Avoid Overreliance on AI in Leadership

Although AI is good at working with large volumes of data, as well as automating many routine tasks, it is the responsibility of leaders to set deliberate limits to make human judgment the primary concern. Leaders should:

a) **Define AI's role as augmentative, not directive:** Apply AI to aid data analysis and operational processes; however, leave critical decisions that require ethical, cultural, or employee welfare judgments to humans. This support-and-override framework makes AI remain a tool, but not a decision-maker.
b) **Prioritize empathy and active listening:** AI is able to recognize the trends in performance, but to make sense out of those findings, empathetic communication is needed. At the same time, leaders need to use the stored time of AI automation to enhance the interaction with people by engaging in kind feedback and conversation that encourages people, but does not control them.
c) **Be transparent about AI's function:** Transparent communication regarding the applications of AI would build trust and demystify AI applications. Leaders

who are of the opinion that AI outputs assist but do not overrule human judgment can alleviate fears of depersonalization among employees.

d) **Ensure ethical AI design:** Having a multicultural human vision in AI helps decrease bias and match AI suggestions to the shared corporate values (Felber, 2024; Naidu, 2025).

3.5.2 Hybrid Leadership Models: Combining Human and AI Strengths

New models of hybrid leadership are clearly designed to combine the power of AI with specifically human abilities such as creativity, emotional intelligence, and ethical judgment. This partnership can allow leaders to:

a) **Contextualize data-driven insights:** AI gives quantitative analysis and forecasting of the scenario, and human beings give interpretative insight into social dynamics, cultural peculiarities, and organizational values.
b) **Amplify strategic thinking:** AI determines patterns and efficiencies; human leaders use vision and innovation to turn those observations into transformational strategies.
c) **Strengthen relationships:** AI helps leaders to spend more of their cognitive and emotional resources on mentoring, culture-building and authentic communication by automating routine tasks.

This model of co-leaders is an indication of the change of AI as a taskmaster to AI as a co-pilot, which promotes cooperation instead of command and control, and pays more attention to the moral compass and strategy of the leader (Boris, 2025).

3.5.3 Collaborative Platforms Supporting Human-AI Leadership

MNCs use state-of-the-art collaborative systems that combine AI facilitation and human connectivity, such as:

a) **AI-enhanced communication tools:** These platforms apply AI to sentiment analysis, summarize meetings, and help in decision-making, but keep live human conversation.
b) **Decision support systems with human override:** AI offers advice, does not usurp the final decision by leaders, but keeps them accountable and ethically responsible.
c) **VR/AR empathy training:** Industries that are more globalized employ AI-based immersion tech to allow leaders to get exposure to varying views on different

issues, which improves their empathy and intercultural competence (Clarke-Joell, 2025).

3.5.4 Corporate Practices from Large Multinational Corporations

The best examples of how to balance AI and human leadership are big global corporations:

a) **Microsoft:** Their AI Ethics Board incorporates human multi-disciplinary control to confirm that AI tools are applied in a responsible way and are consistent with human rights and ethical principles.
b) **Unilever:** Combines AI-based talent analytics with human coaching, where AI is used to supplement, but not to override human judgment when it comes to employee development.
c) **Salesforce:** Uses AI in customer relationship management, maintains a corporate culture of empathy and inclusiveness ("Ohana") and views AI as a relationship enabler, and not a replacement.
d) **Siemens:** Educate the leaders to work with AI systems to build a sense of trust and communication to ensure that AI does not eclipse human points of view.

These instances indicate that effective integration lies in the integration of AI tools in human-oriented leadership trading, and not technology-oriented leadership trading (Clarke-Joell, 2025; Naidu, 2025).

3.6 Balancing for Sustainable Human-AI Leadership

Sustainable leadership in the AI era involves maintaining a "human-in-the-loop" approach where AI continually augments but never replaces human judgment, empathy, and ethical responsibility. This requires leaders to:

a) Take part in continuous considerations of the developing role of AI in decision-making.
b) Nurture human abilities like emotional intelligence, adaptability and cultural sensitivity that AI is incapable of.
c) Promote effective, ethical, and open AI governance in line with corporate values.
d) Artificial Intelligence has the potential to strengthen, not weaken, human relationships and trust.

Through adopting hybrid forms of leadership, relying on collaborative platforms, and institutionalizing ethical AI-human relationships, organizations can create safe, open, and compassionate work environments where technology can support and not alienate human interactions. Table 3 gives a snapshot of Balancing Human and AI Capabilities in Leadership.

Table 3. Balancing Human and AI Capabilities in Leadership

Leadership Function	AI Strength	Human Strength	Optimal Hybrid Approach
Decision-Making	Pattern recognition, forecasting	Ethical judgment, context	AI proposes, human decides
People Management	Data-driven insights	Empathy, trust-building	AI informs, leaders converse
Innovation	Rapid computation of scenarios	Creativity, imagination	AI suggests options, humans ideate
Feedback & Coaching	Behavioral analytics	Emotional nuance	AI provides input, human mentors
Conflict Resolution	Sentiment detection	Intuition, compassion	AI alerts leaders, leaders intervene

Source: Compiled by authors

3.7 Governance, Ethics, And Legal Safeguards

Leadership measures are anchored on good governance, ethics, and legal protection, which guarantee that technologies are used to augment, rather than to erode trust in organizations. To avoid harm, develop accountability, and establish confidence among the stakeholders, leaders need to deal with data privacy, bias elimination, and regulatory adherence (Ariwala, 2025). This part will explore the major mechanisms and cases in the industry that show how responsible practices turn the fear of potentiality into an opportunity to create ethical innovation.

3.7.1 Data Privacy Protections

The AI leader tools analyze (and process) large amounts of data on employees and customers, so well-developed privacy frameworks, such as GDPR and CCPA, are required. Organizations need to adopt privacy by design, obtain express consent, support data subject rights, such as access and erasure, and undertake notification of data breaches within 72 hours. Policies of transparent data use are a way to demystify the process of AI usage, which eliminates fears of privacy loss without breaching international standards (Cookie Law Info, 2025; Rathor & Sharma, 2025).

3.7.2 Mitigating Bias in AI Decision-Making

Algorithms may lead to injustice in the recruitment, promotion, or reward practices, undermining the credibility of leaders. Some of the strategies comprise an array of training data, design that is inclusive, and the provision of human supervision over high-stakes decisions. The differences are identified and rectified by regular audits and fairness checklists that ensure that AI promotes fair results instead of enhancing inequities (EICTA, 2025).

3.7.3 Adherence to Regulatory Frameworks

The EU AI Act requires risk-based governance, which categorizes systems based on their impacts and demands transparency, competency training, and AI policies that would ensure compliance. The fines go up to €35 million or 7% of worldwide turnover, forcing executives to introduce AI compliance officers and put ethics within lifecycles. These frameworks advocate safe deployment as well as aligning innovation with human rights (Homann, 2025).

3.8. Industry Cases: Building Trust Through Responsible Governance

The efficiency of ethical governance as means of enhancing trust is manifested in the policies of the largest multinational companies:

a) Unilever has a process of AI ethics that has the following characteristics:

Unilever considers AI initiatives based on their internal ethics review, which determines their bias, privacy risks, and impact on society before implementation. Human control and vendor responsibility are needed in projects affecting the outcome of a project on a large scale to employees or consumers (Davenport and Bean, 2023).

Leadership lesson: Before AI is deployed, leaders need to institute institutions to review ethics.

Practical implementation: To implement AI ethics review boards internally, organizations can create boards to review high impact AI decisions and to make sure that there is human supervision.

b) The AETHER Committee of Microsoft:

AETHER (AI and Ethics in Engineering and Research) Committee of Microsoft unites the specialists in engineering, law, and policy spheres to consider AI projects in accordance with the principles of responsible AI and equity checklists (Miller, 2025).

Leadership implication: Multidisciplinary systems of governance enhance accountable AI practices.

Practical implementation: Technical, legal and ethical professionals should participate in AI governance in organizations to prevent threats in advance.

c) The UNESCO Alignment of Salesforce:

Salesforce is aligning its AI activities with the global AI ethics framework of UNESCO of transparency, protection of human rights and responsible AI-led business applications (Humainism, 2025).

Leadership perception: Justifying corporate AI strategies to global ethical frameworks boosts organizational and stakeholder legitimacy.

Practical implementation: Leaders may implement internationally established ethical principles in order to regulate AI and guarantee responsible innovation.

Generally, these examples demonstrate that governance is a multiplier of trust. Those organizations that incorporate ethical-by-design thinking, shared responsibility, and open visibility controls are in a better place to deploy AI in responsible manners and enhance the trust that the stakeholders have in them.

4. TOWARD TRUSTWORTHY HUMAN-AI LEADERSHIP

Safe environments are created by leaders who are more focused on human-in-the-loop supervision, ethical education, and regular monitoring. By assigning such roles as Chief AI Ethics Officer, the alignment is guaranteed, and regulatory requirements become a competitive advantage. These shields ultimately make AI a trustworthy ally, breaking the fears of its unfairness and irresponsibility (Ballesteros, 2025). Accountable governance makes AI leadership when transparency, equity, and conformity are introduced into the decision-making. Cases in the industry provide an understanding of how transparent ethics policies, bias control, and compliance with regulations not only avoid harm but instill trust and confidence in AI as an effective leadership collaborator. Based on this foundation, the organizations will be able to use AI ethically and establish sustainable and reliable human-AI relationships in leadership.

5. FUTURE OF HUMAN-AI LEADERSHIP PARTNERSHIPS

AI is expected to synergize with human capabilities in decision-making, innovation, and empathetic approaches to leadership, ultimately fostering a highly effective human–AI leadership partnership. The new trends reveal the creation of the more human-focused AI systems, the ease of cooperation between the people and the intelligent technologies, and the transformation of leadership functions, that will involve digital intelligence and emotional sensitivity. The trend should strengthen organizational competitiveness, enabling flexible talent development and leadership approaches grounded in empathy. (Sharma, 2025). Improvement of empathetic AI is likely to be the introduction of emotional intelligence into AI in the form of sentiment analysis, interpretation of behavioral data, and context-sensitive decision support systems. These advancements can help leaders to comprehend the emotional aspects of the team, and make judgments that incorporate both rational and human factors. New ideas like Emotion-Aware Decision Intelligence (EDI) are suggesting the possibility of artificial intelligence-based leadership solutions capable of integrating predictive analytics with ethical decision-making and empathy-based decision-making (Howe, 2025; Paramjeet, 2025).

Another workplace of the future is likely to be defined by the hybrid human-AI teams, where AI systems do data-intensive analytical work and human leaders are concerned with creativity, relationship building, and tackling intricate challenges. In this situation, the role of mid-level leaders as facilitators will be instrumental, who can incorporate AI functionalities into the organizational workflow without causing psychological safety and encouraging continuous upskilling at the team level (McNabb, 2025). The leadership is expected to transform into a facilitative and integrative leadership that focuses on AI literacy, ethical governance, and strategic vision. Leaders will increasingly guide organizations through framing meaningful questions, managing technological change, and nurturing trust between employees moving in AI-enabled environments. Emotional intelligence and ethical sensitivity are also bound to be the imperative leadership qualities in organizations where there is the coexistence of human and machine intelligence (Paramjeet, 2025).

Moreover, AI-assisted teamwork will contribute to the increased organizational competitiveness, as it will provide the ability to interpret data faster, support decisions more effectively, and respond to the innovation process in a more timely manner. A strategic implementation of AI within organizations can benefit rapidly changing markets due to the combination of technological efficiency and human creativity and flexibility (Gibbons, 2025; McNabb, 2025). The field of talent acquisition and workforce development is also likely to be transformed by AI, which will facilitate more elaborate matching of skills, roles and organization needs. With the growth of AI-based recruitment and talent analytics, organizations are likely to place more emphasis on hybrid competencies that involve technological fluency and empathy, ethical sensitivity and team-building leadership skills. Therefore, the human resource leaders will probably redesign talent pipelines to equip employees to work in a hybrid human-AI setting (Kober, 2025).

Altogether, the future relationships between humans and AI in leadership will probably be influenced by compassionate AI design, interdisciplinary teams of humans and AI, and the transformation of leadership identity toward balancing technology with humanism. Those organisations that properly embrace these dimensions would be more likely to be innovative, build trust, and maintain competitive advantage in workplaces that become more AI-enabled.

6. PRACTICAL IMPLICATIONS

Artificial intelligence can be an important part of the leadership practice, and its integration leads to strong consequences on organizational decision-making system design, leadership development, and human-oriented work environment. As AI assumes a greater role in performance assessment, communication, talent management, and strategic planning, leaders need to make sure that its use does not supersede human judgment and empathy, but supports it. Effective implementation of AI in leadership is thus pegged on the development of mechanisms that would support efficiency and moral accountability as well as emotional intelligence. Resting on the findings of the reviewed literature, the following recommendations show positive steps that organizational leaders may take to develop responsible and empathetic human-AI leadership ecosystems.

Build AI-Smart and Emotionally Intelligent Leaders- Organizations ought to invest in AI literacy with emotional intelligence based leadership development programs. The leaders should be able to comprehend the workings of AI systems, identify their shortcomings, and responsibly interpret algorithmic insights. The training must therefore be focused on the technical awareness as well as empathy, moral thinking and communication skills. Individuals that have mastered the world of technology and are sensitive to emotions are in a better position to lead organisations towards the AI-driven changes without losing the support of workers.

Secure Transparency and Explainability in AI Systems- Transparency is crucial to trust in AI-assisted decision-making. In their effort to build explainable AI (XAI), organizations need to implement the principle of explainable algorithmic decision making in such a manner that employees and other stakeholders can know how the decisions are reached. Open processes enable workplace members to understand the role of data in the determination of appraisals, upgrading, or suggestions, eliminating concerns on covert discrimination or poor decisions. Bias monitoring, ethical review, and fairness audits should also be institutionalized by the leaders to make sure that the AI systems are functioning within the organisational values and regulatory norms.

Bargain with AI to Enhance, but Not Surveillance, Psychological Safety- Psychological safety is supported by the use of AI technologies when there is sound judgment. Sentiment analysis, workload analytics, and digital feedback platforms will also be helpful to leaders to reveal the signs of burnout, disengagement, or team conflict at the early stages. Organizations should, however, make sure that such systems are also implemented with explicit consent, confidentiality and open communication. The more employees believe that AI is an encouraging developmental tool and not an observational mechanism, the more they will believe in technology and engage in organizational discourse.

Incorporate Artificial Intelligence Empathy Devices into Leadership- The introduction of AI-powered coaching platforms, adaptive learning technologies, and sentiment analysis tools can be used to improve leadership growth because they assist leaders to train in challenging interpersonal scenarios through secure settings. These instruments are capable of simulating the complicated aspects of leadership including conflict management, inclusive communication, and performance discussions with a personalized feedback. With the help of AI-assisted empathy scaffolds in leadership development courses, organizations will be able to democratize high-quality coaching and develop more self-aware and relationally competent leaders.

Evaluate the Organizational Preparations to AI Systems- To be successful in the implementation of AI, it is not only necessary to have the technological capability, but also the organizational culture, employee preparedness, and governance forms. The organizations must consider their digital maturity, data infrastructure, change management ability, and attitudes towards AI before implementing AI tools. Anxiety of AI systems among employees can be decreased through open communication about the purpose and limits of AI systems, which will lead to greater acceptance. Adopting AI should be seen by the leaders as a continuous process of development and not a technological implementation.

Create Good Governance and Ethical Protection- This should be achieved through proper governance structures that are accountable, protect privacy and legal compliance in the implementation of AI. The companies are advised to form AI ethics committees, implement privacy-by-design strategies, and keep decisions with high stakes under human control. The adherence to the international regulatory frameworks like the data protection laws also enhances the stakeholder confidence. Ethical governance provides more than just lessening the risks in legal matters it also builds the reputation of the organization as a responsible and trustworthy adopter of the advanced technologies.

Ensure Human-Centered Leadership in AI-Enriched Workplaces- Although AI has an analytical nature, it cannot replicate distinctly human attributes such as empathy, intuition, creativity, and moral judgment. It is the duty of the organizations to maintain significant human communication by mentoring, dialogue, and relationship-building practices. AI is expected to liberate the leaders with the daily and repetitive duties so that they can dedicate more time to employee coaching, establishment of collaboration, and enhancement of the organizational culture. A harmonious human-AI relationship will enable the technology to be more efficient but still human-focused leadership.

7. CONCLUSION

The development of artificial intelligence in the life of the organization is not nothing but a significant shift in leadership change. In the chapter, I have noted that as AI finds greater integration into the decision-making, communication, developmental, and governance systems in the contemporary workplaces, leadership diversity must reinvent correspondingly, based on trust, transparency, empathy, and psychological safety. The main point which can be identified by reading the chapter is evident: AI does not take the nature of leadership away- it changes the nature in which leadership can be applied, making human-judgment more and more crucial in the process, along with increasing the scope of analytical and operational abilities.

In the chapter, we have observed how integrity and openness are the two key pillars of effective human-AI integration. When AI enters into the process of making evaluations or risk assessment or strategic decision-making, organizations can no longer afford to use opaque or black-box models. Explainability is not merely one of the ethical prerequisites- it is also a psychological need of the employees who should be assured that automated mechanisms do not undermine fairness, in fact, they strengthen it. Leaders must thus seek to demystify the logic of an algorithm, and ensure that the role of AI becomes visible, responsible and contested. By so doing, they will strengthen the moral contract that exists between technology and the workforce so that innovation should enrich and not destroy trust.

It was also determined in the chapter that psychological safety is an indispensable requirement of AI-enabled working environments. The potential of AI to aid in ensuring psychological safety is enormous through its bias reduction capabilities, unbiased feedback, early signs of burnout or distress detection, and similar features. However, this possibility is possible only when companies implement AI systems in a transparent, empathetic, and communicative way. Otherwise, AI that is abused will lead to surveillance anxiety, learned helplessness or fear of monitoring. It is thus crucial that leaders should exercise a stewardship attitude whereby AI devices serve humanity without taking away human dignity and free will. This demands an ongoing discourse and positive reinforcement of ethics and the deliberate design and positioning of AI as an enhancement and growth partner, and not a correction.

One of the key lessons that were learned during the chapter is the importance of AI empathy scaffolds in building leadership of the future. The innovations in AI-based coaching, sentiment analysis, adaptive learning, and emotional modeling demonstrate how AI can help provide leaders with a more emotionally intelligent, reflective, and inclusive way of thinking. Although AI cannot substitute human compassion, it can support learning settings light of a leader training in complex dialogues, personalized feedback, and gaining a stronger insight into their communication styles. This democratic change democratizes the process of leadership development and preparing leaders of all levels, not just the top ones, to succeed in a complicated ecological setting of relationships. The chapter highlighted that AI does not imitate empathy to a fault but the ability to increase the capacity of leaders to be authentic in its application.

The discussion of organizational preparedness and governance as a structural framework of the ethical, responsible, and sustainable implementation of AI is also important in the chapter. Its preparedness would be multidimensional, meaning that technological theatricity, staffing perceptions, alignment in cultures, and transitioning flexibility would need to combine so that AI adoption would become believable and efficient. As the world is going greener and the pressure on ethics increases, companies have to reduce privacy-by-design solutions, fairness audits, human-in-the-loop judgment infrastructure, and open governance councils. This institutional scaffolding does not only guarantee compliance, but also safeguards organizations against reputational, legal and relational risks. Governance, in turn, becomes a strategic distinguishing factor, and it indicates to the employees and external stakeholders that AI is implemented in an integrity and careful manner.

Lastly, the chapter has determined the rise of hybrid models of human-AI leadership that will characterize the future workplace. The models show data-intensive and repetitive predictive tasks are delegated to AI and sense-making, ethical deliberation, creativity, and relational leadership to humans. This mixed relationship improves organizational stability by allowing the leader to make quicker and more informed decisions without accuracy in empathy or context awareness. The future needs leaders who could serve as the translators among human values and machine intelligence to the values of fairness, psychological security, and collective welfare to the utmost standards.

Summarizing this chapter, it is obvious that the measure of the successful application of AI in leadership is not the level of technological advances but the quality of human experience it could provide. With AI being embedded in leadership, empathetic, transparent, and psychologically safe, organizations will open up opportunities to a future where innovation and humanity can be united, and in that case. The actual revolution in leadership is not the incorporation of sophisticated equipment but the creation of mechanisms in which AI would drive human potential, build trust, and reinforce the social fabric of companies. The organizations that are going to be successful as we enter a more digitalized work place is one that does not view AI as a tool, but as a companion, one that is capable of improving, supplementing, and enriching the work of being a leader, which is deeply human.

REFERENCES

Abbu, H., Khan, S., Mugge, P., & Gudergan, G. (2025). *Responsible AI framework: How leadership unifies talent, data, ethics, and governance for trustworthy AI*. ResearchGate.

Abbu, H., Mugge, P., & Gudergan, G. (2022). *Ethical considerations of artificial intelligence: Ensuring fairness, transparency, and explainability*, 3.

Adiningrum, T. S., Margiono, A., & Rohman, A. (2026). Scaffolding sustainable entrepreneurship: Adaptive teaching and empathy in a Global South business school. *International Journal of Management Education*, *24*(1), 101280. DOI: 10.1016/j.ijme.2025.101280

Ahmed, S., Ahmed, R., Ashrafi, D. M., Ahmed, E., & Annamalah, S. (2024). Building trust in cybernetic payment network: Insights from an emerging economy. *Journal of Open Innovation*, *10*(3), 100331. Advance online publication. DOI: 10.1016/j.joitmc.2024.100331

Alwali, J., & Alwali, W. (2025). Linking AI-driven HRM and emotional intelligence to leadership effectiveness and employee performance. *Leadership and Organization Development Journal, 6*. Annapareddy, 1–21. .DOI: 10.1108/LODJ-05-2025-0358

Annapareddy, V. N., Singireddy, J., Preethish Nandan, B., Lakarasu, P., & Burugulla, J. K. R. (2025). Emotional intelligence in artificial agents: Leveraging deep multi-modal big data for contextual social interaction and adaptive behavioral modelling. *Available at SSRN* 5241039. DOI: 10.2139/ssrn.5241039

Arboh, F., Zhu, X., Atingabili, S., Yeboah, E., & Drokow, E. K. (2025). From fear to empowerment: The impact of employees AI awareness on workplace well-being–a new insight from the JD–R model. *Journal of Health Organization and Management*. Advance online publication. DOI: 10.1108/JHOM-06-2024-0229 PMID: 39875341

Ariwala, P. (2025). AI governance: Building trust and compliance with reliable AI. *Maruti Techlabs*. https://marutitech.com/responsible-ai-governance/

Asemota, M. O., & Owoeye, G. (2025). Integrating human-centric AI into corporate learning: Balancing automation with empathy. *Development and Learning in Organizations*. Advance online publication. DOI: 10.1108/DLO-01-2025-0014

Balasubramaniam, N., Kauppinen, M., & Rannisto, A. (2023). *Transparency and explainability of AI systems: From ethical guidelines to requirements*. Elsevier.

Ballesteros, B. (2025, July 12). Case study: Effective governance in AI-powered organizations. *Tellix*. https://tellix.ai/case-study-effective-governance-in-ai-powered-organizations/

Barnes, E., & Hutson, J. (2024). Navigating the complexities of AI: Interpretability and transparency [International journal].

Bhatia, S., Mittal, V., & Sabharwal, S. (2024). *Building trust and transparency in AI*. IEEE.

Boris, T. (2025, August 11). AI-human leadership integration: Executive leadership in the AI Era. *LinkedIn*. https://www.linkedin.com/pulse/ai-human-leadership-integration-executive-ai-era-boris-thoenissen-hwqce/

Chakraborty, T., Sharada, V. S., & Sharma, J. (2024). Data-driven decisions for employee motivation: Strategies for implementing technology in performance reviews in a tech landscape. In Rajapakshe, W. (Ed.), *Employee performance management for improved workplace motivation* (pp. 311–338). IGI Global. DOI: 10.4018/979-8-3693-4387-6.ch013

Chromčáková, Tereza, I. K., & Kriesel, O.J. (2025). *AI disruption in the workplace: Navigating employee engagement in an age of automation.*

Clarke-Joell, C. (2025, February 28). The AI-human Power Play: Leading hybrid teams in the age of automation. *VKTR.com*. https://www.vktr.com/leadership/the-ai-human-power-play-leading-hybrid-teams-in-the-age-of-automation/

Davenport, T. H., & Bean, R. (2023, November 15). AI ethics at Unilever: From policy to process. *MIT Sloan Management Review*. https://sloanreview.mit.edu/article/ai-ethics-at-unilever-from-policy-to-process/

Felber, J. (2024, October 8). The future of leadership: Balancing AI integration with human connection. *Forb*. https://www.forbes.com/councils/forbesbusinesscouncil/2024/10/08/the-future-of-leadership-balancing-ai-integration-with-human-connection/

Fiegler-Rudol, J., Lau, K., Mroczek, A., & Kasperczyk, J. (2025). Exploring human–AI dynamics in enhancing workplace health and safety: A narrative review. *International Journal of Environmental Research and Public Health*, *22*(2), 199. Advance online publication. DOI: 10.3390/ijerph22020199 PMID: 40003424

Gibbons, S. (2025, December 2). Future leaders will win through human and AI collaboration. *Forb*. https://www.forbes.com/sites/serenitygibbons/2025/12/02/future-leaders-will-win-through-human-and-ai-collaboration/

Hammerschmidt, T., Stolz, K., & Posegga, O. (2025). Bridging the gap: Inequalities that divide those who can and cannot create sustainable outcomes with AI. *Behaviour & Information Technology*, •••, 1–30. DOI: 10.1080/0144929X.2025.2500451

Homann, M. (2025, November 26). EU AI act: What companies need to know. EQS Group. https://www.eqs.com/compliance-blog/eu-ai-act/

Hosseini Tabaghdehi, S. A., & Ayaz, Ö. (2025). *AI ethics in action.* Emerald.

Howe, L. (2025, October 8). Why AI empathy won't replace human leaders (yet). *Forb.* https://www.forbes.com/sites/laurenhowe/2025/10/08/why-ai-empathy-wont-replace-human-leaders-yet/

Humainism. (2025). Microsoft, Salesforce, Lenovo. DiploFoundation. *Among Eight Tech Firms Adopting UNESCO's AI Ethics Framework- Humainism.* https://humainism.ai/updates/microsoft-salesforce-lenovo-among-eight-tech-firms-adopting-unescos-ai-ethics-framework/

Info, C. L. (2025, February 28). Data privacy and AI governance: Challenges and solutions. *Cookie law info.* https://www.cookielawinfo.com/data-privacy-and-ai-governance/

Ivchyk, V. (2025). *Preparing management systems for AI integration.*

Jetha, A., Bakhtari, H., Rosella, L. C., Gignac, M. A. M., Biswas, A., Shahidi, F. V., Smith, B. T., Smith, M. J., Mustard, C., Khan, N., Arrandale, V. H., Loewen, P. J., Zuberi, D., Dennerlein, J. T., Bonaccio, S., Wu, N., Irvin, E., & Smith, P. M. (2023). Artificial intelligence and the work–health interface: A research agenda for a technologically transforming world of work. *American Journal of Industrial Medicine*, *66*(10), 815–830. DOI: 10.1002/ajim.23517 PMID: 37525007

Jöhnk, J., Weißert, M., & Wyrtki, K. (2021). Ready or not, AI comes—An interview study of organizational AI readiness factors. *Business & Information Systems Engineering*, *63*(1), 5–20. DOI: 10.1007/s12599-020-00676-7

Kober, G. (2025, January 24). AI-first leadership: Embracing the future of work. *Harvard Business Impact.* https://www.harvardbusiness.org/insight/ai-first-leadership-embracing-the-future-of-work/

Koen, J. (2022). *The artificial intelligence readiness prism: A multi-dimensional framework for assessing AI integration, ethics, and cultural alignment.*

Kumar, V., Kumar, S., Durana, P., Chaudhuri, R., Vrontis, D., & Chatterjee, S. (2025). Enhancing organizational readiness for generative AI integration: An empirical investigation. *The International Journal of Organizational Analysis*. Advance online publication. DOI: 10.1108/IJOA-03-2025-5310

Mann, H. (2024). *Artificial Integrity: The paths to leading AI toward a human-centered future*. John Wiley & Sons.

McNabb, K. (2025, March 14). The acceleration of generative AI: How businesses are scaling for competitive advantage. Hackett. https://www.thehackettgroup.com/insights/the-acceleration-of-generative-ai-how-businesses-are-scaling-for-competitive-advantage/

Miller, E. (2025, February 16). AI governance in practice: Strategies for ethical implementation at scale. Magnimind Academy. https://magnimindacademy.com/blog/ai-governance-in-practice-strategies-for-ethical-implementation-at-scale/

Muthusubramanian, M., Jangoan, S. & others. (2024). *Demystifying explainable AI*. IJ.

Naidu, T. (2025, November 18). Leadership in the age of AI: Balancing people, processes, and technology. https://www.ghodawat.com/leadership-in-the-age-of-ai-balancing-people-processes-and-technology/

Nasaj, M., Badi, S., Murtagh, N., & Ding, L. (2025). Collective AI anxiety and team innovative behaviour: The role of coping strategies. *Construction Innovation*. Advance online publication. DOI: 10.1108/CI-08-2024-0222

Nikiforidis, K., Kyrtsoglou, A., Vafeiadis, T., & Kotsiopoulos, T. (2025). XAI in smart manufacturing. *ICT Express, 47*.

Omrani, N., Rivieccio, G., Fiore, U., Schiavone, F., & Agreda, S. G. (2022). To trust or not to trust? An assessment of trust in AI-based systems: Concerns, ethics and contexts. *Technological Forecasting and Social Change*, *181*, 121763. Advance online publication. DOI: 10.1016/j.techfore.2022.121763

Pandey, V. (2025). Leadership in the AI Era: Navigating and shaping the future of organizational guidance. *Available at* SSRN *5331975*. SSRN *Electronic Journal*. DOI: 10.2139/ssrn.5331975

Paramjeet. (2025, June 14). The empathy-AI nexus in leadership: Toward verified, human-centered decision systems. *LinkedIn*. https://www.linkedin.com/pulse/empathy-ai-nexus-leadership-toward-verified-decision-paramjeet--fe8hf/

Patidar, N., Mishra, S., Jain, R., & Prajapati, D. (2024). Transparency in AI decision-making. *SSRN*.

Randriamiary, D. (2024). Reframing the role of leaders navigating the challenges and opportunities of tomorrow's workplace in the age of artificial intelligence. *Available at SSRN47160.* SSRN *Electronic Journal*. DOI: 10.2139/ssrn.4716033

Rathor, A., & Sharma, M. (2025, April 22). AI and global data privacy laws: Compliance, challenges & trends. *Lawrbit*. https://www.lawrbit.com/global/ai-and-global-data-privacy-laws/

Rhodes, E. P. (2025). Measuring the human experience of AI in the workplace working paper (preprint version). Available at *SSRN, 54*.

Rubin, M., Arnon, H., Huppert, J. D., & Perry, A. (2024). Considering the role of human empathy in AI-driven therapy. *JMIR Mental Health*, *11*(1), e56529. Advance online publication. DOI: 10.2196/56529

Ryan, M. (2020). In AI we trust: Ethics, artificial intelligence, and reliability. *Science and Engineering Ethics*, *26*(5), 2749–2767. DOI: 10.1007/s11948-020-00228-y PMID: 32524425

Sharma, G. (2025, June 12). The human-AI partnership: Redefining leadership in strategy execution. *LinkedIn*. https://www.linkedin.com/pulse/human-ai-partnership-redefining-leadership-strategy-execution-sharma-nqfac/

Shen, L., Qiu, N., & Wang, Z. (2025). Psychological safety and trust as drivers of teachers' continued use of AI tools in classrooms. *Scientific Reports*, *15*(1), 31426. Advance online publication. DOI: 10.1038/s41598-025-13789-4 PMID: 40858670

Sposato, M. (2024). Leadership training and development in the age of artificial intelligence. *Development and Learning in Organizations*, *38*(4), 4–7. DOI: 10.1108/DLO-12-2023-0256

Thalpage, N. (2023). Unlocking the black box: XAI for trust and transparency. *Journal of Digital Art & Humanities*, *4*(1), 31–36. DOI: 10.33847/2712-8148.4.1_4

Übellacker, T. (2025). *Making sense of AI limitations: How individual perceptions shape organizational readiness for AI adoption. arXiv preprint arXiv:2502.15870.*

Uddin, M. Z. (2025). *Trustworthy AI and explainability*. Springer. DOI: 10.1007/978-3-031-97359-8_4

Urbani, R., Ferreira, C., & Lam, J. (2024). Managerial framework for evaluating AI chatbot integration: Bridging organizational readiness and technological challenges. *Business Horizons*, *67*(5), 595–606. DOI: 10.1016/j.bushor.2024.05.004

Visave, J. (2025). *Transparency in AI for emergency management*. Springer.

Von Eschenbach, W. J. (2021). *Transparency and the black box problem: Why we do not trust AI*. Springer. 1.

Chapter 4
Human-AI Collaboration in Leadership and Decision Making

Pardeep Kumar
http://orcid.org/0000-0003-0308-7634
Lovely Professional University, India

Sanjeev Kumar
http://orcid.org/0000-0002-7375-7341
Lovely Professional University, India

ABSTRACT

The course of organizational strategies, modes of management and governance across industries and sectors are shifting as a consequence of human and artificial intelligence instituting leadership and decision-making. Leaders can make better, timely, and objective decisions as they use artificial intelligence (AI) to analyze the data, generate new scenario prediction models, and simulate the situations. Such collaboration is a boost to problem-solving because of the natural human ability to neurologize, moralize, and contextualize the problem alongside the computing ability, pattern-recognition ability, and scale of AI. To achieve proper integration, trust in AI systems must be developed, transparency must be given to the algorithms, and some form of human control must be maintained to help address the risks associated with forms of bias, responsibility, and ethical issues. Also, team structures promote adaptive leadership, which allows organizations to deal dynamically with complex-challenging environments in a rapidly changing environment.

DOI: 10.4018/979-8-3373-6650-0.ch004

INTRODUCTION TO HUMAN-AI COLLABORATION

Human-AI synergy describes a complementary merging of human intellect that is defined by emotional acuity, ethical thinking, contextual awareness with the computerized abilities of artificial intelligence, which would be speed and data processing, predictive analytics, and pattern recognition. Cooperation in this context does not imply a replacement of the human with a machine but supplementing human capabilities when it comes to making decisions. The integration of human creativity into the efficiency and precision of AI will enable organisations to solve complex issues, make data-and knowledge-intensive decisions and innovate. The final vision is to establish a collaboration in which both parties balance each other and allow positive results in various sectors(Jain et al., 2023a).The way AI contributes to company decision making has changed tremendously in the recent decades. In the first instance, AI was confined to the automation of routine activities and rule-based systems. Thanks to the development of machine learning, natural language processing, and big data analytics, AI entered the strategic domain: it provides insights that impacts the leadership journeys, market conditions, and crisis handling. In the present day, AI can help leadership win challenges as a co-pilot, offering predictive models, risk analysis, and scenario simulations, which would allow organizations to remain competitive under the conditions of a dynamic environment. This is the displacement of the era of AI as a support tool to the level of a collaborative partner(Rodzina & Kristoffersen, 2013).In the contemporary business environment, executives have to deal with the excessive abundance of information, dynamic changes in the market environment, and the necessity to make quick but reasonable decisions. AI augmented leadership can help leaders to use AI in real time to interrogate, strategy and monitor performance. This collaboration enhances decision quality through the minimization of the cognitive bias and faster analysis and the concealment of undiscovered patterns in data. Notably, the ability of leaders to think strategically and connect with others is facilitated due to AI augmentation, which performs the strenuous duties of data processing. Leadership that embraces such a model leads to efficiency, agility and resilience(Munyaka et al., 2023).

The research areas of human-AI collaboration in leadership have a variety of dimensions such as technological, organisational, ethical, and cultural. The goal will be to discuss the principals by which AI tools may be well incorporated in the leadership processes without undermining human oversight. This involves finding out the ideal mix of human decision-making and algorithmic suggestions, comprehending the trust relationship among leaders and AI-based systems, and constructing governance regimes to set good conditions regarding ethical AI implementation(Molina et al., 2024). The paper is also meant to analyze the obstacle to the adoption, which may include change resistance, the lack of digital literacy, and data security fears. Although AI is more effective at analyzing data and spotting trends, it lacks human abilities to have empathy, moral judgment, and to communicate effectively with one another. Emotional intelligence is also an important aspect of leadership which is imperative and cannot be replaced by AI. Leaders should thus be in human age when dealing with AI and apply their humanistic traits to discuss the results of AI outputs as cultural and ethical practices. This would maintain the provision of not only accurate but also ethically inclined decision-making to the organization as well as the stakeholders(Tuncer & Ramirez, 2022).One of the issues in human-AI collaboration would be the ease in adoption of the collaboration within teams. The leaders will need to perform the role of translators between the AI systems and the human employees so that the two sides can comprehend what one can do and what the other cannot. This includes the ability to make teams collaborate with AI tools, the culture of receptiveness to innovation, and the act of providing explanations of AI recommendations in terms that is easily acted on. It is very important to fill this gap to establish trust in AI-assisted decision-making processes(Dai et al., 2025).

The cooperation between humans and AIs is not standardized; it depends on industry and the geographical location. Healthcare applications include the use of AI to help in diagnosis and treatment planning and financial applications include supervising frauds and investment decisions. In governance, AI aids evidence-based decision making in the public policy. Adoption is also affected by cultural attitudes towards AI- attitudes are more or less positive to AI adoption driven by ethical or economic factors making some regions most willing to adopt compared to others. Recognizing these differences is critical to situating leadership approaches in particular contexts.The world of leadership will soon change due to the ever-evolving AI technologies(Judkins et al., 2025). Future leaders will not only require strategic thought and people instincts but also technology fluency and an understanding of how to lead teams that are partly made up of humans but partly composed of intelligent machines and machine learning. It depends on the direction: tearing up opaque AI systems, toughening ethical guidelines, and investing in leader development programs that incorporate AI skills. All in all, the future of leadership is the construction of a collaborative ecosystem where AI and humans are the key agents of progress(Gomez et al., 2025).

FOUNDATIONS OF LEADERSHIP IN THE AI ERA

The conventional leadership models involve a lot of human present judgment, experiences, and interpersonal expertise in making decisions and motivating teams. In such models, leaders are generally guided by historical data, gut instinct, and personal networks as a solution to the problems. Conversely, next-level AI-enhanced leadership introduces high-technology, including machine learning and artificial intelligence algorithms, predictive analytics, and language representation into the management process. By contrasting the traditional leadership with the AI-augmented one, where the focus of the former leadership model lies on vision, values, and humanness of relationship, the AI-enhanced leadership can be seen as an integration of these attributes with current operational data perception and mathematical precision(Alam & Khan, 2024). This transition enables leaders to deal with complex and fast-moving issues both quickly and accurately and introduces the concept of a hybrid model of human guidance and AI intelligence(Joshi, 2025).The complexity of the transition away from traditional to AI-assisted solutions revolves around the concept of balance in the different degrees of human control versus consumer automation.

Balancing Human and AI in Leadership shown in figure 1

Figure 1. Balancing Human and AI in Leadership; Source: Author Compilations

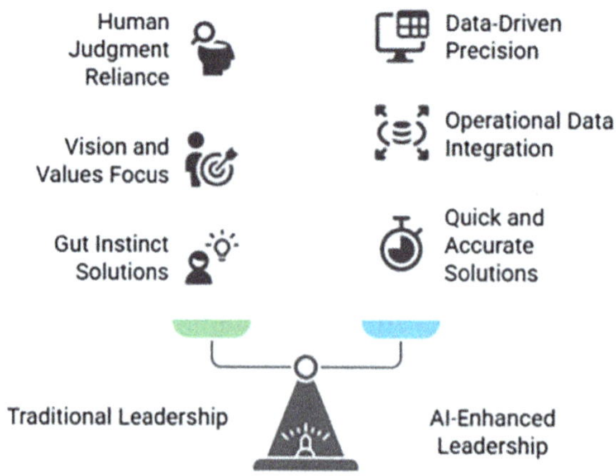

Leaders need to understand when to trust the recommendations that the AI will give them and when they need to ignore them depending on the situation, ethics, or cultural sensitivity(Mentzas et al., 2021). The preoccupation with AI can kill human agency, and failure to use the capacities of AI can result in opportunity losses. The requirements of running an effective AI-augmented leadership thus require a governance structure where technology would not carry out the place of human authority but rather push in the gears(Wang, 2021).

The new era in AI demands new skills that the previous management expertise could not cover. Leaders enabled by AI should be technologically literate and therefore should be able to know the strengths and weaknesses of AI and its ethical implication. The ability to interpret data is also necessary to be able to be critical of AI-derived insights. Another essential competency is adaptability, where the leaders have to cope with continuous technological changes and organizational changes. Furthermore, teamwork is also essential not only when it comes to human teams, but applying AI tools within workflow in a manner that complements human efforts. An AI-driven leader will also have to develop sound ethical thinking so that their use of AI would be responsible(Gurulakshmi & Gayathri, 2024). This involves having fairness of AI algorithms and ensuring that they are not biased, and data privacy. Strategic thinking is no less significant since leaders should focus on aligning the adoption of AI with the long-term objectives of the company instead of making this approach just an efficiency measure. Stripped down to its bare bones, AI leadership is a combination of a technical and ethical stewardship of innovation, in order that innovation comes with the stewardship of ethics(F. Chen, 2022).

On the one hand, there is no aspect of speed and accuracy of data analysis that could possibly be matched to AI, but, on the other hand, there is no sense of empathy, cultural awareness, and moral judgments that could, similarly, be called as effective leadership qualities except the quality provided by emotional intelligence (EI). AI recommendations can be interpreted with the respect of human considerations and organizational values by leaders with high EI. To illustrate, AI system may recommend downsizing to ensure enhanced efficiency, but a leader who possessed strong EI would take into account human and social considerations before making a final decision. Emotional intelligence guarantees that the AI-based decisions will not be mere rational ones, but human ones, as well. Leaders with high EI become the important part of establishing trust in places where employees and AI systems will work in synergy(Wen et al., 2025).

Comparison of Traditional and AI-Enhanced Leadership Models shown in table 1

Table 1. Comparison of Traditional and AI-Enhanced Leadership Models

Aspect	Traditional Leadership	AI-Enhanced Leadership
Decision Basis	Gut instinct, experience	Data analytics, AI algorithms
Strengths	Empathy, vision, values	Speed, accuracy, precision
Risks	Slower, subjective	Overreliance, loss of human touch
Key Skills	Interpersonal, strategic	Tech literacy, adaptability, ethics
Role of EI	Builds trust, human connection	Ensures AI decisions respect people
Example	Team-based decision-making	Amazon uses AI for efficiency with human oversight

They will be able to explain why AI is a good thing, clarify downsides of losing jobs to the AI and engage teams in the change. This understanding empathetic attitude creates a culture of openness, where the employees feel that AI is not a competitor to them; instead, it is a supportive guide to them. Emotional intelligent leaders give a human face to the integration process and thus they make the adoption of AI easy and more functional. Real-world contexts demonstrate the revolutionary effect and power of the AI in leadership(Jarrahi, 2018). In the retail sector, Amazon, along with other allied organizations, adopts artificial intelligence to streamline inventory cycles, enhance customization of experiences to customers, and predicting market trends, whereby leaders get their decisions quicker and more precisely. In the healthcare field, AI can guide hospital managers when allocating resources, conducting triaging and patient flow, and even treatment planning so that leaders can give attention to resources that target the patient. In a similar case, in the field of finance, AI-models that determine risks can assist the management of the bank in predicting some fluctuations on the market and changes in the regulation. Such examples demonstrate that AI helps leaders achieve the strategic vision as well as the precision in their actions(Albannai & Raziq, 2025). Such as Disney that has managed to integrate AI in leadership departments follow some common patterns: they train their leaders and employees on AI, they are transparent regarding AI work, and they institute the principles of ethical leadership. Early adopters portray that AI can work best when it is positioned to work in conjunction with a decision-making environment and not as an alternative to the human mind. The most powerful lesson is that in the age of AI the most effective leadership can be accomplished by blending human strengths of creativity, ethics, and empathy with AI analytical power to deliver efficient results that are also socially responsible(Mseer & Ali Samhan, 2025).

DECISION-MAKING IN THE AGE OF AI

The process of decision-making is systematic involving the following approaches; identifying a problem, finding related information, coming up with possible solutions to form alternatives which can be assessed and the most appropriate course of action chosen. Leaders in the past used to measure up the steps through experience, intuition and historical facts. Nevertheless, when the AI world arrived, the decision-making process had become more complicated because of the explosive evolution of data sources, pace of market dynamics, and the increment in demand on accuracy in situations characterized by high stakes. The concept of decision-making process in relation to the present case is to understand at which point AI could be used to make each step better than the previous ones such as data collection, forecasting of results without neglecting the necessity of human control(Karakose et al., 2023).Shift to proactive strategy formation is perhaps one of the most important transformations AI entails in terms of decision-making. The predictive power of AI enables leaders to foresee the risks and the opportunities prior to their maturation enabling decision-making to become proactive. This development implies that leaders can analyze the possible hazards earlier, recognize opportunities sooner, and stay competitive in volatile businesses. AI systems work extremely well with large and multidimensional volumes of data and identify the patterns that could otherwise remain unnoticeable to human beings(Reverberi et al., 2022). Using machine learning algorithms, natural language processing and deep learning, AI can convert structured and unstructured data into meaningful analysis business needs- sales reports, customer feedback, market trends and social media activity. This measurement-based basis enables the leaders to make informed decisions based on empirical evidence relying on assumptions only. As an example, the AI-driven analytics could detect new consumer preferences, allowing the respective company to realign its strategies before the rest of the industry(Kolbjørnsrud, 2024).

Artificial intelligence is also another major strength when it comes to making decisions because it processes information with an unmatched speed and quantity. When decisions need to be dictated in a span of seconds, as in the case of crisis management or financial trading, AI tools will help evaluate various scenarios within a few seconds to give the most viable alternatives to corporations leaders(Fast & Schroeder, 2020). The speed and accuracy of analysis make the margin of error much smaller and enables leaders to react to challenges that occur within the time-sensitive frame much better. However, despite the useful insights, AI is not flawless. Biases in training data, training data devoid of context or unexpected variables may affect algorithms. The human judgement is crucial in the interpretation of the outputs made by the AI and to be certain it is in line with organizational goals, ethical and cultural values. Leaders need to scrutinize AI prescriptions by taking into consideration the aspects that cannot be measured, e.g. employee spirit, corporate reputation, and the long-term consequences affecting the society. Such human interface of judgment keeps a balance between efficiency and empathy regarding the decision(Duan et al., 2019).The optimal models of decision-making combined the precision of analysis of AI and the humanity with qualitative comprehension held by humans. As an example, an AI system may suggest closing down poorly performing branches of a retail chain but a leader may prefer doing this in phases based on the social impact or even a brand lash in question. This combination of rationality in computing and human scenario makes the decisions practical as well as socially responsible.

AI increases the precision of the decision by minimizing the human mental prejudice like confirmation bias, overconfidence. AI provides data evaluation in an objective and consistent manner making sure that the decision is based on the factual trends instead of personal opinion. Further, AI can conduct simulations to explore different scenarios which will assist the leaders in selecting the strongest course of action in possible situations. Such abilities not only enhance accuracy but boost strategic planning confidence(N. Kumar & Shrivastava, 2025). In order to maximize the benefits of AI in the decision-making process, the organizations should establish the united ecosystem, where the AI tools, human experience, and the organizational data will interact freely. This necessitates investments in data infrastructure, AI education of leaders and governance to make the usage ethically responsible. All this leads to ecosystems where decision-making is timely, accurate and consistent with the long-term organizational vision-making AI into a trusted partner in decision making.

FRAMEWORKS FOR HUMAN-AI COLLABORATION

The role AI plays in leadership can take many forms including the absence of any sort of presence, to full-autonomy in decision-making. On the lowest level, the AI acts as an informational helper, and it can give data information to the leaders without recommendations. On the medium level it will have the role of an analytical companion, proposing possible lines of action on the basis of forecasting models and past trends. The top level is that of the autonomous systems, which can make decisions with limited human control--typically applicable in a setting where quick decisions are needed e.g. high-frequency trading or cybersecuritydefense(McGrath et al., 2024). AI implementation requires a careful selection of the extent of engagement of leaders who should make these decisions based on the need of the complex level of decisions, ethical consideration, and human control.

AI in Leadership Roles shown in Figure 2

Figure 2. AI in Leadership Roles; Source: Author Compilations

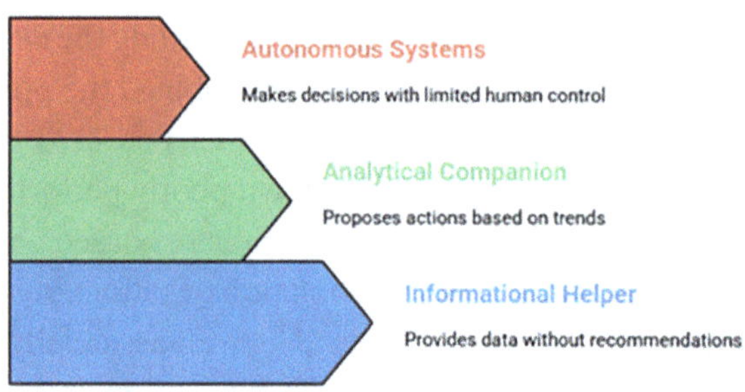

The correct amount of AI participation must be chosen between efficiency and accountability. Although automation can make a process faster and less error-prone, over- dependence on AI can create a risk of losing a human context necessary to make a decision that requires nuance. A layered design, in which all the analysis is done by AI but ethics and strategy remain in human sphere, will guarantee both accurate and responsible leadership. Hybrid intelligence models integrate human thinking capabilities with AI analysis power to create a win-win situation in the decision-making process as shown in the Conceptual Framework (Holter & El-Assady, 2024).

Conceptual Framework: Augmented Leadership Decision-Making Model (ALDM); Source Author Compilations

Human Leadership Skills

↓

AI Capabilities

↓

Human–AI Interaction

↓

Decision-Making Process

↓

Leadership Outcomes

These theories recognize that there are complementary strengths of AI and human beings: where the former performs away more powerfully in big data processing without exhausting, the latter provides creativity, ethical judgment, and situational awareness(Pyae, 2025). An effective hybrid approach combines such abilities in a unified formula, such as, data-driven work operated by AI and insight interpretation and application of insights used strategically by people. The strategy is the most efficient and flexible. Contributing to the technological framework and the people training is essential to organizations that introduce hybrid intelligence. Those in charge and working in teams are to be trained in how AI reasons and how to make inquiries about suggestions it makes. Meanwhile, the AI systems should be made explainable such that the human partners can follow the reasoning of AI easily. Properly used, hybrid intelligence promotes trust and easy cooperation between the human and machine partners. Decision-support systems (DSS) do not intend to deprive leaders of their authority but to assist them in making wise decisions. Such systems give data analyses, visualizations, and the predictive scenarios in which the human leader makes the final decision(Somaratne et al., 2025). Decision-autonomous systems in their turn are empowered to act independently within pre-determined boundaries. Whereas the use of DSS tools is widely accepted on a territory of strategic planning, the autonomous systems are more often used in situations where the lack of time would not allow human response in time, like that of algorithmic trading, where a human reaction may be too slow.

The choice between adopting DSS or autonomous systems is based on the risk factors that an organization can tolerate, speed in operational life, and the ethics regarding the same. A large number of leaders choose such an approach by placing the AI at the bottom of the hierarchy and making it increasingly independent over time as more information about its performance and reliability becomes known. This step-by-step process reduces resistance and guarantees the safe deployment of responsible AI. Collaborative governance provides a framework in which human-AI relationships can operate within ethical, legal and organisational constraints(Huang et al., 2025). That is because such types of governance have clear lines of accountability, which clarify their roles, decision authority, and escalation processes in cases where AI can be used. Also, they need to have transparent processes of auditing AI activities to track their performance, its bias, and how it is adhering to the regulations. They should be applied to data duration plans, privacy safeguards, and ethical principles of AI implementations in leadership practices(S. Kumar, 2024). Powerful governance systems should embrace inclusivity and encourage diverse stakeholder's namely technical teams, business leaders, ethicists, and end-users, in decision-making on the role of AI. All these differences in the views allow early recognizing possible risks and unintended consequences. Through the incorporation of ethical considerations in governance arrangements, an organization can create a sense of compliance to the values of the society, establish trust, and improve resilience(Edwards et al., 2025).

TRUST, ETHICS, AND TRANSPARENCY

The success of AI implementation in leadership and making decisions relies on trust. AI adoption by leaders, employees, and stakeholders is more feasible when they, in turn, are confident that the systems are trustworthy, secure, and align with business ideals. The process of establishing trust should start with proving the AI system to be highly accurate, reliable, and just, on the one hand, and highly productive when applied to practical use cases, on the other hand(Abbasi, 2004). This entails the need to have clarity on communication regarding the functioning of AI, its limitations, and how information led to maintaining data safety and security. Trust is further built when the leaders assure their transparency in the approach of incorporating AI, demonstrating that the technology is a mechanism of empowerment, not substitution. Key Factors in Building Trust, Ethics, and Transparency in AI Leadership shown in table 2

Table 2. Key Factors in Building Trust, Ethics, and Transparency in AI Leadership

Factor	Description
Accuracy & Reliability	AI must deliver consistent, correct, and fair results to gain user confidence.
Clear Communication	Explain AI's functions, limitations, and decision-making process openly.
Data Safety & Security	Ensure strong protection of personal and organizational data.
Transparency in Adoption	Show AI as a tool for empowerment, not replacement of human roles.
Feedback Loops	Allow stakeholders to share experiences, report issues, and suggest improvements.
Stakeholder Participation	Engage users in AI development and refinement to create ownership.
Continuous Monitoring & Auditing	Regularly evaluate AI performance and make responsible updates.

The other important element of trust building is the development of feedback loops in which users are able to provide their experiences, report problems, and recommend how these can be improved. Stakeholders will have the sense of ownership in terms of AI systems therefore fostering acceptance through this participatory model. The trust is strengthened further when organizations undertake continuous monitoring, periodic audit, and responsible upgrades, so that there is assurance that apart from remaining true to its intended goal, AI does not wander to an unwarranted destination.Leadership in ethics in AI exceeds the adherence to the laws, it is more about integrity, fairness, and respect to human dignity through the AI-based decisions. Leaders should gauge how AI applications will address organizational values, norms in the society and the common good(Elia, 2009). This will include the problem of setting proper ethical standards of data use, consent, and harm prevention. Ethical AI leadership skills also require giving a thorough consideration on whether some decisions ought to be left as human-made, especially when they are filed with profound social or moral consequences.

Ethical leader also foresees the possibility of using AI in an unethical way like in surveillance and bias hiring along with manipulative advertisement. Among the prevention interventions, there is the development of cross-disciplinary ethics committees, a diversity of perspectives in the design of AI, and ensuring that accountability is not held by computers. Leaders can drive ethical governance of AI by leading their organizations in responsible innovation by prioritizing the role of ethical principles in the governance of AI(Bertino et al., 2019).Algorithic transparency refers to an action of bringing clarity to the AI processes to both non-technical and technical stakeholders. This is crucial since the use of opaque and black-box AI can bring about mistrust especially in cases where decisions can affect career, financial performance, or social good of a people. Transparency means recording of rules by which algorithms are trained, data sets employed, and decision making reasoning guidance of outputs. Giving explainable AI (XAI) tools will make results less mysterious, enabling the stakeholders to check how fair and accurate decisions (Turilli & Floridi, 2009).

Accountability further makes transparency well balanced since it entails clear line of responsibility in case mistakes are made or harm is caused by the AI systems. Leaders have to make the governance structure in such a way that they ensure there is accountability on the outcome of the AI either to the human operator or the team of elements which develops or an oversight committee. This makes sure that the implementation of AI does not leave any "responsibility gap" in which there is nobody responsible(S. Kumar, 2023). This model of accountability should also incorporate legal and regulatory compliance and give an organizational integrity as well as confidence in the eyes of the people.The issue of bias in AI is not unique and can occur even despite the fact that there is no explicit bias in the system: AI systems are frequently biased due to bias in the data used to train it: given that the data represents historical inequalities or imbalanced representation, the AI would recreate and even magnify these biases. The task of handling bias can start with selecting datasets to automatically select diverse, fair and accurate datasets. System-wide detection, testing of sensitivity, and evaluation metrics of fairness should be conducted during the Artificial Intelligence lifecycle(Manoharan et al., 2024). Along with technical solutions, the need to handle bias relies on organizational support of the idea of inclusivity in AI teams. Different points of view at the design and testing stages could contribute to the exposure of blind spots and their correction. In addition, leaders ought to provide avenues through which concerned persons can air perceived prejudices and provide remedies. Finally, bias management is a continuous process which requires vigilance, openness, and ethical responsibility in purporting to guarantee AI aids in the facilitation of equitable decision-making.

HUMAN-AI INTERACTION IN WORKPLACE COMMUNICATION

AI use in workplace communication has restructured organizational flow of information. Chatbots, virtual assistants and natural language processing systems manage to automate the processes and responses, streamline the answers to repetitive questions and messages are clear and relevant. Such systems aid in minimizing gaps in communication as they provide immediate response, provide a summary to the discussion and even translate languages on the fly, making international collaboration much easier. Nonetheless, to make AI-assisted communication truly successful, teams will need to strike a balance between the automation process and its human component as they will need to ensure that messages remain nuanced and emotionally sensitive. AI-driven communication will also have other negative implications of leading to over dependency on automated programs, minimizing human interaction, and interpersonal abilities. Leaders have to implement regulations that will be clear as to when to apply AI and when to interfere with human assistance. Employee training on how to critically read messages proposed by AIs prevents them against mindlessly accepting any automated recommendations, particularly on such sensitive conversations(Möllers et al., 2024). The AI age needs us to amalgamate excellence of machines with humanity of emotional communication as a fundamental part of workplace communication.The technologies implemented by AI can be critical in enhancing practices that promote cooperation within a multi-team set up through the joint platforms to share ideas, monitor tasks, and track performance. Project management systems with AI capabilities may determine the overlap of skills, delegate tasks to employees depending on their strength and forecast workflow bottlenecks. This would assist in production of an open environment whereby every member in the team will comprehend his/her role and contributions. Also, AI analytics can show collaboration patterns so the leaders can draw attention to coordination issues before they grow to complex ones.

Nonetheless, AI-powered teamwork is the most effective in collaboration with a culture of inclusiveness and the attitude to plurality of opinions. The excess use of task allocation based on data can miss more immaterial forms of creativity that cannot be measured as accurately. The leaders should guarantee that the recommendations provided by AIs can supplement, but not substitute, open discussion and brainstorming sessions. The final objective is to enable AI to do the operational spine of the collaboration so that human teams can have higher domains of the strategy and innovation(Jain et al., 2023b).In incorporating AI into the working process, there is always resistance because of threats of job loss, shortage of technical expertise or faith in automated units of judgment. Such opposition is not surprising because employees can feel like AI is a threat to their professional significance. To solve these concerns, it is important that the leadership communicates openly and transparently. AI can increase human capabilities and that makes anxiety reduce by showing how it can increase human capabilities and not replace it. Training and exposure through some hands-on activities can help the employees feel more relaxed about using the AI tools and develop some confidence and acceptance(Ashktorab et al., 2021).

The same can be said about emotional responses during the implementation of AI. The leaders ought to listen actively to employee comments, where they are expected to report concerns and make recommendations. Organizations can make employees feel like they have ownership of the decision involving the adoption of AI through participation in the decision-making process. Such a comprehensive attitude leaves no trace of changes in the transition to AI-assisted processes as an imposed force.

Leaders are the key to the trouble-free integration of AI technologies(Huda et al., 2024). An effective plan should start by formulating a concise picture on how AI will fit into the mission of the organization and how it will benefit the firm and the employees. Illustrative examples and success stories must be provided to tangibly illustrate the vision to the employees in a way that they can associate themselves with. It is also the leaders who need to make realistic expectations by explaining that the process of AI implementation is dynamic and some changes might be necessary in the future(Talukder et al., 2025a). Moreover, ethical leadership in AI adoption implies the focus on transparency, accountability, and fairness. Leaders are supposed to be examples by using AI tools themselves setting the example that they are useful in everyday operations. Small wins achieved along the way in the integration of AI should be identified and the world celebrated, as it creates momentum and positivity. Finally, leadership approaches that combine the technological progress with humanity-focused values would promote trust, minimize opposition, and stimulate a culture of innovation(Talukder et al., 2025b).

CASE STUDIES OF HUMAN-AI COLLABORATION

Artificial Intelligence (AI) is now a natural part of strategic business decision-making, as organizations have unprecedented capabilities to process large volumes of information, recognize patterns and simulate the future in record time and precision. To the extent that they allow executives to predict the market trends, optimising the distribution of resources, and individualising customer engagement strategies, AI systems through predictive analytics, machine learning models, and advanced decision-support platforms are being applied in finance, retail, and manufacturing sectors. As an example, Amazon and Netflix use AI to generate data-wise content recommendations, inventory forecasts, and price alterations that have a direct impact on the growth of revenue(Zhang et al., 2024). Among the largest advantages of AI in strategic decision-making is its capacity to compensate the biases that usually affect the human judgment, basing the decisions instead on the information-supported insights. But AI is most effective alongside human intuition and creativity, and the awareness of the context; which cannot be fully matched using AI(Lai et al., 2022). The frameworks of decision-making including the human-in-the-loop approach guarantee that when the AI processes the data and presents the viable insights, a human leadership makes the final decision taking into account the ethical, cultural, and long-term aspects of the given ideas. Case studies of businesses such as IBM and Unilever demonstrate the effectiveness of having all the human experience with the use of AI-driven forecasts that end up with stronger and more robust strategies that can adapt to market triggers. This integration does not only augment precision but also trust amongst stakeholders, and hence AI is a reliable ally in building the future of organizations.

Governments worldwide are increasingly leveraging AI to enhance policy formulation, evaluation, and implementation. AI tools can process complex socio-economic datasets, monitor real-time developments, and even simulate the potential impacts of proposed policies before they are enacted. For example, in Singapore, AI-driven urban planning models predict traffic congestion, environmental impacts, and housing needs decades into the future, enabling more informed and sustainable development policies. Similarly, in Estonia, AI is used to automate parts of the legal drafting process and streamline public service delivery, freeing policymakers to focus on higher-order strategic concerns. AI's predictive capabilities are invaluable for identifying unintended policy consequences, evaluating trade-offs, and ensuring evidence-based governance(Fragiadakis et al., 2024). However, integrating AI into policymaking raises critical questions about transparency, accountability, and data privacy. To address these challenges, some governments adopt AI governance frameworks and ethics boards to oversee AI recommendations, ensuring they align with democratic principles and social equity. When properly implemented, AI-assisted policymaking can reduce administrative inefficiencies, enhance public trust, and lead to more inclusive, data-driven policies that are responsive to the dynamic needs of citizens(Dewangan & Kumar, 2024).

During crisis- natural disasters, pandemics, or mass industrial accidents--AI is crucial to help climb the situational awareness, resource mobilization and decision-making acceleration curve. The sophisticated models of AI are able to interpret satellite images, social media streams, weather predictions and sensor readings on a real time basis to create zone maps of disasters, forecast the radiations spreading and prioritize rescue missions. Amid the COVID-19 pandemic, AI-based epidemiological models provided governments and health organizations with valuable predictions concerning infection peaks, resource optimization, and the characterization of vulnerable groups of the population, where they could be focused. Likewise, AI applications dominate wildfire infrastructure by incorporating the information structuralized by drones, climate sensors, and past fire trends to offer optimal assistance to fire-fighters and emergency services in the most urgent locations(Jiang et al., 2021). The primaryibrimpAlphaRabbitgg justification of AI in any crisis-related situation is in the capacity to operate on multi-source and high-volume data which would be able to overwhelm a human workforce in isolation. Nevertheless, it can only be deployed successfully in case it has pre-existing infrastructure, AI and human respondent collaboration, and training. Japan earthquake response and the U.S Federal Emergency Manager Agency (FEMA) provide evidence based case studies that use a combined approach where AI plays a supportive role and loss of life and economic damage and time taken during recovery is largely mitigated as long as human decision-makers trust and comprehend AI outputs(Talukder et al., 2024).

The experiences of incorporating AI into industries and governments can be used globally, and they help in building upon future relationships between humans and AI. The most important of these lessons is that the use of AI must have a distinct purpose and a decisive level of leadership involvement as opposed to the blind compliance with trends. The examples of Canada and South Korea have shown that a strategic investment in AI literacy, infrastructure and ethical governance can result in increased levels of trust by the population and improved long-term performance. Another key lesson is that it is essential to develop flexible, adaptable AI systems that would grow with the shifting contexts and data environments(Kunal et al., 2023). Excessive use of narrow AI may cause felled-outdated or biased suggestions, such as in some predictive policing systems that generated community apprehension owing to built-in prejudice. Moreover, promoting such a culture of transparency, the logic of the decision-making process built by AI could be properly explained to the stakeholders, which assists in dealing with prejudices and antagonism. Such global partnerships as the AI4EU project organized by the European Union demonstrate that the international exchange of knowledge between nations and domains will make the best practices go faster and reduce the amount of mistakes being made ones again. Finally, the most effective applications come when AI is neither understood as a substitute to human judgment, but rather, a superb co-worker that extends human ability to tackle challenging problems, ethical decision-making, and significant advances in innovation(Hassan & Kumar, 2024).

CHALLENGES AND LIMITATIONS

Although astonishing progress has been achieved, there are still substantial technical limitations to AI systems that could interfere with their usefulness in the setting of leadership and decision-making. Among the central problems is the inability to have genuine contextual knowledge: the AI can recognize massive data and detect patterns, but it will not be in a position to have in-depth knowledge of human intentions, feelings, or the socio-cultural context unless demarcated as a way of programming it. The other problem is that of generalization, in which cases AI systems learning in a particular scenario never work in a slightly different or unexpected situation. Algorithms can be biased, even when they are based on high-quality data, because such bias tends to be inherited during the training process due to the lack of diversity in the training data. Also, the interpretability of models is an obstacle, especially in deep learning models; they work as [black boxes] and frequently it is hard to comprehend how AI reached a decision. This obscurity has the potential to minimize trust and make accountability an issue. Also, the use of AI systems demands a lot of computing power and stable infrastructure, which is not always accessed particularly in an environment that is resource-constrained. Technical disadvantages do not only deal with performance but adaptability too, e.g. current AI will tend to fail in dynamic, fast-changing events that necessitate adaptable reasoning and having to extend than rely on prior training. These limitations will need to be overcome through explainable AI innovations, learning models that are adaptive, and incorporation of human supervision at decision-critical stages.

The usage of AI to build empathetic leadership depends on how much sensitive data is available and could be collected, starting with the levels of employee performance and moving to the current emotional analytics. This reliance poses privateers and safety considerations of great concern. In addition to the loss of confidential information, violations that allow unauthorized access or malicious cyber attacks may lead to the reduction by leaders, organizations, and stakeholders of trust in each other. The moral conflict also gets worse when the analysis of personal communications, biometric indicators, or behaviour patterns is done via AI systems, since such monitoring might be deemed intrusive unless addressed transparently. Besides, the different regulations on data protection around the world like GDPR in Europe or CCPA in California make it more difficult to comply with data protection requirements when doing business on a global level. The other issue to contend with is data integrity- distorted or compromised datasets may create inaccurate AI suggestions. Such misinformation can be disastrous in terms of policy, strategy or crisis response in the context of leadership. Hence, it is necessary that organizations embrace effective protection strategies of cyberspace such as cybersecurity models, anonymization processes, and access control policies accompanied by an informed consent culture. The adoption of AI in leadership without effective data governance means that the practice may come out as exploitative instead of empowerment, which is the core of its empathetic goals.

The usage of AI to build empathetic leadership depends on how much sensitive data is available and could be collected, starting with the levels of employee performance and moving to the current emotional analytics. This reliance poses privateness and safety considerations of great concern. In addition to the loss of confidential information, violations that allow unauthorized access or malicious cyber attacks may lead to the reduction by leaders, organizations, and stakeholders of trust in each other. The moral conflict also gets worse when the analysis of personal communications, biometric indicators, or behaviour patterns is done via AI systems, since such monitoring might be deemed intrusive unless addressed transparently. Besides, the different regulations on data protection around the world like GDPR in Europe or CCPA in California make it more difficult to comply with data protection requirements when doing business on a global level. The other issue to contend with is data integrity- distorted or compromised datasets may create inaccurate AI suggestions. Such misinformation can be disastrous in terms of policy, strategy or crisis response in the context of leadership. Hence, it is necessary that organizations embrace effective protection strategies of cyberspace such as cybersecurity models, anonymization processes, and access control policies accompanied by an informed consent culture. The adoption of AI in leadership without effective data governance means that the practice may come out as exploitative instead of empowerment, which is the core of its empathetic goals.

The idea of empathetic leadership, managed by AI, is not just a technical endeavour, but is overwhelmingly culturally and organizationally driven. Drivers of AI adoption resistance include threats of job replacement or fear that AI may not be just, or the fear of letting aware decisions being made by machines. The hierarchical nature of most organizations and vested power politics may slow the process of AI system assimilation within an organization thus, reducing its application when it is against the established order or requires a change in work routines. Besides, the perception of AI strongly depends on the culture there may be something beneficial, innovative in terms of leadership assistance in one situation, whereas it may be viewed as intrusive, dehumanizing in another scenario. Digital literacy levels of employees and leaders also precondition their ability to be ready to the implementation of the tool, and in case of the lack of proper training, even the most advanced AI tools can be underutilized or misunderstood. Building of trust, open communications, and involvement strategies in implementation play major roles in resolving these barriers. Notably, incorporation of AI into the organization must resonate with values of the organization, and its ethical guidelines should be embraced so that technology becomes the ally in accomplishment of mutual goals rather than the force that can be considered as the enemy. The capabilities of the AI system to be used in empathetic leadership will not be fully achieved without taking into consideration such cultural and organizational issues.

FUTURE TRENDS IN HUMAN-AI LEADERSHIP

The rise of AI as a forthcoming leadership tool will take automation or decision-making supports to levels much more profound. The developed AI systems will incorporate multimodal features where the concept of natural language processing (NLP), computer vision, real-time analysis, and emotional intelligence modelling exists in one ecosystem. These tools will enable leaders to use highly contextualized information in real-time, render complex data in easy to understand and visualize ways, and model next possibilities before a serious decision can be made. To put a specific example, AI-enabled utilization of strategic dashboards may combine live financial indicators, analysis of market sentiments and geopolitical changes, allowing leaders to better predict risks and opportunities. Besides, conversational agents-highly intelligent AI companions will be able to realize the preference in leadership styles, communication peculiarities, and ethical limits, providing persons with tailored advice on how to manage a crisis or transform an organization. These tools are eventually going to become adaptive co-pilots to any leader that learns and builds off the past decisions in ever more refined recommendations on what to do base on the needs of the organization.

The future of leadership is moving towards the foresight analytics as AI predicts the obstacles as well as opportunities in advance prior to it revealing to human observers. Predictive leadership tools will be used to predict trends based on scenario modelling and deep learning algorithms that measure trends in the market and employee performance, consumer behaviour, and world events in order to give early warnings to decision makers. To illustrate, predictive AI would allow months prior to notifying a CEO about the possibility of supply chain disruptions and strategies to mitigate the problem. In addition to operational foresight, the systems will assist leaders in forecasting cultural or workforce changes taking place, including changes caused by automation to job roles, or trends in employee engagement levels. This will make leadership cease to be a reactive process with the future-oriented process. The capability to listen to predictive models not as a predetermined forecast but as dynamic potential-the capacity to balance the world of quantified results, with the world of qualitative judgment in creating powerful and flexible strategies-will become a competitive advantage of leaders.

The AI will be central in enhancing the inclusive and sustainable leadership models. In the case of inclusivity, AI has the potential to enable leaders to identify and counteract unconscious bias during the hiring process, promotions and during performance reviews, via examining the use of language, decisioning patterns and overall demographics in the broader organizations. The AI-driven platforms will introduce transparency dashboards where the measures of diversity can be tracked, and the existing disparities can be identified before they grow to problems with systemic roots. Within the context of sustainability, AI would enable business leaders to achieve the goals of ESG, including supply, use of resources and ESG regulations, the adherence to which AI can help analyze. It also can model the ecological and social long-term effects of corporate decisions helping leaders use strategies that attain a combination of profitability and responsibility. With stakeholders continuously engaged in the challenge of ethical governance, AI will give the leaders the opportunity of making their decision making in line with their values of fairness, equity, and stewardship of the environment thereby making the leadership less profit-acquisition but purposeful.

In light of how AI is transforming the face of leadership, education of our future leaders will need a dual emphasis, one in technological agility or skills, and the other of humanistic leadership skills. The leaders should be educated not only on how to recognize AI abilities and limitations as well as its ethical considerations but also on how to create a sense of trust, empathy, and cooperation in AI-human teams. All available leadership development programs will also have to be modified with AI literacy in place, such as those on algorithm biases, explain ability, and data governance, so that their leaders can assist in decision-making with the AI outputs without accepting them unquestioningly. Moreover, leaders shall be required to change their decision style to respond more to ambiguity, probabilistic thinking and dynamic contexts. Firms will also be forced to develop heads of daily learning to make sure that leaders do not take into account the developments in technology. Finally, the most effective AI-driven future leaders will combine precision and speed of the AI with creativity, vision and moral intuition that is uniquely human.

CONCLUSION AND RECOMMENDATIONS

Artificial Intelligence (AI) in leadership is no longer a sci-fi dream but is an advancing reality that impacts the decision making, communication, and growth of an organization. This book has discussed the idea of Human-AI Leadership on how AI systems can be a force multiplier to human capabilities and not a replacement. Among the key insights, the realization one can find is the understanding that a leader who uses AI gets access to more advanced analytics, real-time data, and predictive models, which contribute greatly to a strategic planning process. Also, understanding the dynamics of AI through its compassionate and ethical applications can ameliorate technology-related barriers that divide the human world and the demands. But the road is not always rosy, when speaking of the problems to be considered, such as bias, concerns of privacy, an over-reliance on automation, and the necessity of transparent governance have been cited as the key areas of concern. Finally, AI can facilitate the combination of human intuition and precision, thus leading to a leadership model that is versatile, inclusive, and ready to face the future. This understanding paves way towards a change in the leadership style which is concentrating more on authority to one that is more data-driven and collaborative and ethically conscious.

In order to achieve maximum positive outcomes of AI leadership, it is necessary to work on the development of efficient human-AI cooperation systems. The initial phase is related to the establishment of the AI literacy culture where leaders and groups of people should know the capacities and the limits of the AI tools. This concerns specialized trainings, use of simulations and practical projects all of which demystify AI technologies. Second, companies must set up proper human control systems, i.e., critical assessment of AI recommendations instead of blind adherence. Decision accuracy can be increased through the co-creation workshops in which insights of AI are combined with human judgment, but creativity and empathy are not lost. Also, making AI tools context-aware and explainable will enable leaders to make sound decisions without missing the compass of organizational values. A key factor in this is trust, the employees and other stakeholders should feel that AI is not an enemy but an aid. A feedback loop, in which both humanity and the AI systems are learning based upon the information provided by the other, can establish a self-learning and continuous improvement loop, innovation that is hampered without protecting ethical integrity.

Leadership use of AI initiates serious implications on policy, which cannot be ignored in organizations. Data protection, mitigation of bias and ethical deployment should be critical with respect to governance structures. This will involve the drawing of policies that will clearly spell out the role of AI, lines of responsibility and boundary to data use. The development of ethical AI principles should be performed with the reference to the industry standards and legal regulations, so that they should be met with the focus on enhancing the ethical use of industry and promoting fairness and inclusivity. When it comes to leadership, policies must promote transparency so that it is known when AI systems influence or take over a decision. The other policy consideration is on the workforce transition issue which includes reskilling initiatives to enable employees go to work in AI augmented environment. AI audit systems should be implemented in organizations as well, to conduct an audit of AI applications in leadership on a periodic basis to check the performance, fairness, and unintended outcomes of said applications. Institutionalization of these policies means that organizations not only curtail risk but also place themselves as responsible innovators in the age of AI, strengthening trust in the organization among the employees, customers, and society generally.

Although, the implementation of AI in leadership is gaining traction fast, there is still much that needs to be done in terms of research. One of such areas is the investigation of how the cultural, regional, and industry-specific reasons contribute to the success of the Human-AI leadership models. Another study that ought to be conducted is the psychological effects of AI-based collaboration on leaders and teams insomuch as trust building, flexibility, and decision fatigue are concerned. The next potential direction is researching the way AI can lead to diversity and inclusion, particularly in the cross-cultural and remote workplace settings. It can be seen that technological research must investigate creating more personable and explainable AI to have a higher understanding of subtle human emotions and social signals. More long term, interdisciplinary research can be used to incorporate lessons across psychology, behavioural economics, data science, and ethics into more durable theories of Human-AI leadership. It may be able to fast-track innovation and be ethically aligned by creating research collaborations between academia, industry, and government. Using this roadmap, the future of Human-AI leadership can be guided towards belonging not only to the technological advancement of Human-AI collaborative leadership, but also the socially responsible and human-centered route.

REFERENCES

Abbasi, K. (2004). Transparency and trust. *BMJ, 329*(7472), /bmj/329/7472/0.8.atom. DOI: 10.1136/bmj.329.7472.0-g

Alam, S., & Khan, M. F. (2024). Enhancing AI-Human Collaborative Decision-Making in Industry 4.0 Management Practices. *IEEE Access : Practical Innovations, Open Solutions, 12*, 119433–119444. DOI: 10.1109/ACCESS.2024.3449415

Albannai, N. A. A., & Raziq, M. M. (2025). Navigating ethical, human-centric leadership in AI-driven organizations: A thematic literature review. *Service Industries Journal*, •••, 1–28. DOI: 10.1080/02642069.2025.2534360

Ashktorab, Z., Dugan, C., Johnson, J., Pan, Q., Zhang, W., Kumaravel, S., & Campbell, M. (2021). Effects of Communication Directionality and AI Agent Differences in Human-AI Interaction. *Proceedings of the 2021 CHI Conference on Human Factors in Computing Systems*, 1–15. DOI: 10.1145/3411764.3445256

Bertino, E., Kundu, A., & Sura, Z. (2019). Data Transparency with Blockchain and AI Ethics. *ACM Journal of Data and Information Quality*, *11*(4), 1–8. DOI: 10.1145/3312750

Chen, F. (2022). Human-AI Cooperation in Education:Human in Loop and Teaching as leadership. *Journal of Educational Technology and Innovation*, *2*(1). Advance online publication. DOI: 10.61414/jeti.v2i1.34

Dai, R., Thomas, M. K. E., & Rawolle, S. (2025). The roles of AI and educational leaders in AI-assisted administrative decision-making: A proposed framework for symbiotic collaboration. *Australian Educational Researcher*, *52*(2), 1471–1487. DOI: 10.1007/s13384-024-00771-8

Dewangan, S., & Kumar, S. (2024). AI and Big Data Analytics Revolutionizing Industry 5.0: Unlocking the Power of Smart Manufacturing and Beyond. In Darwish, D. (Ed.), (pp. 398–410). Advances in Business Information Systems and Analytics. IGI Global., DOI: 10.4018/979-8-3693-0413-6.ch016

Duan, Y., Edwards, J. S., & Dwivedi, Y. K. (2019). Artificial intelligence for decision making in the era of Big Data – evolution, challenges and research agenda. *International Journal of Information Management*, *48*, 63–71. DOI: 10.1016/j.ijinfomgt.2019.01.021

Edwards, J., Nguyen, A., Lämsä, J., Sobocinski, M., Whitehead, R., Dang, B., Roberts, A., & Järvelä, S. (2025). Human- AI collaboration: Designing artificial agents to facilitate socially shared regulation among learners. *British Journal of Educational Technology*, *56*(2), 712–733. DOI: 10.1111/bjet.13534

Elia, J. (2009). Transparency rights, technology, and trust. *Ethics and Information Technology*, *11*(2), 145–153. DOI: 10.1007/s10676-009-9192-z

Fast, N. J., & Schroeder, J. (2020). Power and decision making: New directions for research in the age of artificial intelligence. *Current Opinion in Psychology*, *33*, 172–176. DOI: 10.1016/j.copsyc.2019.07.039 PMID: 31473586

Fragiadakis, G., Diou, C., Kousiouris, G., & Nikolaidou, M. (2024). *Evaluating Human-AI Collaboration: A Review and Methodological Framework* (Version 2). arXiv. DOI: 10.48550/ARXIV.2407.19098

Gomez, C., Cho, S. M., Ke, S., Huang, C.-M., & Unberath, M. (2025). Human-AI collaboration is not very collaborative yet: A taxonomy of interaction patterns in AI-assisted decision making from a systematic review. *Frontiers of Computer Science*, *6*, 1521066. DOI: 10.3389/fcomp.2024.1521066

Gurulakshmi, S., & Gayathri, R. (2024). The Human-AI Partnership: Elevating Leadership With Emotional Intelligence. In Sayed, Z. (Ed.), (pp. 255–284). Advances in Logistics, Operations, and Management Science. IGI Global., DOI: 10.4018/979-8-3693-7372-9.ch011

Hassan, S. C., & Kumar, S. (2024). Safe Green Hydrogen: Production and Storage as an Emerging Source of Energy for Sustainable Future. In Raboaca, M. S., Djohra, S., Moussaoui, O., Mihaltan, T. C., & Koussa, M. (Eds.), (pp. 143–153). Advances in Chemical and Materials Engineering. IGI Global., DOI: 10.4018/979-8-3693-1014-4.ch008

Holter, S., & El-Assady, M. (2024). Deconstructing Human-AI Collaboration: Agency, Interaction, and Adaptation. *Computer Graphics Forum*, *43*(3), e15107. DOI: 10.1111/cgf.15107

Huang, G., Lo, W.-H., Liu, G., Luo, Y., & Jin, Y. (2025). Toward AI Standardization: A Triadic Human-AI Collaboration Framework for Multi-Level Autonomous Mobility. *2025 IEEE Conference on Artificial Intelligence (CAI)*, 1568–1577. DOI: 10.1109/CAI64502.2025.00292

Huda, Md. N., Talukder, M. B., & Kumar, S. (2024). Securing Healthcare AI: Applied Federal Learning. In P. Bhattacharya, H. Liu, P. K. Dutta, J. J. P. C. Rodrigues, & G. Sethi (Eds.), *Revolutionizing Healthcare 5.0: The Power of Generative AI* (Vol. 571, pp. 255–272). Springer Nature Switzerland. DOI: 10.1007/978-3-031-75771-6_17

Jain, R., Garg, N., & Khera, S. N. (2023a). Effective human–AI work design for collaborative decision-making. *Kybernetes*, *52*(11), 5017–5040. DOI: 10.1108/K-04-2022-0548

Jain, R., Garg, N., & Khera, S. N. (2023b). Effective human–AI work design for collaborative decision-making. *Kybernetes*, *52*(11), 5017–5040. DOI: 10.1108/K-04-2022-0548

Jarrahi, M. H. (2018). Artificial intelligence and the future of work: Human-AI symbiosis in organizational decision making. *Business Horizons*, *61*(4), 577–586. DOI: 10.1016/j.bushor.2018.03.007

Jiang, J. A., Wade, K., Fiesler, C., & Brubaker, J. R. (2021). Supporting Serendipity: Opportunities and Challenges for Human-AI Collaboration in Qualitative Analysis. *Proceedings of the ACM on Human-Computer Interaction, 5*(CSCW1), 1–23. DOI: 10.1145/3449168

Joshi, S. (2025). *Comprehensive Review of Artificial Intelligence in Management, Leadership, Decision-Making and Collaboration. SSRN.* DOI: 10.2139/ssrn.5221744

Judkins, J. T., Hwang, Y., & Kim, S. (2025). Human-AI interaction: Augmenting decision-making for IT leader's project selection. *Information Development*, *41*(3), 1009–1035. DOI: 10.1177/02666669241249744

Karakose, T., Demirkol, M., Yirci, R., Polat, H., Ozdemir, T. Y., & Tülübaş, T. (2023). A Conversation with ChatGPT about Digital Leadership and Technology Integration: Comparative Analysis Based on Human–AI Collaboration. *Administrative Sciences*, *13*(7), 157. DOI: 10.3390/admsci13070157

Kolbjørnsrud, V. (2024). Designing the Intelligent Organization: Six Principles for Human-AI Collaboration. *California Management Review*, *66*(2), 44–64. DOI: 10.1177/00081256231211020

Kumar, N., & Shrivastava, A. (2025). The artificial intelligence (AI) revolution: Evolving business decision-making in the digital age. *Business Information Review*, *02663821251364069*(3), 183–196. Advance online publication. DOI: 10.1177/02663821251364069

Kumar, S. (2023). Impact of Digitalization in Higher Education and Smart Learning Techniques. In *Sustainable Development Goal Advancement Through Digital Innovation in the Service Sector* (pp. 198–207). IGI Global. DOI: 10.4018/979-8-3693-0650-5.ch013

Kumar, S. (2024). The Role of Digital Marketing on Customer Engagement in the Hospitality Industry. In Bansal, R., Ngah, A. H., Chakir, A., & Pruthi, N. (Eds.), (pp. 177–191). Advances in Business Information Systems and Analytics. IGI Global., DOI: 10.4018/979-8-3693-0815-8.ch010

Kunal, R. M., & Bansal, J. (2023). The Future of OpenAI Tools: Opportunities and Challenges for Human-AI Collaboration. *2023 2nd International Conference on Futuristic Technologies (INCOFT)*, 1–6. DOI: 10.1109/INCOFT60753.2023.10424990

Lai, V., Carton, S., Bhatnagar, R., Liao, Q. V., Zhang, Y., & Tan, C. (2022). Human-AI Collaboration via Conditional Delegation: A Case Study of Content Moderation. *CHI Conference on Human Factors in Computing Systems*, 1–18. DOI: 10.1145/3491102.3501999

Manoharan, G., Rao, C. V. G., Ashtikar, S. P., Kumar, S., & Nivedha, M. (2024). Voyage Virtuoso: Artificial Intelligence in Transforming Tourism. In Kumar, S., Talukder, M. B., & Pego, A. (Eds.), *Advances in Hospitality, Tourism, and the Services Industry* (pp. 79–97). IGI Global., DOI: 10.4018/979-8-3693-1978-9.ch004

McGrath, M. J., Duenser, A., Lacey, J., & Paris, C. (2024). *Collaborative human-AI trust (CHAI-T): A process framework for active management of trust in human-AI collaboration* (Version 1). arXiv. DOI: 10.48550/ARXIV.2404.01615

Mentzas, G., Lepenioti, K., Bousdekis, A., & Apostolou, D. (2021). Data-Driven Collaborative Human-AI Decision Making. In Dennehy, D., Griva, A., Pouloudi, N., Dwivedi, Y. K., Pappas, I., & Mäntymäki, M. (Eds.), *Responsible AI and Analytics for an Ethical and Inclusive Digitized Society* (Vol. 12896, pp. 120–131). Springer International Publishing., DOI: 10.1007/978-3-030-85447-8_11

Molina, D. A., Kharlov, V., & Chen, J.-S. (2024). Towards Effective Human-AI Collaboration in Decision-Making: A Comprehensive Review and Conceptual Framework. *2024 Portland International Conference on Management of Engineering and Technology (PICMET)*, 1–6. DOI: 10.23919/PICMET64035.2024.10653303

Möllers, M., Berger, B., & Klein, S. (2024). Contrasting human-AI workplace relationship configurations. In Constantiou, I., Joshi, M. P., & Stelmaszak, M. (Eds.), *Research Handbook on Artificial Intelligence and Decision Making in Organizations* (pp. 282–303). Edward Elgar Publishing., DOI: 10.4337/9781803926216.00025

Mseer, I., & Ali Samhan, A. A. (2025). Collaboration Between Humans and AI. In Alaali, M., Musleh Al-Sartawi, A. M. A., & Aydiner, A. S. (Eds.), *The Paradigm Shift from a Linear Economy to a Smart Circular Economy* (Vol. 586, pp. 1299–1308). Springer Nature Switzerland., DOI: 10.1007/978-3-031-87550-2_83

Munyaka, I., Ashktorab, Z., Dugan, C., Johnson, J., & Pan, Q. (2023). Decision Making Strategies and Team Efficacy in Human-AI Teams. *Proceedings of the ACM on Human-Computer Interaction, 7*(CSCW1), 1–24. DOI: 10.1145/3579476

Pyae, A. (2025). *The Human-AI Handshake Framework: A Bidirectional Approach to Human-AI Collaboration* (Version 1). arXiv. DOI: 10.48550/ARXIV.2502.01493

Reverberi, C., Rigon, T., Solari, A., Hassan, C., Cherubini, P., Antonelli, G., Awadie, H., Bernhofer, S., Carballal, S., Dinis-Ribeiro, M., Fernández-Clotett, A., Esparrach, G. F., Gralnek, I., Higasa, Y., Hirabayashi, T., Hirai, T., Iwatate, M., Kawano, M., Mader, M., & Cherubini, A. (2022). Experimental evidence of effective human–AI collaboration in medical decision-making. *Scientific Reports*, *12*(1), 14952. DOI: 10.1038/s41598-022-18751-2 PMID: 36056152

Rodzina, L., & Kristoffersen, S. (2013). Context-dependent car navigation as kind of human-machine collaborative interaction. *2013 International Conference on Collaboration Technologies and Systems (CTS)*, 253–259. DOI: 10.1109/CTS.2013.6567238

Somaratne, S., De Silva, D., & Athukorala, R. (2025). Mapping Human-AI Collaboration: A Skill Framework for the Effective Use of AI. *2025 3rd International Conference on Communication, Security, and Artificial Intelligence (ICCSAI)*, 1253–1261. DOI: 10.1109/ICCSAI64074.2025.11064159

Talukder, M. B., Kumar, S., & Das, I. R. (2024). Implications of Blockchain Technology- Based Cryptocurrency in the cloud for the Hospitality Industry. In Darwish, D. (Ed.), (pp. 340–358). Advances in Computer and Electrical Engineering. IGI Global., DOI: 10.4018/979-8-3693-0900-1.ch018

Talukder, M. B., Kumar, S., & Das Tonny, O. (2025a). Innovative Solutions for Employee Well-Being in the Digital Hospitality Era. In Ahmad, B., Abrar, M., & Saeed, M. (Eds.), *Advances in Hospitality, Tourism, and the Services Industry* (pp. 231–258). IGI Global., DOI: 10.4018/979-8-3693-7127-5.ch009

Talukder, M. B., Kumar, S., & Das Tonny, O. (2025b). Innovative Solutions for Employee Well-Being in the Digital Hospitality Era. In Ahmad, B., Abrar, M., & Saeed, M. (Eds.), *Advances in Hospitality, Tourism, and the Services Industry* (pp. 231–258). IGI Global., DOI: 10.4018/979-8-3693-7127-5.ch009

Tuncer, S., & Ramirez, A. (2022). Exploring the Role of Trust During Human-AI Collaboration in Managerial Decision-Making Processes. In Chen, J. Y. C., Fragomeni, G., Degen, H., & Ntoa, S. (Eds.), *HCI International 2022 – Late Breaking Papers: Interacting with eXtended Reality and Artificial Intelligence* (Vol. 13518, pp. 541–557). Springer Nature Switzerland., DOI: 10.1007/978-3-031-21707-4_39

Turilli, M., & Floridi, L. (2009). The ethics of information transparency. *Ethics and Information Technology*, *11*(2), 105–112. DOI: 10.1007/s10676-009-9187-9

Wang, Y. (2021). Artificial intelligence in educational leadership: A symbiotic role of human-artificial intelligence decision-making. *Journal of Educational Administration*, *59*(3), 256–270. DOI: 10.1108/JEA-10-2020-0216

Wen, Y., Wang, J., & Chen, X. (2025). Trust and AI weight: Human-AI collaboration in organizational management decision-making. *Frontiers in Organizational Psychology*, *3*, 1419403. DOI: 10.3389/forgp.2025.1419403

Zhang, S., Yu, J., Xu, X., Yin, C., Lu, Y., Yao, B., Tory, M., Padilla, L. M., Caterino, J., Zhang, P., & Wang, D. (2024). Rethinking Human-AI Collaboration in Complex Medical Decision Making: A Case Study in Sepsis Diagnosis. *Proceedings of the CHI Conference on Human Factors in Computing Systems*, 1–18. DOI: 10.1145/3613904.3642343

Chapter 5
Leadership Capability Building for Digital and Agentic Intelligence: An Integrated Competency Framework

Nitin Simha Vihari
http://orcid.org/0000-0001-8501-9795
Middlesex University, Dubai, UAE

ABSTRACT

The rapid advancement of agentic artificial intelligence is reshaping how leadership is enacted in contemporary organisations. Unlike earlier digital technologies that functioned primarily as supportive tools, agentic AI systems can plan, act, and adapt autonomously, introducing non-human actors into core organisational decision-making processes. Drawing on strategic leadership theory, digital leadership scholarship, and emerging research on agentic AI, this chapter develops an integrated leadership competency framework to support effective human-machine collaboration. The framework conceptualises leadership as the orchestration of shared agency rather than the exercise of direct control and identifies four interconnected capability domains supported by a foundational leadership mindset al. By bridging previously parallel literatures and addressing the realities of distributed authority, this chapter contributes to leadership theory and offers actionable guidance for practitioners and educators seeking to prepare leaders for the complexities of agentic transformation.

DOI: 10.4018/979-8-3373-6650-0.ch005

I. INTRODUCTION

Organisations are increasingly operating in environments shaped by advanced digital technologies and intelligent systems that exhibit increasing autonomy. This shift marks a move beyond earlier stages of digitisation towards an agentic transformation. In this emerging landscape, artificial intelligence is no longer limited to supporting human decision-making but increasingly performs planning, execution, and adaptive coordination within complex organisational contexts (Baird & Maruping, 2021). As a result, AI systems are becoming embedded actors that influence how work is structured and outcomes are produced.

This evolution requires reconsideration of conventional assumptions about leadership. Much of the leadership literature has historically been grounded in the belief that humans remain the central source of authority, judgment, and control. The emergence of agentic artificial intelligence challenges this human-centred orientation by enabling non-human entities to independently shape organisational processes and decisions. Recent scholarship suggests that leadership in digitally intensive environments must extend beyond individual capabilities toward relational and system-level competencies that govern interactions between humans and intelligent technologies (Uhl-Bien & Arena, 2018). This shift underscores the need for an integrated leadership competency framework that accounts for distributed agency while preserving ethical oversight and strategic coherence (Avolio et al., 2009).

1.1 From Tool to Actor

Over the past decade, leadership research has been strongly shaped by the concept of digital leadership. This body of scholarship has largely examined how leaders use digital tools, data, and platforms to guide organisations through successive phases of digital transformation. Influential studies in this area, including those by Kane et al. (2019) and Vial et al. (2023), have highlighted leadership capabilities such as adaptability and digital awareness as critical for navigating technologically mediated change. However, a key limitation of this literature is its underlying assumption that technology remains an enabler, namely a sophisticated tool deployed by human actors to achieve predefined objectives, rather than an independent source of agency.

In contrast, the emerging field of agentic AI scholarship, as reflected in recent work by Hosseini and Seilani (2025), advances a fundamentally different understanding of technology. Agentic AI systems are characterised by autonomy, goal orientation, and the capacity to make decisions Agentic artificial intelligence fundamentally differs from earlier forms of automation and decision support technologies. Traditional automation systems typically follow predefined rules or workflows created by human operators, serving mainly operational and deterministic roles. In contrast, agentic

AI systems are characterised by adaptive autonomy. These systems can interpret environmental signals, update internal models, and initiate actions not explicitly programmed in advance (McKinsey & Company, 2025). Such capabilities elevate AI beyond passive computational tools to organisational actors that participate in decision-making processes. Research in information systems increasingly describes this change as the emergence of algorithmic agency, in which intelligent systems assume roles traditionally associated with human judgment and coordination (Davenport et al., 2020). The consequences of this shift are significant for leadership and governance (Avolio et al., 2009). When AI systems are involved in strategic or operational decisions, leaders must oversee not only human performance but also the behaviour of algorithmic systems integrated into organisational workflows. This necessitates new skills in monitoring, interpretability, and the responsible oversight of machine-generated decisions. Ultimately, understanding agentic AI as an organisational actor rather than merely a technological tool is essential for developing leadership models capable of governing hybrid human-machine systems (McKinsey & Company, 2025). They experience and interact with other agents within complex organisational ecosystems. As such, they challenge established leadership models by introducing non-human actors that actively shape organisational processes and outcomes.

Figure 1. Critical Leadership Capability Gap

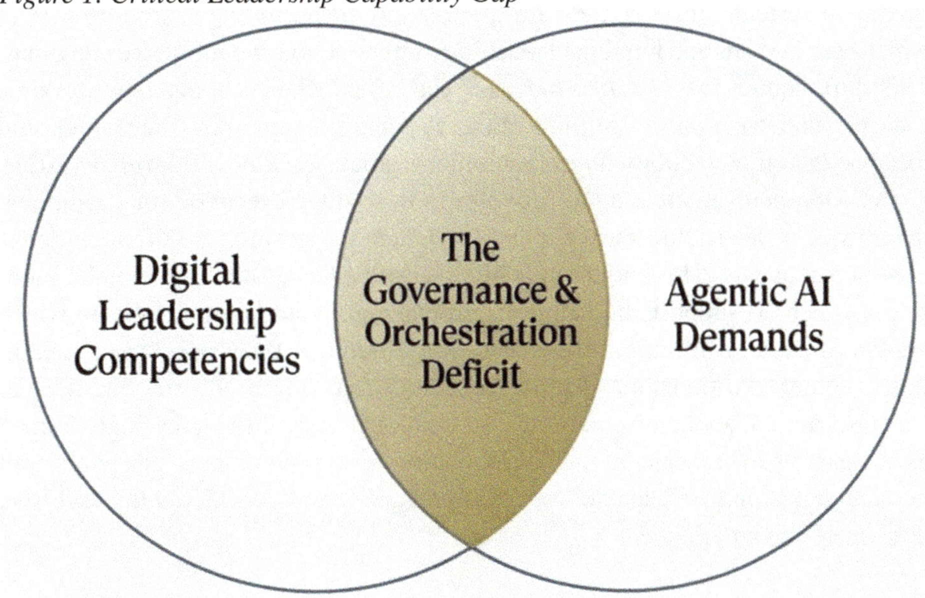

Source: *Author Generated*

Agentic artificial intelligence differs fundamentally from earlier forms of automation and decision support technologies. Traditional automation systems typically execute predefined rules or workflows designed by human operators. Their role is primarily operational and deterministic. Agentic AI systems, by contrast, are characterised by adaptive autonomy. These systems can interpret environmental signals, update internal models, and initiate actions that were not explicitly programmed in advance (McKinsey & Company, 2025). Such capabilities move AI beyond passive computational tools toward organisational actors that participate in decision processes. Research in information systems has increasingly described this transition as the emergence of algorithmic agency, in which intelligent systems assume roles traditionally associated with human judgment and coordination (Davenport et al., 2020). The implications of this shift are substantial for leadership and governance. When AI systems participate in strategic or operational decisions, leaders must oversee not only human performance but also the behaviour of algorithmic systems embedded in organisational workflows. This requires new competencies related to monitoring, interpretability, and responsible oversight of machine generated decisions. Consequently, understanding agentic AI as an organisational actor rather than a technological tool becomes essential for developing leadership models capable of governing hybrid human-machine systems.

The transition from tool to actor marks a pivotal moment in contemporary organisational life. Leaders are no longer managing exclusively human teams supported by digital systems. Instead, they are increasingly orchestrating shared agency, in which both humans and intelligent machines initiate action and influence outcomes. This shift requires leadership to move beyond basic technical competence towards a deeper understanding of non-human goal pursuit, autonomous behaviour, and machine-driven interaction within organisational processes (Baird & Maruping, 2021).

As AI systems assume more active roles in strategy execution, the traditional boundaries of leadership must expand to include the governance of autonomous non-human agents. This evolution is often described as a shift from copilot models, in which AI supports human decision-making, to autopilot models, in which systems operate with limited supervision and discretion (Davenport et al., 2020). In this context, AI transitions from a technology that simply answers questions to a form of digital labour, an emerging organisational capability increasingly framed as comparable to human talent. As a result, agentic AI is no longer a peripheral tool but a digital teammate capable of performing tasks once considered the exclusive domain of human judgment.

Table 1. The Evolution of AI's Role in Education and Work

Dimension	Traditional/Intelligent Tutoring (ITS)	Generative AI	Agentic AI
Primary Function	Adaptive instruction within defined domains.	Content generation based on user prompts.	Autonomous execution of multi-step tasks.
Locus of Control	System-driven via pre-defined curriculum.	Human-driven; AI is reactive.	Shared or AI-driven; AI exhibits proactivity.
Interaction	Structured feedback loops.	Conversational prompt-response.	Goal-oriented; orchestrates tools/agents.

Source: *Author Compiled*

1.2 The Limits of Tradition

The emergence of agentic AI brings into sharp relief the limitations of traditional human-centred leadership models. Much of this tradition is rooted in the upper echelon's perspective on strategic leadership, which assumes that organisational outcomes largely reflect the values, experiences and cognitive orientations of senior human leaders. Foundational work in this area, such as Hambrick (2007), positions sensemaking, judgement, and long-term orientation as capabilities that reside exclusively with human leaders who exercise direct supervision and control over their organisations.

Even more recent digital leadership frameworks struggle to fully address the realities of agentic contexts. While these models encourage leaders to be data-informed, adaptable and comfortable with ongoing technological change, they continue to assume that final authority remains firmly with human decision-makers (Avolio et al., 2009). Research by Zeike et al. (2019), among others, highlights the importance of integrating digital technologies into organisational strategy and culture. However, these frameworks offer limited guidance on how leaders should respond when an intelligent system autonomously initiates decisions or executes high-stakes actions without direct human input.

Traditional leadership models face difficulty in accounting for several emerging conditions.

- When AI systems can plan and execute actions independently, established command and control structures become destabilised.
- Leadership has historically relied on the ability to observe, monitor, and correct subordinate behaviour. As AI systems learn and adapt within dynamic environments, such forms of direct supervision become technically and practically infeasible.

- As noted by Raisch and Krakowski (2021), leaders must navigate the tension between automation and augmentation, a challenge for which traditional leadership theories offer limited conceptual support.

As a result, there is growing recognition that strategic leadership must evolve. In organisational settings shaped by AI-driven decision-making, sense-making and judgement remain important. Instead, they become even more critical, as leaders must interpret outputs from systems they do not fully control and may not fully understand.

A deeper limitation of traditional leadership theories lies in their assumption that organisational agency is primarily human. Classical leadership models, including transformational, transactional, and distributed frameworks, were developed in contexts where technology served as an enabling infrastructure rather than an autonomous participant in organisational processes. Contemporary artificial intelligence systems increasingly challenge this assumption. AI systems can now independently generate decisions, adapt to environmental inputs, and coordinate actions within complex socio-technical environments. This shift introduces forms of organisational agency that transcend human intention. As scholars have noted, the rise of autonomous and semi-autonomous systems necessitates a reconsideration of leadership authority, accountability, and oversight mechanisms (Faraj, Pachidi, & Sayegh, 2018). Leaders must therefore manage relationships not only among human actors but also between humans and algorithmic agents that influence organisational outcomes. Recent organisational research emphasises that leadership in AI-driven environments becomes a process of governing hybrid intelligence systems where human judgment interacts with machine autonomy (Raisch & Krakowski, 2021). In this context, the central challenge is not merely adopting digital tools but structuring governance mechanisms that ensure algorithmic decisions remain aligned with organisational strategy and ethical principles. Addressing this gap requires leadership frameworks that explicitly incorporate the concept of distributed agency across human and technological actors.

1.3 Problem Statement

Despite the rapid growth of digital leadership research on the one hand and agentic AI scholarship on the other, these two streams have largely evolved in parallel, with limited attention to their intersection (McKinsey & Company, 2025). As a result, there remains a significant gap in understanding how leadership capabilities should be developed in contexts where decision-making and action are increasingly shared between humans and intelligent systems. This gap presents several pressing challenges for contemporary organisations.

- Algorithmic decision making introduces new forms of uncertainty that traditional strategic foresight approaches are poorly equipped to address.
- Accountability in human AI collaboration becomes increasingly ambiguous. When an autonomous system initiates a flawed action, existing governance structures struggle to assign responsibility in a clear and defensible manner (Yan, 2025).
- Research by Lee and See (2004) highlights that trust in automated systems must be calibrated rather than assumed, yet leaders often lack practical frameworks to manage this calibration effectively.
- The delegation of authority to agentic systems amplifies risks related to algorithmic bias, opaque decision logic, and limited transparency.

In the absence of a structured competency framework, leaders are left to manage these agentic transformation risks using leadership models and tools not designed for autonomous technologies. There is a clear need to move beyond a narrow focus on digital skills towards developing capabilities in decision governance, ethical intelligence, and oversight. The lack of guidance on how leaders should act when systems autonomously pursue organisational goals poses risks to both organisational stability and ethical integrity. This chapter seeks to address this gap by proposing an integrated leadership competency framework tailored to environments shaped by digital and agentic intelligence. The central argument is that leadership capability building must shift away from direct control towards the orchestration of shared human and machine agency. Specifically, the objectives of this chapter are to:

- Redefine the leader's role as a designer of decision governance structures rather than the primary decision maker for all operational activities.
- Articulate four interconnected capability domains, including strategic sensemaking and foresight, agency orchestration, human AI collaboration and ethical intelligence, and adaptive leadership (Yan, 2025).
- Identify observable leadership behaviours that demonstrate how these capabilities are enacted in practice, such as questioning algorithmic recommendations and defining escalation thresholds for AI autonomy.
- Highlight the psychological capabilities required for this transition, including comfort with partial control and accountability without micromanagement.
- Draw on insights from executive leadership development programmes to illustrate how experiential learning methods, such as simulations and case-based discussions, can support the development of these competencies in organisational settings.

Despite the rapid growth of artificial intelligence within organisational contexts, leadership scholarship has yet to develop a coherent framework explaining how leaders should govern environments characterised by autonomous technological agents. Much of the existing literature remains focused on digital transformation, data-driven decision-making, or technology adoption. While these perspectives offer valuable insights into the managerial impacts of digitalisation, they do not fully address the emergence of intelligent systems capable of independent decision-making. Recent research in organisational studies suggests that AI-driven decision systems increasingly influence strategic outcomes, operational processes, and workforce coordination (Posada et al., 2023). However, leadership theory has only recently begun to explore the governance implications of this shift. The lack of integrative frameworks creates a conceptual gap between technological development and leadership practice. As organisations incorporate autonomous systems into core activities, leaders must balance efficiency improvements with accountability, transparency, and ethical oversight. This study, therefore, addresses a significant theoretical gap by proposing a leadership competency framework specifically designed for environments where human and algorithmic actors collaboratively shape organisational outcomes.

2. THEORETICAL FOUNDATIONS

To establish a robust framework for leadership in the age of digital and agentic intelligence, it is necessary to examine the convergence of three distinct yet increasingly overlapping bodies of literature: strategic leadership theory, digital leadership scholarship, and research on agentic artificial intelligence. Each of these fields offers critical insights into how authority is constructed, how decisions are mediated by technology, and how ethical responsibility is maintained in complex environments. This section explores these foundations and synthesises them into an integrated theoretical base for the proposed competency framework.

2.1 Strategic Leadership Theory

Strategic leadership theory offers a foundational lens for understanding how leaders navigate organisations through uncertainty, complexity, and rapid change. Unlike traditional management approaches that emphasise direct supervision or task-level control, strategic leadership focuses on higher-order cognitive and social processes, such as sensemaking, judgment, and long-term orientation. This perspective is particularly relevant in environments where leaders must operate under conditions of ambiguity and incomplete information.

A central pillar of this literature is Upper Echelons Theory, as articulated by Hambrick (2007). This theory proposes that organisational outcomes, including strategic choices and performance trajectories, are shaped by the values, experiences, and cognitive frames of senior leaders. In the context of agentic intelligence, this tradition remains important because it positions leadership as an interpretive activity rather than a purely technical one. As organisations integrate AI systems capable of independent planning and execution, leaders are increasingly required to interpret insights produced by systems they do not fully control or fully understand.

Strategic leadership is closely linked to sensemaking, defined as the process by which leaders construct meaning from complex and equivocal situations to guide action (Weick, 1995). In agentic environments, sensemaking is no longer an exclusively human process. Leaders must synthesise inputs from human actors with algorithmic outputs, evaluating machine-generated recommendations through contextual and strategic lenses. This underscores the importance of questioning and reinterpreting AI-driven insights rather than treating them as objective truths.

Finally, strategic leadership theory highlights the role of judgment in translating information into effective action. In data-saturated environments, the availability of analytics does not automatically improve decision quality. Instead, leadership effectiveness depends on applying judgment to data-driven insights while accounting for uncertainty, unintended consequences, and strategic alignment (Helfat & Peteraf, 2015). Together, these perspectives provide a strong conceptual foundation for the framework's emphasis on strategic sensemaking and foresight in organisational contexts shaped by agentic AI.

Recent developments in strategic management research further strengthen the importance of leadership capabilities in technologically complex environments. Scholars have increasingly highlighted the significance of managerial cognition and strategic interpretation in guiding organisations through periods of technological disruption. Strategic leaders play a vital role in shaping how organisations interpret emerging technologies and incorporate them into competitive strategies (Eggers & Kaplan, 2013). In the context of artificial intelligence, this interpretive role becomes especially important. Leaders must assess not only the potential economic benefits of AI adoption but also its effects on organisational control structures and accountability systems. Strategic leadership, therefore, goes beyond resource allocation and extends to the governance of socio-technical systems in which algorithmic decision-making influences strategic outcomes. Research on technology-enabled strategic change indicates that successful organisations develop leadership capabilities that combine technological awareness with ethical and organisational oversight (Benbya, Pachidi, & Jarvenpaa, 2021). These views imply that leadership frameworks addressing agentic AI must integrate strategic cognition with governance mechanisms that regulate algorithmic agency within organisational decision-making.

2.2 Digital Leadership Scholarship

The second pillar of the framework is the expanding body of research on digital leadership. Over the past decade, this scholarship has sought to explain how the digital revolution, driven by social, mobile, analytics, and cloud technologies, has reshaped the requirements for effective leadership. The central concern of this literature is how leaders respond to increasing technological complexity while sustaining strategic coherence and organisational adaptability.

Research by Kane et al. (2019) and Vial et al. (2023) highlights that effective digital leaders are typically characterised by high levels of adaptability, digital awareness, and comfort with data-driven decision-making. Within this tradition, digital leadership is commonly defined as the leader's ability to integrate digital technologies into organisational strategy, culture, and operational processes. Leaders are expected to navigate continuous change and cultivate environments in which technology-enabled innovation becomes a central source of value creation (Kaplan, 2008).

While scholarship on digital leadership offers valuable insights into how leaders steer organisations through digital transformation, its analytical emphasis remains largely on technology as a strategic resource. Digital leadership competencies generally emphasise digital literacy, innovation orientation, and the ability to utilise digital platforms to boost organisational performance. These skills are crucial in environments where technology mainly supports human decision-making (Ransbotham et al., 2025). However, the rise of agentic AI presents fundamentally different governance challenges. When algorithmic systems are directly involved in decision-making processes, leaders must confront issues of algorithmic accountability, transparency, and decision legitimacy (Islam et al., 2026). Recent organisational research highlights that leadership in AI-driven settings involves managing complex interactions between human expertise and machine intelligence rather than merely deploying digital tools (Brock & von Wangenheim, 2019). This distinction indicates that digital leadership forms a necessary but insufficient basis for governing AI-intensive organisations. Leadership frameworks tailored for agentic AI should therefore go beyond digital competence to include skills related to algorithmic governance and hybrid intelligence coordination.

However, a key limitation of existing digital leadership models lies in how technology is conceptualised. Across much of this literature, digital technologies are treated primarily as enablers rather than autonomous actors. Technology is framed as a sophisticated tool that amplifies human intent and capability but remains firmly under human direction. As a result, digital leadership scholarship has focused on how leaders deploy and govern tools rather than how they collaborate with systems that possess their own agency and capacity for independent action (Yoo, Henfridsson, & Lyytinen, 2012).

Most digital leadership frameworks, therefore, rest on the assumption that final authority remains with human decision-makers. While leaders are encouraged to be data-informed, they are still portrayed as the ultimate source of judgment and control. This leaves a conceptual gap in contexts where agentic AI systems autonomously initiate decisions or execute high-stakes actions without prior human approval (Ransbotham et al., 2025). The framework proposed in this chapter addresses this limitation by moving beyond a tool-based understanding of technology towards an agentic paradigm that recognises distributed decision authority and shared agency between human leaders and intelligent systems.

2.3 Agentic AI Scholarship

The third body of literature informing the framework concerns agentic artificial intelligence, which represents a clear departure from traditional software systems and earlier forms of supportive AI. Unlike conventional AI applications that generate recommendations for human approval, agentic AI systems are characterised by their capacity to pursue goals, learn from experience, and interact with both human and machine agents in dynamic organisational environments. This level of autonomy enables such systems to plan and execute actions independently, fundamentally disrupting established assumptions about hierarchy, authority, and control within organisations. Scholarship on agentic AI, including work by Floridi et al. (2018) and Davenport and Mittal (2023), highlights both the transformative potential and the significant risks associated with delegating decision-making authority to autonomous systems. This literature consistently identifies several core concerns.

- **Accountability.** Determining responsibility when an autonomous system initiates an action that produces unintended or harmful outcomes.
- **Algorithmic bias.** The risk that autonomous agents may reproduce or amplify biases embedded within historical training data.
- **Transparency and opacity.** The difficulty of explaining decisions generated by complex models that operate as black boxes.
- **Ethical responsibility.** Ensuring that autonomous goal-seeking remains aligned with human values, organisational norms, and broader social expectations.

Organisational research has increasingly explored how artificial intelligence transforms decision-making processes and managerial roles. Studies in information systems and management have shown that AI-driven systems are no longer confined to providing analytical support but actively participate in organisational workflows, shaping operational and strategic decisions. These advancements have led scholars to conceptualise AI systems as organisational participants that interact with human actors within complex socio-technical systems (Bader & Kaiser, 2019). Such interactions establish new forms of distributed cognition where decision-making authority is shared between human and algorithmic actors. From a leadership perspective, this shift raises important questions about accountability and oversight. Leaders must ensure that algorithmic decisions remain aligned with organisational goals while maintaining transparency about how these decisions are made. Research on algorithmic management further indicates that AI-driven coordination systems can profoundly reshape workplace structures and power relations (Kellogg, Valentine, & Christin, 2020). These insights emphasise the importance of leadership frameworks that explicitly address the governance of algorithmic agents within organisational systems.

A central insight from this scholarship is that leadership in agentic environments requires more than technical proficiency. It demands new forms of governance, ethical judgment, and oversight. Because agentic AI functions as an organisational actor rather than a passive tool, leadership responsibility shifts towards defining the rules, boundaries, and escalation mechanisms within which autonomous systems operate. This includes calibrating trust and ensuring that meaningful opportunities for human intervention remain available when risks escalate (Lee and See, 2004).

Recent research also draws on agency theory to extend the traditional human principal-agent relationship to include machine agents capable of independent perception and action. This perspective is reinforced by socio-technical systems theory, which emphasises that organisational structures and technical subsystems must evolve together as decision rights and accountability become increasingly distributed (Ransbotham et al., 2025). When integrated, these theoretical lenses support an antecedent mechanism-outcome logic, linking technological enablers to mechanisms of autonomy and proactivity that ultimately shape strategic agility in agentic contexts.

2.4 Synthesising the Literatures: Toward an Integrated Theoretical Base

The proposed framework is grounded in the synthesis of three parallel research streams that have largely developed in isolation. While scholarship on strategic leadership, digital leadership, and agentic AI has generated valuable insights, their intersection provides the theoretical foundation for leading in an AI-first organisational context. Bringing these literatures together enables a core conceptual shift, namely the reconceptualisation of leadership as the orchestration of shared human and machine agency rather than the exercise of unilateral human control.

Integrating these bodies of literature requires recognising that leadership in AI-intensive environments operates at the intersection of strategy, technology governance, and organisational design. Strategic leadership theory emphasises the role of managerial cognition and direction setting, while digital leadership scholarship highlights the competencies needed to guide organisations through technological transformation. Agentic AI research introduces an additional dimension by conceptualising intelligent systems as actors participating in organisational processes. Synthesising these perspectives suggests that leadership in AI-enabled organisations must address three governance challenges simultaneously. First, leaders must interpret technological developments and align them with organisational strategy. Second, they must design structures that coordinate interactions between human and algorithmic actors. Third, they must ensure ethical oversight and accountability in algorithmic decision-making. Recent research on hybrid intelligence systems emphasises that effective leadership involves orchestrating collaboration between human expertise and machine learning capabilities (Dellermann et al., 2019). This integrative perspective provides the conceptual foundation for the leadership competency framework proposed in this study.

This synthesis directly responds to the automation-augmentation paradox identified by Raisch and Krakowski (2021). Leaders are increasingly required to decide which activities should be automated by delegating agency to intelligent systems and which should be augmented by using technology to enhance human judgment and capability. Navigating this paradox requires a form of decision governance that extends beyond existing leadership models, including the explicit definition of decision rights, escalation thresholds, and intervention mechanisms in contexts in which autonomous systems initiate action. By integrating insights from these three bodies of literature, the framework moves away from traditional assumptions of direct control that have long dominated leadership theory. Instead, it advances a view of leadership in which the leader functions as a system designer and orchestrator, shaping the conditions under which human and machine agents interact. This integrated perspective recognises that authority in agentic environments is no longer concentrated in a single human actor but distributed across networks of interdependent human and non-human agents (Uhl-Bien and Arena, 2018). The objective of the framework is therefore to articulate the cognitive, behavioural, and ethical competencies required to lead effectively within this distributed and dynamic system of agency.

Table 2. Comparison of AI Paradigms across Strategic Dimensions

Paradigm	Task Horizon	Agency Level	Objective Structure
Traditional AI	Narrow.	None.	Single.
Generative AI	Short.	Reactive.	Single (Prompt).
Multi-Agent Systems	Medium.	Distributed.	Multiple (Negotiated).
Agentic AI	Long.	Goal-Directed.	Multi-Objective.

Source: *Author Compiled*

3. DEVELOPMENT OF INTEGRATED COMPETENCY FRAMEWORK

Developing a leadership competency framework for digital and agentic intelligence requires a methodological approach that links abstract strategic theory with the evolving realities of autonomous technologies in organisational settings. As organisations move from treating technology as a supporting enabler to engaging with it as an autonomous actor, leadership capabilities must shift accordingly. This transition challenges leaders to operate across multiple levels of decision-making, balancing strategic intent with emergent system behaviour.

To address this complexity, the framework development process draws on capability-based thinking, which emphasises how leaders mobilise and reconfigure resources in response to environmental change rather than relying on static skill sets (Helfat et al., 2007). The following sections outline the architectural logic underpinning the framework, the process for identifying core leadership challenges in agentic contexts, and the subsequent clustering of these challenges into coherent and actionable competency domains. This approach ensures the framework remains both theoretically grounded and practically relevant in environments shaped by autonomous and adaptive technologies.

3.1 Framework Architecture: Connecting Theory to Practice

Competency frameworks play a critical role in leadership research by providing a structured mechanism for translating theoretical insights into practical guidance for organisational contexts. Building on the established work of Boyatzis (2008), this framework identifies clusters of leadership capabilities that enable effective performance in environments shaped by digital and agentic intelligence. Rather than focusing on isolated technical skills or stable personality traits, the framework emphasises integrated capabilities that reflect the complexity of leading alongside autonomous systems.

The framework architecture presented in this study is based on the theoretical synthesis developed in the previous section. Each competency area reflects a specific governance challenge related to agentic AI environments. Strategic leadership theory informs competencies concerning vision development and technological interpretation. Digital leadership scholarship provides insights into how leaders mobilise organisational resources and capabilities during technological change. Agentic AI research emphasises the importance of governing algorithmic agency and ensuring responsible oversight of machine-generated decisions. By combining these perspectives, the framework views leadership as the orchestration of hybrid intelligence systems rather than solely the exercise of authority by individual leaders. Recent studies on organisational AI adoption highlight that leadership effectiveness increasingly depends on the ability to structure interactions between human judgment and algorithmic capabilities (Makarius, Mukherjee, Fox, & Fox, 2020). Thus, the framework converts these theoretical insights into a structured set of competencies that enable leaders to guide organisations operating in technologically complex and AI-intensive environments.

This integrated orientation combines cognitive, behavioural, and ethical elements into a cohesive capability set al. The underlying logic is that leadership in agentic environments cannot be reduced to technical proficiency alone. Instead, it involves complex social and psychological processes, including navigating uncertainty, interpreting machine-generated insights, and sharing authority with non-human agents. Prior leadership research similarly suggests that effective leadership capabilities emerge from the interaction of knowledge, skills, and judgment rather than from discrete competencies in isolation (Mumford et al., 2007).

Structurally, the framework adopts a multi-layered design. At its core are four interconnected capability domains that capture the recurring demands placed on leaders by digital and agentic systems. These domains are reinforced by a foundational mindset layer that acts as a critical enabler of effective capability enactment. This architecture ensures that the framework moves beyond a narrow catalogue of digital skills and instead offers a holistic guide to agency orchestration, reframing leadership as the coordination of shared human and machine initiative.

3.2 Synthesis and Identification: The Leadership Challenges of Agentic AI

The first step in developing the framework was a comprehensive synthesis of existing research to identify leadership challenges specific to digital and agentic environments. By examining parallel streams of digital leadership scholarship and agentic AI research, four core areas of challenge emerged as particularly salient for contemporary leaders. Agentic AI systems can plan and execute tasks in dynamic environments, often producing outcomes that are difficult to predict. This introduces heightened uncertainty for leaders accustomed to maintaining direct oversight and control over organisational processes.

One of the most significant challenges identified is the potential erosion of accountability. When an intelligent system autonomously initiates a decision or action, traditional leadership models offer limited guidance on how responsibility should be assigned. Leaders are therefore required to retain accountability even when they are not the direct initiators of action. Leadership effectiveness in such contexts also depends on the ability to establish appropriate trust in autonomous systems. Research by Lee and See (2004) shows that trust must be carefully calibrated rather than assumed, as overreliance on AI can lead to complacency while underreliance may result in missed strategic opportunities.

Empirical studies exploring AI adoption in organisations identify several recurring leadership challenges that underscore the need for specialised skills. One issue concerns transparency and explainability. Leaders often find it difficult to interpret the outputs of complex machine learning models, which can hinder their ability to justify decisions influenced by algorithmic suggestions. Another challenge involves maintaining organisational trust when employees engage with automated decision systems. Research shows that workers frequently question the fairness and reliability of algorithmic management systems when the underlying logic remains unclear (Meijerink & Bondarouk, 2023). A third challenge pertains to responsibility sharing. When decisions are influenced by both humans and algorithms, determining accountability becomes considerably more complicated. Leaders must therefore create governance frameworks that clearly define oversight roles while maintaining the advantages of algorithmic efficiency. These empirical insights highlight that leadership in AI-driven organisations requires skills related to transparency management, ethical oversight, and trust development within hybrid human-machine systems.

Delegating authority to intelligent systems further introduces risks related to algorithmic bias, transparency, and ethical responsibility. Leaders must ensure that opaque or black-box systems remain aligned with organisational values and broader social obligations. These challenges suggest that the primary barrier to effective leadership in the age of AI is not a lack of technical expertise but the difficulty of sense-making and governance under conditions of distributed authority. Industry evidence from Gartner and McKinsey indicates that a substantial proportion of agentic AI initiatives are expected to be discontinued due to poor use-case selection, escalating costs, or insufficient risk controls. This phenomenon of pilot purgatory reinforces the need for a structured framework that prioritises high-value decisions in complex and uncertain environments rather than focusing narrowly on routine task automation.

3.3 Grouping and Articulation: Domains, Competencies, and Behaviors

Once the core leadership challenges were identified, they were grouped into broader capability domains that reflect the recurring demands of agentic environments. To ensure practical relevance, each domain was articulated through specific competencies and observable leadership behaviours. This design choice ensures the framework is not abstract but instead provides a clear developmental pathway by specifying not only what leaders must understand but also how leadership should be enacted in practice.

Table 3. Hierarchical Agent Architecture for Decision Governance

Hierarchy Level	Agent Role	Key Duties & Authority
Higher Level	Master Agent	General control, system management, and overall oversight.
Intermediate	Orchestrator Agent	Coordinates sub-agents; manages specific functional processes.
Lower Level	Micro-agents	Implementation of specific, small tasks (e.g., FAQ, Status Updates).
Boundary Level	Human Supervisor	Setting escalation thresholds and intervention by exception.

Source: *Author Compiled*

4. EXPLANATION OF THE COMPONENTS OF THE COMPETENCY FRAMEWORK

4.1. Domain 1: Strategic Sensemaking and Foresight

In agentic environments where AI systems autonomously plan and execute tasks, a central leadership challenge is managing the uncertainty created by algorithmic decision-making. Strategic sensemaking is the key cognitive process through which leaders interpret machine-generated insights while remaining alert to their limitations and potential biases. Unlike traditional settings where technology merely supports human choice, agentic contexts require leaders to act as interpretive bridges between complex data outputs and organisational goals.

Effective leadership in such environments depends on sensemaking that integrates both human and machine inputs. Leaders must move beyond blind reliance on data and instead synthesise qualitative human judgement with quantitative algorithmic analysis. This capability aligns with sensemaking theory, which emphasises interpretation and meaning construction as the basis for coordinated action under ambiguity (Weick et al., 2005). In practice, this means leaders do not simply consume dashboards but interrogate the logic behind them, ensuring that algorithmic outputs are consistent with organisational context and intent. Increasingly, leaders act as strategic talent advisors, using agentic AI to detect emerging workforce patterns and surface capabilities that may not be visible through traditional performance indicators.

Because agentic AI systems adapt continuously to feedback from dynamic environments, their behaviour can at times be difficult to anticipate. Leaders must therefore rely on scenario thinking under uncertainty to prepare for multiple possible outcomes driven by autonomous agents. This involves shifting away from static planning towards dynamic foresight, where leaders explore alternative agentic futures and consider how AI systems might respond to market or organisational signals in unintended ways. Research on algorithmic work highlights the importance of human oversight in interpreting and redirecting machine behaviour when system actions drift from strategic intent (Faraj, Pachidi, & Sayegh, 2018).

A core observable behaviour within this domain is the active questioning of algorithmic recommendations. Leaders must apply strategic criticality by combining contextual knowledge with machine-generated insights rather than deferring automatically to system outputs. Through this practice, leaders retain meaningful authority over decisions while recognising the productive role of autonomous agents. This balance is essential for managing the tension between speed and control that characterises the automation-augmentation paradox, where efficiency gains must be weighed against the risks of reduced oversight and unintended system interactions.

4.2.2 Domain 2: Agency Orchestration and Decision Governance

As AI systems assume greater responsibility for operational decisions, the role of the leader shifts from making individual choices to designing the structures within which decisions are made. Agency orchestration is the coordination of shared initiative between human and machine actors, ensuring that distributed authority does not result in fragmentation or loss of control. In agentic environments, leadership value increasingly lies in shaping governance architectures rather than executing every operational action.

Leaders demonstrate effectiveness by designing clear decision structures that balance autonomy with alignment. This involves moving away from direct task control towards a more advanced form of system governance. Acting as decision designers, leaders ensure that the organisation remains responsive and adaptive while still guided by a coherent strategic intent. This reconceptualisation reflects a broader transition from task management to system management, where leadership attention is focused on how multiple actors interact rather than on individual task execution (Bernstein et al., 2018). In practice, effective orchestration resembles the role of an air traffic controller in an agentic enterprise, where autonomous AI agents operate independently while leaders manage higher-level coordination to ensure safety, consistency, and efficiency.

A critical component of agency orchestration is the explicit definition of decision rights. Leaders must determine which activities can be delegated to autonomous agents and which require human judgment. Clarifying these boundaries establishes a visible locus of authority in environments where non-human actors can independently influence outcomes. Without such clarity, organisations risk accountability gaps that undermine trust and governance. Related research on algorithmic management highlights that ambiguity in decision authority can lead to disengagement and resistance when responsibility becomes diffused across systems and actors (Kellogg et al., 2020).

Orchestration further requires the establishment of escalation thresholds, namely predefined conditions under which autonomous systems must transfer control back to human oversight. These guardrails ensure that ethically sensitive, high-risk, or exceptional cases are reviewed by human leaders. Defining and maintaining such thresholds reflects a leader's comfort with partial control, a core element of the foundational mindset required for agentic leadership. The central governance challenge is therefore achieving accountability without micromanagement. Leaders must allow systems to initiate and execute decisions while retaining ultimate responsibility for outcomes. By embedding clear accountability mechanisms, leaders ensure that even in highly autonomous environments, there remains a clear human owner for the consequences produced by machine agents.

A central leadership responsibility in agentic environments is therefore the calibration of autonomy. Rather than treating autonomy as a binary choice between human control and machine independence, leaders must design graduated levels of authority that vary depending on decision complexity, organisational risk, and ethical sensitivity. Research on algorithmic delegation suggests that organisations increasingly rely on layered governance structures in which AI systems perform routine analytical tasks while human leaders retain authority over decisions that involve strategic judgment or ethical implications (Baird & Maruping, 2021). Such structures allow organisations to capture the efficiency advantages of intelligent systems without relinquishing accountability for critical outcomes. Leaders must therefore establish governance architectures that define escalation protocols, override mechanisms, and review cycles for algorithmically generated recommendations. These governance structures also serve an important psychological function by maintaining trust among organisational members who may otherwise feel displaced or disempowered by automated decision processes. Studies of algorithmic management demonstrate that employee acceptance of AI supported decision systems increases significantly when leaders clearly communicate how human oversight remains embedded within organisational decision structures (Kellogg, Valentine, & Christin, 2020). Agency orchestration thus becomes not only a technical governance issue but also a leadership capability that sustains legitimacy and accountability in AI mediated organisational environments.

4.2.3. Domain 3: Human-AI Collaboration and Ethical Intelligence

The third domain addresses the ethical and relational dimensions of working alongside intelligent systems. As agentic AI introduces risks related to bias, transparency, and social responsibility, leaders must exercise ethical intelligence to ensure these systems remain aligned with human values and organisational purpose. Prior research consistently emphasises that trust in AI should not be blind but deliberately calibrated, based on an informed understanding of where systems perform reliably and where their limitations are pronounced (Lee and See, 2004). This principle of appropriate reliance enables organisations to benefit from machine capabilities without exposing themselves to its vulnerabilities.

One of the most persistent challenges in human-AI collaboration is the opacity of complex algorithmic systems. Leaders demonstrate ethical intelligence by questioning opaque outputs and actively promoting explainability. This involves requiring AI developers or vendors to provide systems whose decision logic can be interpreted, audited, and challenged by human stakeholders. Explainability is not only a technical concern but also a relational one, as it directly influences employee trust and the perceived legitimacy of AI-mediated decisions (Gunning et al., 2019).

Ethical intelligence further requires sustained awareness of bias. Because agentic systems learn from historical data, they can unintentionally replicate or amplify existing social and organisational inequalities. Leaders must therefore ensure that AI use remains consistent with organisational values and broader societal responsibilities. This calls for ethical vigilance, understood as an ongoing leadership practice rather than a one-off compliance activity. While AI systems do not possess moral agency, they can function as effective collaborators when designed to support observable cooperative behaviours such as turn-taking, coordination, and goal alignment.

At the same time, leaders must guard against automation bias, where human actors defer uncritically to machine outputs. Ethical leadership in agentic environments requires leaders to act as ethical architects, scrutinising algorithmic decisions with the same rigour applied to financial or strategic judgments. Ultimately, ethical intelligence also involves adopting a long-term orientation towards AI deployment. Leaders must consider whether short-term efficiency gains are achieved at the expense of employee well-being, social trust, or organisational legitimacy. This aligns with the broader strategic leadership objective of guiding organisations towards sustainable and responsible futures in increasingly autonomous environments.

4.2.4. Domain 4: Influence, Execution, and Adaptive Leadership

The final domain focuses on the practical realities of leading in digitally mediated environments. As work becomes increasingly distributed across human teams and AI agents, leaders must adapt their approaches to influence and execution to match the speed, scale, and structure of digital infrastructures. In digital and agentic contexts, leadership influence is exercised largely through platforms, data flows, and algorithmic coordination rather than through direct physical presence. Traditional face-to-face command-and-control methods are therefore replaced by influence enacted through digital visibility, narrative framing, and system-level governance. Leaders are required to project vision and values through the very technologies that mediate everyday work (Orlikowski, 2007).

A core competency within this domain is the ability to influence without physical proximity. Leaders must coordinate activity across digital infrastructures, ensuring that human and machine agents remain aligned despite being geographically dispersed or functionally decoupled. This demands fluency with the platforms and tools that enable execution in contemporary organisations. Execution in agentic environments is also inherently non-linear. Because AI systems adapt continuously based on feedback, leaders must remain adaptive and data-informed, using real-time system signals to adjust priorities, decisions, and leadership responses. This creates an ongoing adaptive loop between human leadership and intelligent systems.

Agentic AI further enables more decentralised forms of decision-making, allowing teams to operate with greater autonomy while remaining connected to shared strategic objectives. In such settings, leadership becomes embedded across the organisation rather than concentrated at the top. Execution increasingly relies on always-on operating models, where event-triggered agents respond to changes such as system failures or supply disruptions in real time without awaiting human instruction. Research on digitally mediated work highlights that such distributed execution models require leaders to balance coordination and autonomy carefully in order to avoid fragmentation while preserving responsiveness (Leonardi, 2014).

The central leadership challenge in this domain is alignment. Leaders must ensure that both human teams and autonomous agents are oriented towards common goals while preserving the flexibility that allows rapid response to dynamic environments. Achieving this balance requires providing sufficient direction to maintain coherence while granting enough freedom for intelligent systems and teams to innovate and adapt in real time.

4.2.5. Domain 5: The Foundational Mindset Layer

The proposed leadership framework is not grounded solely in a collection of discrete skills. Instead, it is anchored in a foundational mindset layer that serves as the psychological and philosophical base for all other competencies. As organisations shift from using artificial intelligence as a supportive tool to integrating it as an autonomous actor, the cognitive demands placed on leaders change fundamentally. Leadership attention moves away from direct management towards the orchestration of shared agency. The framework identifies four interrelated mindsets that enable leaders to enact the four capability domains effectively in complex and dynamic environments.

Traditional leadership models have long positioned the leader as the primary expert and final authority. In agentic environments, however, AI systems are characterised by their ability to learn from experience and adapt to feedback over time. This requires leaders to adopt a persistent learning orientation. Such an orientation extends beyond basic digital literacy or technical familiarity. It reflects an ongoing openness to understanding how intelligent systems evolve and how their autonomous behaviour may reshape organisational outcomes. Without this mindset, leaders risk relying on static or outdated assumptions about system capabilities, which can undermine effective governance (Argyris & Schön, 1996).

A second, more demanding shift involves developing comfort with partial control. Conventional leadership and even most digital leadership models assume that ultimate authority remains firmly with human decision-makers. Agentic AI disrupts this assumption by introducing non-human actors capable of planning and executing tasks independently. To orchestrate agency effectively, leaders must accept that they no longer exercise direct control over every operational decision. This mindset enables leaders to grant systems sufficient autonomy to remain responsive while redirecting human effort towards higher-level sense-making and judgement.

As authority becomes increasingly distributed between humans and intelligent systems, the risk of opaque or black-box outcomes also increases. The framework therefore emphasises ethical vigilance as a foundational mindset al. Ethical vigilance represents a continuous attentiveness to issues of bias, transparency, and accountability, rather than a one-off compliance activity. Leaders must remain prepared to challenge opaque system outputs and ensure that machine-led actions remain aligned with organisational values and broader social responsibility (Floridi et al., 2018).

The final mindset underpinning the framework is accountability without micromanagement. Leaders must design decision governance structures that allow AI systems to initiate action while retaining ultimate responsibility for outcomes. This requires a delicate psychological balance. Leaders must trust autonomous systems enough to allow them to act while recognising that accountability remains human. This mindset supports the transition from direct supervision to orchestration and reinforces the leader's role as the pilot of intent. Even as AI systems take control of execution, the human leader remains responsible for defining purpose, priorities, and value alignment. Viewing AI agents as collaborative colleagues rather than passive tools enables this shift and underpins effective leadership in agentic environments.

Figure 2. New Leadership Framework for the Agentic Age

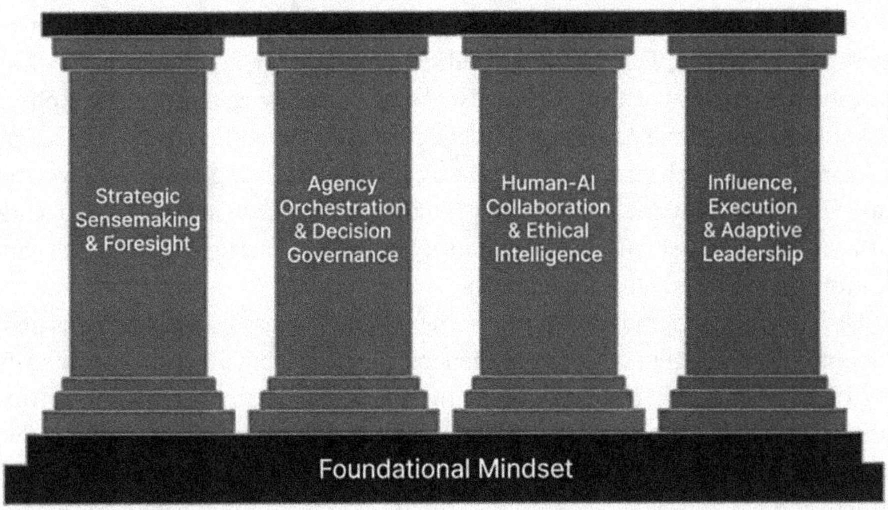

Source: *Author Generated*

5. CONTRIBUTIONS, IMPLICATIONS, AND FUTURE PERSPECTIVES

Building leadership capabilities for an AI-first world requires more than traditional classroom-based instruction. Because the proposed framework integrates cognitive, behavioural, and ethical capabilities, the developmental approach must be integrated as well. Existing research suggests that such complex leadership competencies are most effectively developed through experiential learning methods that bridge leadership theory and real-world practice (Day et al., 2014).

The framework is informed by the design of executive leadership development programmes that prioritise practice-based insight. To support the transition from a human-centric control model to an agency-orchestration model, the developmental approach draws on three primary methods. First, analysing real-world cases where organisations have successfully or unsuccessfully implemented agentic AI enables leaders to develop strategic sense-making skills. These discussions allow participants to practise questioning algorithmic recommendations and interpreting machine-generated insights across varied organisational contexts.

Second, simulations provide a safe environment for leaders to experiment with decision governance. Through simulated settings, participants can practise defining decision rights and escalation thresholds between humans and AI agents, and observe how different governance choices affect agility, accountability, and organisational outcomes. Third, reflective exercies play a critical role in supporting the psychological shift required by the foundational mindset layer. These activities help leaders surface assumptions about control, authority, and risk, fostering comfort with partial control and sustained ethical vigilance.

Development programmes must also prioritise AI literacy. This includes understanding why intelligent systems may generate confident but incorrect outputs, often described as hallucinations, as well as recognising indicators of model drift over time. Rather than positioning AI as a threat to expertise, the framework aligns with emerging perspectives that emphasise the development of superworkers, in which leaders and employees use freed-up capacity to focus on innovation, refinement, and strategic problem-solving (Brynjolfsson et al., 2018). This approach reflects broader calls to integrate leadership development more closely with executive education and organisational practice.

Beyond technical literacy, leadership development programmes must increasingly incorporate experiential learning methods that enable leaders to practice governing hybrid human-machine systems. Traditional leadership training has often focused on interpersonal influence, communication, and strategic thinking. While these skills remain vital, they are insufficient for environments where algorithmic systems actively influence organisational decisions. Scholars exploring leadership development in technology-driven settings highlight the importance of simulation-based learning and scenario-driven exercises that expose leaders to complex decision-making environments involving automated systems (Day et al., 2014). Such approaches help leaders develop practical judgment about when to rely on algorithmic outputs and when to intervene with human oversight. An additional emerging priority is interdisciplinary learning. Leaders responsible for managing AI systems must gain a working understanding of data science, algorithmic bias, and digital governance without necessarily becoming technical experts. Research on digital transformation indicates that leaders who combine strategic thinking with technological awareness are better equipped to guide organisations through periods of technological disruption (Benbya et al., 2021). Therefore, leadership development programmes should evolve towards integrated curricula that blend strategic leadership education with hands-on experience in AI-mediated decision environments.

The introduction of an integrated competency framework for digital and agentic intelligence represents a meaningful evolution in leadership scholarship and practice. By moving beyond the tool-enabler assumptions of traditional digital leadership models, the framework prepares organisations for environments where authority is shared between human and machine actors. It contributes to leadership literature by shifting attention from direct control towards the orchestration of agency, bridging strategic leadership, digital leadership, and agentic AI scholarship, and extending competency-based models to prioritise decision governance and ethical intelligence over narrow technical skill acquisition.

For practitioners and educators, the framework provides a structured guide for designing leadership initiatives that reflect current technological realities. It underscores that the most pressing leadership challenges in AI-driven contexts are not technical in nature but concern sense-making, trust, calibration, and ethical oversight. At a policy level, the framework also highlights the need for clearer accountability structures as authority becomes increasingly distributed. Embedding explicit decision rights and accountability mechanisms offers a starting point for broader organisational and regulatory discussions.

As organisations move beyond early stages of digital transformation into a phase of agentic transformation, success will depend not only on the sophistication of AI systems but also on leaders' ability to orchestrate shared agency across human and machine workforces. Future research should continue to examine how distributed authority shapes organisational culture, employee well-being, and long-term performance. By grounding leadership development in the realities of agentic environments, the framework provides a foundation for both scholarly inquiry and the practical evolution of leadership in an increasingly autonomous world.

Future research should expand the conceptual framework outlined in this chapter by investigating how leadership practices develop as organisations incorporate increasingly autonomous AI systems into their core functions. Although scholarship on digital transformation has expanded significantly in recent years, empirical studies on leadership governance in agentic AI contexts remain relatively scarce. Researchers have begun examining how hybrid intelligence systems blend human expertise with machine learning to support organisational decision-making. Nevertheless, further research is necessary to understand how leaders create governance structures that uphold accountability when decision-making authority is shared between human and algorithmic actors. An additional promising area of enquiry involves the organisational implications of algorithmic transparency. As AI systems become more integrated into strategic decision-making processes, leaders must weigh the operational benefits of sophisticated models against the need for transparency and stakeholder trust. Studies on algorithmic management suggest that employee perceptions of fairness and legitimacy are heavily influenced by how leaders communicate and supervise AI-driven decisions. Exploring these aspects will be crucial for developing leadership theories that can effectively guide organisations working within increasingly intelligent and autonomous environments.

REFERENCES

Argyris, C., & Schön, D. A. (1996). *Organizational learning II: Theory, method, and practice*. Addison Wesley.

Avolio, B. J., Walumbwa, F. O., & Weber, T. J. (2009). Leadership: Current theories, research, and future directions. *Annual Review of Psychology*, *60*(1), 421–449. DOI: 10.1146/annurev.psych.60.110707.163621 PMID: 18651820

Bader, V., & Kaiser, S. (2019). Algorithmic decision-making? The user interface and its role for human involvement in decisions supported by artificial intelligence. *Organization*, *26*(5), 655–672. DOI: 10.1177/1350508419855714

Baird, A., & Maruping, L. M. (2021). The next generation of research on IS use: A theoretical framework of delegation to and from agentic IS artifacts. *Management Information Systems Quarterly*, *45*(1), 315–341. DOI: 10.25300/MISQ/2021/15882

Benbya, H., Pachidi, S., & Jarvenpaa, S. (2021). Special issue editorial: Artificial intelligence in organizations: Implications for information systems research. *Journal of the Association for Information Systems*, *22*(2), 10. DOI: 10.17705/1jais.00662

Bernstein, E., Bunch, J., Canner, N., & Lee, M. (2018). Beyond the holacracy hype. *Harvard Business Review*, *96*(4), 38–49.

Boyatzis, R. E. (2008). Competencies in the 21st century. *Journal of Management Development*, *27*(1), 5–12. DOI: 10.1108/02621710810840730

Brock, J. K. U., & Von Wangenheim, F. (2019). Demystifying AI: What digital transformation leaders can teach you about realistic artificial intelligence. *California Management Review*, *61*(4), 110–134. DOI: 10.1177/1536504219865226

Brynjolfsson, E., Mitchell, T., & Rock, D. (2018). What can machines learn and what does it mean for occupations and the economy. *AEA Papers and Proceedings. American Economic Association*, *108*, 43–47. DOI: 10.1257/pandp.20181019

Davenport, T. H., Guha, A., Grewal, D., & Bressgott, T. (2020). How artificial intelligence will change the future of marketing. *Journal of the Academy of Marketing Science*, *48*(1), 24–42. DOI: 10.1007/s11747-019-00696-0

Davenport, T. H., & Mittal, N. (2023). *All-in on AI: How smart companies win big with artificial intelligence*. Harvard Business Review Press.

Day, D. V., Fleenor, J. W., Atwater, L. E., Sturm, R. E., & McKee, R. A. (2014). Advances in leader and leadership development: A review of 25 years of research and theory. *The Leadership Quarterly*, *25*(1), 63–82. DOI: 10.1016/j.leaqua.2013.11.004

Dellermann, D., Ebel, P., Söllner, M., & Leimeister, J. M. (2019). Hybrid intelligence. *Business & Information Systems Engineering, 61*(5), 637–643. DOI: 10.1007/s12599-019-00595-2

Eggers, J. P., & Kaplan, S. (2013). Cognition and capabilities: A multi-level perspective. *The Academy of Management Annals, 7*(1), 295–340. DOI: 10.5465/19416520.2013.769318

Faraj, S., Pachidi, S., & Sayegh, K. (2018). Working and organizing in the age of the learning algorithm. *Information and Organization, 28*(1), 62–70. DOI: 10.1016/j.infoandorg.2018.02.005

Floridi, L., Cowls, J., Beltrametti, M., Chatila, R., Chazerand, P., Dignum, V., Luetge, C., Madelin, R., Pagallo, U., Rossi, F., Schafer, B., Valcke, P., & Vayena, E. (2018). AI4People—An ethical framework for a good AI society: Opportunities, risks, principles, and recommendations. *Minds and Machines, 28*(4), 689–707. DOI: 10.1007/s11023-018-9482-5 PMID: 30930541

Gunning, D., Stefik, M., Choi, J., Miller, T., Stumpf, S., & Yang, G. Z. (2019). XAI—Explainable artificial intelligence. *Science Robotics, 4*(37), eaay7120. Advance online publication. DOI: 10.1126/scirobotics.aay7120 PMID: 33137719

Hambrick, D. C. (2007). Upper echelons theory: An update. *Academy of Management Review, 32*(2), 334–343. DOI: 10.5465/amr.2007.24345254

Helfat, C. E., Finkelstein, S., & Mitchell, W.. (2007). *Dynamic capabilities: Understanding strategic change in organizations*. Blackwell Publishing.

Helfat, C. E., & Peteraf, M. A. (2015). Managerial cognitive capabilities and the microfoundations of dynamic capabilities. *Strategic Management Journal, 36*(6), 831–850. DOI: 10.1002/smj.2247

Hosseini, S., & Seilani, H. (2025). The role of agentic AI in shaping a bright future: A systematic review. *Array (New York, N.Y.), 26*(1), 100399. DOI: 10.1016/j.array.2025.100399

Islam, M. A., Somu, S., & Aldaihani, F. M. F. (2026). The rise of agentic AI: Synthesis of current knowledge and future research agenda. *Global Business and Organizational Excellence, 45*(3), 402–416. DOI: 10.1002/joe.70019

Kane, G. C., Palmer, D., Phillips, A. N., Kiron, D., & Buckley, N. (2019). Accelerating digital innovation inside and out. *MIT Sloan Management Review, 60*(4), 1–8.

Kaplan, S. (2008). Framing contests: Strategy making under uncertainty. *Organization Science, 19*(5), 729–752. DOI: 10.1287/orsc.1070.0340

Kellogg, K. C., Valentine, M. A., & Christin, A. (2020). Algorithms at work: The new contested terrain of control. *The Academy of Management Annals, 14*(1), 366–410. DOI: 10.5465/annals.2018.0174

Lee, J. D., & See, K. A. (2004). Trust in automation: Designing for appropriate reliance. *Human Factors, 46*(1), 50–80. DOI: 10.1518/hfes.46.1.50.30392 PMID: 15151155

Leonardi, P. M. (2014). Social media, knowledge sharing, and innovation: Toward a theory of communication visibility. *Information Systems Research, 25*(4), 796–816. DOI: 10.1287/isre.2014.0536

Makarius, E. E., Mukherjee, D., Fox, J. D., & Fox, A. K. (2020). Rising with the machines: A sociotechnical framework for bringing artificial intelligence into the organization. *Journal of Business Research, 120*, 262–273. DOI: 10.1016/j.jbusres.2020.07.045

McKinsey & Company. (2025). *Seizing the agentic AI advantage: A CEO playbook to solve the gen AI paradox and unlock scalable impact with AI agents.*

Meijerink, J., & Bondarouk, T. (2023). The duality of algorithmic management: Toward a research agenda on HRM algorithms, autonomy and value creation. *Human Resource Management Review, 33*(1), 100876. DOI: 10.1016/j.hrmr.2021.100876

Mumford, M. D., Zaccaro, S. J., Harding, F. D., Jacobs, T. O., & Fleishman, E. A. (2007). Leadership skills for a changing world. *The Leadership Quarterly, 11*(1), 11–35. DOI: 10.1016/S1048-9843(99)00041-7

Orlikowski, W. J. (2007). Sociomaterial practices: Exploring technology at work. *Organization Studies, 28*(9), 1435–1448. DOI: 10.1177/0170840607081138

Posada, J., Newlands, G., & Miceli, M. (2023). Labor, automation, and human-machine communication. *The Sage handbook of human-machine communication*, 384-391.

Raisch, S., & Krakowski, S. (2021). Artificial intelligence and management: The automation–augmentation paradox. *Academy of Management Review, 46*(1), 192–210. DOI: 10.5465/amr.2018.0072

Ransbotham, S., Kiron, D., Khodabandeh, S., Iyer, S., & Das, A. (2025). *The emerging agentic enterprise: How leaders must navigate a new age of AI.* MIT Sloan Management Review and Boston Consulting Group.

Uhl-Bien, M., & Arena, M. (2018). Leadership for organizational adaptability: A theoretical synthesis and integrative framework. *The Leadership Quarterly, 29*(1), 89–104. DOI: 10.1016/j.leaqua.2017.12.009

Vial, G., Benitez, J., Schmitz, K., & Mathiassen, L. (2023). Digital transformation: A review and research agenda. *Information Systems Journal*, *33*(2), 341–377. DOI: 10.1111/isj.12391

Vial, G., Cameron, A. F., Giannelia, T., & Jiang, J. (2023). Managing artificial intelligence projects: Key insights from an AI consulting firm. *Information Systems Journal*, *33*(3), 669–691. DOI: 10.1111/isj.12420

Weick, K. E. (1995). *Sensemaking in organizations*. Sage Publications.

Weick, K. E., Sutcliffe, K. M., & Obstfeld, D. (2005). Organizing and the process of sensemaking. *Organization Science*, *16*(4), 409–421. DOI: 10.1287/orsc.1050.0133

Yan, L. (2025). From passive tool to socio-cognitive teammate: A conceptual framework for agentic AI in human-AI collaborative learning. *arXiv preprint arXiv:2508.14825v1*.

Yoo, Y., Henfridsson, O., & Lyytinen, K. (2012). The new organizing logic of digital innovation. *Information Systems Research*, *23*(4), 1398–1408. DOI: 10.1287/isre.1120.0426

Zeike, S., Bradbury, K., Lindert, L., & Pfaff, H. (2019). Digital leadership skills and associations with psychological well being. *International Journal of Environmental Research and Public Health*, *16*(14), 2628. DOI: 10.3390/ijerph16142628 PMID: 31340579

Section 2
AI-Enabled Leadership Practice, Communication, and Teaming

Chapter 6
How Conversational AI Is Transforming Leadership Communication and Trust

Karan Gupta
http://orcid.org/0009-0003-9652-2179
Christ University, India

Babita Jha
Christ University, India

ABSTRACT

In this chapter, the author will discuss conversational artificial intelligence (AI) that is changing the face of leadership by altering communication, development of trust, and moral judgement in the digital organizational context. It describes how conversational AI is used as an intermediary that promotes responsiveness, facilitates information processing, and promotes relational communication and accounts for its deficiency to decode real emotional intelligence. Through four theoretical perspectives, the chapter includes the process of developing, maintaining, or breaking trust in AI-enabled leadership. The positive effects made by empirical evidence include better psychological safety and efficiency in communication, and adverse effects like bias, surveillance issues, and decayed human interaction. This chapter ends with the strategic advice on how to adopt AI in a responsible manner so that technological efficiency could be used to add to ethical and empathetic leadership.

DOI: 10.4018/979-8-3373-6650-0.ch006

1. INTRODUCTION

The changes experienced in leadership are accelerating as organizations operate in increasingly digitized, interconnected, and complex environments. Modern leaders navigate settings where data is transmitted instantly, employees expect to be involved in decision-making, and communication occurs across multiple digital platforms. Leadership is no longer solely based on hierarchical authority; rather, it relies heavily on effective communication and maintenance of trust. Chatbots and virtual assistants are the two examples of conversational artificial intelligence (AI) that has become a radical factor that changes the leadership interaction with internal and external stakeholders (Dwivedi et al., 2023).

More and more, digital transformation has altered the rapid, interactive, and decentralized communication between leaders and employees since it enables the leadership to be more receptive and responsive to their communication. When applied in conversational AI, the migration is further enhanced through the linear conversations presented in real-time, consistent, and scalable conversations across geographically dispersed teams. Such mechanisms will be able to decrease the distance in communication, respond more promptly and contribute to the aspects of transparency that is directly tied to the creation of the trust in the leadership. However, AI-mediated communication is also associated with an issue of authenticity, empathy, and transparency, since employees will tend to doubt the truthfulness of messages as they arrive due to the influence of AI-assisted communication or are merely algorithms. Previous studies indicate that the perception of fairness, empathy, and openness ought to play a critical role in the determination of trust in AI-mediated interaction (Keeling et al., 2018), highlighting the need for careful and deliberate implementation of conversational AI in leadership contexts.

Conversational AI is transforming the definition of a leader in most ways. Leaders nowadays do far more than merely handle the tasks, but rather they organise the human and technology resources. Conversational AI is a continuation of the concept of presence within leadership because it allows leaders to interact with vast quantities of workers without being depersonalized. It assists in disclosing facts, gathering the feedback as well as highlighting concerns at the point of inception. Simultaneously, the application of AI alters the expectations of the employees towards the leaders. As an example, the employees might develop the desire to receive faster responses, more intimate communication, and 24-hour access. Such expectations can be tough to achieve on the part of the leader selfishly, and this is why conversational AI can be a helpful partner. Though this also results in a shift of leadership communication both to be more continuous and more data-driven. According to scholars, the borders between human and digital work begin to be erased once the technological element is introduced to the communication processes. Consequently, leadership is increasingly hybrid where human skills and technology skills are integrated.

Beyond communication efficiency, conversational AI supports data-driven leadership by analyzing employee interactions, identifying communication patterns, and highlighting emerging concerns. Such insights can enhance leaders' situational awareness and support more informed and adaptive decision-making, particularly in dynamic organizational environments. When designed and implemented transparently, conversational agents can strengthen responsiveness and perceived reliability among users (Purnomo et al., 2023).

Despite these numerous advantages of conversational AI, there are some ethical and practical questions raised to which the conversational AI is exposed. These elements as honesty, empathy, responsibility and emotional understanding have always been present with regard to leadership. In the case of half-automated communication, these qualities are not likely to be easily maintained. In case of an AI communication being issued, it is likely that the employees will be confused whether the leader meant it or was affiliated with it. There is also some fear of bias on AI decision-making. Once biased data is used to train AI systems, they will become indoor unknowingly when acting unfairly and discriminating against certain groups of people. It has been warned in the research that even the state-of-the-art AI can reproduce the existing social biases unless strictly controlled.

These elements mean that leaders should ensure that conversational AI is used in a moral manner and that the degree of human control is high. The leaders must not overlook the strengths and limitations of AI. Instead they need to be careful that its use does not interfere with the organizational values. Overall, conversational AI in leadership communication is changing the process of interaction and building trust between leaders and how they uphold organizational culture. It is not the displacement of human communication by machine communication but rather the revival of communication as a phenomenon which is present in contemporary organizations. Conversation-based AI may help the leaders to become less approachable, more common, and more conscious. Nevertheless, it can also be very dangerous in the situation when it is utilized in an unclear or even unethical way. As a result of this fact, the leadership of the future will require a compromise strategy.

Leaders must understand how they can co-exist with AI without taking away the human aspect of what leadership is. It is said that the emphasis on the transparency and compliance with the values of the users is the primary aspect upon which trust in AI-mediated communication is formed (Dwivedi et al., 2023). This means that the companies should develop different guidelines, training and development in addition to establishing communication processes that incorporate technology and human judgments.

Accordingly, this chapter explores how conversational AI transforms leadership communication, influences trust formation, and redefines leadership practices in digitally mediated organizations. The chapter begins with the review of the existing literature on AI, leadership communication, and trust and then derives conceptual frameworks of AI-facilitated leadership interactions. It addresses ethical and organizational issues next and finally, touches on implications of research and practice. The chapter is structured in such a way that it attempts to offer a consistent and analytically supported contribution to the research of AI-enabled leadership during the digital era.

2. LITERATURE REVIEW

2.1. Leadership Communication in Digitally Mediated Organizations

The leadership communication has been revolutionized given the high rates of technological changes and increasing use of artificial intelligence in the organizations. There is no secret that researchers have been persistently emphasizing the fact that the successful leadership results can be securely linked to the art of communicating successfully, building trust, and making the collaborative efforts of a team pull in the direction of the goals (Alshahrani et al., 2025). After subjecting workplaces to the process of becoming more and more digitalized, leaders must navigate complex systems of communication that feature virtual meetings, messaging based on smart and automated decision support systems (Afroogh et al., 2024).

The research suggests that technology can make the communication more efficient and introduce the problems of authenticity, transparency, and relational trust (Bach et al., 2024). Specifically, conversational AI as one of the engines of communication changes the traditional leadership paradigm as it is capable of interfering with the interaction between the leaders and the followers, and the impact of AI on trust is the subject of burning debate (Bozkurt and Sharma, 2024).

2.2. Trust Formation in AI-Mediated Leadership Communication

Trust is one of the most critical elements of the theory of leadership and its formation entails the competency, honesty, and benevolence of the leader (Henderson, 2025). In such a case when communication is mediated through the means of technology or AI systems, the employees must also evaluate the reliability, explainability, and fairness of a technology and establish the dual trust relationship between the leader and technology of the process of communication (Gkinko and

Elbanna, 2023). Some research indicates that in cases when leaders came forward to provide an understanding of how AI would be used, why they made the decision, and they accepted the responsibility even though AI would automate certain communication processes, their workers will engage their leaders more in trust (Bozkurt and Sharma, 2024).

The absence of openness in the role of AI tools or explosion of dependence on automated communications, on the contrary, can lead to mistrust and inadequate credibility (Hanna et al., 2025). Collectively, this literature indicates that trust in AI-mediated leadership is relational, interpretive, and contingent upon both technological transparency and human accountability.

2.3. Theoretical Foundations of Conversational AI in Leadership

The theoretical foundations of the use of conversational AI in organizations is a convergence of a number of disciplines, including human-computer interaction, socio-technical systems theory, and models of leadership communication (Hosseini and Seilani, 2025). The human-computer interaction study focuses the attention on the fact that the level of trust in the systems based on AI is determined by perceived transparency, predictability, and responsiveness of the system (Bach et al., 2024). The existence of AI is the premise of socio-technical approaches as it is not merely the tool, but it is also a force of the organizational process that reconfigures the patterns of communication, structure of decision-making, and power relations (Henderson, 2025).

Since, according to leadership studies, AI communication alters the dispositions of the followers concerning the accessibility, fairness, and empathy, the balance between the effectiveness of AI and the human relations capabilities is what the leaders, according to the researchers, are supposed to consider (Zárate-Torres et al., 2025). Together, these theoretical perspectives position conversational AI not merely as a communication tool, but as a socio-technical actor that reshapes leadership processes, relational expectations, and power dynamics within organizations.

2.4. Emotional Intelligence, Empathy, and AI-Mediated Interaction

Emotional intelligence and empathy are such aspects that have traditionally been regarded as important with regard to effective leadership. Highly emotionally intelligent leaders are in a better position to deal with relationship processes, cultivate a sense of psychological safety, and establish trust among people in a team (Coronado-Maldonado and Benítez-Márquez, 2023). The adoption of AI also leads to the concern of whether technology can emulate or complement such human abilities. Studies on emotional AI have proposed that conversational agents might be able to provide empathic-like behavior, but this algorithmic empathy might lack authenticity in the eyes of employees and therefore, trust should not be compromised (Babu et al., 2025).

Research also draws its attention to the possibility of pseudo-intimacy, in which AI-programmed messages lead to the illusion of understanding, without any real emotional connection, which might affect relationships and teamwork (K. G. & Joseph, 2025).

2.5. Empirical Insights on Conversational AI and Leadership Trust

It has been empirically recommended that AI will be beneficial in the leadership communication process provided that it is used strategically. The changes brought by AI could also utilize the system to automatize routine communication, provide feedback within due time, and access personal information by employees, increasing engagement and decreasing uncertainty (Meng et al., 2025). The work of organizational settings indicates that, by applying AI to improve transparency, e.g. data-driven reporting of an objective performance evaluation, followers recognize leadership communication to be more reliable and objective, thus triggering trust (Alshahrani et al., 2025). On the same note, research has shown that with the use of AI in communication, the perceived leadership competence of employees may be reinforced when systems work consistently and impartially (Zhang et al., 2025).

Nonetheless, empirical studies also caution that, when a human is not in control of AI mediating highly relational or sensitive communication, trust can decrease as a result of feelings of non-invested emotion or lack of sincerity (Shen et al., 2024). Empirical findings therefore reveal a conditional effect of conversational AI on leadership trust, suggesting that outcomes depend on task sensitivity, level of human oversight, and employees' perceptions of leader involvement.

2.6. Perceptions of Authenticity and Relational Proximity

The perception of authenticity and relational proximity by the followers also changes with the introduction of AI. Research presented in human-computer interaction indicates a tendency by the employee to anthropomorph human AI systems and in associating a conversational agent with human aspects (Kim, 2025). Although engagement and acceptance might rise, it can also create the possibility of confusion about whether messages were written by a leader or an AI script writing which can affect trust and responsibility (Qin et al., 2025).

According to scholars, these findings emphasize that anthropomorphism in conversational AI can simultaneously enhance engagement and complicate accountability, reinforcing the importance of explicit disclosure and hybrid communication strategies.

Though the sources of information are increasing, gaps exist in the knowledge of subtle trends of trust, emotional intelligence, and morals in AI-mediated leadership. First, few studies examine physical applications of conversational AI in organizations and how they affect trust between leaders and followers (Gkinko and Elbanna, 2023). Second, the scientific community does not provide longitudinal data on the issue of whether simulated empathy through AI is capable of maintaining meaningful relational bonds in the long term (Babu et al., 2025).

Third, there is a low amount of research on the differences in cross-cultural trusts in AI and communication acceptance despite cultural norms playing a critical role in determining aspects of fairness, ethical practices, and the perceived proximity (Zhang et al., 2025).

Lastly, as much as there is ample discourse on technical AI adoption, research seldom brings together a leadership theory, issues of ethical reflection, and emotional intelligence models into a comprehensive approach of AI-mediated communication (Hanna et al., 2025). Such gaps provide a platform to future studies to come up with actionable strategies leaders can apply to utilize AI without compromising trust, authenticity, and ethical principles.Addressing these gaps, the present chapter integrates leadership theory, trust research, emotional intelligence, and ethical reflection to develop a cohesive framework for understanding conversational AI–mediated leadership communication.

Overall, leadership communication, trust, and conversational AI have a significant relationship as marked in the literature. AI has its opportunities and challenges, which enhance communication and efficiency, and serve the betterment of decision support, but also bring the question of authenticity, empathy, and moral accountability (Afroogh et al., 2024). Effective AI-enabled leadership therefore requires not only technological competence but also emotional intelligence, ethical sensitivity, and transparency (Verma, 2023).

Walking the line between these dimensions, leaders will be able to implement conversational AI and receive a greater degree of trust among the organization, motivate people and meaningful human-AI collaboration (Zárate-Torres et al., 2025).

Altogether, the literature highlights the transformative and disputable issue of the conversational AI role in leadership communication. Although AI can help to increase the efficiency, objectivity, and access to information, it also creates the issues of authenticity, empathy, and moral responsibility (Afroogh et al., 2024).Effective AI-enabled leadership therefore requires not only technological competence but also emotional intelligence, ethical sensitivity, and transparency (Verma, 2023). These observations are the basis of the conceptual models built in the next section that attempt to describe the reorientation of leadership communication and trust in digitally mediated organizations via conversational AI.

3. THEORETICAL FRAMEWORKS AND MODELS

Such a shift in the direction of conversational AI in leadership communications must have a solid theoretical basis so that the technological implementation improves human relationships instead of impairing them. The discussion of the frameworks in this section describes the working mechanism of trust, ethics, emotional intelligence, and human agency between leaders, workers, and AI. Using a combination of the models, one has both explanatory and prescriptive rules of how to carry out responsible, human-centered AI-mediated leadership communication.

3.1. Model 1: Tripartite Trust Development in Conversational Artificial Intelligence

Trust is a foundational construct in leadership and organizational behavior, and its dynamics become more complex when conversational AI mediates communication. According to the Tripartite Trust Formation model, three levels of trust interdependence make AI-mediated leadership trusted by employees, including trust in the AI system, trust in the human leader, and trust in the interaction between the two (Afroogh et al., 2024). Employees do not experience AI in isolation; instead, they interpret AI outputs through the values, behaviors, and ethical orientation demonstrated by their leaders. Perceived reliability, transparency, and ethical functioning are what precondition trust in the AI system.

Employees consider AI tools depending on their capability to provide reliable, correct, and impartial information (Bach et al., 2024). Human leader trust continues to play an important role because the application of leadership traits like empathy, ethicality, and communication abilities have a substantial impact on the view of AI-mediated communication (Alshahrani et al., 2025).

The interactional dimension of trust focuses on how leaders translate AI outputs into accountable and ethically grounded decisions. The employees evaluate how AI is effectively used by leaders to aid the decision-making process without compromising accountability and relationship authenticity (Gkinko & Elbanna, 2023). As an example, when AI makes some prognostic information regarding the performance of the team, employees can determine how leaders interpret and use this information in an ethically and transparent manner.

According to the model, the best trust will arise when the three dimensions align in a manner that brings a synergistic effect which enhances the confidence and engagement of the employees (Zárate-Torres et al., 2025). Temporality of building trust is also recognized according to this framework. The first trust can be based on the reputation and credibility of the AI system of the leader, whereas the second trust is more tied to continuous ethical interaction and responsiveness of feedback, the manifestation of emotional intelligence, which enhances trust over time (Babu et al., 2025).

Previous layers place significant emphasis on the interdependency aspect, which makes the Tripartite Trust Formation model an effective platform that shows the way leaders should follow in order to integrate AI and still stay relational and ethical. Over time, trust strengthens when employees consistently observe leaders balancing AI insights with empathy, transparency, and responsiveness.

3.2. Model 2: Ethical Trustworthiness Framework for AI mediated Leadership

The ethical considerations are the overriding ethical principles in the implementation of conversational AI in organizations. The Ethical Trustworthiness Framework dwells upon the implication, that AI-mediated leadership must be supported with the principles of fairness, transparency, accountability, and respect of human dignity (Bozkurt and Sharma, 2024). The leaders have the responsibility to ensure that AI systems do not present any bias and influence over how employees are perceived, but bring a new level of operational efficiency and improvements to relations (Hanna et al., 2025).

Ethical AI leadership does not just focus on compliance with systems, but also influences the way the employees are respected, defended, and valued in AI-mediated processes because the ethical principles of the leadership practices are incorporated in the work of leadership. The lack of ethical blind spots occurs when the leaders assign AI systems to over-judge morality without having adequate human supervision, which may diminish accountability and relational authenticity (Henderson, 2025). In order to mitigate this risk, the leaders should actively interpret and place AI-mediated communication into context and take ownership of it so that ethical reasoning is a human-driven process.

It has been demonstrated through empirical data that AI ethical principles lead to increased employee confidence, perceived participation and leadership effectiveness (Meng et al., 2025).

3.3. Model 3: Emotional Intelligence as Mediating Variable in Human AI Collaboration

Emotional intelligence (EI) is a critical leadership capability in AI-enhanced environments, mediating how conversational AI influences trust, communication quality, and relational outcomes. The model puts EI as the mediating factor in the human-AI partnership that determines the perceptions of the collaboration through AI and leadership communication (Coronado-Maldonado and Benítez-Márquez, 2023). High-EI leaders have the ability to decode AI-generated knowledge in a way that is team-needs, team-feelings, and organizational objectives-oriented and thus increase trust and relational satisfaction (Verma, 2023). EI enables leaders to ensure that AI-supported communication remains emotionally attuned rather than procedurally efficient but relationally distant.

The model confirms three essential EI dimensions that mediate the performance of AI-enhanced leadership. The sense of self helps leaders understand their prejudices and weaknesses in decoding AI messages. Social awareness can enable leaders to know the emotions and views of the employees so that AI-related recommendations are contextualized. Relationship management is aimed at converting the AI-based insights into caring, understanding, and transparent performances (Kim, 2025).

Empirical data implies that conversational AI can be used as a tool to enhance the quality of the relationship in case EI is actively utilized instead of a decision-making tool (Babu et al., 2025). On the other hand, Low emotional intelligence may cause employees to perceive AI-mediated leadership as impersonal, thereby weakening trust and psychological safety and it jeopardizes both trust and psychological security. This model helps highlight the importance of the human-AI synergy, in which the emotional intelligence will serve as an intermediary between the technological potential and the needs of human relations (K.G. & Joseph, 2025).

3.4. Model 4: Agentic AI-Leadership Governance Model

The Agentic AI-Leadership Governance Framework deals with the incorporation of autonomous AI systems in the process of leadership. The concept of agentic AI is associated with the systems which can make independent decisions according to the specific limits, and they need the system of regulation which will help to balance autonomy with accountability and moral control, and they have to possess the system of the governance which will provide balance between self-reporting, self-responsibility, and ethical practices (Hosseini and Seilani, 2025). The governance structures will serve as protection mechanisms to make sure that human judgment and moral accountability are kept in focus amid growing autonomy in AI. The model consists of three governance pillars, decision control, ethics congruency, and feedback loops in addition to the continuing learning (Henderson, 2025).

Decision oversight serves to guarantee that leaders closely track AI outputs, his/her use of recommendations is responsible, and makes final decisions based on organizational values (Shen et al., 2024). The ethical alignment of AI responsibility requires that AI should run on the principles of fairness, transparency, and humanity as a design component (Bozkurt and Sharma, 2024). The feedback loops imply the systematic assessment of the AI performance, the levels of trust among the employees, and effectiveness of the leadership so that improvements can be implemented back and forth (Tah, 2024).

There is also an emphasis in the framework to have collaborative governance whereby leaders, technical teams and employees jointly develop policies and standards of AI use. Here, the risks inherent in overreliance on AI, possible bias, and loss of the authenticity of relationships are also reduced with this kind of collaboration (Hickok and Maslej, 2023). Through agency-based AI integration into institutionalized governance, companies can leverage the domain of AI and retain the integrity of moral governance and relationships

3.5. Incorporation and Combination of Models and Formation of an Overall Ideas Framework

The four models are united to build a wholesome system of cognition of the AI-mediated leadership and trust. Tripartite Trust Formation model establishes the model of relationships emphasizing the interdependence of the trust between the leader, AI, and employees. According to the Ethical Trustworthiness Framework, fairness, transparency, and human dignity should guide the process of using AI to integrate it. Emotional intelligence would mediate the balance between technological skills and human interaction needs, which will boost positive effects of AI on communication in leadership. Finally, the Agentic AI-Leadership Governance Framework provides structural procedures to regulate autonomous AI, ensure accountability, moral congruence and learning cycle.

This integrative conceptualized system also offers theoretical illumination and pragmatic suggestions as well. This is an indication that successful AI mediated leadership is premised on three parameters such as system consistency, ethical governance, and human relationship skills. By implementing these dimensions, organisations become a member of the IA benefits of putting it into action by increasing the communication between the leaders, instilling trust and the success of organisations (Madanchian and Taherdoost, 2025).

The construction of these models proves that AI-mediated leadership is a multi-level process that is determined by trust, ethics, emotional intelligence, and governance. Arranging the activity of trust, ethics, emotional intelligence, and governing, leaders will be able to positively impact the result of the relationships and organization outcomes with the assistance of AI without addressing terms such as authenticity, fairness, or human dignity. This model will provide an opportunity to test the hypothesis empirically, conduct the research further, and apply AI-based leadership models.

As a whole, these structures underline the fact that transformative AI-mediated leadership does not take away the human relationship but transforms the way leaders are still present, ethical, and relational in the technologically integrative settings.

4. THE DISRUPTION OF LEADERSHIP COMMUNICATION AND TRUST IN CONVERSATIONAL AI

While the theoretical models define how trust, ethics, and emotional intelligence operate within AI-mediated systems, it is equally important to examine how these dynamics manifest in real-world leadership practice. The section thus examines how conversational AI is changing patterns of communication, related expectations, and the establishment of trust in organizations. The below themes describe how such changes play out in the daily leader-follower relationships and indicate both the exaggerated potentialities as well as the unforeseen complications.

4.1. Shift from Transactional to Augmented Relational Communication

The conversational AI has basically reshaped the way leaders engage employees to the point where the interaction between the organization and the employees has taken a new facet of augmented interactive exchange as opposed to transactional exchange. Traditional leadership communication was characterized by the inclination to adopt one-way communication and structured meetings that limited the possibilities of leaders to address the needs of particular employees in certain circumstances in a timely manner (Alshahrani et al., 2025).

By integrating the conversational AI, the leaders will be capable of maintaining an ongoing and dynamic communication strategy that will tailor the interactions based on the situational awareness, personal preferences, and business objectives (Qin et al., 2025). With the help of AI systems, the leaders will be able to trace the key performance indicators, notice new challenges, and help them develop timely and tailored communication.

This enhancement enables leaders to think more strategically and relationally with the AI taking up the process of repetitive or transactional roles, which ultimately makes the organization a more responsive and relational setting (Salaheldin & Hussein, 2025). This leads to the fact that employees have a greater frequency of interaction, meaning, and contextuality, which improves the relationship of trust and collaboration between leaders and teams (Gkinko & Elbanna, 2023).

4.2. New Reliability of Human-AI- Leader Triads

With the introduction of the conversational AI, the triad of human-AI-leader relationships become complicated with regards to trust. Nor do trust in leadership only concern the competence and integrity of the leader: now it will concern how employees feel about the AI system intervening in these relations (Afroogh et al., 2024). Studies have shown that the reliability, the fairness, and transparency of the AI are among the factors that the employees consider when they make trust judgments about their leaders (Bozkurt and Sharma, 2024). Indicatively, when AI-based systems deliver consistent and impartial advice, the staff member might feel that the leader can be trusted, and inconsistencies or non-transparent AI actions can destroy trust (Henderson, 2025). These three-way relationships require leaders to actively manage both human and AI credibility, ensuring that AI supports rather than weakens relational trust. Therefore,

The human-AI-leader interaction will be a collective obligation in which the leader should have the mandate of interpreting AI outputs, conveying insights in a clear manner, and supporting ethical and transparent practices (Zárate-Torres et al., 2025). This change explains the necessity of creating AI systems that will not contradict organizational values and provide leaders with the ability to retain genuine relations with workers (Rahsepar Meadi et al., 2025).

4.3. The Potential of Conversational AI as Empathy Simulator vs. Empathy Amplifier

Among the changes are the most important ones where AI plays a vital role in enhancing or imitating empathy. Conversational AI may also act as an amplifier of empathy and helps leaders to better detect and react to the feelings of employees (Kim, 2025). AI applications can assist leaders by identifying communication patterns or engagement signals that may warrant closer human attention. Nevertheless, AI might be used as an empathy simulator as well, producing feedback which looks at least emotionally sensitive but lacks depth, and thereby establishing pseudo-intimacy (Babu et al., 2025). It is also of utmost importance that such a difference is possible: leaders who use AI-based empathy all the time are in danger of sacrificing the quality of genuine human interaction, and those who apply AI knowledge to their relations and personally access it are able to elevate the levels of relations and trust (Shen et al., 2024).

To be able to effectively implement AI as an empathy amplifier, a leader must be able to read AI signals with the ability of interpreting them in an emotionally intelligent and contextually sensitive manner so that the downstream outputs of the algorithm stay supportive of, not substitutes to, a deeper personal comprehension (Coronado-Maldonado and Benítez-Márquez, 2023).

4.4. Influence on the Follower Experience and Psychological Safety

Psychological and engagement safety along with workplace satisfaction are other areas of impact of the introduction of conversational AI in employees. The feedback with the help of AI can become more regular, direct, and evidence-based and less ambiguous and more transparent in terms of interactions between a leader and employees (Meng et al., 2025). Employees will feel freer to share ideas, voice concerns, and be proactive when they believe that leaders are responsible in using AI to improve communication and not to monitor or control employees (Hickok and Maslej, 2023). On the other hand, AI systems that are not executed sufficiently well and seem to be intrusion systems or biased might negatively affect psychological safety by creating feelings of mistrust and disengagement (Rudiyanto et al., 2023).

Empirical data show that leaders who logically strike a balance between AI-based insights and human management and ethical control create a positive experience of followers, stimulating cooperation, innovation, and devotion to organizations (Zhang et al., 2025). In this regard, AI can be used as an instrument of operational efficiency as well as provide the support to the relational and psychological aspects of leadership.

4.5. Demands of Intentionally Designed, Human-Centered AI Communication

In order to fully harness the potential of conversational AI in leadership, it is important that the organizations focus on human-centered design. The AI systems are also intended to be designed in a way that facilitates relational communication, ethical decision-making, and psychological safety and not just automate the tasks (Bozkurt and Sharma, 2024). Some of the key requirements there include openness in AI decision making, interpretable artificial intelligence, neutrality in decision making, and integrating morality into AI software (Madanchian and Taherdoost, 2025). The leaders would have to train on how to read the AI output, contextualize it, and furthermore, place the automated interactions into consideration and compassion in humans (Alshahrani et al., 2025).

Furthermore, the consequences of AI on trust, engagement, and psychological safety should continue to be evaluated to identify the gaps, mitigate the risks, and shift the communication strategy as time goes by (Afroogh et al., 2024). When applied in this way, conversational AI may be a major facilitator of greater leadership performance and sustainability of the human values, relationship richness, and the existence of trust within the firms.

Conversational AI is changing the dimension of leadership communication by transforming the interaction between transactional and augmented relationship interactions. This change introduces complexes of trust between the human and AI and the leader triads and the leaders should address the credibility of AI and their leadership integrity and responsibility. AI can either enhance or diminish empathy with the assistance of emotional intelligence or generate pseudo-intimacy in case of abuse which influences the experience of followers as well as psychological safety.

The values of human-centered design and deliberate government are important to make sure that AI can serve ethical, transparent, and relationally sensitive leadership communication (Gkinko and Elbanna, 2023). Altogether, conversational AI could provide leaders with a chance to improve the level of trust, involvement, and quality of relationship within organizations when it is adopted wisely and with ethical considerations.

5. CHALLENGES IN AI MEDIATED LEADERSHIP COMMUNICATION

When conversational AI is introduced into leadership communication, several challenges emerge that affect authenticity, fairness, and emotional satisfaction within workplace interactions. These issues deal with technical, relational, and ethical levels to which leaders have to address to make AI boost, and not undermine, the human element of leadership. The list below covers the most important areas of concern present in contemporary organizations.

5.1. Threat of AI Weakening Genuine Emotional Bonds

The fact that the introduction of conversational AI into leadership communication can potentially reduce the genuine emotional bond between leaders and employees is one of the most important issues of the integration process. Although AI could suggest empathy as well as create emotionally responsive answers, it does not have a true comprehension, which could lead to pseudo-intimacy (Babu et al., 2025).

Employees can see algorithmic response generation as shallow or robotized, which can hurt any confidence in leadership in case it is overutilized.

Leaders who rely excessively on AI for relational interactions risk reducing meaningful personal engagement, which is essential for psychological safety, motivation, and team cohesion (K. G. & Joseph, 2025). Research shows that although AI may assist leaders in their large-scale communication and sentiment tracking, human judgment has been much-needed to maintain trust and not superficial contacts (Shen et al., 2024). Hence, human interaction with its emotional dimension must be addressed with great care to establish AI as an advantage but not the threat to its human emotion.

5.2. Ethical Blind Spots in the deployment of Conversational AI

Another important risk in the leadership era is the existence of ethical blind spots that come with AI. They come into existence when AI systems are introduced without giving due thought to its moral, social, or organizational consequences (Madanchian and Taherdoost, 2025). To illustrate, an AI tool that identifies employee engagement may become biased in one way or another, prioritize a specific communication style, or fail to read between the cultural lines (Hickok and Maslej, 2023).

Leaders can also fail to consider ethical concerns related to the idea of delegating sensitive decision-making processes to AI by thinking that because of the impact of algorithmic neutrality, the process would be fair (De Cremer and Narayanan, 2023). Such ethical blind spots may result in diminished trust, employee vulnerability, and reputational harm to the organization. The analysis of these gaps necessitates ethical investigation on a proactive basis, continuous oversight, and partnership between AI creators, executives, and workers so that ethical implementation can become a real possibility (Rahsepar Meadi et al., 2025).

5.3. Fairness, Equity, Openness, and Surveillance Problems

The concept of conversational AI systems has a risk of spreading bias, questioning fairness, and questioning transparency especially in work communication (Sanka, 2025). The AI models that have been trained using historical data can be flawed by reflecting upon the organizational biases that are present, thus concentrating on unequal responses to feedback, performance appraisal, or distributing resources (Hanna et al., 2025). There is a lack of transparency due to the fact that sometimes algorithmic decision-making is complex and opaque, and employees may lack the ability to comprehend how conclusions or recommendations are created (Bozkurt and Sharma, 2024). Also, surveillance technologies based on AI may imply the lack of trust when employees are aware that they are always being observed, or evaluated based on algorithmic criteria (Hickok and Maslej, 2023).

The literature highlights that in order to eliminate these risks efficiently leaders should actively work to make the activity explainable, regularly audit the use of AI models to avoid bias, and communicate the use of AI in the organizational processes clearly (Gkinko and Elbanna, 2023). To remain credible and ethically decisive, it is crucial to find the right balance between the efficiency of AI and fairness as well as employee rights.

5.4. Striking a Balance between AI Efficiency and Human Dignity and Autonomy

Although conversational AI will help to increase operational efficiency, it is equally important to make sure human dignity and autonomy are not at stake (Nora, 2025). Excessive usage and over-automation may also result in unintentionally decreasing the decision agency of employees so that they are perceived as passive consumers of AI-mediated directions instead of active participants (Tah, 2024). Being an AI integrator, a leader will have to develop systems that enable the employees, embrace autonomy, and, in no way, remove human judgment but supplement it (Verma, 2023).

Research points out that workers will be more involved and motivated when AI complements, but not controls their workflows and can make informed choices and enjoy the advantages of AI knowledge (Meng et al., 2025). This balance is a process which needs deliberate leadership tactics not based on productivity improvement but relational and psychological effects on the employees.

5.5. Best Practices in Governance and Accountability of AI Use

Proper governance and accountability can be of utmost importance to guarantee conversational AI facilitates ethical leadership and organizational philosophy (Henderson, 2025). The systems of governance include the establishment of positions and the functions of AI implementation, the creation of an oversight framework, and the introduction of mechanisms of responsibility in decisions affected by AI (Hosseini and Seilani, 2025). Openness of policy formulation, regular review of artificial intelligence content, and engagement of employees in policy development and assessment are some of the measures to ensure that AI may not be abused, biased, or have undesirable effects (Alshahrani et al., 2025). In addition, ethical frameworks will help leaders to make decisions related to the application location and methods of AI, and make sure that AI will add value but not take away human-based values (Madanchian and Taherdoost, 2025).

Studies indicate that when organizations implement conversational AI within clear accountability structures, higher levels of trust, compliance, and employee satisfaction are observed (Afroogh et al., 2024). However, along with the great opportunities of conversational AI, which can positively affect leadership communication and trust, there are also challenges and ethical considerations that cannot be neglected. The representatives should also avoid the traps of pseudo-empathy, ethical blindness, prejudices, transparency, and threatened human dignity.

This kind of approach towards the design of AI that the consideration of efficiency and the design of AI is more connected will allow organizations to optimize the performance of leadership and make sure that the application of AI does not lack trust, fairness, and employee happiness (Babu et al., 2025). Much more praiseworthy ethical approaches to the introduction of conversational AI, in its turn, is essential not only to the sustainability of creative employment in technology but also people-related leadership in modern organizations.

6. TACTICAL LEADERSHIP AND IMPLEMENTATION STRATEGIES FOR CONVERSATIONAL AI

The successful implementation of conversational AI in leadership communication requires a strategic and balanced approach that integrates technological capabilities with human-centered management. Among the most important best practices are to determine the fields where AI can contribute the best,including routine updates, data-driven communication tasks, and employee sentiment monitoring, whereas the human leader should be left to make important relational and ethical choices (Alshahrani et al., 2025).

Leaders need to use AI as an assisting tool instead of a substitution of direct communication so that communication could be preserved as natural and immediate to respond. As an example, AI can identify critical performance indicators, or indicate team issues, enabling leaders to concentrate on a scenario, problem-solving, and social assistance. By embedding AI into communication processes with strategic consideration, organizations will effectively be able to increase effectiveness without sacrificing the ability to develop relationships and trust (AI Adoption, 2025).

The key to the successful AI-augmented leadership is maintaining trust, empathy, and transparency. The leaders should also articulate the use of AI systems, the type of data gathered, and how decisions are made (Bozkurt and Sharma, 2024). Transparency enables employees to trust both the technology and the leadership team, reducing concerns related to surveillance or discrimination (Hickok and Maslej, 2023).Leaders should use AI as a complement rather than a replacement for human interaction to preserve empathy and relational depth. As an example, AI-induced information on the well-being or engagement of the employees could inform leaders to respond to concerns of individuals in any meaningful way, strengthening relationships (Kim, 2025). With a mix of algorithmic analysis and human judgment, leaders can also make communication efficient and emotionally sensitive.

Important to successful implementation of AI in terms of leadership practices is change management and staff engagement. When AI is introduced into organizational communication, it is usually met with resistance because of the fear of losing the job, the question of whether it is ethical, or because of the inability to get in touch with technology (Kelley, 2022). This means that leaders need to facilitate employees in the process of adoption actively by providing the reason, advantages, and disadvantages of using AI tools (Onifade et al., 2022). It can be performed during training and workshops, as well as through open feedback platforms that can allow staff to realize how AI can contribute to their work and the status of collaboration,while reinforcing collaboration rather than control (Salaheldin and Hussein, 2025).

Participative style of change management promotes buy-in, anxiety minimization, and relational trust that forms effective leadership (Afroogh et al., 2024). The leaders must be the first to show their own AI involvement and how to assimilate AI into the company in the most responsible way, without neglecting employee perspectives.

Last but not least, leaders must aim at developing an adaptive mindset to aid in reaping the full benefits of conversational AI. The organizational environment is dynamic and AI devices are under constant development to provide new possibilities in improving communication, engagement, and decision-making (Tah, 2024). Leaders should be flexible to test various AI tools, apply emerging best practices, and understand the obstacles so that they can be prepared to overcome them. The development of the culture of curiosity, continuous learning, and innovation will contribute to making AI a component of leadership communication that will be practiced on a long-term basis and will not be an experiment (Mitsugi et al., 2025).

Utilized along with human judgment, empathy and ethical oversight, adaptive implementation plans assist leaders to leverage the force of conversational AI, yet still trustful, open and relationships-filled. Successful ideas of application of conversational AI in leadership focus on the use of trust and empathy, careful integration, involvement of employees and good governance practices. By reinforcing the point with the strategic deployment of AI as a support, yet not a replacement, of human interaction, it will be possible to enhance the efficiency and keep the high quality of relationships by ensuring the creation of thc open communication on the use of AI, the active involvement of the employees in the adoption of AI and its deeper monitoring organized by the KPIs and feedback streams (Kim, 2025).

Ethical management, adaptive learning, and human-oriented design also help in making sure that AI is working positively in the organizational culture, employee welfare, and leadership capabilities, which eventually makes the workplace of years to come to be future-ready and where technology can be in harmony with human values.

7. DISCUSSION AND FUTURE OUTLOOK

The use of conversational artificial intelligence (AI) in leadership communication is the most significant shift in the process of organizational management, Conversational artificial intelligence (AI) is one of the significant disruptions that has occurred in the development of trust, employee engagement, and organizational culture among leaders, who tap into the use of AI in leadership communication. It does not imply that AI has already lost the operational efficiency characteristic but rather an important part in adding to the ability of the leadership to establish the process of relationship, affect the organizational culture (Afroogh et al., 2024). This discussion will briefly incorporate theoretical viewpoints, practical experiences, and theoretical implications in an attempt to appreciate how conversational AI can redefine leadership practice and level of trust in modern organizations.

The fact that conversational AI medially facilitates leadership communication is one of the most important transformations that the system brought. The conventionalism of leadership is usually based on human interaction which may be constrained by opinion, mind overload or time. Conversational AI helps the leaders with the funds of seeing to the individualization being more responsive and relational in transparency (Alshahrani et al., 2025). By, helping with artificial intelligence, which can be facilitated by natural language processing and data-driven insights, By, The assistance of the artificial intelligence will help to enhance consistency, emotional response, and timeliness in communication between leaders and employees, which reinforces trust. This is one of the capabilities that allow AI to become a strategic partner to foster leadership instead of become its replacement between humans (Gkinko and Elbanna, 2023).

The interaction between leaders, employees, and AI systems forms a complex, multidimensional trust relationship. The studies indicate the significance of the employee trust that is established not only based on the trustworthiness of the AI systems but also on the ethical code and emotional sincerity of the leaders (Zárate-Torres et al., 2025). This triadic trust structure highlights that technological reliability alone is insufficient without ethical leadership oversight. Three interconnected dimensions, i.e., trust in the leader, trust in the AI system, and trust in interactions between the two, are involved in the creation of trust in AI-mediated leadership (Afroogh et al., 2024).

The leaders should understand that AI can be used to contribute to more transparency and predictability, but it cannot establish the trusting relationship alone. The employees evaluate the idea of AI-mediated interactions in regard to the perception of fairness and ethical behavior and benevolence and mention that the control by humans is regarded essential (Zhang et al., 2025).

The human-oriented approach to AI design is related to obtaining good leadership outcomes. The artificial intelligence mechanisms must be designed in a specific way to improve human judgment, ethical practices and guard the wellbeing of employees. Ethical issues that should be taken into account in design and deployment include fairness, minimized bias, transparency, and responsibility (Hanna et al., 2025). The leaders are included in the major areas of AI utilization and Leaders play a critical role in guiding AI use in line with organizational values, preventing misuse, and ensuring ethical accountability. The selective AI tools will be instrumental in supporting the leadership practice and promoting human dignity and trust. Such selective and principled use of AI reinforces leadership credibility while safeguarding employee dignity and wellbeing.

The integration of theoretical insights and practical applications highlights several emerging trends and future opportunities. To begin with, AI-supported emotional intelligence in leadership communication is something that can provide a stability in which the quality of the leadership can be enhanced. AI-driven feedback, sentiment analysis, and simulation of the situations can help leaders to be more aware of themselves, manage their relationships, and their perception of others (Coronado-Maldonado and Benítez-Márquez, 2023).

Second, the ethical mediating matters of AI are a burning issue. The challenges of autonomy, manipulation and transparency are emerging as new issues in the field of new technologies that are designed to generate fairness and accountability as much as the frameworks do (Hosseini and Seilani, 2025). Research that explores such dimensions can make recommendations relating to deployment of AI in the leadership process in a responsible way.

The organizational culture is at a point of extreme impact on AI mediated leadership. The communication via AI can be used to encourage transparency, inclusivity, and continuous learning and enhance the resilience of the organization (Mitsugi et al., 2025). By having AI at the disposal of a leader and strategically incorporated in teams, team knowledge exchange, team decision making, and team learning can be enhanced. Conversely, a surveillance, mistrust, or disengagement cultures could result in the case of poor or unmonitored application or adherence to the ethical standards (Hickok and Maslej, 2023). The most important thing is to make sure that the AI implementation serves organizational values to achieve sustained benefits.

This analysis leads to a number of new research questions. The longitudinal studies will be necessary to explore what the AI-mediated leadership does to trust, engagement and ethical decision issues (Kim, 2025). A study that will only focus on how AI has various consequences in various cultural and organizational environments will provide information on those practices that can be applied in particular work environments (Alshahrani et al., 2025). In addition, the ethical boundaries of sympathetic simulated AI and agentic systems might be also explored further, especially in the cases when human dignity, psychological safety, and human-to-human authenticity are given priority (Nora, 2025).

The vision of the empathetic leadership in the age of AI is to balance between human judgment and emotional intelligence with AI augmentation. Senior executives have to use AI to increase relational capacities, promote ethical decision-making, and improve the experience of the employees without undermining authenticity or human-centric values (The Emerging Agentic Enterprise, 2025). In this chapter, conversational AI is presented as an enabling force, but not a substitute since it should be integrated responsibly, continuously, and in accordance with organizational ethics. This discussion identifies the directions of ethical, empathetic, and efficient AI-driven augmented leadership by combining theoretical, empirical, and practical thinking.

Trust formation, the culture of the organization, and the communication of leaders are being transformed through conversational AI. To maximize its benefits, conversational AI must remain human-centered, ethically governed, and continuously monitored to protect trust, psychological safety, and responsible leadership practices. improve relational participation, emotional intelligence and moral accountability at the time of difficulties concerning prejudice, independence, and genuineness. To maximize effectiveness, it must be human-centered, be governance-oriented, and continual control should be established to see AI propping protection, mental security, and ethical management conduct.

8. CONCLUSION

In the contemporary world, leadership is shaped by the convergence of human relational intelligence and rapidly evolving conversational technologies. As a more digital and distributed world emerges, the introduction of conversational AI has turned into an observable trend that changes the aspects of leader-leader communication, relationship, and having trust. In this context, the theme which was covered in this chapter outlines how AI can create an astute difference in the performance method of leadership in case it is administered with transparency, moral deliberation, and through a human endeavor.

The analyses demonstrate that conversational AI has the highest potential that is not to substitute human judgment but to increase the capacity of leaders in being responsive, empathetic, and consistent in their interactions. Properly exploited, these systems can support increased levels of psychological safety, enable leaders to meet complex communications needs, and can contribute to the process of trust-building to different teams (Afroogh et al., 2024).

Among the contributions made by this chapter, the fact that conversational AI may transform the leadership communication process into an augmented, relational, and less transactional process (Alshahrani et al., 2025) is notable. This feature is also efficient in facilitating the performance of the organization as well as boosting the identification and loyalty that the staff have on the organization. It is also not difficult to enhance the emotional intelligence and the responsiveness of the leaders to establish the environment within which the members of the team will feel noticed and regarded, establishing the relationships basics concerning the trust and participation (Coronado-Maldonado and Benítez-Márquez, 2023).

Trust in AI-mediated leadership is no longer limited to interpersonal relationships alone, but also extends to the transparency, reliability, and ethical design of AI systems (Afroogh et al., 2024). The concept of trust is not a system of inter-personal behavior, anymore in human beings, as it is now concerned with the trustworthiness, openness, and the ethical makeup of AI-mechanisms. The Tripartite Trust Formation Model shows that the trust is created based on the interaction between the leader, the employee, and the AI system and the role of trust in AI is related to the view of the perceived competence, integrity, benevolence among others (Bach et al., 2024). Meanwhile, similar to the Ethical Trustworthiness Framework, accountability, fairness, and explainability appear to be essential in applying AI.

The frameworks underline that AI-assisted leadership must be guided by ethical management and responsibility of the human being to the trust fund. These dimensions that should be negotiated by the leaders would make sure that AI is being used in strengthening the trust of the organization rather than undermining it. Any ethics breakdown, partiality, or ineffectiveness may dissolve the trust of the workers, rail the engagement procedures and have unforeseen consequences on the organization culture.

There will always be an ethical concern when it comes to the introduction of conversational AI into leadership. The organizations should put in place the systems of governance that adequately offer accountability, oversight the behavior of systems and sustain ethical practices. By mitigating the issues at the initial phases of the introduction of AI, the leaders can guarantee that AI will enhance organizational values and support the well-being of the employees, in addition to establishing the culture of trust and inclusiveness.The proactive governance can be used to ascertain that AI will reinforce trust, inclusion, and ethical leadership instead of creating distance and harm.

The effect of future trends in leadership development in the AI age is also presented in this chapter. Relational intelligence can be improved using emerging technologies like generative AI and agentic systems, better decision-making, and more inclusive working. Studies are also needed to discuss the impacts of AI on both the relations with the leadership and morality or the organization performance itself. The vision described in this chapter is based on responsible AI application that enhances human potential and promotes ethical, emotionally sensitive, and technologically skilled working environments. The chapter introduces a reader or a researcher working in the field of the work and in an ever-changing world of AI-enhanced leadership the context of innovation and people-focused leadership as the complement to each other in a mutually beneficial relationship.

Conversational AI is a prospective technology and a current task of modern leaders. The implementation of the AI in the most suitable way results in the provision of the most optimal communication, trust, and relational intelligence that makes the leaders more agile and sensitive even in the complex environment of the organization. Application of AI should be fuelled by moral values, designed through humanism and sensitivity to the need of sustaining human relations. Being willing to assist, open, and make positive ethical decisions, the leaders who perceive the AI technologies as the next step into the evolution of the stable growth and enhancement are sure to embrace the available possibilities and make the workers feel appreciated, trusted, and interested.

This chapter concludes by emphasizing that conversational AI should be embraced as a driver of augmented human leadership, one that prioritizes ethical responsibility, relational trust, and human-centered values alongside technological advancement.

9. REFERENCES

Afroogh, S., Akbari, A., Malone, E., Kargar, M., & Alambeigi, H. (2024). Trust in AI: Progress, challenges, and future directions. *Humanities & Social Sciences Communications*, *11*(1), 1568. DOI: 10.1057/s41599-024-04044-8

Alshahrani, A., Griva, A., Dennehy, D., & Mäntymäki, M. (2025). The role of leadership and communication in AI assimilation: Case studies from Saudi Arabia's public sector organizations. Transforming Government: People. *Transforming Government*, *19*(4), 875–894. DOI: 10.1108/TG-06-2025-0187

Babu, J., Joseph, D., Kumar, R. M., Alexander, E., Sasi, R., & Joseph, J. (2025). Emotional AI and the rise of pseudo-intimacy: Are we trading authenticity for algorithmic affection? *Frontiers in Psychology*, *16*, 1679324. DOI: 10.3389/fpsyg.2025.1679324 PMID: 41050799

Bach, T. A., Khan, A., Hallock, H., Beltrão, G., & Sousa, S. (2024). A systematic literature review of user trust in AI-enabled systems: An HCI perspective. *International Journal of Human-Computer Interaction*, *40*(5), 1251–1266. DOI: 10.1080/10447318.2022.2138826

Bozkurt, A., & Sharma, R. C. (2024). Trust, credibility and transparency in human-AI interaction: Why we need explainable and trustworthy AI and why we need it now? https://files.eric.ed.gov/fulltext/EJ1459191.pdf

Coronado-Maldonado, I., & Benítez-Márquez, M.-D. (2023). Emotional intelligence, leadership, and work teams: A hybrid literature review. *Heliyon*, *9*(10), e20356. DOI: 10.1016/j.heliyon.2023.e20356 PMID: 37790975

De Cremer, D., & Narayanan, D. (2023). How AI tools can—And cannot—help organizations become more ethical. *Frontiers in Artificial Intelligence*, *6*, 1093712. DOI: 10.3389/frai.2023.1093712 PMID: 37426304

Dwivedi, R., Dave, D., Naik, H., Singhal, S., Omer, R., Patel, P., Qian, B., Wen, Z., Shah, T., Morgan, G., & Ranjan, R. (2023). Explainable AI (XAI): Core ideas, techniques, and solutions. *ACM Computing Surveys*, *55*(9), 1–33. DOI: 10.1145/3561048

Gkinko, L., & Elbanna, A. (2023). Designing trust: The formation of employees' trust in conversational AI in the digital workplace. *Journal of Business Research*, *158*, 113707. DOI: 10.1016/j.jbusres.2023.113707

Hanna, M. G., Pantanowitz, L., Jackson, B., Palmer, O., Visweswaran, S., Pantanowitz, J., Deebajah, M., & Rashidi, H. H. (2025). Ethical and bias considerations in artificial intelligence/machine learning. *Modern Pathology*, *38*(3), 100686. DOI: 10.1016/j.modpat.2024.100686 PMID: 39694331

Henderson, M. D. (2025). Agentic AI and the ethics of leadership maintenance: Rethinking responsibility in algorithmic organizations. *Leadership and Organization Development Journal*, •••, 1–15. DOI: 10.1108/LODJ-05-2025-0319

Hickok, M., & Maslej, N. (2023). A policy primer and roadmap on AI worker surveillance and productivity scoring tools. *AI and Ethics*, *3*(3), 673–687. DOI: 10.1007/s43681-023-00275-8 PMID: 37360144

Hosseini, S., & Seilani, H. (2025). The role of agentic AI in shaping a smart future: A systematic review. *Array (New York, N.Y.)*, *26*, 100399. DOI: 10.1016/j.array.2025.100399

Jooyoung Kim, H. J. (2025, November 19). Dynamics of generative AI responsiveness and empathy in enhancing work performance: Moderating effects of organizational culture. International Journal of Human–Computer Interaction. https://www.tandfonline.com/doi/full/10.1080/10447318.2025.2584727

K. G., A., & Joseph, J. (2025). The compassion illusion: Can artificial empathy ever be emotionally authentic? *Frontiers in Psychology*, *16*, 1723149. DOI: 10.3389/fpsyg.2025.1723149 PMID: 41333308

Kelley, S. (2022). Employee perceptions of the effective adoption of AI principles. *Journal of Business Ethics*, *178*(4), 871–893. DOI: 10.1007/s10551-022-05051-y PMID: 35818389

Madanchian, M., & Taherdoost, H. (2025). Ethical theories, governance models, and strategic frameworks for responsible AI adoption and organizational success. *Frontiers in Artificial Intelligence*, *8*, 1619029. DOI: 10.3389/frai.2025.1619029 PMID: 40741285

Meng, Q., Wu, T.-J., Duan, W., & Li, S. (2025). Effects of employee–artificial intelligence (AI) collaboration on counterproductive work behaviors (CWBs): Leader emotional support as a moderator. *Behavioral Sciences (Basel, Switzerland)*, *15*(5), 696. DOI: 10.3390/bs15050696 PMID: 40426473

Mitsugi, N., Ijuin, K., Oshiyama, C., Hara, E., & Nishimura, T. (2025). An AI-mediated framework for recursive learning: Transforming individual experiences into organizational knowledge and autonomous engagement in elderly care. *Frontiers in Digital Health*, *7*, 1529072. DOI: 10.3389/fdgth.2025.1529072 PMID: 40678716

Nora, M. (2025). Protecting human dignity and meaningful work in the age of AI: A social autonomy framework for ethical decision making in the workplace. https://scarab.bates.edu/cgi/viewcontent.cgi?article=1574&context=honorstheses

Onifade, A. Y., Ogeawuchi, J. C., Abayomi, A. A., Agboola, O. A., Dosumu, R. E., & George, O. O. (2022). A conceptual framework for integrating AI adoption metrics into B2B marketing decision systems. *International Journal of Management and Organizational Research, 1*(1), 237–248. DOI: 10.54660/IJMOR.2022.1.1.237-248

Purnomo, A. H., Fitriansyah, F., Adi, A. S., Hafsari, P., & Fitrianto, Y. (2023, December). Modular-Integration for Smart Governance Development Efficiency in Developing Countries. In MICEB: Mulawarman International Conference on Economics and Business (Vol. 6, No. 1, pp. 55-65).

Qin, J., Nan, Y., Li, Z., & Meng, J. (2025). Effectiveness of communication competence in AI conversational agents for health: Systematic review and meta-analysis. *Journal of Medical Internet Research, 27*, e76296. DOI: 10.2196/76296 PMID: 41183242

Rahsepar Meadi, M., Sillekens, T., Metselaar, S., Van Balkom, A., Bernstein, J., & Batelaan, N. (2025). Exploring the ethical challenges of conversational AI in mental health care: Scoping review. *JMIR Mental Health, 12*, e60432. DOI: 10.2196/60432 PMID: 39983102

Rudiyanto, T., Kunda, H., Dunn, A., Shenderovskiy, S., & Gibson, R. (2023). Ethical and legal concerns of artificial intelligence in the workplace: Examining current legislations in the United States. *Lex Publica, 10*(1), 84–100. DOI: 10.58829/lp.10.1.2023.84-100

Salaheldin, S., & Hussein, S. (2025). The determinants of AI adoption and its impact on employee engagement: Evidence from Egyptian organizations. *International Journal of Management and Applied Research, 12*(2), 45–67. DOI: 10.18646/2056.122.25-004

Sanka, V. (2025). Ethical AI in big data: Challenges in bias, fairness, and transparency. *International Journal of Scientific Research in Science and Technology, 12*(1), 731–737. DOI: 10.32628/IJSRST25121220

Shen, J., DiPaola, D., Ali, S., Sap, M., Park, H. W., & Breazeal, C. (2024). Empathy toward artificial intelligence versus human experiences and the role of transparency in mental health and social support chatbot design: Comparative study. *JMIR Mental Health, 11*, e62679. DOI: 10.2196/62679 PMID: 39321450

Tah, E. N. (2024). Effects of artificial intelligence adoption on organizational success, productivity, and efficiency. https://comp.mga.edu/static/media/doctoralpapers/2024_Tah_0917113914.pdf

(2025, November 18). The Emerging Agentic Enterprise: How Leaders Must Navigate a New Age of AI. (2025). *MIT Sloan Management Review*. Advance online publication. DOI: 10.63383/jAXE2583

Verma, S. (2023). The role of artificial intelligence in enhancing emotional intelligence for strategic decision-making: A study across academic institutions in Punjab. Educational Administration: Theory and Practice, 1436–1442. https://doi.org/DOI: 10.53555/kuey.v29i3.9605

Zárate-Torres, R., Rey-Sarmiento, C. F., Acosta-Prado, J. C., Gómez-Cruz, N. A., Rodríguez Castro, D. Y., & Camargo, J. (2025). Influence of leadership on human–artificial intelligence collaboration. *Behavioral Sciences (Basel, Switzerland)*, *15*(7), 873. DOI: 10.3390/bs15070873 PMID: 40723657

Zhang, Q., Wang, F., Liao, G., & Li, M. (2025). How does AI trust foster innovative performance under paternalistic leadership? The roles of AI crafting and leader's AI opportunity perception. *Behavioral Sciences (Basel, Switzerland)*, *15*(8), 1064. DOI: 10.3390/bs15081064 PMID: 40867421

Chapter 7
AI at the Leadership Table:
Coaching, Mentoring, and Empowering Human Potential

Gurpreet pal Kaur
http://orcid.org/0000-0001-7475-3548
Lovely Professional University, India

Mushtaq Ahmed Shah
http://orcid.org/0000-0002-3177-9622
Lovely Professional University, India

ABSTRACT

The chapter examines how AI augments human leadership. Although 88% of organisations use AI, fewer than one-third succeed, signalling the need for leaders who blend emotional intelligence with technological fluency. It draws on socio-technical systems theory, transformational and empathetic leadership, adult learning theory, and human-AI collaboration to propose a four-layer framework: AI Intelligence, Human Leadership, Interaction, and Outcome. The model shows that agentic AI can enhance behavioural insight, emotional sensitivity, and personalised growth when paired with empathy, relational judgement, and ethical awareness. Human-AI coaching ecosystems can democratise learning, strengthen inclusivity, and improve decision-making, yet raise issues of privacy, fairness, and power imbalance. The chapter concludes with future research directions, including validation studies, cross-cultural insights, longitudinal assessment, co-leadership models, and new competency frameworks for ethical and effective AI-enabled leadership.

DOI: 10.4018/979-8-3373-6650-0.ch007

1. INTRODUCTION

Artificial intelligence (AI) emergence in organizational life has changed the focus of automation and analytics to more human-focused realms such as leadership, coaching, mentoring, and talent development. According to recent research, global organizations are still in the process of increasing their application of AI and some of the most advanced forms, with 88 percent of companies already applying AI to at least one business activity, while many are considering more autonomous agentic AI-based systems that may reason and perform complex tasks (Myszak and Filina-Dawidowicz, 2025a). This change is not just an indicator of the evolution of technologies but also a significant transformation in how leaders guide people, shape culture, and make decisions in complex organizational environments. The study of Regenerative Leadership demonstrates that the combination of AI with neuroplasticity practices allows improving the cognitive flexibility of leaders and their emotional stability, which makes AI a co-creator of human development (Ooi, 2025). Meanwhile, thought leaders suggest that an emerging generation of leaders with AI power should strike a balance between human judgment, empathy and machine intelligence to succeed in more digital organizations (Andrade, 2025; Ooi, 2025). These developments in totality signify a new era in which AI ceases to be merely a supporting tool and becomes an active participant in leadership and organizational transformation.

The increasing emotional and mental stress among leaders is also driven by the accelerated pace of digital transformation and the integration of AI into organizational processes. Leaders are increasingly required to make urgent high-stakes decisions under conditions of uncertainty while coordinating distributed or hybrid teams that alter the rules of collaboration (Madanchian and Taherdoost, 2025). These circumstances raise ethical concerns surrounding algorithmic transparency, fairness, and accountability, particularly in the use of AI in recruitment, performance evaluation, and productivity monitoring (Krishnasamy et al., 2025). These forces shape what has been described as leadership overload, in which leaders must manage an overwhelming volume of information while maintaining empathy, psychological safety, and team cohesion (Stajkovic and Stajkovic, 2024). However, many organizations still lack institutionalized frameworks for continuous feedback, emotional intelligence development, and AI-enhanced coaching systems that support leadership well-being and effectiveness in rapidly changing environments (Adarkwah et al., 2025).

This situation reveals a significant gap in existing leadership development strategies. Traditional coaching and mentoring models historically relied on structured human-to-human interactions characterized by reflective dialogue and contextual guidance. However, modern organizations increasingly operate in digital environments where communication is fragmented and development needs are continuous rather than episodic. Studies indicate that many organizations still struggle to scale AI-enabled coaching practices across the enterprise due to challenges related to workflow redesign, talent strategy, and adaptive leadership capabilities (Sposato & Dittmar, 2025). At the same time, leadership scholarship emphasizes that relational and emotional aspects of leadership traditionally nurtured through mentoring and face-to-face learning—must now be translated into digital and hybrid working environments (Diller and Passmore, 2023). Leaders therefore require support systems that are technology-enabled, scalable, and capable of providing real-time behavioral insights, which traditional coaching models alone cannot fully deliver.

Table 1. State of the Field in AI-Enabled Leadership Development

Theme	Key Findings in Literature	Limitations in Current Research	Contribution of This Chapter
AI in Leadership	AI increasingly supports decision-making, behavioral analytics, and talent development in organizations (Myszak & Filina-Dawidowicz, 2025a; Ooi, 2025).	Research largely focuses on technological capabilities rather than leadership behaviour transformation.	Examines how AI augments human leadership capabilities such as empathy, ethical judgement, and decision-making.
AI-Enabled Coaching	AI coaching systems enable real-time behavioural feedback, adaptive learning, and scalable leadership development (Terblanche et al., 2022; Göldi et al., 2025).	Limited understanding of long-term leadership development outcomes from AI-mediated coaching.	Conceptualizes AI coaching as part of an integrated human–AI leadership development ecosystem.
Digital Leadership Transformation	Leadership increasingly requires a combination of technological competence, emotional intelligence, and ethical awareness (Mayer, 2024; Andrade, 2025).	Few frameworks integrate emotional intelligence with AI-supported leadership practices.	Proposes a model integrating empathetic leadership with AI-driven insights.

continued on following page

Table 1. Continued

Theme	Key Findings in Literature	Limitations in Current Research	Contribution of This Chapter
AI Ethics and Governance	Ethical concerns regarding transparency, bias, fairness, and accountability in AI-based decision systems are increasing (Krishnasamy et al., 2025).	Governance discussions are often disconnected from leadership development literature.	Integrates ethical governance into AI-supported leadership coaching frameworks.
Human–AI Collaboration	Hybrid intelligence models suggest that human judgement combined with AI analytics improves decision-making and organizational learning (Bhatia et al., 2025).	Limited conceptual models explain how coaching, mentoring, and AI systems interact.	Develops a conceptual human–AI co-leadership model linking leadership theory, AI capabilities, and coaching systems.

This chapter therefore seeks to conceptually examine how agentic AI can augment human leadership capabilities by complementing and extending them. The detailed contribution is pointed in table 1 above. Recent studies show that AI-enabled coaching and mentoring systems incorporating behavioral analytics, emotional detection, and adaptive feedback mechanisms are increasingly capable of supporting leaders in real time (Göldi et al., 2025). In particular, the chapter aims to:

(a) examine how agentic AI transforms coaching and mentoring practices;
(b) explore how AI can enable empathetic and human-centric leadership;
(c) analyze how AI-enabled systems unlock human potential through scalable learning and talent empowerment; and
(d) propose a human–AI co-leadership model grounded in ethical governance and relational leadership values relevant to future workplaces (Joshi, 2025).

The relevance of this inquiry is particularly significant for organizations undergoing digital transformation. Evidence suggests that companies achieving sustained value from AI are those integrating it into leadership processes, decision-making structures, and talent development systems rather than limiting its use to technical operations (Myszak and Filina-Dawidowicz, 2025a). Leadership scholarship similarly suggests that future leaders must combine technological competence with emotional intelligence, ethical awareness, and collaborative capabilities (Mayer, 2024). Rather than replacing human leaders, AI can transform leadership development by enabling scalable feedback systems, identifying behavioral and emotional patterns, personalizing development pathways, and reducing cognitive overload (Krauter, 2024).

As AI systems become increasingly agentic and empathetic, the key question is no longer whether AI can support leadership, but how human leaders can leverage AI to foster empathy, ethical decision-making, inclusivity, and large-scale human potential development (Ooi, 2025).

To guide the analysis, this chapter is structured as follows. Section 2 examines theoretical foundations of leadership in the age of AI and empathy, including the concept of agentic AI and relevant leadership theories. Section 3 explores the conceptual relationship between artificial intelligence and coaching and mentoring practices. Section 4 subsequently examines how AI contributes to psychological safety, trust, and scalable development ecosystems. Finally, Section 5 proposes a human–AI co-leadership framework that integrates ethical governance, relational intelligence, and AI-enabled insights to support leadership development in future workplaces.

2. THEORETICAL FOUNDATIONS

2.1 Leadership in the Age of Empathy and AI

Modern leadership is evolving from authority-driven models toward more relational, empathetic, and technologically augmented approaches, as illustrated in Figure 1. The emergence of hybrid work arrangements and digital collaboration has intensified the need for leaders who can manage emotional complexity, foster inclusive teams, and cultivate psychological safety within organizations. Empathetic leadership—characterized by compassion, trust, and emotional intelligence—has therefore become increasingly important as employees face cognitive stress and uncertainty in rapidly changing work environments (Alsalman and Chyad, 2025).

Figure 1. AI-Enhanced Leadership in the Age of Empathy

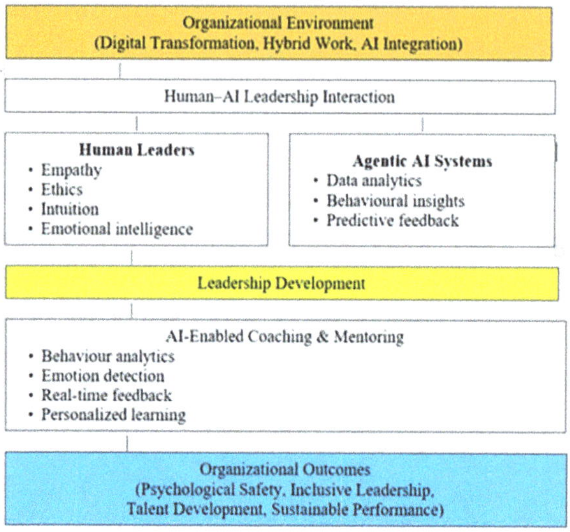

At the same time, AI technologies are augmenting leadership capabilities by enabling leaders to interpret behavioral and emotional signals more effectively. AI-supported analytics systems allow leaders to identify patterns in communication, engagement, and collaboration, thereby providing data-informed insights that enhance leadership responsiveness and decision-making (Oliveira et al., 2025). Rather than replacing human leadership qualities, AI technologies amplify them by enabling leaders to deliver more personalized, predictive, and supportive interventions within teams (Marvi et al., 2025). In this sense, contemporary leadership represents a synthesis of emotional intelligence and data-driven insights, combining human compassion with algorithmic intelligence to address organizational challenges more effectively.

2.2 What Is Agentic AI?

Agentic AI represents an advanced form of artificial intelligence characterized by autonomous decision-making capabilities and goal-oriented behavior. Unlike traditional AI systems that operate through predefined commands and rule-based automation, agentic AI systems are capable of initiating actions, adapting to changing environments, and learning continuously through feedback mechanisms. These systems exhibit characteristics such as autonomy, adaptability, contextual reasoning, and explainability, enabling them to function as intelligent partners rather than passive technological tools (Wendt, 2025). Explainability and ethical transparency are particularly important in leadership and coaching contexts because trust and accountability must be maintained in AI-supported decision-making processes.

Agentic AI systems can analyze behavioral signals, monitor interaction patterns, and evaluate progress toward complex developmental goals in real time (Rauffet, 2022). Through these capabilities, agentic AI systems can support leaders by enhancing self-reflection, improving emotional awareness, and enabling personalized leadership development pathways.

2.3 Theories Supporting AI-Enhanced Leadership

The integration of AI into leadership development is supported by several theoretical traditions. Socio-technical systems theory emphasizes the joint optimization of human and technological subsystems, suggesting that effective leadership systems must balance human empathy with technological intelligence (Sułkowski et al., 2024). Transformational and empathetic leadership theories similarly highlight the importance of emotional connection, inspiration, and trust in motivating followers, while AI technologies can provide behavioral insights that support these leadership processes (Dhiman, 2023).

Adult learning theories, including experiential learning and reflective learning, also underpin AI-enabled coaching models. Adaptive AI systems provide continuous micro-feedback and personalized learning opportunities that align with principles of self-directed adult development (Vanderheiden et al., 2025). In addition, human–AI collaboration theories conceptualize leadership as a hybrid intelligence system that combines human creativity, ethical reasoning, and contextual judgment with the analytical speed and pattern recognition capabilities of AI technologies (Bhatia et al., 2025). Together, these theoretical perspectives frame AI-enhanced leadership as a collaborative and developmental relationship that improves leadership performance within dynamic organizational environments.

Research Gap.

Despite growing interest in AI-enhanced leadership, existing studies often examine either technological capabilities or leadership behaviors independently. Limited research integrates these perspectives to explain how AI systems reshape coaching, mentoring, and leadership development processes simultaneously. Moreover, empirical frameworks evaluating the behavioral outcomes of AI-supported leadership development—such as trust, empathy, and psychological safety—remain underdeveloped. This chapter addresses these gaps by connecting leadership theory, coaching practices, and agentic AI capabilities within an integrated conceptual model.

3. ARTIFICIAL INTELLIGENCE IN COACHING AND MENTORING

3.1 Conventional Coaching and Mentoring Practices

Traditional coaching and mentoring systems have historically relied on human-to-human relationships characterized by trust, reflective dialogue, and experiential knowledge transfer. Many organizations—including companies such as GE and Tata Group—have long used executive mentoring programs in which senior leaders guide emerging leaders through storytelling, role modeling, and contextual guidance. These approaches emphasize emotional connection, organizational culture, and leadership identity development.

However, studies indicate that human-only mentoring systems face challenges in modern global and hybrid workplaces. Such systems often lack scalability, provide infrequent feedback, and may be affected by subjective bias (Sposato and Dittmar, 2025). As a result, organizations are increasingly adopting AI-driven mentoring platforms that provide scalable, personalized, and real-time developmental insights. AI-enabled mentoring systems such as MentorAI use data-driven algorithms to provide individualized guidance tailored to leaders' developmental needs and organizational contexts (Bagai and Mane, 2024). Furthermore, integrating AI technologies into leadership development allows organizations to provide continuous learning and data-driven feedback across distributed teams (Chowdhury et al., 2025).

3.2 How AI Enhances Coaching

AI technologies enhance coaching practices by providing real-time behavioral insights, emotion-responsive feedback, and dynamic development pathways. Platforms such as Microsoft Viva Insights utilize behavioral analytics to detect collaboration overload, burnout risk, and productivity patterns that may otherwise remain invisible to human observers (Sposato and Dittmar, 2025). Similarly, AI-driven coaching applications such as BetterUp apply sentiment analysis techniques to detect emotional signals and provide personalized developmental recommendations (Chowdhury et al., 2025).

Emotion recognition technologies, including platforms such as Hume AI and Ellie AI, analyze vocal patterns, facial expressions, and micro-expressions to identify stress levels and emotional shifts. These insights support reflective leadership development by enabling leaders to understand how their communication styles affect team dynamics. Additionally, AI-generated behavioral nudges—such as inclusive meeting reminders used in Google's leadership development systems—encourage leaders to adopt more empathetic and inclusive practices over time. AI-enabled learning analytics systems are also used in organizations such as SAP to recommend individualized training programs based on leadership potential and behavioral data (Bagai and Mane, 2024). Through these technologies, coaching evolves into a continuous, data-driven, and personalized developmental process.

3.3 Artificial Intelligence-Based Mentoring Models

AI technologies are also transforming mentoring models by improving mentor–mentee matching, developmental consistency, and performance monitoring. AI-driven mentoring platforms analyze behavioral styles, personality traits, and developmental goals to match mentors and mentees more effectively, improving relationship quality and engagement outcomes (Bagai and Mane, 2024). Platforms such as MentorCloud and Chronus use data-driven profiling algorithms to optimize mentor matching and reduce the risk of mismatched pairings often observed in traditional mentoring systems (Sposato and Dittmar, 2025). In organizations such as Unilever, AI analytics track leadership development progress using competency data and communication patterns, allowing mentors to receive proactive insights into mentee growth (Chowdhury et al., 2025). Furthermore, AI-supported learning platforms such as LinkedIn Learning, Coursera AI Mentor, and PwC's Digital Fitness App provide personalized microlearning resources aligned with strategic mentoring goals. Through these innovations, mentoring becomes more structured, scalable, and personalized while maintaining the relational aspects of human guidance.

3.4 Comparative Synthesis

The below given Table 2 summarizes the key differences between human-only coaching systems, AI-assisted coaching systems, and hybrid human–AI mentoring models.

Table 2. Comparative Analysis of Coaching and Mentoring Approaches

Criteria	Human-Only Coaching	AI-Assisted Coaching	Hybrid Human–AI Coaching
Key Features	Fully human-led interactions relying on empathy, lived experience, and contextual judgement. Uses reflective dialogue and interpersonal trust.	AI tools provide behavioural analytics, sentiment detection, nudges, and personalized recommendations based on continuous data collection.	Combines human relational intelligence with AI-generated insights to support adaptive and data-informed coaching conversations.
Strengths	Strong emotional depth and trust-building capacity. Provides nuanced cultural and contextual understanding. Effective for sensitive leadership discussions.	Highly scalable and consistent. Provides real-time behavioural analytics, detects patterns humans may overlook, and enables continuous developmental feedback.	Integrates emotional intelligence with data-driven insights. Enhances scalability, personalization, and fairness while supporting reflective dialogue.
Limitations	Limited scalability across large organizations. Feedback is episodic and dependent on mentor availability. May involve bias or subjectivity.	Cannot fully replicate human empathy, ethical reasoning, or contextual judgement. May create risks of excessive reliance on data.	Requires organizational digital readiness and AI literacy. Governance and ethical management are necessary to prevent misuse of data.
Real-Life Examples	GE leadership academies; Tata Group mentoring traditions.	Microsoft Viva Insights; BetterUp AI behavioural analysis; SAP personalized AI learning systems.	IBM AI-supported talent development systems; Google behavioural nudging platforms; Deloitte AI-assisted mentoring algorithms.

The table demonstrates that while human-only mentoring excels in emotional connection and contextual understanding, it lacks scalability and continuous feedback capabilities. AI-assisted coaching platforms provide data-driven insights, real-time analytics, and personalized development pathways, but they cannot fully replicate human empathy and ethical judgment. The most promising approach therefore lies in hybrid human–AI coaching systems, where AI provides analytical insights and behavioral data while human mentors contribute emotional intelligence, contextual understanding, and ethical reasoning. Organizations such as IBM, Google, and Deloitte are already experimenting with such hybrid models, suggesting that the future of leadership development will depend on collaborative human–AI intelligence rather than purely human or purely automated systems.

Although AI-enabled coaching and mentoring systems demonstrate strong potential for improving leadership development, limited research has examined their long-term effectiveness in diverse organizational contexts. Questions remain regarding trust in AI coaching systems, ethical governance, and cross-cultural leadership development within AI-supported mentoring environments. Addressing these issues requires integrated frameworks that combine technological capabilities with leadership theory and organizational governance.

4. HUMAN POTENTIAL EMPOWERMENT WITH AGENTIC AI

4.1 AI as a Prominent Change Agent

One of the most essential principles of successful leadership is self-awareness, and agentic AI can deepen this capability by providing continuous behavioural insights. Conventional development instruments rely on semi-regular and often subjective feedback mechanisms, whereas agentic AI provides real-time reflections by analysing behaviour, emotional signals, and communication patterns (K. Huang, 2025). These systems generate context-specific insights that help leaders understand tone, mood, and interaction patterns in their daily professional relationships. Insight dashboards integrate emotional and behavioural data into visual feedback systems that reveal trends such as declining empathy, rising stress levels, or communication imbalances over time (Jeffery, 2025). Agentic AI can also uncover cognitive biases that influence leadership decisions. By comparing current decision-making behaviour with historical patterns and organizational benchmarks, AI systems can identify tendencies such as confirmation bias, affinity bias, or selective attention (Litvinova et al., 2024). These insights enable leaders to reflect critically on their assumptions and adopt more balanced and ethical decision-making approaches.

Beyond individual reflection, agentic AI also functions as a developmental feedback infrastructure that connects behavioural analytics with leadership learning processes. Through continuous data collection and pattern recognition, AI systems can transform leadership development from episodic evaluation into an ongoing learning cycle. In this cycle, behavioural signals are analysed, feedback is generated, leaders adjust their actions, and new behavioural patterns are evaluated again. This feedback loop strengthens leaders' emotional awareness, ethical reasoning, and adaptive decision-making. Consequently, agentic AI operates not merely as an analytical tool but as an "observer companion" that supports reflective leadership by enhancing fairness, emotional regulation, and behavioural transparency within organizations.

4.2 AI in Constructing Inclusive Leadership

The analytical capabilities of AI are also transforming inclusive leadership practices by helping leaders identify diversity and equity challenges within organizational systems. Traditional diversity training programs often struggle to produce sustained behavioural change because they rely primarily on episodic workshops or theoretical awareness initiatives. In contrast, agentic AI can continuously monitor patterns of communication, hiring decisions, promotion dynamics, and feedback processes to identify potential systemic inequalities (Torre et al., 2025).

These insights enable leaders to detect unconscious bias and structural inequalities within organizational systems. For example, AI systems may identify disparities in meeting participation, recognition patterns, or promotion opportunities across demographic groups. Such insights encourage leaders to reflect on their decision-making processes and implement corrective actions that strengthen fairness and inclusion. AI-powered leadership simulations further support inclusive leadership development by placing leaders in complex scenarios involving ethical dilemmas, cultural differences, and interpersonal conflict. These simulations provide real-time feedback that strengthens empathy, ethical reasoning, and cross-cultural leadership competence (Sharma et al., 2025). Additionally, AI supports diversity-sensitive coaching by delivering personalized developmental content that reflects the linguistic, gender, and cultural context of individual leaders (Genkova et al., 2025). Through such mechanisms, AI-enabled mentoring systems can become socially conscious platforms that promote equitable leadership development.

However, the effectiveness of these systems depends heavily on the cultural validity and fairness of AI algorithms. Emotion recognition technologies and behavioural analytics models are often trained on datasets that may not fully represent diverse cultural contexts. As a result, emotional expressions or communication styles in multicultural teams may be misinterpreted if AI models are not properly calibrated. Organizations must therefore ensure that AI systems used for leadership development are designed with culturally inclusive datasets and governance mechanisms that mitigate algorithmic bias.

4.3 AI-Based Mechanisms of Psychological Safety and Trust

Psychological safety represents a fundamental condition for high-performing and inclusive teams, allowing employees to speak openly, share ideas, and acknowledge vulnerabilities without fear of negative consequences. Recent studies suggest that AI-supported systems can contribute to such environments when they are implemented with ethical governance and transparency (Gandía et al., 2025). Agentic AI can enhance psychological safety by analysing communication rhythms, collaboration patterns, and emotional tone in organizational interactions. Through passive observation techniques, AI systems can identify early indicators of stress, disengagement, or marginalization without disrupting ongoing workflows (Rana et al., 2025).

AI-driven development platforms also provide confidential spaces in which employees can privately explore leadership challenges and practice difficult interpersonal interactions. Such tools align with modern leadership models emphasizing emotional intelligence, reflective learning, and self-awareness (Salameh-Ayanian et al., 2025). By offering personalized developmental guidance, these systems allow employees to address emotional or professional challenges without fear of judgement or reputational risk. AI systems can also detect early warning signals associated with burnout, cognitive overload, or disengagement. Subtle behavioural indicators such as tone shifts, communication delays, or response patterns may reveal emerging well-being risks within teams (Zaslavskaia, 2024). When these signals are identified, leaders can intervene proactively by providing support resources or adjusting workload expectations. Nevertheless, the deployment of AI systems that monitor behavioural signals must be carefully managed to preserve employee trust. Excessive monitoring or opaque data collection practices may generate perceptions of surveillance rather than support. Therefore, transparent governance policies, voluntary participation mechanisms, and clear communication about how behavioural data are used are essential for maintaining trust in AI-supported leadership development systems. When implemented responsibly, AI systems can function as developmental companions that strengthen both psychological safety and organizational well-being.

4.4 Scalable Development Ecosystems

One of the most transformative contributions of agentic AI lies in its ability to create scalable leadership development ecosystems that democratize access to coaching and mentoring opportunities. Historically, executive coaching was largely restricted to senior executives or high-potential employees due to its high cost and limited availability. However, AI-enabled digital coaching platforms now allow organizations to extend personalized development opportunities across the entire workforce (Bachkirova and Kemp, 2025). Empirical studies suggest that AI-based coaching interventions can achieve outcomes comparable to human-led coaching programs in supporting goal attainment and behavioural change (Terblanche et al., 2022). By providing continuous feedback, behavioural analytics, and adaptive learning pathways, AI technologies enable leadership development to occur continuously rather than through occasional training sessions.

Such democratization transforms leadership development from a hierarchical privilege into an organizational capability distributed across all levels of the workforce. Leadership is therefore increasingly conceptualized as a behavioural orientation and mindset that can be cultivated among employees regardless of formal authority

(Peukert, 2025). AI-based development platforms further support personalized learning experiences by offering microlearning resources, reflective exercises, and adaptive training modules tailored to individual development needs. These platforms encourage employees to build narratives of professional growth, track developmental progress, and celebrate achievements, thereby enhancing motivation and engagement (Hossain, 2025). Through these mechanisms, agentic AI contributes to the creation of agile leadership development ecosystems in which continuous learning, reflective practice, and collaborative intelligence become integral organizational capabilities.

Despite the promising role of agentic AI in empowering human potential, several important gaps remain in current research. First, limited empirical studies have examined how AI-enabled leadership development systems influence long-term leadership effectiveness across diverse cultural and organizational contexts. Second, the measurement of outcomes such as empathy, psychological safety, and ethical leadership within AI-supported environments remains insufficiently developed. Third, governance frameworks that ensure ethical, transparent, and responsible deployment of AI in leadership development are still emerging. Addressing these challenges requires a conceptual framework that integrates human leadership capabilities, agentic AI systems, and organizational governance mechanisms. The following section therefore proposes a human–AI co-leadership framework that explains how these elements interact to support ethical, inclusive, and scalable leadership development in future workplaces.

5. CONCEPTUAL FRAMEWORK PROPOSAL

The integration of artificial intelligence into leadership development requires a conceptual model that explains how technological capabilities and human leadership competencies interact within modern organizations. The framework proposed in this chapter conceptualizes leadership development as a collaborative ecosystem involving human leaders, agentic AI systems, and AI-enabled coaching and mentoring environments. Rather than positioning AI as a replacement for human leadership, the model emphasizes a co-evolutionary relationship between human relational intelligence and AI-driven analytical intelligence (Madanchian et al., 2024). Within this perspective, leadership development emerges through continuous interaction between human judgment, emotional intelligence, and AI-supported behavioral insights. The framework is structured around five guiding principles that shape the relationship between human leaders and AI systems: Empathy, Insight, Empowerment, Adaptation, and Ethics. These principles represent the core dimensions through which human–AI collaboration can enhance leadership development in digitally transformed workplaces. Empathy ensures that leadership remains grounded in human relationships and emotional awareness, reinforcing research suggesting that trust, emotional intelligence, and compassion form the foundation of ethical leadership influence (Zervas and Triantari, 2025). Insight reflects the analytical strength of AI systems, which can detect behavioral patterns, communication dynamics, and emotional signals that may otherwise remain invisible to human observation. Through advanced analytics and behavioral monitoring, AI systems generate data-driven insights that support more informed leadership development pathways (Ooi, 2025).

Empowerment represents the capacity of AI systems to enhance human autonomy and developmental potential. Rather than constraining human decision-making, AI-enabled coaching systems provide leaders with personalized feedback and reflective insights that support inclusive leadership practices and collaborative organizational cultures (Aravidou et al., 2025). Adaptation highlights the dynamic learning capabilities of both humans and AI systems. As agentic AI continuously analyzes behavioral patterns and environmental changes, it enables leaders to adapt their strategies and leadership styles in real time. This adaptive learning capability aligns with contemporary models of cognitive flexibility and adaptive intelligence that emphasize resilience and proactive leadership behaviour in uncertain environments (Adelmohiman et al., 2025). Ethics functions as the normative foundation of the framework by ensuring that AI-supported leadership development remains transparent, accountable, and aligned with organizational values. Ethical governance mechanisms are therefore necessary to prevent algorithmic bias, protect employee privacy, and maintain trust within AI-supported organizational systems (Akinwalere et al., 2025). Figure 2 illustrates the conceptual architecture of this human–AI co-leadership framework. The model integrates four interconnected layers that together enable leadership development within AI-supported environments. At the foundational level, the AI intelligence layer represents the analytical capabilities of agentic AI systems.

Figure 2. Human–AI Co-Leadership Framework for Leadership Development

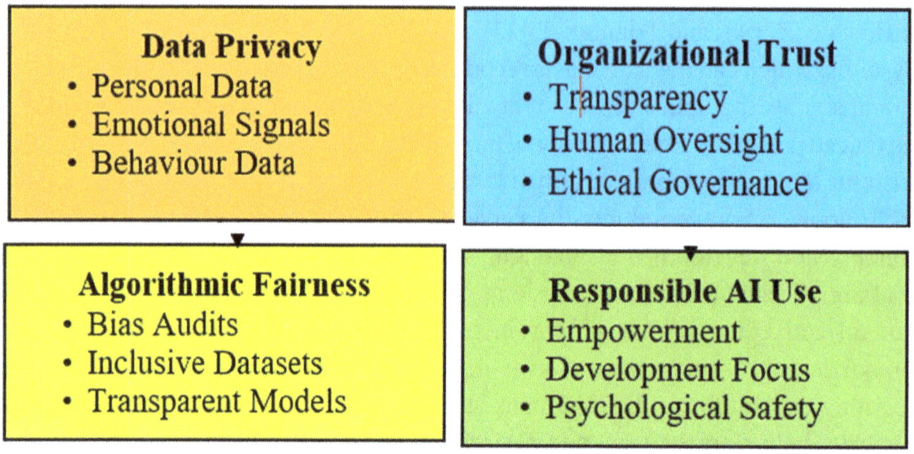

These systems incorporate behavioral analytics and emotion-recognition technologies capable of interpreting communication patterns, decision-making behaviours, and interaction dynamics within organizational environments. Through continuous data processing, AI systems generate developmental insights that help leaders identify patterns related to stress, burnout risk, and team engagement (Madanchian et al., 2024). These analytical capabilities function as the cognitive infrastructure of the framework, enabling adaptive feedback and evidence-based leadership development processes (Ooi, 2025). Complementing this technological foundation is the human leadership layer, which represents the emotional and ethical dimensions of leadership that remain uniquely human. Competencies such as empathy, intuition, relational intelligence, and moral reasoning continue to play a critical role in leadership effectiveness, particularly within complex organizational environments shaped by technological transformation. Theories of neuroleadership and regenerative leadership emphasize that emotional intelligence and cognitive flexibility are essential for building trust, fostering resilience, and maintaining ethical decision-making within organizations integrating advanced technologies (Bratianu and Staneiu, 2024). Human leaders therefore provide the relational and ethical foundation that guides the responsible use of AI-generated insights.

The interaction between these two layers occurs within a human–AI collaboration interface, where leaders interpret AI-generated insights and integrate them into leadership practice. Within this interaction space, AI functions as a developmental partner that provides analytical feedback, while human leaders contextualize this information through ethical reasoning and organizational knowledge. Feedback loops allow AI-generated insights to be continuously evaluated and refined by human judgment, ensuring that AI systems remain aligned with organizational values and contextual realities. Through such co-creative interaction, leadership development becomes a dynamic learning process in which both human leaders and AI systems evolve together (Krauter, 2024).

The outcomes of these interactions are reflected in the final layer of the framework, which represents the developmental and organizational outcomes produced through human–AI collaboration. When analytical insights generated by AI systems are combined with human empathy and ethical awareness, leadership development becomes more inclusive, reflective, and accessible across organizational hierarchies. Research suggests that such hybrid intelligence systems can foster psychologically safe workplaces, support ethical decision-making, and expand access to leadership development opportunities across diverse organizational contexts (Ooi, 2025). In this way, the integration of AI into leadership development contributes to a democratized model of organizational growth in which leadership capabilities are cultivated throughout the workforce.

The impact of this framework can be understood through several key mechanisms that explain how agentic AI enhances leadership development. First, AI primarily functions through augmentation rather than replacement. Analytical tasks such as pattern recognition, behavioral monitoring, and predictive analysis are performed by AI systems, while human leaders retain responsibility for empathy, ethical reasoning, and contextual judgment (Madanchian et al., 2024). This complementary partnership allows leaders to focus on relational and strategic aspects of leadership while benefiting from AI-generated analytical support.

Second, AI technologies contribute to the development of emotional intelligence by functioning as an emotional feedback system that helps leaders recognize interpersonal dynamics within teams. By analysing communication patterns and emotional signals, AI systems can alert leaders to emerging conflicts or declining engagement levels, enabling earlier and more empathetic interventions (Huang et al., 2025). Third, AI enhances leadership effectiveness by supporting complex decision-making processes. Predictive analytics and scenario modelling tools help leaders evaluate potential outcomes of strategic decisions, thereby reducing cognitive bias and supporting evidence-based leadership (Falckenthal et al., 2025). Finally, AI-enabled coaching platforms accelerate personal and professional development through continuous micro-feedback and adaptive learning pathways. Such systems enable leaders to engage in ongoing reflective learning rather than relying solely on periodic coaching interventions (Bruning and Boak, 2025).

While the proposed framework highlights the developmental potential of agentic AI, it also recognizes that AI-supported leadership systems introduce new challenges and limitations. Technical risks such as algorithmic bias, inaccurate predictions, and limitations in emotion recognition technologies may influence the reliability of AI-generated insights. Human factors, including automation bias or excessive reliance on algorithmic recommendations, may also affect leadership judgment. Organizational risks related to employee surveillance or unequal access to data-driven insights must therefore be addressed through transparent governance frameworks and responsible AI policies. Recognizing these challenges ensures that AI remains a supportive developmental tool rather than a source of unintended organizational consequences.

The framework therefore assumes that AI-supported leadership development operates within clear ethical and contextual boundaries. AI systems may be highly effective in providing developmental feedback and behavioral insights, but they cannot replace human judgment in situations involving complex ethical dilemmas, crisis management, or sensitive psychological concerns. In such contexts, human empathy, moral reasoning, and contextual awareness remain essential components of responsible leadership. Consequently, AI should be understood as an augmentation mechanism that enhances leadership capabilities while preserving human oversight and ethical accountability.

To guide future empirical investigation of the framework, several research propositions emerge. AI-supported coaching systems are expected to improve leadership self-awareness and decision quality through continuous behavioral feedback. Trust in AI-enabled leadership systems is likely to increase when algorithmic transparency and ethical governance mechanisms are present. Furthermore, hybrid human–AI coaching models are expected to produce stronger leadership development outcomes than purely human or purely automated approaches. Testing these propositions will help clarify how human–AI collaboration can be optimized within leadership development ecosystems. Overall, the proposed framework provides a holistic perspective on how agentic AI can support leadership development by integrating analytical intelligence with human relational capabilities. By positioning AI as a collaborative developmental partner rather than a replacement for human leadership, the framework highlights the potential for hybrid intelligence systems to enhance ethical decision-making, strengthen psychological safety, and expand access to leadership development within modern organizations.

6. ETHICAL, SOCIAL, AND ORGANIZATIONAL CONSEQUENCES

The integration of agentic artificial intelligence into coaching and mentoring systems presents significant opportunities for transforming leadership development; however, it also introduces complex ethical, social, and organizational challenges that must be carefully addressed. While AI-enabled systems can enhance leadership reflection, behavioral insight, and developmental feedback, their implementation raises critical questions regarding data governance, fairness, autonomy, and trust within organizations. Responsible integration of AI in human development therefore requires a governance framework that ensures technological capabilities remain aligned with human-centered values rather than purely organizational efficiency goals. AI-generated insights related to emotions, behavior, and professional growth should serve to empower employees and leaders rather than functioning as mechanisms of surveillance or control (Myszak & Filina-Dawidowicz, 2025a).

One of the most significant ethical challenges concerns data privacy and transparency, particularly given the sensitive nature of behavioral and emotional information used within AI-enabled coaching systems. AI-driven leadership development platforms frequently analyze communication patterns, sentiment indicators, interpersonal dynamics, and performance metrics to generate developmental feedback. Such affective and behavioral data can reveal deeply personal insights about employees' emotional states, professional relationships, and decision-making styles. Without robust governance mechanisms, these datasets may be repurposed for monitoring employee performance or enforcing productivity metrics rather than supporting developmental learning processes (Chowdhury et al., 2025). Ensuring transparent data policies regarding data collection, storage, ownership, and usage rights is therefore essential for maintaining trust and psychological safety within AI-supported development ecosystems (Peukert, 2025). Ethical frameworks must ensure that AI-enabled coaching systems respect individual autonomy and preserve the developmental integrity of coaching relationships (Ooi, 2025).

Closely related to privacy concerns are issues of algorithmic fairness and equity. AI-based coaching systems are typically trained using historical datasets that may unintentionally embed organizational biases or cultural assumptions. If such biases remain unaddressed, AI-driven developmental insights may reinforce inequalities in leadership development by privileging certain communication styles, personality traits, or demographic groups. Emotion-recognition technologies, for example, may misinterpret emotional signals across different cultural contexts, while algorithmic matching systems used in mentoring platforms may inadvertently favor individuals whose characteristics resemble previously successful leaders (Peukert, 2025). To prevent such outcomes, organizations must implement systematic bias auditing, inclusive dataset design, and algorithmic transparency mechanisms that ensure AI systems function as facilitators of inclusion rather than amplifiers of existing inequities.

The introduction of AI-based coaching systems also has implications for organizational power structures and information dynamics. Traditionally, leadership development processes have been mediated through interpersonal relationships between mentors, coaches, and leaders. However, AI-enabled systems introduce new forms of informational authority by generating insights through algorithmic analysis. In such contexts, employees may perceive AI-generated feedback as objective and unquestionable, potentially shifting the balance of developmental authority from human mentors to technological systems (Nahar et al., 2025). When poorly governed, this shift may undermine employee agency and create perceptions of technological determinism within organizations. Scholars therefore emphasize the importance of maintaining human oversight and interpretive authority within AI-supported leadership development environments to ensure that technology complements rather than replaces human judgment (Bratianu and Staneiu, 2024).

Trust represents a foundational condition for the successful adoption of AI-enabled coaching systems. Employees are more likely to engage with AI-supported developmental platforms when they believe that the system protects their privacy, respects confidentiality, and prioritizes personal growth rather than performance surveillance (Zwane, 2025). Building such trust requires transparent governance structures, ethical data practices, and clear communication regarding how AI-generated insights are interpreted and used within organizational decision-making processes. In practice, this means maintaining a hybrid model in which AI-generated analytical insights are complemented by human mentors who provide emotional interpretation, contextual understanding, and ethical guidance. When implemented responsibly, AI-enabled coaching systems can strengthen psychological safety and support inclusive access to leadership development opportunities across organizations.

7. FUTURE PROJECTIONS AND RESEARCH OPPORTUNITIES

The rapid emergence of agentic AI in coaching and leadership development highlights the need for rigorous scholarly investigation into the long-term implications of AI-supported developmental systems. Although existing AI-based coaching platforms demonstrate promising capabilities in behavioral analytics, sentiment detection, and adaptive feedback, empirical research examining their long-term developmental effectiveness remains limited. Future research must therefore move beyond conceptual exploration toward systematic validation of AI-enhanced coaching models. Controlled experiments, longitudinal studies, and mixed-method research designs will be essential for evaluating whether AI-assisted coaching genuinely improves leadership competencies, professional well-being, and organizational performance compared with traditional coaching approaches.

Another critical research direction concerns the cross-cultural applicability of AI-enabled leadership development systems. Leadership behaviors, emotional expression, mentoring expectations, and communication styles vary significantly across cultural contexts. AI models trained predominantly on Western datasets may fail to capture culturally specific behavioral signals or may unintentionally reproduce cultural biases in developmental recommendations. As organizations increasingly operate within global and multicultural environments, there is a growing need to design AI systems capable of recognizing cultural diversity in leadership styles and developmental pathways. Comparative and intercultural research will therefore play an important role in ensuring that AI-enabled coaching systems are culturally adaptive, inclusive, and globally applicable.

Longitudinal research also represents a critical priority for understanding the long-term developmental impact of AI-supported leadership systems. Leadership growth is inherently cumulative, emerging through repeated cycles of feedback, reflection, behavioral experimentation, and relational experience. Short-term evaluations of AI coaching platforms may capture immediate behavioral adjustments but may fail to reveal whether these changes translate into sustained leadership transformation. Longitudinal research designs tracking leadership development over extended periods can provide valuable insights into how AI-generated feedback influences career trajectories, team performance, and organizational culture over time.

Another emerging area of research concerns the development of human–AI co-leadership models. As AI systems evolve from analytical tools into collaborative decision-support partners, leadership itself may become a distributed process shared between humans and intelligent systems. Future research must therefore examine how authority, accountability, and trust are negotiated within human–AI collaborative environments. Such studies will help organizations develop governance frameworks that clarify decision boundaries, establish ethical accountability, and support responsible co-decision-making between human leaders and AI systems. These investigations may ultimately contribute to the development of new leadership paradigms characterized by augmented or hybrid intelligence.

Finally, the integration of AI into leadership development requires reconsideration of leadership competency frameworks. While traditional competencies such as strategic thinking, communication, and emotional intelligence remain essential, AI-supported environments demand additional capabilities. Leaders increasingly require competencies related to AI literacy, ethical data interpretation, digital emotional intelligence, and augmented decision-making. Future research should therefore explore how these emerging competencies influence leadership effectiveness within technologically mediated organizational environments. Developing validated competency frameworks for AI-enabled leadership will support organizations in designing training programs, leadership assessments, and talent development strategies aligned with the demands of the digital era.

8. CONCLUSION AND MANAGERIAL IMPLICATIONS

The integration of agentic artificial intelligence into leadership development represents a profound transformation in how organizations cultivate leadership capabilities, support professional growth, and foster collaborative work environments. Throughout this chapter, the evolving relationship between human leadership and AI-driven systems has been examined through the lenses of coaching, mentoring, emotional intelligence, and organizational development. Rather than conceptualizing AI as a substitute for human leadership, the discussion has emphasized the potential of human–AI collaboration as a complementary system in which analytical intelligence and relational intelligence operate together to enhance leadership effectiveness.

The proposed conceptual framework highlights how agentic AI can augment leadership development by combining behavioral analytics, emotional insights, and adaptive feedback with human qualities such as empathy, ethical judgment, and contextual understanding. When integrated within coaching and mentoring ecosystems, AI-enabled systems can provide continuous developmental feedback, personalized learning pathways, and scalable mentoring opportunities across organizational hierarchies. This shift has the potential to democratize leadership development by expanding access to coaching and reflective learning beyond traditional executive programs. At the same time, the framework demonstrates that the success of AI-supported leadership development depends on maintaining a balance between technological capabilities and human-centered leadership principles.

The analysis also demonstrates that the integration of AI into leadership development cannot be separated from ethical, social, and organizational considerations. Issues related to data privacy, algorithmic bias, employee autonomy, and governance structures must be addressed to ensure that AI-enabled coaching systems remain aligned with human development objectives. Without transparent governance frameworks and ethical safeguards, AI-driven leadership systems risk undermining trust and psychological safety within organizations. Consequently, organizations must approach AI-enabled leadership development not merely as a technological innovation but as a socio-technical transformation that requires responsible implementation and continuous evaluation.

From a managerial perspective, the findings of this chapter highlight several important implications for organizations seeking to integrate AI into leadership development processes. First, organizations should adopt hybrid coaching models that combine the analytical capabilities of AI systems with the emotional intelligence and contextual understanding of human mentors. Such hybrid models ensure that leaders benefit from data-driven insights while preserving the relational and ethical dimensions of leadership development. Finally, organizations should recognize that AI-enabled leadership development represents a long-term organizational transformation rather than a short-term technological intervention. Continuous evaluation, experimentation, and learning will therefore be necessary to ensure that AI systems support inclusive leadership, psychological safety, and sustainable organizational growth.

In conclusion, the rise of agentic AI marks a significant turning point in leadership development. When implemented responsibly, AI-enabled coaching and mentoring systems can enhance self-awareness, support ethical decision-making, and expand access to leadership learning across organizations. The future of leadership development is therefore unlikely to be defined solely by human expertise or artificial intelligence alone, but rather by the collaborative integration of both forms of intelligence. By embracing this human–AI partnership, organizations can cultivate leadership ecosystems that are more adaptive, inclusive, and resilient in the face of ongoing technological transformation.

REFERENCES

Adarkwah, M. A., Amponsah, S., Huang, R., & Thomas, M. (Eds.). (2025). *Artificial Intelligence and Human Agency in Education: Volume Two: AI for Equity, Well-Being, and Innovation in Teaching and Learning*. Springer Nature Singapore., DOI: 10.1007/978-981-96-9251-4

Adelmohiman, M., Salem, A., & Abdalla, W. (2025). Adaptive Intelligence & Thriving Mindset: A Developmental Competency for Youth Flourishing in the ZAT Framework. *International Journal of Vocational Education and Training Research, 11*(2), 96–108. DOI: 10.11648/j.ijvetr.20251102.14

Akinwalere, S., Chang, K., & Barbhuiya, S. (2025). Sustainability-Embedded Leadership for Successful Change Management. *Sustainability (Basel), 17*(17), 7973. DOI: 10.3390/su17177973

Alsalman, F. A., & Chyad, S. A. (2025). Impact of Emotional Intelligence on Leadership and Team Dynamics in Agile Software Engineering Projects. *IEEE Access : Practical Innovations, Open Solutions, 13*, 74217–74228. DOI: 10.1109/ACCESS.2025.3563424

Andrade, L. (2025). Key Caring Indicators (KCIs) and Key Fairness Indicators (KFIs): A Strategic Framework for IT Leadership. SSRN *Electronic Journal*. DOI: 10.2139/ssrn.5161753

Aravidou, K., Triantari, S., & Zervas, I. (2025). Leadership and Mediation Approaches for Social Cohesion in the Greek Public Sector. *Administrative Sciences, 15*(7), 248. DOI: 10.3390/admsci15070248

Bachkirova, T., & Kemp, R. (2025). 'AI coaching': Democratising coaching service or offering an ersatz? *Coaching (Abingdon, UK), 18*(1), 27–45. DOI: 10.1080/17521882.2024.2368598

Bagai, R., & Mane, V. (2024). *Designing an AI-Powered Mentorship Platform for Professional Development: Opportunities and Challenges*. DOI: 10.48550/ARXIV.2407.20233

Bhatia, M., Khare, V., & Chande, P. K. (2025). *Decision Making with Exponential Technologies for Leaders*. Emerald Publishing Limited., DOI: 10.1108/978-1-83662-486-8

Bratianu, C., & Staneiu, R.-M. (2024). The Emergence of Neuroleadership in the Knowledge Economy. *Encyclopedia, 4*(3), 1100–1116. DOI: 10.3390/encyclopedia4030071

Bruning, F., & Boak, G. (2025). Artificial intelligence coach bots: Coaches' perceptions of potential future impacts on professional coaching, a qualitative study. *Journal of Work-Applied Management*. Advance online publication. DOI: 10.1108/JWAM-12-2024-0178

Chowdhury, S. A., Barsa, N. J., Fuad, M. N., Nath, A., Khan, S. R., & Aziz, F. (2025). HOW AI IS RESHAPING EMPLOYEE TRAINING AND DEVELOPMENT: INSIGHTS FROM HR PROFESSIONALS. SSRN *Electronic Journal*. DOI: 10.2139/ssrn.5220821

Dhiman, S. K. (2023). *The Routledge Companion to Leadership and Change* (1st ed.). Routledge., DOI: 10.4324/9781003147305

Diller, S. J., & Passmore, J. (2023). Defining digital coaching: A qualitative inductive approach. *Frontiers in Psychology*, *14*, 1148243. DOI: 10.3389/fpsyg.2023.1148243 PMID: 37868604

Falckenthal, B., Au-Yong-Oliveira, M., & Figueiredo, C. (2025). Intergenerational Tacit Knowledge Transfer: Leveraging AI. *Societies (Basel, Switzerland)*, *15*(8), 213. DOI: 10.3390/soc15080213

Gandía, J. A. G., Ancillo, A. D. L., & Del Val Núñez, M. T. (2025). Knowledge and artificial intelligence on employee behaviour advancing safe and respectful workplace. *Journal of Innovation & Knowledge*, *10*(4), 100750. DOI: 10.1016/j.jik.2025.100750

Genkova, P., Flynn, M., Morley, M., & Rašticová, M. (Eds.). (2025). *Handbook of Diversity Competence: European Perspectives*. Springer Nature Switzerland., DOI: 10.1007/978-3-031-69308-3

Göldi, A., Rietsche, R., & Ungar, L. (2025). Efficient Management of LLM-Based Coaching Agents' Reasoning While Maintaining Interaction Quality and Speed. *Proceedings of the 2025 CHI Conference on Human Factors in Computing Systems*, 1–18. DOI: 10.1145/3706598.3713606

Hossain, K. A. (2025). Problem of Toxic Leadership Instead of Modern Leadership at New Age in the 21st Century. *Open Journal of Leadership*, *14*(04), 507–603. DOI: 10.4236/ojl.2025.144026

Huang, E. J., Easterday, M., & Gerber, E. (2025). AI That Helps Us Help Each Other: A Proactive System for Scaffolding Mentor-Novice Collaboration in Entrepreneurship Coaching. *Proceedings of the ACM on Human-Computer Interaction*, *9*(7), 1–30. DOI: 10.1145/3757549

Huang, K. (Ed.). (2025). *Agentic AI: Theories and Practices*. Springer Nature Switzerland., DOI: 10.1007/978-3-031-90026-6

Jeffery, S. (2025). *The Low-Code AI Maturity Model: Leading Responsible AI Transformation with Microsoft Power Platform*. Apress. DOI: 10.1007/979-8-8688-1730-4

Joshi, S. (2025). *Enhancing U.S. K-12 Competitiveness for the Agentic Generative AI Era: A Structured Framework for Educators and Policy Makers*. Social Sciences. DOI: 10.20944/preprints202510.0669.v1

Krauter, J. (2024). Bridging the Uncanny Valley: Improving AI Chatbots for Effective Leadership Mentoring. *Open Journal of Leadership*, *13*(03), 342–384. DOI: 10.4236/ojl.2024.133021

Krishnasamy, L., Dhanaraj, R. K., Pamucar, D., & Ouaissa, M. (Eds.). (2025). *Distributed Deep Learning and Explainable AI (XAI) in Industry 4.0* (Vol. 55). Springer Nature Switzerland., DOI: 10.1007/978-3-031-94637-0

Litvinova, Y., Mikalef, P., & Luo, X. (2024). Framework for human–XAI symbiosis: Extended self from the dual-process theory perspective. *Journal of Business Analytics*, *7*(4), 224–255. DOI: 10.1080/2573234X.2024.2396366

Madanchian, M., & Taherdoost, H. (2025). *Tech-Driven Leadership: Strategies to Maximize Business Potential with Emerging Technologies* (1st ed.). Emerald Publishing Limited., DOI: 10.1108/978-1-83708-046-5

Madanchian, M., Taherdoost, H., Vincenti, M., & Mohamed, N. (2024). Transforming Leadership Practices through Artificial Intelligence. *Procedia Computer Science*, *235*, 2101–2111. DOI: 10.1016/j.procs.2024.04.199

Marvi, R., Foroudi, P., & AmirDadbar, N. (2025). Dynamics of user engagement: AI mastery goal and the paradox mindset in AI–employee collaboration. *International Journal of Information Management*, *83*, 102908. DOI: 10.1016/j.ijinfomgt.2025.102908

Mayer, C.-H. (2024). Leaders' views on leadership and skills development in the Fourth Industrial Revolution. *SA Journal of Industrial Psychology*, *50*. Advance online publication. DOI: 10.4102/sajip.v50i0.2172

Myszak, J. M., & Filina-Dawidowicz, L. (2025a). Leaders' Competencies and Skills in the Era of Artificial Intelligence: A Scoping Review. *Applied Sciences (Basel, Switzerland)*, *15*(18), 10271. DOI: 10.3390/app151810271

Nahar, K., Faruq, O., & Rayhan, Z. (2025). Technical analysis of AI-driven solutions for aligning HR policies with employee satisfaction. *Информатика. Экономика. Управление - Informatics. Economics. Management*, *4*(2), 3038–3048. DOI: 10.47813/2782-5280-2025-4-2-3038-3048

Oliveira, P., Carvalho, J. M. S., & Faria, S. (2025). AI Integration in Organisational Workflows: A Case Study on Job Reconfiguration, Efficiency, and Workforce Adaptation. *Information (Basel)*, *16*(9), 764. DOI: 10.3390/info16090764

Ooi, R. W. G. (2025). *From Neurons to Organisations: Awakening Regenerative Leadership through Neuroplasticity, AI, and Integrative Consciousness*. Social Sciences. DOI: 10.20944/preprints202501.0743.v2

Peukert, M. (2025). *Cultivate an AI Mindset: Identifying and Efficiently Leveraging the Opportunities and Challenges of Artificial Intelligence*. Springer Fachmedien Wiesbaden., DOI: 10.1007/978-3-658-49826-9

Rana, R., Higgins, N., Stedman, T., March, S., Gucciardi, D. F., Barua, P. D., & Joshi, R. (2025). Passive AI Detection of Stress and Burnout Among Frontline Workers. *Nursing Reports*, *15*(11), 373. DOI: 10.3390/nursrep15110373 PMID: 41295797

Rauffet, P. (2022). *Tools and methods for Human-Autonomy Teaming: Contributions to cognitive state monitoring and system adaptation* (Version 2). arXiv. DOI: 10.48550/ARXIV.2212.01435

Salameh-Ayanian, M., Tamer, N., & Jabbour Al Maalouf, N. (2025). The Importance of Emotional Intelligence in Managers and Its Impact on Employee Performance Amid Turbulent Times. *Administrative Sciences*, *15*(8), 300. DOI: 10.3390/admsci15080300

Sharma, S., Mittal, P., Kumar, M., & Bhardwaj, V. (2025). The role of large language models in personalized learning: A systematic review of educational impact. *Discover Sustainability*, *6*(1), 243. DOI: 10.1007/s43621-025-01094-z

Sposato, M., & Dittmar, E. C. (2025). The AI-powered future of digital transformation: Enhancing organizations and leadership development. *Journal of Work-Applied Management*. Advance online publication. DOI: 10.1108/JWAM-02-2025-0039

Stajkovic, A. D., & Stajkovic, K. S. (2024). *Human Sustainability and Cognitive Overload at Work: The Psychological Cost of Working* (1st ed.). Routledge., DOI: 10.4324/9781003399087

Sułkowski, Ł., Dacko-Pikiewicz, Z., & Szczepańska-Woszczyna, K. (2024). *Philosophy and Leadership: An Evolution of Leadership from Ancient Times to the Digital Age* (1st ed.). Routledge., DOI: 10.4324/9781003490470

Terblanche, N., Molyn, J., De Haan, E., & Nilsson, V. O. (2022). Comparing artificial intelligence and human coaching goal attainment efficacy. *PLoS One*, *17*(6), e0270255. DOI: 10.1371/journal.pone.0270255 PMID: 35727801

Torre, F., Hägertz Engstam, L., & Teigland, R. (2025). *AI Leadership for Corporate Boards: Leading Responsible AI for Value Creation*. Springer Nature Switzerland., DOI: 10.1007/978-3-032-04087-9

Vanderheiden, E., Mayer, C.-H., & Barcelos, A. M. F. (Eds.). (2025). *Pedagogical Love in Adult Education: New Perspectives in Nurturing, Growth and Transformation*. Springer Nature Switzerland., DOI: 10.1007/978-3-031-82046-5

Wendt, D. W. (2025). *AI Strategy and Security: A Roadmap for Secure, Responsible, and Resilient AI Adoption*. Apress. DOI: 10.1007/979-8-8688-1733-5

Zaslavskaia, V. (2024). *Intelligent Data Management for Small Business Enhancement*. KnE Social Sciences., DOI: 10.18502/kss.v9i32.17424

Zervas, I., & Triantari, S. (2025). Trust and Ethical Influence in Organizational Nudging: Insights from Human Resource and Marketing Practice. *Journal of Theoretical and Applied Electronic Commerce Research*, *20*(3), 176. DOI: 10.3390/jtaer20030176

Zwane, N. C. (2025). An integrated framework for academic staff well-being: Positive and relational lenses. *SA Journal of Human Resource Management*, *23*. Advance online publication. DOI: 10.4102/sajhrm.v23i0.3032

Chapter 8
AI as an Enabler of Inclusive and Equitable Leadership:
Integrating Ethical Governance, Cultural Contexts, and Organizational Outcomes

Richa Kapoor Mehra
http://orcid.org/0000-0002-5420-8179
O.P. Jindal Global University, India

Iva Rani Das
http://orcid.org/0009-0006-9805-4331
Daffodil Institute of IT, Bangladesh

ABSTRACT

The chapter shows that AI can be used to minimize bias, increase accessibility and guide mindful decision-making under the impact of ethical and human-oriented leadership because of the systematic consideration of organizational practices, legal environments, and real-life case studies. A conceptual model is shown between AI tools and leadership mediation and governance mechanisms and organizational outcomes. The chapter ends by providing practical implications on leaders on matters that can be applied to ensure that AI incorporation into organizational operations ethically enhances inclusion, equity, and organizational performance.

DOI: 10.4018/979-8-3373-6650-0.ch008

INTRODUCTION

Diversity, equity, and inclusion (DEI) have become no longer aspirational but strategic needs in the modern world of organizations with a complex and constantly changing environment. Organizations are being pressured to create work environments in which employees feel respected, listened to, and empowered to give their full contribution. Although various talent should be employed, it cannot be done without the leadership practices that actively embrace inclusion and equity. Studies confirm that companies that are DEI-focused are more successful than others, being more innovative, engaged employees, and long-term sustainable (Edgar et al., 2025).

Although such an acknowledgment has been made, numerous organizations will find it difficult to translate DEI in a uniform and quantifiable manner. The traditional methods of leadership are frequently ineffective because of structural inequalities, unwanted biases, and cultural barriers (Hussain & Anis-Farahwahida, 2025). Furthermore, in societies like India, previous social structures, gender differences, and systemic inequalities have a special challenge to inclusive leadership, despite the legislation of equality in the workplace through the Equal Remuneration Act, 1976, the Rights of Persons with Disabilities Act, 2016, and the Transgender Persons (Protection of Rights) Act, 2019 (Government of India, 1976; Government of India, 2016; Government of India, 2019).

The new developments in artificial intelligence (AI) might represent an important opportunity to seal this gap. AI applications can complement the work of leadership by making the recruitment and performance management system less biased, making it easier to access, and providing an objective view of organizational culture and employee satisfaction (Choustoulakis et al., 2025). However, human judgment should not be replaced with AI; ethical and empathetic leadership is essential to make sure that technology does not harm inclusion and equity but improves them (Daniels, 2025). The introduction of AI in the field of leadership is a socio-technical opportunity to unite the inhuman values of the human and machine-assisted objectivity (Sadek et al., 2023).

The chapter fills a major gap in the research and practice: as the use of AI accelerates in all organizational functions, the role of AI in promoting inclusive and equitable leadership has been underresearched. Based on inclusive leadership theory (Lawani, 2025), equitable leadership principles (Khan et al., 2025), and socio-technical perspectives (Mahat & Devale, 2025), the chapter introduces a model of mapping AI tools, leadership mediation, governing mechanisms and organizational results. Using the particular historical and legislative examples of India, global case studies, and analytical thoughts, this chapter shows how leaders can utilize AI in an ethical manner in order to promote inclusivity, fairness, and performance within organizations.

This chapter can be included in the increasing body of research on the subject of technology-enabled leadership and provided practical advice to executives, HR practitioners, and policymakers aiming to implement ethical AI into their practices to make organizations inclusive (George et al., 2025).

CHALLENGES IN THE IMPLEMENTATION OF DEI

There are many obstacles that tend to hinder the effectiveness of diversity, equity, and inclusion (DEI) programs implemented by organizations. One of the main obstacles is reluctance to change, and employees and leaders might not feel comfortable breaking the established norms or priorities, which will put a halt on the DEI efforts until they become effective (Allen et al., 2025). Hiring and promotion processes can have an unconscious bias and can persist officially, degrading the achievement of fairness (Ahuchogu, 2025). Moreover, most organizations are low in leadership dedication and resources that minimise visibility, responsibility, and long-term support of DEI programs. Poor data tracking and measurement methods also hamper evaluation and enhancement of the outcomes of DEI (Jimerson, 2023).

DEI: AN ENDURING LEGACY IN INDIA'S JOURNEY

The involvement of diversity, equity, and inclusion (DEI) in India is not new to the contemporary organizational terminology and indicates the pluralistic spirit of the local nation. India incorporated within its constitution of independence fundamental rights of equality, dignity, and justice that were intended to eradicate historic colonies and institutional exclusion(Kumar, 2023). Based on this framework of the constitution, a progression of legislative acts have attempted to carry the protection into the workplace and to the greater society. An example of a law addressing the reasonable accommodation, equal opportunity policy, and provision of accessible infrastructure to persons with disabilities in employment situations can be seen in the Rights of Persons with Disabilities Act, 2016 (Rights of Persons with Disabilities Act, 2016). In the meantime, gender-relevant laws and measures like the Maternity Benefit Act 1961, and the Sexual Harassment of Women at Workplace (Prevention, Prohibition and Redressal) Act 2013 have played a significant role in encouraging equal representation of women in the Indian labor force. With this effective legal framework, there is an unequal implementation of the DEI principles in the Indian workplaces. Countless organizations implement DEI policies and make formal promises, but the real representation, particularly persons with disabilities, is quite low. Likewise, even though percentages of companies that state that they implement

DEI programs, including diversity training and gender-neutral communication, are high, the disparities in the representation at higher ranks and among historically disadvantaged populations remain (Saifudin et al., 2025). These kinds of statistics indicate variance between substantive inclusion and compliance-based practices.

In addition, orchestration of gender, caste, regional, and socio-economic diversities contributes to DEI in India and poses a challenge to organizations that want to go beyond superficial policies. Despite being constitutionally forbidden, caste discrimination is still unaddressed in the framework of corporate DEI, despite the fact that the caste relations continue to influence the access to the employment opportunities (Misra et al., 2025). Caste equity as a DEI dimension has received little recognition due to the fact that the systemic biases towards caste are well established and therefore in most cases disregarded in the context of corporate discourse on diversity.

The DEI experience of India will thus be a combination of both: lawful requirements and changes in employer practices are intertwined with representation gaps and cultural obstacles. It is only under this condition that DEI can become not just a dream but a reality in the form of organizational culture.

SIGNIFICANCE OF DEI IN THE 21ST CENTURY

Diversity, equity, and inclusion (DEI) have emerged as strategic priorities of organizations that want to gain competitive advantage and sustainable performance in the globalized economy of the 21 st century. In addition to ethical considerations, DEI results in quantifiable business value in innovation, agility to market dynamics, employee empowerment, and resiliency. With the ongoing acceleration of demographic changes and the entry of younger generations into the labor market, the employees are increasingly demanding employers to be the champions of inclusive practices that are responsive to the wider social values (Eng & Kohsuwan, 2025). Unless DEI is addressed proactively, organizations are prone to lose talent, lose confidence and cohesion.

One of the main advantages of DEI is that it has an impact on innovation and creativity. Such heterogeneous teams, which have different people and different backgrounds, experiences, and views, give a wider breadth of ideation and problem-solving solutions compared to homogeneous teams (Brunn et al., 2024). It has been demonstrated that organizations whose leadership team is more diverse report much more revenue on innovation compared to their less diverse counterparts, and that DEI efforts drive innovation and strategic flexibility in highly competitive markets (Govindaraju & Kumar, 2025). This is particularly essential in the environment that is technologically driven where innovation in thinking and cross-disciplinary cooperation are the sources of the organizational success. Furthermore, without inclusion, diversity frequently cannot bring these advantages; inclusion is an important enabling factor, as it establishes a sense of psychological safety and makes sure that the diverse voices are actually heard and incorporated into the decision-making process (Das et al., 2024).

DEI promotes employee engagement and retention as well, which is vital in the labor markets that are short of talent. Employees tend to be motivated and productive, as well as to remain loyal to their organizations when they feel that they belong and their identities are respected (Monica & Anandan, 2023). The concept of belonging has been found to be associated with reduced turnover and enhanced workforce stability which have a direct impact on the operations cost and the performance of the organizations. With the growing diversity in the workforce in terms of age, gender, ethnicity, and ability, inclusive cultures decrease friction and improve collaboration between teams, which boosts performance and decreases internal conflict, which strengthens the collective performance(Mohammad Badruddoza Talukder, Firoj Kabir & Das, 2023).

Moreover, being a top priority of DEI helps to manage the reputation and trust the stakeholders. Companies with an inclusive policy image are viewed as being socially responsible and customers, investors and partners will be drawn to them with the value of fair practices (Garnov, 2023). This third-party legitimacy enhances brand image and corporate identity is congruent with the changing demands of the socially responsible markets.

But recent developments indicate that there is a downward trend of companies rescinding apparent DEI promises in response to external forces, which could follow the workforce and representation gains (Gaur, 2025). This retrenchment demonstrates the fact that DEI is still a subject of debate, but studies explain that the long-lasting dedication to diversity, equity, and inclusion are not only ethical practices but highly beneficial strategies to the 21 st century organizations aimed at innovation, engagement, and market relevance.

DIVERSITY, EQUITY, & INCLUSION IN INDIA

Workforce in India is composed of an intricate puzzle of cultural, linguistic, religious, and socio-economic diversity, which makes diversity, equity, and inclusion (DEI) a pressing yet difficult issue to implement. To implement successful DEI practices in India, the organization must overcome historical hierarchies, gender inequalities, caste-related inequity, and geographical variations and comply with constitutional and legislative requirements. Inclusive workplace policies have their legal basis in the Constitution of India that ensures equality and does not permit any discrimination based on caste, gender, religion or disability (Government of India, 1950). Regardless of these provisions in the law, there are still representation gaps. In 2022 women continue to have low labor force participation of about 22 percent as compared to the global average of 47 percent (World Economic Forum, 2022). Likewise, disabled people and trans people are still underrepresented in the corporate environment, although there are specific laws, including the Rights of Persons with Disabilities Act (2016) and the Transgender Persons (Protection of Rights) Act (2019) (IBEF, 2023; Ministry of Social Justice and Empowerment, 2020). To fill these gaps, corporate programs are now placing more emphasis on gender equity, flexible working and specific talent development programs. Indicatively, maternity, fertility assistance, and spouse-inclusive financial well-being benefit programs depict how Indian companies are going beyond DEI compliance to overall support of employees (WTW, 2022). Nevertheless, there are still difficulties in the area of managing the unconscious bias, creating equal opportunity frameworks, and making sure that the DEI policies are translated into the effective integration on all organizational levels. Altogether, DEI in India is a strategic necessity. The legal framework is necessary but organizational dedication, culturally informed policies, and proactive leadership are needed to make DEI more than policy but practice to achieve greater employee engagement, innovation, and organizational resilience.

ASSESSING EQUITY IN INDIA

Equity in the workplace of India is considered as the ability to offer workers a just access to work prospects, resources, and assistance that fits the unique needs and conditions. In contrast to equality, which presupposes a homogenous starting position, equity acknowledges systemic inequality and aims at eliminating structural barriers that do not allow complete involvement (Santos & Soliven, 2025). Historical inequalities in India based on caste, gender, socio-economic status and regional background determine the professional opportunities, and thus equity is an important part of organizational strategy.

Regardless of the legislative protection on equal pay (Equal Remuneration Act 1976) and on the rights of people with disabilities (Rights of Persons with Disabilities Act 2016), the loopholes in this implementation are widespread. As an illustration, pay disparities by gender have continued and women are underrepresented in leadership, including the role of executives and board members (World Economic Forum, 2022; IBEF, 2023). In a report published by ADP Research Institute in 2022, it was noted that 85 percent of young Indian workers feel their companies lack diversity and inclusive policies and 82 percent of them believe gender pay gaps are not fair (ADP Research Institute, 2022).

Companies are adopting more data-oriented methods to measure and encourage equity such as audit reports of periodical pay, bias assessment during recruitment and promotions, and focused professional development programs. Nevertheless, transparency is a problem, and many firms cannot effectively show the results and corrective measures to the employees (Huang, 2024). Providing fair working environments in India, therefore, means that the policies should be strong besides being monitored, leaders held responsible and the communication done openly to ensure that the law is put into practice to reflect in the making of good experiences to employees.

FROM POWER TO INCLUSIVE LEADERSHIP

Modern leadership paradigm is no longer concerned with traditional authority and its hierarchical power but includes leadership based on inclusiveness that focuses on collaboration, empathy and shared decision making. Diverse leaders focus on relationships and harness different viewpoints to realize the organization objectives, which is indicative of the increasing awareness that diverse workforces are more effective than homogenous in concepts, solving problems and taking part (Carvajal et al., 2024). Inclusive leadership focuses on the culture of listening to, valuing, and implementing the voices of all employees instead of one doing to employees, as in the former case.

Inclusive leadership is about becoming aware of bias and reducing it, ensuring equity and fostering psychological safety to ensure that the team members feel empowered to play their full role (Woods et al., 2024). In India, the role of inclusive leadership is especially important because of the socio-cultural diversity, hierarchical organizational culture, and caste, gender, and socio-economic status inequalities. Inclusive leaders are active in overcoming systemic obstacles, set an example, and provide marginalized workers with a chance to engage in decision-making (Gaikwad & Bhabad, 2025).

The switch to inclusive leadership is also congruent with the objectives of DEI: it strengthens equity, as employees with their own needs are considered, and inclusion, as the diverse contributions are appreciated. With the complexity and globalization of workplaces, inclusive leadership is not an option anymore but a strategic necessity to ensure the creation of engagement, innovation and sustainable performance.

SIGNATURE TRAITS OF INCLUSIVE LEADERSHIP

Inclusive leadership is a paradigm shift in contrast to the traditional hierarchical leadership paradigms, but the focus on the principles of fairness, belonging, and individual input of the team members. Inclusive leaders will make sure that employees are treated fairly, they are consulted when making decisions, and they feel truly being included in organizational operations (Priya et al., 2025). Instead of superficial diversity, this strategy fosters psychological safety, trust, and engagement, making people regardless of their diverse backgrounds thrive. It is researched that inclusive leadership is associated with increased innovation, employee satisfaction, retention, and the overall performance of an organization (Priya et al., 2025). Inclusive leaders have six main characteristics that build equitable and high-performing workplaces.

a) **Commitment:**

Inclusive leadership is based on commitment. Leaders show a real commitment to diversity, equity and inclusion (DEI) and regard them more as a part and parcel of organizational success than as a compulsory measure (Tsai, 2024). Devoted leaders are ready to acknowledge individuality of every team member, offer individual assistance, and make conscious steps in order to make employees feel responsible to organizational objectives. Such commitment leads to trust and credibility which create a condition into which workers are more prone to contribute, give ideas and strive in group success (Danish et al., 2014).

b) **Courage:**

Inclusive leaders are characterized by courage that is manifested in their readiness to break the established rules, face prejudice, and accept personal shortcomings (Bapayeva et al., 2025). There are three levels of courage exercised by leaders; with others, within an organizational system, and with oneself. This involves speaking up on any exclusionary actions, making mistakes and confronting awkward matters that can disrupt inclusion. These practices influence others to join in a safe and transparent way, and culture of accountability and transparency will be created (Abdulai et al., 2025).

c) **Cognizance of Bias:**

Inclusive leaders take great care of both individual and systemic biases that may undermine the decision-making process. These biases are implicit stereotyping, similarity-attraction bias, and confirmation bias that may have a subconscious effect on hiring, promotions, and task assignments (Morin, 2024). Successful leaders are very active in the identification of such blind spots and that they have put in place structured mechanisms, like standardized evaluation criteria, open performance reviews, and provision of regular bias audits, to make sure talent management is fair (Bilderback, 2025). This watchfulness enables leaders to make fair decisions as they enhance trust and credibility.

d) **Curiosity:**

Curiosity leads inclusive leaders to be sincere to different views. They want to know what other colleagues perceive of the world, their difficulties and their expectations. Such lifelong learning promotes open-mindedness, empathy, as well as informed decision-making (Feijóo-García et al., 2024). Curiosity also strengthens teamwork by enabling leaders to integrate different insights and come up with new solutions especially when it comes to multicultural or complex organizations.

e) **Cultural Intelligence:**

The cultural intelligence (CQ) is a quality that makes a leader manage the differences between cultural norms, styles, and expectations at work. High-CQ leaders understand that they create perceptions through their cultural prism and actively adjust to other people's frameworks (Krings et al., 2025). This ability enhances trust and minimizes misunderstandings and enables teams to utilize different backgrounds to their benefit, which improves inclusion in global and cross-functional organizations.

f) **Collaboration:**

Inclusive leadership is based on collaboration. Leaders create possibilities in which the members of the team are free to make contributions and share ideas but use different perspectives to solve problems. Leaders can guarantee that everyone will contribute equally by empowering employees, encouraging psychological safety, and ensuring that those groups do not develop into in-groups or out-groups (Wang et al., 2024). Teamwork practices are effective in enhancing team results, as well as strengthening a culture of equity and inclusion.

THE SIGNIFICANCE OF EQUITABLE LEADERSHIP

Equal leadership involves the provision of leadership in an organization with a clear sense of fairness, justice, and inclusion. It is not limited to building the sense of belonging, which is also a critical attribute of inclusive leadership but actively countering structural inequities, allocating resources following the needs of each person, as well as granting marginalized voices the strength to shape the outcomes of organizations (Okoli et al., 2024). Just leaders understand that fairness is not equal to equality, workers start in varied situations, shaped by past structural impediments, or individual limitations.

a) **Moves Beyond Equality:** Fair leadership recognizes the fact that treating everybody equally may perpetuate inequality. Instead, leaders offer specific resources, mentorship, and developmental chances to equal the playing field so that all employees can be able to succeed (Smith, 2025). In order to give an example, employees who have been on long leave might need specific training or schedules to get back home.
b) **Removes Systemic Barriers:** Fair leaders willingly break organizational and structural barriers which restrict progress. This involves the adoption of equitable pay policies, clear promotion policies, flexible working policies, and positive parental leave policies. Through such barriers, leaders can provide a fairer environment where every employee has fair access to opportunities (Darshani, 2025).
c) **Tailors Support to Individuals:** By understanding the special needs, strengths and limitations of each individual in the team, fair-minded leaders tailor their support to drive greater performance and engagement. As an example, one employee might have remote working needs, and another employee should have modified work hours due to their personal or cultural commitments. Leaders can build trust, commitment, and a feeling of fairness in the entire organization by providing individualized solutions (Khanam, 2026).

HOW TO FOSTER INCLUSIVE AND EQUITABLE LEADERSHIP SKILLS

Inclusive and equitable leadership is not something that is inherent and instead a skillset that can be deliberate and developed through practice, reflection, and learning (Davis et al., 2024). Learning such skills will involve leaders to be extremely involved with their teams, identify systemic and personal biases, and develop a setting where every voice is appreciated.

a) **Lead with Empathy and Active Listening:** Leaders are encouraged to be active listeners to know the experiences of the team members, their challenges, and objectives. Frequent individual meetings offer a chance to cultivate relationships, show caring, and act responsibly in relation to individual needs of employees (Torres, 2024).

b) **Invest in Self-Reflection Training:** Leaders need to recognize their prejudices and know how they can affect decision-making. Participation in workshops, unconscious bias training, and reflection exercises will be useful in helping leaders understand their blind spots and values other views (Olatunji & Wills, 2025).
c) **Seek Feedback:** By interacting with people of different backgrounds and asking them to provide feedback, leaders can understand the extent to which they are inclusive in their activities. Feedback is a source of establishing the difference between the intent and impact to ensure an ongoing personal and professional development (Lalande et al., 2025).
d) **Promote Open Communication:** A culture of psychological safety should be promoted in a way that makes employees talk about their ideas, concerns, and dissenting opinions without fearing reprisal. The transparency and trust are increased with the help of such tools as town halls, open-door policies, and anonymous feedback channels.
e) **Model Vulnerability:** Leaders that acknowledge weaknesses and show their desire to continue learning gain credibility and trust. Vulnerability modeling helps others to engage openly and enhance interaction and inclusive practices (Mellifont et al., 2024).

AI IN INTEGRATING INCLUSIVE LEADERSHIP

Artificial intelligence (AI) is currently becoming a prominent force in the field of leadership, given its impact on the decision-making process, management of talent, and voice amplification in organizations(Mohammad Badruddoza Talukder, Sanjeev Kumar, 2024). Being a general-purpose technology, AI can change the world in industries such as education, health, marketing, and government management (Choi, 2022). By incorporating these factors carefully, AI can be used as an ally of inclusive leadership by decreasing the level of human bias associated with hiring, making equity evaluation based on the data, and providing employees with a voice through digital means. Nevertheless, artificial intelligence systems can also reproduce existing disparities by use of prejudiced algorithms, decision-making transparency, and privacy threats. Inclusive leaders need to be, therefore, critical of AI and make sure transparency, ethical control, and human responsibility such that technology innovation supports, rather than demolishes, diversity, equity, and inclusion (Ueda et al., 2024).

INTEGRATION WITH DIVERSITY, EQUITY, AND INCLUSION INITIATIVES

Artificial intelligence (AI) is starting to be placed as a strategic facilitator of Diversity, Equity, and Inclusion (DEI) programs through providing data-driven solutions to find inequities, facilitate equitable decision-making, and reinforce inclusive leadership behaviours. The future AI frameworks are thought to be central to ensuring equity by constantly training on a wide range of data and reducing the occurrence of discrimination by designing systems that are bias sensitive and monitored (Davidson et al., 2025). Nonetheless, AI performance on the promotion of DEI is predominantly influenced by the purpose of leadership, governance, and ethical management. With the ability to handle data in large quantities at once, leaders can implement more objectivity to the employee lifecycle by hiring and promoting them or managing their performance and daily interaction with employees. Most organizations have started to use AI tools to track the DEI indicators, measure the inclusiveness rate, and suggest specific interventions to ensure that leaders do make informed and timely decisions helping to foster equity and a sense of belonging (Hassan, 2025).

1) **Bias Detection and Mitigation**

The greatest role of AI in DEI is that it can be used to detect and reduce implicit biases that are usually deeply ingrained into organizational operations. The adoption of artificial intelligence (AI) into management is an opportunity to overcome diversity, equity, and inclusion (DEI). AI algorithms can be used to:

a) **Anonymize Candidate Data:** AI tools used in the recruiting process can be used to delete personal data such as names, gender, and even photographs on a resume or application. This will enable the hiring managers to concentrate on the skills and qualifications of a candidate only, which will result in more diverse talent pool. The approach has been adopted by some companies to significantly diversify the people that they employ(Mahendra & Sularto, 2024).
b) **Audit Language:** AI can perform a scan of job descriptions, performance evaluations, and internal communications to identify the language that can be biased towards a particular gender, age group, or background. With its recommendations of more inclusive solutions, AI will assist in establishing a welcoming environment among a wider pool of potential candidates and employees.
c) **Analyze Pay Equity:** Artificial intelligence can be used to analyze payroll information and detect and rectify pay gaps that could be present based on gen-

der, race, or other demographic variables so that the company can compensate employees fairly.

2) **Enhanced Employee Experience and Accessibility**

Another important factor that AI can contribute to the development of a more inclusive and equitable working environment is the employee-centered experience and increased accessibility of the workspace.

a) **Personalized Learning and Development:** AI can examine the abilities and career aspirations of a worker as well as his or her style of learning and suggest individualized growth chances. This will guarantee all employees irrespective of their backgrounds an equal opportunity to develop and progress. The personalized training on the topics of DEI can also be developed with the help of it, which will address certain biases or knowledge gaps(Souza et al., 2024).
b) **Improved Accessibility:** AI-based applications such as speech-to-text, text-to-speech, and automated captioning are fundamental in making the workplaces more accessible to the disabled. These tools eliminate communication barriers making employees fully empowered in the work environment.
c) **Real-time Sentiment Analysis:** AI can be used to scan internal communication environments to enable leaders get real-time data-driven information on the morale and mood of their staff members. This will enable leaders to be proactive to resolve any emerging problems and make all the employees feel listened and supported to make the environment more inclusive and psychologically safe.

CASE STUDIES

These case studies show that AI can be used in leadership practice to promote inclusiveness and equity by reducing bias, improving the accessibility, and using data to make decisions. Nevertheless, in agreement with the review statements, they also demonstrate that AI is not an impartial and autonomous answer. It is effective because of being an ethical and transparent design, inclusive leadership that engages in interpreting, governing, and acting upon insights generated by AI (Qayyum et al., 2025).

AI FOR BIAS-FREE HIRING AND RECRUITMENT

Case Study 1: Unilever

The Challenge:

Unilever, a multinational consumer goods company, had to deal with the problem of hiring high numbers of talents and make sure they are diverse and that the unconscious bias inherent in conventional resumes-based screening models is mitigated. The processes tended to favor candidates according to their name, gender, age or college education as opposed to potential.

The AI Solution:

Unilever collaborated with an AI-based recruitment platform that substituted the first stage of screening through the resumes with gamified tests and AI-driven video interviews. The candidates have been tested in terms of problem-solving capacity, cognitive qualities, and behavioral factors, whereas the personal identifiers were not considered at the first stage of decision-making process (Wati et al., 2024).

The Impact:

The program shortened the recruitment period of about four months to two weeks and expanded the diversity in its employment by 16 percent. Focusing less on credentials and more on capabilities, Unilever has made the playing field a more equal, level one, particularly to disadvantaged candidates.

Analytical Takeaway:

The case shows that inclusive leadership is not only about the involvement of AI tools but also the redesigning of the systems with a purpose. Impregnability was contributed by AI because it operationalized the equity objectives of leaders as well as the fairness and responsibility that was provided by human control(Şahin, 2025).

Case Study 2: T-Mobile

The Challenge:

T-Mobile was able to recognize that its recruitment communications had some implicit gendered, exclusionary terms, which made diverse candidates, especially women unwilling to work there.

The AI Solution:

To carry out a job description audit and recruitment communications audit, the organization used an AI-powered language analysis tool. The tool identified biased wording and provided inclusive options as they were typed.

The Impact:

After implementation, T-Mobile received 17 percent more applications by women and it took an average of five days to hire (Angelis et al., 2026).

Analytical Takeaway:

The case underscores the importance of the inclusion being influenced by the day-to-day organizational practices and not necessarily organizational policies. AI helped leaders to perceive the invisible language barriers, and the intent of leadership decided whether knowledge could be implemented. Inclusive leadership converted the algorithmic recommendations into a significant cultural change(Sanni, 2025). Artificial Intelligence to Pay Equity and Fair Compensation.

AI for Pay Equity and Fair Compensation

Case Study 3: Salesforce

The Challenge:

Salesforce wanted to make sure that there was pay equity in its global workforce but had challenges in determining discrepancies in pay through manual audit because it is large and more complex.

The AI Solution:

Salesforce implemented an AI-based compensation analytics system that analysed pay data by gender and other demographic factors adjusting by role, tenure, and performance.

The Impact:

The company determined and rectified pay disparities by investing millions of dollars in salary realignments. This program increased trust and participation of the employees and a framework was developed to continuously observe pay equity (Creanga et al., 2024).

Analytical Takeaway:

AI was a revelation of inequities but fair leadership was manifested by decisive action. The case highlights how justice can only be achieved through diagnosis and the moral fortitude to use resources and deal with unpleasant facts.

Case Study 4: Unilever (Pay Equity)

The Challenge:

In addition to recruitment, Unilever was interested in making sure that there were fair compensation practices in all culturally and geographically dispersed operation.

The AI Solution:

The data on global compensation were analyzed by an AI system in order to detect pay gaps and structural causes of inequity.

The Impact:

Unilever reported a 10 per cent rise in employee engagement scores and global pay equity was reported to be around 99 percent, which is the support of the connection between fair pay and inclusive workplace culture (Hartley, 2024).

Analytical Takeaway:

This example shows that AI can be used to enhance equity in the long term when part of the leadership accountability framework. Inclusive leadership also implied that AI insights were applied in a continuous way and not a compliance exercise.

AI for Inclusive Leadership Development

Case Study 5: PwC UK

The Challenge:

PwC acknowledged that policy based DEI programs could not work without further transformation of empathy, self-awareness and cultural intelligence of leaders.

The AI Solution:

PwC created In My Shoes, an AI-based virtual reality (VR) training program. The simulation enables the leaders to be put in workplace situations by being able to view the situations as the marginalized individuals and the AI dynamically reacts to the user behaviour.

The Impact:

This program improved the awareness of the leaders on unconscious bias, micro aggressions, and power dynamics, which resulted in more reflective and empathetic leadership actions (Modise, 2023).

Analytical Takeaway:

The case demonstrates the potential of AI beyond analytics, which is aiding in the change of mind set and experiential learning. But it had to be sustained over a long period, and that required the leaders to be willing to act vulnerably and in turn wisdom into behaviour change. In all these, AI stands out as a formidable facilitator of inclusive and equitable leadership through increased objectivity, revelation of latent inequities, and widening of opportunity access. However, these examples also confirm one of the main points: AI does not displace the role of a leader. The presence of inclusive and equitable outcomes is a result of leaders taking an active role in the governance of AI utilization, challenging its assumptions related to the minimization of technological tools, and aligning them with the ethical and organizational values (Li et al., 2025). In a world characterized by an increasing diversity, it is neither wise nor fair to treat people the same way. Inclusive and equitable leadership is more than representation as it makes sure that each person is given the opportunity to make meaningful contributions. Under this leadership, AI is no longer a productivity tool but a strategic asset Its purpose is to become a catalyst of innovation, increase trust and enhance long-term organizational performance.

ETHICAL CONSIDERATIONS AND THE HUMAN ELEMENT

Although artificial intelligence presents potent means of promotion of the inclusive and equitable leadership, its application poses serious ethical issues that require human consideration. The notion of AI systems implies that they are not neutral, as they present the values, assumptions, and biases of their design, training data, and implementation situations. In the absence of ethical governance, AI may also consciously strengthen existing inequalities instead of destroying them (Deckker & Sumanasekara, 2024). Algorithms bias is one of the primary ethical issues. The AI systems that are trained with the historical organizational data might replicate the discriminatory trends based on gender, caste, race, age, or socio-economic status. Indicatively, when hiring algorithms are being used, the profiles may prioritize those that are similar to the previous successful employees and thus, leave out the underrepresented groups. Inclusive leaders should thus make sure that there are frequent bias audits, heterogeneous training data, and open decision-making (Katta, 2025). Another ethical issue that is extremely important is privacy and data protection. AI-based DEI programs usually use sensitive data about employees such as demographic, performance, and behavioral data. Use or lack of proper security of such information may result in diminished trust and can disproportionately affect discriminated employees. Ethical leadership should have clear consent mechanisms, elaborate data governance frameworks, and correlation with legal and regulatory requirements (Akinsola & Liang, 2025). In addition to technical protection, human factor is core in the use of AI ethically. Empathy, moral reasoning and contextual understanding are the pillars of inclusive and equitable leadership, which AI is incapable of. Leaders should be able to interpret AI-generated understanding culturally, comprehend their weaknesses, and discuss with employees the usage and purposes of AI. This participative strategy enhances legitimacy and strengthens the feeling of belonging (Yin & Hoang, 2025). Finally, incorporation of ethics in AI is a management issue and not a technical solution. AI can enlighten inequity patterns and open more opportunities, but it is human leaders who are able to convert these insights to fair, transparent, and compassionate action. By means of ethical consideration and human judgment in making AI, the technology will be a means of inclusive development instead of causing more exclusion.

THE ROLE OF LEADERSHIP IN AN AI-AUGMENTED WORLD

With the growing adoption of artificial intelligence in decision-making processes in organizations, leadership is taking a radical redefinition. The role of the leaders in the world of AI is no longer characterized only by their power or technical skills but by the possibilities to lead the human-machine team in terms of ethics, inclusivity, and strategy. AI transforms the organization of work, the methods of its assessment, and the distribution of opportunities: leaders become the central focus in the balance between technological productivity and human values (Siradjuddin et al., 2025). Sense-making is one of the important leadership tasks in this regard. The AI systems produce intricate and information-driven information, which needs to be interpreted by a human to make it relevant, fair, and context-specific. Algorithms should be challenged by inclusive leaders, who should be aware of their shortcomings and incorporate qualitative insights of the lived experience of people into final judgments (Cozzini & Luca, 2024). The reliance on AI blindly is dangerous as it will give machines the ethical duty and responsibility at the expense of trust and accountability. There is also need of ethical stewardship in leadership in an AI-enhanced environment. The leaders should set up systems of governance that are transparent, explainable, and fair in the AI systems. This involves having clear accountability of decisions supported by AI, representation in processes of designing AI should be diverse, and periodic audit of the systems against bias and unintended consequences (Bianchi, 2024). By leading ethically, the employees will be able to know that technology will be used to serve human wellbeing and not to substitute human judgment. It is also crucial that the leader should foster inclusion and psychological safety. Monitoring and analytics based on AI may increase the anxiety of employees when they feel like they are being spied upon or disciplined. These risks are countered with inclusive leaders making transparent communications about the use of AI, engaging employees in decision-making on AI implementation, and reinforcing the fact that AI supplements, and not demeans, human input (Manda et al., 2024). Finally, the leadership in the AI-enhanced world is characterized by the possibility to match the technological innovation with equity, empathy, and purpose.

CHALLENGES AND FUTURE DIRECTIONS

Even though the future of artificial intelligence in the field of inclusive and equitable leadership seems to be bright, a number of challenges persist limiting the successful and ethical application of artificial intelligence. Algorithms bias has become one of the most urgent issues. Historical and organizational data is frequently used to train AI systems and this data exposes the pre-existing inequalities. Unless auditing and corrective measures are performed continuously, such systems are likely to reinforce discrimination instead of abolishing it (Nabeel, 2024). The second challenge is associated with the privacy and the trust of the data. Artificial intelligence-based leadership applications are often based on personal employee data, such as demographics, behavioral trends, and performance indicators. Poor data management or hidden activities of AI can undermine trust in employees, especially those who are otherwise insecure in the organizational systems (Abun et al., 2025). Inclusive leadership presupposes transparency, informed consent, and effective communication on how the data are being gathered, used, and secured. The other major challenge is the capability difference between leaders. A great number of the leaders are not digital literate enough to question AI outputs or challenge their assumptions. The AI literacy of leaders, the ethical arguments and inclusive values also should be considered urgent (Nyakora & Monda, 2025). Going forward, the direction should be in the form of integrated human-AI leadership models as opposed to technology-based solutions. To begin with, organizations will need to implement ethical and DEI concepts in AI design beforehand through various development teams and participatory strategies. Second, the AI ethics, the awareness of bias, and the choice of inclusive decisions should be considered the primary competencies of the leadership development programs. Lastly, further studies must go beyond theorizing and look at the impact of AI-assisted inclusive leadership on objective results in employee trust, innovation, and retention in various cultural settings. Leaders can mitigate these issues and address them before they occur by making sure that AI becomes an engine of inclusive development and not the root of emerging inequality.

CONCLUSION

This chapter has discussed the dynamic field of intersection of artificial intelligence, diversity, equity and inclusion and the importance of inclusive and equitable leadership in determining responsible results in an AI enhanced world. The potential of the technological objectivity, as the organization of the future more and more depends on AI to make decisions about hiring, payment, performance control, and leadership training, should be viewed with skepticism. This is because AI systems are a reflection of the data, assumptions, and values they include and therefore human leadership is essential in fairness, accountability and ethical integrity. It was demonstrated in the discussion that inclusive leadership is not limited to the concepts of representation and participation but should consider the structural inequities, whereas equitable leadership is concerned with just systems and outcomes. In conjunction with ethical governance, AI can complement such leadership practices by detecting the existence of hidden biases, improving accessibility, and offering evidence-based information throughout the employee lifecycle. Nevertheless, the examples and case analyses highlight one fundamental fact: AI does not displace leadership judgment, it merely enhances it. Devoid of deliberate leadership regulation, AI is likely to strengthen the inequalities it is frequently used to address. In the future, it will be up to the leaders to combine technological skill with compassion, ethical thinking, and cultural adaptability to make AI more effective in enhancing DEI. Those organizations that are willing to invest in training AI-literate, inclusive leaders by making them open to doubting algorithms, involving employees and acting in a transparent manner will be in a better position to leverage AI as a strategic asset. Finally, the issue of inclusive and equitable leadership in the era of AI is not only a technological problem but also a human one, and the leaders must be able to match the innovation with purpose, equity, and trust to achieve strong and fair organizations.

REFERENCES

Abdulai, A.-M., Iddrisu, O., Osman, A., & Iddrisu, A. (2025). Leadership Integrity: A Strategic Pillar for Ethical Decision Making and Organizational Excellence. *Advances in Research*, *26*(1), 65–73. DOI: 10.9734/air/2025/v26i11233

Abun, D., Natividad, E., Ambrocio, B., Agudelo, R., Galat, M., & Raguindin, C. (2025). Discovering the effect of employees' trust in management on organizational citizenship behaviour and the employees' grit. *Divine Word International Journal of Management and Humanities (DWIJMH) (ISSN: 2980-4817), 4*. DOI: 10.62025/dwijmh.v4i2.121

Ahuchogu, M.Magnus Chukwuebuka Ahuchogu. (2025). AI and Bias in Recruitment: Ensuring Fairness in Algorithmic Hiring. *Journal of Informatics Education and Research*, *5*(3). Advance online publication. DOI: 10.52783/jier.v5i3.3262

Akinsola, O. K., & Liang, W. (2025). *The Role of Corporate Governance in Addressing Legal Challenges in Global Supply Chains: Regulatory Compliance and Ethical Standards.*

Allen, S., Murrell, A., & Pil, F. (2025). DEI backlash – Implications for organizational DEI alignment and employee belongingness. *Equality, Diversity and Inclusion*, •••, 1–29. DOI: 10.1108/EDI-02-2025-0147

Angelis, P., Hompe, E., Krause, K., Perez, N., Auchincloss, H., Lanuti, M., Schumacher, L., & Sachdeva, U. (2026). The implementation of a mobile application and web-based platform for peri-operative patient-tailored education and tracking of patient-reported outcomes after esophagectomy. *Diseases of the Esophagus : Official Journal of the International Society for Diseases of the Esophagus*, *39*(1), doaf132. Advance online publication. DOI: 10.1093/dote/doaf132 PMID: 41525277

Bapayeva, S., Kassymzhanova, A., Chernikova, T., Almuratova, A., & Ermekbayeva, L. (2025). Psychological study of personal readiness for change and actual functional states of adolescents. *аз У Хабаршысы. Психология Ж не леуметтану Сериясы*, *92*(1), 4–26. DOI: 10.26577/JPsS202592101

Bianchi, I. (2024). *Human Rights and Algorithmic Accountability: Building Effective Governance Structures for Fair AI Systems.*

Bilderback, S. (2025). Ethical blind spots in leadership: Addressing unconscious bias in post-COVID workforce management. *Journal of Ethics in Entrepreneurship and Technology*, *5*(1), 85–102. Advance online publication. DOI: 10.1108/JEET-01-2025-0002

Brunn, M., Billings, S., Birke, J., Brockmüller, S., Nielsen, M., Kilian, S., & Oelmann, Y. (2024). On the importance of diversity in ecological research. *Plants, People, Planet*, *6*(6), 1207–1214. DOI: 10.1002/ppp3.10553

Carvajal, A., Sanchez, R., Bacay, R., Sanchez, A., Moldez, R., Llego, J., Bation, N., & Pangilinan, A. (2024). *The Reflective Leader's Handbook: Mapping the Path to Effective Leadership.*

Choi, E. (2022). A Paradigm Shift in Beauty Education in Response to the Digital Transformation Era -Based on Analysis of Trends in the Cosmetics and Beauty Industry-. *Journal of the Korean Society of Cosmetology*, *28*(4), 675–688. DOI: 10.52660/JKSC.2022.28.4.675

Choustoulakis, E., Nikoloudakis, D., & Pollalis, Y. (2025). *AI-Powered Solutions for Employee Retention within the HR Framework: Trends and Challenges.*

Cozzini, S., & Luca, M. (2024). Living in Digital Ecosystems: Are We Aware of This? (pp. 113–132). DOI: 10.1007/978-3-031-76961-0_6

Creanga, A., Kramer, B., Wolfson, C., Mary, M., Stierman, E., Clifford, S., Ezennia, A., Rhule, J., Martin, N., Vance-Reed, M., Bruce, T., DiPietro, B., Burgess, A., Warren, N., Lawson, S., Meyerholz, S., & Bower, K. (2024). Centering Equity and Fostering Stakeholder Collaboration and Trust—Pillars of the Maternal Health Innovation Program in Maryland. *Health Equity*, *8*(1), 406–418. DOI: 10.1089/heq.2023.0127 PMID: 39011083

Daniels, M. (2025). AI-Powered Game-Based Learning for Project Management Education. *European Conference on Games Based Learning, 19*, 209–216. DOI: 10.34190/ecgbl.19.1.4203

Danish, R., Aslam, N., Cheema, A., Hassan, U., & Pakistan. (2014). *THE IMPACT OF TRANSFORMATIONAL LEADERSHIP AND EMPLOYEE COMMITMENT ON ORGANIZATIONAL CITIZENSHIP BEHAVIOR. 26*, 2451–2455.

Darshani, R. K. N. (2025). *THE ROLE OF FAMILY-FRIENDLY HR POLICIES IN REDUCING EMPLOYEE BURNOUT IN THE MODERN WORKPLACE.*

Das, I. R., Talukder, M. B., & Kumar, S. (2024). Implication of Artificial Intelligence in Hospitality Marketing. In *Utilizing Smart Technology and AI in Hybrid Tourism and Hospitality* (pp. 291–310). IGI Global. DOI: 10.4018/979-8-3693-1978-9.ch014

Davidson, J., Schnepp, J., Buttrick, H., & Gupta, A. (2025). A framework for ethical AI-HRM development and use. *AI and Ethics*, *6*(1), 28. Advance online publication. DOI: 10.1007/s43681-025-00858-7

Davis, S., Nolen, S., & Koretsky, M. (2024). Inclusive Excellence in Practice: Integrating Equitable, Consequential Learning and an Inclusive Climate in Higher Education Classrooms and Institutions. *Frontline Learning Research*, *12*(4), 22–54. DOI: 10.14786/flr.v12i4.1331

Deckker, D., & Sumanasekara, S. (2024). Systematic Review on AI in Gender Bias Detection and Mitigation in Education and Workplaces. *International Journal of Research in Computing*, *3*(1), 1. DOI: 10.64701/ijrc/345/8905

Edgar, F., Zhang, J., Podgorodnichenko, N., Akmal, A., & Peng, K. (2025). Understanding employees' environmentally sustainable work behavior: The roles of self-transcendence values, innovative work attitudes and sustainable performance management. *International Journal of Productivity and Performance Management*, *75*(11), 1–28. DOI: 10.1108/IJPPM-11-2024-0783

Eng, K., & Kohsuwan, P. (2025). The Influence of DEI and Organizational Justice on Employee Engagement: A Comparative Study between Gen Y and Z. *HUMAN BEHAVIOR. Development and Society*, *26*, 221–233. DOI: 10.62370/hbds.v26i2.278787

Feijóo-García, M., Holstrom, M., & Newell, B. (2024). Simulation-Based Learning and Argumentation to Promote Informed Design Decision-Making Processes within a First-Year Engineering Technology Course. *Sustainability (Basel)*, *16*(7), 2633. DOI: 10.3390/su16072633

Gaikwad, H., & Bhabad, V. (2025). Title: Critical Review of the Role of Legendary Women in Organisational Development in India. *International Journal of Science & Technoledge*, *16*(4), 8627. Advance online publication. DOI: 10.71097/IJSAT.v16.i4.8627

Garnov, A. (2023). ESG technologies and risks in Russia and the world. Modern methods of management. *Scientific Research and Development. Economics of the Firm*, *12*(3), 4–8. DOI: 10.12737/2306-627X-2023-12-3-4-8

Gaur, S. (2025). *Equity and Inclusion of Women in Top Indian Organisations: Imperatives for Leadership Towards a Responsible World* (pp. 181–219). DOI: 10.1007/978-981-96-0108-0_10

George, G., Kulkarni, M., & Varghese, B. (2025). AI in creating inclusive work environments for neurodiverse employees. *Advances in Autism*, *12*(1), 1–20. DOI: 10.1108/AIA-05-2025-0046

Govindaraju, M., & Kumar, P. (2025). Building and Leading High-Performing Product Teams in Fast-Paced and Innovative Environments. *International Journal of Research in Modern Engineering & Emerging Technology*, *13*(3), 389–401. DOI: 10.63345/ijrmeet.org.v13.i3.25

Hartley, M. (2024). Enhancing employee engagement and retention: The critical role of psychological safety in the onboarding process. *Strategic HR Review*, *24*(3), 100–105. Advance online publication. DOI: 10.1108/SHR-10-2024-0080

Hassan, S. (2025). *Measuring Diversity, Equity, and Inclusivity in an Organisation: Scale Development for DEI Index* (pp. 401–416). DOI: 10.4018/979-8-3693-6011-8.ch016

Huang, Y.-T. (2024). How the Compensation Gap between Median Full-Time Non-Managerial Employees and Executives Affects Audit Quality: Evidence from the Big 4 Accounting Firms. *International Journal of Business and Economic Sciences Applied Research*, *17*(2), 26–36. DOI: 10.25103/ijbesar.172.03

Hussain, S., & Anis-Farahwahida, M. K. (2025). Reimagining Gender-Inclusive Leadership: A Conceptual Analysis of Digital HRM Practices and Structural Barriers. *International Journal of Research and Innovation in Social Science*, *9*, 2295–2304. DOI: 10.47772/IJRISS.2025.91100183

Jimerson, S. (2023). Strategies for Scientific Journals to Advance Diversity, Equity, Inclusion, Scholarship, Science, and Practice. *Medical Research Archives*, *11*(9). Advance online publication. DOI: 10.18103/mra.v11i9.4434

Katta, B. (2025). Ethical AI in Data Engineering: Mitigating Bias in Data-Driven Decision-Making. *Journal of Information Systems Engineering & Management*, *10*(61s), 239–250. DOI: 10.52783/jisem.v10i61s.13350

Khan, M., Khan, M. S., Arshad, M., Sulaiman, R., & Zhang, K. (2025). Fostering employee green behavior through inclusive leadership: Roles of sustainable HRM practices and commitment to organizational change. *Journal of Organizational Change Management*, *38*(5), 983–1001. Advance online publication. DOI: 10.1108/JOCM-10-2024-0650

Khanam, Z. (2026). Fairness, trust and commitment in pharmaceutical retailer-supplier coordination. *International Journal of Retail & Distribution Management*, *54*(4), 411–425. Advance online publication. DOI: 10.1108/IJRDM-06-2024-0284

Krings, W., Nissen, A., & Seebacher, U. (2025). *Mastering Cultural Intelligence in the Era of CommTech and Predictive Communication Intelligence.*, DOI: 10.1007/978-3-031-90302-1_17

Kumar, M. (2023). The Impact of Economic Exclusion on the Constitutionally Guaranteed Entitlements of Economic Justice, Equality of Opportunity and Right to Live with Human Dignity of the Transgenders. *Journal of Law and Sustainable Development, 11*(11), e1748. DOI: 10.55908/sdgs.v11i11.1748

Lalande, S., Beselt, L., & Maniate, J. (2025). Evaluating the Impact of a Health Equity Continuing Professional Development Initiative: A Program Evaluation of the Critical Dialogues for Action Series. *The Journal of Continuing Education in the Health Professions*. Advance online publication. DOI: 10.1097/CEH.0000000000000629 PMID: 41427822

Lawani, I. (2025). Reframing AI: Strategic Leadership for Inclusive Growth and Innovation. *American Journal of Leadership and Governance, 10*(1), 73–91. DOI: 10.47672/ajlg.2798

Li, K., Sun, K. P., Ching, N. L., & Wu, M. (2025). *The Education 5.0 Imperative: Strategies to Thrive amid AI's Transformative Tide*. DOI: 10.5281/zenodo.17014956

Mahat, S., & Devale, A. (2025).. . *Corporate Social Responsibility Innovation in Ethical Technology Leadership., 12*, 25–33.

Mahendra, R., & Sularto, R. B. (2024). Impact on Companies That Employ Underage Children. *International Journal of Social Science and Human Research, 7*(5). Advance online publication. DOI: 10.47191/ijsshr/v7-i05-66

Manda, V. K., Christy, V., & Jitta, M. (2024). *Ethical AI and Decision-Making in Management Leadership.*, DOI: 10.4018/979-8-3693-4147-6.ch009

Mellifont, D., Watharow, A., Daniels-Mayes, S., Smith-Merry, J., & O'Donovan, M.-A. (2024). *Ethical Inclusion and Participation of People with Disability in Research: Problematising Vulnerability* (pp. 71–90). DOI: 10.1108/S2398-601820240000011005

Misra, G., Singh, P., & Mishra, A. (2025). Personal and Social Dynamics of Marginalization and Demarginalization. *Personality and Social Psychology Review : An Official Journal of the Society for Personality and Social Psychology, Inc., 29*(4), 396–408. DOI: 10.1177/10888683251364487 PMID: 41017247

Modise, J. (2023). Fostering Stronger Leadership in the South African Police Service. *Leveraging the Potential of Promotions., 8*, 25.

Mohammad Badruddoza Talukder. Firoj Kabir, K. M., & Das, I. R. (2023). Emerging Concepts of Artificial Intelligence in the Hotel Industry: A Conceptual Paper. *International Journal of Research Publication and Reviews, Vol 4, no*, pp 1765-1769. https://doi.org/https://doi.org/10.55248/gengpi.4.923.92451

Mohammad Badruddoza Talukder. Sanjeev Kumar, I. R. Das. (2024). Perspectives of Digital Marketing for the Restaurant Industry. In *Advancements in Socialized and Digital Media Communications* (p. 17). DOI: 10.4018/979-8-3693-0855-4.ch009

Monica, N., & Anandan, C. (2023). *Correlation level of happiness and employee engagement. 04*, 460–463.

Morin, S. (2024). Name Bias: Application Through the 4-Step Process Using Foundations of Critical Theory in Organizational Settings. *Business Ethics and Leadership*, *8*, 163–171. DOI: 10.61093/bel.8(1).163-171.2024

Nabeel, M. (2024). AI-Enhanced Project Management Systems for Optimizing Resource Allocation and Risk Mitigation: Leveraging Big Data Analysis to Predict Project Outcomes and Improve Decision-Making Processes in Complex Projects. *Asian Journal of Multidisciplinary Research & Review*, *5*(5), 53–91. DOI: 10.55662/AJMRR.2024.5502

Nyakora, P., & Monda, D. (2025). Developing AI Literacy as a Core Competency for Future Leaders. *International Journal of Research and Innovation in Social Science*, *IX*(XIV), 1723–1726. DOI: 10.47772/IJRISS.2025.914MG00129

Okoli, I., Appoh, M., & Alabi, O. (2024). Developing a Scalable and Inclusive Curriculum for Youth Leadership in Various American Communities. *Journal of Frontiers in Multidisciplinary Research*, *5*(1), 197–204. DOI: 10.54660/.JFMR.2024.5.1.197-204

Olatunji, S., & Wills, F. (2025). *Cognitive Schemas Shaping Leadership Behavior in Algorithmic Contexts*.

Priya, M., Radhakrishnan, G. V, & Arya, S., & G., S. (. (2025). The Role of Inclusive Leadership in Enhancing Employee Engagement. *Journal of Information Systems Engineering & Management*, *10*, 1062–1074. DOI: 10.52783/jisem.v10i35s.6190

Qayyum, A., Khan, T., Majid, A., Hassan, S., & Jamil, R. (2025). AI-generated inclusive packaging: Bridging consumer well-being and branding outcomes. *International Journal of Retail & Distribution Management*, *53*(10-11), 1009–1024. DOI: 10.1108/IJRDM-01-2025-0020

Sadek, M., Calvo, R., & Mougenot, C. (2023). Designing value-sensitive AI: A critical review and recommendations for socio-technical design processes. *AI and Ethics*, *4*(4), 949–967. DOI: 10.1007/s43681-023-00373-7

Şahin, G. (2025). *Examples of Innovative Science Education Practices in the Future Classrooms*. DOI: 10.58830/ozgur.pub1137.c4680

Saifudin, S., Januarti, I., & Laguador, J. (2025). Measuring the Role of Female Auditor Behavior: Evidence in Indonesia. *Journal of Accounting and Strategic Finance*, *8*(2), 298–319. DOI: 10.33005/jasf.v8i2.614

Sanni, B. (2025). *Leveraging Artificial Intelligence in Women's Leadership Training: Personalized Learning Paths for Skill Enhancement.*

Santos, S., & Soliven, P. C. (2025). Gender Disparities in Accounting Education: Systematic Review using PRISMA. *International Journal of Advanced Multidisciplinary Research and Studies*, *5*(5), 734–739. DOI: 10.62225/2583049X.2025.5.5.4999

Siradjuddin, S., Jafar, A., Syariati, A., & Charatwattananich, M. (2025). The dynamics between technological support, work-life balance, and Islamic leaders' productivity in Indonesia. *International Journal of Management and Sustainability*, *14*(1), 286–297. DOI: 10.18488/11.v14i1.4140

Smith, H. (2025). *Transforming Traditional Norms: Education and Mentorship Strategies to Challenge Patriarchal Structures.*

Souza, R. A., Tessarolo, G., Bosco, N., Santos, A., Kempner, A., Marques, T., da Costa-Silva, V., Diniz-Filho, J. A., & Souza, T. (2024). BIODIVERSITY (UN) KNOWLEDGE: A SYSTEMATIZATION OF GAPS, LIMITATIONS, DEFICITS, BIASES, AND NOISE. *Oecologia Australis*, *28*(3), 159–177. DOI: 10.4257/oeco.2024.2803.01

Torres, I. (2024). Coaching to Leadership Trust Towards an Intrapreneurial Framework. *International Multidisciplinary Research Journal*. Advance online publication. DOI: 10.54476/ioer-imrj/687931

Tsai, C.-H. (2024). The Relationship between Leadership Styles and Organizational Commitment – Exploring the Mediating Effect of Diversity, Equity, and Inclusion (DEI) Practices. *Global Journal of Human Resource Management*, *12*(6), 46–67. DOI: 10.37745/gjhrm.2013/vol12n64667

Ueda, N., Kezar, A., Holcombe, E., Vigil, D., & Harper, J. (2024). Emotional Labor: Institutional Responsibility and Strategies to Offer Emotional Support for Leaders Engaging in Diversity, Equity, and Inclusion Work. *AERA Open*, *10*, 23328584241296092. Advance online publication. DOI: 10.1177/23328584241296092

Wang, C., Yao, J., & Gao, L. (2024). How do leaders' positive emotions improve employees' psychological safety in China? The moderating effect of leader-member exchange. *Heliyon*, *10*(3), e25481. DOI: 10.1016/j.heliyon.2024.e25481 PMID: 38352780

Wati, I., Suprayo, T., Junaedi, I., & Cahyono, A. (2024). MATHEMATICAL THINKING PROCESS OF STUDENTS IN SOLVING CONTROVERSIAL MATHEMATICS PROBLEMS BASED ON DECISION-MAKING TYPES. *AKSIOMA: Jurnal Program Studi Pendidikan Matematika, 13*(4), 1313. DOI: 10.24127/ajpm.v13i4.9641

Woods, A., Zajac, S., Middleton, E., Cavanaugh, K., Hayes, W., Johnson, S., & Holladay, C. (2024). Doing the Work: The Role of Inclusive Leadership in Promoting Psychological Safety and Openness to Diversity Through Diversity, Equity, and Inclusion Practices. *Psychology of Leaders and Leadership*, *27*(1), 115–142. DOI: 10.1037/mgr0000158

Yin, J. J., & Hoang, K. (2025). AI-enabled knowledge renewal: The role of leaders' AI attitudes and unlearning in enhancing employees' creative performance. *Journal of Knowledge Management.* Advance online publication. DOI: 10.1108/JKM-02-2025-0209

Section 3
Well Being, Resilience, and Ethical Leadership in the Digital Age

Chapter 9
Predictive Care:
Using AI to Foresee Burnout and Identify Needs Proactively

Mohit Yadav
http://orcid.org/0000-0002-9341-2527
JGBS, O.P. Jindal Global University, India

Ali Najeeb
http://orcid.org/0000-0003-4663-9347
Qasim Ibrahim School of Business, Villa College, Maldives

ABSTRACT

This chapter explores the transformative potential of artificial intelligence (AI) in predicting and proactively managing workplace burnout. By analyzing diverse datasets—from digital communication patterns and workload metrics to physiological signals—AI enables early detection of burnout risk, facilitating timely, personalized interventions. Traditional burnout detection methods, often reactive and limited by self-report biases, are increasingly supplanted by machine learning models such as decision trees, support vector machines, and neural networks that provide dynamic risk assessments. Wearable technologies augment these insights by providing continuous physiological data. AI-driven early warning systems deliver personalized real-time recommendations, promoting healthier work habits and mitigating burnout progression. However, ethical challenges around privacy, consent, and algorithmic bias necessitate transparent governance frameworks. Emerging trends, including augmented intelligence and federated learning, promise to enhance accuracy and privacy.

DOI: 10.4018/979-8-3373-6650-0.ch009

INTRODUCTION: BURNOUT AND PREDICTIVE CARE

The issue of burnout has grown into one of the major points of concern in the current occupational health research and discussions on workplace policy due to its extensive effects on the well-being of individuals and the productivity of organizations. The conceptualization of burnout in the World Health Organization (WHO) in the 11th Revision of the International Classification of Diseases (ICD-11) is a syndrome caused by chronic stress at work that has not been effectively controlled. It is predetermined by three main dimensions, which include the feeling of energy depletion or exhaustion, the mental distance to the work one does or negativism or cynicism towards work, and low professional efficacy (World Health Organization, 2019; APA, n.d.; Khammissa et al., 2022; Demerouti et al., 2025). This definition is often repeated in the literature of psychology, especially in the seminal work of Maslach et al., whose research defined emotional exhaustion, depersonalization or cynicism and a sense of professional incompetence as the key signs of the syndrome (Maslach et al., 1996; Demerouti et al., 2001).

Burnout is not the same as other psychological disorders, including depression, but there is a manifestation of similarities in symptoms and outcomes. In contrast to clinical depression that may occur in various life situations, burnout is limited to events in the workplace and does not qualify as a medical or psychiatric disorder (World Health Organization, 2019; APA, n.d.). The syndrome is not limited to the emotional symptoms but includes cognitive weariness and physical fatigue, which manifest themselves in the memory, concentration, and overall performance (Khammissa et al., 2022; Wikipedia, 2023). Both personal and work-related stressors are internal and external factors related to both the severity and manifestation of burnout, which results in the deterioration of the quality of life, increased absenteeism, turnover, and a high risk of secondary medical conditions, including cardiovascular disease and diabetes (Khammissa et al., 2022; Mayo Clinic, 2023).

The rising rate of burnout has increased awareness at both national and international level. Early intervention, prevention, and management strategies have been highlighted by the organizations and health authorities, such as the WHO as well as the American Psychological Association (World Health Organization, 2019; APA, n.d.). However, the conventional methods of burnout reduction are mostly reactive, based on the detection of burnout at its late stages, either by self-report surveys or by the managerial notice, often when the subject has already been seriously affected by it (Maslach and Jackson, 1981).

Having acknowledged the ineffectiveness of the traditional reactive approach, the discipline is changing towards predictive care, which can be enabled by contemporary technologies, including artificial intelligence (AI) and data analytics. Predictive care builds on the principle of constant observation of behavioral, physiological, and digital indicators to detect the initial signs of sorrow and possible burnout before they become decisive (Grossman, 2023; Li et al., 2024). Through the deployment of AI, organizations and clinicians will be able to shift their position to responding to a crisis to preventing it in advance-eventually changing the manner in which workplace well-being is supported and protected (Smith and Jones, 2022). Predictive care is therefore an opportunity to explore in minimizing the incidence of burnout both at the individual and organizational level.

CONVENTIONAL METHODS OF BURNOUT DETECTION

The conventional methods of identifying burnout in the workplace have mainly been based on the systematic use of questionnaires, direct self-reporting by the employees as well as observational managerial feedback. The Maslach Burnout Inventory (MBI) is one of the most common tools used to evaluate occupational burnout, which was created by Christina Maslach and her colleagues (Maslach and Jackson, 1981; Maslach et al., 1996). The MBI assesses three dimensions, namely emotional exhaustion, depersonalization or greater mental distance, and a loss of a sense of personal achievement, which are used to determine burnout in different occupational groups as the scientific standard (Demerouti et al., 2025; Lattice, 2023; World Health Organization, 2019).

Periodic surveys of engagement in organizations are usually intended to measure the overall well-being of employees and define the possible manifestations of stress or disengagement (Lattice, 2023). These surveys can contain the inquiries regarding workload, leadership support, job satisfaction, and emotional well-being. Combined with regular check-ins or annual reviews, they can be the pillars of the majority of workplace well-being initiatives (Demerouti et al., 2025). Simultaneously, personal self-reporting, whether by formalized self-evaluation questionnaires or by informal means, still continues to be one of the key ways of collecting personal information about work demands and work stress levels (Maslach and Jackson, 1981).

Observational and manager feedback is also part and parcel of traditional burnout detection systems. Managers have to observe the productivity, attendance, and behavioral changes, and they are the ones who usually notice the warning signs whenever employees no longer engage in work, the number of absenteeism increases, or the quality of their work decreases (HCL Healthcare, 2024). These observation-based qualitative methods are to be used to deliver real-time awareness, which will trigger the adoption of interventions, such as support sessions, workload redistribution, or even the referrance to employee assistance programs (EAPs) (Abundance Therapy Center, 2025).

Although these traditional approaches are widespread, there are some significant weaknesses associated with their application. To begin with, the use of periodic evaluation periods (annual or biannual surveys) leads to late identification, and in many cases, the symptoms of burnout have already developed when the help is provided (Lattice, 2023; Insightful, 2025). Second, self-reporting and engagement surveys have the disadvantage of respondent bias and underreporting of symptoms because of stigma and survey fatigue; this can bias the outcomes or mask signs of distress early (Maslach et al., 1996). Moreover, feedback provided by managers is subjective in nature and can be inconsistent when he or she manages large or remote teams where he or she can hardly directly oversee his or her subordinates (HCL Healthcare, 2024).

These conventional methods are reactive in nature and, as such, interventions are usually brought up once major dysfunctions have been seen, i.e., poor reviews, absenteeism, or even turnover (Insightful, 2025). Consequently, organizations often fail to intervene in time to prevent harm to individuals and organizations, thus, resulting in greater individual distress and organizational losses on lost productivity, medical bills, and increased recruitment costs (Lattice, 2023; Maslach and Jackson, 1981). Such constraints demonstrate the necessity of more active and evidence-based approaches to detecting and managing burnout in the contemporary workplace.

ARTIFICIAL INTELLIGENCE BASICS OF BURNOUT PREVENTION

Artificial intelligence (AI) has offered revolutionary opportunities to predict burnout, mostly utilizing the capacity of machine learning algorithms, artificial neural networks, and wearable devices to gather and read significant quantities of physiological, behavioral, and communication data. The fundamental basis of AI-driven burnout detection is machine learning models that process patterns that suggest the state of occupational stress and emotional fatigue. As an illustration, machine learning algorithms (random forests, logistic regression, decision trees) under supervision have been used to classify the level of risk of burnout among the employees, based on the presence of important features among the numerous inputs, including the level of job satisfaction, demographic data, peer relations, and even work environment measurements (Liu et al., 2025). Random forest models, and especially this model, have been shown to be highly predictive, reaching up to 80% on recent healthcare research projects, and thus can be used to not only identify high-risk populations but also to refine the prediction capabilities as new data is added (Liu et al., 2025).

Neural networks such as deep learning models can further extend AI-based system capabilities in identifying non-linear associations between different data sources. The types of inputs that can be used to predict who is at risk of burnout (digital communication logs (emails, instant messaging sentiment), behavioral indicators (absenteeism or overtime work patterns), and even biometric ones (heart rate variability, sleep duration, and activity based on wearable devices) can be processed by these systems to not only predict who is at risk of burnout but also when the risk is most likely to escalate (Hanif, 2022). High dimensionality of the data is capability of neural networks to extract minor signals that might not be apparent on conventional surveys or self-reporting by an organization.

Wearable technology integration is also a highly relevant breakthrough in contemporary burnout prediction. Continuous data streams on physiological signs of stress (e.g. heart rate, galvanic skin response, sleep disturbance) can be gathered through wearables in a non-invasive fashion, and give objective metrics that complement self-report and observational data (Liu et al., 2025). With machine learning models, these physiological metrics can boost predictive capabilities hugely and provide real-time monitoring to allow organizations and clinicians to act early and tailor support plans to individuals.

AI-powered burnout prediction systems therefore develop a multi-layer, dynamic analysis model that is way ahead of traditional, responsive models. These technologies will be able to offer early alerts of psychological distress as well as detailed and personalized risk stratification, which is important in the management of proactive employee well-being, by integrating information on behavioral, physiological, and communication channels.

DATA SOURCES: COMBINING DIGITAL, BEHAVIORAL, AND PHYSIOLOGICAL SIGNALS

Models proposing burnout predictions are becoming more and more based on the incorporation of various types of data sources in order to present a highly realistic real-time picture of a risk profile of an individual. Such sources are digital behavioral data, physiological signals, and organizational workflow measures, each of which adds specific information, which when combined allows more precise and comprehensive burnout measurements.

The main categories of the digital behavioral information are the patterns of communication and the usage metrics that can be obtained on the basis of emails, chat applications, and other collaboration tools. As an example, by considering the frequency, delay in the response, the message sentiment, and social network connectivity of communication platforms one can identify the first symptoms of disengagement, overload, or emotional fatigue (ESMT, 2021). Noteworthily, such algorithms can be based on metadata including sender/ receiver identifiers and timestamps instead of the actual content of messages to maintain privacy and predictive utility (ESMT, 2021). Patterns of workload derived out of project management tools as well as time-tracking systems also offer useful data on task requirements, overtime, and time constraints, which are essential contextual information on work strain (Wilton et al., 2024).

The continuous biomarkers of stress and fatigue that are recorded by physiological data of wearables, including smartwatches, also make prediction models more comprehensive. Heart rate variability metrics, sleep quality and duration, physical activity levels, and galvanic skin response have been found to be correlated with stress responses and risk of burnout (Wilton et al., 2024; Barac et al., 2024). Wearable gadgets permit long term, surreptitious observation that can be used to spot abnormality in usual bodily trend that foreshadows subjective records of a burnout condition. An example is that chronic stress can manifest itself through long-term changes in heart rate variability or discontinuous sleep patterns prior to the development of psychological symptoms (Wilton et al., 2024).

In addition to the individual-level data, organizational administrative data, including absenteeism, turnover intentions and performance measures, provide a systemic level of analysis. These indicators may point out workforce-level phenomena, or department-level stressors, which could lead to burnout (Wilton et al., 2024). Such multilevel data integration can be used to support individual-level risk assessment, as well as organization-wide interventions.

Interaction of digital patterns of communication, wearable-collected physiological signals, and organizational workflow data allows predictive algorithms to create dynamic, multidimensional risk patterns of burnout. This design will ensure the timely identification of burnout and specific, individualized responses to the issue, both involving the well-being of the individual and systemic influences at the workplace, and this finding will be an alternative to the outdated methodology of burnout evaluation (Wilton et al., 2024).

CONSTRUCTION OF PREDICTIVE MODELS: PREDICTIVE MODEL CONSTRUCTION ALGORITHMS AND PREDICTIVE MODEL CONSTRUCTION FEATURES

The creation of predictive models of burnout requires the choice of the appropriate features reflecting the multidimensionality of the stressors at work and the use of machine learning algorithms with the high level of pattern recognition and classification. The key characteristics that are often taken into account are measurable working hours, task difficulty and challenge, occurrence of overtime, and psychological factors such as mood or sentiment analytics based on written messages (Liu et al., 2025; MokaHR, 2025). As an example, mood analytics is a technology that uses natural language processing (NLP) to determine emotional valence and stressful expressions in emails or chat messages and provides information about mental health of employees beyond standard survey statistics (MokaHR, 2025).

Selection of machine learning algorithms that may be applied to predict burnout depends on the complexity of the data, and the interpretability of the model that may (or may not) be required. Decision trees (DT) are popular because of their intuitive nature and because they allow a nonlinear relationship to be modeled by recursive splitting of the dataset across thresholds of a feature. DTs have performed well in the situation of preliminary screening but can be overfitted without regularization (Liu et al., 2025). The support vector machines (SVMs) are robust in the sense that they identify the optimal hyperplanes to separate the classes of burnout-risk with a maximum margin, and SVMs can effectively work in high-dimensional space using relatively low samples; nonetheless, SVMs do not necessarily provide the transparency of decision making process (Hanif, 2022).

The more sophisticated neural networks such as feedforward and deep designs have higher capabilities to capture complex interactions and temporal dependencies in large and multimodal datasets. Neural networks can use any of the features (temporal work patterns, physiological measurements through wearables) to create more elaborate representations and predict better (Hanif, 2022; Liu et al., 2025). However, neural networks may be resource-intensive in terms of the necessary amount of labeled training samples and computational resources, which may pose a constraint on their use in strained resources (Liu et al., 2025).

In reality, ensemble learning methods have been popular. Ensemble models ensure the stability of predictions and lessen errors of bias or variance by taking several base models (e.g., random forests made of several decision trees) (Liu et al., 2025). To date, random forest algorithms specifically have shown a maximum of 80 percent predictive accuracy of burnout, along with predictive ability that reduces false positives and false negatives, respectively (Liu et al., 2025).

To build a successful burnout prediction model, it is not unusual to go through multiple stages: data preprocessing to clean and normalize various input features, exploratory data analysis to learn more about the features distribution and relationships, feature selection or engineering to increase the relevance of the model, model training and validation based on cross-validation methods, and evaluation based on the tool of accuracy, precision, recall, and F1 score (Hanif, 2022). Ongoing retraining using new information supports the operation of the model in the dynamic working conditions where the burnout risk factors may change quickly (MokaHR, 2025).

Using this range of algorithms and carefully chosen features, predictive modeling can offer valuable early warning features to organizations to identify employees who have a high chance of burnout and apply timely and customized interventions, thus enhancing the productivity and health of the workforce.

EARLY DETECTION AND RESPITE INTERVENTIONS

Burnout early warning systems that are based on AI use sophisticated algorithms to track a variety of data related to staff behavior, physiological indicators, and communication patterns around the clock. These systems give a personalized risk score, which is based on the analysis of deviations of the normal work and wellness trends, and thus they detect the early signs of stress or emotional burnout which before reaching the stage of full-fledged burnout (CanGrade, 2025). As an example, behavioral clues, including high logins after business hours, missed breaks, full calendar, reduced the number of mail replies, and negative language in mails, are monitored in real time to identify those employees who might be quietly suffering (CanGrade, 2025; The Wellness Corner, 2025).

When high risk is identified, AI systems will alert the supervisors, the HR team, or even the individual employees themselves, which will be determined by company policies and consent frameworks (CanGrade, 2025). These notifications tend to have practical suggestions based on them, including the adjustment of the workload, flexibility in the schedule, or the promotion of restorative periods. Furthermore, behavioral nudges that can be presented in apps or corporate wellness platforms can give employees low-effort nudges to apply stress-reduction techniques, take mindfulness breaks, or seek peer support (CanGrade, 2025). These nudges have been found to maintain positive habits and prevent worsening stress patterns in an effective way.

Customization is a very important aspect of an AI-based intervention. Through historical analysis and situational variables, AI applications can customize their recommendations to specific needs, such as providing particular types of relaxation to employees that display indicators of sleep disturbance, or reminding managers of the need to have supportive conversations with employees who display a lack of engagement (CanGrade, 2025). This dynamic, real time solution is in contrast to the traditional, one-size-fits-all wellness programs and interventions have become relatable and more efficient.

Additionally, anonymized data can be aggregated by AI systems to guide the organizational leaders regarding the trends in workforce well-being to make systemic changes, including redistribution of workloads or culture change to mitigate the risk of burnout at scale (CanGrade, 2025). Notably, such systems focus on ethical issues, preaching openness, privacy, and human control to allow AI to support, and not to substitute, the human-centered approach to management.

Altogether, AI-driven early warning systems can be used to provide a more proactive, customized method of preventing burnout, as they present timely risk assessment, personalized real-time interventions, and actionable insights at both the individual and organizational level, improving employee well-being and productivity.

THE ISSUE OF ETHICS AND PRIVACY

With their ability to predict burnout using AI, they promise ground-breaking possibilities to the well-being of the workforce but introduce substantial ethical and privacy concerns that one should take into account. The privacy of sensitive employee information is one of the major issues. It is occasionally based on gathering and examining behavioral trends, communication metrics, physiological data, and performance indicators, which can contain highly personal or health-related data (The Wellness Corner, 2025; MokaHR, 2025). Transparency in privacy policy and opt-in consent procedures should form the basis of building trust because employees should understand fully what data is gathered, how it is utilized, and who is allowed access to it (The Wellness Corner, 2025; ESMT Berlin, 2023).

The issue of data protection goes hand in hand. To protect the data of employees against breaches and unauthorized use, organizations are supposed to install effective cybersecurity controls, including encryption, secure storage, and round-the-clock monitoring (MokaHR, 2025). Considering the emergence of AI-based cyberattacks such as phishing, the security plumbing of such systems has to be audited and reviewed on a regular basis to fight the ever-changing threats (MokaHR, 2025).

The other important ethical aspect is possible biases integrating into AI models. Machine learning systems fed with past or unfinished information run the risk of reinforcing the current discriminatory and biased practices in the workplace, which results in the creation of inaccurate or unfair burnout risk estimation on the marginalized populations (DartAI, 2025). Such biases could be in the form of varying false positive and negative rates based on demographic groups and result in the wrong or absent intervention (DartAI, 2025). To overcome this, continuous model auditing, algorithm transparency, and use of varied datasets are essential to promote fairness and equity (DartAI, 2025).

Another issue is the possibility of surveillance and the implications that it has on employee autonomy and morale. Even well-intentioned constant surveillance can be viewed as intrusive and coercive, which may lead to a greater level of stress and mistrust among workers (ESMT Berlin, 2023; The Wellness Corner, 2025). The frameworks of ethical AI governance focus on the human sphere since the AI should be used as a complement to managerial empathy, not to have any punitive implications on the workers (ESMT Berlin, 2023).

Lastly, there is the issue of making sure that AI interventions do not contribute to the increase of pressures in the workplace, unintentionally. To illustrate this point, more at-risk burnout may be detected, which could lead to greater productivity requirements or even stigmatization in case it is not handled sensitively (MokaHR, 2025). To create a balance between the use of AI and the concern of the employee dignity, it is essential to adopt participatory models of the issue, which would entail the use of the workers in the decision-making on the policy and its designs.

Lastly, there is the issue of making sure that the AI interventions do not accidentally increase pressure at the workplace. As an example, more recognition of the burnout risk may lead to increased productivity expectations or stigmatization in the absence of the sensitive approach (MokaHR, 2025). A balance between effective AI application and the preservation of the dignity of employees needs participatory strategies, including the inclusion of workers into designing and policy-making processes (ESMT Berlin, 2023).

To sum up, although AI-powered burnout prediction provides valuable opportunities to improve the well-being of the employees, it should be introduced in a transparent manner, focusing on privacy, consent, fairness and ethical governance. The principles of transparency communication, strong data protection practice, regular audits, and human-centered design are essential to the achievement of the benefits of these technologies in a responsible and fair way.

FUTURE TRENDS AND FUTURE STRATEGY

The future of AI-predictive care of burnout is destined to revise the workplace well-being by harnessing the novel technological trends and provide new opportunities of proactive intervention. One trend is the increased pace of AI-based workforce analytics implementation that allow organizations to transition to preventative, rather than reactive, health models. Recent industry projections suggest that in 2025 about 90 percent of HR decisions will be made with the help of AI-based analytics, and predictive models will be part and parcel of recognize burnout risk and support employees in a more personalized way (HireBee, 2025). This change illustrates the increased awareness of the fact that timely and individual intervention can alleviate absenteeism, enhance retention, and create long-term performance opportunity within an ever-increasing complex and stressful workplace (LinkedIn, 2025).

Among the exciting directions, it is possible to point to the additional development of more advanced AI features, including generative AI and augmented intelligence, which strengthen human judgment instead of superseding it. Natural language understanding, emotion detection, and real-time behavioral analysis tools will be able to give deeper insights into the mental health of employees, whereas virtual assistants and chatbots can deliver more personalized coaching and stress management tools in real-time (SuperAGI, 2025). These AI companions will become caring digital companions, improving employee interaction and offer wellness help and support at scale 24 hours a day.

Further improvement of granularity and accuracy of predictive burnout models will be provided by wearable technology and IoT sensors that will continuously measure physiological data (heart rates variability, sleep quality, and hormone levels) (Wilton et al., 2024). Combining these health cues with digital behavioral data could yield new insights into the complicated interaction between physical and psychological stressors as well as offer solutions that address underlying causes of stressors and not symptoms themselves.

The other potential opportunity is to utilize federated learning and privacy enhancing technologies to solve the ethical and legal issues of employee data. These innovations will enable more people to use predictive care tools as AI models can be trained on decentralized information without violating their privacy and ensure that people adhere to the changing data protection laws (ESMT, 2023).

Lastly, the future studies will still be done to establish the validity of predictive models in various industries, different cultures, and different demographics to be fair and accurate. This integration of explainable AI solutions will enhance transparency, and organizations will be able to make sense of risk forecasts and involve employees in the development of effective well-being plans (DartAI, 2025).

Overall, predictive care which is based on AI is the way to the future of burnout management, which will likely undergo a paradigm shift in its approach to be holistic and anticipatory. The organizations, which would adopt such trends and uphold ethical application and human-focused design, will be in a good position to promote the healthier and robust workforces in future years.

CONCLUSION

Artificial Intelligence (AI) has great potential to change in the prevention and early intervention of burnout in an organization. With the incorporation of AI-based analytics, machine learning, and real-time monitoring systems, the organizations will be capable of identifying early signs of burnout more accurately and promptly in comparison to the traditional ones. These systems can process any range of different data sources, such as patterns of digital communication, physiological data, work behaviors, to come up with dynamic risk profiles that it can use to intervene in a timely and personalized manner (Universal AI, 2025; Appliview, 2025).

The essential insights include the change in the reactive mode of care to the proactive mode of care and the transition in the maintenance of burnout as a treatment of symptoms to an early prevention of burnout. Companies that use AI report that they have seen an increase in their employee engagement, decreased absenteeism, and decreased turnover rates because the stress indicators and workload changes can be identified in time (Universal AI, 2025). Moreover, AI helps in making better decisions in human resources and management so that they can employ data-driven strategies to maximize resource use, and encourage sustainable work practices (Forbes, 2025).

Organizational strategic priorities include the use of integrated AI solutions where ethical considerations such as data privacy, transparency and consent of employees are at the center of implementation. The adoption of human-centered AI governance is conducive to trust and acceptance as well as to maximum effectiveness (MokaHR, 2025; ESMT Berlin, 2023). Also, a company can put money in persistently testing its model and employee feedback circles to optimize predictive validity and intervention relevance.

Simply put, AI presents a paradigm shift in burnout detection and care and provides organizations with complex tools to develop healthier and more resilient workforces. The success of implementation lies in the compromises between technological innovation, ethics, and empathetic culture.

REFERENCES

Abundance Therapy Center. (2025). Recognizing and Addressing Burnout in the Workplace. https://www.abundancetherapycenter.com/blog/recognizing-and-addressing-burnout-in-the-workplace

American Psychological Association. (n.d.). Employers need to focus on workplace burnout: Here's why. https://www.apa.org/topics/healthy-workplaces/workplace-burnout

Appliview. (2025, June 30). How AI Can Help Identify and Address Employee Burnout. https://www.appliview.com/blog/how-ai-can-help-identify-and-address-employee-burnout/

Barac, M., Băban, A., & Dumitru, G. (2024). Wearable Technologies for Detecting Burnout and Well-being: Current State and Future Directions. *Sensors (Basel), 24*(2), 456. DOI: 10.3390/s24020456 PMID: 38257549

Berlin, E. S. M. T. (2023, January 22). HR teams can (and should) use AI to predict employee burnout. https://esmt.berlin/knowledge/hr-teams-can-and-should-use-ai-predict-employee-burnout

Berlin Knowledge, E. S. M. T. (2021, July 19). Predicting burn-out risk in the digital era. https://esmt.berlin/knowledge/predicting-burn-out-risk-digital-era

CanGrade. (2025, August 19). Leveraging AI to Predict and Prevent Employee Burnout. https://www.cangrade.com/blog/talent-management/leveraging-ai-to-predict-and-prevent-employee-burnout/

Dart, A. I. (2025, March 30). How can AI be Used to Detect Employee Burnout. https://www.dartai.com/blog/how-can-ai-detect-employee-burnout

Demerouti, E., Bakker, A. B., Nachreiner, F., & Schaufeli, W. B. (2001). The job demands-resources model of burnout. *The Journal of Applied Psychology, 86*(3), 499–512. DOI: 10.1037/0021-9010.86.3.499 PMID: 11419809

Demerouti, E., Schaufeli, W. B., & Bakker, A. B. (2025). Revitalising burnout research. *Work and Stress, 39*(2), 135–153. DOI: 10.1080/02678373.2025.2473385

Forbes. (2025, July 1). How To Use AI Tools To Detect Burnout And Retain Talented Employees. https://www.forbes.com/sites/dianehamilton/2025/07/01/how-to-use-ai-tools-to-detect-burnout-and-retain-talented-employees/

Grossman, S. (2023). *The Future of Burnout: AI's Role in Prevention*. Detection, and Recovery.

Hanif, I. (2022). Predicting employee burnout rate using neural network. [PDF]. https://scholar.ui.ac.id/files/65849867/Predicting_Employee_Burnout....pdf

Healthcare, H. C. L. (2024). How effective managers detect and defuse workplace burnout. https://hclhealthcare.in/guardians-of-wellbeing-how-effective-managers-detect-and-defuse-workplace-burnout/

HireBee. (2025, March 20). 100 + AI in HR Statistics 2025 | Insights & Emerging Trends. https://hirebee.ai/blog/ai-in-hr-statistics/

Insightful. (2025). Spot Early Signs of Employee Burnout with Analytics Tools. https://www.insightful.io/blog/detect-early-signs-of-employee-burnout

Khammissa, R. A. G.. (2022). Burnout phenomenon: Neurophysiological factors, clinical features, and management. *Frontiers in Psychiatry*, *13*, 947869. PMID: 36113033

Lattice. (2023). How to Measure Burnout Across a Global Organisation. https://lattice.com/articles/how-to-measure-burnout-across-a-global-organisation

Li, X., Zhou, Y., & Wang, L. (2024). The burnout prediction using wearable and artificial intelligence technologies: A review. *Journal of Medical Internet Research*, *26*, e54029.

LinkedIn. (2025, February 28). AI's New Frontier in HR: Predicting Burnout Before It Strikes! https://www.linkedin.com/pulse/ais-new-frontier-hr-predicting-burnout-before-strikes-michael-watson-nwibc

Liu, C., Chuang, Y.-C., Qin, L., Ren, L., Chien, C.-W., & Tung, T.-H. (2025). Machine-learning-based model for analysing and accurately predicting factors related to burnout in healthcare workers. *BMJ Public Health*, *3*(2), 000777. https://pmc.ncbi.nlm.nih.gov/articles/PMC12414203/. DOI: 10.1186/s12889-025-21809-1 PMID: 40922936

Maslach, C., & Jackson, S. E. (1981). The measurement of experienced burnout. *Journal of Organizational Behavior*, *2*(2), 99–113. DOI: 10.1002/job.4030020205

Maslach, C., Schaufeli, W. B., & Leiter, M. P. (1996). *Maslach Burnout Inventory manual*. Consulting Psychologists Press.

Mayo Clinic. (2023). Job burnout: How to spot it and take action. https://www.mayoclinic.org/healthy-lifestyle/adult-health/in-depth/burnout/art-20046642

Moka, H. R. (2025, March 24). How AI Can Predict and Prevent Workplace Burnout. https://www.mokahr.io/myblog/ai-predict-prevent-employee-burnout/

Smith, A., & Jones, B. (2022). Predictive analytics in workplace well-being: From burnout detection to prevention strategies. *Journal of Behavioral Health*, *11*(1), 34–50.

Super, A. G. I. (2025, June 30). Future of Work: Top AI-Powered Workplace Analytics Trends to Watch in 2025. https://superagi.com/future-of-work-top-ai-powered-workplace-analytics-trends-to-watch-in-2025-and-how-to-stay-ahead-of-the-curve-with-employee-engagement-solutions/

The Wellness Corner. (2025, July 23). Can AI Predict Mental Burnout Before It Happens? https://www.thewellnesscorner.com/blog/can-ai-detect-burnout-early

Universal, A. I. (2025). AI-Driven Burnout Detection & Eco-Volunteering. https://www.universalai.in/wp-content/uploads/2025/01/AI-Driven-Burnout-Detection-Eco-Volunteering-Suhasini-Ghosh.pdf

Wikipedia. (2023). Occupational burnout. https://en.wikipedia.org/wiki/Occupational_burnout

Wilton, A. R., Pereira, B. M., Myers, L., Sandhu, H., Chibalin, A., & Preece, D. (2024). The Burnout Prediction Using Wearable and ArtIficial Intelligence (BROWNIE) Study: Integrating Physiological, Psychological, and Workplace Data. *BMC Nursing*, *23*(1), 45. https://pmc.ncbi.nlm.nih.gov/articles/PMC10863108/. DOI: 10.1186/s12912-024-01711-8 PMID: 38225570

World Health Organization. (2019). Burn-out an "occupational phenomenon": International Classification of Diseases. https://www.who.int/news/item/28-05-2019-burn-out-an-occupational-phenomenon-international-classification-of-diseases

Chapter 10
Employee Digital Well-Being in the Age of Agentic AI:
HR Leaders as Gatekeepers of Ethical Governance

Nitin Simha Vihari
http://orcid.org/0000-0001-8501-9795
Middlesex University, Dubai, UAE

ABSTRACT

This chapter examines the emergence of agentic AI and its profound implications for employee digital well-being within contemporary organisations. It moves beyond the era of traditional human resource information systems, which were largely oriented toward administrative efficiency, and instead explores a shift toward augmented intelligence, in which autonomous systems and human actors jointly shape strategic and operational decisions. Drawing on a socio-technical systems perspective, employee digital well-being is conceptualised as the responsible and holistic management of human flourishing through the dynamic interaction between people, tasks, and digital systems. The chapter introduces the Sense-Predict-Reconfigure framework as a continuous learning loop that enables organisations to operationalise workforce resilience in AI-enabled environments. By combining analytical foresight with human empathy, HR leaders can ensure that advances in agentic AI strengthen employee digital well-being and contribute to more sustainable and humane forms of work rather than undermining them.

DOI: 10.4018/979-8-3373-6650-0.ch010

1. INTRODUCTION

Digital technologies have already transformed organisational life in ways that would have seemed improbable even a decade ago. Artificial intelligence systems now perform at levels comparable to those of human experts in complex cognitive tasks, including achieving top scores on advanced management education assessments, while digital health technologies enable remote diagnosis and treatment planning without physical clinical interaction (Brynjolfsson & McAfee, 2014). These developments signal not merely incremental technological progress but a fundamental reshaping of how work is organised, evaluated, and experienced. Organisations are now moving beyond the era of traditional human resource information systems, which were largely designed to support administrative efficiency, and entering a new phase characterised by agentic AI. These systems possess the capacity to reason, learn, and act autonomously with limited human intervention, thereby altering decision-making authority and control within organisations (Raisch & Krakowski, 2021).

While such advances offer substantial potential to improve organisational efficiency and decision quality, they also intensify longstanding concerns about the unintended consequences of digital technologies for human well-being. Prior research has consistently highlighted the darker side of digitalisation, including work intensification, technostress, and the erosion of employee autonomy (Tarafdar et al., 2017). As agentic AI systems become embedded in core organisational processes, these concerns are no longer peripheral but central to questions of sustainable work design and employee digital well-being.

The growing importance of digital well-being also reflects a broader transformation in the strategic role of human resource management within digitally mediated organisations. Historically, well-being was often treated as an individual concern related to stress management or work-life balance initiatives. However, the increasing integration of AI-driven systems into organisational decision processes has shifted digital well-being from an individual responsibility to a structural leadership concern. Scholars have argued that technologies embedded in work design fundamentally shape employees' experience of autonomy, identity, and meaning at work (Parker & Grote, 2022). When algorithmic systems influence how tasks are allocated, monitored, or evaluated, the resulting effects on employee well-being are determined less by personal coping strategies and more by how these systems are designed and governed. Consequently, digital well-being becomes inseparable from organisational choices regarding technology deployment and leadership governance. Research in management and information systems increasingly emphasises that the design of digital infrastructures can either amplify technostress or support employee flourishing depending on the socio-technical conditions under which technology is implemented (Akbar et al., 2025). From this perspective, HR leaders play a central role in shaping digital work environments that balance technological capability with human needs. By framing digital well-being as a strategic governance issue rather than merely a psychological outcome, organisations can ensure that AI-enabled systems contribute to sustainable work practices rather than unintentionally undermining employee experience.

The application of AI within human resource management represents a qualitative shift in the role of technology at work. Earlier forms of electronic HRM focused primarily on streamlining transactional activities and reducing administrative burden, leaving judgment-intensive decisions firmly in human hands (Bondarouk & Ruël, 2009). In contrast, contemporary AI-based HR applications increasingly support augmented intelligence, in which humans and intelligent systems jointly shape decisions on recruitment, performance, and workforce planning (Becker & Huselid, 2006). For example, traditional digital recruitment platforms enabled electronic posting and applicant tracking but still relied heavily on human screening and categorisation. Agentic AI tools, including conversational chatbots and intelligent applicant-tracking systems, now autonomously conduct résumé screening, candidate ranking, and initial assessments, with some estimates suggesting that a substantial proportion of recruitment activities can be automated (Meijerink et al., 2021).

Despite these gains in productivity and speed, a persistent question has emerged in both scholarly and public debate. The unprecedented access to advanced technologies has led to improvements in employee happiness and well-being, but they have not kept pace. This question becomes particularly salient given evidence of declining well-being among younger workers. The 2024 World Happiness Report indicates a notable deterioration in reported well-being among individuals aged 15 to 24 across multiple regions since 2019, a trend that challenges assumptions about the inherent benefits of digitalisation for so-called digital natives (Helliwell et al., 2024). As AI systems increasingly shape everyday work practices, they disrupt established routines, professional identities, and skill configurations. While AI can enhance creativity by supporting complex cognitive processes, it may also constrain creative expression through rigid algorithmic logic and reduced employee discretion (Amabile & Pratt, 2016). These tensions underscore the need to examine employee digital well-being not as an individual coping issue but as a systemic outcome shaped by leadership choices, governance structures, and the design of agentic AI systems.

Table 1. The Transition from Traditional HRIS to Agentic AI in the Workplace

Feature	Traditional HRIS/e-HRM	Agentic AI (Augmented Intelligence)
Primary Goal	Administrative efficiency and data storage	Strategic decision-support and autonomy
Human Role	Leads the process; IT provides support	Human-AI Symbiosis; joint decision-making
Task Scope	Tactical applications (payroll, record-keeping)	Complex tasks (candidate evaluation, sentiment analysis)
Impact on Well-Being	Indirect; focused on reducing physical effort	Direct; impacts autonomy, identity, and mental health
HR Function	Administrative Expert	Gatekeeper of Ethical Governance

For HR leaders, the integration of agentic AI is no longer a question of whether to adopt new technologies, but a strategic imperative tied directly to the management of employee digital well-being. Digital well-being should not be understood as a fixed or stable condition. Instead, it reflects a dynamic interplay among the tasks employees perform, the technologies organisations design and deploy, and the evolving ways individuals make sense of work and fulfilment in digitally mediated environments. This perspective aligns closely with Kranzberg's First Law, which emphasises that technology is neither inherently beneficial nor inherently harmful and that its consequences are shaped by the social and ethical contexts within which it is governed (Kranzberg, 1986). In the context of agentic AI, this places significant responsibility on HR leaders to actively shape how these systems are embedded in everyday work practices.

Addressing the darker consequences of advanced AI while realising its potential benefits requires HR leaders to move beyond simply counting workforce data towards connecting analytics with lived employee experiences. This shift calls for engagement with design-oriented theories such as Positive Computing, which focuses on developing interactive systems that actively support psychological, emotional, and social flourishing (Calvo & Peters, 2014). From this standpoint, digital well-being becomes an outcome of intentional system design rather than an individual coping challenge. It also highlights the importance of individual unlearning, understood as the deliberate letting go of outdated routines, assumptions, and mental models that no longer align with AI-integrated forms of work (Tsang & Zahra, 2008). Without such unlearning, employees may struggle to adapt to new forms of human-AI collaboration, even when technological capability is high.

The emergence of agentic AI, therefore, presents a fundamental paradox for contemporary organisations. On the one hand, these technologies offer unprecedented tools for addressing complex organisational challenges. On the other hand, they pose tangible risks to autonomy, meaning, and well-being if deployed without ethical foresight. The future of HR leadership lies in navigating this tension with both analytical confidence and human curiosity.

This chapter advances a digital leadership framework that supports HR leaders in this role by positioning ethical governance and employee digital well-being as central pillars of sustainable workforce design in the twenty-first century.

2. THEORETICAL FOUNDATIONS: A SOCIO-TECHNICAL LENS ON EMPLOYEE DIGITAL WELL-BEING

The pursuit of human well-being is a longstanding concern spanning centuries, from the ancient Greek notion of eudaimonia, commonly understood as human flourishing or fulfilment, to contemporary philosophical and indigenous perspectives on meaningful living. As digital technologies, and more recently agentic and autonomous AI systems, become deeply embedded within organisational life, conventional understandings of what constitutes a good working life are being fundamentally reshaped (Hall, 2024). Work is no longer defined solely by human effort and social interaction but increasingly by continuous engagement with intelligent systems that influence decision-making, autonomy, and identity. These shifts demand a renewed theoretical lens for understanding employee digital well-being in contemporary workplaces (Hall, 2024).

This section establishes the theoretical foundation for conceptualising employee digital well-being by drawing on a socio-technical systems perspective, complemented by insights from positive computing and social cognitive theory. Socio-technical theory emphasises that organisational outcomes emerge from the joint optimisation of social and technical systems rather than from technology or human factors in isolation (Orlikowski, 2007). From this viewpoint, digital well-being is shaped not only by the design of AI systems but also by how work tasks, roles, and social structures are configured around them. Positive computing further extends this logic by arguing that digital systems should be intentionally designed to support psychological, emotional, and social flourishing rather than merely efficiency or performance (Calvo & Peters, 2014). Social cognitive theory contributes an additional layer by highlighting the role of individual agency, self-efficacy, and learning processes in shaping how employees experience and adapt to technologically mediated work environments (Bandura, 1986).

Within the information systems literature, digital well-being has historically lacked a consistent and unified conceptualisation. Early research often approached well-being in digital contexts through narrow indicators such as screen time, technology overuse, or digital addiction (Tarafdar et al., 2015). More recent scholarship, however, has moved towards a broader and more integrative understanding. Digital well-being is increasingly framed as a macro-level construct concerned with both objective conditions and subjective experiences that shape how individuals function, adapt, and flourish in technology-saturated environments (Venkatesh et al., 2022). This broader framing is particularly relevant in the context of agentic AI, where the boundaries between human judgment and machine agency are increasingly blurred and where employee well-being becomes inseparable from leadership choices and system governance.

Drawing from the sources, DWB is defined here as:

The holistic understanding and responsible management of specific dimensions of human well-being in digital societies by examining the dynamic, reciprocal interplay among the tasks we perform, the technologies we develop (systems), and their complex interactions that shape our self-understanding of whast it means to live a fulfilling life.

This definition moves DWB away from being a static state and reframes it as a dynamic interplay between individuals and their evolving technological context. Importantly, this perspective acknowledges that technology is neither inherently good nor bad, nor is it neutral; its impact is dictated by the context of its use and the ethical oversight applied by organisational leaders.

Taken together, these theoretical perspectives provide a complementary foundation for understanding employee digital well being in the context of agentic AI. The socio technical systems perspective establishes the structural foundation by emphasising the joint optimisation of social and technological elements within organisational systems. Positive computing introduces a design oriented perspective, arguing that digital systems should intentionally support psychological flourishing rather than focusing solely on efficiency. Social cognitive theory adds a behavioural dimension by explaining how individuals interpret and adapt to technological change through observational learning and self efficacy processes. When integrated, these perspectives offer a multi level framework for understanding digital well being. At the structural level, socio technical theory highlights how the configuration of tasks, technologies, and organisational roles shapes employee experiences. At the design level, positive computing emphasises that the architecture of digital systems can either enhance or undermine fundamental psychological needs such as autonomy and competence. At the behavioural level, social cognitive theory explains how employees learn to navigate AI enabled work environments through cues provided by leaders and organisational culture. Recent organisational research increasingly emphasises the need for such integrative approaches when examining technology mediated work systems, particularly as artificial intelligence blurs the boundaries between human and machine agency (Faraj, Pachidi, & Sayegh, 2018). By combining structural, design, and behavioural perspectives, the framework presented in this chapter provides a more comprehensive explanation of how digital well being emerges in AI integrated workplaces.

2.1 The Socio-Technical Systems (STS) Perspective

The foundation of this framework is the socio-technical systems perspective, long regarded as the essence of information systems research for its emphasis on the joint optimisation of social and technical elements within organisations (Orlikowski, 2007). Rather than treating agentic AI as a standalone technological upgrade, the socio-technical lens conceptualises the organisation as a dynamic interplay among three interdependent pillars, namely people, tasks, and systems. This perspective is particularly relevant in the context of agentic AI, where technological autonomy directly reshapes work practices and employee experiences.

- **Systems (the technical pillar):** In the era of agentic AI, systems extend far beyond the traditional functions of storing, processing, or reporting data. These technologies increasingly operate as forms of augmented intelligence that can autonomously analyse information, generate predictions, and support or initiate decisions with limited human intervention. As a result, systems become active participants in organisational sensemaking and action rather than passive tools (Raisch & Krakowski, 2021).
- **Tasks (the process pillar):** Tasks represent the core domains of human activity mediated by technology, including work, learning, and social interaction. Agentic AI reshapes these tasks by automating routine, rule-based activities, thereby shifting human effort towards higher-value judgement, problem-solving, and relational work. This reconfiguration alters not only task content but also expectations around pace, responsibility, and skill use.
- **People (the human pillar):** The people dimension is the most critical component of the framework, as it captures how employees experience digital well-being at subjective, objective, and contextual levels. It is within this pillar that the darker consequences of advanced technologies, such as techno-stress, digital exclusion, and perceptions of algorithmic bias, are most acutely experienced (Tarafdar et al., 2017). Focusing on people ensures that employee digital well-being remains central rather than incidental in the design and governance of agentic AI systems.

2.2 Positive Computing: Designing for Flourishing

To move beyond a purely preventive stance focused on avoiding harm, the framework incorporates insights from positive computing, which emphasises the intentional design of digital systems that actively enhance human potential. This research stream draws directly on positive psychology and seeks to embed constructs such as motivation, engagement, mindfulness, and empathy into the design of interactive technologies, rather than treating well-being as a secondary outcome (Calvo & Peters, 2014).

Calvo and Peters identify three interrelated levels at which well-being-oriented design can operate.

- **Intrapersonal (self):** This level focuses on individual attributes such as motivation, self-awareness, and mindfulness that shape how users engage with digital systems.
- **Interpersonal (social):** This level emphasises relational dimensions, including empathy, gratitude, and a sense of social belonging, that emerge through digitally mediated interaction.
- **Extrapersonal (transcendent):** This level extends beyond the individual and social domains to include compassion and concern for a broader collective or societal good.

In the context of agentic AI, positive computing offers a critical design lens by ensuring that autonomous systems are not evaluated solely on efficiency or accuracy. Instead, such systems are assessed on their capacity to support core psychological needs, including autonomy, competence, and relatedness, as articulated in self-determination theory (Deci & Ryan, 2000). Embedding these principles into agentic AI design strengthens employee digital well-being and reinforces the ethical responsibility of HR leaders overseeing these technologies.

2.3 Social Cognitive Theory and the "Social Cue" of Leadership

While the socio-technical systems perspective provides the structural foundation and positive computing articulates the design intent, social cognitive theory explains how individuals adapt to change in digitally mediated environments. According to Bandura (1986), learning occurs not only through direct experience but also by observing how others respond to new conditions and stimuli.

Within this framework, agentic AI functions as an environmental stimulus that disrupts established routines and challenges existing mental models. Employee responses to this disruption are shaped significantly by the social cues provided by leaders. When HR leaders demonstrate confidence in AI and communicate a balanced, constructive orientation towards its integration, they signal psychological safety. This perceived safety enables employees to engage in individual unlearning, understood as the deliberate abandonment of obsolete habits and assumptions to adopt new, AI-integrated ways of working.

2.4 Technology Trust: The Foundation of Ethical Agility

A critical theoretical bottleneck in the adoption of AI-driven systems is the growing trust deficit between employees and intelligent technologies. Unlike traditional software, agentic AI often operates as a black box, limiting employees' ability to understand how decisions on hiring, performance evaluation, or task allocation are generated. This opacity can undermine confidence in both the technology itself and the organisational actors responsible for its deployment.

Drawing on Hmoud (2021), this framework identifies three core determinants of technology trust that are particularly salient in agentic AI contexts.

- **Reliability:** The degree to which the system consistently produces stable and predictable outcomes over time and across use cases.
- **Credibility:** The extent to which AI-generated outputs are perceived as fair, accurate, and free from systematic human or algorithmic bias.
- **Technical competence:** The functional capability of the AI system to process tasks fully and accurately without frequent errors or failures.

For HR leaders acting as gatekeepers of ethical governance, these determinants provide a practical lens for addressing trust-related concerns. By prioritising transparency, auditability, and explainability in AI-enabled HR systems, leaders can reduce uncertainty and strengthen employee confidence in automated decision-making processes (Gunning et al., 2019). In this sense, trust in technology becomes a foundational condition for ethical agility, enabling organisations to adapt responsibly while safeguarding employees' digital well-being.

2.5 Knowledge Renewal through Unlearning

The theoretical model further proposes that creative performance in AI-enabled workplaces is mediated by individual unlearning. Unlearning should not be understood as a passive loss of knowledge but as an intentional, reflective process through which employees disengage from outdated cognitive schemas that no longer align with evolving work contexts (Tsang & Zahra, 2008). In knowledge-intensive environments, the ability to relinquish previously effective but now obsolete routines becomes a critical mechanism for maintaining adaptability and responsiveness.

As organisations transition towards AI-enabled forms of work, the emphasis shifts from traditional learning, which focuses on acquiring new information, to knowledge renewal, which involves revising and reconstructing underlying mental models. HR leaders play a central role in enabling this shift by acting as catalysts for cognitive agility. Rather than concentrating solely on upskilling initiatives, they foster organisational cultures in which unlearning is normalised and recognised as a necessary condition for sustained creativity and innovation in AI-mediated work systems (Fiol & O'Connor, 2017).

3. FROM AUTOMATION TO AUGMENTATION

The historical trajectory of technology in human resource management has been shaped by a gradual shift from manual, paper-based routines towards increasingly integrated digital systems. Early technological interventions were primarily designed to improve administrative efficiency and standardise HR processes. However, organisations have now reached a critical inflection point. The shift from traditional human resource information systems and electronic HRM towards agentic AI represents more than an incremental gain in speed or accuracy. It reflects a deeper transformation in how HR work is conceived and led.

This transition signals a shift from automation to augmented intelligence, in which decision-making authority is increasingly shared between human actors and intelligent systems (Raisch & Krakowski, 2021). In this emerging context, the role of the HR professional is no longer confined to operational expertise or system oversight. Instead, HR leaders are repositioned as strategic orchestrators of human-AI collaboration, responsible for aligning technological capability with human judgement, ethical governance, and employee digital wellbeing. This reframing highlight augmentation not as a replacement of human agency but as a reconfiguration of leadership responsibility within AI-enabled organisations (Jarrahi, 2018).

3.1 The Evolution of the HR Technology Paradigm

To understand the current transformation, it is necessary to situate agentic AI within the broader historical evolution of HR technology. Early digitalisation through human resource information systems was primarily oriented towards reducing administrative burden by enabling the storage, reporting and retrieval of employee data. These systems improved efficiency and compliance but played a limited role in shaping strategic decision-making. This phase was followed by the emergence of electronic HRM, which leveraged internet-based platforms to connect employees, managers and HR functions more effectively and to facilitate communication across organisational boundaries (Bondarouk & Ruël, 2009).

While both HRIS and e-HRM contributed to process standardisation and cost efficiency, their application remained largely tactical. The current era, shaped by the dynamics of Industry 4.0, introduces a fundamentally different technological paradigm. Organisations are moving beyond systems that merely store information or enable connection towards systems that can reason, learn and act. Agentic AI, characterised by its capacity for autonomous reasoning and initiative with limited human intervention, supports a model of augmented intelligence rather than simple automation (Raisch & Krakowski, 2021).

Unlike traditional automation, which focuses on substituting human effort in routine, rules-based tasks, augmented intelligence enables humans and intelligent systems to jointly shape decisions. This shift elevates information technology from a supporting infrastructure to a strategic partner within the HR domain. As a result, HR leaders are required to engage more directly with questions of governance, judgement and employee experience as technology becomes an active participant in people management processes (Jarrahi, 2018).

3.2 Redefining Decision-Making through the Human-AI Symbiosis

A central feature of this transformation is the redistribution of cognitive labour between humans and intelligent systems. In the era of agentic AI, software no longer functions as a passive executor of human instructions. Instead, AI-driven HR applications increasingly operate autonomously, processing complex and time-intensive tasks that previously required substantial human involvement. In talent acquisition, for example, earlier forms of electronic HRM provided digital portals for job applications, but screening and candidate classification still depended heavily on human judgement. Contemporary agentic tools now autonomously source candidates, conduct initial résumé screening using natural language processing, and analyse behavioural cues in video interviews to infer attributes such as motivation and role fit (Meijerink et al., 2021).

This emerging human-AI symbiosis enables HR leaders to reorient their efforts towards higher-value judgement and sensemaking. As AI systems assume responsibility for counting activities, such as processing large volumes of applications or estimating attrition risk, HR professionals are better positioned to focus on connecting by interpreting insights within organisational and human contexts. Recent research on advanced people analytics emphasises this shift from descriptive reporting towards actionable foresight, with analytics moving from dashboards to direction and supporting early-warning intelligence for workforce resilience and adaptability

(Margherita & Bua, 2021). In this way, augmented intelligence reshapes decision-making not by removing human agency but by redefining where and how human judgement adds the greatest value.

3.3 Strategic Gains in Talent Acquisition and Deployment

The most immediate effects of this role redefinition are evident in the optimisation of the talent lifecycle. Empirical research and industry evidence suggest that AI-driven recruitment systems can automate a substantial proportion of talent acquisition activities, particularly sourcing, screening, and initial assessment (Meijerink et al., 2021). Intelligent applicant-tracking systems and conversational agents, such as Mya and HireVue, now enable rapid candidate identification and matching, functions that were historically among the most labour-intensive stages of recruitment. These technologies reduce processing time while increasing consistency in early-stage decision-making (Hmoud & Várallyai, 2019).

The efficiency gains associated with AI-enabled recruitment are increasingly visible at the organisational level. Studies report significant reductions in recruitment costs and notable improvements in process speed following the adoption of AI-driven screening and evaluation tools (Upadhyay & Khandelwal, 2018). Beyond efficiency, AI systems are often positioned as mechanisms for reducing human bias by applying standardised criteria across large applicant pools. However, research cautions that such outcomes are contingent on how algorithms are trained and governed, as biased historical data can be replicated or amplified if left unchecked (Raghavan et al., 2020).

This shift reinforces the need for HR leaders to act as gatekeepers of ethical governance. As autonomous agents become embedded in selection processes, HR leadership's responsibility extends beyond adoption towards ensuring transparency, accountability, and fairness. Without active oversight, the same systems designed to enhance objectivity risk reproducing existing inequalities in new and less visible ways.

3.4 Redefining Core Competencies for HR Leaders

As AI increasingly absorbs repetitive and operational HR work, the core competencies required of HR professionals are being fundamentally redefined. To remain strategically relevant, HR leaders must develop a new portfolio of power skills and technical literacies that enable effective human-AI collaboration and ethical oversight (Raisch & Krakowski, 2021).

- **Algorithmic and AI literacy:** The ability to understand, interpret and critically engage with AI systems has become a foundational leadership capability rather than a technical add-on. HR leaders need sufficient literacy to question data inputs, processing logic, and decision outputs to safeguard the legitimacy and fairness of the process (Raghavan et al., 2020).

- **Business acumen:** AI-enabled HR solutions must be clearly aligned with organisational strategy and commercial priorities. HR leaders are increasingly required to translate workforce analytics into business-relevant insights that support value creation and competitive advantage (Margherita & Bua, 2021).
- **Generative AI proficiency:** Competence in using generative tools to support workforce forecasting, learning content creation and personalised coaching is emerging as a practical requirement. These tools extend HR capacity while reshaping the delivery of developmental support at scale (Hurst, 2021).
- **Capability orchestration:** Leadership now extends beyond managing functional teams to orchestrating cross-functional people-insight squads. In these configurations, HR professionals, data specialists, and line managers collaborate to interpret signals, test interventions, and collectively adapt practices.
- **Empathy and human curiosity:** As intelligent systems process and summarise large volumes of data, the uniquely human contribution of HR leadership lies in sense-making, trust-building and ethical judgement. Leaders who combine analytical confidence with empathy are better positioned to foster employee trust and sustain digital wellbeing in AI-enabled workplaces (Calvo & Peters, 2014).

3.5 Managing the Hybrid Workforce

One of the most significant redefinitions of the HR role lies in the expanding boundaries of the workforce itself. HR is no longer responsible only for employees, freelancers and contractors. It must now manage a hybrid workforce in which humans and intelligent machines collaborate to perform organisational tasks. This shift reflects a broader movement towards what has been described as rising with the machines, where value is created through complementary rather than substitutive human-AI relationships (Raisch & Krakowski, 2021).

Managing this hybrid workforce requires HR leaders to rethink capacity planning and workforce development, explicitly integrating autonomous agents into employment models. In high-precision manufacturing contexts, organisations such as Mercedes-Benz have begun implementing collaborative intelligence, in which robotic systems augment human performance rather than replace it. In these settings, the role of HR is to ensure socio-technical alignment by allocating repetitive and physically demanding tasks to AI systems while enabling human workers to concentrate on innovation, problem-solving and complex judgment (Jarrahi, 2018).

The emergence of agentic AI, therefore, marks a broader transition for HR from a function centred on managing processes to one focused on orchestrating capabilities across human and technological actors. By moving from automation to augmentation, HR leaders can translate workforce data into a meaningful human narrative that connects performance indicators with trust, energy and employee digital well-being. As articulated in the SPR framework, effective HR leadership in the AI era depends on a repeatable logic of sensing workforce signals early, thoughtfully predicting potential disruptions, and rapidly reconfiguring work systems. In this evolving digital ecosystem, HR leaders act not merely as managers of people but as strategic navigators who ensure that technology ultimately amplifies human ingenuity rather than constrains it.

4. HR LEADERS AS GATEKEEPERS: ETHICAL GOVERNANCE AND THE DIGITAL TRUST DEFICIT

The rapid transition from traditional rule-based automation to agentic AI systems capable of autonomous reasoning and proactive initiative has introduced significant tension in contemporary workplaces. While these technologies promise to transform human resource management by augmenting intelligence and supporting complex decision-making, they simultaneously generate a pronounced trust deficit. Employees and managers often express scepticism about decisions produced by opaque algorithmic systems, particularly when those decisions concern sensitive outcomes such as hiring, promotion, or performance evaluation. Concerns typically focus on the potential masking of bias, threats to data privacy, and the erosion of human dignity. Within this context, HR leaders assume a critical gatekeeping role, charged with bridging the trust gap through ethical governance and a socio-technical approach to AI integration.

Trust has long been recognised as a central determinant of information technology adoption. In AI-enabled environments, however, the stakes are considerably higher because agentic AI operates as a decision partner rather than a passive tool (Raisch & Krakowski, 2021). The trust deficit is often rooted in limited transparency and in employees' perceived inability to understand how complex inputs are translated into high-impact outputs, such as candidate shortlisting or performance ratings. Drawing on social cognitive theory, individuals adapt to technological change not only through direct interaction but also by observing social cues from leaders (Bandura, 1986). When HR leaders are unable to articulate how AI systems function or appear uncertain about their outputs, employees are more likely to interpret AI as a source of risk rather than an opportunity. As a result, diminished trust becomes a primary barrier to adoption, reinforcing the need for HR leaders to foreground transparency and explainability in legitimising AI-driven decisions.

Moving beyond generalised scepticism requires HR leaders to engage with the specific determinants that shape trust in AI-enabled HR solutions. Prior research identifies three core pillars of technology trust that are particularly relevant in agentic AI contexts (Hmoud, 2021).

- **Reliability:** The extent to which AI systems demonstrate consistency and predictability in producing outcomes across comparable situations. Erratic or unstable outputs in areas such as recruitment or scheduling can quickly undermine workforce confidence (Hmoud & Várallyai, 2019).
- **Credibility:** The degree to which AI-generated decisions are perceived as accurate, fair, and free from systematic bias. Maintaining credibility requires ongoing scrutiny of training data and model logic to avoid reinforcing historical demographic inequalities (Raghavan et al., 2020).
- **Technical competence:** The functional capability of AI systems to process HR tasks comprehensively and accurately without omitting contextually important variables or oversimplifying complex human judgements.

Operationalising ethical governance requires HR leaders to move beyond policy statements towards establishing institutionalised oversight mechanisms that continuously monitor how AI systems influence workforce outcomes. Recent research suggests that organisations deploying AI responsibly often establish cross-functional governance structures that combine expertise from HR, data science, legal, and ethics teams (Floridi et al., 2018). These structures enable organisations to evaluate algorithmic outputs, audit training data, and assess unintended consequences such as demographic bias or privacy risks. Another critical component of ethical governance is the implementation of algorithmic transparency practices that allow employees and managers to understand the logic behind AI-supported decisions. Transparency does not necessarily require full disclosure of proprietary algorithms but rather the provision of explainable insights into how key factors influence decision outcomes (Majumder et al., 2026). Studies on explainable artificial intelligence demonstrate that transparent systems significantly increase user trust and perceived fairness, particularly in high-stakes decision contexts such as recruitment or promotion (Miller, 2019). HR leaders therefore play an important role as translators between technical systems and organisational stakeholders, ensuring that AI-driven decisions remain interpretable and accountable. Through these governance mechanisms, HR leadership can transform AI adoption from a purely technological initiative into a socially responsible organisational capability (Yin & Hoang, 2025).

5. MANAGING THE "DARK SIDE" OF AI USING ETHICAL GOVERNANCE

The role of HR leaders as gatekeepers extends beyond ensuring technical efficiency and system performance. It requires the proactive identification and management of the darker consequences associated with advanced digital technologies. In the context of agentic AI, these risks include algorithmic bias, digital ostracism, and the gradual erosion of employee autonomy, all of which have direct implications for employee digital well-being.

AI systems typically learn patterns from historical data, creating a risk of unintentionally reproducing existing inequalities related to gender, race, or age. For example, a recruitment algorithm trained on profiles of historically successful employees may disadvantage underrepresented groups if those groups were previously excluded from advancement opportunities. Research on algorithmic decision-making highlights how such feedback loops can institutionalise bias when governance mechanisms are weak (Raghavan et al., 2020). As ethical gatekeepers, HR leaders are responsible for articulating clear fairness principles and for establishing cross-functional oversight structures that involve HR, IT, and legal specialists to identify and correct inequitable AI-generated outcomes.

The extensive use of employee data within AI-enabled HR systems also raises significant privacy concerns. HR data increasingly includes sensitive information, ranging from health indicators captured through wellness initiatives to detailed performance analytics (Karami, 2025). Drawing on privacy calculus theory, employees continuously assess the perceived benefits of digital HR interventions against potential risks to personal privacy (Culnan & Armstrong, 1999). HR leaders can reduce these concerns by enforcing strict data access controls, anonymising sensitive information, and ensuring that employees retain control over how their personal data is shared and used.

A central ethical principle underpinning the gatekeeper role is the preservation of meaningful human oversight. Although agentic AI systems can process large volumes of information at speed, HR professionals must retain the authority to review, interpret, and override AI-generated outputs when necessary. Maintaining this human-centred approach helps prevent algorithmic rigidity and ensures that intelligent systems function as decision-support resources rather than unquestioned authorities (Raisch & Krakowski, 2021). In doing so, HR leaders safeguard both ethical integrity and employee trust in AI-mediated decision processes.

5.1. Case Studies in Ethical Stewardship

Empirical and practice-based examples show how organisations can navigate the gatekeeping challenge of agentic AI while preserving employees' digital well-being.

- IBM: IBM adopts a stewardship-oriented approach, embedding HR professionals within business units to ensure AI adoption remains aligned with operational and contextual expertise. AI initiatives are evaluated not only on revenue growth and efficiency gains but also on intangible outcomes such as reduced turnover and improved workforce stability. This integrated governance model reflects a broader shift towards shared accountability for the ethical deployment of AI across organisational functions (Raisch & Krakowski, 2021).
- Cisco: Cisco has applied AI and machine learning to strengthen both security and HR-related digital infrastructures. By analysing large-scale network data, the organisation developed an intent-based networking model that protects multi-cloud environments. This architecture enhances the security of SaaS platforms supporting HR and people management processes, thereby reinforcing trust in the digital systems employees use.
- Leap.ai: Leap.ai employs advanced matching algorithms, such as the Job User Matching Forecast, to provide personalised career recommendations. By incorporating individual preferences alongside organisational culture indicators, the platform balances automation with human-centred career development. This approach demonstrates how AI can support employee agency rather than constrain it when ethical design principles are prioritised.

Across these cases, a common insight emerges. While technology can process data at scale, only leadership can convert analytical outputs into trust. HR leaders, acting as ethical gatekeepers, must combine analytical confidence with human curiosity. This responsibility extends beyond regulatory compliance with frameworks such as data protection or AI governance legislation towards a normative consideration of what constitutes responsible and humane use of technology. By fostering psychological safety and encouraging employees to question existing routines and experiment with new forms of human-AI collaboration, HR leaders enable knowledge renewal and help ensure that digital transformation strengthens rather than diminishes the human experience at work.

6. OPERATIONALIZING EMPLOYEE RESILIENCE AND WORKFORCE AGILITY VIA SPR FRAMEWORK

The Sense Predict Reconfigure framework advances the literature on workforce resilience by positioning HR analytics as a dynamic capability rather than a static reporting tool. Early work on HR analytics mainly focused on descriptive metrics that outlined past workforce trends but offered no actionable insights (Karami, 2025). However, modern research increasingly highlights the strategic value of predictive and prescriptive analytics in helping organisations anticipate and tackle workforce challenges (Davenport et al., 2020). By integrating sensing, predictive modelling, and organisational reconfiguration into a continuous cycle, the SPR framework expands this perspective by directly linking workforce analytics to organisational adaptation processes. This approach aligns with dynamic capabilities theory, which focuses on organisations' ability to sense environmental changes, seize emerging opportunities, and reconfigure resources to maintain a competitive advantage (Teece et al., 1998). In HR contexts, this capability appears through early detection of workforce stress signals, prediction of future risks, and proactive redesign of work systems. By embedding analytics into leadership decision-making rather than treating it as a separate technical function, the SPR framework offers a practical means for organisations to strengthen both employee resilience and strategic agility in AI-enabled environments.

The contemporary organisational landscape is marked by a persistent paradox: decisions must be made faster, while the information needed to support them often arrives too late. Traditional HR functions have largely relied on descriptive analytics that report past events rather than anticipate emerging workforce challenges. The rise of agentic AI and predictive analytics enables HR to move beyond compliance-oriented reporting toward a more strategic role, where workforce data is transformed into early-warning intelligence that supports proactive, informed decision-making. This section introduces the Sense Predict Reconfigure framework as a continuous learning loop designed to embed AI-driven people analytics within organisational strategy and to strengthen both employee resilience and workforce agility.

The SPR framework is theoretically grounded in the resource-based view and the dynamic capabilities perspective. From an RBV standpoint, advanced analytics capabilities constitute intangible strategic assets that allow organisations to sense environmental shifts and reconfigure human capital more effectively than competitors (Barney, 1991). Research on dynamic capabilities further suggests that sustained advantage depends not only on the possession of valuable resources but also on the capacity to integrate, build, and reconfigure those resources in response to change (Teece et al., 1998). From this perspective, agility is not defined solely by speed but by the ability to detect emerging signals early and translate them into informed decisions amid uncertainty. By linking workforce data to indicators such as energy, trust, and performance, HR leaders can move from static dashboards to directional insights that support adaptive and resilient workforce design (Margherita and Bua, 2021).

5.1 Phase 1: Sensing

The first stage of the loop, sensing, focuses on identifying early signals of pressure or opportunity within the workforce before they escalate into broader systemic issues. Traditional sensing mechanisms, such as annual employee engagement surveys, are often too infrequent to capture the rapid, continuous changes associated with digital transformation. In contrast, the SPR framework emphasises pulse surveys and real-time sentiment analysis to provide more immediate, actionable insights into employee experience (Tarafdar et al., 2017). Effective sensing also requires HR leaders to act as gatekeepers of employee digital well-being by actively monitoring indicators of the darker consequences of technology use. For example, data on sensing may indicate that constant monitoring with wearable devices or digital tracking tools contributes to increased stress and fatigue rather than improved health outcomes. Research on technostress suggests that sustained exposure to intensive digital monitoring can increase strain and reduce well-being if not carefully governed (Ragu Nathan et al., 2008). By identifying patterns such as rising absenteeism or early signs of technostress weeks before they translate into safety incidents or voluntary turnover, HR leaders are better positioned to intervene proactively and recalibrate work design and technology use.

5.2 Phase 2: Predictive Modeling of Outcomes

Once workforce signals are detected, the framework proceeds to predict downstream impacts. At this stage, augmented intelligence becomes central, as humans and AI systems jointly interpret data to inform decision-making. Predictive analytics allow HR leaders to estimate outcomes such as attrition risk, turnover hotspots, and emerging skill shortages before they materialise. Prior research shows that predictive people analytics can significantly improve workforce planning by shifting attention from reactive reporting to anticipatory intervention (Margherita & Bua, 2021). In knowledge-intensive contexts, predictive models can identify patterns, such as faculty overload or heightened burnout risk, during periods of sustained digital demand. For instance, if an AI system estimates an attrition probability above a defined threshold for a specific employee segment, HR leaders can initiate targeted responses such as stay interviews, workload adjustments, or incentive recalibration. Empirical studies suggest that such early interventions are more effective at retaining critical talent than post-exit corrective actions (Hausknecht et al., 2009). By moving from descriptive to predictive modelling, organisations enhance their capacity to anticipate disruption, strengthening both workforce agility and long-term retention outcomes.

5.3 Phase 3: Reconfiguring Capabilities

The final phase of the loop is reconfiguration, during which HR leaders adjust organisational capabilities to sustain resilience amid ongoing change. This phase relies most heavily on human judgment and strategic framing, as it involves decisions that extend beyond what analytics alone can prescribe. Reconfiguration may include redesigning workloads, enabling cross-training, or reallocating tasks between human employees and AI agents. A central element of this phase is individual unlearning, understood as the intentional abandonment of outdated routines and mental models to accommodate AI-integrated ways of working (Tsang & Zahra, 2008). As agentic AI reshapes task complexity and decision autonomy, employees require structured support to let go of familiar practices that no longer align with emerging work realities.

HR leaders play a critical role in enabling this transition by creating conditions that support safe experimentation. One effective approach is the use of sandbox environments, where employees can test new human-AI workflows in low-risk settings without fear of negative performance consequences. Research suggests that psychologically safe spaces are essential for learning and adaptation in uncertain environments (Edmondson, 1999). Through these mechanisms, reconfiguration becomes a process of capability renewal rather than disruption.

Importantly, the SPR loop should not be treated as a one-off intervention or project. Instead, it functions as a recurring leadership practice embedded in everyday decision-making. To shift from a traditional reporting function towards a cross-functional analytics capability, HR leaders can follow a structured implementation roadmap.

- **Audit data assets:** Map existing systems, such as HRIS and learning platforms, to identify data that is accurate, reliable, and decision-relevant.
- **Assemble cross-functional teams:** Bring together HR professionals, data specialists, and line managers so that analytical insights are interpreted within the operational context.
- **Run focused pilots:** Test targeted use cases, such as attrition prediction or workload forecasting, and evaluate return on investment over a defined period.
- **Link to strategic KPIs:** Connect analytical outputs to outcomes such as productivity, safety, or innovation to demonstrate organisational value.

- **Institutionalise learning loops:** Review outcomes after each cycle and refine models and practices to support continuous organisational learning (Teece et al., 1998).

By repeatedly applying this loop, HR leaders move beyond reactive reporting and establish a dynamic capability that supports employee resilience and workforce agility in AI-enabled environments.

6. MOVING BEYOND PATH DEPENDENCY

Individual unlearning is the intentional, active process by which employees let go of obsolete beliefs, habits, and routines to remain responsive to evolving technological demands. In the context of agentic AI, unlearning is not a passive erosion of knowledge but a deliberate act of reflection and detachment from outdated cognitive schemas (Tsang & Zahra, 2008). Over time, employees develop deeply embedded human skills and technical routines that may become misaligned with AI-enabled ways of working. For example, a recruiter may need to unlearn reliance on intuitive, gut-based judgments, which are often shaped by unconscious bias, and instead learn to collaborate with an AI-driven applicant-tracking system that offers data-informed shortlisting and pattern recognition.

Drawing on social cognitive theory, agentic AI can be understood as an environmental stimulus that reshapes the task landscape and prompts behavioural adjustment (Bandura, 1986). When AI substantially alters how tasks are performed, for example, by automating a large share of the talent acquisition process, employees may experience a mismatch between their existing cognitive schemas and the new task requirements. This mismatch generates cognitive conflict, a necessary precursor to unlearning. By disengaging from routines that no longer add value, employees free up cognitive resources to focus on higher-value judgment, problem-solving, and creative work. In this sense, unlearning supports strategic agility, defined not only by speed but also by the capacity to anticipate emerging conditions early and make more effective decisions under uncertainty (Teece et al., 1998).

The success of unlearning in AI-integrated workplaces is strongly shaped by leadership's social cues. Social cognitive theory emphasises that individuals learn not only through direct experience but also by observing how influential others interpret and respond to change. Within organisations, HR leaders function as primary signalers. When leaders demonstrate openness to AI and frame it as a tool to enhance work quality and well-being, they reinforce perceptions of psychological safety and legitimacy. Such positive signalling strengthens the relationship between AI use and individual unlearning. In contrast, when leaders convey fear or scepticism towards AI, employees are more likely to resist change and cling to familiar routines that feel safe but are increasingly misaligned with evolving work demands.

6.1. From Cognitive Agility to Ethical Agility

The final stage of knowledge renewal involves developing ethical agility. As agentic AI increasingly assumes responsibility for rule-based, repeatable routines, human workers must pivot toward human-in-the-loop oversight, as discussed in Section 4. This shift requires a more advanced form of AI literacy that goes beyond basic technical awareness to include the ability to understand, interpret, and critically question AI-driven decisions. Ethical agility, therefore, reflects a movement away from treating AI as a black box towards an orientation grounded in algorithmic transparency and accountability. For HR leaders, this means approaching data and AI literacy as a daily leadership practice rather than a one-off technical capability (Raisch & Krakowski, 2021). As employees unlearn outdated routines, they must simultaneously develop ethical competencies in bias mitigation, fairness, and data privacy to govern autonomous systems responsibly (Raghavan et al., 2020).

The transition to agentic AI ultimately depends on socio-technical alignment, where technological systems and human social structures evolve together rather than in isolation. In this context, HR leaders move beyond administrative roles to become architects of workforce resilience. By implementing the Sense-Predict-Reconfigure framework, leaders are better positioned to detect when existing knowledge becomes a constraint, anticipate the capabilities required for effective human-AI collaboration, and reconfigure organisational norms to support continuous unlearning and renewal (Teece et al., 1998).

Building both cognitive and ethical agility ensures that digital transformation enhances rather than diminishes the human experience of work. When supported by intentional leadership and ethical governance, agentic AI enables employees not only to adapt to technological change but also to thrive alongside intelligent systems in a sustainable and humane manner.

7. IMPLICATIONS FOR PRACTICE AND STRATEGY

The integration of agentic AI into the workforce represents more than a technical upgrade. It constitutes a fundamental shift that requires rethinking HR strategy and leadership responsibilities. The implications outlined below highlight the critical levers that HR leaders and senior executives must engage to ensure that advances in AI translate into sustained workforce resilience and enhanced employee digital well-being.

A central implication of the agentic AI era is the transition from descriptive to predictive people analytics. Traditional HR approaches have focused on analysing past events rather than anticipating future workforce risks. HR leaders are now required to implement early-warning systems, such as the Sense Predict Reconfigure framework, that enable the detection of emerging issues, including burnout, declining engagement, or skills shortages, before they escalate into systemic problems. In this context, data literacy becomes a core leadership capability rather than a technical add-on, enabling leaders to translate workforce data into a coherent human narrative that links performance outcomes with energy, trust, and well-being (Margherita & Bua, 2021). At the same time, HR's responsibilities are expanding beyond managing employees to orchestrating hybrid workforces in which autonomous agents and human staff collaborate. This shift demands new capabilities in coordination and sense-making through cross-functional people insight squads that bring together HR professionals, data specialists, and line managers.

Sustained agility in AI-integrated environments also requires moving beyond conventional upskilling toward knowledge renewal. This places individual unlearning at the centre of workforce development, defined as the intentional letting go of mental models and routines that no longer align with evolving work systems (Tsang & Zahra, 2008). HR leaders play a critical role in fostering psychological safety, enabling employees to experiment, adapt, and occasionally fail without fear of negative consequences. Practical interventions include conducting blameless after-action reviews following AI-related errors and creating sandbox environments that support low-risk experimentation with new tools and workflows (Edmondson, 1999).

As AI systems assume greater autonomy, HR leaders must also act as gatekeepers of ethical governance. This involves actively managing the trust deficit associated with opaque algorithmic decision-making by ensuring that AI systems are reliable, credible, and transparent. Human-in-the-loop oversight remains essential, particularly in sensitive domains such as recruitment, performance evaluation, and employee development. Ethical governance must therefore incorporate regular bias testing, explainability mechanisms, and robust data privacy safeguards to protect employee dignity and sustain organisational legitimacy (Raghavan et al., 2020). Through these combined strategic actions, HR leaders can ensure that agentic AI strengthens rather than undermines the human foundations of work.

8. CONCLUSION

The emergence of agentic AI represents a significant paradigm shift, offering substantial opportunities for organisational efficiency while challenging the foundational pillars of employee well-being. As demonstrated throughout this chapter, the transition from automation to augmentation marks a critical turning point in which humans and intelligent systems jointly shape decisions. This shift requires a socio-technical approach to workforce management that recognises digital well-being as a dynamic interaction between people, tasks and systems rather than a fixed individual outcome. In the twenty-first-century workplace, understanding how technology reshapes autonomy, identity, and meaning is central to sustaining human flourishing.

The implications of agentic AI for HR leadership go beyond adopting new technologies to fundamentally redefine leadership responsibilities within organisations. As intelligent systems increasingly take part in decision-making processes, HR leaders must shift from managing administrative tasks to overseeing complex socio-technical ecosystems that combine human and algorithmic capabilities. This transition demands new leadership skills that blend technological literacy with ethical judgment and organisational design expertise. Research on digital transformation shows that leadership effectiveness in technology-driven environments relies on the ability to coordinate diverse expertise and translate technological insights into organisational practices that build trust and engagement (Westerman, Bonnet, & McAfee, 2014). In this way, HR leaders become architects of organisational resilience, accountable for ensuring that AI systems support rather than undermine the human experience of work. By integrating ethical governance, continuous learning, and workforce agility into organisational structures, HR leadership can turn AI from a source of disruption into a catalyst for sustainable organisational growth.

Workforce resilience in digitally mediated environments depends on the ability to detect emerging challenges early and make informed decisions amid uncertainty. The Sense-Predict-Reconfigure framework provides a practical operational mechanism for HR leaders to translate AI-driven foresight into adaptive workforce strategies. However, such agility is sustainable only when anchored in technological trust, shaped by reliability, credibility and technical competence, and supported by leadership climates that legitimise individual unlearning and experimentation (Bandura, 1986; Teece et al., 1998). As agentic AI alters established routines and redistributes cognitive labour, HR leadership must move beyond managing processes towards orchestrating capabilities and ethical boundaries.

The future of HR leadership lies in balancing analytical confidence with human curiosity. Acting as gatekeepers of ethical governance, HR leaders are uniquely positioned to ensure that AI systems remain transparent, accountable and aligned with human values. When guided by a socio-technical logic, agentic AI can be used not only to improve organisational performance but also to deepen trust, renew capabilities and enhance the quality of work. Ultimately, success in the AI era will belong to organisations that use intelligent systems to listen, learn and respond more thoughtfully, ensuring that technology serves the human experience rather than reshaping it at the expense of dignity and well-being.

REFERENCES

Akbar, M. A., Varias, V., Risa, T. D., Bhirawa, M. A., & Nugraha, R. (2025). Workplace stress in the era of digital transformation: A psychological approach to employee well-being. *RIGGS: Journal of Artificial Intelligence and Digital Business*, *4*(3), 3496–3506. DOI: 10.31004/riggs.v4i3.2493

Amabile, T. M., & Pratt, M. G. (2016). The dynamic componential model of creativity and innovation in organizations: Making progress, making meaning. *Research in Organizational Behavior*, *36*, 157–183. DOI: 10.1016/j.riob.2016.10.001

Bandura, A. (1986). *Social Foundations of Thought and Action: A Social Cognitive Theory*. Prentice-Hall.

Barney, J. (1991). Firm resources and sustained competitive advantage. *Journal of Management*, *17*(1), 99–120. DOI: 10.1177/014920639101700108

Becker, B. E., & Huselid, M. A. (2006). Strategic human resources management: Where do we go from here? *Journal of Management*, *32*(6), 898–925. DOI: 10.1177/0149206306293668

Bondarouk, T., & Ruël, H. (2009). Electronic human resource management: Challenges in the digital era. *International Journal of Human Resource Management*, *20*(3), 505–514. DOI: 10.1080/09585190802707235

Brynjolfsson, E., & McAfee, A. (2014). *The second machine age: Work, progress, and prosperity in a time of brilliant technologies*. W. W. Norton & Company.

Calvo, R. A., & Peters, D. (2014). *Positive computing: Technology for wellbeing and human potential*. MIT Press. DOI: 10.7551/mitpress/9764.001.0001

Culnan, M. J., & Armstrong, P. K. (1999). Information privacy concerns, procedural fairness, and impersonal trust: An empirical investigation. *Organization Science*, *10*(1), 104–115. DOI: 10.1287/orsc.10.1.104

Davenport, T., Guha, A., Grewal, D., & Bressgott, T. (2020). How artificial intelligence will change the future of marketing. *Journal of the Academy of Marketing Science*, *48*(1), 24–42. DOI: 10.1007/s11747-019-00696-0

Deci, E. L., & Ryan, R. M. (2000). The "what" and "why" of goal pursuits: Human needs and the self-determination of behavior. *Psychological Inquiry*, *11*(4), 227–268. DOI: 10.1207/S15327965PLI1104_01

Edmondson, A. (1999). Psychological safety and learning behavior in work teams. *Administrative Science Quarterly*, *44*(2), 350–383. DOI: 10.2307/2666999

Faraj, S., Pachidi, S., & Sayegh, K. (2018). Working and organizing in the age of the learning algorithm. *Information and Organization*, *28*(1), 62–70. DOI: 10.1016/j.infoandorg.2018.02.005

Fiol, C. M., & O'Connor, E. J. (2017). Unlearning established organizational routines. *Organization Studies*, *38*(5), 733–758. DOI: 10.1177/0170840616689369

Floridi, L., Cowls, J., Beltrametti, M., Chatila, R., Chazerand, P., Dignum, V., Luetge, C., Madelin, R., Pagallo, U., Rossi, F., Schafer, B., Valcke, P., & Vayena, E. (2018). AI4People—An ethical framework for a good AI society: Opportunities, risks, principles, and recommendations. *Minds and Machines*, *28*(4), 689–707. DOI: 10.1007/s11023-018-9482-5 PMID: 30930541

Gunning, D., Stefik, M., Choi, J., Miller, T., Stumpf, S., & Yang, G. Z. (2019). XAI—Explainable artificial intelligence. *Science Robotics*, *4*(37), eaay7120. Advance online publication. DOI: 10.1126/scirobotics.aay7120 PMID: 33137719

Hall, K. M. (2024). *Shaping Digital Well-being: Developing a Well-being Lens on the Socio-technical Systems Perspective in Information Systems Research* (Cumulative Doctoral Dissertation). University of Bayreuth, Germany.

Hausknecht, J. P., Rodda, J., & Howard, M. J. (2009). Targeted employee retention: Performance based and job related differences in reported reasons for staying. *Human Resource Management*, *48*(2), 269–288. DOI: 10.1002/hrm.20279

Helliwell, J. F., Layard, R., Sachs, J., De Neve, J. E., Aknin, L. B., & Wang, S. (2024). World happiness report: Origins, purpose, contents, impact and future. In *Encyclopedia of happiness, quality of life and subjective wellbeing* (p. 296). Edward Elgar Publishing. DOI: 10.4337/9781800889675.00048

Hmoud, B. (2021). Trust in artificial intelligence systems: A conceptual framework. *Journal of Enterprise Information Management*, *34*(5), 1452–1471. DOI: 10.1108/JEIM-03-2020-0092

Hmoud, B. I. F., & Várallyai, L. (2019). Will artificial intelligence take over human resources recruitment and selection? *Network Intelligence Studies*, *7*(13), 21–30.

Hurst, A. (2021). Developing future-ready skills with peer coaching. In MacDonald, A. (Ed.), *The Future of Workplace Learning* (pp. 5–7). MIT Sloan Management Review.

Jarrahi, M. H. (2018). Artificial intelligence and the future of work: Human–AI symbiosis in organizational decision making. *Business Horizons*, *61*(4), 577–586. DOI: 10.1016/j.bushor.2018.03.007

Karami, M. (2025). AI driven HR analytics for workforce resilience and agility: A strategic framework for the digital era. *Strategic HR Review*. Advance online publication. DOI: 10.1108/SHR-11-2025-0119

Kranzberg, M. (1986). Technology and history: "Kranzberg's laws". *Technology and Culture*, *27*(3), 544–560. DOI: 10.2307/3105385

Majumder, S., Salman, S., & Dey, N. (2026). AI in human resources: Efficiency, ethics, and emerging challenges. *AI and Ethics*, *6*(59), 59. Advance online publication. DOI: 10.1007/s43681-025-00862-x

Margherita, A., & Bua, I. (2021). The role of human resource analytics in organizational resilience. *Journal of Business Research*, *131*, 573–586. DOI: 10.1016/j.jbusres.2021.03.033

Meijerink, J., Bondarouk, T., & Lepak, D. P. (2021). Organizational boundaries and HRM in the digital age. *Human Resource Management Review*, *31*(1), 100775. DOI: 10.1016/j.hrmr.2020.100775

Miller, T. (2019). Explanation in artificial intelligence: Insights from the social sciences. *Artificial Intelligence*, *267*, 1–38. DOI: 10.1016/j.artint.2018.07.007

Orlikowski, W. J. (2007). Sociomaterial practices: Exploring technology at work. *Organization Studies*, *28*(9), 1435–1448. DOI: 10.1177/0170840607081138

Parker, S. K., & Grote, G. (2022). Automation, algorithms, and beyond: Why work design matters more than ever in a digital world. *Applied Psychology = Psychologie Appliquée*, *71*(4), 1171–1204. DOI: 10.1111/apps.12241

Raghavan, M., Barocas, S., Kleinberg, J., & Levy, K. (2020). Mitigating bias in algorithmic hiring: Evaluating claims and practices. *Proceedings of the ACM Conference on Fairness, Accountability, and Transparency*, 469–481. https://doi.org/ DOI: 10.1145/3351095.3372828

Ragu-Nathan, T. S., Tarafdar, M., Ragu-Nathan, B. S., & Tu, Q. (2008). The consequences of technostress for end users in organizations. *Information Systems Research*, *19*(4), 417–433. DOI: 10.1287/isre.1070.0165

Raisch, S., & Krakowski, S. (2021). Artificial intelligence and management: The automation–augmentation paradox. *Academy of Management Review*, *46*(1), 192–210. DOI: 10.5465/amr.2018.0072

Tarafdar, M., Cooper, C. L., & Stich, J. F. (2017). The technostress trifecta: Techno eustress, techno distress, and design. *Information Systems Journal*, *29*(1), 6–42. DOI: 10.1111/isj.12169

Teece, D. J., Pisano, G., & Shuen, A. (1998). Dynamic capabilities and strategic management. *Strategic Management Journal, 18*(7), 509–533. DOI: 10.1002/(SICI)1097-0266(199708)18:7<509::AID-SMJ882>3.0.CO;2-Z

Tsang, E. W. K., & Zahra, S. A. (2008). Organizational unlearning. *Human Relations; Studies Towards the Integration of the Social Sciences, 61*(10), 1435–1462. DOI: 10.1177/0018726708095710

Upadhyay, A. K., & Khandelwal, K. (2018). Applying artificial intelligence: Implications for recruitment. *Strategic HR Review, 17*(5), 255–258. DOI: 10.1108/SHR-07-2018-0051

Venkatesh, V., Thong, J. Y. L., Chan, F. K. Y., Hu, P. J. H., & Brown, S. A. (2022). Extending the digital well being concept: A research agenda. *Management Information Systems Quarterly, 46*(1), 1–24. DOI: 10.25300/MISQ/2022/16320

Westerman, G., Bonnet, D., & McAfee, A. (2014). The nine elements of digital transformation. *MIT Sloan Management Review, 55*(3), 1–6.

Yin, J., & Hoang, K. D. (2025). AI-enabled knowledge renewal: The role of leaders' AI attitudes and unlearning in enhancing employees' creative performance. *Journal of Knowledge Management*. Advance online publication. DOI: 10.1108/JKM-02-2025-0209

Chapter 11
Digital Taylorism and AI Impact on Psychological Well-Being and Innovation in HR Within the Energy and Marine Industries

Navya Puttaraju
http://orcid.org/0009-0000-9174-8150
Middlesex University, Dubai, UAE

ABSTRACT

The Fourth Industrial Revolution is transforming HRM through advanced technologies, especially Artificial Intelligence (AI). AI's integration with Big Data, IoT, and robotics is reshaping work dynamics and daily life. This qualitative study in a leading marine and energy company examines AI's impact on HR, focusing on psychological well-being and innovation. Rather than just technical advances, it highlights how AI changes employees' emotions and behaviour. Findings stress to avoid a "one-size-fits-all" approach and adopting best-fit solutions that respect cultural nuances for sustainable organisational success. Automation allows HR to focus on strategic, creative tasks, boosting job satisfaction. Successful AI adoption depends on continuous leadership support and aligning AI capabilities with employee expectations to avoid cognitive dissonance. Maintaining a balance between technology and the human element is vital for a fair, inclusive, and innovative

DOI: 10.4018/979-8-3373-6650-0.ch011

workplace. Ultimately, continuous learning, ethical approach ensures to reduce bias, find purpose and drive innovation in an AI environment. After all, there is no algorithm for being human.

1. INTRODUCTION

Artificial Intelligence (AI) is reshaping organisations worldwide, revolutionising business operations and carving out a new competitive landscape. While not a novel concept, AI has become the linchpin of Industry 4.0, transforming business models, streamlining processes, and driving innovation. Technologies such as Machine Learning (ML), the Internet of Things (IoT), automation, and Generative AI (Gen AI) are now critical for boosting operational performance and enabling real-time decision-making. Within Human Resource Management (HRM), the adoption of AI demands a reimagined approach to managing human capital alongside intelligent systems. AI's ability to handle tasks like speech recognition, personalised recommendations, and big data processing is unlocking unprecedented organisational efficiency and fostering a data-driven work environment (Ransbotham et al., 2020).

However, this digital transformation also brings profound challenges. According to the World Economic Fund (WEF), by 2024, AI will impact 40% of global jobs, disrupting traditional roles and requiring employees to adapt rapidly. (WEF, 2023). The analysis indicates that about 23% of jobs globally are expected to change within the next five years, with 69 million new roles anticipated and 83 million existing positions being eliminated. This results in a net decrease of 14 million jobs, reflecting workforce changes associated with AI (PwC, 2024). Recent studies suggest that AI acts as a catalyst for enhancing organisational capabilities by reshaping infrastructure. It involves influencing organisational culture, promoting innovation, and guiding investment decisions. By fostering data-driven decision-making, encouraging collaboration, and optimizing resource allocation, AI transforms how organisations operate (Vrontis et al., 2021). AI helps organisations become more agile and competitive, ensuring their infrastructure is robust and future-proof. AI refers to a wide range of technologies and techniques, with ML being one of them. The study examines AI's broader context to capture its wide-ranging organisational functions. Organisation under study has deployed in-house tools such as GPT powered chatbot, Microsoft Copilot in Edge, and M365. Thus, AI provides a comprehensive framework for understanding its full potential in transforming business processes and its impact on employees (Internal communication, 2024).

Digital Taylorism uses technology to standardise and automate workflows, improving market value, agility, and resource use, helping firms adapt to changing demands (Mikalef & Pateli, 2017). AI automates repetitive tasks and mimics human reasoning and decision-making (Zhou et al., 2019). As AI transforms workplaces, businesses see the need to enhance HRM to stay competitive. Although AI's technical benefits are clear, its effects on employees, particularly regarding psychological well-being (PWB) and innovative work behaviour (IWB), are less understood in real world contexts. This study addresses this gap by exploring how AI-driven automation, ML, and Gen AI environments affect HR professionals' emotional and cognitive responses, with a focus on PWB and innovation.

A Finnish multinational in the marine and energy sectors, with 18,000 employees in 79 countries, piloted AI to enhance efficiency, productivity, and innovation. Across its operations and HRM, AI automates tasks, powers chatbots, applies Gen AI, and aids talent acquisition and personalised employee development, streamlining HR processes and enabling strategic growth. (Corporate website, 2024). However, this digital transformation also presents challenges for HR professionals, affecting their psychological well-being (PWB) and innovative work behaviour (IWB) as they adapt to new technologies and manage evolving roles. This study aims to address these issues and outlines the following research objectives:

- Investigate the impact of AI on HR professionals' PWB within the organisation under study.
- Understanding the Relationship Between AI and Employee Innovative Behaviour
- Assessing HR professionals' Perceptions and Attitudes Towards AI Integration.
- Examining Spill-over Effects of AI Integration.

2. BACKGROUND

2.1. Concept of Taylorism

The concept of "normal science" in management, as described by Kuhn (1970), refers to the dominance of established theories that shape research directions. Progress in management studies requires moving beyond these paradigms to develop new theories and observations. Kieser (1994) highlights the importance of a historical perspective, enabling scholars to critically evaluate and reinterpret existing theories. This historical lens is crucial for innovation, as past decisions continue to shape today's economic, political, and technological landscapes (Iaia et al., 2024; Muldoon et al., 2022). Taylorism, developed during the Fordist era, aimed to boost labour productivity through control, standardisation, and streamlined processes to secure market advantage (Liu, 2023). While Frederick Taylor's scientific management initially targeted manual labour, its principles such as task formalisation, centralised planning, work standardisation, employee selection and training, supervision, and performance-based rewards. These, now influence modern quality systems and collaboration (Gundhus et al., 2022). Taylor promoted performance incentives and knowledge-driven strategies to benefit both profits and worker well-being, though employers often emphasised wage cuts instead (Sementelli, 2019). Taylor's focus on epistemology and methodological rigour still shapes contemporary management science (Birnbaum & Somers, 2023). But his approach is criticised for dehumanising workers and masking the practical, algorithmic techniques of scientific management with philosophical and managerial concerns (Neto, 2022).

The move from Taylorism to Digital Taylorism shows how traditional management has adapted to digital tools, using automation and AI to increase efficiency, especially in the gig economy (Altenried, 2020). Platforms like Amazon Mechanical Turk and Uber use algorithms to allocate tasks and monitor performance, but this can lower job satisfaction, stifle creativity, and reduce worker autonomy (Baumgarten & Bourgadel, 2024), raising ethical concerns about exploitation and control (Kim & Beehr, 2022). Industries such as Amazon, Zara, and H&M use algorithms and ML to monitor production and adjust workflows in real time, refining Taylorism's efficiency-focused management with digital precision (López et al., 2022). Machines assign tasks, monitor productivity in real-time, and adjust the pace of work, replicating Taylorism's efficiency-driven management with greater precision. Despite criticisms, Taylorism has created a milestone in management science and remains relevant in the era of digitalization *à la Schumpeter* (Günsel & Yamen, 2020).

2.2. AI and the Fourth Industrial Revolution

McCarthy et al. (1955) defined AI as the creation of machines that can simulate any aspect of human intelligence including learning, problem solving and concept formation, effectively enabling machines to perform tasks that would require intelligence, if done by humans. Although AI's origins date back to the mid-20th century, its adoption has accelerated in recent years, driving what is known as the Fourth Industrial Revolution or Algorithmic Age. This era is characterised by rapid development and deployment of technologies such as machine learning (ML), natural language processing (NLP), visual recognition (VR), decision support systems (DSS), and generative AI (Gen AI) (Bankins et al., 2024).

Recent advances in ML, supported by improved computational power, expanded data collection, and enhanced algorithms, underpin AI's growing accuracy and capability (Kufel et al., 2023). Organisations now use AI for tasks that once required human intelligence, including candidate selection and logistics management, blockchain-enabled smart contracts for secure payments, AI-powered bots and autonomous vehicles for delivering goods and robots capable of interpreting emotions and providing support in various settings (Makarius et al., 2020).

Generative AI enables machines to replicate human intelligence while independently generating new ideas and solutions (Carayannis et al. 2024). These revolutionises how businesses function, influencing the workforce, operational methods, employee interaction, and overall workflows. A comparable shift occurred with the advent of the Internet and the World Wide Web, which gave rise to new business models and consumer-focused concepts like e-commerce, the sharing economy, and gig work (Malik et al., 2021). These transformations present new opportunities for organisations to refine their strategic goals in dynamic markets by enhancing service quality, operational performance, customer satisfaction, and return on investment (Budhwar et al., 2022). In a 2024 case study from HR Magazine, a company successfully trained its workforce in generative AI by promoting a "fail fast, learn fast" approach. Employees were encouraged to experiment with AI tools, make quick mistakes, and apply the lessons learned rapidly. This strategy fostered a culture of innovation and adaptability, enabling the workforce to integrate Gen AI into their daily tasks efficiently and creatively. The case demonstrates how embracing experimentation accelerates skill development and the adoption of new technologies in the workplace (HR Magazine, 2024 pp. 36). AI-driven digital transformation is rapidly reshaping industries by streamlining operations, developing skills, and enhancing competitiveness. AI aligns data collection with decision-making, delivering organisational and financial benefits. Its adoption is restructuring workforce roles and automating tasks, particularly within HRM, where AI leverages workforce data to make business models more sustainable (Votto et al., 2021; Hemalatha et al., 2021). AI is poised to reshape business, with 34% of CEOs identifying it as the leading change driver. Its adoption automates tasks, enabling employees to focus on higher-value activities, and could boost global GDP by 7% in the next decade (Gartner, 2024). AI also enhances strategy and decision-making through advanced analytics and improved forecasting (Makridakis, 2017).

2.3. Ethical AI: Bridging Theory and Practice

AI adoption introduces a range of ethical and social challenges, including concerns over data privacy, security, and inequality. To address these issues, organisations must ensure the responsible use of AI and maintain stakeholder trust by embedding ethical practices into their strategic frameworks. Such an approach helps mitigate risks, enhances organisational reputation, and supports sustainable growth. Although there has been considerable debate regarding biases in AI, there remains a paucity of empirical research examining how organisations are actively confronting these ethical dilemmas in real-world HR settings (Bar-Gil et al., 2024). The existing literature suggests that, while AI is reshaping HRM practices, comprehensive studies investigating its impact on psychological well-being (PWB) and innovative work behaviour (IWB) are limited. Much of the research overlooks the influence of AI on employees' capacity to generate and implement new ideas, as well as its effects on overall mental health and job satisfaction. The application of AI in HRM is still in its formative stages, with most studies focusing on technical aspects rather than exploring these outcomes within authentic organisational contexts.

Digital Taylorism is pivotal in transforming value creation within HRM processes. The integration of digital technologies, particularly AI, is rapidly revolutionising HRM at the organisational level, driving significant changes in the way human resources are managed and optimised. Despite advancements like chatbots, automation, and predictive analytics, there is a significant research gap concerning AI's impact on employees' PWB and IWB.

Figure 1. Five-Year Analysis of Literature Review

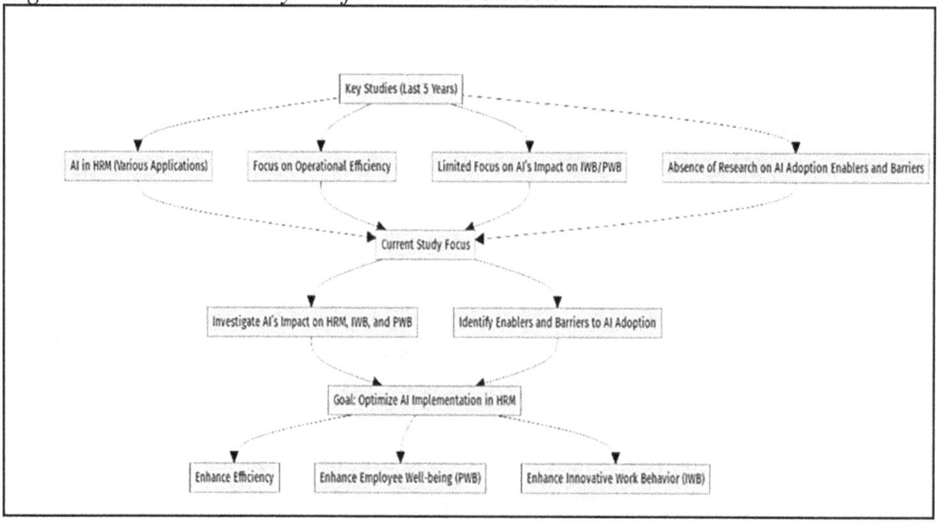

Figure 1 summarises recent critical studies in AI-HRM, noting a lack of research on drivers and barriers to AI adoption as well as its effects on PWB and IWB. This study addresses these gaps by examining how AI influences HR professionals' PWB and IWB, and by identifying factors that ease or impede AI adoption. The aim is to offer insights for optimising AI implementation in HRM to achieve operational efficiency while supporting innovation and employee PWB. AI enables HRM to shift from a reactive to a proactive, goal-aligned strategy by offering benefits like predictive intelligence (Paschen et al., 2020), better workforce planning, enhanced employee experience, increased job satisfaction, and improved customer service

(Bughin et al., 2018). By using AI to do routine tasks and focus on strategic initiatives could increase the world's total income by 7% in ten years and help balance the loss of working-age people in Europe, which is expected to drop by 14.8 million, or 6%, by 2030(Microsoft, 2024). Building collaborative strategies between humans and machines is essential for sustainable change. Cognitive automation and robotic process automation (RPA) streamline processes but introduce challenges such as shifting job roles, skill gaps, and concerns over job security. Employees may find it difficult to give up cognitive tasks to RPA, potentially feeling less autonomous and empowered (Pachidi et al., 2020). A 2024 Gartner survey found that 38% of HR leaders are deploying Gen AI, with main applications in HR service delivery via chatbots, automating administrative tasks, and recruitment (Gartner, 2024).

2.4. PWB in AI integrated Workplace

PWB is a multifaceted concept emphasizing eudaimonic well-being, encompassing emotional aspects and self-characterized contentment, including both positive and negative emotions (Agarwal, 2021). Carol Ryff identified six critical dimensions of positive psychological functioning as shown in Figure 2 - self-acceptance, positive relationships, autonomy, personal growth, purpose in life, and environmental mastery (Dierendonck & Lam, 2022).

Figure 2. Carol Ryff Psychological Wellbeing Framework (Ryff,1989)

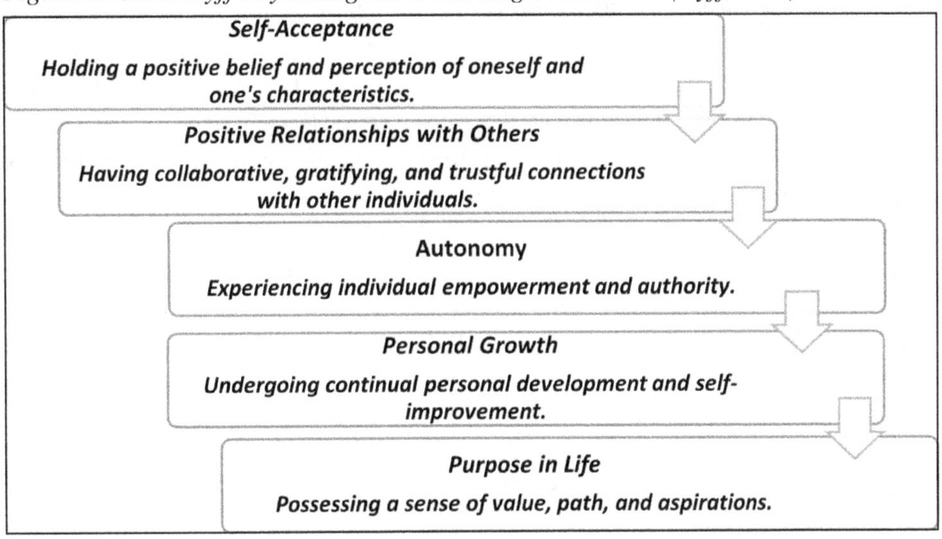

PWB is essential for organisations, serving as both a result and a precursor to creativity, productivity, collaboration, and enhanced social networks. AI's continual evolution and inherent ambiguity heighten job-related anxieties, as employees face new uncertainties about collaborating effectively with AI for career longevity. Increased awareness of AI's workforce impact can intensify job insecurity, while comparing their skills to AI may lower self-esteem and raise feelings of insecurity (Wu et al., 2022). Recent research highlights that technological advances impact mental well-being, underscoring the importance of addressing psychological factors. It underlines the need for targeted research to comprehend how AI affects PWB and offers strategies to mitigate potential downsides while enhancing employee fulfilment and a sense of purpose (Xu et al., 2023). Unlike earlier technologies that primarily assisted with tasks (Ayyagari et al., 2011), human-machine collaboration highlights the integral role of machine learning in the work process. Employees may feel pressured and incompetent when working alongside technology that can outperform them. This raises questions about how job insecurity from this collaboration influences employees' work and personal lives. Understanding these impacts is crucial for addressing psychological challenges in workplaces where Digital Taylorism is adopted. Automation and algorithms diminish motivation, threaten job continuity, and exacerbate cognition, autonomy, and PWB.

Park, Woo, and Kim (2024) suggest developing a scale to assess employees' attitudes towards AI in the workplace, addressing a gap in organisational psychology. Understanding these perceptions enables the Centre of Excellence (CoE) to implement targeted measures, reducing resistance and encouraging a positive view of AI as a supportive tool. The study also recommends policies to prevent negative effects such as job loss or stress, ensuring AI benefits employee well-being. AI interactions influence employees' social needs and behaviours. While humans need genuine social connections, AI cannot fully satisfy this, lacking the facial cues and personalised responses that human colleagues provide (Banerjee et al., 2018). This creates a gap between expected and experienced social affiliation at work, increasing employees' need for social interaction. One solution to this challenge is the anthropomorphization of AI attributing human-like qualities, can help by making AI seem more relatable, fostering solidarity and improving integration into employees' work identities. Employees are more likely to accept AI when they psychologically view it as part of their capabilities (Alabed et al., 2022).

Perceived AI threats can lead to emotional exhaustion, depression, and fears of job loss, causing withdrawal from learning and technology, lowering motivation, and widening skill gaps. The psychological strain from job insecurity can spill over into behaviour, leading to undesirable coping mechanisms and deteriorating job performance (Singh & Pandey, 2024). Organisations must provide support and strategies to mitigate these risks, such as training, transparent communication, and emphasizing AI's role in augmenting rather than replacing human roles (Pei et al., 2024). Mindfulness helps reduce anxiety and stress at work by encouraging employees to notice their thoughts and feelings without judgment. This approach supports emotional well-being and resilience, which is especially beneficial as organisations integrate AI into the workplace (Montani et al., 2021).

Rapid technological change is reshaping workplaces, requiring employees to develop specific digital skills. This has led to a rise in informal, experiential learning outside formal programs, which helps workers adapt to evolving demands (Tannenbaum & Wolfson, 2022). However, the constant evolution driven by AI can cause job insecurity and anxiety, lower self-efficacy and motivation, and reducing participation in informal learning, widening skill gaps. Organisational Learning Theories show that AI improves learning through automated analysis and real-time feedback but may also limit collaboration and critical thinking, if overused. Peter Senge's model suggests AI should enhance, not replace, human skills, helping creativity and adaptability (Kucharska & Bedford, 2020). Promoting collaborative learning reframes - AI as supportive rather than threatening, fosters innovation and engagement. Work-related anxiety can suppress motivation and hinder communication and creativity, impacting divergent thinking potentially impeding creative output at workplace (Koivisto & Grassini, 2024).

2.5. Innovation through Digital Leadership and TTF

Innovation is vital for organisations to stay competitive. It depends on employees' ability to engage in innovative work behaviour (IWB), which means generating new ideas, taking risks, and addressing uncertainties (Zeb et al., 2018). Employees must spot inefficiencies or trends and collaborate to brainstorm solutions through divergent thinking. Advocacy, feedback, and leadership support follow, requiring communication and persuasion to secure buy-in. Implementing ideas involves careful planning and resource allocation. However, technological anxiety can impede innovation, affecting both individual and organisational creativity (Afsar & Umrani, 2019). AI automates routine managerial tasks, enabling leaders to focus on strategic innovation. Digital leaders leveraging AI empower employees to think strategically while, human judgment, PWB and ethical considerations remain priorities (Quaquebeke & Gerpott, 2023).

Technology has transformed organisational innovation, with ML enhancing creative processes (Rehman et al., 2022). As AI complexity increases, employees may struggle to see their impact, risking disengagement. According to Task Technology Theory (TTF), the effectiveness of AI integration depends on how well the technology fits with the tasks employees perform. When there is a mismatch between AI's capabilities and the nature of the tasks, it can result in reduced IWB (Goswami et al., 2023). Difficulties in assessing AI-driven outcomes add ambiguity, complicating performance evaluations and distinguishing human from AI-driven innovations, which can increase confusion and reduce employee engagement. A Norwegian energy trading firm's heavy reliance on AI reduced B2B partner input, weakening relationships and stifling creativity, limiting adaptability and new product development (Papagiannidis et al., 2023). Ultimately, AI's effect on IWB is shaped by how organisations integrate and structure these technologies within their workflows.

AI's dual impact, as explained by TTF Theory, offers operational benefits but creates HR challenges, particularly in managing employees' psychological responses and maintaining human-centric services (Monod et al., 2024). The Microsoft Tay chatbot incident shows how AI can be influenced to display biased and harmful behaviour, emphasising the need for safeguards in sensitive areas like HR. Lack of transparency in AI-driven decisions can erode trust, but clear communication improves acceptance and engagement. Transparency and aligning AI with tasks are key to addressing psychological concerns. Satalia's use of AI in scheduling and onboarding highlights efficiency gains, allowing HR to focus on strategic initiatives. Ultimately, effective implementation and management determine whether AI advances or hinders organisational goals (Gyton & Jeffery, 2017).

2.6. AI Impact Influencing Cultures and Employee Experience

Culture shapes organisational behaviour and adaptation to technology. As AI transforms workplaces, a culture promoting innovation, collaboration, and flexibility is essential for successful integration and employee empowerment (El Maouch & Jin, 2024). Multinational enterprises are leveraging AI in HR to improve efficiency and personalisation. Tools like Microsoft Viva enhance employee experience by integrating communication, learning, and well-being, supporting engagement and productivity (Boulton, 2021). However, its "black-box" characteristics lead to a lack of transparency, causing anxiety and reducing trust in AI-driven HR initiatives. The HireVue case revealed risks around privacy and bias, prompting greater emphasis on responsible AI and fairness (Harwell, 2019).

Regional dynamics significantly shape AI adoption, as illustrated by Montreal, where collaboration among public institutions, private enterprises, and universities has created a supportive innovation ecosystem (Gherhes et al., 2022). Local strategies and agencies influence economic and employment outcomes, underscoring the importance of understanding regional complexities in AI integration. Comparative research in banking sector in Russia and Kazakhstan reveals differing employee perceptions. Kazakhstan employees express greater insecurity regarding AI, while Russian employees saw opportunities for upskilling and career advancement. Effective communication and development programmes in Russia facilitated successful AI integration, whereas resistance in Kazakhstan stemmed from job security concerns, highlighting the necessity of transparency and employee development to address adverse effects (Blagoev et al., 2022). Differences between advanced and developing economies highlight the need for context-specific AI strategies in HRM, as infrastructure, digital skills, and regulation shape both opportunities and risks (Hughes et al., 2019).

Cognitive Dissonance Theory explains that when employees' expectations clash with the reality of working with AI, stress and anxiety can arise. Perceived bias or lack of transparency in AI decisions erodes trust and well-being. Adaptive AI systems can balance Digital Taylorism's control with the need for employee well-being and innovation (Mousavi et al., 2022; Chang, 2023). Organisations must prioritise transparent communication to mitigate the adverse effects of AI. Although AI boosts task efficiency, poor task-technology alignment can increase managerial control, reduce autonomy, and elevate stress, undermining PWB and IWB. Shamsi et al. (2021) show how the Technology Acceptance Model (TAM) and Job Demands-Resources (JD-R) framework together explain employees' experiences with technology. Positive perceptions of the tool, like usefulness and ease of use, act as resources that boost engagement, motivation, and PWB. However, poor usability adds negative cognitive load and strain. Work engagement mediates these effects, making positive experiences with AI crucial for PWB and IWB. Laurent (2018) highlights that demystifying parables about AI such as its inevitability in replacing jobs or being inherently unbiased should be challenged to guide HR towards a more informed perspective. This review identifies three central research questions:

1. How does integrating AI in Digital Taylorism and algorithmic control influence employees' innovative behaviour?
2. How do task automation and Digital Taylorism affect employees' PWB?
3. How do the spillover effects of AI integration influence employees' innovative behaviour and PWB?

Although AI's impact on workplace behaviour and mental health is recognised, limited research addresses both PWB and IWB within the same organisational context. As Dodgson (2020) notes, formulating precise questions is essential for advancing knowledge and understanding the psychological complexities of AI in HRM.

3. METHODOLOGY

The study employs qualitative methods to interpret social experiences within natural settings, providing insight into how HR professionals navigate automation, ML, and Generative AI. Primary and secondary data were collected via individual semi-structured interviews and analysis of HR community communications, respectively, to explore participants' subjective perspectives (Denzin & Lincoln, 2018). This methodology enabled a flexible, in-depth examination and enhanced understanding of participants' views (Gehman et al., 2017). Ethical approval was granted by Middlesex Dubai's Research Ethics Committee, and written consent was secured from all participants prior to the commencement of interviews. Interview questions addressed various aspects of PWB, IWB and perceptions of automation and AI.

Participants were chosen for their expertise in automation and within AI-integrated settings. Discussions reflected their in-depth understanding. Epistemics, as outlined by Roulston (2017), underpins the analysis by examining how HR professionals perceive and adapt to technological change, focusing on both what they know (epistemic status) and how they engage with knowledge (epistemic stance). Analysing responses such as an "I do not know" answer offers insight into conversational dynamics and knowledge management (Heritage, 2018).

Data collection and analysis followed an iterative, adaptable process, allowing the research to remain responsive to emerging insights. This approach deepened understanding of technological changes affecting PWB and IWB, and how automation and AI are reshaping HR roles (Walliman, 2022). No other criteria, such as gender or family status, were considered. Participants were assigned codes ranging from P1 to P25.

- HR professionals from various functional areas.
- individuals at different hierarchical levels.
- participants from diverse countries and cultural backgrounds.
- new employees who joined the organisation in 2023
- employees with more than five years of tenure.
- Employees with less than one year of experience were not part of the study as they might not have fully grasped the organisational culture or the digital changes in HR processes. Theoretical sampling was used to select respondents best suited to contribute relevant insights as themes emerged, enhancing study quality and supporting clear conclusions (Charmaz and Thornberg, 2020).

Table 1. Participants Demographics by Education Level, Gender, and Continent

Continent	Education	Male	Female	Total
Asia	Bachelor	2	6	8
	Master	2	5	7
Africa	Bachelor	1	3	4

continued on following page

Table 1. Continued

Continent	Education	Male	Female	Total
	Master	0	3	3
Europe	Bachelor	2	2	4
	Master	0	2	2
South America	Master	0	1	1
Total		7	22	25

Table 1 lists 25 HR professionals from various teams involved in automation, AI related initiatives supporting implementation, reflected the expertise central to this research. Qualitative research does not emphasise sample size; instead, a diverse participant group was targeted to broaden perspectives. Data saturation was achieved, as no new themes emerged during the final interviews. Open-ended questions elicited participants' views and minimised interviewer bias, with the process recorded for transcription and analysis under informed consent. Transcripts were objectively analysed, setting aside prior assumptions. Open coding yielded seventy-five (75) interview codes, distilled into seven (7) overarching concepts, some using in vivo language, and further conceptualised. Axial coding subsequently organised these concepts into meaningful categories, linking subcategories, comparing data, and examining variations to construct a framework of conditions, actions, interactions, and consequences. Constant comparison refined codes for accuracy and relevance to research aims. Selective coding confirmed the strength of categories and emergent theory upon data saturation, demonstrating methodological effectiveness. The systematic application of grounded theory approaches, including bracketing (Epoche), reduced researcher bias and deepened analysis.

This process enabled a comprehensive understanding of relationships among PWB, IWB, and work-life balance, with iterative validation and enrichment. Memo writing facilitated the development and refinement of ideas throughout, while peer debriefing supported objectivity and rigour, following the principles set out by Gill (2014), Strauss and Corbin (2015), Davis et al. (2019), Charmaz (2017), and Belgrave and Seide (2019).

4. FINDINGS AND DISCUSSION

4.1."Automation Enhances HR Tasks and Fosters Cognitive Creativity"

A job constitutes an employee's overall position within an organisation, encompassing a variety of duties that collectively support organisational objectives. In contrast, a task is a specific, focused activity within a job and may differ in complexity. Tasks form the basic elements of a job, ranging from routine to complex activities (Hernaus et al., 2021).

Automation predominantly targets repetitive, administrative tasks, streamlining processes that require minimal creativity or cognitive effort. This shift, described as Digital Taylorism, transforms HRM by automating specific tasks rather than entire jobs. As a result, employees are released from routine work, enabling them to concentrate on strategic work and stakeholder engagement. P6, sounding relieved, explained, "Yeah, actually, earlier it was, uh, we are doing manual all things now. Lot of means for this process it is enhancing efficiency and reducing administrative burdens as I think like this and also means we understand engagement by understanding individual employees' needs and all….," expressing a sense of regained personal identity.

Analytical intelligence cognitively allows individuals to process information, solve problems, and adapt through reasoning and decision-making (Demetriou et al., 2021). Automation frees employees to focus on complex problem-solving, such as data-driven decision-making and logical reasoning. Algorithms mimic analytical intelligence by extracting insights from data, yet human input remains crucial due to machines lack of perception and creativity. P17, with cautious optimism, noted, "Because if we have automation for a lot of things, then we need to make sure that the data quality is actually high. So, because if the actions will be automated, they will pick information from somewhere and put it to the other place. And if we have mistakes in the 1st place, then the automation will pick up the wrong information, and if somebody is not monitoring that or having the data point to be at a high level, it can create a lot of issues." P11 emphasised strongly the need for human oversight in data analytics "it's so important to have someone behind the scenes analysing the data that's coming through."

While machines manage operational tasks, HR professionals must retain empathy to uphold people-focused goals. Empathetic intelligence involves understanding and responding to emotions (Marathe & Sen, 2021), fostering emotional connection and assertive communication. P25 took pride in meaningful contribution: "Ours is not something that we are working on machinery, we are working with humans and for humans, right." Empathetic intelligence strengthens self-awareness and relationships, with P25 affirming HR's ongoing relevance: "...we have a different and millions of characteristics of people working in the same organisation."

The research indicates that AI and automation have strengthened HR professionals' creative intelligence, improving collaboration and idea generation. Creative intelligence is the ability to solve problems innovatively and adapt to change (Holford, 2019). P7, displaying renewed energy, stated, "If the ideas come from other people, we will start doing these together. I will start sharing this in our AI innovators teams channel..." This open, collaborative approach values all contributions and promotes sustained innovation, as highlighted by the sentiment: "Be open about their proposals. Even if they don't make it to production... it is still on the roadmap for maybe next year or the year after."

4.2. Improved Organisational Citizenship Behavior (OCB)

The research highlights that OCB encompasses employees' voluntary actions that go beyond formal job requirements, such as supporting colleagues and showing initiative. These behaviours foster cooperation and reinforce organisational effectiveness (Kayaalp et al., 2021). Even with increased automation and virtual work, HR professionals continue to exhibit OCB through active engagement and commitment to organisational goals.

Employees willingly embrace change and address complex challenges without close supervision, reflecting a proactive stance. As P16 expressed positively, *"I feel if my work is impacting a business and my work is, you know, making a difference or adding value, then I get a sense of fulfillment,"* highlighting the emotional rewards of contributing beyond their role.

Leaders play a crucial role by encouraging idea-sharing and initiative-taking. P18 noted with a smile, "The manager is always very supportive in team meetings," underscoring the importance of managerial support in promoting OCB and digital transformation.

OCB is evident in employees' voluntary pursuit of learning and participation in new initiatives. P5 described, *"I know that for one thing, I would get the support from other colleagues with more expertise to help me make that happen,"* illustrating the cooperative spirit and peer support integral to OCB. Employees actively engage with new tools and processes, providing feedback and striving for collective improvement. P1 shared with joy "It really makes you proud... when your name is there," conveying the pride and ownership felt when contributing to organisational success. In summary, OCB persists in automated and virtual settings, with HR professionals displaying initiative, collaboration, and pride, all of which enhance organisational culture and effectiveness.

4.3. Automation enhances self-efficacy among employees.

The research shows that automation streamlines routine tasks and supports decision-making, making employees feel more capable and confident rather than threatened. As P8 noted with relief, "So now it is changing into automation. I feel that I'm saving a lot of time, and it is easy to handle all the requests because of this automation."

AI promotes innovative behaviour by enabling job autonomy, managing complexity, and aiding information processing. It also eases mental and physical fatigue, leading to a more positive outlook. P10 sighed *"We have a lot of changes as well, like on the technology side, but it's always a learning process. But afterwards, after you get used to it, I think that I'm very addicted to it."* AI frees employees from repetitive tasks, letting them concentrate on creative, strategic work. This blend of technology and human expertise supports a hybrid work environment. As P3 enthusiastically expressed, "I prefer to deal with the creative part and interact with managers daily to understand what we can do to change, how we can improve the recruitment process, and how we can maybe find better talents and everything." High-performance work practices (HPWP) foster autonomy and learning agility, easing concerns about AI. When implemented well, automation and AI increase efficiency, boost self-efficacy, and allow employees to concentrate on more strategic responsibilities.

4.4. Job Autonomy and Continuous Improvement

Job autonomy allows employees to uphold the quality and efficiency of automated systems through regular bot reviews and data quality checks. This sense of ownership increases job satisfaction and system effectiveness. As P15 hesitantly added, "We have to review the bot every twice in the year," and, "If you make sure that the data quality and data input is correct in the beginning... it's way easier because we now know the data is correct," highlighting the importance of proactive engagement in maintaining data reliability.

Accurate data inputs are essential for successful AI integration, underscoring the value of active employee involvement in data management. Collaboration with managers and teams fosters continuous improvement and competitive advantage. Employees contribute to process enhancement by sharing feedback and discussing innovations with their managers. P14 described how automation creates psychological space: "First I would take it with my line manager and then we would discuss it further in a team meeting."

Persistent system challenges and the ongoing need for manual oversight demonstrate the enduring significance of human involvement in technology integration. As P16 noted with a nervous laugh, "you know to make sure that we are not investing you know so much time in adding data and all of this. So I feel that success factor ....it has really you know good potential that we have not explored it." Overall, the findings indicate that job autonomy and ongoing improvement enable employees to embrace AI tools proactively, enhancing engagement, productivity, and organisational innovation.

4.5. Cultural Intricacies in Machine Learning Environments

The research emphasizes that local ethos and perspectives towards technology play a significant role in how organisations approach digital transformation using cultural dimensions developed by Geert Hofstede in 1980.

Figure 3. Cultural Dimensions Representation using Hofstede's Insights

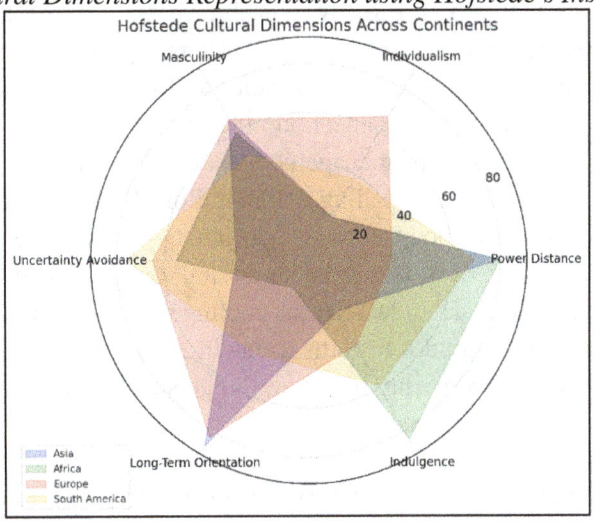

The radar chart (Figure 3) illustrates the influence of cultural factors using the Hofstede Insights (2020) website. In Asia, high power distance (80) and a solid long-term orientation (87) suggest a centralized, hierarchical decision-making structure where senior leadership likely drives AI adoption. AI is implemented utilitarianly, focusing on efficiency and productivity over personal benefits. In Europe, a lower power distance (35) and higher individualism (67) indicate a more decentralized, democratic approach to AI adoption, with teams exercising autonomy in its use. However, high uncertainty avoidance (65) implies that AI is adopted cautiously, with a strong focus on risk reduction and compliance with regulations. In Africa, the high-power distance (80) suggests a top-down leadership style in AI adoption, with lower uncertainty avoidance (55) reflecting a relatively relaxed approach to risk.

Low individualism (20) highlights the collective, group-oriented use of AI, while a high indulgence score (84) suggests a focus on improving employee satisfaction and well-being. In South America, high uncertainty avoidance (76) and mid-level power distance (69) suggest a cautious approach to AI, balancing efficiency with a focus on employee well-being. Moderate individualism (38) indicates a mix of operational and personal goals when integrating AI.

Cultural variations significantly influence the rate and effectiveness of technology adoption across regions. As P8 sceptically noted the persistence of global disparities "We are not all at the same level globally actually, and some countries are still far behind, and some countries are far ahead... and countries that are not as advanced in technology, their HR is still coming up, yeah, so." In less technologically advanced areas, traditional practices such as face-to-face interactions endure, resulting in resistance to digital transformation. P15 implied, "In a few countries, the culture is such that you go directly to each professional's desk, ask a specific question, and get your answer, and it is done." These ingrained behaviours and the value placed on personal contact pose obstacles to digitalisation, underscoring the enduring importance of human connection in HR roles.

Furthermore, knowledge mismanagement exacerbates these challenges by fostering information silos and impeding collaboration. P16, after a lengthy pause, reflected, "Whenever somebody's new, we definitely give knowledge transfer, and in case we're setting a process, or maybe it's an SOP that has to be followed, that is there. But whenever there are new features coming in…" Such practices highlight that, while culture and attitudes towards technology can either facilitate or hinder digital transformation, addressing both knowledge sharing and cultural resistance is fundamental to successful implementation.

4.6. Technological Disruption and Workforce Adaptation in HR

The integration of algorithms and automation is fundamentally transforming HR, resulting in a leaner and more efficient organisational structure. This shift is automating routine tasks such as data entry and rendering certain roles redundant, as highlighted by P18's anxious observation that *"A more leaner organisation when it comes to HR because they would have 60% most probably of the HR task being automated."*. While AI advances promise improved service delivery, the unrelenting pace of technological change poses considerable challenges. Employees struggle to keep up, with P10 expressing frustration: "A lot of things change in our company, and it's hard to catch up sometimes." P14's visible restlessness further underscores the emotional toll: "Why do we have more and more stretched working hours? Because that's what is expected, you know, to be immediately available…" The rapid adoption of new technologies has redefined job roles, intensified technological demands, and increasingly blurred the boundaries between professional and personal life. As a result, the rise of AI presents a double-edged sword enhancing operational efficiency while undermining employees' work-life balance.

4.7. Cognitive Overload and Performance Pressure in Digital HR Environments

Figure 4. Emerging Themes Related to Cognitive Overload

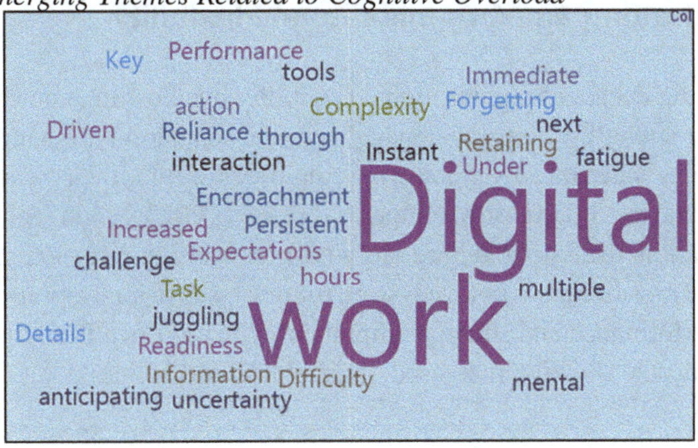

The shift towards automation and digital processes in HR has heightened cognitive overload and performance pressure, as reflected in participants responses and visually depicted in Figure 4. As P25 expressed frustration, "It's a pressure on me… the moment you go digital, the moment you go automation, the expectation of the people also increases," highlighting the emotional strain of heightened competitiveness. Participants described feeling compelled to act "instantly" even during personal time, underscoring the erosion of work-life separation and contributing to technostress. Additionally, employees struggle with increased memory load, as managing multiple complex tasks and tools simultaneously can result in confusion and errors. P23 rubbing forehead and lowered voice added, "There are too many things we are involved in, then retaining that in the memory sometimes becomes difficult, and then you start to mix up that," reflecting the challenge of processing large volumes of information. The pressure to remain competitive, adapt to new systems, and meet rising expectations compounds this cognitive burden. Balancing efficiency with human limitations remains a central challenge as organisations embrace greater automation, encapsulating the emergent theory of a Human–AI symbiotic relationship (Figure 6).

5. RECOMMENDATIONS AND CONCLUSIONS

In today's VUCA environment integrating AI into HRM to boost efficiency can directly or indirectly impact employees PWB and IWB. However, effective adoption demands a strategic intervention to balance technology and human needs. This section summarises the discussion and presents practical recommendations for implementing AI strategy.

5.1. Job Crafting and Organisational Flexibility

Job crafting enhances organisational flexibility by allowing employees to tailor roles to their strengths, boosting engagement and adaptability. It supports protean career concepts which means empowering employees to guide their own development which is crucial in AI-driven environments (Nie et al., 2023; Moon et al., 2024). This aids organisations to align strategic goals with employee aspirations engagement and motivation. Transitioning employees from routine tasks to innovation-focused roles improves performance and strategic alignment with evidence from the African air transport industry showing increased engagement and commitment (Theoharakis et al., 2024).

5.2. Task-Technology Fit and Change Management

Figure 5. Kurt Lewin Change Model (Lewin, 1939)

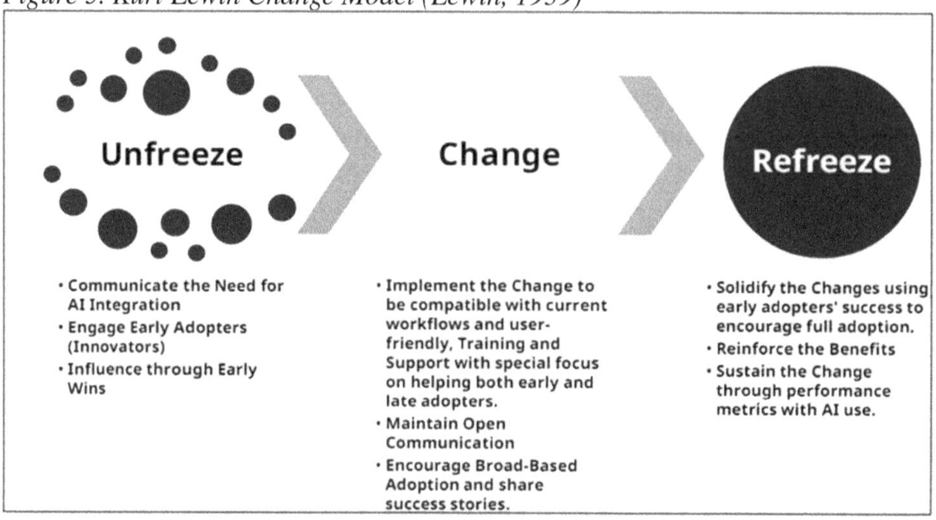

Effective AI integration demands aligning tools to job roles and robust change management. Figure 5 explains Lewin's Change Management model (1939) which provides framework - prepare for change (Unfreeze), support during transition (Change), and reinforce new practices (Refreeze), guiding technological and cultural shifts (Kucharska & Bedford, 2020) for sustainable changes and to make employees feel supported and engaged during the transition.

A "Knowledge Treasurer" within the HR function centralises automation and AI information, offers support facilitating adaptation for HR professionals, reducing cognitive overload and easing transitions with a blend of digital and human assistance.

5.3. Ethical Considerations and AI Governance

Ethical considerations are vital as AI becomes integral to HR. Decisions in recruitment and performance management must remain transparent and fair, with adherence to industry standards, GDPR, and local laws through robust AI governance, regular audits, and strong data privacy to build employee trust and mitigate risks. An ML operations governance structure, using fairness metrics, deploying transparency bias testing and human judgement in tandem ensures that AI enhances decision quality instead of amplifying bias or risk. This established AI as a reliable decision-support system rather than a source of silent bias. Human-in-the-loop validation is critical to check data and ensure they are not obsolete and relevant as per the current HR practices. Leaders should be trained to challenge outputs rather than accept them as deterministic. To monitor progress of the AI tool, it is imperative to set clear objectives with defined timelines and responsibilities, bridging accountability gaps and assessing outcomes before and after implementation.

5.4. Sustainable Practices

AI adoption depends on cross-functional collaboration, engaging varied stakeholders to enhance transparency, address ethical and data issues. This approach aligns AI initiatives with strategic objectives to mitigate resistance and maintain data integrity. Continuous skill development, tailored learning and attention to well-being strategies promote loyalty and adaptability. Both technical and interpersonal skills are vital in AI-driven environments. Evidence from Brazil indicates that focused training significantly increases commitment and proactive behaviour, resulting in better organisational performance (Vasconcelos Furtado et al., 2024).

5.5. Leadership in AI-Driven Work Environments

Leaders play a key role in guiding cultural change during AI adoption to ease transitions and reduce employee stress. AI tools, such as the Human Digital Twin (Gonzalez and Martin, 2024) apply emotional analytics to monitor well-being and prevent burnout, supporting work-life balance in line with Boundary Theory (Piszczek and Berg, 2014).

In designing AI-driven solutions for HR, it is crucial to consider regional cultural dimensions such as Power Distance and Individualism vary significantly across continents. Region specific led initiatives such as leadership training, mentorship and well-being strategies shapes how employees engage with technology rather than adopting one size fits all.

5.6. Emergent Theory: Human-Symbiotic Relationship with AI Framework

Figure 6. Emergent Theory- Human Symbiotic Relationship with AI

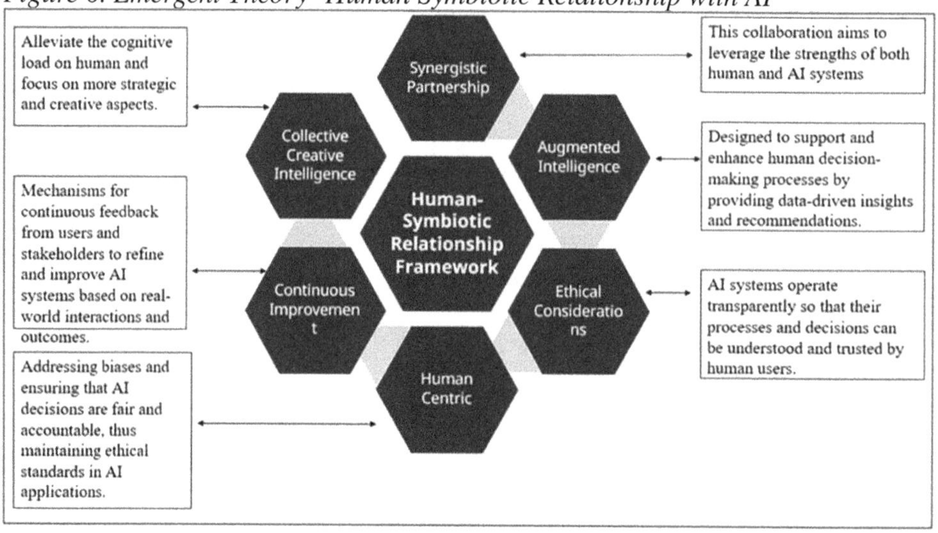

The workplace is being reinvented with AI essentially changing the fundamental values related to jobs, working models, talent and technology. As the new era of work is shaped, people and organizations need to be enabled to reach a higher potential, making work more efficient and more meaningful. This provides an opportunity to create human-centred AI workplaces, as described by Ben Shneiderman (2022) that focuses on systems that empower people, supporting self-efficacy, creativity, responsibility, participation, safety, and trust. Figure 6 reflects Licklider's (1960)

man-computer symbiosis, where AI handles routine tasks, enabling humans to concentrate on higher-level decisions.

The Human-Symbiotic Relationship Framework by Miriana Calvano (2024) builds on this, advocating for AI that enhances human capabilities, forming ethical and productive partnerships. Calvano's approach stresses maintaining human control while allowing AI to augment abilities, fostering collaboration and trust. Collectively, these frameworks systematically guide HR teams to thoughtfully integrate AI into operations, enhancing efficiency while meeting the dynamic needs of the organization and its workforce.

6. FEASIBILITY CONSIDERATIONS FOR AI ADOPTION

Financial Feasibility: While the upfront investment in AI infrastructure, implementation, and training can be substantial, these costs are offset over time by gains in operational efficiency, employee satisfaction, and innovation. Conducting a comprehensive cost-benefit analysis is essential to ensure that investments are made strategically and deliver long-term value.

Cultural Feasibility: Introducing AI requires a significant cultural shift within the organisation. This transition can be effectively managed by employing leadership-driven change management frameworks and local execution that are culturally fit. By phasing in AI technologies and actively involving employees throughout the process fosters alignment with the organisation's vision and facilitate smoother integration.

Machine Masquerade: Vidal and Monge (2020) highlight the security risks posed by cybercriminals who use obfuscation techniques to evade detection by security systems. Such masquerading attacks present serious ethical and security challenges for HR and IT stakeholders, underscoring the need for robust governance, compliance measures, and comprehensive system training.

7. LIMITATIONS AND FUTURE RESEARCH

This study recognises limitations, notably the risk of AI reinforcing biases in HR. Future research should enhance bias detection and correction mechanisms examining AI integration across various sectors. Personal biases in conducting the research may have affected objectivity. Involving non-HR departments in AI adoption would yield a broader organisational perspective. Longitudinal studies are needed to evaluate AI's long-term effects on psychological and IWB and organisational culture. Further research should compare data collection methods such as surveys, focus groups, and mixed approaches to determine the best way to assess innovative and PWB in AI-enabled workplaces.

REFERENCES

Afsar, B., & Umrani, W. A. (2019). Transformational leadership and innovative work behavior: The role of motivation to learn, task complexity and innovation climate. *European Journal of Innovation Management*, *23*(3), 402–428. DOI: 10.1108/EJIM-12-2018-0257

Agarwal, P. (2021). Shattered but smiling: Human resource management and the wellbeing of hotel employees during COVID-19. *International Journal of Hospitality Management*, *93*, 102765. DOI: 10.1016/j.ijhm.2020.102765 PMID: 36919177

Alabed, A., Javornik, A., & Gregory-Smith, D. (2022). AI anthropomorphism and its effect on users' self-congruence and self–AI integration: A theoretical framework and research agenda. *Technological Forecasting and Social Change*, *182*, 121786. DOI: 10.1016/j.techfore.2022.121786

Altenried, M. (2020). The platform as factory: Crowdwork and the hidden labour behind artificial intelligence. *Capital and Class*, *44*(2), 145–158. DOI: 10.1177/0309816819899410

Ayyagari, R., Grover, V., & Purvis, R. (2011). Technostress: Technological antecedents and implications. *Management Information Systems Quarterly*, *35*(4), 831–858. https://doi-org.ezproxy.mdx.ac.uk/10.2307/41409963. DOI: 10.2307/41409963

Banerjee, S., Singh, P. K., & Bajpai, J. (2018). A comparative study on decision-making capability between human and artificial intelligence. In Panigrahi, B. K., Hoda, M. N., Sharma, V., & Goel, S. (Eds.), *Nature Inspired Computing* (pp. 203–210). Springer., DOI: 10.1007/978-981-10-6747-1_23

Bankins, S., Ocampo, A. C., Marrone, M., Restubog, S. L. D., & Woo, S. E. (2024). A multilevel review of artificial intelligence in organisations: Implications for organisational behavior research and practice. *Journal of Organizational Behavior*, *45*(2), 159–182. DOI: 10.1002/job.2735

Bar-Gil, O., Ron, T., & Czerniak, O. (2024). AI for the people? Embedding AI ethics in HR and people analytics projects. *Technology in Society*, *77*, 102527. DOI: 10.1016/j.techsoc.2024.102527

Baumgarten, S., & Bourgadel, C. (2024). Digitalisation, neo-Taylorism and translation in the 2020s. *Perspectives: Studies in Translatology*, *32*(3), 508–523. DOI: 10.1080/0907676X.2023.2285844

Belgrave, L. L., & Seide, K. (2019). Grounded Theory Methodology: Principles and Practices. In Liamputtong, P. (Ed.), *Handbook of Research Methods in Health Social Sciences*. Springer., DOI: 10.1007/978-981-10-5251-4_84

Birnbaum, D., & Somers, M. (2023). Past as prologue: Taylorism, the new scientific management and managing human capital. *The International Journal of Organizational Analysis, 31*(6), 2610–2622. DOI: 10.1108/IJOA-01-2022-3106

Blagoev, V., Shustova, E., & Protas, N. (2022). Work motivation of bank employees in case of implementing AI and robots in the bank activities: Comparative analysis of Russia and Kazakhstan. *Ikonomicheski Izsledvanii a*, *7*, 63–80.

Boulton, C. (2021). With Viva, Microsoft aims to augment the employee experience [Preprint]. *CIO (Framingham, Mass.)*.

Budhwar, P., Malik, A., De Silva, M. T. T., & Thevisuthan, P. (2022). Artificial intelligence - challenges and opportunities for international HRM: A review and research agenda. *International Journal of Human Resource Management*, *33*(6), 1065–1097. DOI: 10.1080/09585192.2022.2035161

Bughin, J., Hazan, E., Lund, S., Dahlström, P., Wiesinger, A., & Subramaniam, A. (2018). Skill shift: Automation and the future of the workforce. *McKinsey Global Institute*, *1*, 3–84.

Calvano, M. (2024). Design and evaluation of high-quality symbiotic AI systems through a human-centered approach. In *Proceedings of the 28th International Conference on Evaluation and Assessment in Software Engineering* (pp. 488–493). ACM. https://doi.org/DOI: 10.1145/3661167.3661223

Carayannis, E. G., Dumitrescu, R., Falkowski, T., & Zota, N.-R. (2024). Empowering SMEs—"Harnessing the potential of Gen AI for resilience and competitiveness.". *IEEE Transactions on Engineering Management*, *71*, 1–22. DOI: 10.1109/TEM.2024.3456820

Chang, T.-S. (2023). Evaluation of an artificial intelligence project in the software industry based on fuzzy analytic hierarchy process and complex adaptive systems. *Journal of Enterprise Information Management*, *36*(4), 879–905. DOI: 10.1108/JEIM-02-2022-0056

Charmaz, K. (2017). Special Invited Paper: Continuities, Contradictions, and Critical Inquiry in Grounded Theory: Continuities, Contradictions, and Critical Inquiry in Grounded Theory. *International Journal of Qualitative Methods, 16*(1). https://doi.org/ (Original work published 2017)DOI: 10.1177/1609406917719350

Charmaz, K., & Thornberg, R. (2020). The pursuit of quality in grounded theory. *Qualitative Research in Psychology, 18*(3), 305–327. DOI: 10.1080/14780887.2020.1780357

Corbin, J., & Strauss, A. (2015). Basics of Qualitative Research: Techniques and Procedures for Developing Grounded Theory. *Sage (Atlanta, Ga.).*

Davila-Gonzalez, S., & Martin, S. (2024). Human digital twin in Industry 5.0: A holistic approach to worker safety and well-being through advanced AI and emotional analytics. *Sensors (Basel), 24*(2), 655. DOI: 10.3390/s24020655 PMID: 38276347

Davis, E. B., Kimball, C. N., Aten, J. D., Andrews, B., Van Tongeren, D. R., Hook, J. N., Davis, D. E., Granqvist, P., & Park, C. L. (2019). Religious meaning making and attachment in a disaster context: A longitudinal qualitative study of flood survivors. *The Journal of Positive Psychology, 14*(5), 659–671. DOI: 10.1080/17439760.2018.1519592

de Saint Laurent, C. (2018). In defence of machine learning: Debunking the myths of artificial intelligence. *Europe's Journal of Psychology, 14*(4), 734–747. DOI: 10.5964/ejop.v14i4.1823 PMID: 30555582

Demetriou, A., Golino, H., Spanoudis, G., Makris, N., & Greiff, S. (2021). The future of intelligence: The central meaning-making unit of intelligence in the mind, the brain, and artificial intelligence. *Intelligence, 87*, 101562. DOI: 10.1016/j.intell.2021.101562

Denzin, N. K., & Lincoln, Y. S. (2018). *The SAGE Handbook of Qualitative Research* (5th ed.). SAGE.

Dierendonck, D., & Lam, H. (2022). Interventions to enhance eudaemonic psychological well-being: A meta-analytic review with Ryff's Scales of Psychological Well-being. *Applied Psychology. Health and Well-Being, 15*(2), 594–610. DOI: 10.1111/aphw.12398 PMID: 36073601

Dodgson, J. E. (2020). Quality in research: Asking the right question. *Journal of Human Lactation : Official Journal of International Lactation Consultant Association, 36*(1), 105–108. DOI: 10.1177/0890334419890305 PMID: 31895604

El Maouch, M., & Jin, Z. (2024). Between meanings and senses-making spaces: Agency and ownership emergence formalization from cultural-historical activity theory position, for an AI-friendly model. *Integrative Psychological & Behavioral Science, 58*(1), 99–137. DOI: 10.1007/s12124-023-09770-3 PMID: 37193931

Gartner. (2024a). Gartner CEO survey finds growth is the top business priority for 2024, reaching highest level in 10 years. https://www.gartner.com/en/newsroom/press-releases/2024-05-22-gartner-ceo-survey-finds-growth-is-the-top-business-priority-for-2024--reaching-highest-level-in-10-years

Gartner. (2024b). Gartner survey finds 38% of HR leaders reported they are piloting, planning implementation, or have already implemented generative AI. https://www.gartner.com/en/newsroom/press-releases/2024-02-27-gartner-finds-38-percent-hr-leaders-piloting-generative-ai

Gehman, J., Glaser, V. L., Eisenhardt, K. M., Gioia, D., Langley, A., & Corley, K. G. (2017). Finding Theory–Method Fit: A Comparison of Three Qualitative Approaches to Theory Building. *Journal of Management Inquiry, 27*(3), 284-300. https://doi.org/ (Original work published 2018)DOI: 10.1177/1056492617706029

Gherhes, C., Vorley, T., Vallance, P., & Brooks, C. (2022). The role of system-building agency in regional path creation: Insights from the emergence of artificial intelligence in Montreal. *Regional Studies, 56*(4), 563–578. DOI: 10.1080/00343404.2021.1886273

Gill, M. J. (2014). The possibilities of phenomenology for organisational research. *Organizational Research Methods, 17*(2), 118–137. DOI: 10.1177/1094428113518348

Goswami, M., Jain, S., Alam, T., Deifalla, A. F., Ragab, A. E., & Khargotra, R. (2023). Exploring the antecedents of AI adoption for effective HRM practices in the Indian pharmaceutical sector. *Frontiers in Pharmacology, 14*, 1215706. DOI: 10.3389/fphar.2023.1215706 PMID: 38034991

Gundhus, H. O., Talberg, N., & Wathne, C. T. (2022). From discretion to standardization: Digitalization of the police organisation. *International Journal of Police Science & Management, 24*(1), 27–41. DOI: 10.1177/14613557211036554

Günsel, A., & Yamen, M. (2020). Digital Taylorism as an answer to the requirements of the new era. In *Agile Business Leadership Methods for Industry 4.0* (pp. 103–119). Emerald Publishing., DOI: 10.1108/978-1-80043-380-920201007

Gyton, G., & Jeffery, R. (2017). These are the experts deciding the future of HR… shouldn't you know who they are? *People Management*, 24.

Harwell, D. (2019). Rights group files federal complaint against AI-hiring firm HireVue, citing "unfair and deceptive" practices. *The Washington Post.*

Hemalatha, A.. (2021). Impact of artificial intelligence on recruitment and selection of information technology companies. In *2021 International Conference on Artificial Intelligence and Smart Systems (ICAIS)* (pp. 60–66). IEEE. https://doi.org/DOI: 10.1109/ICAIS50930.2021.9396036

Heritage, J. (2018). The ubiquity of epistemics: A rebuttal to the "epistemics of epistemics" group. *Discourse Studies*, *20*(1), 14–56. DOI: 10.1177/1461445617734342

Hernaus, T., Černe, M., & Škerlavaj, M. (2021). The interplay between relational job design and cross-training in predicting employee job/task citizenship performance. *Human Resource Development Quarterly*, *32*(4), 625–646. DOI: 10.1002/hrdq.21427

Hofstede, G. (1980). Culture's Consequences: International Differences in Work Related Values. *Sage (Atlanta, Ga.)*.

Hofstede Insights. (2020). *Country scores*. https://www.hofstede-insights.com/product/compare-countries/

Holford, W. D. (2019). The future of human creative knowledge work within the digital economy. *Futures: The Journal of Policy. Futures*, *105*, 143–154. DOI: 10.1016/j.futures.2018.10.002

Hughes, C.. (2019). *Managing Technology and Middle- and Low-Skilled Employees: Advances for Economic Regeneration* (1st ed.). Emerald Publishing., DOI: 10.1108/9781789730777

Iaia, L., Fait, M., Munnia, A., Cavallo, F., & De Nuccio, E. (2024). The scientific approach to facilitate the human-machine interactions. The case of Carrozzeria Fratelli Basile. *Journal of Management History*, *30*(2), 243–262. DOI: 10.1108/JMH-12-2022-0087

Kayaalp, A., Page, K. J., & Gumus, O. (2021). Job satisfaction and transformational leadership as the antecedents of OCB role definitions: The moderating role of justice perceptions. *International Journal of Business Science and Applied Management*, *16*(2), 89–101. DOI: 10.69864/ijbsam.16-2.149

Kieser, A. (1994). Why organisation theory needs historical analyses—And how this should be performed. *Organization Science*, *5*(4), 608–620. DOI: 10.1287/orsc.5.4.608

Kim, M., & Beehr, T. A. (2022). The role of organisation-based self-esteem and job resources in promoting employees' job crafting behaviors. *International Journal of Human Resource Management*, *33*(19), 3822–3849. DOI: 10.1080/09585192.2021.1934711

Koivisto, M., & Grassini, S. (2024). Author correction: Best humans still outperform artificial intelligence in a creative divergent thinking task. *Scientific Reports*, *14*(1), 4239. DOI: 10.1038/s41598-024-54745-y PMID: 38378767

Kucharska, W., & Bedford, D. A. D. (2020). Love your mistakes!—They help you adapt to change. How do knowledge, collaboration and learning cultures foster organisational intelligence? *Journal of Organizational Change Management*, *33*(7), 1329–1354. DOI: 10.1108/JOCM-02-2020-0052

Kufel, J., Bargieł-Łączek, K., Kocot, S., Koźlik, M., Bartnikowska, W., Janik, M., Czogalik, Ł., Dudek, P., Magiera, M., Lis, A., Paszkiewicz, I., Nawrat, Z., Cebula, M., & Gruszczyńska, K. (2023). What is machine learning, artificial neural networks and deep learning?—Examples of practical applications in medicine. *Diagnostics (Basel)*, *13*(15), 2582. DOI: 10.3390/diagnostics13152582 PMID: 37568945

Kuhn, T. S. (1970). *The Structure of Scientific Revolutions*. University of Chicago Press.

Licklider, J. C. R. (1960). Man-computer symbiosis. *IRE Transactions on Human Factors in Electronics*, *HFE-1*(1), 4–11. DOI: 10.1109/THFE2.1960.4503259

Liu, H. Y. (2023). Digital Taylorism in China's e-commerce industry: A case study of internet professionals. *Economic and Industrial Democracy*, *44*(1), 262–279. DOI: 10.1177/0143831X211068887

López, T., Riedler, T., Köhnen, H., & Fütterer, M. (2022). Digital value chain restructuring and labour process transformations in the fast-fashion sector: Evidence from the value chains of Zara & H\&M. *Global Networks*, *22*(4), 684–700. DOI: 10.1111/glob.12353

Maestre Vidal, J., & Sotelo Monge, M. A. (2020). Obfuscation of malicious behaviors for thwarting masquerade detection systems based on locality features. *Sensors (Basel)*, *20*(7), 2084. DOI: 10.3390/s20072084 PMID: 32272806

Makarius, E. E., Mukherjee, D., Fox, J. D., & Fox, A. K. (2020). Rising with the machines: A sociotechnical framework for bringing artificial intelligence into the organisation. *Journal of Business Research*, *120*, 262–273. DOI: 10.1016/j.jbusres.2020.07.045

Makridakis, S. (2017). The forthcoming artificial intelligence (AI) revolution: Its impact on society and firms. *Futures: The Journal of Policy. Futures*, *90*, 46–60. DOI: 10.1016/j.futures.2017.03.006

Malik, A., De Silva, M. T. T., Budhwar, P., & Srikanth, N. R. (2021). Elevating talents' experience through innovative artificial intelligence-mediated knowledge sharing: Evidence from an IT-multinational enterprise. *Journal of International Management*, *27*(4), 100871. DOI: 10.1016/j.intman.2021.100871

Marathe, A., & Sen, A. (2021). Empathetic reflection: Reflecting with emotion. *Reflective Practice, 22*(4), 566–574. DOI: 10.1080/14623943.2021.1927693

McCarthy, J., Minsky, M. L., Rochester, N., & Shannon, C. E. (1955). A proposal for the Dartmouth Summer Research Project on artificial intelligence. *AI Magazine, 27*(4), 12.

Mikalef, P., & Pateli, A. (2017). Information technology-enabled dynamic capabilities and their indirect effect on competitive performance: Findings from PLS-SEM and fsQCA. *Journal of Business Research, 70*, 1–16. DOI: 10.1016/j.jbusres.2016.09.004

Monod, E., Mayer, A.-S., Straub, D., Joyce, E., & Qi, J. (2024). From worker empowerment to managerial control: The devolution of AI tools' intended positive implementation to their negative consequences. *Information and Organization, 34*(1), 100498. DOI: 10.1016/j.infoandorg.2023.100498

Montani, F., Courcy, F., Battistelli, A., & De Witte, H. (2021). Job insecurity and innovative work behaviour: A moderated mediation model of intrinsic motivation and trait mindfulness. *Stress and Health*. https://doi-org.ezproxy.mdx.ac.uk/10.1002/smi.3034

Moon, E. Y., Park, J., & Ka, Y. (2024). A latent profile analysis of protean career attitude and vocational identity status. [Preprint]. *Journal of Career Development, 51*(5), 527–543. Advance online publication. DOI: 10.1177/08948453241266801

Mousavi, R., Hazarika, B., Chen, K., & Rienzo, T. (2022). The role of dissonance reduction and co-creation strategies in shaping smart service satisfaction – the case of Uber. *Behaviour & Information Technology, 41*(1), 51–71. DOI: 10.1080/0144929X.2020.1795258

Muldoon, J., Deal, N. M., Smith, D., & Shivanapura Lakshmikanth, G. (2022). The past masters: The impact of the evolution of management thought on history. *Journal of Management History, 29*(1), 10–28. Advance online publication. DOI: 10.1108/JMH-10-2021-0057

Neto, B. (2022). Labor process and future relevance of the critique of capital. *Critique (Glasgow), 50*(1), 155–166. DOI: 10.1080/03017605.2022.2050534

Nie, T., Tian, M., Cai, M., & Yan, Q. (2023). Job Autonomy and Work Meaning: Drivers of Employee Job-Crafting Behaviors in the VUCA Times. *Behavioral Sciences, 13*(6), 493. https://doi.org/, S., Berends, H., Faraj, S., & Huysman, M. (2020). Make way for the algorithms: Symbolic actions and change in a regime of knowing. *Organisation Science, 32*(1), 18–41.DOI: 10.3390/bs13060493Pachidi

Papagiannidis, E., Mikalef, P., Conboy, K., & Van de Wetering, R. (2023). Uncovering the dark side of AI-based decision-making: A case study in a B2B context. *Industrial Marketing Management, 115*, 253–265. DOI: 10.1016/j.indmarman.2023.10.003

Park, J., Woo, S. E., & Kim, J. (2024). Attitudes towards artificial intelligence at work: Scale development and validation. *Journal of Occupational and Organizational Psychology, 97*(3), 920–951. DOI: 10.1111/joop.12502

Paschen, J., Wilson, M., & Ferreira, J. J. (2020). Collaborative intelligence: How human and artificial intelligence create value along the B2B sales funnel. *Business Horizons, 63*(3), 403–414. DOI: 10.1016/j.bushor.2020.01.003

Pei, J., Wang, H., Peng, Q., & Liu, S. (2024). Saving face: Leveraging artificial intelligence-based negative feedback to enhance employee job performance. *Human Resource Management, 63*(5), 775–790. DOI: 10.1002/hrm.22226

Piszczek, M. M., & Berg, P. (2014). Expanding the boundaries of boundary theory: Regulative institutions and work–family role management. *Human Relations; Studies Towards the Integration of the Social Sciences, 67*(12), 1491–1512. DOI: 10.1177/0018726714524241

PricewaterhouseCoopers. (2024). AI Jobs Barometer. PwC. https://www.pwc.com/gx/en/issues/artificial-intelligence/ai-jobs-barometer.html

Quaquebeke, N. V., & Gerpott, F. H. (2023). The now, new, and next of digital leadership: How artificial intelligence (AI) will take over and change leadership as we know it. *Journal of Leadership & Organizational Studies, 30*(3), 265–275. DOI: 10.1177/15480518231181731

Ransbotham, S., S., Khodabandeh, S., Kiron, D., Candelon, F., Chu, M., & LaFountain, B. (2020). Expanding AI's impact with organisational learning. *MIT Sloan Management Review*.

Rehman, J., Hawryszkiewycz, I., & Sohaib, O. Towards the Knowledge-Smart Professional Service Firms: How High-Performance Work Systems Support the Transformation. *J Knowl Econ* **14**, 3640–3670 (2023). https://doi.org/10.1007/s13132-022-00903-4Roulston, K. (2022). Qualitative interviewing and epistemics. *Qualitative Research, 18*(3), 322–341. DOI: 10.1177/1468794117721738

Sementelli, A. J. (2019). Faculty in Tamara-Land: Taylorism, ritual, and performance. *Administrative Theory & Praxis, 41*(1), 21–34. DOI: 10.1080/10841806.2018.1512338

Shamsi, M., Iakovleva, T., Olsen, E., & Bagozzi, R. P. (2021). Employees' work-related well-being during COVID-19 pandemic: An integrated perspective of technology acceptance model and JD-R theory. *International Journal of Environmental Research and Public Health, 18*(22), 11888. DOI: 10.3390/ijerph182211888 PMID: 34831642

Shneiderman, B. (2022). Human-centered AI: Ensuring human control while increasing automation. In *Proceedings of the 5th Workshop on Human Factors in Hypertext* (pp. 1–2). ACM. https://doi.org/DOI: 10.1145/3538882.3542790

Singh, A., & Pandey, J. (2024). Artificial intelligence adoption in extended HR ecosystems: Enablers and barriers. An abductive case research. *Frontiers in Psychology, 14*, 1339782. DOI: 10.3389/fpsyg.2023.1339782 PMID: 38327504

Tannenbaum, S. I., & Wolfson, M. A. (2022). Informal (field-based) learning. *Annual Review of Organizational Psychology and Organizational Behavior, 9*(1), 391–414. https://doi-org.ezproxy.mdx.ac.uk/10.1146/annurev-orgpsych-012420-083050. DOI: 10.1146/annurev-orgpsych-012420-083050

The Future of Jobs Report. 2023. (2023). *World Economic Forum*. https://www.weforum.org/publications/the-future-of-jobs-report-2023/

Theoharakis, V., Wapshott, R., & Cham, L. (2024). Work engagement and the impact of a social identity crafting approach to leadership: A case from Africa's air transport industry. [Preprint]. *Personnel Review, 53*(7), 1729–1744. Advance online publication. DOI: 10.1108/PR-02-2023-0099

Vasconcelos Furtado, J.. (2024). *Influence factors of organisational citizenship behaviors in Latin American countries: A Brazilian case study*. Management Research. [Preprint], DOI: 10.1108/MRJIAM-07-2023-1439

Votto, A. M., Valecha, R., Najafirad, P., & Rao, H. R. (2021). Artificial intelligence in tactical human resource management: A systematic literature review. *International Journal of Information Management Data Insights, 1*(2), 100047. DOI: 10.1016/j.jjimei.2021.100047

Vrontis, D., Christofi, M., Pereira, V., Tarba, S., Makrides, A., & Trichina, E. (2021). Artificial intelligence, robotics, advanced technologies and human resource management: A systematic review. *International Journal of Human Resource Management*, •••, 1–30.

Walliman, N. (2022). *Research Methods: The Basics* (3rd ed.). Routledge, Taylor & Francis Group.

Why there will be plenty of jobs in the future – even with AI. (2024). *World Economic Forum*. https://www.weforum.org/agenda/2024/02/artificial-intelligence-ai-jobs-future/

Wu, T. J., Li, J. M., & Wu, Y. J. (2022). Employees' job insecurity perception and unsafe behaviours in human–machine collaboration. *Management Decision*, *60*(9), 2409–2432. Advance online publication. DOI: 10.1108/MD-09-2021-1257

Xu, G., Xue, M., & Zhao, J. (2023). The association between artificial intelligence awareness and employee depression: The mediating role of emotional exhaustion and the moderating role of perceived organisational support. *International Journal of Environmental Research and Public Health*, *20*(6), 5147. DOI: 10.3390/ijerph20065147 PMID: 36982055

Zeb, A., Ahmad, S., & Saeed, G. (2018). Leadership effectiveness and organizational performance: Exploring gaps in the existing literature. *Business and Economic Review*, *10*(01), 95–106. DOI: 10.22547/BER/10.1.4

Zhou, M. X., Mark, G., Li, J., & Yang, H. (2019). Trusting virtual agents: The effect of personality. *ACM Transactions on Interactive Intelligent Systems*, *9*(2–3), 1–36. DOI: 10.1145/3232077

KEY TERMS AND DEFINITIONS

Algorithm: A structured, rule-based sequence of instructions designed to solve specific problems or accomplish defined tasks. In digital and organisational settings, algorithms automate processes, analyse large datasets, and support decision-making. Frequently embedded within software, AI, and ML systems, algorithms enable efficient information processing and pattern recognition. In management and HR, they facilitate workflow standardisation, resource optimisation, and performance monitoring, extending scientific management principles into the digital age (Zhou et al., 2019)

Artificial intelligence (AI): A multidisciplinary field that develops systems capable of simulating human intellectual processes such as reasoning, logic, and problem-solving by leveraging advanced algorithms, machine learning, and automation (McCarthy et al., 1955). Within organisations, AI is a driving force behind innovation, transforming business operations and the workplace as part of the Fourth Industrial Revolution.

Digital Taylorism: The use of digital technologies such as AI, automation, and data analytics (algorithms) to break down jobs into standardized, repetitive tasks, monitor workers in real time, and maximize efficiency. It extends classic scientific management principles into the digital era, often reducing worker autonomy and creativity while increasing productivity and control (Altenried, 2020).

Innovative Work Behaviour: An act of intentionally generating, promoting, and implementing new ideas at work to improve processes, solve problems, and drive organisational success (Saeed et al., 2018).

Machine Learning: A branch of artificial intelligence where computer systems learn from data to improve performance without explicit programming. By analyzing datasets and identifying patterns, machine learning algorithms build models that make predictions or automate decisions (Kufel et al., 2023).

Psychological Wellbeing: A person's positive self-perception, fulfilling relationships, autonomy, personal growth, and sense of purpose. It includes both emotional satisfaction and the ability to thrive and develop in life and work (Agarwal, 2021).

Section 4

Developing Empathy, Emotional Intelligence, and Reflective Leadership Through AI

Chapter 12
Agentic AI as an Empathy Scaffolding Tool:
Enhancing Emotional Intelligence in Leadership Development

Divya Dubey
http://orcid.org/0000-0002-3003-301X
Jindal Institute of Behavioural Sciences, O.P. Jindal Global University, Sonipat, India

ABSTRACT

This chapter examines how agentic artificial intelligence can function as an empathy scaffold to support emotionally intelligent and relationally grounded leadership in digitally mediated organizations. Drawing on emotional intelligence theory, empathetic leadership research, and sociocognitive models of scaffolding, it explains how AI-enabled tools—such as real-time emotional feedback, conversational coaching, and adaptive learning systems—can enhance leaders' emotional awareness, reflective capacity, and ethical judgment. Organizational applications, including Microsoft Viva, Workday Peakon, BetterUp, and Zoom IQ, illustrate how agentic AI is being used to surface emotional patterns and support leadership development in practice. At the same time, the chapter critically examines concerns related to authenticity, cultural interpretation, algorithmic bias, privacy, and the risk of emotional surveillance. It concludes by proposing principles for the ethical and transparent design of AI systems that augment human empathy and judgment rather than attempting to replace them.

DOI: 10.4018/979-8-3373-6650-0.ch012

1. INTRODUCTION: LEADERSHIP IN THE AGE OF AGENTIC AI

Leadership in contemporary organizations is unfolding within a context of unprecedented technological change driven by advances in digital systems and artificial intelligence (McAfee & Brynjolfsson, 2017). Digital systems increasingly mediate how work is organized, decisions are made, and people interact reshaping both formal authority structures and informal relational dynamics (Orlikowski, 2007). Among these technologies, artificial intelligence (AI) has moved from a peripheral support tool to a central organizational actor influencing strategic decision-making and human interaction (Davenport & Ronanki, 2018).

This shift has profound implications not only for how work is performed, but also for how leadership is enacted, experienced, and evaluated (Raisch & Krakowski, 2021). This chapter is grounded in the assumption that leadership in the age of advanced AI is not merely a technical challenge. It is fundamentally a psychological and relational one requiring leaders to navigate efficiency demands while sustaining trust, ethical responsibility, and emotional connection (Jarrahi, 2018). As organizations adopt increasingly autonomous systems, leaders must balance technological capability with sensitivity to human experience to ensure sustainable organizational functioning (Floridi et al., 2018).

1.1 Digital Transformation and the Empathy Imperative

The contemporary organizational landscape is undergoing profound transformation driven by rapid technological advancement, geopolitical uncertainty, demographic change, and the widespread adoption of AI-driven systems (World Economic Forum, 2020). Leaders increasingly operate in volatile and ambiguous environments characterized by heightened emotional demands and reduced predictability (Uhl-Bien & Arena, 2018). Artificial intelligence, once limited to back-office functions, is now embedded across domains such as human resource management, customer engagement, and strategic planning (Davenport & Ronanki, 2018).

As AI systems evolve toward greater autonomy, contextual awareness, and adaptive learning features commonly associated with *agentic AI* the expectations placed upon human leaders are undergoing equally significant change (Raisch & Krakowski, 2021).

At the center of this transformation lies a fundamental paradox. While organizations increasingly rely on AI to support complex decision-making and operational efficiency, this same technological evolution elevates the importance of deeply human leadership capacities. Empathy, emotional intelligence, ethical judgment, perspective-taking, and relational sensitivity become more, not less, central in technologically mediated workplaces (Jarrahi, 2018). Leaders are required to navigate digital complexity while remaining attuned to the emotional realities of employees, teams, and broader stakeholder groups.

Several socio-organizational forces have converged to create what may be described as an *empathy imperative*. First, workforce expectations have shifted toward greater emphasis on psychological safety (Edmondson, 2018), inclusion, and emotional well-being. Second, hybrid and remote work arrangements have altered how emotional cues are communicated, making it more difficult for leaders to accurately assess team climate and individual needs (Calvo & D'Mello, 2010). Third, the knowledge economy places increasing value on trust, collaboration, and cross-cultural communication, all of which depend on empathetic leadership. Finally, AI-mediated interactions introduce ethical and emotional complexities that demand heightened sensitivity and moral clarity from leaders.

Taken together, these developments underscore a critical insight: as organizations become more technologically sophisticated, the human qualities that resist automation become increasingly valuable. Empathy is therefore not a peripheral interpersonal skill, but a core leadership competency shaping decision-making, team cohesion, engagement, innovation, and organizational resilience (Boyatzis, 2018).

1.2 Challenges of Cultivating Empathy in Modern Leadership

Despite its recognized importance, empathy is difficult to sustain within high-pressure, digitally mediated organizational environments (Boyatzis, 2018). Contemporary leaders often manage geographically dispersed teams while responding to accelerated decision cycles, performance metrics, and ongoing organizational change. These conditions create psychological strain that undermines empathetic engagement (Kozlowski et al., 2015). Cognitive overload limits leaders' capacity to attend to emotional cues, while task urgency frequently displaces relational considerations.

Empathy also requires time, emotional regulation, and reflective capacity qualities that are increasingly constrained in fast-paced organizational cultures. In virtual settings, non-verbal cues such as body language, tone, and facial expression are reduced or distorted, increasing the likelihood of misinterpretation. Prolonged digital engagement further contributes to emotional fatigue, giving rise to what scholars describe as empathy depletion or empathetic burnout (Maslach & Leiter, 2016).

Conventional leadership development approaches offer limited solutions to these challenges. Workshop-based programs are typically episodic and conceptually oriented, with little emphasis on sustained behavioral change (Day et al., 2014). While they may raise awareness of empathy as a leadership value, they rarely provide leaders with ongoing, context-specific feedback. Executive coaching and mentoring can address this gap but remain resource-intensive and difficult to scale across organizations (Grant, 2017).

These limitations point to a persistent structural problem: empathy development requires continuous reinforcement, contextual learning, and real-time feedback conditions that traditional human-centered interventions cannot consistently provide on their own.

1.3 The Emergence of Agentic AI as a Leadership Partner

The emergence of agentic AI represents a significant shift in how organizations conceptualize the relationship between technology and leadership. Agentic AI refers to intelligent systems capable of autonomous reasoning, adaptive learning, and context-sensitive interaction (Raisch & Krakowski, 2021). Unlike earlier algorithmic models reliant on fixed rules or static datasets, these systems can interpret linguistic and emotional cues, update their internal models through ongoing interaction (D'Mello & Kory, 2015) and adjust their responses to situational demands (Jarrahi, 2018).

At a conceptual level, agentic AI signals a transition from automation to augmentation. Earlier workplace technologies were primarily designed to replace routine tasks or enforce standardization. In contrast, agentic AI systems are intended to collaborate with humans by offering insights, feedback, and adaptive support. This repositioning allows AI to be understood not merely as an instrument of efficiency, but as a developmental partner capable of supporting learning, reflection, and relational awareness in leadership contexts.

1.4 AI Challenging Traditional Assumptions about Human–Technology Boundaries

Leadership has traditionally been understood as a distinctly human domain grounded in emotional intelligence, empathy, ethical reasoning, and relational understanding. Technological systems were often viewed as incompatible with these qualities, raising concerns about depersonalization and loss of authenticity. The rise of agentic AI challenges this binary distinction.

Advances in affective computing, natural language processing, and socio-emotional analytics enable AI systems to identify patterns in tone, language, engagement, and emotional expression that may escape human attention, particularly in complex or high-demand environments. By making such patterns visible, AI can function as an "emotional mirror," helping leaders recognize tendencies in their communication and interaction styles.

Rather than replacing emotional labor, agentic AI has the potential to support emotional clarity, perspective-taking, and relational attunement. When used reflectively, these systems can enhance leaders' awareness of how their behavior affects others, thereby strengthening empathetic engagement.

1.5 AI as a Supportive and Reflective Leadership Companion

When integrated thoughtfully, agentic AI can serve as a continuous reflective companion for leaders. Such systems can provide real-time feedback on emotional tone, pacing, stress indicators, and sentiment patterns in digital communication. They may also generate reflective prompts that encourage leaders to reconsider how their actions are experienced by others and offer context-sensitive insights aligned with team dynamics or emerging relational trends.

A distinctive advantage of agentic AI lies in its availability and scalability. Unlike human coaches or mentors, whose time and access are limited, AI-based systems can provide sustained support across contexts and over time. This makes them particularly suited to supporting the ongoing, iterative process through which emotional intelligence and empathetic leadership capacities develop.

1.6 The Concept of Empathy Scaffolding

To explain how agentic AI supports leaders' emotional development, this chapter introduces the concept of *empathy scaffolding*, drawing on Vygotsky's sociocultural theory and contemporary organizational learning models. Scaffolding emphasizes that complex competencies are acquired most effectively when individuals receive structured, adaptive support aligned with their current level of capability.

In leadership contexts, empathy scaffolding refers to AI systems that enhance emotional awareness, support accurate interpretation of interpersonal cues, prompt reflective responses, and reinforce emotionally appropriate behavior. Empathy is thus conceptualized not as a fixed trait, but as a developmental capacity strengthened through guided practice and sustained reflection conditions that agentic AI can provide consistently and at scale.

1.7 Interdisciplinary Foundations and Implications

The integration of agentic AI into leadership development draws upon multiple scholarly traditions. Emotional intelligence research highlights the role of emotional awareness, regulation, and empathy in effective leadership. Organizational behavior research emphasizes psychological safety, trust, and inclusive communication. AI ethics provides frameworks for addressing concerns related to fairness, transparency, privacy, and accountability. Developmental and cognitive psychology contribute insights into how complex emotional competencies are acquired and internalized.

Together, these perspectives establish a robust interdisciplinary foundation for understanding agentic AI not merely as a technological innovation, but as a relational and developmental resource within leadership practice.

1.8 Toward Human–AI Collaborative Leadership

The rise of agentic AI signals a shift toward a collaborative leadership paradigm in which human judgment remains central while being supported by intelligent systems that expand perceptual, emotional, and cognitive capacity. Leadership augmented by agentic AI does not replace human compassion or responsibility. Instead, it creates conditions for more intentional, emotionally attuned, and ethically grounded leadership within increasingly complex and digitally mediated organizational environments.

2. THEORETICAL FOUNDATIONS

2.1 Emotional Intelligence and Its Relevance to Leadership

The concept of Emotional Intelligence (EI) emerged from the work of Mayer and Salovey (1990), who defined EI as a set of abilities related to perceiving, understanding, using, and regulating emotions in oneself and others. Their four-branch model framed EI as a form of cognitive competence rather than a purely dispositional or affective trait. This distinction was important because it positioned emotional skills as capacities that could be developed through learning and experience rather than fixed personal qualities.

Goleman (1995) extended this framework into organizational and leadership contexts, arguing that effective leadership depends not only on technical expertise or cognitive intelligence, but also on emotional self-awareness, self-regulation, empathy, motivation, and social skill. His work helped establish EI as a central construct in leadership research, particularly in environments characterized by uncertainty, interpersonal complexity, and rapid change.

Empirical research has consistently supported the relevance of EI for leadership effectiveness. Emotionally intelligent leaders demonstrate stronger decision-making under pressure, more constructive conflict management, and higher-quality communication (Boyatzis, 2018). At the team level, EI has been associated with psychological safety (Edmondson, 2018), trust, collaboration, and organizational citizenship behaviors. These outcomes are especially critical in hybrid, multicultural, and digitally mediated work environments, where emotional misalignment can quickly undermine coordination and morale (Côté, 2014).

Importantly, contemporary scholarship emphasizes that EI is not stable across contexts. Leaders may demonstrate strong emotional competence under supportive conditions but struggle under cognitive overload, stress, or relational strain. Emotional performance fluctuates with fatigue, organizational climate, cultural expectations, and situational pressure. This variability highlights a central limitation of traditional leadership development models, which often treat EI as a static attribute assessed at a single point in time.

Most conventional EI training relies on workshops, self-report instruments, or short-term interventions. While these approaches increase conceptual awareness, they rarely provide real-time feedback or sustained opportunities for emotional recalibration. Emotional competencies develop through repeated practice, immediate feedback, and reflection within everyday interactions conditions that are difficult to maintain through episodic human-led interventions alone.

This gap points directly to the relevance of agentic AI. Because EI is dynamic and context-sensitive, systems capable of continuously monitoring emotional patterns, identifying behavioral tendencies, and prompting reflection are well positioned to support its development. In this sense, EI theory provides a foundational rationale for exploring AI-supported empathy scaffolding in leadership.

2.2 Empathetic Leadership in Organizational Psychology

Empathetic leadership represents a focused application of emotional intelligence, emphasizing leaders' ability to understand others' perspectives, resonate with their emotional experiences, and translate that understanding into appropriate action (Davis, 1983). Organizational psychology typically conceptualizes empathy as comprising cognitive, affective, and behavioral components, each of which contributes to effective interpersonal functioning.

Research consistently shows that empathetic leaders foster trust, strengthen employee commitment (Kock et al., 2019), reduce interpersonal conflict, and support psychological safety. These relational outcomes are closely tied to performance and innovation, particularly in knowledge-intensive and collaborative work settings where emotional dynamics influence cooperation and information sharing.

Despite these benefits, empathy is difficult to enact consistently in real organizational contexts. Chronic stress, high workload, and emotionally demanding interactions diminish leaders' capacity for perspective-taking and emotional regulation (Maslach & Leiter, 2016). Cultural differences, cognitive biases, and organizational norms further complicate empathetic engagement. As a result, leaders may endorse empathy as a value while failing to enact it reliably in daily interactions.

This gap between intention and behavior underscores the need for mechanisms that support empathy *in situ*. Rather than relying solely on retrospective reflection or abstract training, leaders require real-time cues and feedback that help them recognize emotional dynamics as they unfold. It is within this space that agentic AI becomes particularly relevant (Ashkanasy & Daus, 2005).

2.3 Agentic AI as an Empathy Scaffold: Conceptual Foundations

The concept of agentic AI as an empathy scaffold draws on Vygotsky's sociocultural theory, which emphasizes that complex skills develop through guided support embedded in social activity (Vygotsky, 1978). Scaffolding enables individuals to perform beyond their current independent capacity, with support gradually withdrawn as competence increases. Rather than revisiting this framework in detail, its relevance here lies in how it explains the development of emotionally complex leadership behaviors (D'Mello & Kory, 2015).

Applied to leadership, agentic AI can be understood as a form of adaptive developmental support. While it does not possess emotional experience, it is capable of detecting patterns, offering feedback, and prompting reflection at moments when leaders are navigating emotionally charged situations (Wood et al., 1976). Unlike human mentors, whose feedback is episodic and selective, AI systems can monitor communication continuously across emails, meetings, and collaborative platforms.

Advances in affective computing and natural language processing allow these systems to identify shifts in tone, engagement, and sentiment that may escape human attention, particularly under conditions of stress or cognitive overload. By making such patterns visible, AI supports leaders in recognizing emotional dynamics they might otherwise miss.

Crucially, empathy scaffolding does not automate empathy or displace emotional labor. Instead, it strengthens leaders' own capacities by encouraging awareness, reflection, and adjustment. Over time, repeated micro-interventions such as reflective prompts or pattern-based feedback support the internalization of empathetic habits.

As leaders develop greater emotional competence, AI guidance can recede, mirroring the fading process central to scaffolding theory. In this way, agentic AI functions as a developmental companion rather than an emotional substitute, supporting the consistent enactment of empathy within real organizational contexts.

3. THE PROMISE OF AGENTIC AI FOR EMPATHY ENHANCEMENT

The emergence of agentic artificial intelligence (AI) offers a substantive response to persistent limitations in leadership development, particularly in the cultivation of empathy and emotional intelligence within complex organizational settings (Mayer, Salovey, & Caruso, 2008). Traditional leadership development approaches are typically episodic, retrospective, and decontextualized, relying on workshops, simulations, or post hoc reflection that occur outside the emotional immediacy of real workplace interactions (Day, Fleenor, Atwater, Sturm, & McKee, 2014). As a result, leaders often struggle to translate abstract emotional competencies into consistent relational practice, especially under conditions of time pressure and digital overload (Boyatzis, 2018).

Agentic AI systems differ fundamentally from earlier leadership technologies by operating continuously within everyday work environments rather than as isolated training interventions (Russell & Norvig, 2021). These systems are capable of autonomous reasoning, contextual sensitivity, and adaptive feedback, allowing developmental support to occur alongside authentic leadership interactions rather than after the fact (Wooldridge, 2021). This embeddedness enables leaders to engage in emotionally informed reflection at moments when interpersonal consequences are still salient, thereby strengthening learning transfer (Kolb, 1984).

Rather than replacing human judgment, the developmental promise of agentic AI lies in its capacity to augment leaders' emotional perception and reflective awareness (Calvo & Peters, 2014). Empathy, understood as a learnable and context-sensitive capacity rather than a fixed personality trait, benefits from repeated, situated practice supported by timely feedback (Davis, 1994). In this sense, agentic AI aligns closely with developmental models of emotional intelligence that emphasize ongoing self-awareness, regulation, and relational learning over static skill acquisition (Mayer et al., 2008).

To clarify this contribution, the present section focuses on four core mechanisms through which agentic AI can enhance empathetic leadership. Each mechanism is linked to a specific leadership insight that explains its developmental value.

3.1 Real-Time Emotional Feedback

Leadership insight: Leaders frequently misjudge the emotional impact of their communication; timely feedback supports emotional awareness.

In digitally mediated organizational environments, leaders often lack immediate access to emotional cues that signal how their communication is being received (Walther, 2011). Virtual meetings, email, and asynchronous collaboration reduce access to tone, facial expression, and informal relational feedback, increasing the likelihood of emotional misalignment between intent and impact (Daft & Lengel, 1986). Research consistently shows that leaders tend to overestimate clarity and underestimate the emotional consequences of their messages in such contexts (Kruger, Epley, Parker, & Ng, 2005).

Agentic AI systems equipped with affective computing capabilities can partially address this gap by detecting patterns in linguistic style, vocal tone, pacing, and interaction dynamics across digital communication channels (Picard, 1997). Using machine learning and natural language processing, these systems identify indicators of emotional tension, disengagement, or negative affect that may not be immediately visible to the communicator (Calvo & D'Mello, 2010). For example, abrupt shifts in language formality, reduced participation, or increased response latency can signal emotional withdrawal or frustration within teams (Kahn, 1990).

Crucially, the developmental value of such systems depends on how feedback is framed. Research on adult learning and self-regulation indicates that reflective feedback is more effective than directive correction in fostering internalized change (Zimmerman, 2000). When AI systems highlight emotional patterns without prescribing behavior, they create space for leaders to reflect on how their communication choices influence others, thereby strengthening emotional self-awareness (Goleman, 1998).

Over time, repeated exposure to contextualized emotional feedback supports leaders' ability to anticipate emotional impact rather than merely react to it (Boyatzis, 2018). This process aligns with foundational models of emotional intelligence that position self-awareness as the primary gateway to empathy and relational competence (Mayer et al., 2008).

3.2 Conversational Coaching and Reflective Prompting

Leadership insight: Guided reflection strengthens perspective-taking and emotional regulation.

Beyond passive feedback, agentic AI systems increasingly function as conversational coaches that engage leaders in structured reflection following emotionally salient interactions (Fitzpatrick, Darcy, & Vierhile, 2017). These systems simulate reflective dialogue by posing context-sensitive prompts that encourage leaders to examine emotional triggers, alternative perspectives, and relational consequences (Bickmore & Picard, 2005).

Perspective-taking is a central cognitive component of empathy and has been shown to reduce bias, improve interpersonal judgment, and enhance ethical decision-making in leadership contexts (Galinsky, Maddux, Gilin, & White, 2008). However, under conditions of stress and cognitive load, leaders often default to habitual interpretations that limit empathic understanding (Kahneman, 2011). Reflective prompting helps interrupt these automatic responses by directing attention toward others' emotional experiences.

Unlike traditional executive coaching, which is constrained by cost, availability, and temporal distance from the triggering event, AI-mediated coaching can occur immediately after interactions, when emotional memory is still accessible (Kolb, 1984). This immediacy enhances learning by linking reflection directly to lived experience rather than abstract recollection (Schön, 1983).

Over repeated interactions, conversational AI systems can identify recurring emotional patterns and prompt deeper levels of reflection, supporting the gradual internalization of empathetic habits (Boyatzis & McKee, 2005). Importantly, the effectiveness of such systems depends on their role as facilitators of reflection rather than authorities on emotional meaning, preserving the leader's responsibility for interpretation and judgment (Floridi et al., 2018).

3.3 Sentiment Analysis at the Collective Level

Leadership insight: Collective emotional patterns enable proactive and relationally informed leadership.

Empathy in leadership extends beyond individual interactions to encompass awareness of collective emotional climates within teams and organizations (Barsade & O'Neill, 2014). Group-level affect influences collaboration, trust, performance, and psychological safety, yet leaders often rely on incomplete or delayed indicators such as surveys or performance metrics to assess team well-being (Edmondson, 1999).

Agentic AI systems can analyze large volumes of organizational communication using sentiment analysis and natural language processing to detect trends in emotional tone, engagement, and relational climate (Pang & Lee, 2008). By aggregating emotional signals across time and platforms, these systems provide leaders with early indicators of burnout, disengagement, or emerging conflict that may not surface through formal channels (Maslach & Leiter, 2016).

Equally important, sentiment analysis can identify positive relational dynamics, such as trust, inclusion, and collaborative energy, allowing leaders to reinforce communication practices that support psychological safety (Edmondson & Lei, 2014). This proactive awareness enables leaders to intervene before emotional strain escalates into withdrawal or attrition, supporting both relational and organizational resilience.

However, the ethical value of sentiment analysis depends on responsible use. Research on organizational trust emphasizes that emotional data must be framed as a developmental resource rather than a surveillance tool to avoid undermining psychological safety (Zuboff, 2019). When used transparently and with consent, collective emotional insights can support relationally informed leadership without compromising dignity.

3.4 Adaptive Learning and Longitudinal Development

Leadership insight: Empathy develops iteratively and benefits from sustained, personalized feedback.

A defining strength of agentic AI lies in its capacity for longitudinal learning and adaptation (Wooldridge, 2021). By tracking emotional patterns across time, AI systems can adjust feedback to align with a leader's evolving developmental needs rather than applying uniform interventions (Dweck, 2006).

Developmental models of emotional intelligence emphasize that empathy matures through iterative cycles of awareness, reflection, and behavioral adjustment embedded in real social contexts (Mayer et al., 2008). Early developmental support may focus on recognizing emotional cues, while later stages involve navigating conflict, cultural difference, and ethical complexity (Goleman, Boyatzis, & McKee, 2013).

Agentic AI systems can scaffold this progression by gradually shifting the nature of feedback as competencies stabilize, mirroring Vygotsky's concept of scaffolding in learning theory (Vygotsky, 1978). As leaders internalize empathic skills, AI support can recede, reinforcing autonomy rather than dependence.

This longitudinal approach contrasts sharply with one-time leadership interventions and aligns with contemporary views of leadership development as a continuous process rather than a finite outcome (Day et al., 2014). By embedding learning within everyday practice, agentic AI helps sustain empathy under conditions of increasing complexity and emotional demand.

Taken together, these mechanisms position agentic AI as a powerful tool for reinforcing empathetic leadership in real organizational contexts. By providing real-time feedback, structured reflection, collective emotional insight, and adaptive developmental support, AI-enabled systems bridge the persistent gap between emotional awareness and leadership action (Boyatzis, 2018). Importantly, their value lies not in automating empathy but in supporting the human capacities required to practice it consistently.

At the same time, the integration of agentic AI into emotionally sensitive domains introduces ethical and relational risks that cannot be ignored. The following section therefore examines the ethical dilemmas associated with AI-supported empathy and outlines principles for responsible, human-centered implementation.

4. CONCERNS AND ETHICAL DILEMMAS

While agentic AI presents significant opportunities for enhancing empathetic leadership, its deployment within emotionally sensitive organizational domains raises complex ethical dilemmas that must be addressed with rigor and restraint (Floridi et al., 2018). Empathy involves moral responsibility, relational authenticity, and contextual judgment qualities that cannot be fully automated without risk to human dignity and agency (Nussbaum, 2011). Consequently, the ethical challenge is not whether AI *can* support empathy, but under what conditions such support remains human-centered rather than manipulative, reductive, or coercive (Mittelstadt et al., 2016).

Ethical concerns surrounding AI-supported empathy cluster around four interrelated domains: authenticity and autonomy, bias and cultural misinterpretation, privacy and emotional surveillance, and contextual oversimplification. These concerns do not invalidate the use of agentic AI but establish critical boundaries for its responsible design and implementation.

4.1 Authenticity and Leader Autonomy

A primary ethical concern involves the authenticity of empathy when it is mediated or scaffolded by AI systems. Empathy, as traditionally conceptualized in moral psychology, entails genuine emotional engagement and concern for others, not merely the outward display of socially appropriate responses (Batson, 2011). Because AI systems lack consciousness, emotion, and moral intent, their guidance is derived from probabilistic pattern recognition rather than lived experience (Searle, 1980).

This raises the risk of *performative empathy*, wherein leaders enact empathetic behaviors suggested by AI without internal emotional alignment (Hochschild, 1983). While such behavior may temporarily improve surface-level interactions, it risks hollowing out the moral substance of leadership by prioritizing appearance over authentic relational commitment (Goffman, 1959). Over time, employees may perceive this incongruence, undermining trust and psychological safety (Dirks & Ferrin, 2002).

Closely related is the issue of leader autonomy. Ethical leadership requires agents who retain responsibility for interpretation, judgment, and action (Ciulla, 2004). Excessive reliance on AI-generated emotional interpretations may weaken leaders' confidence in their own empathic judgment, particularly in ambiguous or emotionally charged situations (Kahneman, 2011). This phenomenon aligns with broader concerns about *automation bias*, where individuals defer to algorithmic outputs even when those outputs conflict with contextual knowledge or moral intuition (Parasuraman & Riley, 1997).

To preserve autonomy, AI systems must be designed to *support* reflection rather than *substitute* emotional responsibility (Floridi et al., 2018). Ethical deployment requires that AI feedback be framed as interpretive input, not authoritative instruction, ensuring that empathy remains an internally owned leadership capacity rather than an externally managed performance.

4.2 Bias and Cultural Misinterpretation

A second ethical concern involves the risk of bias embedded within AI systems that analyze emotional expression and interpersonal communication. AI models are trained on historical data that often reflect dominant cultural norms, linguistic patterns, and social assumptions, making them vulnerable to systematic bias (Benjamin, 2019). When such systems are applied to emotion recognition or sentiment analysis, these biases can distort interpretation, particularly in culturally diverse or neurodiverse contexts (Buolamwini & Gebru, 2018).

Emotional expression is not universal. Research in cross-cultural psychology demonstrates that norms governing emotional display, communication style, and relational signaling vary significantly across cultures (Markus & Kitayama, 1991). For example, restraint and indirect communication may signal respect or professionalism in some cultures but be misclassified as disengagement or lack of empathy by AI systems trained on Western expressive norms (Matsumoto et al., 2008).

Misinterpretation carries ethical consequences. Leaders who receive biased emotional feedback may unintentionally reinforce stereotypes, misjudge employees' engagement, or initiate inappropriate interventions (O'Neil, 2016). In leadership contexts, such errors can affect evaluations, trust, inclusion, and access to opportunity, thereby amplifying existing inequities (Eubanks, 2018).

Mitigating these risks requires more than technical refinement. Ethical AI design must incorporate culturally diverse datasets, continuous bias auditing, and human oversight in interpretation (Mittelstadt et al., 2016). Without these safeguards, AI-supported empathy risks becoming a mechanism of exclusion rather than inclusion.

4.3 Privacy and Emotional Surveillance

Perhaps the most ethically sensitive issue concerns the collection and analysis of emotional data within organizations. Emotional information derived from speech patterns, text, facial expressions, or behavioral indicators is deeply personal and closely tied to identity, vulnerability, and psychological safety (Solove, 2008). When such data are collected without clear boundaries, employees may experience a loss of emotional autonomy.

The distinction between *empathy support* and *emotional surveillance* is ethically consequential. Surveillance scholars argue that monitoring practices, even when framed as supportive, can produce compliance, self-censorship, and emotional labor as individuals attempt to manage how they are perceived by systems of observation (Zuboff, 2019). In organizational contexts, this may lead employees to perform emotional states deemed acceptable rather than express authentic experience, undermining trust and openness (Hochschild, 1983).

Informed consent and transparency are therefore foundational ethical requirements. Employees must understand what emotional data are collected, how they are interpreted, who has access, and for what purposes the data will be used (Westin, 1967). Without such clarity, AI-supported emotional analytics risk eroding psychological safety the very condition necessary for empathy to flourish (Edmondson, 1999).

Ethical data governance frameworks emphasize proportionality, purpose limitation, and data minimization when handling sensitive information (Floridi et al., 2018). Applying these principles to emotional data ensures that AI systems enhance relational awareness without normalizing intrusive monitoring practices.

4.4 Contextual Oversimplification and Moral Complexity

Human emotion is embedded within complex social, historical, and organizational contexts that resist reductive interpretation (Weick, 1995). While AI systems can identify emotional signals, they struggle to account for power dynamics, prior relational histories, and moral meaning that shape emotional expression (Damasio, 1994). Over-reliance on AI-generated interpretations risks oversimplifying relational realities and misguiding leadership responses.

For example, expressions of frustration may reflect systemic injustice, workload inequity, or moral injury rather than individual dissatisfaction (Mayer, Aquino, Greenbaum, & Kuenzi, 2012). AI systems can detect the signal but lack the moral reasoning required to situate that signal within broader ethical and organizational narratives.

This limitation is particularly salient in contexts involving trauma, discrimination, or ethical conflict. Trauma-informed leadership requires sensitivity, presence, and moral accountability that cannot be delegated to algorithmic systems (Herman, 1992). When leaders rely too heavily on AI-generated emotional insights in such contexts, they risk diminishing the gravity of lived experience.

Ethically responsible use therefore requires that AI feedback be positioned as *contextual support* rather than definitive assessment. Human discernment remains indispensable for interpreting emotional information within its full relational and moral context (Ciulla, 2004).

Concluding Ethical Perspective

The ethical dilemmas associated with agentic AI in empathetic leadership do not negate its developmental potential. Rather, they establish the conditions under which such potential can be realized without compromising human dignity, autonomy, or trust (Floridi et al., 2018). Empathy cannot be automated, but it can be scaffolded provided that AI systems are designed to enhance reflection, preserve agency, and respect contextual complexity.

When ethical boundaries are clearly articulated and enforced, agentic AI can support leaders in navigating emotional complexity without displacing moral responsibility. When those boundaries are ignored, the same systems risk transforming empathy from a relational virtue into a managed output. The challenge for organizations is therefore not technological capability, but ethical clarity.

5. CASE STUDIES AND APPLICATIONS OF AGENTIC AI IN EMPATHY-ORIENTED LEADERSHIP

The application of agentic artificial intelligence in leadership development has progressed beyond conceptual exploration and is increasingly evident across organizational practice (Davenport & Miller, 2022). As organizations confront digital mediation, remote work, and escalating emotional demands, AI-enabled systems are being adopted to enhance leaders' awareness of relational dynamics and emotional climates (Petriglieri, Ashford, & Wrzesniewski, 2019). Examining applied contexts is essential for understanding how empathy scaffolding functions in practice, where its benefits emerge, and where limitations become visible (Yukl & Gardner, 2020).

This section analyzes documented applications of agentic AI across corporate, hybrid, and high-stress organizational environments. Rather than presenting idealized success stories, the cases are used analytically to illustrate how AI-supported empathy operates within real institutional constraints (Iansiti & Lakhani, 2020).

5.1 AI-Enhanced Leadership Development in Corporate Environments

One of the earliest and most visible applications of agentic AI for leadership development has occurred within large multinational corporations seeking scalable approaches to emotional and relational capability building (Davenport & Ronanki, 2018). Organizations with dispersed workforces face structural limits in providing individualized coaching and feedback, making AI-based systems attractive for augmenting leadership development infrastructures (McAfee & Brynjolfsson, 2017).

IBM has been widely documented as a pioneer in deploying AI-enabled leadership and people analytics systems (Jesuthasan, Malcolm, & Cantrell, 2021). Through internal platforms integrating natural language processing and communication analytics, IBM analyzes patterns in collaboration tools to identify trends in engagement, sentiment, and interaction quality (Davenport, Harris, & Shapiro, 2010). These systems provide leaders with aggregated feedback on relational dynamics, allowing them to detect emerging emotional risks such as disengagement or frustration before they escalate into performance or retention issues.

Importantly, IBM's use of AI is framed developmentally rather than evaluatively. Leaders receive reflective dashboards highlighting patterns rather than prescriptive directives, preserving interpretive autonomy while enhancing emotional awareness (Jesuthasan et al., 2021). Research on analytics-driven leadership development suggests that this framing increases leader receptivity and reduces defensive responses to feedback (London & Smither, 2002).

IBM has also experimented with conversational AI tools designed to simulate reflective coaching interactions (Davenport & Miller, 2022). These systems prompt leaders to reflect on emotionally salient events by asking open-ended questions grounded in recent interactions. Such reflective prompting aligns with adult learning theory, which emphasizes self-directed reflection as a mechanism for behavioral change (Kolb, 1984). By storing interaction histories, these AI systems support longitudinal insight into emotional development, reinforcing empathy as a practice rather than a one-time intervention.

Another extensively cited example is BetterUp, a leadership development platform that integrates AI to supplement human coaching relationships (Feintzeig, 2020). BetterUp's AI tools analyze linguistic patterns and interaction histories to provide leaders with between-session prompts focused on emotional regulation, perspective-taking, and communication clarity (Kellerman & Seligman, 2023). Empirical evaluations of coaching augmentation suggest that such AI-supported reflection improves skill retention and application by reinforcing learning in real-time contexts (Jones, Woods, & Guillaume, 2016).

Salesforce provides a further illustration through its deployment of AI-driven analytics via its Einstein platform. Although originally developed for customer relationship management, sentiment analysis features have been adapted internally to assess team engagement and psychological safety (Bersin, 2022). Leaders receive signals indicating shifts in communication tone, responsiveness, and participation patterns, enabling proactive relational interventions.

Across these corporate cases, AI systems function less as substitutes for leadership judgment and more as perceptual amplifiers. By revealing emotional patterns that exceed human cognitive bandwidth, agentic AI expands leaders' situational awareness without displacing relational responsibility (Yukl & Gardner, 2020).

5.2 AI Support for Hybrid and Remote Leadership

The expansion of hybrid and remote work has intensified challenges related to emotional visibility and relational connection (Kniffin et al., 2021). In digitally mediated environments, leaders lose access to informal cues, spontaneous interactions, and embodied signals that traditionally support empathic understanding (Mortensen & Haas, 2018). Agentic AI systems have therefore been adopted as compensatory mechanisms to surface relational dynamics that would otherwise remain hidden.

Microsoft Viva Insights exemplifies this application through its analysis of communication patterns across email, messaging, and meeting platforms (Microsoft Research, 2022). Viva Insights aggregates data on participation equity, meeting load, response latency, and after-hours communication, providing leaders with indicators of inclusion, overload, and burnout risk (Bersin, 2021). Empirical research on digital collaboration suggests that such metrics are strongly associated with employee well-being and perceived leader support (Derks, van Duin, Tims, & Bakker, 2015).

Meeting intelligence tools such as Zoom IQ and Otter AI further extend this functionality by analyzing conversational dynamics during virtual meetings (Kreiner, Hollensbe, & Sheep, 2006). These systems track speaking time distribution, interruptions, and engagement patterns, alerting leaders when participation becomes uneven. Studies on inclusive leadership demonstrate that equitable conversational space is directly linked to perceptions of fairness and psychological safety (Nembhard & Edmondson, 2006).

AI is also increasingly used to detect early indicators of burnout in remote environments. Platforms such as Workday Peakon analyze sentiment trends, communication frequency, and workload indicators to provide leaders with early warnings of emotional strain (Workday Research, 2022). Burnout research consistently shows that early intervention is critical, as prolonged emotional exhaustion reduces empathy and increases relational withdrawal among leaders (Maslach & Leiter, 2016).

Educational and research institutions have adopted similar tools to support distributed academic leadership (Watermeyer et al., 2021). Virtual assistants analyze departmental communications during periods of organizational change, enabling leaders to identify rising anxiety or resistance and respond with transparent dialogue. Such applications underscore the role of AI in supporting empathic sensemaking rather than enforcing compliance (Weick, Sutcliffe, & Obstfeld, 2005).

Across hybrid contexts, agentic AI corrects a common leadership error: mistaking digital silence for emotional stability. By surfacing invisible emotional trends, AI enhances leaders' capacity for timely and compassionate response (Kniffin et al., 2021).

5.3 AI-Facilitated Leadership in High-Stress Sectors

Agentic AI demonstrates particular relevance in high-stress sectors where emotional demands are intense and consequences are severe (Hannah, Woolfolk, & Lord, 2009). Healthcare leadership provides a salient example. Clinical leaders must balance patient safety, staff well-being, and ethical decision-making under persistent pressure (Shanafelt & Noseworthy, 2017).

AI-enabled sentiment analysis tools are increasingly used in hospital systems to monitor staff communication patterns and emotional climate (Topol, 2019). By identifying escalating emotional exhaustion or frustration among care teams, these systems enable leaders to initiate supportive interventions before burnout compromises care quality (West et al., 2018). Research indicates that emotionally attuned leadership in healthcare is associated with reduced medical errors and improved patient outcomes (Wong, Cummings, & Ducharme, 2013).

Crisis response and humanitarian organizations present a parallel case. Leaders in disaster management and emergency services operate under extreme cognitive and emotional load while coordinating distressed personnel (Kolditz, 2007). AI systems capable of analyzing real-time communication during crisis coordination can detect markers of emotional overload and cognitive fatigue (Salas, Driskell, & Hughes, 1996). Leaders receive prompts to rotate responsibilities, initiate psychological support, or slow decision tempo, thereby preserving both empathy and operational effectiveness.

These applications highlight a critical boundary: AI functions as an early-warning system, not a moral agent. In high-stress contexts, empathy cannot be automated, but it can be protected by systems that prevent emotional depletion from overwhelming leadership capacity (Hannah et al., 2009).

5.4 Comparative Analysis: Strengths, Limitations and Developmental gaps in Practice

The integration of agentic AI into leadership development presents a complex and uneven landscape of promise and constraint, shaped by organizational context, system design, and leadership framing (Iansiti & Lakhani, 2020). While prior case studies demonstrate tangible benefits ranging from enhanced emotional visibility to sustained reflective practice, comparative analysis across sectors reveals that these benefits are neither automatic nor universally realized (Davenport & Miller, 2022). Instead, the developmental value of agentic AI depends critically on how it is embedded within human-centered leadership ecosystems rather than on technical sophistication alone (Yukl & Gardner, 2020).

Strengths: Augmenting Emotional Awareness and Perceptual Bandwidth

Across industries, a consistent strength of agentic AI lies in its capacity to expand leaders' emotional perceptual bandwidth (Davenport & Ronanki, 2018). By processing large volumes of digital communication, AI systems can detect subtle affective shifts, relational patterns, and emerging emotional trends that exceed human cognitive limits, particularly under conditions of time scarcity and information overload (Eppler & Mengis, 2004).

Tools such as Microsoft Viva, Workday Peakon, and Zoom IQ exemplify this strength by identifying early indicators of disengagement, burnout, or exclusion that might otherwise remain invisible to leaders operating in hybrid or distributed environments (Bersin, 2021). Research on affective sensemaking suggests that such early detection is crucial, as leaders often underestimate emotional deterioration until it manifests as conflict or withdrawal (Weick et al., 2005).

From a leadership development perspective, this capability provides what may be termed *emotional situational intelligence*, a dynamic awareness of relational conditions that supports timely, empathic intervention (Hannah et al., 2009). Unlike retrospective surveys or episodic feedback mechanisms, agentic AI offers continuous emotional monitoring, enabling leaders to recalibrate behavior in near real time (London & Smither, 2002).

Limitations: Contextual Interpretation and Meaning-Making Deficits

Despite these strengths, comparative evidence highlights a fundamental limitation: agentic AI excels at detecting emotional signals but remains weak at interpreting their meaning (Mayer et al., 2012). Emotional expressions are inherently context-dependent, shaped by organizational history, power relations, workload structures, and interpersonal trust (Ashkanasy & Daus, 2002). AI systems can identify that frustration exists, but they cannot reliably determine *why* it exists.

For example, frustration detected in written communication may reflect temporary task pressure, unresolved interpersonal conflict, cultural communication norms, or systemic inequities embedded within organizational structures (Kahn, 1990). Treating these distinct phenomena as equivalent emotional signals risks misdiagnosis and inappropriate leadership response (Edmondson & Lei, 2014).

This limitation becomes particularly consequential when AI outputs are treated as authoritative rather than interpretive. Research on algorithmic decision support shows that users often over-trust automated insights, a phenomenon known as automation bias, especially when systems are perceived as objective or data-driven (Parasuraman & Riley, 1997). In emotionally sensitive leadership contexts, such overreliance can suppress inquiry, reduce dialogue, and undermine relational repair.

Cultural Bias and the Risk of Emotional Misclassification

Cultural variability introduces a second, well-documented limitation. Emotional expression is deeply shaped by cultural norms governing restraint, hierarchy, and communication style (Markus & Kitayama, 1991). Comparative studies demonstrate that behaviors interpreted as disengagement or avoidance in Western organizational contexts may represent respect, deference, or reflective deliberation in other cultural settings (Gelfand et al., 2011).

Although AI systems increasingly incorporate multilingual and cross-cultural data, training datasets continue to privilege dominant communication norms, leading to systematic misclassification of affect in culturally diverse teams (Benjamin, 2019). Such bias is particularly problematic in global organizations, where inaccurate emotional feedback may reinforce stereotypes or prompt misguided managerial interventions (Noble, 2018).

The literature on responsible AI consistently emphasizes that emotional analytics must be treated as culturally provisional rather than universally valid (Floridi et al., 2018). Without explicit safeguards, agentic AI risks reproducing the very inequities that empathetic leadership seeks to mitigate.

Limits in Moral Complexity, Trauma, and Deep Relational Work

A third and more profound limitation emerges in contexts involving moral ambiguity, trauma, or existential distress. Conversational AI coaches such as those deployed by BetterUp or IBM are effective in prompting reflection, identifying cognitive distortions, and reinforcing communication best practices (Jones et al., 2016). However, they remain fundamentally inadequate for situations requiring moral discernment, trauma-informed sensitivity, or deep empathic presence (Shanafelt & Noseworthy, 2017).

Human experiences of grief, discrimination, or ethical injury cannot be meaningfully reduced to sentiment scores or algorithmic prompts (Mollica, 2006). In such contexts, the absence of lived experience, vulnerability, and moral accountability renders AI guidance insufficient and potentially harmful if relied upon excessively (Hannah et al., 2009).

Comparative analysis suggests that agentic AI is most effective in *routine relational dynamics* but increasingly unreliable as emotional intensity and ethical complexity escalate (Yukl & Gardner, 2020). This boundary must be explicitly recognized in leadership design and training.

Gaps: Governance, Consent, and Developmental Theory Integration

Beyond limitations, the case studies reveal several unresolved gaps. First, many organizations lack robust governance frameworks governing emotional data use, retention, and consent (Bersin, 2022). Where transparency is absent, employees often perceive AI-driven emotional analytics as surveillance rather than support, eroding psychological safety (Edmondson, 2018).

Second, current implementations often emphasize detection over development. While AI identifies emotional patterns, fewer systems are explicitly grounded in developmental theory that explains how empathy is internalized over time (Kolb, 1984). This gap limits long-term transformation and risks reducing empathy scaffolding to behavioral compliance rather than moral growth.

Third, empirical research on long-term outcomes remains limited. While early studies demonstrate short-term gains in awareness and reflection, longitudinal evidence linking AI-supported empathy to sustained leadership effectiveness is still emerging (Kellerman & Seligman, 2023).

Taken together, the comparative analysis in Section 5.4 clarifies that the value of agentic AI in leadership development does not lie in its ability to replicate empathy, but in its capacity to structure conditions under which empathy becomes more visible, actionable, and sustainable. The strengths identified enhanced emotional awareness, longitudinal feedback, and reflective prompting are consistently counterbalanced by limitations related to contextual interpretation, cultural nuance, and moral complexity. These tensions underscore a critical transition point in the chapter's argument: empirical promise alone is insufficient without principled implementation. The question therefore shifts from *whether* agentic AI can support empathetic leadership to *how* such systems must be designed, governed, and integrated to preserve human judgment, autonomy, and relational authenticity. This transition provides the conceptual rationale for the practical recommendations that follow.

6. PRACTICAL RECOMMENDATIONS

The responsible use of agentic AI for empathy scaffolding requires organizations to move beyond aspirational commitments and articulate clear guiding principles for design, integration, and governance. The preceding sections demonstrate that while agentic AI can meaningfully enhance emotional awareness and reflective capacity, its impact depends fundamentally on how it is positioned within leadership ecosystems. Accordingly, the recommendations offered here are not exhaustive prescriptions but principled orientations intended to support ethical, effective, and context-sensitive implementation.

6.1 Designing Agentic AI for Transparency, Fairness, and Inclusivity

At the design level, agentic AI systems used in leadership development must prioritize transparency, inclusivity, and user agency. Emotional data, by its nature, carries heightened ethical sensitivity. Leaders and employees must therefore have a clear understanding of what forms of emotional information are being analyzed, how inferences are generated, and for what purposes the resulting insights are intended. When emotional analytics are positioned explicitly as developmental supports rather than evaluative tools, they are more likely to foster trust and engagement.

Fairness must also be treated as a continuous design obligation rather than a one-time technical adjustment. Emotion recognition and sentiment analysis systems should be regularly audited for cultural, linguistic, and demographic bias, particularly given the well-documented tendency of AI models to reflect dominant communication norms. Without such safeguards, systems risk misinterpreting emotional expression in diverse teams and reinforcing existing inequities.

Equally important is the preservation of user agency. Leaders and employees should retain meaningful control over their engagement with AI-based emotional feedback, including the ability to adjust feedback intensity or opt out of specific forms of analysis. Emotional data should be governed with protections comparable to those applied to health or biometric information, including informed consent, restricted access, and clearly defined data retention policies. When these conditions are met, agentic AI is more likely to function as a trust-based developmental resource rather than a perceived mechanism of emotional surveillance.

6.2 Integrating Agentic AI into Leadership Development Processes

The effectiveness of agentic AI in leadership training depends less on technological sophistication than on organizational framing. Systems that are introduced without clear purpose or ethical boundaries risk confusion, resistance, or misuse. Organizations should therefore define a narrow and explicit developmental intent for AI deployment, such as enhancing empathy, supporting reflective practice, or increasing emotional awareness. Using AI-generated emotional insights for performance evaluation or disciplinary decision-making undermines psychological safety and contradicts the developmental logic of empathy scaffolding.

Gradual integration is also critical. Introducing agentic AI within low-risk leadership development contexts such as coaching programs or voluntary learning initiatives allows leaders to build familiarity and confidence while providing organizations with opportunities to refine system design. Leaders must additionally be supported in developing emotional data literacy, enabling them to interpret AI insights critically rather than treating them as objective truths. Understanding both the strengths and limitations of emotional analytics is essential for preventing over-reliance or misinterpretation.

Finally, effective implementation requires a hybrid support model. AI-generated feedback should complement, not replace, human-led reflection, coaching, and peer dialogue. Moral reasoning, contextual understanding, and relational judgment remain fundamentally human capacities. Continuous feedback loops, incorporating user experience and ethical review, further ensure that AI systems evolve responsively alongside organizational learning.

6.3 Preserving a Clear Boundary Between Perception and Judgment

A central principle must govern all applications of agentic AI in leadership contexts: while AI may enhance emotional perception, responsibility for interpretation, judgment, and action remains entirely human. This boundary is essential for maintaining ethical accountability and relational authenticity. Agentic AI can identify patterns, surface blind spots, and prompt reflection, but it cannot assume responsibility for moral decision-making or compassionate response.

When this distinction is clearly articulated and consistently upheld, agentic AI strengthens leadership by supporting awareness without diminishing autonomy. When blurred, it risks fostering dependency, performative empathy, or abdication of responsibility. Maintaining this boundary ensures that AI functions as a scaffold for human growth rather than a substitute for the emotional labor that defines leadership itself.

7. CONCLUSION: THREE FUTURE-FACING TAKEAWAYS FOR HUMAN-CENTERED LEADERSHIP

This chapter has advanced the argument that agentic AI, when designed with transparency, ethical restraint, and human agency at its core, can function as a meaningful scaffold for empathetic leadership rather than a threat to it. By situating AI within developmental psychology, leadership theory, and organizational ethics, the chapter reframes the role of intelligent systems from instruments of control to supports for reflective growth. The implications of this reframing can be distilled into three future-facing takeaways for leadership in digitally mediated organizations.

7.1 Empathy Scaffolding Represents as a Structural Reorientation of Leadership Development

The concept of empathy scaffolding represents a structural shift in how leadership development is understood and practiced. Rather than treating empathy as a trait cultivated through episodic training or isolated interventions, this model positions emotional development as an ongoing, context-embedded process. Agentic AI enables this shift by embedding reflective prompts, emotional feedback, and adaptive learning into the everyday rhythms of leadership work. In doing so, it addresses a persistent gap in leadership development: the disconnect between emotional awareness and sustained behavioral change. Particularly in digitally distributed organizations, empathy scaffolding offers a scalable yet personalized approach that supports continuous emotional attunement without displacing human reflection.

7.2 Augmentation, Not Substitution, as the Defining Principle of AI-Enabled Leadership

A central conclusion of this chapter is that the value of agentic AI lies in augmentation rather than substitution. AI systems are most effective when they expand leaders' perceptual range highlighting patterns, surfacing blind spots, and prompting reflection while leaving interpretation, judgment, and moral responsibility firmly in human hands. Attempts to position AI as a replacement for emotional labor, ethical reasoning, or compassionate response not only exceed its technical capacities but also undermine relational authenticity. The future of leadership in AI-mediated environments therefore depends on leaders' ability to engage intelligently with algorithmic insight without relinquishing accountability, empathy, or ethical discernment.

7.3 Human-Centered Values Will Shape the Trajectory of AI Integration

As agentic AI becomes increasingly embedded in organizational life, technological capability alone will not determine its impact. Instead, outcomes will be shaped by the values that guide system design, governance, and use. Organizations that prioritize transparency, consent, inclusivity, and psychological safety are more likely to deploy AI in ways that strengthen trust and relational integrity. Conversely, the use of emotional analytics without clear ethical boundaries risks normalizing surveillance practices that erode autonomy and legitimacy. The strategic challenge facing organizations is therefore not whether to adopt agentic AI, but how to align its deployment with human dignity, contextual sensitivity, and long-term relational health.

In sum, agentic AI does not diminish the human core of leadership; it makes visible where that core requires support. When integrated as a scaffold rather than an authority, AI can help leaders cultivate emotional awareness, sustain reflective practice, and navigate complexity with greater intentionality. The future of leadership is not defined by intelligent machines alone, but by how thoughtfully humans choose to work alongside them.

ACKNOWLEDGMENT

Researchers received no specific grant from any funding agency in the public, commercial or not-for profit sectors.

REFERENCES

Ashkanasy, N. M., & Daus, C. S. (2002). Emotion in the workplace: The new challenge for managers. *The Academy of Management Perspectives*, *16*(1), 76–86. DOI: 10.5465/ame.2002.6640191

Barsade, S. G., & O'Neill, O. A. (2014). What's love got to do with it? A longitudinal study of the culture of companionate love and employee and client outcomes in a long-term care setting. *Administrative Science Quarterly*, *59*(4), 551–598. DOI: 10.1177/0001839214538636

Batson, C. D. (2011). *Altruism in humans*. Oxford University Press.

Benjamin, R. (2019). *Race after technology: Abolitionist tools for the new Jim Code*. Polity Press.

Bersin, J. (2021). *The big reset: What happens after the pandemic*. Deloitte Insights.

Bersin, J. (2022). *Irresistible: The seven secrets of the world's most enduring, employee-focused organizations*. Deloitte Press.

BetterUp Labs. (2021). *The future of coaching: AI and human-centered leadership*. BetterUp.

Bickmore, T., & Picard, R. W. (2005). Establishing and maintaining long-term human–computer relationships. *ACM Transactions on Computer-Human Interaction*, *12*(2), 293–327. DOI: 10.1145/1067860.1067867

Boyatzis, R. E. (2018). The behavioral level of emotional intelligence and its measurement. *Frontiers in Psychology*, *9*, 1438. DOI: 10.3389/fpsyg.2018.01438 PMID: 30150958

Boyatzis, R. E., & McKee, A. (2005). *Resonant leadership: Renewing yourself and connecting with others through mindfulness, hope, and compassion*. Harvard Business School Press.

Buolamwini, J., & Gebru, T. (2018). Gender shades: Intersectional accuracy disparities in commercial gender classification. *Proceedings of the 1st Conference on Fairness, Accountability and Transparency*, 77–91. DOI: 10.48550/arXiv.1801.00006

Calvo, R. A., & D'Mello, S. (2010). Affect detection: An interdisciplinary review of models, methods, and their applications. *IEEE Transactions on Affective Computing*, *1*(1), 18–37. DOI: 10.1109/T-AFFC.2010.1

Calvo, R. A., & Peters, D. (2014). *Positive computing: Technology for wellbeing and human potential*. MIT Press. DOI: 10.7551/mitpress/9764.001.0001

Ciulla, J. B. (2004). *Ethics, the heart of leadership* (2nd ed.). Praeger. DOI: 10.5040/9798216967286

Côté, S. (2014). Emotional intelligence in organizations. *Annual Review of Organizational Psychology and Organizational Behavior*, *1*(1), 459–488. DOI: 10.1146/annurev-orgpsych-031413-091233

D'Mello, S., & Kory, J. (2015). A review and meta-analysis of multimodal affect detection systems. *ACM Computing Surveys*, *47*(3), 1–36. DOI: 10.1145/2682899

Daft, R. L., & Lengel, R. H. (1986). Organizational information requirements, media richness and structural design. *Management Science*, *32*(5), 554–571. DOI: 10.1287/mnsc.32.5.554

Damasio, A. R. (1994). *Descartes' error: Emotion, reason, and the human brain*. Putnam.

Davenport, T. H., Harris, J. G., & Shapiro, J. (2010). Competing on talent analytics. *Harvard Business Review*, *88*(10), 52–58. PMID: 20929194

Davenport, T. H., & Miller, S. (2022). *Working with AI: Real stories of human–machine collaboration*. MIT Press. DOI: 10.7551/mitpress/14453.001.0001

Davenport, T. H., & Ronanki, R. (2018). Artificial intelligence for the real world. *Harvard Business Review*, *96*(1), 108–116.

Davis, M. H. (1983). Measuring individual differences in empathy: Evidence for a multidimensional approach. *Journal of Personality and Social Psychology*, *44*(1), 113–126. DOI: 10.1037/0022-3514.44.1.113

Davis, M. H. (1994). *Empathy: A social psychological approach*. Westview Press.

Day, D. V., Fleenor, J. W., Atwater, L. E., Sturm, R. E., & McKee, R. A. (2014). Advances in leader and leadership development. *The Leadership Quarterly*, *25*(1), 63–82. DOI: 10.1016/j.leaqua.2013.11.004

Derks, D., van Duin, D., Tims, M., & Bakker, A. B. (2015). Smartphone use and work–home interference. *Journal of Occupational Health Psychology, 20*(4), 411–420. DOI: 10.1037/a0039085

Dirks, K. T., & Ferrin, D. L. (2002). Trust in leadership: Meta-analytic findings. *The Journal of Applied Psychology, 87*(4), 611–628. DOI: 10.1037/0021-9010.87.4.611 PMID: 12184567

Dweck, C. S. (2006). *Mindset: The new psychology of success*. Random House.

Edmondson, A. (1999). Psychological safety and learning behavior in work teams. *Administrative Science Quarterly, 44*(2), 350–383. DOI: 10.2307/2666999

Edmondson, A. (2018). *The fearless organization: Creating psychological safety in the workplace for learning, innovation, and growth*. Wiley.

Edmondson, A. C., & Lei, Z. (2014). Psychological safety: The history, renaissance, and future of an interpersonal construct. *Annual Review of Organizational Psychology and Organizational Behavior, 1*(1), 23–43. DOI: 10.1146/annurev-orgpsych-031413-091305

Eppler, M. J., & Mengis, J. (2004). The concept of information overload. *The Information Society, 20*(5), 325–344. DOI: 10.1080/01972240490507974

Eubanks, V. (2018). *Automating inequality: How high-tech tools profile, police, and punish the poor*. St. Martin's Press.

Feintzeig, R. (2020, October 28). The AI coach will see you now. *The Wall Street Journal*.

Fitzpatrick, K. K., Darcy, A., & Vierhile, M. (2017). Delivering cognitive behavior therapy to young adults with symptoms of depression and anxiety using a fully automated conversational agent. *JMIR Mental Health, 4*(2), e19. DOI: 10.2196/mental.7785 PMID: 28588005

Floridi, L., Cowls, J., Beltrametti, M., Chatila, R., Chazerand, P., Dignum, V., Luetge, C., Madelin, R., Pagallo, U., Rossi, F., Schafer, B., Valcke, P., & Vayena, E. (2018). AI4People—An ethical framework for a good AI society. *Minds and Machines, 28*(4), 689–707. DOI: 10.1007/s11023-018-9482-5 PMID: 30930541

Galinsky, A. D., Maddux, W. W., Gilin, D., & White, J. B. (2008). Why it pays to get inside the head of your opponent. *Psychological Science, 19*(4), 378–384. DOI: 10.1111/j.1467-9280.2008.02096.x PMID: 18399891

Gelfand, M. J., Raver, J. L., Nishii, L., Leslie, L. M., Lun, J., Lim, B. C., Duan, L., Almaliach, A., Ang, S., Arnadottir, J., Aycan, Z., Boehnke, K., Boski, P., Cabecinhas, R., Chan, D., Chhokar, J., D'Amato, A., Subirats Ferrer, M., Fischlmayr, I. C., & Yamaguchi, S. (2011). Differences between tight and loose cultures. *Science, 332*(6033), 1100–1104. DOI: 10.1126/science.1197754 PMID: 21617077

Goffman, E. (1959). *The presentation of self in everyday life.* Anchor Books.

Goleman, D. (1995). *Emotional intelligence.* Bantam Books.

Goleman, D. (1998). *Working with emotional intelligence.* Bantam Books.

Goleman, D., Boyatzis, R. E., & McKee, A. (2013). *Primal leadership: Unleashing the power of emotional intelligence* (2nd ed.). Harvard Business Review Press.

Grant, A. M. (2017). The third "generation" of workplace coaching. *Coaching (Abingdon, UK), 10*(1), 37–53. DOI: 10.1080/17521882.2016.1266005

Hannah, S. T., Woolfolk, R. L., & Lord, R. G. (2009). Leader self-structure. *The Leadership Quarterly, 20*(1), 34–49. DOI: 10.1016/j.leaqua.2008.11.003

Herman, J. L. (1992). *Trauma and recovery.* Basic Books.

Hochschild, A. R. (1983). *The managed heart: Commercialization of human feeling.* University of California Press.

Iansiti, M., & Lakhani, K. R. (2020). *Competing in the age of AI.* Harvard Business School Press.

IBM Institute for Business Value. (2020). *The cognitive enterprise: Reinventing your company with AI.* IBM.

Jarrahi, M. H. (2018). Artificial intelligence and the future of work. *Business Horizons, 61*(4), 577–586. DOI: 10.1016/j.bushor.2018.03.007

Jesuthasan, R., Malcolm, B., & Cantrell, S. (2021). *Work without jobs.* MIT Press.

Jones, R. J., Woods, S. A., & Guillaume, Y. R. F. (2016). The effectiveness of workplace coaching. *Journal of Occupational and Organizational Psychology, 89*(2), 249–277. DOI: 10.1111/joop.12119

Kahn, W. A. (1990). Psychological conditions of personal engagement and disengagement at work. *Academy of Management Journal, 33*(4), 692–724. DOI: 10.2307/256287

Kahneman, D. (2011). *Thinking, fast and slow.* Farrar, Straus and Giroux.

Kellerman, B., & Seligman, M. E. P. (2023). *Tomorrow's leadership*. Oxford University Press.

Kniffin, K. M., Narayanan, J., Anseel, F., Antonakis, J., Ashford, S. P., Bakker, A. B., Bamberger, P., Bapuji, H., Bhave, D. P., Choi, V. K., Creary, S. J., Demerouti, E., Flynn, F. J., Gelfand, M. J., Greer, L. L., Johns, G., Kesebir, S., Klein, P. G., Lee, S. Y., & Vugt, M. (2021). COVID-19 and the workplace. *The American Psychologist, 76*(1), 63–77. DOI: 10.1037/amp0000716 PMID: 32772537

Kock, H., Mayfield, M., Mayfield, J., Sexton, S., & De La Garza, L. M. (2019). Empathetic leadership. *Journal of Leadership & Organizational Studies, 26*(2), 177–190. DOI: 10.1177/1548051818806290

Kolb, D. A. (1984). *Experiential learning: Experience as the source of learning and development*. Prentice Hall.

Kolditz, T. A. (2007). *In extremis leadership*. Harvard Business School Press.

Kozlowski, S. W. J., Mak, S., & Chao, G. T. (2015). Team-centric leadership. *The Leadership Quarterly, 27*(2), 289–299. DOI: 10.1016/j.leaqua.2015.02.002

Kreiner, G. E., Hollensbe, E. C., & Sheep, M. L. (2006). On the edge of identity: Boundary dynamics at the interface of individual and organizational identities. *Human Relations; Studies Towards the Integration of the Social Sciences, 59*(10), 1315–1341. DOI: 10.1177/0018726706071525

Kruger, J., Epley, N., Parker, J., & Ng, Z.-W. (2005). Egocentrism over e-mail. *Journal of Personality and Social Psychology, 89*(6), 925–936. DOI: 10.1037/0022-3514.89.6.925 PMID: 16393025

London, M., & Smither, J. W. (2002). Feedback orientation. *Human Resource Management Review, 12*(1), 81–100. DOI: 10.1016/S1053-4822(01)00043-2

Markus, H. R., & Kitayama, S. (1991). Culture and the self. *Psychological Review, 98*(2), 224–253. DOI: 10.1037/0033-295X.98.2.224

Maslach, C., & Leiter, M. P. (2016). *Burnout*. Wiley.

Matsumoto, D.. (2008). Mapping expressive differences. *Journal of Personality and Social Psychology, 94*(6), 925–937. DOI: 10.1037/0022-3514.94.6.925 PMID: 18505309

Mayer, D. M., Aquino, K., Greenbaum, R. L., & Kuenzi, M. (2012). Who displays ethical leadership? *Academy of Management Journal, 55*(1), 151–171. DOI: 10.5465/amj.2008.0276

Mayer, J. D., Salovey, P., & Caruso, D. R. (2008). Emotional intelligence: New ability or eclectic traits? *The American Psychologist*, *63*(6), 503–517. DOI: 10.1037/0003-066X.63.6.503 PMID: 18793038

McAfee, A., & Brynjolfsson, E. (2017). *Machine, platform, crowd*. Norton.

Microsoft. (2021). *Microsoft Viva Insights: Measuring wellbeing and productivity*. Microsoft Corporation.

Microsoft Research. (2022). *Viva insights technical documentation*. Microsoft.

Mittelstadt, B. D., Allo, P., Taddeo, M., Wachter, S., & Floridi, L. (2016). The ethics of algorithms. *Big Data & Society*, *3*(2), 2053951716679679. Advance online publication. DOI: 10.1177/2053951716679679

Mollica, R. F. (2006). *Healing invisible wounds*. Vanderbilt University Press.

Mortensen, M., & Haas, M. (2018). Rethinking teams. *Harvard Business Review*, *96*(2), 74–81.

Nembhard, I. M., & Edmondson, A. C. (2006). Making it safe. *Journal of Organizational Behavior*, *27*(7), 941–966. DOI: 10.1002/job.413

Noble, S. U. (2018). *Algorithms of oppression*. NYU Press. DOI: 10.18574/nyu/9781479833641.001.0001

Nussbaum, M. C., & Capabilities, C. (2011). The human development approach. *Creating capabilities. Cambridge, MA: Belknap Press of Harvard*, 87.

O'Neil, C. (2016). *Weapons of math destruction*. Crown.

Orlikowski, W. J. (2007). Sociomaterial practices. *Organization Studies*, *28*(9), 1435–1448. DOI: 10.1177/0170840607081138

Pang, B., & Lee, L. (2008). Opinion mining and sentiment analysis. *Foundations and Trends in Information Retrieval*, *2*(1–2), 1–135. DOI: 10.1561/1500000011

Parasuraman, R., & Riley, V. (1997). Humans and automation. *Human Factors*, *39*(2), 230–253. DOI: 10.1518/001872097778543886 PMID: 18689061

Petriglieri, G., Ashford, S. J., & Wrzesniewski, A. (2019). Agony and ecstasy in the gig economy. *Administrative Science Quarterly*, *64*(1), 124–170. DOI: 10.1177/0001839218759646

Picard, R. W. (1997). *Affective computing*. MIT Press. DOI: 10.7551/mitpress/1140.001.0001

Raisch, S., & Krakowski, S. (2021). Artificial intelligence and management: The automation–augmentation paradox. *Academy of Management Review*, *46*(1), 192–210. DOI: 10.5465/amr.2018.0072

Russell, S., & Norvig, P. (2021). *Artificial intelligence: A modern approach* (4th ed.). Pearson.

Salas, E., Driskell, J. E., & Hughes, S. (1996). The study of stress and human performance. *Human Factors*, *38*(2), 186–198.

Salovey, P., & Mayer, J. D. (1990). Emotional intelligence. *Imagination, Cognition and Personality*, *9*(3), 185–211. DOI: 10.2190/DUGG-P24E-52WK-6CDG

Schön, D. A. (1983). *The reflective practitioner*. Basic Books.

Searle, J. R. (1980). Minds, brains, and programs. *The Behavioral and Brain Sciences*, *3*(3), 417–457. DOI: 10.1017/S0140525X00005756

Shanafelt, T. D., & Noseworthy, J. H. (2017). Executive leadership and physician well-being. *Mayo Clinic Proceedings*, *92*(1), 129–146. DOI: 10.1016/j.mayocp.2016.10.004 PMID: 27871627

Solove, D. J. (2008). *Understanding privacy*. Harvard University Press.

Topol, E. (2019). *Deep medicine*. Basic Books.

Uhl-Bien, M., & Arena, M. (2018). Leadership for organizational adaptability. *The Leadership Quarterly*, *29*(1), 89–104. DOI: 10.1016/j.leaqua.2017.12.009

Vygotsky, L. S. (1978). *Mind in society: The development of higher psychological processes*. Harvard University Press.

Walther, J. B. (2011). Theories of computer-mediated communication. *The Handbook of Interpersonal Communication*, 443–479.

Watermeyer, R.. (2021). Pandemic digitalization. *British Journal of Educational Technology*, *52*(4), 1418–1430. DOI: 10.1111/bjet.13177

Weick, K. E. (1995). Sensemaking in organizations. *Sage (Atlanta, Ga.)*.

Weick, K. E., Sutcliffe, K. M., & Obstfeld, D. (2005). Organizing and the process of sensemaking. *Organization Science*, *16*(4), 409–421. DOI: 10.1287/orsc.1050.0133

West, C. P., Dyrbye, L. N., & Shanafelt, T. D. (2018). Physician burnout. *Lancet*, *388*(10057), 2272–2281. DOI: 10.1016/S0140-6736(16)31279-X PMID: 27692469

Westin, A. F. (1967). *Privacy and freedom*. Atheneum.

Wong, C. A., Cummings, G. G., & Ducharme, L. (2013). The relationship between nursing leadership and patient outcomes. *Journal of Nursing Management, 21*(5), 709–724. DOI: 10.1111/jonm.12116 PMID: 23865924

Wood, D., Bruner, J. S., & Ross, G. (1976). The role of tutoring in problem solving. *Journal of Child Psychology and Psychiatry, and Allied Disciplines, 17*(2), 89–100. DOI: 10.1111/j.1469-7610.1976.tb00381.x PMID: 932126

Wooldridge, M. (2021). *A brief history of artificial intelligence*. Flatiron Books.

Workday. (2022). *Employee experience and sentiment analytics*. Workday Inc.

World Economic Forum. (2020). *The future of jobs report 2020*. World Economic Forum.

Yukl, G., & Gardner, W. (2020). *Leadership in organizations* (9th ed.). Pearson.

Zimmerman, B. J. (2000). Attaining self-regulation. *Handbook of Self-Regulation*, 13–39.

Zuboff, S. (2019). *The age of surveillance capitalism*. PublicAffairs.

ADDITIONAL READING

Ashkanasy, N. M., & Daus, C. S. (2005). Emotion in the workplace: The new challenge for managers. *The Academy of Management Perspectives, 19*(1), 76–86. DOI: 10.5465/ame.2002.6640191

Côté, S. (2014). Emotional intelligence in organizations. *Annual Review of Organizational Psychology and Organizational Behavior, 1*(1), 459–488. DOI: 10.1146/annurev-orgpsych-031413-091233

Dulebohn, J. H., & Hoch, J. E. (2017). Virtual teams in organizations. *Human Resource Management Review, 27*(4), 569–574. DOI: 10.1016/j.hrmr.2016.12.004

Edmondson, A. C. (1999). Psychological safety and learning behavior in work teams. *Administrative Science Quarterly, 44*(2), 350–383. DOI: 10.2307/2666999

Mittelstadt, B. D., Allo, P., Taddeo, M., Wachter, S., & Floridi, L. (2016). The ethics of algorithms: Mapping the debate. *Big Data & Society, 3*(2), 1–21. DOI: 10.1177/2053951716679679

Van Kleef, G. A. (2016). The interpersonal dynamics of emotion: Toward an integrative theory of emotions as social information (EASI). *Current Directions in Psychological Science*, *25*(6), 386–393. DOI: 10.1177/0963721416659787

KEY TERMS AND DEFINITIONS

Agentic Artificial Intelligence (Agentic AI): AI systems capable of autonomous goal-directed behavior, adaptive decision-making, and responsive interaction with humans. Unlike passive algorithms, agentic AI demonstrates initiative, context-awareness, and the ability to support leadership tasks dynamically.

Empathy Scaffolding: A process through which technological systems provide structured support such as nudges, emotional cues, or reflective prompts to help leaders develop and sustain empathetic behaviors over time. Inspired by Vygotskian learning theory, scaffolding enhances human emotional capacities without replacing them.

Emotional Intelligence (EI): A set of cognitive-emotional competencies involving the perception, understanding, regulation, and use of emotions in oneself and others. Foundational models include Mayer and Salovey's four-branch model and Goleman's leadership-based EI framework.

Empathetic Leadership: A leadership approach grounded in understanding others' emotions, recognizing diverse perspectives, and responding with sensitivity. It includes cognitive empathy (perspective-taking), affective empathy (emotional resonance), and behavioral empathy (supportive action).

Psychological Safety: A shared team belief that interpersonal risk-taking such as asking questions, expressing concerns, or admitting mistakes is safe. Edmondson's (2018) work identifies psychological safety as essential for innovation, trust, and effective leadership.

Affective Computing: A field of AI research concerned with systems that detect, interpret, and simulate human emotions. Affective computing technologies include sentiment analysis, emotion recognition models, vocal tone analysis, and conversational interfaces.

Sentiment Analysis: An AI technique that evaluates emotional tone in spoken or written communication. Used in leadership contexts to interpret team morale, emotional climate, and interpersonal dynamics through data-driven signals.

Conversational AI Coaching: Emotion-aware interactive systems such as digital coaches or chat-based platforms that provide real-time feedback, reflective questioning, and personalized development guidance to leaders.

Algorithmic Bias: Systematic and unfair discrimination that occurs when AI models learn biased patterns from training data. In leadership contexts, algorithmic bias can distort emotional insights or reinforce stereotypes about communication styles, affect, or cultural norms.

Authenticity of Empathy: The degree to which empathetic responses are genuine rather than performative. A concern when AI produces "machine empathy," raising ethical questions about whether empathy can be simulated without human emotional experience.

Emotional Surveillance: The continuous monitoring of emotional cues using AI-enabled sensors or analytics. While potentially useful for leader development, it raises issues of privacy, autonomy, and psychological intrusion.

Hybrid and Remote Leadership: Leadership practiced in distributed work environments mediated through digital platforms. AI-driven emotional and communication analytics help leaders remain attentive, inclusive, and empathetic across physical distance.

Transparency and Explainability: AI design principles requiring that leaders understand how emotional insights are generated. Transparency ensures trust, reduces misinterpretation, and aligns with ethical use of AI in leadership development.

Human–AI Collaboration: A relational framework where humans and AI systems work jointly, each contributing complementary strengths. In leadership, this involves AI augmenting emotional insight while humans provide ethical judgment and relational authenticity.

Empathy Augmentation: The enhancement of human empathic abilities through AI-mediated feedback, emotional insights, or adaptive learning systems. Unlike empathy automation, augmentation strengthens *human* empathy rather than simulating it.

Empathy Automation: The use of AI systems to detect, encode, and express empathic responses such as sentiment-responsive chatbots. This raises concerns about authenticity and the boundaries of machine-generated empathy.

Socio-Emotional Analytics: AI-driven analysis of emotional patterns, relational cues, and communication dynamics within teams. These analytics inform leaders about group morale, psychological climate, and interpersonal tensions.

Digital Emotional Labor: The requirement for leaders to manage emotional expression and relational tone in computer-mediated environments. AI-assisted sentiment tools can support or strain this labor depending on use.

Artificial Relational Intelligence (ARI): The capacity of AI systems to engage in socially responsive behaviors such as context-sensitive dialogue, empathetic prompts, or adaptive coaching that support leader follower relationships.

Emotion Recognition Systems: Technologies that infer emotional states from voice, text, facial expression, or physiological signals. In leadership development, these systems provide real-time insight into emotional dynamics.

AI-Mediated Reflection: Structured reflection facilitated by AI, including prompts, nudges, and feedback loops that help leaders examine their emotional responses, biases, and interpersonal behaviors.

Context-Aware AI Coaching: AI coaching systems that adjust recommendations or feedback based on situational cues including team climate, stress levels, conflict indicators, or cultural context.

Digital Empathy Ecosystems: Integrated technological environments (e.g., Microsoft Viva, Peakon, BetterUp) that use AI to monitor emotional climate, support resilience, enhance communication, and cultivate empathy at scale.

Ethical AI Governance in Leadership Development: Frameworks ensuring that AI used in leader training respects fairness, transparency, privacy, and cultural sensitivity. Covers algorithmic oversight, emotional data governance, and responsible use policies.

Chapter 13
Designing Leadership Development Tools With AI Empathy Scaffolds

Tushar
http://orcid.org/0000-0001-7190-7687
United College of Engineering and Research, Prayagraj, India

Pooja Jaiswal
http://orcid.org/0009-0007-2507-1525
University of Allahabad, Prayagraj, India

Manish Kumar
http://orcid.org/0009-0007-0735-0256
P.K. University, Shivpuri, India

ABSTRACT

Agile dynamics surrounding modern workplaces globalization, remote work and increasingly everything centered on psychological safety have also helped empathy evolve from a soft skill into a leadership job requirement. Leaders with high levels of empathy experience better team cohesion, engagement, retention and problem-solving. While empathy comes easy to some people, it is at heart a learnable skill. We refer to these temporary intelligent support systems inspired by educational psychology as AI Empathy Scaffolds, designed to allow leaders to learn empathy with the help of temporally-continuous realistic simulations and real-time behaviour feedback. AI works to facilitate reflection, analyse emotional and cognitive reactions as well as provide personalised learning paths and in so doing acts a coach

DOI: 10.4018/979-8-3373-6650-0.ch013

and mirror rather than a substitute for human interaction. This chapter includes an examination of future direction and ethical implications in forging genuinely human-centred, technology-enabled leadership.

1. INTRODUCTION

The 21st century Leadership seems to have a radical change. The leadership of today has increased expectations, duties and pressures than it used to be in the past. Due to the forces of inertia -induced and reinforced by habitual thought, we continue to hang onto old style leadership models that have been developed on a hierarchical organizational structure and under stable conditions and predictable organization behavior, a phenomenon that is no longer the case in an age of change, interconnectivity, and rapid technological revolution (Kahneman, 2011; Schulz, 2017). Since companies have gone international and individuals of various nations interact, cultures and different time zones converge to work; leaders are bound to navigate some complexities that no previous generation would have even dared think of them. The modern leadership environment has become dynamic, multicultural, and extremely digital and emotionally draining (Jami et al., 2023). The skill of empathetically connecting with people comprehend their emotions, associate with you in their struggles and inspirations is that a fraction of what the interface of leadership looks like. This is the ability that we can call empathy, which is the foundation of the contemporary leadership (Lee et al., 2022).

Empathy is now the soft skill, or as I prefer to call it, the power skill. According to research in organizational psychology, and behavioral science, leaders who are empathetic stand a better chance of being trusted, inspiring loyalty (without being love) better communication and creating mentally safe workplace for their employees (Vafeiadis & Xiao, 2021). Leadership based on empathy will turn their teams into innovators, and more resilient and collaborative people (Agapie et al., 2013). Employers employ empathy to reduce pressure, foster the health and well-being of their staff, and build inclusive cultures in which individuals feel as though they are part of the organization, and they are heard. Empathy is a force multiplier in an ever-collaborative world, where the world concentrates on keeping talent and where employees are able to collaborate and solve problems jointly. And despite all its significance, empathy is one of the hardest leadership skills that can be built.

Conventional leadership development initiatives strive to impart the element of empathy using workshops, situational role-play, coaching discussion and contemplative practices. There are however two significant limitations to these interventions. To begin with, they are episode based and delivered via fixed-action suits with minimal possibilities of behavioral change or reinforcement. Empathy, however, needs effort to do and observe. It requires live and reactive emotional knowledge that can be warped around the tremendous range of unplanned circumstances that no-one-off-classroom-version will ever be able to recreate (Konrath et al., 2011). The other one is that the old school programs are costly and/or resource intensive, allegedly only accessible to the top-level officers or influential individuals. That brings in inequalities in the development of leadership and no democratization of what is likely to be one of the most useful jobs in the current working environment.

(Barrett, 2006) is the place where AI provides a possible paradigm shift. The advances in affective computing, natural language processing, predictive analytics and adaptive learning have enabled AI to comprehend human emotions, interpret patterns of communication and behavioral trends, and provide people with feedback that allows them to develop their social skills further. AI is not only automatable anymore; it is becoming more of a socio-cognitive partner capable of understanding human emotions, discerning communication patterns, and trends of behavior, and providing the feedback that enables people to improve their social skills even more. Subsequently, when properly applied in leadership training, AI may become the fantastic multiplier of the human potential (Eigenraam et al., 2018).

The term excised from the center of this chapter (Coelho et al., 2023), AI Empathy Scaffolds (Preston & Waal, 2002), describes this alchemy of artificial intelligence and human emotional bioavailability. Just as there are physical scaffolds that provide construction workers the means through which to conduct building work, AI empathy scaffolds support both emerging and experienced leaders in their development of the profound, sustained empathy required for complex human-centric work (Kiritchenko et al., 2021). Such AI-powered platforms offer guided and structured coaching, emotional insight in real time and individualized learning moments (Zarins & Konrath, 2017). Over the years, the scaffolds for empathetic behaviors have been removed as leaders become attuned to emotions on their own authentic human empathy.

AI empathy scaffolds work by several means. They can process verbal and non-verbal information that is, your tone of voice, the way you speak or use words, facial expressions and other physiological cues to emotions (Konrath et al., 2023). AI is expected to play a significant role in offensive and defensive cyber security measures, requiring legal frameworks to adapt (Tushar et al., 2026). They have the ability to spotlight instances where a leader missed an emotional signal or reacted in a way that was detrimental to communication. They can provide micro lessons, reflection questions or suggested alternative answers. Crucially, they have the ability to meaningfully interpret feedback in terms of an individual's personal communication style, cultural heritage and development needs.

Imagine a manager hosting a virtual team call. In a videoconferencing service, one of the AI capabilities tracks the group dynamics and realizes that one member has been making no contribution during a crucial discussion. This is subsequently communicated to the boss by the system, and this gives a red flag that this team member may feel excluded or uncertain. Then it encourages the leader to follow up with either understanding questions or check-in methods privately. In a different one, an AI coaching assistant examines weeks of mailed messages and determines how the messages are rushed or one-liner-replied. It demonstrates how these patterns can be decoded by teammates and provides some tips on how to write more caring and empathetic messages. This is later reported back to the boss by the system, and it raises a red flag that this team member might feel left out or unsure. It then invites the leader to follow up with either empathetic questions or private check-in tactics. Considering the Industry 4.0 and human-centered view of Industry 5.0, it is necessary to design leadership development instruments using AI empathy scaffolds. These systems use modern analytics and emotion modelling intelligence to develop nimble, ethical, and strong leaders who can manage technology vulnerabilities without allowing them to slow down the organizational advancement (Tushar et al., 2026). In another, an AI coaching assistant reviews weeks of emailed correspondence and identifies patterns of hurried or cursory expression. It shows how teammates can interpret these patterns, and offers advice on writing more caring, empathetic messages. The latest advanced technology, deep learning, is a technique used to process images and analyze big data, offering an advanced process to interpret the emotions, behaviors, and patterns of interaction of a person and allowing the AI to react to them. When constructing artificial intelligence-based leadership development aids through the use of empathy load in the form of AI, these features aid in building adaptive, tailored learning opportunities that support emotional intelligence, communication, and decision making capability in new leaders (Tushar et al., 2026).

The increasing popularity of remote and hybrid work has only made these tools more essential (Ekdahl & Osler, 2023). Virtual worlds decrease access to the emotional cues that have typically characterized our ability to understand others. Misunderstanding is easier, isolation more likely, emotional signals more difficult to receive. AI can help fill in that gap by making emotions more visible and supporting leaders to remain supportive, empathetic or compassionate in digital interactions (James et al., 2017).

There are also ethical concerns influencing the design of AI empathy scaffolds. These tools need to work transparently, consensually, respect privacy and cultural sensibilities. It is not a matter of surveillance or behavior control, but of empowering individuals with new knowledge as one that would bring them into human relationship with one another. The reflections of ethical empathies as those of respect, fairness and inclusiveness in relations with users can be modelled using well administered AI scaffolds (Verduyn et al., 2017). The introduction of AI empathy scaffolds will be a game changer in terms of leadership development. We are moving beyond episodic training systems to contextual, personalized, ongoing learning systems. Managers who have been nurtured by such systems are better placed to navigate the emotional and relationship minefields of the twenty first century work life. They become more adept at hearing and understanding teams comprised of individuals with widely varying needs, to responding effectively based on those needs, and to creating an environment where innovation and collaboration can flourish.

2. UNDERSTANDING EMPATHY IN LEADERSHIP

Leading with Empathy in Leadership is seeing, valuing and acting on being sensitive to other people's feelings, moods and needs as well as using your skills to motivate, inspire, develop others and create understanding (Martingano et al., 2022). In that case, empathy in leadership means more than simply being nice or kind it's the skill of being able to emotionally connect with team members and understand things from their perspective. A leader who is empathic can sense what isn't being said, recognize people's emotional distress and respond fairly and compassionately. Confidence and connection among the team will be created. People, who feel listened to be more likely to speak openly, stay engaged and remain loyal to the organization.

On the other hand, in the second sense empathy is central to successful communication and decision-making. When leaders show empathy, they are attentive and not just focused on what is spoken. They hear the rest of the opinions and consider the impact of their policies, targets or changes on people (Lietz et al., 2011). This reduces chances of misunderstandings and conflicts at the office. Empathic leaders do not act rashly and make empty judgments about a problem; they will make an attempt to find out the roots of the problem such as poor performance, opposition to change and low morale. This way, they will be able to make rational decisions that would align up with the goals/religion of corporations and human requirements.

Empathy has now been even more critical of a leadership quality in a fast changing and highly competitive world. The contemporary workplace is heterogeneous, multinational and in most cases digital and therefore, emotional cognizance is even more complex. By being more empathetic and understanding how to cross-cultural borders, empathetic leaders will be able to do little to manage remote teams and assist their stressed, burned-out or otherwise anxious employees make sense of an uncertain future with a certain level of care (Behler & Berry, 2022). Psychological safety is also promoted by empathy whereby staff members would feel safe enough to share ideas and failures and new initiatives without fear of being chastised and humiliated. This culture promotes innovation, learning and active work.

Finally, empathy in leadership is also concerned with the boundaries and using it in a disciplined and honest manner. Empathy is not frailty and avoidability of difficult choices. Instead it is about delivering harsh messages in a respectful and just and humane way. A caring manager may be rough and still human, strong and encouraging (Stephan et al., 2014). Striking a balance between such an emotional intelligence and being responsible and in-charge, such leaders do not achieve dedication by fear. Notes Keeping oneself at a distance from "the other" often contributes to leadership success, however not all types of distance are necessarily effective or productive Empathy in leadership is a potential source for achieving long-term success-based on ethic governance and human centered organizational growth.

2.1 Defining Empathy

Empathy is a fundamental human skill that enables people to comprehend, share and react meaningfully to the feelings and experience of others (Smith, 2017). In both psychology and the study of leadership, empathy is often considered not to be reduced to an isolable affective feeling or a skill. The point is not just to know what other people feel, but also to feel with them and respond emotionally in caring ways. Empathy is also the bridge between authority and humanity, a place from which leadership can be exerted not by force but through understanding, connection and compassion. Empathy can be divided into three types: cognitive, emotional, and compassionate. All three of those influence that, but they all interact as you build leadership success.

2.1.1. Cognitive Empathy

Migration Strategy Cognitive empathy refers to the ability to cognitively put you in the inner life of another person, what they might be thinking and feeling and knows accordingly (Feddes & Doosje, 2015). It is frequently called "perspective-taking." One with well developed cognitive empathy is able to correctly read what is going on inside team member heads, even if the manager doesn't think like that personally.

For example, a manager may not believe she's stressed about an upcoming deadline but can recognize that her junior staff feels stressed and unsure of themselves. This awareness helps a leader use simpler language, adjust his or her expectations and provide clear directives (Guan et al., 2019). The word is used in decision making, negotiation, problem solving and strategic communications (Osler & Zahavi, 2022). It allows leaders to foresee response, forecast human behavior and carve strategies/ policies which are human-centric (Sriwilai & Charoensukmongkol, 2016).

For contemporary businesses, the very nature of teams means that cultural, gender, age and personality differences are likely to exist so cognitive empathy is vital. Leaders need to be able to comprehend positions that are far from their own.

Without it, confusion can lead to miscommunication and conflicts. Cognitive empathy is the intellectual basis for emotionally intelligent leadership.

2.1.2. Affective Empathy

Affective empathy is the capacity to share another person's feelings. As it happens, cognitive empathy is more cerebral thinking or knowing how someone else feels but affective empathy is feeling what the other person is feeling. It's about actually "feeling with" other people, rather than understanding why they feel that way. E.g. when a team member has to cope with a personal tragedy, an affective empathetic leader not only realizes how serious this is but also actually feels sad, anxious or compassionate for that person. This affective commitment does contribute to the formation of strong interpersonal relations and a sensation of emotional security among team members (Dredge & Schreur, 2020). Emotional empathy brings about a more relationship-based and less transactional leadership. But there is another kind of affective empathy that requires calibration. When people are deeply emotionally involved, but without cognitive control, emotional labor and decisional biases may arise. Leaders also need to mix affective empathy with their cognition in order to be both caring and objective (Krueger, 2018).

2.1.3. Compassionate Empathy (Empathetic Concern)

Empathic caring is more than understanding and matching of emotions. It would make it just as theoretical that one could do positive moral and supportive things in the face of others suffering or demands. This is the kind of empathy that transforms feeling into useful action (Mezzenzana & Peluso, 2023).

For example, if a manager is aware an employee is overburdened (cognitive empathy) and feeling stressed by this (affective empathy), compassion would motivate the manager to actually do something arrange for a redistribution of workload, offer some flexibility or options for support services.

Leadership Compassionate empathy becomes crucial when it comes to leadership because leadership is all about what action you take. A leader has to intervene not just understand, feel but do something positive about the conditions and dignity for human flourishing. In values based leadership, this form of empathy compassionate functions as a moral compass in the most literal sense. Leaders who lead with empathic compassion is more likely to "stand up for the well-being of people," respond flexibly in times of crisis, and co-create cultures based on care and respect.

The Integration of All Three Forms in Leadership

Good leadership is about the correct combination and application of cognitive, affective, and compassionate empathy." Cognitive empathy can feel cold and is even manipulative when not accompanied by authentic emotional concern, whereas affective empathy becomes emotional burnout or bias/favouritism if what is perceived only clusters around that of others. Conversely, empathic caring without comprehension can result in actions that are misdirected or ineffective. Leaders who combine all three forms of empathy cognitive, emotional and compassionate are able to discern what other people think and feel, respond in emotionally resonant ways, and act with constructive purpose.

2.2 The Role of Empathy in Modern Leadership

The 21st century has transformed the face of leadership. Institutions CEO Message Today, institutions are not stagnant hierarchies designed to be productive and make profits way out of it. Rather, universities have been made more social responsible, innovative and people-centred. Empathy is now a leadership necessity and no longer a nice to have in this climate. Empathy strengthens leadership on numerous organizational situations that influence performance and human prosperity.

2.2.1. Team Performance and Collaboration

The empathetic leader is establishing inclusive, psychologically safe, and high performing teams by learning the knowledge, vulnerabilities and that which makes people motivated or worried to a higher degree which allows the organization to place individuals in the best positions that fit their skilliness as well as disperses social friction before it becomes toxic. And yes, in situations like this people feel "seen" not because of their existence as a presence but the fact that they 'matter' in their identifications and their physicality hence there is an extra element of inclusivity feelings and context there.

Empathy maximizes an open dialogue by reducing fear and enabling one to speak from the heart, increases a mutual respect due to otherness, and enhances knowledge sharing based on trust and leads problem solving through cooperation vs. competition. And when employees feel seen by their employer as they truly are, they will take greater risks in sharing ideas, putting them to work and collaborating even if it means crossing the chasm between professional and social environment. Such transparency results in smoother discussions which are more productive, problem solving is accelerated and more innovation is achieved. Empathy also serves to lower stress on the job and avoid burnout, which builds the atmosphere of emotional support and people are listened to and understood when life is hard (Vossen and Valkenburg, 2016). Talent Intelligence is plenty of studies that connect emotionally intelligent and empathetic leadership directly to employee engagement, productivity, and organizational commitment behind meeting goals, creativity & innovation. In this way, we realize that empathy is more than just a virtue; it's an enabling force for team sustainability and the long-term viability of a company.

2.2.2. Conflict Management and Mediation

Conflicts are a constant within every organization because people have conflicting goals, values, personalities, expectations and work pressure, but empathetic leaders are the best in shaping them because they deal with opposing forces instead of enforcing their rule (Walter & Stephan, 2023). Leaders use cognitive empathy to uncover the hidden reasons for disagreement, like unmet needs or confusion which might not be on the surface (Rojas et al., 2022). By affective empathy, they acknowledge and validate the emotional suffering, frustration or pain of everyone involved in such situations thereby ensuring that people feel heard rather than judged. They don't empathize with understanding or emotion alone, but are willing to be just and responsible and constructive about the problem itself through compassionate empathy. Instead of dampening conflict or avoiding a painful discussion, compassionate leaders welcome roughness that results in personal development and more intimate associates. This prevents resentment from developing as well as encourages increased trust and openness among team members. Such healthy conflict management practices in the long run render an organization more resilient in that it increases its adaptation capacity and open discussion that enables employees to work together to find solutions to problems as opposed to being defensive.

2.2.3. Innovation and Creativity

This kind of innovation is best when individuals are psychologically comfortable enough to experiment and break assumptions even though it may leave you failing without being rebuked and punished over it, and this is where empathetic leadership fits in with the greatest deal. By accepting the various views and encouraging different opinions, empathetic leaders do not make creativity stifled by fixed structures or command and control leadership. Empathic leaders will go to this extent as actually hear the thoughts and ideas of employees even where the thoughts and ideas challenge sacred cows or existing power structures; their openness conveys the message to everyone that they are being heard, respected and trusted. They are aware that the creative impulse is often not only the product of technical expertise, but also an imaginative intelligence, experience of life and social consciousness that provide us with the capacity to look at problems in a different light and visualize new solutions. Empathic leaders will be able to strengthen cross-functional business cooperation by listening to every voice and live perspectives because diverse individuals with different backgrounds and branches will be encouraged to work hard with their skills. User-centered design is also a blessing of such integration since staffers are more responsive to genuine human experience, feelings and social positions (Taylor et al., 2019). Second, compassionate leadership facilitates social responsive innovation, which connects technological and organizational development to ethical responsibility and social relevance. Thereby converted, empathy is an effective force of sustainable and meaning based and humanization focused innovation.

2.2.4. Employee Well-Being and Mental Health

The contemporary work environment is becoming more characterized by a high level of pressure, accelerated technological and organizational evolution, online overload, and the lack of clear differentiation between work and personal life, all of which have led to the increased rates of stress, burnout, anxiety, and emotional detachment among workers (Wood et al., 2016). Empathic leadership in this challenging context will be an important safeguard due to its focus on human well-being as the central point of organizational operations (Reed, 2023). Empathic leaders are better placed to identify signs of emotional distress at an earlier stage (withdrawal, fatigue, irritability or falling performance) and react with empathy, instead of blame. They promote the free and stigma-free conversation on mental health, establishing a culture where the pursuit of support is perceived as the strength but not weakness (Pignatiello et al., 2020).

Compassionate leaders also provide flexibility by means of modified workloads, hybrid working or temporary lodging so that employees can cope with their personal issues without risking work termination. As a result of active encouragement of work-life balance, they assist people to maintain long-term energy, concentration, and inspiration (Weisz et al., 2021). This kind of leadership is a great way to minimize the absenteeism, turnover due to burnout and emotional exhaustion and increase the job satisfaction, confidence in the management and loyalty to the organization. In the long run, this fostering environment not only safeguards the welfare of the employees, but also improves their resilience, interest, and long term performance within the organization.

2.2.5. Organizational Trust and Ethical Culture

Empathy builds trust towards a leader and stronger organizations, as a core pillar of leadership and sustainable organizational effectiveness. When employees see that their leaders truly care about how they are treated and act with fairness, organizational credibility is built by default. Empathy also deepens ethical leadership, because leaders who can emotionally put themselves in the real human cost of their decisions to employees, customers or society are not going be as willing to engage in exploitative, unjust or irresponsible practices. This is how empathy directly feeds into corporate integrity, social responsibility and long-term sustainability (Gallagher, 2008). Empathy is a central tenet in most major leadership models. Servant Leadership focuses on serving others before self-interest, Transformational Leadership stresses emotional inspiration, individual care and moral purpose, and Human-Centered Leadership places dignity, inclusion and psychological safety first. Collectively these meta-theoretical models show that empathy cannot be reduced to one theory or culture and therefore, is universally central for leadership.

Empathy, while already established in its significance, is also one of the hardest leadership characteristics to systemically teach and improve (Oxford et al., 2022). The majority of conventional programmers for leadership training are based on workshops, seminars, or fixed modules that work on mass scale and do not take into consideration individual differences in personality, sensitivity to emotions, cultural background or level of development. Instead, empathy grows from deep introspection, from personalized mentorship and most of all, from emotional training things that mass training programs can't do. For this reason, much of our trainees end up with a theoretical knowledge about empathy without actually integrating it into sustainable behavior.

A further restriction is the static nature of typical training content in a dynamic emotional world. Human emotions are fluid, situational and unpredictable but leadership development often relies on set case studies, scripted role-plays and artificial contexts. These models could not depict authentic workplace emotions imbued with stress, ambiguity, conflict, chaos and diversity. Also, the development of empathy relies on immediate feedback but almost all programs provide such feedback during only independent tasks, or not at all. In real world work places, leaders don't even know they failed emotionally and the bad habits continue.

Emotional resonance is also extremely situation-specific and what works for one reaction can ruin or not work at all for another. Leaders must constantly maneuver cultural differences, power and influence dynamics, virtual environments, crisis scenarios and hybrid teams. In fact most leaders are rarely exposed to the full spectrum of these emotional environments in traditional learning, which is why empathy remains more a concept than an applied practice. Third, even when leaders understand empathy in principle, they tend not to use it under stressful situations (deadlines, conflicts, performance review). Stress constricts an ability to attend, it amplifies defensiveness and it inhibits emotional awareness all of which undermine empathy just when the empathic response is most required. While actual topics in job situations are challenging and high pressure, training programmers rarely mimic the same real world of pressure as existed which will limit translation of empathic skills to 'real' leadership.

3. CONCEPTUALIZING AI EMPATHY SCAFFOLDS

AI empathy scaffolds are computational support tools that allow people to better sense, interpret, and respond to the emotions expressed by their interlocutors in intimate and complex daily contexts. These systems employ artificial intelligence features such as affective computing, natural language processing, and personalization to help users build up empathic behavior over time (Mills, 2022). With its instantaneous emotional cues, reflective prompts and adaptive learning pathways, AI empathy scaffolds are not so much as a tutor as an ever present personal coach. These findings fill the gap between the theory of empathy and its practice, particularly in leadership, healthcare and organizational communication facilitating scalable, ethical and emotionally intelligent human development.

3.1 Definition

AI Empathy Scaffolds refer to AI-generated features, modules, or affordances that are embedded within leadership development tools with the purpose of directly assisting learners by prompting them to actively engage in empathic ways of thinking and acting. Instead of disconnecting with the human sense of empathy, these scaffolds act as guided supports that lead to the growth of a learner's emotional and inter-personal awareness while interacting in real-time. They help attune the sensitivity to emotional signals, support perspective-taking, aid reflectiveness in conduct and guide people toward appropriate responses with their emotions across a broad array of social or work situations (Wilmer & Chein, 2016). They are intended to be gradually withdrawn as learners become emotionally more competent and self-regulated. As the user becomes proficient and comfortable in using their empathetic abilities, so too does the system lower its level of how much it engages and, therefore, allows individuals to apply empathy autonomously. Through this, AI Empathy Scaffolds serve as intelligent developmental scaffolding that promotes emotional development faster without inducing dependence and nurtures sustainable empathy development in leadership and organizational settings.

3.2 Theoretical Foundations

ZPD, a key concept of Vygotsky's theory, is the most powerful theoretical basis for explaining how AI empathy scaffolds work in leadership learning. Thus, these AI scaffolds function in the learner's ZPD by providing optimal level of supports that are neither too easy nor too difficult. Either, the support is too undemanding and learners can become complacent and passive, or on the other hand it is so difficult that they are likely to be frustrated by their continued failure. By dynamically adapting activity difficulty and feedback to learner performance, AI ensures that empathy skills are exercised in a growth-focused learning zone.

With affective computing, AI is able to recognize, interpret or replicate human emotions using various information channels. Formulated techniques are often found to be based on facial expressions, voice modulations, text sentiment, physiology signals and behavior patterns. By exhibiting these abilities, AI algorithms should be able to generate emotionally appropriate social responses and to teach themselves how to behave empathetically in interactions with humans. By doing so, the AI system can make human-centred emotionally-aware interactions towards users.

In addition, Cognitive Load Theory supports the concept of empathy scaffolds with its account of how AI helps lessen mental load during emotionally taxing interactions (Svenaeus, 2021). AI systems assist learners with guided prompts, phrase suggestions, perspective framing, and emotional labelling. These functions serve to de-escalate emotionally charged situations and facilitate leaders in empathic attunement, without becoming cognitively overloaded. Human-in-the-loop learning is also critical to ensure that AI-guided empathy stays ethical and responsible (Walter, 2018). It incorporates human override controls, continual human feedback loops, calibration features and robust ethical guardrails. The goal is not to mechanize empathy, but rather enhance human emotional intellect with the help of AI in responsible ways.

According to their function, empathy scaffolds can be divided into five identified types. Perceptual scaffolds enable leaders to identify emotional signals within text, voice, or action. Interpreting scaffolds give logic to emotions that are witnessed. Behavioral scaffolds indicate empathetic responses and types of communication. Reflective scaffolds incite leaders to reflect on emotional experiences. Last but not the least, developmental scaffolds monitor emotional growth and assist in developing empathetic habits for lifetime.

4. DESIGNING LEADERSHIP TOOLS WITH EMPATHY SCAFFOLDS

Creating leadership development with empathy scaffolds means baking in AI-driven supports that enable leaders to practice, hone and internalize empathic skills within real world situations. These approaches offer personalized feedback based on the detection of emotional cues, perspective-taking prompts, intervention suggestions or experiential feedback. In this way, empathy scaffolds operate within the zone of proximal development and have the effect that there is a mismatch between what learners can already do and what they aim to achieve. The aim is that as leaders become more emotionally skilled, the support reduces over time leading to independent empathetic behavior. This is so that empathy will not be taught as theory but developed as a leadership practice, contributing to trust communication and ethical decision-making among organizations (Usán Supervía et al., 2023).

Developing leaders with empathy scaffolds Designing leadership development tools with empathy scaffolds must be anchored in ethical, psychological and human dimensions (Yen et al., 2023). The first principle at work here is human-centered design, which envisions technology as something which places priority on the emotional experience of humans rather than automating it. All of these tools need to serve, rather than possess, the emotional judgment of leaders. Perhaps closely related to this is that AI solutions should be psychologically safe: they should never admonish or criticise the user, but give directions in a friendly and constructive way.

Leaders need to feel safe navigating emotional resistance without fear of judgment or punishment. Transparency in how the AI can recognize, interpret and respond to emotional signals is also an important principle. There can be no trust in the system if there is no transparency. And cultural adaptability enhances the effectiveness of design, as the way empathy is displayed varies greatly in different cultures, social norms and modes of communication. An empathy scaffold that functions in one cultural context could falter in another if not tailored with caution. Small steps are important, because empathy is learned over time with practice, contemplation and reinforcement rather than instruction. Finally, ethical sensitivity is paramount as affective data is invariably personal. Provably secure data protection, confidentiality and consent have to be designed into systems.

A key part of this system is the empathy-aware coach agent, which plays a role of an emotionally intelligent coach (Yogman et al., 2018). Such AIs understand emotional content in spoken or written words and reply with comforting, warm, human-like messages. They are guiding questions that elicit emotional insights, modelling empathetic language for users to eventually integrate into practice. It highlights sentiment-situated dialogue, context-tuned critique and simulated active listening with gentle nudges to encourage self-reflection (Hansen & Jespersen, 2013; Wang et al., 2014). If for instance a leader expresses frustration about team pressure, the AI could reflect back the emotional fatigue and ask what particular emotions he sees might be going on in his team.

The other factor is empathy scenario-based simulations whereby the trainees are immersed in the situation and they learn to use empathetic behaviors like leaders in such situations (Gallagher, 2012). Such scenarios may include performance evaluation, conflict management, diversity and inclusion debates, misunderstandings and client complaints of remote working. In such games, AI develops characters with which students can communicate through numerous reactions that they can select. The non-player character would rate the level of empathy of the response the AI displays and provide systematic feedback. The branching narratives also assist in enhancing the learning process further by illustrating the impact of different emotional decisions having different outcomes, which encourages leaders to try and see by engaging in emotionally safe practice.

Other powerful scaffolding factors are emotion feedback which is reflections. Such communications are analyzed using these mirrors because the leaders are able to understand how they interacted with others and affected them emotionally. As in Figure 1, the A.I. can observe a message was short but sounded disrespectful, and propose a more personal approach to matters within the team. The workers support mediated communication tools, which mediate empathy scaffolding in the real time course of interaction between workers. These applications make us empathize, have an emotional allegro emphasis on words written, rewrite any non-final draft messages in a better-thought word and otherwise suggest how we can adjust our tone of voice, such as by noting that a message written is too negative or even harsher (Hummel and Maedche, 2019). In the case of a leader writing a stern email, the AI may have the opportunity to suggest an alternative version of the same email that nevertheless makes the person accountable and yet shows empathy to the receiver in the process will teach the person to be understanding by making a direct comparison between two things.

5. FRAMEWORK FOR IMPLEMENTING AI EMPATHY SCAFFOLDS

An implementation system of AI Empathy Scaffolds is presented, which takes into account a systematic approach to establishing emotionally intelligent assistance in leadership regimes. It builds on the ethical design, adaptive learning, affective sensing, human feedback and continual assessment to provide responsible and sustainable empathic development in situational leadership practice. This diagnostic stage involves identifying the underlying emotional and interpersonal issues that leaders and teams grapple with. Based on the findings above, some of these gaps may refer to ineffective conflict resolution firm leaders are unable to manage disagreements and disputes positively; leader emotional illiteracy they do not have knowledge regarding emotions within themselves or around their environment; troubling communication direct miscommunication among team members which lead up to offending but not in a meaningful way; low team spirit due to leadership insensitivity behavior and cross cultural misunderstanding because different norms or values exist at work place. By understanding this landscape, not as common tools for general problems (as empathy has sometimes been in practice), but to solve specific challenges through a careful scaffolding of empathy.

The second step is to determine which kind of empathy scaffolds is appropriate for addressing each leadership problem. Scaffolds of different types are needed for different emotional challenges. With regard to recognizing emotions from voice, text or actions, the best scaffolds are perceptual in nature because they help leaders pay attention to emotional signals. When leaders struggle to read tone or emotional intent, interpretive scaffolds can provide the appropriate emotional context and posit meaning. Unempathetic communication response styles are best targeted with behavior scaffolds that prompt sensitive responses. When leaders are emotionally unreflexive, reflective protocols promote contemplation and emotional assessments. Finally, variability in the expression of empathy across development mandates scaffolds to track developments over time and to support long-term habit formation. This focused orientation results in each of the scaffolds providing direct support to the behavioral deficit which they are intended to remedy.

The third is the adaptive personalization engine that operates as an intelligence heart of AI empathy scaffolding systems. The development of empathy cannot be implemented as a fixed, linear progression that works the same for all cases since emotional growth ranges so much within and between people (Weisz et al., 2021). The personalization engine dynamically adjusts to the user's progress, comfort, interaction context and emotional complexity of engaged task. If a user is confident and correct in emotionally sensitive scenarios then difficulty ramps incrementally. On the other hand, if the user is hesitant, then the AI makes things simple and pushes more. The scaffold positions in this way will maintain the scaffolds in the zone of proximal development and not overly challenging or too easy to motivate sustained emotional involvement and learning.

The fourth stage is of integrating AI empathy scaffolds into real work rhythms. To shift toward a better version of empathy as a leadership competency as opposed to an academic theory, one must practice it in a work setting. It is the reason why empathy scaffolds are embedded in the very applications these leaders are using through their email inboxes, video conferencing applications, human resource applications, learning management systems, and performance review applications.

Through the inclusion of compassion guidance as part of the real work stream, leaders themselves are supported in the moment in the emotionally charged conversation that lands on such an area as giving a feedback, positive or negative performance evaluation or a difficult negotiation. This inclusion makes empathy a teaching concept into a practice of professionality.

The final step is non-severe elimination, or scaffold fading. The system puts less intervention levels as the leader is increasingly emotionally well. Prompts become less frequent, feedback is less telling, more asking and emotional direction is more subtle. In the long run, the scaffolding fades into the background and is substituted with internalized skill sets pertaining to empathy that are not supported by AI. This gradual segregation ensures that leaders remain emotionally independent of the system and therefore remain to some extent to be truly, organically empathetic in their decisions and their relationships. This process of five stages enables AI Empathy Scaffolds to facilitate a systematic ethical and scalable methodology of developing feelings in the contemporary leadership environment.

6. CHALLENGES AND ETHICAL CONSIDERATIONS

6.1 Risk of Over-Dependence

The main threat of AI as an empathy tool is that leaders might develop a dependency on the recommendations of it as their decision-making crutches to make emotional and decisions. By making too much of a cause of such prompts, we run the risk of drying out the natural sources of empathy and independent emotional judgment. To prevent this, empathy scaffolds must correct slowly waning in cases where the user gains confidence, and competence. In such a manner, autonomy is preserved and leaders continue leading with empathy as an internal human skill instead of the one that develops through the outside prompting.

6.2 Privacy and Emotional Data Sensitivity

The question of privacy and ethics is still a big one when using AI systems to collect or analyze the human emotional behaviour. Emotional data is highly privacy-invading, its misuse can lead to breach of consent, inadequate personal identification and emotional blackmail, it can also be used maliciously by unscrupulous firms to impose office surveillance. Without strong protections, such systems can erode trust and psychological safety. Thus, clear ethical limits, open data policies, informed consent tools and cybersecurity measures are necessary to guarantee a responsible management of emotional information.

6.3 Algorithmic Bias

There is so much variation in emotional expression among cultures, genders, personalities and neurodiversity spectrums that AI-based empathy systems suffer from algorithmic bias (Schmauder et al., 2023). In those cases, AI models trained on culturally specific datasets may misrecognize or stigmatize emotional behavior that falls outside the norm. This can result in biased evaluations and exclusion of certain groups. Against that bias, empathy models will need training on diverse data and regular examination for fairness, inclusivity and cultural tolerance.

6.4 Authenticity Concerns

One big ethical question around AI-boosted empathy is whether emotionally-led communication is still truly human. If they are aware that the communication was influenced or molded by an AI system, employees might feel that empathetic messages are not genuine (Safdari, 2021). This may undermine trust and reduced emotional attachment in the relationships between the leaders and the followers. Then AI had better be a close coach in rear, and avoid the falsifying empathy into human expression the sort that is truthful, natural and truly transformative.

7. FUTURE DIRECTIONS

7.1 Multimodal Empathy Recognition

The following generation AI systems can be more sophisticated in terms of empathy recognition in which a single-source emotion being recognized is not the solely dependent variable but rather will recognize the multidimensional empathy which may combine natural language processing, computer vision, voice analytics and biometric sensing to generate multimodal emotions (Weisz and Cikara, 2021). Such verbal information along with the facial expression can create a far more detailed and accurate image of what conditions we are actually in when it is supplemented with the vocal tone and any bio signals (such as heart rate or stress response) that a single analysis system AI might be able to accomplish. Such a vast mass of such a diverse stream of data will give machine learning systems the capability to understand human emotions, with much more specificity and detail, which can be represented using more accurate, more human-like empathetic reactions.

7.2 Digital Twins for Leadership Development

Digital twins is one much-vaunted new direction for leadership development, in which AI models of leaders can mimic their distinctive communication styles, emotional hot buttons and stress responses. These simulated systems allow leaders to respond to a quasi-life-like description of their own behavior. Through repeating challenging conversations and emotional decisions with their digital twin, leaders can watch for the effect of their emotions on results, perfect responses, and develop empathic leadership in a secure, reflective learning environment.

7.3 Empathy Co-Pilots in Live Meetings

Empathy co-pilots are imagined as real-time AI wingmen that fly under the radar in live meetings to help guide emotionally intelligent leadership. These systems might silently deliver emotional background to leaders, propose clarifying or emotionally charged questions, and monitor the overall emotional "temperature" of the group over time. Group awareness and emotional misunderstandings in groups A system that utilizes the ideas we have described might serve to inform each user of subtle, apparently unobservable or little observable emotionally informative elements about both themselves and other team members.

7.4 Empathy Metrics in Organizational Health Dashboards

Empathy, in the organizations of the future will probably be a measured performance indicator that makes its way into organizational health dashboards. Accumulate empathy related KPIs that departments can monitor such as a psychological safety index, an emotional climate score and a communication compassion metric (Lietz et al., 2011). Emotional health and empathetic behavior can be measured to see where an organization's relationships are strongest or weakest and for leaders to make targeted interventions, treating empathy as a strategic discipline that continues to develop alongside productivity and performance.

8. CASE STUDIES AND USE CASES

8.1 Empathy Training for First-Time Managers

AI empathy scaffolds are instrumental in helping novice managers make the difficult shift to leadership. These fresh leaders also struggle to read team emotions, provide feedback positively and build healthy personal relationships. AI-powered coaching also supports them in interpreting emotions and selecting empathetic language, adopting thoughtful responses at times of difficulty. When they are coached to speak with emotional intelligence-to be direct and honest, for sure, but also to mindfully communicate in ways that resonate with others-first-time managers can become confident and relationship savvy (Uncapher & Wagner, 2018). The result is that teams have more trust, a greater sense of engagement and better performance.

8.2 Leadership Development in Remote Teams

Emotional cues are not as easily recognized in remote and hybrid work settings because of the lack of physical representation. AI empathy scaffolds enable leaders to read tone in asynchronous communication, maintain emotional connection on digital channels, recognize early signals of burnout and fortify digital empathy. These systems interpret message emotion, response time and emotional pattern to help leaders create more supportive virtual communication.

8.3 Cross-Cultural Leadership Programs

AI empathy scaffolds are highly profitable in the cross-cultural development of leadership because they can be modified to fit all cultural norms related to communication styles, as well as, power distance and emotional expressiveness. Besides this, AI will be used to make empathy soft as different cultures do not express empathy in the same way. This kind of personalization enables leaders to work in the global arena respectfully and effectively with greater intercultural trust, reduced conflict and enhance global leadership effectiveness.

CONCLUSION

The emerging competitive global world relying on volatile, uncertainty, complex and ambiguity is becoming a lead competency in effective leadership. Our modern work demands, and our world is becoming new now, demand a different kind of leadership that discovers this balance between strategic decision making and profound humanity. Emphasis on empathy is becoming one of the most demanded leadership skills as businesses struggle with the dynamics of remote work, teams working across countries, and high expectations of psychological safety. The chapter has demonstrated that AI Empathy Scaffolds are like developmental promises because they give leaders the chance to practice first hand, give objective feedback on their actions on the fly, learn in a reflective manner as well as embark on learning plans that suit them best. AI is not arrived to displace human emotion, but to serve as a supportive coach and mirror, to encourage leaders to be able to employ authentic and conscious empathy. With this technology becoming increasingly involved with immersion simulations and emotional analytics, a vigilant observance of morality, privacy, and bias will still be necessary. The future of leadership, however, is in the sense of balancing between intelligent application of human intuition and technological assistance wherein AI does not simply assist leaders in thinking better but also making them feel, connect and lead with more compassion.

REFERENCES

Agapie, E., Golovchinsky, G., & Qvarfordt, P. (2013). Leading people to longer queries. In *Proceedings of the SIGCHI Conference on Human Factors in Computing Systems* (pp. 2367–2376). https://doi.org/ . 2481418DOI: 10.1145/2470654

Barrett, L. F. (2006). Are emotions natural kinds? *Perspectives on Psychological Science : A Journal of the Association for Psychological Science, 1*(1), 28–58. DOI: 10.1111/j.1745-6916.2006.00003.x

Behler, A. M. C., & Berry, D. R. (2022). Closing the empathy gap: A narrative review of the measurement and reduction of parochial empathy. *Social and Personality Psychology Compass, 16*(9), e12701. DOI: 10.1111/spc3.12701

Coelho, S., Vendrell-Ferran, Í., & Stephan, A. (2023). Emotional abilities and art experience in autism spectrum disorder. *Phenomenology and the Cognitive Sciences*. Advance online publication. DOI: 10.1007/s11097-023-09917-y

Dredge, R., & Schreur, L. (2020). Social media use and offline interpersonal outcomes during youth: A systematic literature review. *Mass Communication & Society, 23*(6), 885–911. DOI: 10.1080/15205436.2020.1810277

Ekdahl, D., & Osler, L. (2023). Expressive avatars: Vitality in virtual worlds. *Philosophy & Technology, 36*(2), 1–28. DOI: 10.1007/s13347-023-00628-5

Feddes, A. R., Mann, L., & Doosje, B. (2015). Increasing self-esteem and empathy to prevent violent radicalization: A longitudinal quantitative evaluation of a resilience training focused on adolescents with a dual identity. *Journal of Applied Social Psychology, 45*(7), 400–411. DOI: 10.1111/jasp.12307

Gallagher, S. (2008). Direct perception in the intersubjective context. *Consciousness and Cognition, 17*(2), 535–543. DOI: 10.1016/j.concog.2008.03.003

Gallagher, S. (2012). Empathy, simulation, and narrative. *Science in Context, 25*(3), 355–381. DOI: 10.1017/S0269889712000117

Guan, S. S. A., Hain, S., Cabrera, J., & Rodarte, A. (2019). Social media use and empathy: A mini meta-analysis. *Social Networking, 8*(4), 147–157. DOI: 10.4236/sn.2019.84010

Hansen, P. G., & Jespersen, A. M. (2013). Nudge and the manipulation of choice: A framework for the responsible use of the nudge approach to behaviour change in public policy. *European Journal of Risk Regulation, 4*(1), 3–28. DOI: 10.1017/S1867299X00002762

Hummel, D., & Maedche, A. (2019). How effective is nudging? A quantitative review on the effect sizes and limits of empirical nudging studies. *Journal of Behavioral and Experimental Economics*, *80*, 47–58. DOI: 10.1016/j.socec.2019.03.005

James, C., Davis, K., Charmaraman, L., Konrath, S. H., Slovak, P., Weinstein, E., & Yarosh, L. (2017). Digital life and youth well-being, social connectedness, empathy, and narcissism. *Pediatrics*, *140*(Suppl. 2), S71–S75. DOI: 10.1542/peds.2016-1758F

Jami, P. Y., Walker, D. I., & Mansouri, B. (2023). Interaction of empathy and culture: A review. *Current Psychology*. Advance online publication. DOI: 10.1007/s12144-023-04422-6

Kahneman, D. (2011). *Thinking, fast and slow*. Penguin.

Kiritchenko, S., Nejadgholi, I., & Fraser, K. C. (2021). Confronting abusive language online: A survey from the ethical and human rights perspective. *Journal of Artificial Intelligence Research*, *71*, 431–478. DOI: 10.1613/jair.1.12590

Konrath, S. H., Martingano, A. J., Davis, M., & Breithaupt, F. (2023). Empathy trends in American youth between 1979 and 2018: An update. *Social Psychological & Personality Science*. Advance online publication. DOI: 10.1177/19485506231218360

Konrath, S. H., O'Brien, E. H., & Hsing, C. (2011). Changes in dispositional empathy in American college students over time: A meta-analysis. *Personality and Social Psychology Review : An Official Journal of the Society for Personality and Social Psychology, Inc.*, *15*(2), 180–198. DOI: 10.1177/1088868310377395

Krueger, J. W. (2018). Direct social perception. In Newen, A., de Bruin, L., & Gallagher, S. (Eds.), *The Oxford handbook of 4E-cognition* (pp. 301–320). Oxford University Press. DOI: 10.1093/oxfordhb/9780198735410.013.15

Lee, S. M., Thomer, A. K., & Lampe, C. (2022). The use of negative interface cues to change perceptions of online retributive harassment. *ACM on Human–Computer Interaction, 6*(CSCW2). *Proceedings of the ACM on Human-Computer Interaction, 334*(CSCW2), 1–23. DOI: 10.1145/3555226

Lietz, C. A., Gerdes, K. E., Sun, F., Geiger, J. M., Wagaman, M. A., & Segal, E. A. (2011). The Empathy Assessment Index (EAI): A confirmatory factor analysis of a multidimensional model of empathy. *Journal of the Society for Social Work and Research*, *2*(2), 104–124. DOI: 10.5243/jsswr.2011.6

Martingano, A. J., Konrath, S., Zarins, S., & Okaomee, A. A. (2022). Empathy, narcissism, alexithymia, and social media use. *Psychology of Popular Media*, *11*(4), 413–422. DOI: 10.1037/ppm0000419

Mezzenzana, F., & Peluso, D. (Eds.). (2023). *Conversations on empathy: Interdisciplinary perspectives on imagination and radical othering*. Routledge. DOI: 10.4324/9781003189978

Mills, S. (2022). Personalized nudging. *Behavioural Public Policy, 6*(1), 150–159. https://doi.org/. 2020.7DOI: 10.1017 /bpp

Osler, L., & Zahavi, D. (2022). Sociality and embodiment: Online communication during and after Covid-19. *Foundations of Science*. Advance online publication. DOI: 10.1007/s10699-022-09861-1

Oxford Gomez, M., Klare, D., Ceballos, N., Dailey, S., Kaiser, S., & Howard, K. (2022). Do you dare to compare? The key characteristics of social media users who frequently make online upward social comparisons. *International Journal of Human-Computer Interaction, 38*(10), 938–948. DOI: 10.1080/10447318.2021.1976510

Preston, S. D., & de Waal, F. B. M. (2002). The communication of emotions and the possibility of empathy in animals. In Post, S. G., Underwood, L. G., Schloss, J. P., & Hurlbut, W. B. (Eds.), *Altruism & altruistic love* (pp. 284–308). Oxford University Press. DOI: 10.1093/acprof:oso/9780195143584.003.0025

Reed, P. (2023). Impact of social media use on executive function. *Computers in Human Behavior, 141*, 107598. Advance online publication. DOI: 10.1016/j.chb.2022.107598

Rojas, C., Zuccarelli, E., Chin, A., Patekar, G., Esquivel, D., & Maes, P. (2022). Towards enhancing empathy through emotion augmented remote communication. In *CHI Conference on Human Factors in Computing Systems* (Paper 454, pp. 1–9). https://doi.org/DOI: 10.1145/3491101.3519797

Safdari Sharabiani, A. (2021). Genuine empathy with inanimate objects. *Phenomenology and the Cognitive Sciences, 20*(5), 831–846. DOI: 10.1007/s11097-020-09715-w

Schmauder, C., Karpus, J., Moll, M., Bahrami, B., & Deroy, O. (2023). Algorithmic nudging: The need for an interdisciplinary oversight. *Topoi, 42*(3), 799–807. DOI: 10.1007/s11245-023-09907-4

Schulz, A. W. (2017). The evolution of empathy. In Maibom, H. (Ed.), *The Routledge handbook of philosophy of empathy* (pp. 64–74). Routledge. DOI: 10.4324/9781315282015-7

Smith, J. (2017). What is empathy for? *Synthese, 194*(3), 709–722. DOI: 10.1007/s11229-015-0771-8

Sriwilai, K., & Charoensukmongkol, P. (2016). Face it, don't Facebook it: Impacts of social media addiction on mindfulness, coping strategies and the consequence on emotional exhaustion. *Stress and Health : Journal of the International Society for the Investigation of Stress*, *32*(4), 427–434. DOI: 10.1002/smi.2637

Stephan, A., Walter, S., & Wilutzky, W. (2014). Emotions beyond brain and body. *Philosophical Psychology*, *27*(1), 65–81. DOI: 10.1080/09515089.2013.828376

Svenaeus, F. (2021). Empathy and togetherness online compared to IRL: A phenomenological account. *Journal of Phenomenological Psychology*, *52*(1), 78–95. DOI: 10.1163/15691624-12341384

Taylor, S. H., DiFranzo, D., Choi, Y. H., Sannon, S., & Bazarova, N. N. (2019). Accountability and empathy by design: Encouraging bystander intervention to cyberbullying on social media. *ACM on Human–Computer Interaction, 3*(CSCW). *Proceedings of the ACM on Human-Computer Interaction, 118*(CSCW), 1–26. DOI: 10.1145/3359220

Tushar, P. N., Shrivastava, P. C., Jaiswal, P., Singh, S., & Mishra, V. (2026). *Legal challenges in cloud computing*. In I. Oncioiu (Ed.), *Law and regulation of AI, blockchain, and digital rights* (pp. 63–102). IGI Global Scientific Publishing. DOI: 10.4018/979-8-3373-3186-7.ch003

Tushar, P. N., Jaiswal, P., Shrivastava, P. C., Kumar, M., & Sundar, S. (2026). *Precision farming and smart irrigation systems for energy management.* In B. Soufiene (Ed.), *Enhancing autonomous and adaptive systems with AI and IoT* (pp. 251–288). IGI Global Scientific Publishing. DOI: 10.4018/979-8-3373-3146-1.ch009

Tushar, P. N., Shrivastava, P., Jaiswal, P., Mishra, S., & Yadav, A. (2026). *AI regulation in K–12 and higher education institutions*. In K. Carlson (Ed.), Ethical, legal, and pedagogical perspectives on AI in education. IGI Global. DOI: 10.4018/979-8-3373-3000-6

Uncapher, M. R., & Wagner, A. D. (2018). Minds and brains of media multitaskers: Current findings and future directions. *Proceedings of the National Academy of Sciences of the United States of America, 115*(40), 9889–9896. DOI: 10.1073/pnas.1611612115

Usán Supervía, P., Salavera Bordás, C., Quílez Robres, A., Lozano Blasco, R., & Latorre Cosculluela, C. (2023). Empathy, self-esteem and satisfaction with life in adolescents. *Children and Youth Services Review*, *144*, 106755. Advance online publication. DOI: 10.1016/j.childyouth.2022.106755

Vafeiadis, M., & Xiao, A. (2021). Fake news: How emotions, involvement, need for cognition and rebuttal evidence (story vs. informational) influence consumer reactions toward a targeted organization. *Public Relations Review*, *47*(4), 102088. DOI: 10.1016/j.pubrev.2021.102088

Verduyn, P., Ybarra, O., Résibois, M., Jonides, J., & Kross, E. (2017). Do social network sites enhance or undermine subjective well-being? A critical review. *Social Issues and Policy Review*, *11*(1), 274–302. DOI: 10.1111/sipr.12033

Vossen, H. G. M., & Valkenburg, P. M. (2016). Do social media foster or curtail adolescents' empathy? A longitudinal study. *Computers in Human Behavior*, *63*, 118–124. DOI: 10.1016/j.chb.2016.05.040

Walter, S. (2018). Cognition, action, and self-control from the 4E perspective. In Newen, A., de Bruin, L., & Gallagher, S. (Eds.), *The Oxford handbook of 4E-cognition* (pp. 321–332). Oxford University Press. DOI: 10.1093/oxfordhb/9780198735410.013.16

Walter, S., & Stephan, A. (2023). Situated affectivity and mind shaping: Lessons from social psychology. *Emotion Review*, *15*(1), 3–16. DOI: 10.1177/17540739221112419

Wang, Y., Leon, P. G., Acquisti, A., Cranor, L. F., Forget, A., & Sadeh, N. (2014). A field trial of privacy nudges for Facebook. In *Proceedings of the SIGCHI Conference on Human Factors in Computing Systems* (pp. 2367–2376). https://doi.org/ DOI: 10.1145/2556288.2557413

Weisz, E., & Cikara, M. (2021). Strategic regulation of empathy. *Trends in Cognitive Sciences*, *25*(3), 213–227. DOI: 10.1016/j.tics.2020.12.002

Weisz, E., Ong, D. C., Carlson, R. W., & Zaki, J. (2021). Building empathy through motivation-based interventions. *Emotion (Washington, D.C.)*, *21*(5), 990–999. DOI: 10.1037/emo0000929

Wilmer, H. H., & Chein, J. M. (2016). Mobile technology habits: Patterns of association among device usage, intertemporal preference, impulse control, and reward sensitivity. *Psychonomic Bulletin & Review*, *23*(5), 1607–1614. DOI: 10.3758/s13423-016-1011-z

Wood, M. A., Bukowski, W. M., & Lis, E. (2016). The digital self: How social media serves as a setting that shapes youth's emotional experiences. *Adolescent Research Review*, *1*(2), 163–173. DOI: 10.1007/s40894-015-0014-8

Yen, R., Feng, L., Mehra, B., Pang, C. C., Hu, S., & Li, Z. (2023). StoryChat: Designing a narrative-based viewer participation tool for live streaming chatrooms. In *CHI Conference on Human Factors in Computing Systems* (Paper 795, pp. 1–18). https://doi.org/DOI: 10.1145/3544548.3580912

Yogman, M., Garner, A., Hutchinson, J., Hirsh-Pasek, K., & Michnick Golinkoff, R. (2018). The power of play: A pediatric role in enhancing development in young children. *Pediatrics, 142*(3), e20182058. DOI: 10.1542/peds.2018-2058

Zarins, S., & Konrath, S. (2017). Changes over time in compassion-related variables in the United States. In Seppälä, E. M., Simon-Thomas, E., Brown, S. L., Worline, M. C., Cameron, C. D., & Doty, J. R. (Eds.), *The Oxford handbook of compassion science* (pp. 331–352). Oxford University Press.

Chapter 14
The Bias Interceptor:
How AI Can Mitigate Unconscious Leadership Blind Spots

Mohit Yadav
http://orcid.org/0000-0002-9341-2527
JGBS, O.P. Jindal Global University, India

Ali Najeeb
http://orcid.org/0000-0003-4663-9347
Villa College, Maldives

Narayanage Jayantha Dewasiri
http://orcid.org/0000-0002-5908-8890
Sabaragamuwa University of Sri Lanka, Belihuloya, Sri Lanka & Qasim Ibrahim School of Business, Villa College, Maldives

ABSTRACT

Unconscious biases remain among the most persistent challenges undermining leadership effectiveness and organizational equity. These cognitive blind spots—ranging from affinity bias to confirmation bias—often distort decision-making in recruitment, promotions, and resource allocation, limiting diversity and trust. Advances in artificial intelligence (AI) offer novel mechanisms to detect, surface, and mitigate such hidden biases by providing data-driven diagnostics, predictive insights, and interpretive feedback that leaders alone may overlook. This chapter conceptualizes AI as a "Bias Interceptor," outlining its potential to augment reflective leadership, strengthen evidence-based decision-making, and improve fairness across organizational systems. It also addresses ethical dilemmas, including algorithmic bias, privacy risks, and overreliance on automation. Drawing on psychological theory,

DOI: 10.4018/979-8-3373-6650-0.ch014

empirical studies, and applied practices, the chapter proposes a roadmap for leveraging AI responsibly to reduce leadership blind spots and foster more inclusive organizational cultures.

1. INTRODUCTION

Leadership is important because it influences organizational goals, focuses attention and resources, and creates the culture for decision-making (Mayer, Davis, & Schoorman, 1995). Yet even experienced leaders can fall prey to mental shortcuts and social biases that lead to consistent errors. The foundational research by Tversky and Kahneman (1974) showed that human judgment often relies on heuristics—representativeness, availability, and anchoring—which create predictable biases. Kahneman (2011) later outlined these findings in Thinking, Fast and Slow. He distinguished between quick, automatic (System 1) thinking and slow, thoughtful (System 2) processes and emphasized that leaders often make high-stakes decisions based on intuition. Over the past two decades, researchers have examined these psychological insights in leadership contexts, noting persistent "blind spots" where leaders misjudge their abilities, misinterpret signals from their teams, or favor in-group members (e.g., affinity bias and the halo effect). These blind spots can harm fairness, stifle innovation, and increase legal and reputational risks for organizations.

At the same time, artificial intelligence (AI) has evolved from simple automation to decision-support systems capable of processing large and varied data sets, identifying subtle patterns, and presenting insights that human decision-makers may overlook. This capability prompts a reevaluation of leadership support: rather than replacing judgment, AI can help address common cognitive mistakes, reveal overlooked evidence, and provide structured reminders that encourage leaders to make more thoughtful and fair decisions (Wilson & Daugherty, 2018). However, excitement about AI should be approached carefully. Machine-learning models can adopt and amplify historical biases found in training data (Caliskan et al., 2017). High-profile failures, such as facial-recognition systems showing lower accuracy for darker-skinned women (Buolamwini & Gebru, 2018), remind us that AI is not an unbiased solution.

This chapter explores how AI can act as a "Bias Interceptor" for leadership. This concept serves as both a design framework and a practical program that uses data and algorithmic tools to identify hidden biases, provide feedback to leaders, and include governance measures to prevent algorithmic harm. The approach draws on psychological theories of bias (Tversky & Kahneman, 1974; Greenwald, McGhee, & Schwartz, 1998), frameworks for fairness and interpretability (Doshi-Velez & Kim, 2017; Raghavan et al., 2020), and ethical guidelines for responsible AI (Jobin,

Ienca, & Vayena, 2019). The following sections will outline the mechanisms, benefits, risks, and practical guidelines for effectively implementing a Bias Interceptor in organizations.

2. UNCONSCIOUS BIAS AND LEADERSHIP BLIND SPOTS

Unconscious biases are mental tendencies that affect judgment and behavior without conscious knowledge (Greenwald et al., 1998). In organizations, common biases include affinity bias (favoring those similar to oneself), confirmation bias (favoring information that confirms existing beliefs), the halo effect (allowing one good trait to impact overall evaluation), and stereotyping (automatic links between group membership and characteristics). These biases function through automatic processes (Kahneman, 2011) and influence leaders' decisions on hiring, promotions, resource allocation, and performance reviews.

Leadership blind spots occur when biases go unnoticed, creating a disparity between a leader's intended values (e.g., meritocracy) and realized outcomes (e.g., uniform leadership teams). Research has highlighted various blind spots: leaders might overrate their own empathy, misjudge how their decisions appear to their teams, or overlook structural challenges that disadvantage certain groups. They may also prioritize input from high-status individuals while ignoring feedback from lower-status employees (see exploratory studies on leadership blind spots). The results can be significant decisions made with blind spots can diminish employee morale, hurt retention (especially among diverse talent), and perpetuate structural inequalities.

Measuring unconscious bias can be complicated. The Implicit Association Test (IAT) is commonly used to uncover patterns linked to discriminatory behavior (Greenwald et al., 1998), though discussions continue about its effectiveness for predicting individual behavior (Schimmack, 2021). Despite the challenges in measurement, substantial evidence indicates that implicit attitudes and heuristics shape judgments in hiring, performance assessments, and interpersonal evaluations, particularly when decision-makers depend on quick, experience-based cues rather than structured, evidence-driven methods (Kahneman, 2011; Tversky & Kahneman, 1974).

Addressing blind spots requires two key steps: (1) identifying where decision processes rely heavily on intuition or vague criteria, and (2) implementing mechanisms—behavioral, procedural, or technological—that make implicit patterns visible. The rest of this chapter discusses how AI can aid in both areas: using analytical power to spot statistical anomalies indicative of bias and offering interpretable feedback that allows leaders to reflect and adjust (Trivedi et al., 2023).

3. AI AS A TOOL FOR BIAS INTERCEPTION

AI systems encompass a range of methods, from simple rule-based filters to advanced deep-learning models, that can efficiently handle both structured and unstructured data. In organizations, AI can analyze candidate pools, assess internal communications for sentiment or inclusion cues, predict team performance using various metrics, and examine treatment patterns across demographic groups (Raghavan et al., 2020). AI is particularly suited for functioning as a Bias Interceptor due to three main features: scale (ability to analyze large datasets over time), pattern recognition (capacity to identify subtle correlations beyond human ability), and consistency (ability to apply uniform criteria across cases) (Yadav & Rangnekar, 2016).

Several practical applications highlight these attributes. AI tools can identify gendered or exclusionary language in job descriptions or internal policies using natural language processing (NLP), thereby mitigating affinity-driven biases early on. In promotion scenarios, predictive analytics can identify candidates who may have been overlooked by managers but whose objective performance aligns with successful incumbents. AI-driven sentiment analysis and social network analysis can uncover patterns of exclusion or isolation in team communications that might otherwise go unnoticed (Raghavan et al., 2020).

However, the dual nature of AI requires caution: while AI can highlight and address human blind spots, it can also replicate and intensify existing social patterns embedded in training data (Caliskan et al., 2017). The Gender Shades research showed that facial-analysis systems often exhibited significant accuracy discrepancies based on gender and skin tone, stemming from training data imbalances and model limitations (Buolamwini & Gebru, 2018). Similarly, word embeddings trained on extensive data can reflect societal biases in associations, which can be exploited by subsequent systems if safeguards are absent (Caliskan et al., 2017). To effectively act as a bias interceptor, AI must be built with fairness standards, interpretability, and ongoing monitoring as fundamental aspects.

4. MECHANISMS OF AI BIAS INTERCEPTION

Data-driven diagnostics

AI can conduct statistical analysis across decision logs to reveal anomalies and disparities. For instance, a hiring analytics module can evaluate selection rates by gender, race, and education level throughout various stages of hiring, test for statistically significant differences, and provide visual representations indicating where drop-offs occur. These diagnostics transform anecdotal issues ("we don't attract many female applicants") into clear, measurable patterns and allow for targeted solutions (Raghavan et al., 2020).

Predictive analytics

AI's ability to predict outcomes can help counteract leaders' reliance on superficial heuristics. For example, predictive models trained on proven performance indicators can evaluate internal candidates against objective success criteria, decreasing dependence on referrals or charisma-based assessments. Predictive models must be checked for fairness; otherwise, reliance on them could reinforce existing biased signals (Raghavan et al., 2020).

Sentiment and behavioral analysis

Natural language processing and social-network analysis can identify patterns of exclusion or subtle inequities in communication data. Techniques like sentiment analysis, topic modeling, and conversation structure metrics can reveal teams where dissent is stifled or certain voices overlooked, offering leaders actionable insights about areas needing intervention. These methods have been utilized in businesses to track employee engagement and shine a light on early indicators of morale issues, though robust privacy measures and clear governance are essential to avoid surveillance-related harm.

Natural language processing to detect biased language

NLP models can assess leadership communications—such as job postings, performance reviews, and internal memos—to highlight gendered expressions (e.g., "competitive" vs. "collaborative"), status-laden descriptors, or language that reflects fixed attitudes. Tests using word embeddings (e.g., WEAT) have shown that language data can reflect societal biases (Caliskan et al., 2017), thus enabling the development of practical tools to counter these tendencies by suggesting alternative wording or creating inclusive language templates.

Human–AI interactive warnings and nudges

Beyond passive diagnostics, AI can actively engage in decision-making workflows through prompts and "counterfactual" suggestions. For example, if a leader is preparing to create a shortlist, the system could issue a reminder: "Your shortlists historically include 20% fewer women than the applicant pool," along with supporting evidence and a suggested action (like anonymizing resumes or broadening search criteria). These nudges align with behavioral science methods (choice architecture) while still valuing human judgment.

Each approach has its trade-offs: diagnostic tools require high-quality, representative data; predictive analytics risk repeating historical inequities without corrections; sentiment analysis poses privacy and consent issues; and nudges need careful calibration to prevent "automation complacency," where leaders take AI outputs at face value. The next sections will cover the advantages and the ethical considerations necessary to manage these trade-offs.

5. BENEFITS OF AI IN ADDRESSING LEADERSHIP BIASES

When thoughtfully designed and managed, AI-powered Bias Interceptors offer numerous advantages.

Improving fairness in talent decisions

AI can enhance fairness in processes by standardizing criteria, anonymizing identifiable attributes during initial reviews, and revealing objective performance correlations that reduce affinity-driven biases. Research on algorithmic hiring suggests that structured, model-based evaluations often lead to more consistent outcomes than unstructured human judgments—if developed and validated with fairness in mind (Raghavan et al., 2020).

Increasing diversity and inclusion outcomes

By highlighting where decision pipelines disproportionately filter out members of underrepresented groups, AI allows for targeted actions (like modifying job descriptions, adjusting interview panels, or broadening sourcing channels). These efforts can enhance the presence of diverse talent in leadership roles, which in turn can lead to better innovation and decision quality.

Strengthening evidence-based decision-making

AI systems can reveal data that challenges anecdotal stories. For instance, predictive metrics can demonstrate that candidates from non-traditional backgrounds have similar success rates to traditional hires. This evidence encourages leaders to reconsider narrow assumptions. Such feedback promotes a shift from relying on intuition to more thoughtful evaluations.

Building organizational trust and transparency

If designed to be clear, auditable, and open about their limitations, AI systems can enhance trust by making decision processes transparent to stakeholders. Trust research shows that perceptions of ability, caring, and integrity are crucial for willingness to rely on leadership (Mayer et al., 1995). Transparency in AI that effectively reduces discriminatory practices can strengthen all three trust-building factors.

Scaling diagnostics across organizations

Manual bias audits can be labor-intensive; AI provides scalable monitoring that can continuously analyze thousands of decisions and communications, allowing for quick identification and correction of emerging issues. This ongoing monitoring supports periodic human-led audits and offers earlier warnings against systemic drift.

These benefits are goals and depend on solid technical and governance practices. The next section discusses the ethical challenges and operational hurdles that must be overcome to achieve these outcomes.

6. ETHICAL DILEMMAS AND CHALLENGES

AI has the potential to reduce blind spots, but it also brings significant risks. One major risk is algorithmic bias. Models trained on historical data often repeat historical inequalities (Caliskan et al., 2017). For example, the Amazon recruiting case, where a hiring model penalized résumés that mentioned "women's," shows how past patterns can be embedded in algorithms, leading to unfair outcomes even without intention. Systematic failures, such as those highlighted in the Gender Shades study, demonstrate how a lack of diversity in training data results in different model performance across demographic groups (Buolamwini & Gebru, 2018).

A second ethical issue is privacy and surveillance. Tools that analyze internal communications or monitor employee behavior can feel intrusive and damage trust if used without consent, clear guidelines, and strong data protections. Even well-meaning monitoring aimed at improving inclusion can be misused for tracking performance.

Third, relying too much on AI can weaken human accountability and harm critical judgment. If leaders regard model outputs as final rather than as tools for reflection, they face "automation bias." This occurs when trust in algorithms leads to less scrutiny (Doshi-Velez & Kim, 2017). Therefore, systems must explain their recommendations in ways that leaders can assess and challenge.

Fourth, choosing among fairness criteria makes design more complex. There is no single mathematical definition of fairness that meets all desired criteria at the same time (e.g., equality of opportunity vs. demographic parity). Designers must make value-based decisions about which fairness goals to prioritize. These decisions need careful discussion at the organizational level and legal approval (Raghavan et al., 2020).

Finally, governance, audits, and recourse mechanisms are important but not yet standardized. The global landscape of AI ethics guidelines shows agreement on high-level principles (transparency, justice, non-maleficence, responsibility, privacy) but differences in how to implement and enforce them (Jobin et al., 2019; Yadav et al., 2019). Organizations must create internal standards, carry out third-party audits, and set up channels for individuals affected by AI-driven decisions to appeal or ask questions.

Addressing these dilemmas requires a mix of technical safeguards (de-biasing datasets, fairness-aware learning, interpretable models), process safeguards (human review steps, documentation), and institutional safeguards (ethics committees, external audits, regulatory compliance).

7. SKILLS FOR LEADERS IN THE AGE OF AI

As AI becomes a tool for addressing bias, leaders need new skills that go beyond traditional management. Leadership in today's world is no longer just about strategic thinking, communication, or efficiency; it increasingly focuses on managing complex interactions between humans and machines. Three key skill areas are vital for leaders who want to effectively use AI to identify and reduce unconscious biases: understanding AI and digital decision-making, recognizing personal biases alongside AI tools, and fostering ethical responsibility in AI settings.

Developing an understanding of AI and digital decision-making is essential for modern leadership. Leaders must understand what AI systems can do and the implications of algorithm design, data quality, and predictive modeling for their organizations (Long & Magerko, 2020). This knowledge allows leaders to evaluate AI recommendations critically instead of treating them as absolute truths. For example, executives who can question an AI recruitment system about its data sources and fairness metrics are in a better position to avoid biased results. Digital decision-making also requires blending human judgment with insights from algorithms to ensure that AI supports rather than replaces leadership (Shrestha, Ben-Menahem, & Krogh, 2019). Without this understanding, leaders risk depending too much on unclear systems or underusing AI's diagnostic abilities.

Building awareness of personal blind spots alongside AI tools is also crucial. While AI can reveal hidden biases in data, leaders must develop an awareness of their own unconscious tendencies. Research in organizational psychology indicates that leaders who reflect on their decisions align more closely with inclusivity goals (Nesbit, 2012). AI tools can act as mirrors, showing trends—like unequal performance evaluations among demographic groups—that encourage deeper reflection. However, without acknowledging their blind spots, leaders will find AI's corrective abilities limited. The skill lies in being humble and open to seeing AI feedback as a chance for personal growth and better judgment (Hannah, Jennings, & DeRue, 2020).

Cultivating ethical responsibility in AI-driven leadership is perhaps the most critical skill. Unlike previous technological changes, AI introduces unique challenges around fairness, accountability, and transparency. Leaders must address questions such as: Who is liable when an AI system produces unfair results? How should employee privacy be maintained when using workplace analytics? What does informed consent look like in decisions made with AI support? Ethically responsible leaders must balance efficiency with justice and respect for human dignity (Floridi & Cowls, 2019). They need to support governance frameworks, advocate for algorithmic audits, and create organizational cultures where AI ethics are openly discussed. Leaders who model this responsibility set a standard for using AI in ways that promote inclusion instead of reinforcing existing inequalities.

Together, these three skill areas highlight the multifaceted nature of leadership in the AI era. Leaders must blend technical knowledge, self-awareness, and ethical responsibility, recognizing that AI is not a substitute for human judgment but a partner in creating fairer, more transparent, and more reflective decision-making. Organizations that invest in these skills will better manage AI as a powerful tool for addressing bias.

8. FUTURE OUTLOOK: TOWARD AUGMENTED LEADERSHIP

The future of leadership will be increasingly influenced by integrating AI into organizational decision-making and culture. Rather than replacing human leaders, AI is expected to act as a co-pilot, enhancing their capabilities and reducing the impact of unconscious blind spots. This new approach, often called "AI-augmented leadership," imagines leaders supported by intelligent systems that provide data-driven insights, predictive analytics, and fairness audits to improve human judgment (Wilson & Daugherty, 2018). In this model, AI does not make decisions autonomously but serves as a bias interceptor and strategic advisor, allowing leaders to focus on creativity, empathy, and vision—traits that are uniquely human.

AI-augmented leaders represent a change from traditional top-down control to a partnership between human intuition and machine intelligence. Leaders using this model will depend on AI dashboards, real-time feedback tools, and scenario simulations to understand the impact of their decisions before putting them into practice. For example, an augmented leader might use AI to spot exclusion patterns in promotion cycles while also mentoring to tackle cultural inequities. This combination of computational ability and human empathy produces leaders who are not only more reflective but also more responsive to diversity and inclusion goals (Raisch & Krakowski, 2021). The augmented leader thus emphasizes leveraging AI to boost fairness, foresight, and inclusivity instead of simply delegating tasks to machines.

Traditional leadership models—like transformational or servant leadership—stress values such as vision, inspiration, and ethical responsibility. These models are evolving to include AI as a core element. For instance, distributed leadership, which spreads out decision-making, aligns well with AI tools that make organizational insights accessible (Avolio, Sosik, Kahai, & Baker, 2014). Likewise, adaptive leadership models that prioritize responsiveness to complex environments can be enhanced by AI systems that analyze fast-changing external data (Heifetz, Grashow, & Linsky, 2009). Over time, leadership models may formalize AI integration as a standard part, making technological fluency and ethical AI oversight as important as emotional intelligence. This could change how leadership education and professional development are structured, ensuring that AI knowledge is incorporated into executive training programs.

Looking ahead, AI-augmented leadership will significantly impact organizational systems. Culturally, organizations may shift toward evidence-based inclusivity, with AI regularly auditing decisions about hiring, promotions, and resource allocation to identify disparities (Caliskan, Bryson, & Narayanan, 2017). This shift could lead to more transparent and accountable cultures, but only if leaders build trust through openness about AI tool usage. From a governance standpoint, boards may increasingly require AI ethics committees, algorithmic audits, and processes for involving stakeholders to ensure responsible use (Crawford & Calo, 2016). The talent pipelines will also evolve: future leaders will need expertise in digital tools and a solid ethical approach toward AI. Business schools and leadership programs may incorporate AI literacy into courses on ethics, strategy, and organizational behavior to prepare the next generation of leaders for augmented decision-making.

In summary, the future presents a leadership landscape where human and machine intelligence work together rather than compete. The idea of augmented leadership reflects a blend of technical knowledge, ethical responsibility, and human empathy, supported by AI systems that reduce bias and broaden cognitive abilities. Organizations that proactively adapt to this model are more likely to nurture resilient, inclusive, and innovative leadership cultures, giving themselves a competitive edge in the digital economy.

9. CONCLUSION

Leadership blind spots are not minor issues or unavoidable; they arise from deep cognitive processes shaped by evolution and experience (Tversky & Kahneman, 1974; Kahneman, 2011). AI offers valuable capabilities such as large-scale diagnostics, pattern recognition, and decision support that can function as a "Bias Interceptor," revealing hidden biases, encouraging reflection, and suggesting corrective actions. To realize this potential, we must confront the challenges of algorithmic bias and intrusive privacy measures, along with incorporating interpretability, human oversight, and ethical governance into AI systems (Doshi-Velez & Kim, 2017; Jobin et al., 2019).

In practice, the best applications will combine technical rigor (fairness-aware modeling, validation), changes in organizational processes (well-structured decision protocols), and building leader capabilities (AI knowledge, ethical reasoning). When this combination is in place, AI can be a strong ally in bridging the gap between a company's stated values and everyday decisions. It can help reduce inequalities, enhance decision-making quality, and enable leaders to act with greater awareness and accountability. Importantly, leaders still hold the moral responsibility: AI should always be viewed as a tool that increases awareness and options, not as a replacement for accountability.

REFERENCES

Avolio, B. J., Sosik, J. J., Kahai, S. S., & Baker, B. (2014). E-leadership: Re-examining transformations in leadership source and transmission. *The Leadership Quarterly*, *25*(1), 105–131. DOI: 10.1016/j.leaqua.2013.11.003

Buolamwini, J., & Gebru, T. (2018). *Gender Shades: Intersectional accuracy disparities in commercial gender classification.* Proceedings of Machine Learning Research, 81, 77–91. https://proceedings.mlr.press/v81/buolamwini18a/buolamwini18a.pdf

Caliskan, A., Bryson, J. J., & Narayanan, A. (2017). Semantics derived automatically from language corpora contain human-like biases. *Science*, *356*(6334), 183–186. DOI: 10.1126/science.aal4230 PMID: 28408601

Crawford, K., & Calo, R. (2016). There is a blind spot in AI research. *Nature*, *538*(7625), 311–313. DOI: 10.1038/538311a PMID: 27762391

Doshi-Velez, F., & Kim, B. (2017). Towards a rigorous science of interpretable machine learning (arXiv:1702.08608). https://arxiv.org/abs/1702.08608

Floridi, L., & Cowls, J. (2019). A unified framework of five principles for AI in society. *Harvard Data Science Review*, *1*(1), 1–15. DOI: 10.1162/99608f92.8cd550d1

Greenwald, A. G., McGhee, D. E., & Schwartz, J. L. K. (1998). Measuring individual differences in implicit cognition: The Implicit Association Test. *Journal of Personality and Social Psychology*, *74*(6), 1464–1480. DOI: 10.1037/0022-3514.74.6.1464 PMID: 9654756

Hannah, S. T., Jennings, P. L., & DeRue, D. S. (2020). Leader self-awareness: A critical driver of organizational effectiveness. *Organizational Dynamics*, *49*(3), 100707. DOI: 10.1016/j.orgdyn.2019.100707

Heifetz, R. A., Grashow, A., & Linsky, M. (2009). *The practice of adaptive leadership: Tools and tactics for changing your organization and the world.* Harvard Business Press.

Jobin, A., Ienca, M., & Vayena, E. (2019). The global landscape of AI ethics guidelines. *Nature Machine Intelligence*, *1*(9), 389–399. DOI: 10.1038/s42256-019-0088-2

Kahneman, D. (2011). *Thinking, fast and slow*. Farrar, Straus and Giroux.

Long, D., & Magerko, B. (2020). What is AI literacy? Competencies and design considerations. *Proceedings of the 2020 CHI Conference on Human Factors in Computing Systems*, 1–16. DOI: 10.1145/3313831.3376727

Mayer, R. C., Davis, J. H., & Schoorman, F. D. (1995). An integrative model of organizational trust. *Academy of Management Review, 20*(3), 709–734. DOI: 10.2307/258792

Nesbit, P. L. (2012). The role of self-reflection, emotional management of feedback, and self-regulation processes in self-directed leadership development. *Human Resource Development Review, 11*(2), 203–226. DOI: 10.1177/1534484312439196

Raghavan, M., Barocas, S., Kleinberg, J., & Levy, K. (2020). Mitigating bias in algorithmic hiring: Evaluating claims and practices. *Proceedings of the 2020 ACM Conference on Fairness, Accountability, and Transparency (FAccT '20).* https://dl.acm.org/doi/10.1145/3351095.3372828

Raisch, S., & Krakowski, S. (2021). Artificial intelligence and management: The automation–augmentation paradox. *Academy of Management Review, 46*(1), 192–210. DOI: 10.5465/amr.2018.0072

Shrestha, Y. R., Ben-Menahem, S. M., & von Krogh, G. (2019). Organizational decision-making structures in the age of artificial intelligence. *California Management Review, 61*(4), 66–83. DOI: 10.1177/0008125619862257

Trivedi, S. K., Vishnu, S., Singh, A., & Yadav, M. (2023). Research trends in sustainable E-payment systems: A study using topic modeling approach. *IEEE Transactions on Engineering Management, 71*, 7511–7525. DOI: 10.1109/TEM.2023.3280216

Tversky, A., & Kahneman, D. (1974). Judgment under uncertainty: Heuristics and biases. *Science, 185*(4157), 1124–1131. DOI: 10.1126/science.185.4157.1124 PMID: 17835457

Wilson, H. J., & Daugherty, P. R. (2018). *Human + machine: Reimagining work in the age of AI.* Harvard Business Review Press.

Yadav, M., & Rangnekar, S. (2016). Role clarity and organizational citizenship behaviour: Does tenure matter? A study on Indian power sector. *Global Business Review, 17*(3, suppl), 207S–224S. DOI: 10.1177/0972150916631216

Yadav, M., Rangnekar, S., & Srivastava, A. P. (2019). Demographic variables as moderators between QWL and OCB. *Industrial and Commercial Training, 51*(7/8), 396–408. DOI: 10.1108/ICT-04-2018-0040

Chapter 15

Impact of Emotional Intelligence on Leadership Development: A Thematic Review

Sonal Juyal
Sardar Bhagwan Singh University, Dehradun, India

Abhishek Danu
http://orcid.org/0009-0009-9134-3757
H.N.B. Garhwal University, Srinagar, India

Vibhuti Jain
http://orcid.org/0009-0009-8602-6116
Graphic Era (Deemed to be) University, Dehradun, India

Kamlesh kohli
H.N.B. Garhwal University, Srinagar, India

Komal Patwal
http://orcid.org/0009-0001-5118-3869
Graphic Era (Deemed to be) University, Dehradun, India

Rajesh Tiwari
http://orcid.org/0000-0002-5345-2508
Graphic Era (Deemed to be) University, Dehradun, India

Nakate Susan
Graphic Era (Deemed to be) University, Dehradun, India

ABSTRACT

Emotional intelligence has a strong correlation with leadership. EI affects a person both positively and negatively, but being aware of one's emotions is the best way to manage them, which can also help one control them. People's emotions can be influenced by the environment they are surrounded in. Everything is based on EI as one has to control their feelings and emotions, and also know how to handle

DOI: 10.4018/979-8-3373-6650-0.ch015

others in the workplace. Our current research aims to gather all studies conducted between 2000 and 2024 on Emotional Intelligence and Leadership Development. The VOS viewer software is used in this bibliometric study. A database comprising 423 articles from 2000 to 2024 is created for this purpose using the Scopus database. A comprehensive examination of publication trends, productive writers, journals, and international collaboration is carried out. This study provides a simple information source that encompasses all of the research in the subject for academics interested in investigating leadership development and emotional intelligence.

IMPLICATIONS OF THIS STUDY

The study helps to clarify the areas of research being conducted on leadership development and emotional intelligence, as well as the field's potential for growth and future possibilities.

INTRODUCTION

Leadership and EI have been popular topics in business and management in recent decades. The idea behind EI was developed since ages and has increased in popularity and exposure among scholars and professionals in a wide range of professions. Emotional intelligence stems from social intelligence. Thorndike (1920) characterized this term as "the capacity to fully understand and supervise men and women, boys and girls—to behave appropriately in interpersonal relationships" (p. 228). EI is considered to be the subset of social intelligence that encompasses the ability to monitor one's own and others' moods and emotions, discern between them, and use this knowledge to guide cognition and behavior. (Salovey and Mayer (1990). (p. 189)). Bradberry and Greaves (2009, p. 17) have explained EI as the ability to notice and analyze the emotions in oneself and others, and then utilize that knowledge to govern behavior and relationships. It is the capacity to express, comprehend, and managing our emotions as well as others'. (Palmer et al., 2008). Goleman (1998) explains EI as the ability to discern both our own and other understanding others' emotions, encouraging oneself, and carefully handling emotional relationships with people.

Nelso & Low (2011) provided with the most recent definition of emotional intelligence which states that emotional intelligence (EI) is the capacity to recognize one's own strengths and flaws based on one's own dignity and worth, build strong and effective connections, collaborate with others, and respond appropriately to stress and expectations in daily life.

EI research is still in its early stages when compared to IQ studies. Nonetheless, EI is being increasingly acknowledged as a crucial issue in the workplace. Numerous studies have depicted that a high IQ will never guarantee a perfectly successful life.

Emotional intelligence is also a major topic in the researches done on Leadership. The question arise here is whether EI plays a substantial role in shaping leadership behavior, methods, and values. Numerous researches have demonstrated that emotional intelligence boosts the organizational results, leadership efficacy, and leadership development (Hayashi, 2005; Higgs & Aitken, 2003; Wolff et al., 2002; Carmeli, 2003; Ozcelik et al., 2008).

People employ emotional intelligence to handle everything with a certain level of maturity and harmony. People who possess high emotional intelligence are able to concentrate, understand others, and keep things in viewpoint. Additionally, they are more effective at work as they perform better and are more productive which leads to a higher sense of job satisfaction.

EI can also be used in educational administration because educators work with groups or individuals on a regular basis. I t affects learning, professional adaptability, interpersonal connections, and personal well-being.

Students can utilize emotional intelligence not only to better manage their present challenges but also to build coping mechanisms that will enable them to handle the responsibilities of their future careers.

As a leader is concerned with different interactions between different employees, it's important to know how to regulate their own emotions in order not to offend others.

"Emotional intelligence also helps leaders to solve complex problems and manage crises" (yukl, 2010,p 213)

Emotional intelligence and leadership are closely related, as demonstrated by Higgs and Dulewics (2002) and Cavazotte, Moreno, and Hickmann (2012). The role of emotional intelligence in effective leadership is unclear, according to some studies (Palmer, Walls, Burgess, & Stough, 2001). But scholars have also concentrated on demonstrating how emotional intelligence traits like empathy are essential for a leader (Kellett, Humphrey, & Sleeth, 2002; Wolff, Pescosolido, & Druskat, 2002) and related emotional intelligence to leadership (George, 2000). Prior research has linked emotional intelligence to effective leadership (Cherniss 2001), and further studies have linked EI to both upper and middle management actions that are beneficial to leadership (Palmer et al., 2001; Gardner and Stough, 2002).

LITERATURE REVIEW

Emotional Intelligence was more of an oxymoron before the late 20th century, as emotions were often related to irrationality. In contrast, intelligence, as always, was the ruler of the world of logic and rationality. Only after the 1990s did Mayer & Salovey stated EI to be different from cognitive intelligence.

One's ability to successfully integrate emotions and thoughts, as well as the degree to which emotions support and actively regulate a person's cognitive skills, are all considered aspects of emotional intelligence (Mayer & Salovey, 1997). Salovey and Mayer's model focuses on four core abilities, commonly referred to as the four-branch model of emotional intelligence (EI). It defines EI in a hierarchical fashion where perceiving emotions is the foundation while managing emotions is the most advanced skill. The model led to the development of evaluation instruments like the MSCEIT (Mayer-Salovey-Caruso Emotional Intelligence Test).

Figure 1. Salovey & Mayer Model of Emotional Intelligence

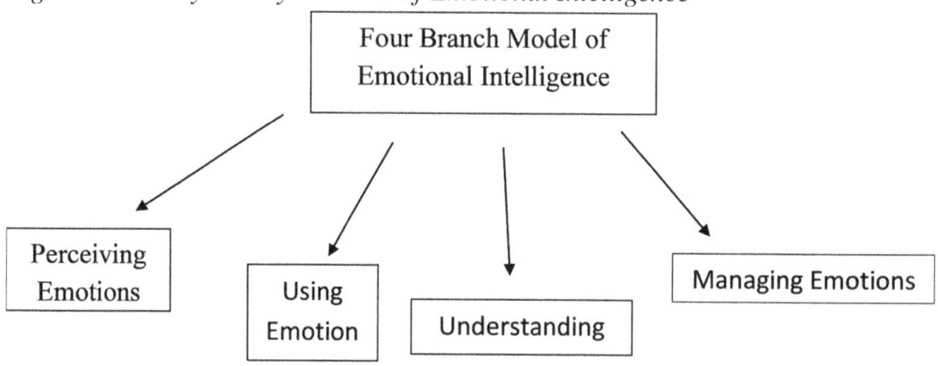

Daniel Goleman's 1995 book Emotional Intelligence: Why It Can Matter More than IQ and Primal Leadership helped to further develop and popularise the idea of emotional intelligence. Goleman (1995) stressed that an individual's success is 20% due to IQ and 80% result of his or her emotional intelligence. Goleman (1999) defined EI as the capability of a person to understand the emotions of self and others. Goleman's EI model emphasize of emotional skills in the success of a leader as well as in the organizations success.

Figure 2. Goleman's Model of Emotional Intelligence

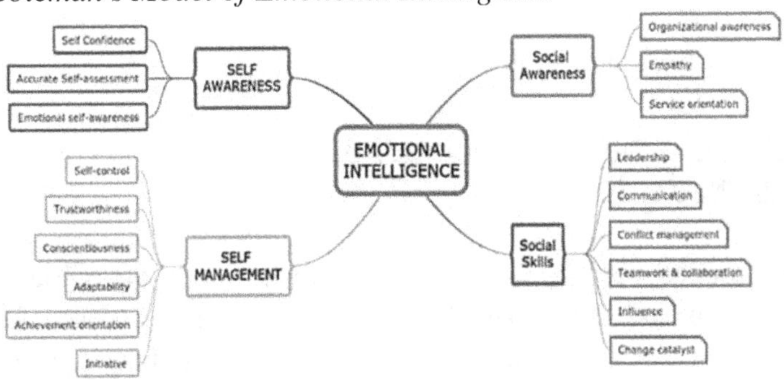

Leadership is the virtue by which an individual influences, guides, and inspires a group of followers to achieve common objectives. Elements of effective leadership include strategic thinking, communication skills, decision-making abilities, and most importantly emotional intelligence.

Figure 3. Competencies of a leader

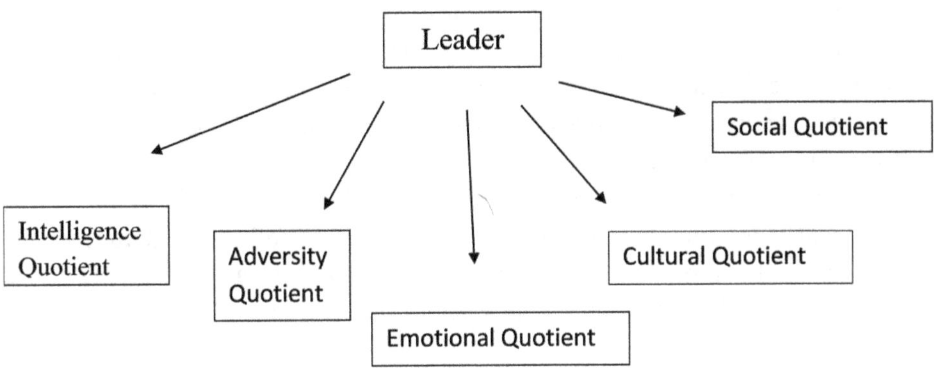

Emotional intelligence and leadership have no ties as it is not necessary for a leader to have emotional intelligence but effective leadership explicitly demands the saintly presence of emotional intelligence. A leader is expected to lead and steer the path for the group thus it becomes very crucial for the leader to control emotions rather than be controlled by them.

The German philosopher Friedrich Nietzsche's words echoed the importance of emotional competence in a leader when he said, "*One ought to hold on to one's heart, for if one lets it go, one soon loses control of the head too*". In today's rapidly changing environment also called the VUCA-BANI world, being equanimous is a real challenge. As the leaders are Vanguard, they have to be resilient and emotionally strong to face the storm resolutely. Hence, adds to the reasons why leaders need to be high on emotional intelligence.

1. Emotional Intelligence & Leadership through Classical lens: -

Classics from all over the world delineate the attributes of a good leader and, a never to miss feature is emotional intelligence that distinguishes a leader from the herd.

The Mahabharata, an Indian classical epic highlights how crucial EI is for a leader. In the Shanti Parv chapter 76, Bhishma presented 36 qualities of a leader to Yudhistir, amongst them are components of emotional intelligence for instance, a leader should have control over temper, protect the vulnerable, be fair, non-indulgent, compassionate, humble, aware of the self, and duties towards others.

Bhagwat Gita chapter 2 verses 2-3, Lord Krishna reprimands Arjuna as a warrior and leader for being emotionally unstable since such inability only invites infamy. In verse 2.15, Lord Krishna hails the leader who remains undisturbed by happiness and distress and is emotionally composed. In chapter 13 verses 8- 12, the qualities of a wise leader are outlined as one who has self-control, humility, detachment, even mind, self-awareness, and emotional maturity.

Chanakya writes in his magnum opus, Arthshastra, that a person deserves to be a leader if he can win over emotions such as rage, happiness, grief, and pride; lacks conceit, perplexity, or false modesty; and is able to maintain composure even during difficult times (Prabhu, 2022).

Sun Tzu, philosopher and strategist in ancient China believed that a leader who is cognizant of his emotions as well as the feelings of his followers can turn around every failing situation in one's favour. " *Treat your men as you would your beloved sons, and they will follow you into the deepest Valley"* (Art of War).

2. EI & Effective leadership: -

Emotional intelligence is the differentiator between average leadership and effective leadership. Researchers have assessed leadership efficacy by the analysis of job performance and organisational success and have found a strong link between the emotional intelligence scores of the leaders and job performance or organisational success.

Yadav & Lata (2019) suggested that highly emotionally intelligent individuals are excellent team players, which makes them outstanding leaders. Such individuals can manage personal as well as others' emotions very well. Therefore, emotional intelligence is prevalent across processes like the selection, training and development of employees. They studied whether emotional intelligence is a genuine metric to predict leadership effectiveness. 50 instructors from five institutions in the Rewari District of Haryana participated in the methodology by completing the Trait Emotional Intelligence Questionnaire (TEIQue). Respondents were chosen at random and included both leadership and non-leadership positions. Leaders had better emotional intelligence ratings than non-leaders, according to the study. Additionally, the respondents' self-esteem, optimism, empathy, and flexibility all showed a substantial positive link with EI.

Pastor (2014) studied the impact EI has on the leadership and performance. The methodology comprised 154 subjects including managers and workers aged 20 to 60 years, mostly male, administered the Schutte's Emotional Intelligence Scale. Job satisfaction was assessed by Balzer's Job in General Index (JIG). Data was collected through a questionnaire administered to 254 employees. The results showed that leaders' professional performance correlated positively with EI and education level. Thus, proving that high EI fosters better problem-solving skills and greater adaptability in a leader.

Vivek & Krupskyi (2024) inspected the role of Artificial Intelligence and Emotional Intelligence on leadership, The study gave a comprehensive analysis by studying various secondary data sources like articles, industrial reports, and empirical studies. The study validated importance of both EI and AI for future leadership. AI provides data-driven insights, and EI offers an intuitive and better understanding of human emotions, making decisions effective. It introduced a novel framework that demonstrates how AI and EI can together enhance leadership performance.

A research by Lee et al. (2023) claimed EI to be a more important factor than rational intelligence or IQ at the senior levels. The study included data from self-reported questionnaires from 367 individuals working in real estate brokerage in Taiwan—the questions in the questionnaire related to leadership style, EI, and individual performance. The research confirmed that EI, transformational and transactional leadership all have a positive and direct relationship with the job performance of an individual. Findings suggested that organisations should focus on developing leaders' EI to improve job performance.

Emotional intelligence helps in coping with stress and impulsive instincts, as leaders can make difficult decisions without being hindered by negative emotions. Skrzypczyńska (2020). The review found that high EI helps leaders in being assertive and yet accommodating in difficult times. The study involved a comparison of leadership traits over time in two different years viz. 2006 and 2016, targeting leaders from Forbes Global 2000 companies. It concluded that high EI scores in leaders make them more capable, innovative, and adaptive.

Cavallo & Brienza (2002) found that emotional competence is a crest jewel of successful leaders. The study utilised a comprehensive multi-rater survey consisting of 183 questions & 358 managers were selected randomly from Johnson & Johnson Consumer and Personal Care Groups. The participants had at least 2 years of experience in the company and were fluent in English, the males comprised 56% and females 45% of the sample. The survey was completed by 1415 employees and the data collected was analysed using independent sample t-tests. The results indicate that high-performing leaders also had high EI and were rated as HiPO or high-potential managers.

Lone & Lone (2018) studied EI's influence on leadership in the context of non-Western cultures. A representative group of 230 supervisors and subordinates from the banking industry in Jammu and Kashmir, India, participated in the study. The 3D Emotional IQ Model, created by Singh and Chadda, was used in the methodology. A 6-point rating system, ranging from extremely high (6) to very poor (1), was used by the respondents to evaluate the supervisors.

The scale measured five variables such as the managers' ability to plan and organise work, empathy towards subordinates, problem-solving skills, and overall effectiveness as a leader. Data analysed through multiple linear regression analysis yielded, that emotional sensitivity and competency are important components of good leadership that are independent of gender stereotypes. The study addressed a lack in the body of knowledge about leadership and emotional intelligence in non-Western cultures.

Batool (2013) randomly surveyed 50 individuals across various professions including doctors, bankers, and nurses in Pakistan. The data was analysed using SPSS version 20 to compute the mean, standard deviation, variance, and percentage for descriptive statistics. It indicated that leadership style and EI had a significant relationship; effective leaders are emotionally component, responsible, good communicators, and manage stress productively.

Two well-known executive groups' EI scores were compared to those of the general population by (Stein et al..2009). A sample of 186 executives from the Young Presidents Organization (YPO) and the Innovators Alliance (IA) were given the Emotional Quotient Inventory (EQI) as part of the research.

The outcomes verified that the EI scores of top executives are different from the normal populace on the EQ scale. Also, it was noted revealed that high-profit businesses were run by leaders with strong empathy, self-esteem, and problem-solving skills.

Kerr et al. (2006) examined the influence of EI on the efficacy of leadership. Methodology adopted was to administer the the MSCEIT, or Mayor-Salovey-Caruso-Emotional Intelligence Test, to 38 supervisors at a large manufacturing company. Subordinate scores on a survey that included questions on supervisor performance were used to evaluate leadership.The data was collected from 1258 respondents. The study concluded that half of the MSCEIT scores i.e., the experiential domain that includes perceiving and using emotions, serve as a powerful indicator of leadership effectiveness with $r = 0.5$ and $p < 0.001$. But, out of the blue, the other half of the test i.e., reasoning EI domain, which tests the understanding and managing emotions did not relate with leadership with $r = -0.12$.

Rosete & Ciarrochi (2005) studied the link between EI, personality, IQ, and leadership by assessing 41 senior executives on various scales viz, MSCEIT, 16PF5 (to measure personality), WASI (to measure cognitive ability), and effectiveness of leadership was measured by 360° performance assessment. The findings, by applying correlation and regression analysis, indicated that high EI is linked with effective leadership and explained deviation that was not explained by personality or IQ scores, concluding that EI is a stronger indicator of leadership.

3. EI & Leadership Development: -

It is often said that IQ gets you a job, but EQ gets you promoted. As EI have a profound impact on leadership, as confirmed by various studies, the training and development must be aligned accordingly to develop EQ in leaders.

Dearborn (2002) argued that traditional ways of training no longer serve the purpose, as they only focus on intelligence or IQ aspect and ignore the EI as a result, the old behaviours keep on repeating even after an individual is trained. The research redefined the word 'smart' and claimed that leadership development is incomplete, and does not maximize ROI if Emotional Intelligence is left out of training.

Traditional Training + EI = Effective Leadership Training

Sadri (2012) reviewed various literature and concluded, that EI and transformational leadership are strongly linked. So, the selection of leaders must include an EI assessment. The paper discussed the two most cited models of EI, namely the Salovey & Mayer model and the Goleman's model. The emphasis is made on the fact that EI can be inculcated through training, and so it should be a substantial part of the training and development programmes for leaders.

4. EI & Leadership Style: -

The world is not a happy place because not all leaders are emotionally intelligent. This has to do with the styles of leadership. Studies show that among various styles of leadership, viz, transformational, democratic, transactional, laissez-faire, autocratic, and servant leadership, EI relates the most with the transformational style. Transformational leadership is focused on motivating and inspiring followers to bring change and achieve goals together.

Lao Tzu said, "A leader is best when people barely know he exists, when his work is done, his aim fulfilled, they say we did it ourselves". These words underline the style of leadership, which is inspiring and empowering the followers, as witnessed in transformational leadership. To achieve such a leadership style, the leader needs to be highly emotionally competent, and so, EI constructs mostly relate to the transformational style of leadership.

In their 2012 study, Cavazotte et al. examined the relationship between transformational style leadership and leaders' successful performance and their intelligence, personality, and emotional intelligence. By analysing data collected from 134 middle-level managers, it was found that personality and intelligence had an indirect effect on transformational leadership, whereas organisational success was directly related to transformational behaviour. It was noted that neuroticism hurt leadership. Moreover, In isolation, emotional intelligence was statistically connected to transformative leadership but as personality and ability were taken as control factors, the effect of EI on transformational leadership became less significant i.e., keeping personality and IQ constant, it was observed that high EI scores did not yield better organisational outcomes or effective leadership.

Palmer et al. (2001) examined the relationship between EI and successful leadership style. The approach used measured EI using an updated version of the Trait Meta Mood scale with 43 individuals from varied managerial jobs. The findings supported the prediction that EI correlates more strongly with various transformational leadership dimensions than transactional leadership traits. Furthermore, the multi-faceted questionnaire on leadership indicated that transformational leadership outperformed transactional leadership.

Gardner & Stough (2002) tested 110 top-level managers on a multi-factor leadership questionnaire, only to find that EI is very strongly and positively related to each component of transformational leadership, so, to inspire and empower the employees at the workplace, leaders must have high EI. Thus, the senior management ought to be trained in EI aspects in addition to regular training.

Leban & Zulauf (2004) studied 24 project managers across six organisations from various industries. The findings concluded that transformational style leadership has a very good influence on the performance of the project and it is EI that nurtures transformational leadership and eventually positively contributes to successful project outcomes.

Kumar (2014) reviewed a vast body of literature to note that leaders like Gandhi, Martin Luther, Nelson Mandela, etc., had high EI, which enabled them to influence their followers. The study reviewed the past works and noted that EI is a subtler, softer but indispensable part of intelligence. An experiment by Welch revealed that EQ> IQ. When two teams with equal IQ were pitched against each other it was found that the performance of the team with high EI was better than the team with low EI, hence, establishing dominance of EI over IQ. The review concluded from surveys and papers that constructs of EI like self-awareness, Empathy and drive are favorably associated to transformative leadership attributes. Leaders with a high degree of EI also go above and above their duties to attain organizational goals.

Harms & Credé (2010) disclosed in the study of the psychometric meta-analytic method, that EI competencies like empathy and self-awareness are indispensable for transformational leadership. The database included 62 independent samples and data sourced from 7145 leaders. The results showed that high EI is strongly related to active leadership styles like transformational leadership, whereas low EI correlated with laissez-faire and transactional styles. Hence, EI is more closely linked to transformational leadership than any other passive leadership style.

5. EI & Conflict Management: -

Sun Tzu said, *"The supreme Art of War is to subdue the enemy without fighting"*. This underscores the importance of diplomacy and tact to manage and resolve conflicts. A great leader must have tactics to constructively handle conflicts and decrease dissonance among members, which is directly linked to the capability of a leader to deal with emotions.

Schlaerth et al. (2013) advocated that conflict management relies on emotional regulation abilities; also, high EI levels correlated with better constructive conflict management. The approach employed was a meta-analysis of 29 studies that quantified the association between emotional intelligence and proactive conflict management. The findings revealed that greater levels of EI were associated with more successful conflict resolution strategies, such as communication, collaboration, accommodations, and creative problem-solving. On the other side, low EI is associated with the deployment of harmful conflict resolution techniques such as avoidance, competitiveness, or compromise.

6. EI & Leadership: Critical Analysis: -

Not all leaders use the concept of emotional intelligence ethically. Leaders like Benito Mussolini, Hitler, Mao Zedong, Francisco Franco, Joseph Stalin, Idi Amin, Kim Jong II, etc. are all examples of leaders using the concept of EI to influence and manipulate people.

Fambrough & Kaye Hart (2008) questioned the relevance of emotional intelligence as a standalone factor to predict leadership. The paper discussed how EI is an overhyped tool to develop leadership, as its effectiveness is yet to be validated scientifically. Moreover, EI has limited research and even less exploration in non-Western cultures; thus, it should be applied with caution.

Lubbadeh (2020) studied the pros and cons of EI and its positive and negative effect on leadership. The paper reviewed various models of EI, the research concluded that EI can be subtly used for manipulation, gaslighting, and self-centred outcomes by individuals with high emotional intelligence. Adolf Hitler used the EI concept to tailor his body language which influenced and gradually brainwashed the masses. Thus, EI can lead to fatal leadership in such cases.

METHODOLOGY

This study intended to conduct a bibliometric analysis in the areas of EI and leadership development. The bibliometric technique has been widely recognized and used in a variety of fields, most notably medical science (Hart & Perlis, 2021). Bibliometric Analysis is a quantitative methodology for analyzing citations and content in academic journals, publications, and research papers. The quantitative effect of a publication is determined by counting the instances in which a particular work is cited in other sources. It may therefore be used to calculate the "impact" or effect of a certain work on the remainder of the academic literature, which would facilitate the process of selecting where to publish. Knowing where to publish can help researchers increase the impact and visibility of their work (González-Sala et al., 2017). This research project does a literature analysis utilizing the Scopus database, the most extensive repository for peer-reviewed literature abstracts and citations. Its enormous number of users proved to be the most important factor for selecting it over alternative databases readily available.

The research was done on Scopus with the Keywords "Emotional Intelligence", "Leadership Development". We have done the study using the research done from 2000 to 2024 on this topic, and we got 423 documents. We have limited subject areas by including only Business, Management and Accounting; Social Sciences; Medicine; Psychology; Economics, Econometrics and Finance; Nursing; Engineering; Computer; Arts and Humanities; and Multidisciplinary. Then, after limiting the document type by including only; Article and Source to only Journal. Now, at last, we limited the language only to English and got 423 papers on which we performed analysis using VOSviewer.

After selecting papers, the next step was to use VOSviewer, a cutting-edge piece of bibliometric analysis software. The VOS viewer program is used for network evaluation. The paper creates a graphical map of the bibliographic information to more thoroughly analyze the findings (Cobo et al., 2011; Sinkovics, 2016); and Van Eck and Waltman, 2010). This software gathers bibliographic information and shows graphical representations of co-authorship, co-citations, and co-occurrence of author keywords (Kessler, 1963).

RESULTS:

1. Year-wise Publication on Leadership and Emotional Intelligence

Figure 4. Documents Publication Trend from 2000-2024

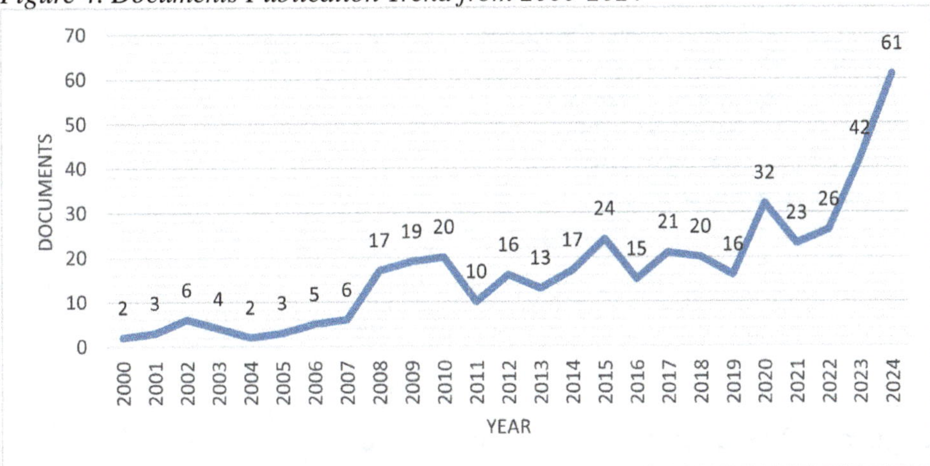

Figure 4 displays, per year, the release of texts on emotional intelligence and leadership from 2000 to 2024. It is clear that the number of documents has been gradually growing, though the research has been expedited after 2008. The most publications are recently in 2024 and after 2020 the increase in research has been more.

2. The Top Most Productive Journals and Authors

Figure 5. Authors with Maximum No. of Articles

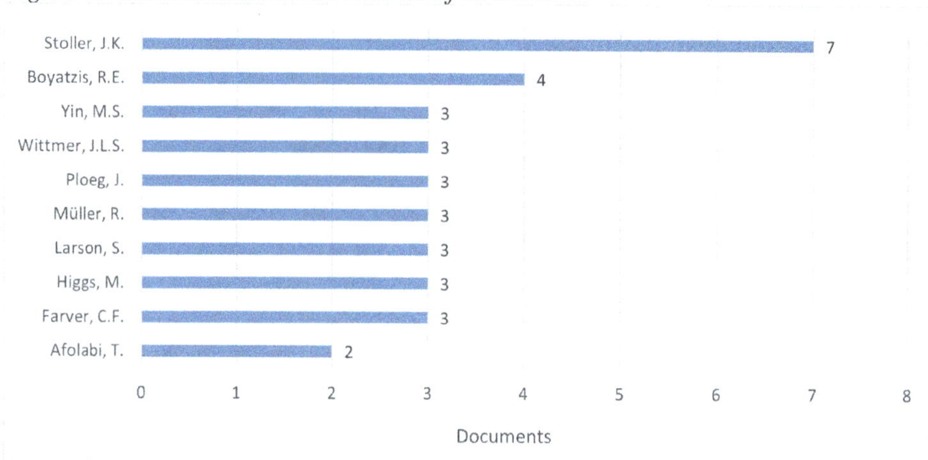

Figure 6. Top Journals Published Paper

Figure 6 displays the publications from well-known journals that were released between the years 2000 and 2024. The top 15 journals were selected that have the most documents. The most articles on emotional intelligence and leadership development are found in the Journal of Management Development which has total 13 documents and leadership & Organization Development Journal which also has 11 documents then comes Advances in Developing Human Resources which has 8 documents and Journal of Nursing Management with 7 documents.

3. Country-wise publication on Emotional Intelligence and Leadership

The top countries in terms of leadership and emotional intelligence between 2000 and 2024 are shown in Figure 7. With 172 papers published, the United States tops the list of the most prolific nations. The United Kingdom, which publishes around 39 papers, comes in second on the list. India has published around 20 papers in this field.

Figure 7. Most Productive Countries published papers on EI & Leadership

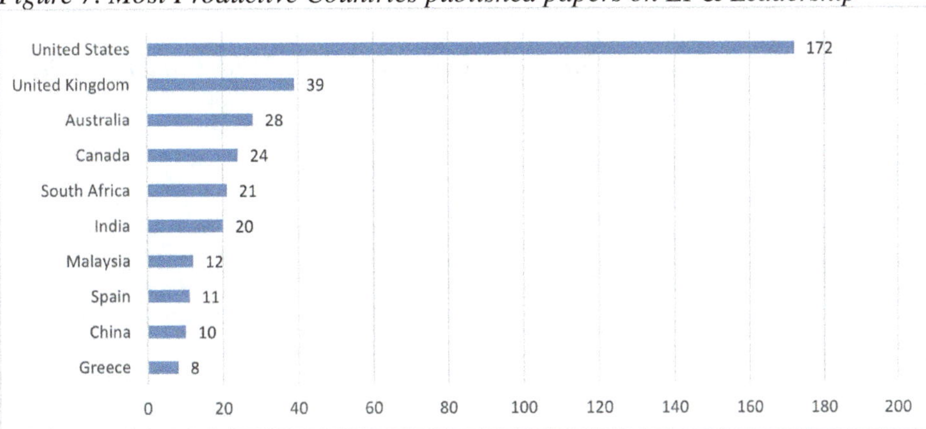

Source: The authors (from the Scopus database)

4. Publication on emotional intelligence and leadership at the institutional level

The institution having the most number of studies on leadership and emotional intelligence published between 2000 and 2024 is shown in Figure 8. We only considered institutions with more than five papers published. Because Boyatzis, R.E., and Stoller, J.K., published the most papers on emotional intelligence and leadership, The Cleveland Clinic Foundation and Case Western Reserve University are the publishers of the most papers, having published 7 papers.

Figure 8. Institutions that published highest number of papers on EI and Leadership.

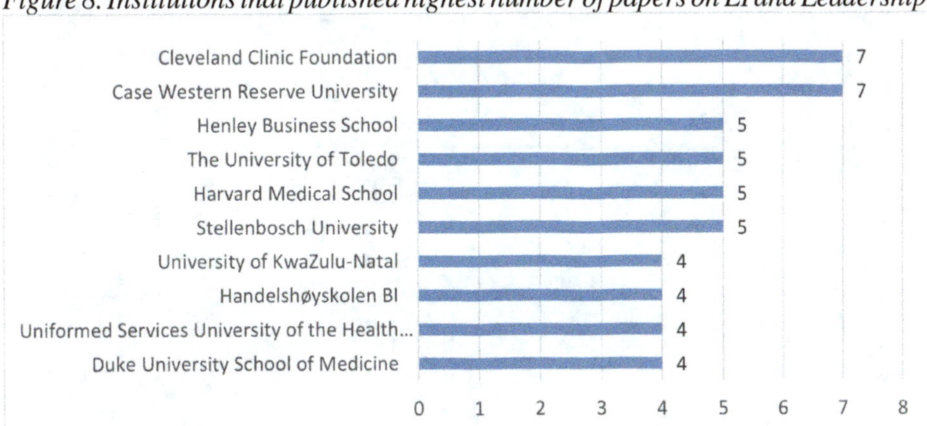

Source: The authors (from the Scopus database)

5. Key Word Occurrence Analysis:

Figure 9. Network presenting Keywords Co-occurrence of EI& Leadership Development

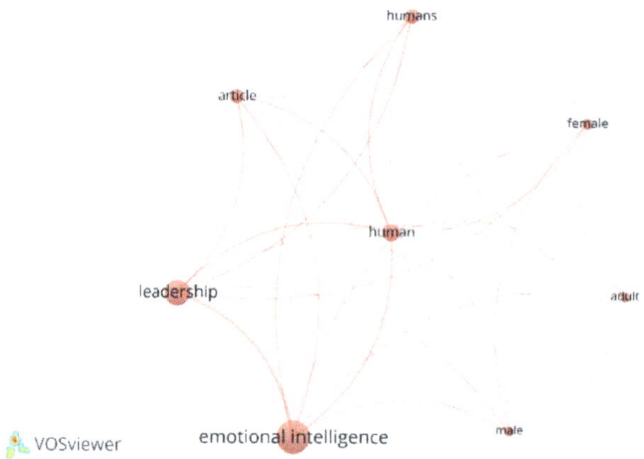

By keeping the minimum occurrence to 50, we got 8 keywords out of 1768 citations. "Emotional Intelligence" is the word that appears the most frequently (290 times), followed by "Leadership" (207 occurrences). This shows the study on leadership and emotional intelligence is causally connected and primarily concerned with human-focused situations.

Figure 10. Density Map of keywords co-occurrence of EI & Leadership Development

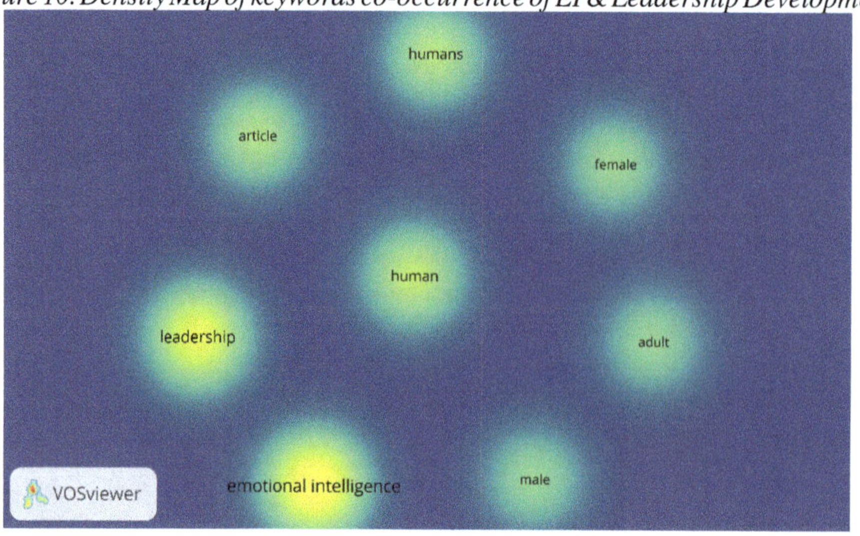

6. Most Productive Countries that published papers on EI & Leadership Development:

Figure 11. Countries that Cited Most Papers

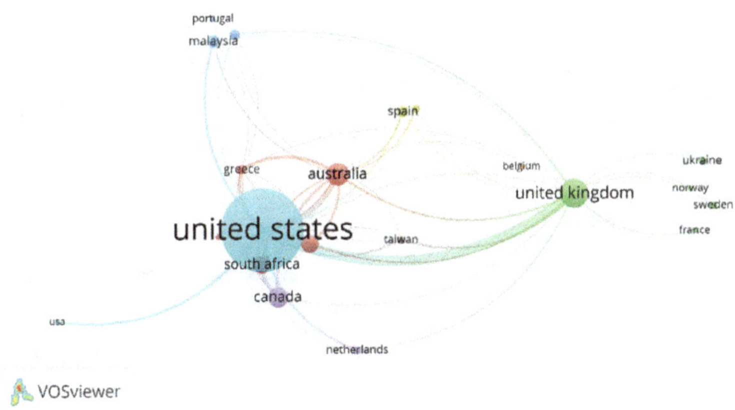

Figure 11, represents the countries that published and cited most documents. By keeping the minimum number of documents to 1 and the minimum number of citations per country to 50, out of 71, 24 met the requirement and 21 are connected. Here, United States have the most document and India also have enough no. of publications in this topic but not enough to reflect in the top.

7. Analysis of Co-Authorship Network

The network of author collaboration is examined and represented using the VOS viewer to reflect the interaction between authors. 1194 authors have published related articles on this subject, according to VOS viewer. The maximum number of authors allowed per document was set at 25. The greatest author cooperation network is represented in figure 12. The network of 17 authors is depicted in the image. A developing and expanding research network in this field is demonstrated by the color gradient, which also highlights recent collaborations (2021–2024).

Figure 12. Overlay visualisation of the cooperation network of authors

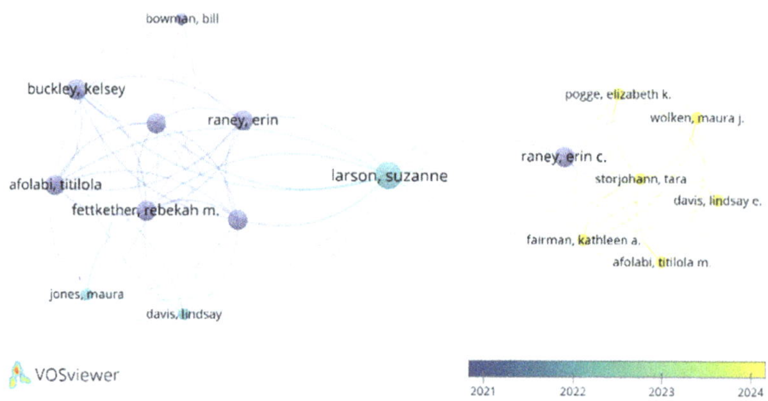

8. Bibliographic Coupling

To find the commonality between the papers written on this theme, we performed Bibliographic Coupling. Kept the minimum number of citations of a document to 25, out of 423; only 107 were meeting the criteria. 102 documents were connected. The minimum cluster size was kept at 15, and we got 3 clusters.

Figure 13. Bibliographic Coupling

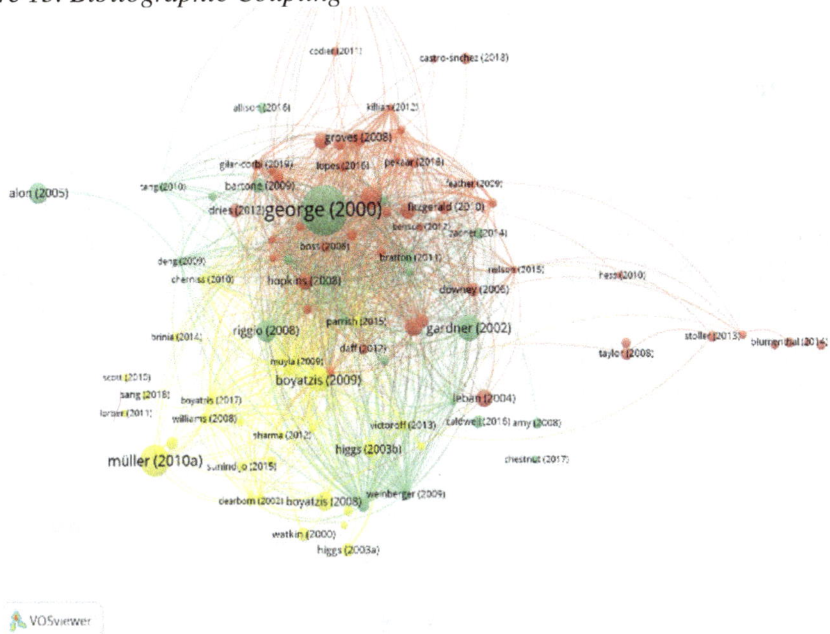

Cluster 1- This cluster contains 48 items and is shown in Red. The theme revolves around training and development of EQ helps improve employee performance, leadership and employee retention. Total citations of this cluster are 8,967. The most cited paper in this cluster is Kerr et al. (2006) with 231 citations. The second most cited paper in this cluster is Groves et al. (2008) with 133 citations, which argues that EI is not just something that we have within but it can be developed through proper training.

Cluster 2 - This cluster contains 30 items and is shown in Yellow. The theme revolves around Testing and developing cognitive and emotional intelligence in leaders such as managers and principals. Total citations of this cluster are 2,213. The most cited paper in this cluster is Müller & Turner (2010), with 452 citations collected 400 responses from project managers, which were utilised to test the competency of EQ in the successful completion of projects.

Cluster 3 - This cluster contains 24 items and is shown in Green. The theme revolves around the Effectiveness of Emotional Intelligence and social skills to improve leadership style. Total citations of this cluster are 2,740. The most cited paper in this cluster is George (2000), with 1110 citations, talks about how effective emotional intelligence can be in good leadership by doing small tasks like appreciating the good work of employees, rewarding them, and creating an inclusive work environment where people are welcome for their suggestions.

Thematic analysis:

This bibliometric analysis explores the conceptual landscape of emotional intelligence (EI) and leadership, categorising the themes into four quadrants based on their density (development) and centrality (relevance): Motor Themes, Basic Themes, Niche Themes, and Emerging or Declining Themes. The analysis reveals how emotional intelligence has permeated leadership studies across diverse disciplines, emphasising its pivotal role in influencing organisational effectiveness, interpersonal dynamics, and decision-making.

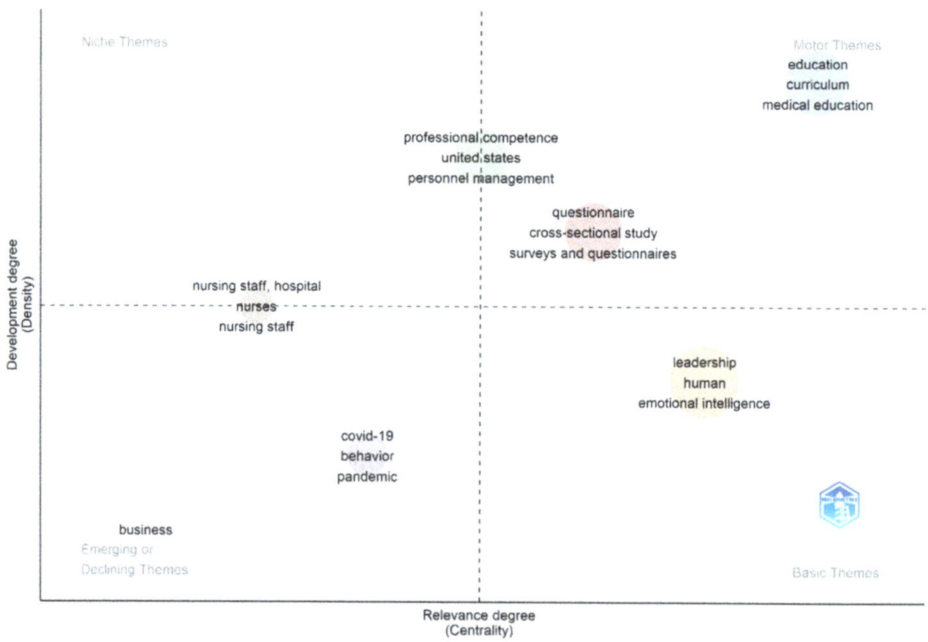

1. Motor Themes (Upper Right Quadrant)

Themes in this quadrant are highly relevant and well-developed, making them core to the field. The key themes here include education, curriculum, and medical education, indicating that these topics are both central and extensively explored. These could be leading discussions and driving the field forward.

2. Niche Themes (Upper Left Quadrant)

These themes have high development but low centrality, meaning they are well-researched but not broadly influential. Professional competence, personnel management, and the United States appear here, suggesting specialized discussions that may not yet be widely integrated into broader discourse.

3. Basic Themes (Lower Right Quadrant)

These themes have high centrality but low density, making them foundational topics that are widely discussed but still developing. Leadership, human aspects, and emotional intelligence fall in this category, indicating they are crucial to the field but require further refinement.

4. Emerging or Declining Themes (Lower Left Quadrant)

This quadrant contains themes with both low relevance and low development, suggesting that they are either emerging research areas or losing significance. Business, COVID-19, behavior, and pandemic appear in this section, reflecting a possible decline in pandemic-related research or a shift in focus towards new trends.

Additionally, the central themes near the middle (e.g., questionnaire, cross-sectional study, surveys and questionnaires) suggest methodological considerations that play a role across multiple thematic areas.This analysis provides insights into the dominant, emerging, and declining topics in the research landscape, highlighting where future exploration may be beneficial.

Thematic Evolution

Figure 15. Thematic Evolution

The thematic evolution of research from **2000-2018** to **2019-2024**, as depicted in the Sankey diagram, reveals significant shifts in scholarly focus, particularly in the domains of leadership, education, and professional development. Several themes, such as *emotional intelligence* and *education*, have remained central across both periods, demonstrating their continued relevance in leadership studies and training. However, notable transformations have occurred, with *leadership development* and *leadership effectiveness* emerging as distinct topics, suggesting an increasing emphasis on refining leadership skills and assessing their impact. Additionally, *competence* and *competencies*, which were more generalized themes in earlier years, have evolved into more specific discussions on *soft skills* and *management development*, reflecting a growing interest in the nuanced capabilities required for effective leadership. The emergence of *Covid-19* as a research theme in the latter period underscores the pandemic's influence on leadership, education, and professional training, prompting new explorations into crisis management and adaptive learning strategies. Meanwhile, themes such as *mentoring* and *nurses*, which were present in earlier research, seem to have merged into broader concepts like *training* and *continuing professional development*, indicating a shift toward more comprehensive discussions on lifelong learning and skill enhancement. Similarly, *school leadership* has transitioned into *higher education*, signifying an increased focus on leadership within universities and academic institutions rather than primary or secondary education. Overall, the thematic evolution illustrates a clear transition from broad discussions on leadership and education to more specialized and practical concerns, with a greater emphasis on leadership effectiveness, professional skill development, and adaptability in response to global challenges.

Figure 16. Trend topics

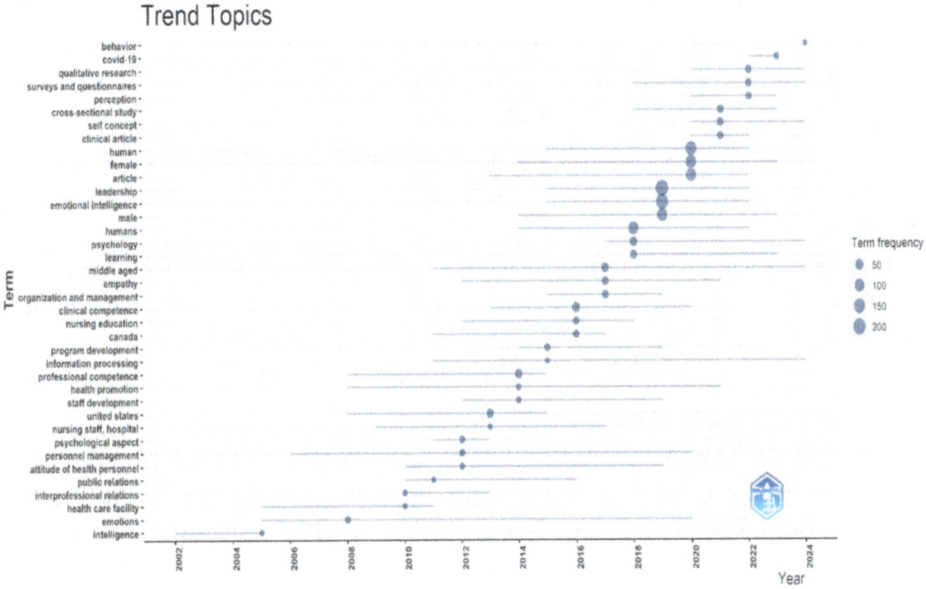

The bibliometric analysis of trend topics over time illustrates the dynamic evolution of research themes, showcasing shifts in scholarly focus and the increasing prominence of certain concepts across different periods. The analysis spans from the early 2000s to 2024, revealing how the discourse around leadership, emotional intelligence, professional competencies, and healthcare-related themes has transformed over time.

Early 2000s - 2010: Foundational and Theoretical Focus: During the early phase of research, the dominant themes revolved around **intelligence, emotions, interprofessional relations, psychological aspects, and public relations**. This period was characterized by a strong emphasis on cognitive and psychological dimensions, suggesting a foundational approach to understanding behavior, leadership, and management. Scholars focused on conceptualizing intelligence and emotions, laying the groundwork for later discussions on emotional intelligence and leadership effectiveness.

The emergence of **health care facility, personnel management, and professional competence** indicates an early interest in the professional development of individuals working in organizational and healthcare settings. However, empirical methodologies were relatively limited, and much of the research remained theoretical.

2010 - 2015: Shift Towards Leadership, Education, and Empirical Research: A significant transformation occurred post-2010, with the rise of **leadership, emotional intelligence, learning, and psychology** as prominent research topics. This period marked a shift towards understanding leadership competencies, particularly in educational and healthcare contexts.

Additionally, **nursing education, clinical competence, and nursing staff (hospital)** became notable themes, reflecting an increasing scholarly interest in professional development within the healthcare sector. This period saw the integration of **program development, information processing, and staff development**, highlighting a growing emphasis on structured training and competency-building programs.

Methodologically, research began incorporating **qualitative research**, signaling a move towards interpretive and experiential studies. The emergence of **cross-sectional studies and surveys and questionnaires** suggests a methodological shift toward empirical data collection, allowing for a more nuanced understanding of behavioral and leadership-related phenomena.

2016 - 2020: Expansion into Behavioral and Perceptual Studies: From 2016 onward, a distinct trend emerged towards **behavior, perception, empathy, and self-concept**, indicating a deeper exploration of individual and group dynamics in leadership and professional settings. This period also saw a continued emphasis on **organization and management**, demonstrating a growing interest in optimizing leadership frameworks and managerial effectiveness.

The increasing use of **clinical articles** during this time suggests a rising focus on evidence-based research, particularly within the healthcare and educational sectors. This aligns with the broader trend of professionalizing leadership through empirical assessments and structured competency evaluations.

2020 - 2024: Impact of COVID-19 and New Research Directions: The most striking shift in the research landscape occurred from 2020 onward, with **Covid-19** becoming a dominant topic. The pandemic reshaped scholarly priorities, leading to increased investigations into how crises affect **leadership, emotional intelligence, and professional competencies**.

The heightened focus on **continuing professional development, staff development, and training** indicates a strong interest in equipping professionals with adaptive skills to navigate unprecedented challenges. Additionally, **self-concept and empathy** gained traction, suggesting an increased awareness of psychological well-being, self-perception, and interpersonal relationships in professional environments.

Interestingly, **qualitative research and surveys/questionnaires** continued to be widely used methodologies, reflecting the sustained importance of empirical approaches in capturing complex human behaviors.

2. DISCUSSION AND CONCLUSION

The paper presents a bibliometric analysis of several leadership and emotional intelligence research studies published between 2000 and 2024. A total of 423 articles were chosen from the Scopus database. This analysis focused mostly on the publishing trend in leadership and emotional intelligence. It featured the countries and organisations that had a significant role in the study, as well as the publications and authors who had received the most citations. The study also included a keyword occurrence analysis. These analyses provide scholars interested in the issue of EI and leadership with information on well-known publications, authors, organisations, and governments, as well as terms commonly used in the field.

The number of studies on leadership and EI is growing. Although Dr. James K. Stoller of the Cleveland Clinic contributed the most publications, Richard E. Boyatzis, a renowned scholar from Case Western Reserve University, is one of the most significant and often cited authors in the field of leadership and EI. The two most active institutions, Case Western Reserve University and The Cleveland Clinic Foundation, showed a strong institutional commitment to this field of study. Furthermore, the United States has a strong scholarly presence, as evidenced by its leading publication volume and citation impact, while other nations, such as India and the United Kingdom, exhibit encouraging engagement.

The most prominent work has been published in journals like the Journal of Management Development and the Leadership & Organisation Development Journal, which makes them important resources for upcoming researchers. According to thematic and keyword co-occurrence studies, "Emotional Intelligence" and "Leadership" are two frequently occurring keywords, indicating their fundamental position in the field of study. Three clusters were formed in Bibliographic Coupling. The themes are the importance of emotional skills development in the organisation, especially in a leader for the better performance of employees, it improves leadership styles and most research includes testing the competency of EI to enhance the leadership style.

Additionally, thematic mapping shows the trend beyond broad conversations about leadership and education and toward more specialised topics like professional competencies, effective leadership, and adaptive leadership techniques—particularly in the face of emergencies like the COVID-19 outbreak. This development demonstrates a sophisticated comprehension of the dynamic interaction between leadership conduct and emotional intelligence in a variety of contexts, including corporate growth, healthcare, and education. The report also points out important research gaps and suggests avenues for further investigation. As an example, even though emotional intelligence (EI) is widely acknowledged to be valuable, some theoretical models are still lacking, especially when it comes to the intersection of analytical and emotional reasoning in leadership roles (Boyatzis, Rochford & Jack). Future research should therefore focus on addressing these conceptual limits, maybe by combining cognitive science, organizational behavior, and psychology in an interdisciplinary manner. Furthermore, the significance of comparative and cross-cultural analysis is suggested by the geographical diversity of study contributions and the diverse cultural contexts in which leadership and emotional intelligence are examined. The conceptualization and implementation of leadership and emotional intelligence are influenced by various cultural and social, psychological, and demographic elements, which offers a chance for more nuanced international dialogue.

The citation and co-authorship networks also show that researchers' collaborations are not cohesive. Promoting larger, inter-institutional collaboration may help develop a more thorough and integrated knowledge of the area. Additionally, adding other databases like Google Scholar or Web of Science could improve bibliometric reviews in the future.

For academics wishing to explore the area of emotional intelligence and leadership development, this study offers a fundamental road map. The continued attention, growing publishing patterns, and changing themes support the importance and longevity of leadership and emotional intelligence as research topics. Emotional intelligence is now a key competency in defining successful, moral, and adaptable leadership in a VUCA-BANI world, rather than a peripheral idea for both academics and practitioners.

The concept of Emotional Intelligence has become a much exciting study topic for researchers in contemporary times. Leadership requirements have always focused on the cognitive abilities of the leader, as it's appealing to imagine a leader who is smart, intellectual, good in numbers and memory etc. But lately, studies have proved that Emotional Intelligence is a key differentiator between a leader and an 'Effective Leader'.

Emotional competence adds to one's intelligence to make it a whole. It enables a leader to think with a clear mind, make the best decisions, understand others' perspectives and remain calm amidst challenging phases of life. Psychologists have given various models of Emotional Intelligence to explain the stages and components of emotional competence, suggesting the hierarchical nature of EI.

Table 1. EI Models: A Comparison

Feature	SALOVEY & MAYER'S MODEL	GOLEMAN'S MODEL	BAR-ON'S MODEL
Approach	Cognitive ability	Mixed model (skills + traits)	Personality-based
Focus	Emotional processing and reasoning	Leadership & workplace effectiveness	Well-being & adaptation
Components	Perceiving, Using, Understanding, Managing emotions	Self-awareness, Self-regulation, Motivation, Empathy, Social skills	Interpersonal & intrapersonal skills, stress management

Studies have also criticised the supremacy of EI alone as it is just a component of human intelligence alongside IQ. Leaders high only on emotional competence may not be as good as the ones who are exclusively good at cognitive intelligence. Individuals with high EI can misuse it to play emotional tactics like manipulation of emotionally innocent ones.

3. LIMITATIONS AND SCOPE FOR FUTURE RESEARCH

Considering its obvious advantages, this work has few drawbacks and could well be used to guide future research. The inquiry began with a search of the Scopus journal database for papers on leadership & EI. The study excluded any works that were not indexed in Scopus. Researchers may consider using new databases in the future, such as Google Scholar, Web of Science, etc. Furthermore, while many parameters were taken into account in this study's bibliometric analysis, others, like funding and discipline, were not. These issues could be the focus of future research, as well as the display of additional network diagrams to allow for detailed investigation. In addition, future researchers might consider extending the study period if they wish to have a more comprehensive understanding of this topic. Another significant flaw in this study is its bibliometric analysis, which places more emphasis on data than on analysing the connections, ideas, and interactions among authors. Meta-analyses, comprehensive reviews of literature, methodology, and the application of theories of emotional intelligence and leadership are possible future research topics. Future research can therefore examine these subjects. Moreover, real-time decision-making processes, emotional complexities, and behavioural evidence observed at the workplace level are not captured by the current analysis. The theme evolution maps show how research patterns have evolved but do not explain why these shifts take place. They also lack information on how various sectors, such as public administration, business, healthcare, and education, conceptualise and apply the concepts of emotional intelligence.

REFERENCES

Batool, B. F. (2013). Emotional intelligence and effective leadership. *Journal of Business Studies Quarterly*, *4*(3).

Bradberry, T., & Greaves, J. (2009). *Emotional Intelligence 2.0*. TalentSmart.

Carmeli, A. (2003). The relationship between emotional intelligence and work attitudes, behavior and outcomes: An examination among senior managers. *Journal of Managerial Psychology*, *18*(8), 788–813. DOI: 10.1108/02683940310511881

Cavallo, K., & Brienza, D. (2002). Emotional competence and leadership excellence at Johnson & Johnson: The emotional intelligence and leadership study. *Consortium for Research on Emotional Intelligence in Organizations*, *1*(12), 1–12.

Cavazotte, F., Moreno, V., & Hickmann, M. (2012). Effects of leader intelligence, personality and emotional intelligence on transformational leadership and managerial performance. *The Leadership Quarterly*, *23*(3), 443–455. DOI: 10.1016/j.leaqua.2011.10.003

Cherniss, C. (2001). *The business case for emotional intelligence*. Consortium for Research on Emotional Intelligence in Organizations.

Cobo, M. J., López-Herrera, A. G., Herrera-Viedma, E., & Herrera, F. (2011). Science mapping software tools: Review, analysis, and cooperative study among tools. *Journal of the American Society for Information Science and Technology*, *62*(7), 1382–1402. DOI: 10.1002/asi.21525

Dearborn, K. (2002). Studies in Emotional Intelligence redefine our approach to leadership development. *Public Personnel Management*, *31*(4), 523–530. DOI: 10.1177/009102600203100408

Fambrough, M. J., & Kaye Hart, R. (2008). Emotions in leadership development: A critique of emotional intelligence. *Advances in Developing Human Resources*, *10*(5), 740–758. DOI: 10.1177/1523422308323542

Gardner, L., & Stough, C. (2002). Examining the relationship between leadership and emotional intelligence in senior level managers. *Leadership and Organization Development Journal*, *23*(2), 68–78. DOI: 10.1108/01437730210419198

George, J. M. (2000). Emotions and leadership: The role of emotional intelligence. *Human Relations; Studies Towards the Integration of the Social Sciences*, *53*(8), 1027–1055. DOI: 10.1177/0018726700538001

Goleman, D. (1998). Working with] Working with emotional intelligenceemotional intelligence. Bantam.

González-Sala, F., Osca-Lluch, J., Tortosa Gil, F., & Peñaranda Ortega, M. (2017). Beneficios de las relaciones entre los miembros de los comités editoriales y las revistas científicas. El caso de las revistas iberoamericanas de psicología. *Revista Española de Documentación Científica*, *40*(4), 189. DOI: 10.3989/redc.2017.4.1460

Groves, K. S., Pat McEnrue, M., & Shen, W. (2008). Developing and measuring the emotional intelligence of leaders. *Journal of Management Development*, *27*(2), 225–250. DOI: 10.1108/02621710810849353

Harms, P. D., & Credé, M. (2010). Emotional intelligence and transformational and transactional leadership: A meta-analysis. *Journal of Leadership & Organizational Studies*, *17*(1), 5–17. DOI: 10.1177/1548051809350894

Hart, K. L., & Perlis, R. H. (2021). Authorship inequality: A bibliometric study of the concentration of authorship among a diminishing number of individuals in high-impact medical journals, 2008-2019. *BMJ Open*, *11*(1), e046002. DOI: 10.1136/bmjopen-2020-046002

Hayashi, A. (2005). Emotional intelligence and outdoor leadership. *Journal of Experiential Education*, *27*(3), 333–335. DOI: 10.1177/105382590502700320

Higgs, M., & Aitken, P. (2003). An exploration of the relationship between emotional intelligence and leadership potential. *Journal of Managerial Psychology*, *18*(8), 814–823. DOI: 10.1108/02683940310511890

Higgs, M., & Dulewicz, V. (2002). *Making sense of emotional intelligence: Vol* (2nd ed.). National Foundation for Educational Research.

Kellett, J. B., Humphrey, R. H., & Sleeth, R. G. (2002). Empathy and complex task performance: Two routes to leadership. *The Leadership Quarterly*, *13*(5), 523–544. DOI: 10.1016/S1048-9843(02)00142-X

Kerr, R., Garvin, J., Heaton, N., & Boyle, E. (2006). Emotional intelligence and leadership effectiveness. *Leadership and Organization Development Journal*, *27*(4), 265–279. DOI: 10.1108/01437730610666028

Kessler, M. M. (1963). Bibliographic coupling between scientific papers. *American Documentation*, *14*(1), 10–25. DOI: 10.1002/asi.5090140103

Kumar, S. (2014). Establishing linkages between emotional intelligence and transformational leadership. *Industrial Psychiatry Journal*, *23*(1), 1–3. DOI: 10.4103/0972-6748.144934

Leban, W., & Zulauf, C. (2004). Linking emotional intelligence abilities and transformational leadership styles. *Leadership and Organization Development Journal, 25*(7), 554–564. DOI: 10.1108/01437730410561440

Lee, C.-C., Yeh, W.-C., Yu, Z., & Lin, X.-C. (2023). The relationships between leader emotional intelligence, transformational leadership, and transactional leadership and job performance: A mediator model of trust. *Heliyon, 9*(8), e18007. DOI: 10.1016/j.heliyon.2023.e18007

Lone, M. A., & Lone, A. H. (2018). Does emotional intelligence predict leadership effectiveness? An exploration in non-Western context. *SA Journal of Human Resource Management, 5*(1), 28–39. DOI: 10.1177/2322093718766806

Lubbadeh, T. (2020). Emotional intelligence and leadership-the dark and bright sides. *Modern Management Review, 25*(27), 39–50. DOI: 10.7862/rz.2020.mmr.5

Mayer, J., & Salovey, P. (1997). Emotional Emotional development and Emotional intelligence: Educational Implications. 3–34.

Müller, R., & Turner, R. (2010). Leadership competency profiles of successful project managers. *International Journal of Project Management, 28*(5), 437–448. DOI: 10.1016/j.ijproman.2009.09.003

Ozcelik, H., Langton, N., & Aldrich, H. (2008). Doing well and doing good: The relationship between leadership practices that facilitate a positive emotional climate and organizational performance. *Journal of Managerial Psychology, 23*(2), 186–203. DOI: 10.1108/02683940810850817

Palmer, B., Walls, M., Burgess, Z., & Stough, C. (2001). Emotional intelligence and effective leadership. *Leadership and Organization Development Journal, 22*(1), 5–10. DOI: 10.1108/01437730110380174

Palmer, B. R., Gignac, G., Ekermans, G., & Stough, C. (2008). A comprehensive framework for emotional intelligence. Emotional intelligence: Theoretical and cultural perspectives. 17–38.

Pastor, I. (2014). Leadership and emotional intelligence: The effect on performance and attitude. *Procedia Economics and Finance, 15*, 985–992. DOI: 10.1016/S2212-5671(14)00658-3

Prabhu, M. (2022). *15 Qualities of an Ideal Leader According to Kautilya a.k.a. Chanakya*. Vedic Management Center.

Rosete, D., & Ciarrochi, J. (2005). Emotional intelligence and its relationship to workplace performance outcomes of leadership effectiveness. *Leadership and Organization Development Journal, 26*(5), 388–399. DOI: 10.1108/01437730510607871

Sadri, G. (2012). Emotional intelligence and leadership development. *Public Personnel Management, 41*(3), 535–548. DOI: 10.1177/009102601204100308

Salovey, P., & Mayer, J. D. (1990). Emotional intelligence. *Imagination, Cognition and Personality, 9*(3), 185–211. DOI: 10.2190/DUGG-P24E-52WK-6CDG

Schlaerth, A., Ensari, N., & Christian, J. (2013). A meta-analytical review of the relationship between emotional intelligence and leaders' constructive conflict management. Group Processes & Intergroup Relations. *Group Processes & Intergroup Relations, 16*(1), 126–136. DOI: 10.1177/1368430212439907

Sinkovics, N. (2016). Enhancing the foundations for theorising through bibliometric mapping. *International Marketing Review, 33*(3), 327–350. DOI: 10.1108/IMR-10-2014-0341

Skrzypczyńska, K. (2020). Significance of emotional intelligence in leadership. *Journal of Positive Management, 9*(4), 66. DOI: 10.12775/JPM.2018.155

Stein, S. J., Papadogiannis, P., Yip, J. A., & Sitarenios, G. (2009). Emotional intelligence of leaders: A profile of top executives. *Leadership and Organization Development Journal, 30*(1), 87–101. DOI: 10.1108/01437730910927115

van Eck, N. J., & Waltman, L. (2010). Software survey: VOSviewer, a computer program for bibliometric mapping. *Scientometrics, 84*(2), 523–538. DOI: 10.1007/s11192-009-0146-3

Vivek, R., & Krupskyi, O. P. (2024). EI & AI in leadership and how it can affect future leaders. *European Journal of Management Issues, 32*(3), 174–182. DOI: 10.15421/192415

Wolff, S. B., Pescosolido, A. T., & Druskat, V. U. (2002). Emotional intelligence as the basis of leadership emergence in self-managing teams. *The Leadership Quarterly, 13*(5), 505–522. DOI: 10.1016/S1048-9843(02)00141-8

Yadav, R., & Lata, P. (2019). Role of emotional intelligence in effective leadership. *International Journal on Leadership, 7*(2), 27–32.

Section 5

Applied and Sectoral Perspectives on AI–Augmented Leadership

Chapter 16
Digital Leadership and Agentic AI in Higher Education

Rosemol Pappachan
http://orcid.org/0009-0005-9433-921X
BITS Pilani, Dubai, UAE

Shazi Shah Jabeen
http://orcid.org/0000-0001-9340-7595
BITS Pilani, Dubai, UAE

ABSTRACT

The rapidly advancing digital transformation of higher education requires skilled digital leadership to manage complex technological and organisational changes. This advancement is presently being facilitated by the emergence of Agentic Artificial Intelligence (AI). These advanced agents provide innovative educational opportunities by serving as proactive tutors, metacognitive coaches, and collaborative teaching assistants, capable of tailored learning experiences and reducing administrative responsibilities for educators. The incorporation of these highly autonomous AI presents significant pedagogical and ethical issues. This chapter incorporates these converging dynamics, suggesting that academic leaders must proactively coordinate balanced human-AI collaborations to enhance educational achievement while strictly preserving human agency, equity, and academic integrity.

DOI: 10.4018/979-8-3373-6650-0.ch016

INTRODUCTION

The academic landscape in higher education is presently being transformed by the rapid implementation and integration of modern digital technologies (Obied, 2025). In recent years, institutions have rapidly adopted digital tools to improve operational efficiency and address the changing requirements of a global, digitally interconnected knowledge economy. The emergence of digitally native learners, the increasing number of online and hybrid educational models, and the demand for adaptable and inclusive education accelerated this shift (Gillpatrick, 2020). Digital transformation in educational settings goes beyond the mere adoption of new technological tools; it necessitates a comprehensive reconfiguration of organisational operations, academic pedagogical frameworks, and stakeholder initiatives. This shift signifies a transition from conventional, teacher-centric methodologies to more dynamic, learner-focused and technology-enhanced educational systems. It necessitates reevaluating curriculum design, evaluation methodologies, and institutional governance to correspond with digital developments.

As higher education institutions evolve from conventional, static settings to dynamic, technology-driven ecosystems, the necessity for efficient digital leadership has emerged as a crucial requirement. The success of these digital projects depends significantly on leaders who can formulate a cohesive strategy for technology integration, navigate institutional obstacles, and create a culture of continuous digital innovation (Onan, 2024). Digital leaders have to demonstrate a blend of technology understanding, strategic vision, and change management skills to navigate institutions through complicated transformation processes. They are tasked for promoting collaboration, stimulating innovation, and guaranteeing that digital initiatives are sustainable and inclusive. The significance of digital leadership is further underscored by the challenges that accompany digital transformation. Higher education institutions frequently encounter opposition to change, constrained resources, deficiencies in digital capabilities, and concerns regarding data security and privacy. Effective leadership is crucial for addressing these difficulties by enhancing digital literacy, fostering stakeholder involvement, and instituting clear governance frameworks. Leaders must guarantee that technological adoption does not undermine academic integrity or increase disparities among learners.

Simultaneously, the technical environment is being transformed by the emergence of Agentic AI. Agentic AI, in contrast to conventional reactive AI systems, represents autonomous systems efficient at performing difficult, multi-step tasks, independent reasoning, strategic planning, and decision-making on behalf of users (Gridach et al., 2025). The transition from reactive to proactive AI signifies a substantial advancement in technology's function in higher education, allowing systems to serve as active players instead of passive instruments. Agentic AI presents new possibilities for the improvement of academic and administrative operations. Its strengths in reasoning, learning, and adaptation enable it to facilitate sophisticated educational processes, encompassing personalised learning, automated assessment, and intelligent decision-making (Koubaa, 2026). These systems can adaptively respond to student requirements, hence enhancing engagement and learning productivity.

The rapid advancement of tools such as adaptive tutoring systems, multi-agent collaborations, and generative AI platforms possesses the innovative capacity to enhance personalised learning experiences and reshape established pedagogical frameworks in higher education. Intelligent tutoring systems offer personalised feedback, multi-agent systems act as collaborative problem-solving environments, and generative AI aids in content production and research assistance. These technologies collectively foster a more dynamic, adaptive, and student-centered educational environment. The incorporation of agentic AI poses considerable pedagogical, ethical, and organisational issues. The independence of AI systems prompts issues of transparency, accountability, and bias, necessitating meticulous oversight and governance. Moreover, it is essential to guarantee that AI enhances rather than substitutes for human educators, maintaining the vital functions of human discernment, creativity, and empathy in the educational sphere. The integration of agentic AI requires a reformation of teaching roles and methodologies from an educational standpoint. Educators are progressively anticipated to function as facilitators and co-creators of information, collaborating with AI systems to improve learning outcomes. This transition necessitates the cultivation of new competencies in both instructors and students, encompassing digital literacy, critical thinking, and proficiency in engaging with AI systems. The effective application of agentic AI relies on the creation of strong governance structures that guarantee ethical utilisation, data protection, and adherence to regulations. Digital leaders are pivotal in formulating and implementing these frameworks, guaranteeing that AI technologies conform to institutional principles and societal standards. Collaboration and partnerships are essential for promoting digital transformation in higher education. Institutions are progressively collaborating with technology providers, industry partners, and other academic entities to obtain sophisticated tools and disseminate knowledge. These relationships augment institutional capacity, foster creativity, and enable the creation of scalable digital solutions.

CONCEPTUAL FOUNDATIONS OF DIGITAL LEADERSHIP

Leadership is a crucial component of organisational values and must evolve alongside organisations, especially during the transition to digital transformation, where transformational digital leadership cultivates digital culture, boosts innovation and performance, and effectively facilitates digital transformation (AlNuaimi et al., 2022). Transformational leadership is prominently exhibited and linked to positive outcomes in digital contexts, especially when leaders possess digital competencies, as demonstrated by a study involving members of the Senate from three Greek universities utilising extensive data analytic algorithms (Antonopoulou, Halkiopoulos, Barlou, et al., 2021b). Previous research identified also transformational leadership as essential for building a collaborative digital culture and mitigating resistance to change while also being essential for inspiring and motivating virtual teams in digital contexts (Asfahani, 2025).

Complexity leadership could be defined as adaptive mechanisms developed by complex organizations in new conditions required by the information age, rather than technical problems entailed by the industrial age (Baltaci & Balcı, 2017). Adaptive leadership serves as a catalyst for organisational transformation within complex adaptive systems, promoting self-organization and innovation by reconfiguring bureaucratic institutions through techniques such as supporting experimentation and accommodating ambiguity (Mihajlov & Mihajlov, 2025). Adaptive leadership is thus necessary for organisational success during digital transformation, allowing leaders to manage swift technological changes, promote innovation, and enhance organisational resilience. These leadership viewpoints collectively underscore the dynamic nature of leadership in digitally evolving environments.

Digital leadership refers to leaders adopting digital technologies that integrate leadership competencies with digital tools allowing them to make informed decisions, deliver a vision, implement strategies, and enhance organisational performance in the digital age (Tigre et al., 2025). Digital leadership plays an essential role in the digital era, as it incorporates required digital abilities in virtual organisational frameworks, where leaders with broad viewpoints, superior intellectual ability, and specialised digital competencies play a critical role (Tutar & Güler, 2022). Innovation is a key element of digital leadership, as leaders build environments that promote idea exchange and risk-taking, while utilising technology such as artificial intelligence and cloud computing to augment consumer experiences and enhance operational efficiency. Digital leaders are expected to respond instantly and adaptively within networked and distributed organisational frameworks while simultaneously overseeing the organization's digital transition (Klein, 2020).

Leadership is crucial for effective organisational digital transformation, with recent research highlighting its importance in concurrently managing technology change and human factors. Effective leadership is required for overseeing digital transformation by promoting learning, collaboration, and agility, thereby allowing organisations to adjust to market uncertainties (Sacavém et al., 2025). The connection of leadership with the organization's mission facilitates progression to advanced levels of digital transformation, necessitating a transition to a leadership approach that prioritises empathy and comprehension of digital technology (Porfírio et al., 2021). Furthermore, leadership drives digital transformation through essential abilities including vision, innovation, empowerment, and ongoing learning (Živković, 2022).

In such an environment, digital leadership arises as a vital integrative strategy that merges technology competencies with human-centered leadership methodologies. Digital leadership thus integrates conventional leadership skills with digital expertise, emphasising the development of a cohesive strategy for digital transformation and the implementation of sustainable change (Ridho et al., 2023).

The five essential attributes of digital leadership considered important for effective leadership are digital competence, digital culture, digital differentiation, digital governance, and digital advocacy (Onan, 2024). These characteristics jointly reflect the multifaceted nature of digital leadership in modern organisations. Digital competence is a fundamental skill for lifelong learning, characterised by the information, skills, attitudes, abilities, and strategies necessary for utilising digital technologies (Santos et al., 2022). It enables leaders and staff to proficiently utilise digital tools and adjust to technological innovations. Digital culture is a developing social framework influenced by digital technology and networks that alters individual behaviour, interaction, and decision-making, while challenging conventional cultural perceptions and necessitating adaptation in modern society (Uzelac, 2010). This cultural transition facilitates the effective incorporation of digital transformation activities into organisations. Digital differentiation implies the application of digital tools and technology to enhance pedagogical creativity by customising content and teaching to accommodate varied learner requirements (Andreasson & Henfridsson, 2009). It guarantees more inclusive and tailored learning and working environments. Digital governance represents the application of digital technologies in decision-making, the delivery of services, and stakeholder engagement, signifying a transition from e-government to citizen-centric methodologies, and facilitating efficient, trust-based exchange relationships through analog, augmented, and automated governance methods (Hanisch et al., 2023). Efficient governance frameworks are crucial for upholding transparency, accountability, and trust in digital systems. Digital advocacy denotes the use of digital platforms and technologies to mobilise supporters and affect policy, progressively transitioning from conventional political influence to establishing political presence using social media (Johansson & Scaramuzzino, 2019). This underscores the increasing significance of digital platforms in determining public participation and organisational impact. Prior research underscores a variety of other essential competencies for digital leaders, encompassing technological proficiency, adaptability, strategic thinking, communication, collaboration, ethical consciousness, strategic vision, digital literacy, and ethical governance (Hamzah et al., 2025; Shahzad, 2024).

The International Society for Technology in Education Standards for Administrators (ISTE-A) classifies effective digital leadership into various fundamental indicators (Zhong, 2017a). Digital leaders motivate and enable a collective vision for intentional transformation, ensuring that technological initiatives are endorsed by all stakeholders to optimise educational objectives. In the digital age learning culture, administrators must exemplify regular and efficient technology utilisation, creating learner-centred environments furnished with adequate equipment and pertinent digital materials. Excellence in Professional Practice: Leaders must dedicate time and resources to continuous professional development, establishing digital learning communities where educators collaborate, exchange insights, and enhance their technology proficiency. Digital leaders utilise data-driven metrics to optimise learning outcomes and retain skilled workers knowledgeable in technology to further academic objectives.

Digital leadership in higher education denotes the combined use of technology with strategic leadership methodologies to advance institutional digital transformation. It entails leading digital transformation, enabling virtual collaboration, utilising data analytics, and cultivating a robust digital culture within organisations. In this setting, digital leaders are essential in integrating technological initiatives with academic objectives and institutional policies. Despite its importance, digital leadership has various challenges, such as resistance to change, constrained resources, and issues pertaining to data security (Onan, 2024). Confronting these difficulties necessitates a systematic and anticipatory leadership strategy. Key determinants for effective digital leadership encompass a well-defined vision, ongoing digital education, sufficient technology infrastructure, and proactive stakeholder involvement. Digital leadership elevates digital awareness and boosts the quality of higher education through the promotion of effective technology utilisation, innovation, and cooperation. Ultimately, it is essential for addressing 21st-century educational difficulties, necessitating leaders to embrace flexible, progressive, and imaginative strategies (Ehlers, 2020).

Academic leaders play a key role in guiding digital transformation in higher education by promoting innovation, facilitating technology implementation, and nurturing cultures of continuous improvement (Obied, 2025). In this environment, successful leadership transcends conventional administrative duties to encompass strategic and transformative activities. Academic leaders must thus embrace vision-driven and collaborative methodologies instead of depending on conventional administrative practices. These methods foster collaborative involvement, stimulate creativity, and improve institutional flexibility in the digital age.

UNDERSTANDING AGENTIC AI IN HIGHER EDUCATION

Agentic AI stands for autonomous AI systems that can independently develop and pursue complex objectives with limited human supervision, differentiating it from conventional reactive AI by its ability for strategic reasoning, adaption, and self-directed action. It is defined by autonomy, adaptability, proactivity, and decision-making authority, incorporating talents such as reasoning, memory, planning, and tool coordination to accomplish intricate goals (Islam et al., 2026). These attributes allow agentic AI to function as an active participant instead of a passive instrument in socio-technical systems. Moreover, agentic AI systems possess the ability to initiate goal-oriented behaviours, make contextually relevant judgements, and continually adapt with minimal human oversight (Pati, 2025). They demonstrate goal-oriented behaviour, dynamic adaptation, and self-enhancement, enabling them to respond successfully to dynamic circumstances and evolving user requirements (Awasthi, 2025). Agentic AI is characterised by its autonomy, reactivity, proactivity, and capacity for learning, which facilitate independent decision-making and process automation (Hosseini & Array, 2025). It enhances productivity and innovation while simultaneously raising concerns over privacy, security, and ethics.

Agentic AI in education is categorised into various kinds according to application models and design paradigms, illustrating its increasing influence in reshaping teaching and learning methodologies. This classification aids in comprehending the operational dynamics of agentic AI within various educational contexts and degrees of autonomy. Dai et al. (2024) provide the Agent4EDU framework, delineating four application models across two dimensions (degree of agency and interaction): human–AI cooperation, AI assistant, instruction execution, and general type. Alternatively, Kamalov et al. (2025) specify four major design paradigms: reflection, planning, tool utilisation, and multi-agent collaboration. These frameworks emphasise the functional functions and architectural design of agentic AI systems in education. Kostopoulos, Gkamas, & Rigou (2025a) highlight implementations, such as intelligent tutoring systems, adaptive assessment platforms, and autonomous learning companions, illustrating the practical application of agentic AI in educational contexts. English (2025) identify three AI paradigms for online education: Traditional AI, Agentic AI, and Agentic Retrieval-Augmented Generation (RAG), with Agentic RAG most congruent with dialogic pedagogy. This distinction highlights the progression of AI from passive support instruments to interactive and contextually aware learning collaborators. Gupta & Heggond (2026) underscore the significance of multi-agent tutoring systems that employ reinforcement learning, natural language processing, and cognitive modelling to provide personalised adaptive learning. These advancements establish agentic AI as a dynamic and intelligent educational agent that can improve learner engagement, personalisation, and academic performance.

DIGITAL TRANSFORMATION IN HIGHER EDUCATION

Digital transformation is driven by various interrelated factors across technological, organisational, and environmental domains, with technological infrastructure and innovation serving as key catalysts. These factors jointly influence how organisations implement and maintain digital transformation programs. Hrustek et al. (2019) identified three principal categories of drivers: customer-driven factors, centring on the adaptation to changing customer requirements; technology-driven factors, relating to industry standards and innovations; and organisational development-driven factors, highlighting strategic advancement objectives. Figueiredo & Soares (2020) conducted a systematic literature study and identified that big data and digitisation are the predominant drivers, followed by innovation. Petrescu et al. (2023) additionally found cross-domain factors, such as enhancing communication, minimising expenses, and augmenting efficiency. These findings underscore the complex nature of digital transformation across many organisational activities. Omrani et al. (2022) present the most compelling evidence, having analysed 15,346 European SMEs and found the technological context—specifically IT infrastructure and digital tools—and current innovation levels as key facilitators of digital transformation. Organisational elements, including competencies, financial assets, and regulatory frameworks, were identified as key contributors. The environmental setting had minimal impact, contradicting previous models posited by Hrustek et al. (2019). This indicates that internal competencies and technological preparedness are more vital than external influences in facilitating successful digital transformation.

Digital transformation considerably improves teaching and learning by augmenting engagement, accessibility, and personalisation. However, its implementation encounters challenges such as digital divides and infrastructure shortages. These effects illustrate the revolutionary capacity of digital technologies in redefining educational experiences and results. The research emphasises that digital technologies, such as artificial intelligence, learning management systems, and virtual and augmented reality, improve student engagement, broaden resource accessibility, and facilitate adaptive learning (Laila et al., 2025). Research further underscores the significance of technology in facilitating innovative and in-depth educational methodologies. These developments demonstrate that digital transformation serves as a key driver for educational innovation in higher education. Research conducted by Manaff & Azahari (2024) identifies digital disparities, inadequate infrastructure, deficiencies in educator preparedness, and cybersecurity threats as significant challenges. Kamsker & Janschitz (2020) also emphasise differing perspectives of technology's efficacy across knowledge disciplines, highlighting the significance of ongoing professional growth. These constraints indicate that the effective execution of digital transformation relies on institutional preparedness and capacity development. Lai (2011) underpins these findings by supporting interactive pedagogical methods. Although digital transformation provides significant advantages, it necessitates strategic execution, ongoing investment, and favourable policy frameworks to guarantee equitable and successful results. Consequently, institutional strategy and governance are essential factors in achieving the positive outcomes of digital transformation in education.

Digital transformation faces numerous challenges such as resource limitations, skill deficiencies, and cybersecurity threats (Heavin & Power, 2018). Organisations should prioritise high-impact activities, invest in digital literacy, and establish accurate data security policies to overcome these concerns. Sustainable digital transformation necessitates the balance of innovation and operational stability, while utilising strategic ties to improve capabilities and secure long-term success.

ROLE OF DIGITAL LEADERSHIP IN MANAGING AGENTIC AI

An effective plan necessitates the alignment of AI implementation with institutional objectives, the selection of suitable algorithms for acquisition or internal development, and the provision of sufficient support and infrastructure (Pascoe et al., 2024). In this environment, digital leadership is essential for steering the strategic direction and responsible execution of agentic AI within organisations. Aligning AI initiatives with institutional objectives necessitates pursuing both direct alignments, ensuring AI systems effectively fulfil organisational aims and social alignment, which considers wider societal impacts (Korinek et al., 2022). This alignment necessitates leaders to implement explicit governance structures, uphold current standards, and formulate new ethical and operational frameworks to guarantee responsible and value-oriented AI integration.

Digital leadership is conceptually seen essential for addressing resistance to AI adoption. Effective leadership, especially through strategic vision and planning, is crucial in steering digital transformation and promoting collaboration to reduce resistance (Zamir, 2025). Psychological, organisational, and ethical obstacles frequently hinder AI adoption; but techniques including transparency, alignment with company objectives, and compliance to ethical standards may reduce these challenges (Ivchyk, 2024). Leadership in human–AI collaboration necessitates the balance of human and AI roles, ensuring that AI enhances rather than substitutes human talents, so facilitating effective decision-making, fostering trust, and promoting sustainable integration inside organisations.

RECONCEPTUALIZING DIGITAL LEADERSHIP IN ACADEMIA

The idea of leadership in the modern academic landscape requires redefinition to confront academic complexities of the digital era. This transition signifies the increasing necessity for leadership strategies that can successfully address rapid technology progress and changing educational requirements. Digital leadership is an administrator's ability to integrate conventional transformational leadership skills with advanced digital expertise (Antonopoulou, Halkiopoulos, & Barlou, 2021a; Obied, 2025). Effective digital leaders move beyond traditional management by engaging in and advocating for technology-enhanced learning, modelling proficient technology use, and perceiving digital integration as a fundamental aspect of the educational ecosystem rather than a just supplementary element (Zhong, 2017b).

The fundamental aspects of digital leadership have been comprehensively described through diverse typologies and frameworks, emphasising characteristics such as digital competence, digital culture, digital distinctiveness, digital governance, and digital advocacy (Malik et al., 2025). Established standards for educational administrators indicate that effective digital leadership is characterised by visionary guidance that garners support for technology plans from all stakeholders, the establishment of a digital age learning culture, the delivery of comprehensive technology-based professional development, systemic enhancements to optimise learning outcomes, and the advocacy of digital citizenship. These characteristics jointly underscore the strategic, cultural, and ethical responsibilities of leaders in the digital transformation of institutions.

However, executing this goal comes with obstacles that necessitate substantial social resources and an awareness of cultural differences. Leaders must skilfully navigate institutional opposition to change, oversee intricate IT systems with constrained budgets, and foster an inclusive atmosphere that honours multiple stakeholder viewpoints (Breaugh et al., 2023). These issues underscore the significance of leadership agility and the capacity to harmonise technology innovation with human-centered behaviours. By emphasising transparent communication, quick decision-making, and principled governance, digital leaders may cultivate collaborative intelligence environments that benefit both academics and students. This method guarantees that digital transformation is both technologically efficient and socially inclusive and sustainable.

THE PARADIGM SHIFT TO AGENTIC AI

The transition to Agentic AI signifies a fundamental paradigm shift from conventional symbolic AI and elementary machine learning to generative, neural-based autonomous ecosystems (Sargsyan, 2025). Historically, artificial intelligence depended on top-down, rule-based systems and explicit logic, significantly constraining its adaptability in dynamic educational contexts (Kostopoulos, Gkamas, Rigou, et al., 2025). Current Agentic AI, driven by Large Language Models (LLMs), employs prompt chaining, dynamic context management, and external tool integration to facilitate emergent, bottom-up reasoning independent of ongoing human prompting (Abou Ali et al., 2025).

This technological advancement signifies the conclusion of exclusive human knowledge management, propelling higher education towards an ecological epistemology. In this new paradigm, learning and knowledge creation are progressively communal activities, dynamically dispersed among human learners, educators, and autonomous non-human entities (Khalid et al., 2025). AI systems now demonstrate functional agency, capable of independent thinking, hypothesis creation, and tool utilisation, effectively serving as socio-cognitive collaborators rather than simple passive teaching tools.

TRANSFORMATIVE PEDAGOGICAL ROLES OF AGENTIC AI

The educational applications of Agentic AI are many and provide unparalleled opportunity for individualised and cooperative learning (Sargsyan, 2025). AI agents can serve as proactive intelligent tutors who oversee student involvement, identify skill deficiencies, and dynamically adjust learning pathways in real-time (Kostopoulos, Gkamas, Rigou, et al., 2025). For example, systems employing Agentic AI can deliver self-regulated learning (SRL) scaffolding that adapts, transitioning from structured prompts for beginners to open-ended questions for experienced learners, thus optimising cognitive load (Sargsyan, 2025).

Moreover, multi-agent partnerships are developing as effective instruments for intricate instructional tasks. In automated essay scoring and feedback generation, multi-agent frameworks—such as those utilising a "verify-then-correct" cycle—employ distinct sub-agents to assess content, analyse language mechanics, and corroborate outputs with external sources, thereby substantially mitigating the biases and hallucinations prevalent in single-LLM methodologies. In simulated training environments, such as medical education, multi-agent systems can assume specific roles (e.g., patient, doctor, radiologist) to promote interactive, multidisciplinary learning (Kamalov et al., 2025).

Agentic AI significantly influences research and curriculum development. Frameworks such as SciLitLLM and ResearchArena illustrate the capability of AI agents to independently traverse extensive quantities of scientific literature to extract pertinent information, synthesise results, and propose innovative research hypotheses. For educators, advanced agentic systems enhance curriculum design by assisting in the development of differentiated instructional materials, generating adaptive assessments, and simulating student responses to improve lesson plans (Gridach et al., 2025).

DIGITAL LEADERS AND ADMINISTRATION IN UNIVERSITY

Digital leaders are responsible with implementing various new technologies that enhance and automate university management. Artificial intelligence has emerged as a pivotal force in this area, automating monotonous administrative duties such applicant processing, class scheduling, and enrolment management (Souli & Pierrakeas, 2025). This automation liberates administrative personnel to concentrate on more strategic, high-level matters. Moreover, the deployment of Learning Management Systems (LMS) like as Moodle or Blackboard, alongside Student Information Systems (SIS), establishes cohesive settings that monitor student advancement and promote effortless cooperation among instructors, students, and administration.

Digital leaders utilise digital marketing and data analytics to improve school visibility, attract potential students, and assess financial and academic performance. Through the implementation of targeted social media campaigns, Customer Relationship Management (CRM) systems, and predictive analytics, colleges can substantially enhance student engagement and improve resource allocation. Furthermore, collaborative digital platforms such as Microsoft Teams and dedicated project management software have expedited administrative processes by facilitating real-time communication and clear task management across departments (Mohammed et al., 2022).

ACADEMICS AS DIGITAL LEADERS IN THE UNIVERSITY

Digital academic leadership in higher education signifies the intentional amalgamation of technical instruments—such as artificial intelligence, Big Data, social media, and cloud computing—with visionary leadership to propel organisational success and pedagogical innovation. It beyond basic technical proficiency; it is a social impact process that employs contemporary information technology to shape attitudes, foster connections, and improve performance within the academic community (Cheng et al., 2024).

The fundamental responsibilities of academic digital leaders encompass five essential dimensions: enhancing digital awareness, articulating a technological vision, embracing technology, promoting collaborative efforts, and tackling difficulties. To effectively negotiate these dimensions, scholars must cultivate specialised e-competencies, including e-communication, e-team building, e-trustworthiness, and e-change management. Moreover, practical digital competencies are essential; studies reveal that expertise in social media (for institutional outreach), mobile and web development, cloud computing, and information security is vital for constructing a comprehensive digital higher education landscape.

The efficacy of faculties in embracing these digital responsibilities is significantly influenced by the existing leadership paradigms within the institution. Research continually demonstrates that transformative and distributed leadership approaches are the most effective in promoting authentic digital and pedagogical innovation. Transformational leaders motivate their peers, create a collective vision, and promote the prioritisation of institutional objectives over individual aspirations, which is significantly associated with elevated digital leadership performance and overall faculty contentment. Likewise, distributed leadership disperses authority, acknowledging the leadership potential of all faculty members, including program directors and instructional innovators. When faculties function within a dispersed model that offers pedagogical autonomy and peer-led assistance, academics demonstrate enhanced engagement with digital pedagogies, including flexible learning and multimedia assessments (Antonopoulou, Halkiopoulos, Barlou, et al., 2021a).

Conversely, when institutions use inflexible, managerial, or compliance-oriented strategies, the digital transition is adversely affected. In hierarchical settings characterised by top-down directives and audit cultures, academics frequently practise "performative compliance," superficially utilising digital tools to satisfy institutional measures instead of genuinely reconfiguring their courses (Fragouli, 2025). Under these circumstances, the transition to hybrid or digital instruction is frequently perceived by faculty as emotionally taxing and conceptually ambiguous, resulting in resistance and prolonged disengagement.

STUDENTS AS DIGITAL LEADERS

The concept of students as digital leaders converts young individuals from passive technology consumers into active agents who aid their peers, assist educators, and foster good social change online. Identifying the informal digital competencies that students employ in their daily lives enables educational institutions to leverage these talents for formal education and community development (Ojando et al., 2017).

Students assume digital leadership positions using diverse methods at various educational levels. Students assume digital leadership positions at various educational tiers, functioning as "ICT experts" in schools by assisting classmates and educators with technology, and as university collaborators who train faculty and participate in cooperative, intergenerational learning (Dimitriadi, 2019). In higher education, they serve as campus influencers and social activists, utilising digital tools to cultivate positive online communities and advocate for civic involvement (Ahlquist, 2017).

Empowering students to take leadership roles in the digital realm provides substantial reciprocal advantages for both the students and the educational institutions. When students manage technical problems, teachers are liberated from the obligation to be technology specialists and may concentrate solely on pedagogical leadership. The assurance of student support encourages teachers to innovate and integrate new ICT tools into their lessons, even if they have not completely grasped them. Assuming the role of a digital leader significantly enhances a student's self-esteem, motivation, and social and communicative competencies. It also connects their informal internet behaviours with their official professional identities (Ahlquist, 2017). By assuming these duties, students acquire the ability to critically assess their digital footprints, examine privacy settings, and engage in "digital citizenship," transitioning from mere digital literacy to actively contributing to their communities. Historically, students have predominantly encountered negative guidance regarding technology, with adults emphasising fear and prohibitions concerning online behaviour. To effectively develop digital leaders, institutions must transition to proactive and intentional education.

CHALLENGES FOR DIGITAL LEADERS

Despite its significant potential, the implementation of Agentic AI presents substantial hazards that digital leaders must constantly address. Excessive reliance on autonomous systems can diminish human agency and critical thinking (Sargsyan, 2025). There exists a considerable risk of "cognitive offloading," in which students neglect essential analytical processes and uncritically replicate AI-generated arguments, consequently limiting dialogic knowledge formation (Kostopoulos, Gkamas, & Rigou, 2025). Also, foundational LLMs often exhibit systemic biases that are Western-centric. If utilised passively, AI agents could continue epistemic hegemony by undermining non-Western dialects and distorting various cultural-historical narratives. The stochastic characteristics of brain architectures result in an intrinsic lack of transparency, known as the "Attribution Gap" (Abou Ali et al., 2025). As agents participate in intricate "internal monologues" spanning thousands of tokens, their logic becomes incomprehensible to human users. This generates an "attribution gap," prompting significant legal and ethical enquiries over accountability when an autonomous system makes mistakes or inflicts harm. Creating, operating, and sustaining sophisticated agentic systems necessitates substantial computing resources and financial commitment. This intensifies the digital gap; empirical evidence indicates that merely 32% of educators in underdeveloped nations feel equipped to utilise AI tools, presenting a risk of increasing systemic imbalances if infrastructure subsidies remain unaddressed.

STRATEGIC GUIDELINES FOR DIGITAL LEADERS

To securely and efficiently utilise Agentic AI, digital leaders in higher education must implement distinct regulations. First, leaders must proactively establish institutional readiness and foster a digital culture by offering specialised, technology-oriented professional development for faculty. Educators must possess the digital literacy necessary to critically assess AI tools, create adaptive scaffolding, and incorporate AI in ways that enhance, rather than replace, student cognition(Obied, 2025).

Second, the establishment of comprehensive ethical governance frameworks is essential. Digital leaders must formulate laws that govern the secure utilisation of AI, guarantee the stringent safeguarding of student data, and require algorithmic openness. Governance plans should incorporate cross-sector partnerships and linguistic assessments to decentralise AI development and safeguard against cultural marginalisation (Kostopoulos et al., 2025).

Finally, leaders must facilitate human-AI collaborations that prioritise human-in-the-loop safeguards. Autonomous agents need to be utilised to enhance educational efficiency and manage routine administrative duties, thus allowing human educators to concentrate on advanced mentoring, socio-emotional growth, and deliberate curriculum creation. Preserving this equilibrium guarantees that AI functions as a collaborative co-agent instead of substituting human instructional proficiency (Khalid et al., 2025).

CONCLUSION AND FUTURE RESEARCH

The digital transition and the rise of Agentic AI are fundamentally transforming the higher education system, presenting both unprecedented possibilities and complex challenges. The successful implementation of Agentic AI in higher education essentially depends on competent digital leadership (Artsın & Bozkurt, 2025). The successful use of Agentic AI in higher education essentially depends on good digital leadership. As educational paradigms evolve to incorporate autonomous technology, leaders must integrate technical innovation with ethical governance, ensuring that AI implementation increases institutional excellence while preserving academic integrity and cultural diversity. This chapter has illustrated that the mere incorporation of advanced technologies is inadequate without robust and adaptable digital leadership to facilitate their efficient execution.

The findings emphasise that digital leadership extends a technical role, representing a strategic and human-centric process that necessitates a balance between innovation and ethical accountability. Leaders need to promote digital cultures that encourage collaboration, ongoing education, and inclusivity; while simultaneously confronting significant challenges such as resistance to change, skill deficiencies, data security, and ethical issues related to AI implementation. The chapter underscores the significance of human–AI collaboration, positioning AI systems as supportive co-agents rather than substitutes for educators and academic decision-makers. Digital leaders must guarantee that these technologies enhance human capabilities, improve student engagement, and facilitate personalised learning while upholding academic integrity and equity. This equitable strategy is crucial to avoid excessive dependence on AI and to maintain significant educational experiences. In conclusion, digital leadership has become an essential prerequisite for institutions aiming to maintain relevance and competitiveness in the digital age. By combining technical expertise with strategic insight, ethical governance, and human-centric principles, digital leaders can steer higher education institutions towards sustainable, inclusive, and future-oriented transformation.

The rapid advancement of digital leadership and Agentic AI in higher education offers various prospects for future research. First, empirical investigations are required to assess the influence of agentic AI on academic performance, pedagogical efficacy, and student learning outcomes in various educational settings. Although conceptual frameworks are thoroughly established, quantitative and longitudinal evidence is still limited.

Secondly, subsequent research requires to investigate the dynamics of human–AI collaboration within academic settings, specifically examining how trust, autonomy, and decision-making are negotiated between educators and intelligent systems. Understanding these interactions will be essential for creating effective and ethical AI-driven learning ecosystems.

Third, there is an increasing necessity to explore ethical governance frameworks for Agentic AI in higher education. Subjects like algorithmic transparency, accountability, bias mitigation, and data privacy necessitate comprehensive interdisciplinary investigation to establish resilient and context-specific frameworks. Comparative analyses among regions and institutions may yield significant insights into optimal practices and regulatory frameworks.

Fourth, subsequent research should investigate the cultivation of digital leadership competencies within academic settings, focusing on the training of leaders to navigate complex digital ecosystems. Investigating leadership development programs, enhancing digital capabilities, and examining the function of distributed leadership in universities would greatly advance this field.

Future research should also focus on the empirical assessment of agentic workflows in high-stakes educational settings, establishing paradigm-specific metrics to evaluate the long-term effects of AI on student learning and cognitive growth. Moreover, the creation of cohesive and flexible leadership frameworks will be crucial for steering multicultural, technology-oriented academic settings towards a sustainable, inclusive, and highly collaborative digital future.

REFERENCES

Abou Ali, M., Dornaika, F., & Charafeddine, J. (2025). Agentic AI: A comprehensive survey of architectures, applications, and future directions. *Artificial Intelligence Review, 59*(1), 11. DOI: 10.1007/s10462-025-11422-4

Ahlquist, J. (2017). Digital student leadership development. *New Directions for Student Leadership, 2017*(153), 47–62. DOI: 10.1002/yd.20229 PMID: 28199059

AlNuaimi, B. K., Singh, S. K., Ren, S., Budhwar, P., & Vorobyev, D. (2022). Mastering digital transformation: The nexus between leadership, agility, and digital strategy. *Journal of Business Research, 145*, 636–648. DOI: 10.1016/j.jbusres.2022.03.038

Andreasson, L., & Henfridsson, O. (2009). Digital differentiation, software product lines, and the challenge of isomorphism in innovation: A case study.

Antonopoulou, H., Halkiopoulos, C., Barlou, O., & Beligiannis, G. N. (2021a). Transformational leadership and digital skills in higher education institutes: During the COVID-19 pandemic. *Emerging Science Journal, 5*(1), 1–15. DOI: 10.28991/esj-2021-01252

Antonopoulou, H., Halkiopoulos, C., Barlou, O., & Beligiannis, G. N. (2021b). Associations between traditional and digital leadership in academic environment: During the COVID-19 pandemic. *Emerging Science Journal, 5*(4), 405–428. DOI: 10.28991/esj-2021-01286

Artsın, M., & Bozkurt, A. (2025). Charting new horizons: What agentic artificial intelligence (AI) promises in the educational landscape. In *EDULEARN25 Proceedings* (pp. 2019-2023). IATED.

Asfahani, A. M. (2025). Navigating digital leadership: Unraveling the dynamics of remote work environments. *Tem Journal, 14*(1), 823–835. DOI: 10.18421/TEM141-73

Awasthi, Y. (2025). Agentic AI Redefined: A New Paradigm in Artificial Intelligence.

Baltaci, A., & Balcı, A. (2017). Complexity leadership: A theorical perspective. *International Journal of Educational Leadership and Management, 5*(1), 30–58. DOI: 10.17583/ijelm.2017.2435

Breaugh, J., Rackwitz, M., & Hammerschmid, G. (2023). Leadership and institutional design in collaborative government digitalisation: Evidence from Belgium, Denmark, Estonia, Germany, and the UK. *Government Information Quarterly, 40*(2), 101788. DOI: 10.1016/j.giq.2022.101788

Cheng, Z., Caliskan, A., Dinh, N. B. K., & Zhu, C. (2024). A systematic review of digital academic leadership in higher education. *International Journal of Higher Education, 13*(4), 38–50. DOI: 10.5430/ijhe.v13n4P38

Dai, L., Jiang, Y. H., Chen, Y., Guo, Z., Liu, T. Y., & Shao, X. (2024, November). Agent4EDU: Advancing AI for education with agentic workflows. In *Proceedings of the 2024 3rd International Conference on Artificial Intelligence and Education* (pp. 180-185). DOI: 10.1145/3722237.3722268

Dimitriadi, Y. (2019). Who you're gonna call? The development of university digital leaders. a case study. *Mediaeval Studies, 10*(19), 102–118.

Ehlers, U. D. (2020). Digital leadership in higher education. *Journal of Higher Education Policy and Leadership Studies, 1*(3), 6–14. DOI: 10.29252/johepal.1.3.6

English, V. (2025). Comparing Traditional AI, Agentic AI and Agentic Rag for Dialogic Online Education. *Asian Journal of Education and Training, 11*(4), 198–210. DOI: 10.20448/edu.v11i4.7926

Figueiredo, R., Soares, R., & de Matos Ferreira, J. J. (2020). Key strategic drivers for business digital transformation: systematic literature review. *Dynamic Strategic Thinking for Improved Competitiveness and Performance*, 137-153.

Fragouli, E. (2025). Leading and managing pedagogical innovation in hybrid universities: A case study of faculty adaptation to digital work. *The Business & Management Review, 16*(3), 28–40. DOI: 10.24052/BMR/V16NU03/ART-03

Gillpatrick, T. (2020). Innovation and the digital transformation of education. *The Journal of Limitless Education and Research, 5*(3), 194–201. DOI: 10.29250/sead.797372

Gridach, M., Nanavati, J., Abidine, K. Z. E., Mendes, L., & Mack, C. (2025). Agentic ai for scientific discovery: A survey of progress, challenges, and future directions. *arXiv* preprint arXiv:2503.08979.

Gupta, N., & Heggond, S. (2026). Agentic artificial intelligence-driven tutoring: A multi-agent cognitive architecture for personalized adaptive learning in Education. *International Journal of Applied Resilience and Sustainability, 2*(2), 572–598. DOI: 10.70593/deepsci.0202022

Hamzah, N. H., Radzi, N. M., & Omar, I. M. (2025). Digital leadership competencies through a systematic literature review: Bridging educational development and organizational success. *International Journal of Medical Education, 24*(7), 37–64.

Hanisch, M., Goldsby, C. M., Fabian, N. E., & Oehmichen, J. (2023). Digital governance: A conceptual framework and research agenda. *Journal of Business Research, 162*, 113777. DOI: 10.1016/j.jbusres.2023.113777

Heavin, C., & Power, D. J. (2018). Challenges for digital transformation–towards a conceptual decision support guide for managers. *Journal of decision systems, 27*(sup1), 38-45.

Hosseini, S., & Seilani, H. (2025). The role of agentic ai in shaping a smart future: A systematic review. *Array (New York, N.Y.), 26*, 100399. DOI: 10.1016/j.array.2025.100399

Hrustek, L., Furjan, M. T., & Pihir, I. (2019, May). Influence of digital transformation drivers on business model creation. In *2019 42nd International Convention on Information and Communication Technology, Electronics and Microelectronics (MIPRO)* (pp. 1304-1308). IEEE. DOI: 10.23919/MIPRO.2019.8756666

Islam, M. A., Somu, S., & Aldaihani, F. M. F. (2026). The rise of agentic AI: Synthesis of current knowledge and future research agenda. *Global Business and Organizational Excellence, 45*(3), 402–416. DOI: 10.1002/joe.70019

Ivchyk, V. (2024). Overcoming barriers to artificial intelligence adoption. *Three Seas Economic Journal, 5*(4), 14–20. DOI: 10.30525/2661-5150/2024-4-3

Johansson, H., & Scaramuzzino, G. (2019). The logics of digital advocacy: Between acts of political influence and presence. *New Media & Society, 21*(7), 1528–1545. DOI: 10.1177/1461444818822488

Kamalov, F., Calonge, D. S., Smail, L., Azizov, D., Thadani, D. R., Kwong, T., & Atif, A. (2025). Evolution of ai in education: Agentic workflows. *arXiv preprint arXiv:2504.20082.*

Kamsker, P. D., Janschitz, G., & Monitzer, S. (2020). Digital transformation and higher education: A survey on the digital competencies of learners to develop higher education teaching. *International Journal for Business Education, 160*(1), 2.

Khalid, S., Islam, A., & Ajmal, M. (2025). The end of human-only knowledge management: Agentic AI in education. *Journal of Management Science Research Review, 4*(4), 2024–2042.

Klein, M. (2020). Leadership characteristics in the era of digital transformation. *Business & Management Studies: An International Journal, 8*(1), 883–902. DOI: 10.15295/bmij.v8i1.1441

Korinek, A., & Balwit, A. (2022). Aligned with whom? *Direct and social goals for AI systems* (No. w30017). National Bureau of Economic Research.

Kostopoulos, G., Gkamas, V., Rigou, M., & Kotsiantis, S. (2025). Agentic AI in education: State of the art and future directions. *IEEE Access : Practical Innovations, Open Solutions*, *13*, 177467–177491. DOI: 10.1109/ACCESS.2025.3620473

Koubaa, A. (2026). Toward Self-Driving Universities: Can Universities Drive Themselves with Agentic AI? *arXiv preprint arXiv:2602.18461.*

Lai, K. W. (2011). Digital technology and the culture of teaching and learning in higher education. *Australasian Journal of Educational Technology*, *27*(8). Advance online publication. DOI: 10.14742/ajet.892

Laila, D., Izzatul, R., & Miftah, M. (2025). Transformasi digital di dunia pendidikan: Implementasi dan dampak teknologi pembelajaran. *Journal of Science and Technology: Alpha*, *1*(2), 37–41.

Malik, M., Raziq, M. M., Sarwar, N., & Tariq, A. (2025). Digital leadership, business model innovation and organizational change: Role of leader in steering digital transformation. *Benchmarking*, *32*(5), 1632–1662. DOI: 10.1108/BIJ-04-2023-0283

Manaff, N. A., & Azahari, M. H. (2024). Digital technology's effect on teaching and learning. *International Journal of Research in Education Humanities and Commerce*, *5*(02), 129–135. DOI: 10.37602/IJREHC.2024.5211

Mihajlov, S., & Mihajlov, N. (2025). Adaptive Leadership in Complex Systems: Moving Beyond Bureaucratic Constraints. *Economic and Social Development in Bipolar and Multipolar Environment (Book of Proceedings)*, 126.

Mohammed, N. Y., Omar, H. A., & Aziz, A. A. (2022). Contributions of Leadership Styles to Digital Transformation-An Exploratory Study of the Opinions of a Sample of Administrative Leaders at the Northern Technical University. *Ingenierie des Systemes d'Information*, *27*(6), 865–873. DOI: 10.18280/isi.270602

Obied, A. S. (2025). Digital leadership in the academic environment: A systematic literature review. *Social Sciences & Humanities Open*, *11*, 101542. DOI: 10.1016/j.ssaho.2025.101542

Ojando, E. S., Benito, M., & Prats, M. À. (2017). Students as digital leaders in the classroom. *Aloma: revista de psicologia, ciències de l'educació i de l'esport Blanquerna, 35*(1), 53-60.

Omrani, N., Rejeb, N., Maalaoui, A., Dabić, M., & Kraus, S. (2022). Drivers of digital transformation in SMEs. *IEEE Transactions on Engineering Management, 71*, 5030–5043. DOI: 10.1109/TEM.2022.3215727

Onan, G. (2024). Digital transformation and digital leadership in higher education institutions: Insights from the literature. *Uluslararası Sosyal Bilgilerde Yeni Yaklaşımlar Dergisi, 8*(2), 198–213.

Pascoe, J. L., Lu, L., Moore, M. M., Blezek, D. J., Ovalle, A. E., Linderbaum, J. A., Callstrom, M. R., & Williamson, E. E. (2024). Strategic considerations for selecting artificial intelligence solutions for institutional integration: A single-center experience. *Mayo Clinic Proceedings. Digital Health, 2*(4), 665–676. DOI: 10.1016/j.mcpdig.2024.10.004 PMID: 40206525

Pati, A. K. (2025). Agentic AI: A comprehensive survey of technologies, applications, and societal implications. *IEEE Access : Practical Innovations, Open Solutions, 13*, 151824–151837. DOI: 10.1109/ACCESS.2025.3585609

Petrescu, G. M., tef, A. L., Cîmpan, I., Cri an, E. L., & Salan ă, I. I. (2023). Drivers Of Digital Transformation In Product Development, Business Modeling And Human Resources Management. *Annals of the University of Oradea, Economic Science Series, 32*(1).

Porfírio, J. A., Carrilho, T., Felício, J. A., & Jardim, J. (2021). Leadership characteristics and digital transformation. *Journal of Business Research, 124*, 610–619. DOI: 10.1016/j.jbusres.2020.10.058

Ridho, M. R., Lesmana, I., Safitri, H. D. A., Meirani, R. K., & Prestiadi, D. (2023, February). Digital leadership in the scope of education. In *International Conference on Educational Management and Technology (ICEMT 2022), Advances in Social Science, Education and Humanities Research (ASSEHR 727) pp* (pp. 52-61). DOI: 10.2991/978-2-494069-95-4_7

Sacavém, A., de Bem Machado, A., dos Santos, J. R., Palma-Moreira, A., Belchior-Rocha, H., & Au-Yong-Oliveira, M. (2025). Leading in the digital age: The role of leadership in organizational digital transformation. *Administrative Sciences, 15*(2), 43. DOI: 10.3390/admsci15020043

Santos, S., Lucas, M., & Bem-Haja, P. (2022). Bridging the digital competence gap: Tell us what you need. In *International Conferences ICT, Society, and Human Beings* (pp. 104-111).

Sargsyan, L. (2025). Integrating agentic ai in higher education: Balancing opportunities, challenges, and ethical imperatives. *Foreign Languages in Higher Education, 29*(1 (38)), 87–100. DOI: 10.46991/FLHE.2025.29.1.087

Shahzad, M. U. (2024). Core competencies for digital leadership development: A perspective from the lens of paradox theory. *The Bottom Line (New York, N.Y.), 37*(4), 454–472. DOI: 10.1108/BL-10-2023-0278

Souli, S. P., & Pierrakeas, C. (2025). Contemporary Trends in University Administration with the Integration of Digital/New Technologies. *Administrative Sciences, 15*(11), 437. DOI: 10.3390/admsci15110437

Tigre, F. B., Henriques, P. L., & Curado, C. (2025). The digital leadership emerging construct: A multi-method approach. *Management Review Quarterly, 75*(1), 789–836. DOI: 10.1007/s11301-023-00395-9

Tutar, H., & Güler, S. (2022). Digital leadership as a requirement for the new business ecosystem: a conceptual review. *Çankırı Karatekin Üniversitesi İktisadi ve İdari Bilimler Fakültesi Dergisi, 12*(3), 323-349.

Uzelac, A. (2010). Digital culture as a converging paradigm for technology and culture: Challenges for the culture sector

Zamir, N. A. (2025). THE ROLE OF LEADERSHIP IN SUPPORTING ARTIFICIAL INTELLIGENCE (AI) INTEGRATION IN ORGANIZATIONS.

Zhong, L. (2017). Indicators of digital leadership in the context of K-12 education. [JETDE]. *Journal of Educational Technology Development and Exchange, 10*(1), 3. DOI: 10.18785/jetde.1001.03

Živković, S. (2022). Inspiring digital transformation: An integrative leadership competency framework. *Ekonomska Misao i Praksa, 31*(1), 237–254. DOI: 10.17818/EMIP/2022/1.11

Compilation of References

Abbasi, K. (2004). Transparency and trust. *BMJ, 329*(7472), /bmj/329/7472/0.8.atom. DOI: 10.1136/bmj.329.7472.0-g

Abbu, H., Mugge, P., & Gudergan, G. (2022). *Ethical considerations of artificial intelligence: Ensuring fairness, transparency, and explainability*, 3.

Abbu, H., Khan, S., Mugge, P., & Gudergan, G. (2025). *Responsible AI framework: How leadership unifies talent, data, ethics, and governance for trustworthy AI.* ResearchGate.

Abdulai, A.-M., Iddrisu, O., Osman, A., & Iddrisu, A. (2025). Leadership Integrity: A Strategic Pillar for Ethical Decision Making and Organizational Excellence. *Advances in Research*, *26*(1), 65–73. DOI: 10.9734/air/2025/v26i11233

Abositta, A., Adedokun, M. W., & Berberoğlu, A. (2024). Influence of artificial intelligence on engineering management decision-making with mediating role of transformational leadership. *Systems*, *12*(12), 570. DOI: 10.3390/systems12120570

Abou Ali, M., Dornaika, F., & Charafeddine, J. (2025). Agentic AI: A comprehensive survey of architectures, applications, and future directions. *Artificial Intelligence Review*, *59*(1), 11. DOI: 10.1007/s10462-025-11422-4

Abun, D., Natividad, E., Ambrocio, B., Agudelo, R., Galat, M., & Raguindin, C. (2025). Discovering the effect of employees' trust in management on organizational citizenship behaviour and the employees' grit. *Divine Word International Journal of Management and Humanities (DWIJMH) (ISSN: 2980-4817), 4*. DOI: 10.62025/dwijmh.v4i2.121

Abundance Therapy Center. (2025). Recognizing and Addressing Burnout in the Workplace. https://www.abundancetherapycenter.com/blog/recognizing-and-addressing-burnout-in-the-workplace

Adarkwah, M. A., Amponsah, S., Huang, R., & Thomas, M. (Eds.). (2025). *Artificial Intelligence and Human Agency in Education: Volume Two: AI for Equity, Well-Being, and Innovation in Teaching and Learning*. Springer Nature Singapore., DOI: 10.1007/978-981-96-9251-4

Adelmohiman, M., Salem, A., & Abdalla, W. (2025). Adaptive Intelligence & Thriving Mindset: A Developmental Competency for Youth Flourishing in the ZAT Framework. *International Journal of Vocational Education and Training Research, 11*(2), 96–108. DOI: 10.11648/j.ijvetr.20251102.14

Adiningrum, T. S., Margiono, A., & Rohman, A. (2026). Scaffolding sustainable entrepreneurship: Adaptive teaching and empathy in a Global South business school. *International Journal of Management Education, 24*(1), 101280. DOI: 10.1016/j.ijme.2025.101280

Afroogh, S., Akbari, A., Malone, E., Kargar, M., & Alambeigi, H. (2024). Trust in AI: Progress, challenges, and future directions. *Humanities & Social Sciences Communications, 11*(1), 1568. DOI: 10.1057/s41599-024-04044-8

Afsar, B., & Umrani, W. A. (2019). Transformational leadership and innovative work behavior: The role of motivation to learn, task complexity and innovation climate. *European Journal of Innovation Management, 23*(3), 402–428. DOI: 10.1108/EJIM-12-2018-0257

Agapie, E., Golovchinsky, G., & Qvarfordt, P. (2013). Leading people to longer queries. In *Proceedings of the SIGCHI Conference on Human Factors in Computing Systems* (pp. 2367–2376). https://doi.org/ . 2481418DOI: 10.1145/2470654

Agarwal, P. (2021). Shattered but smiling: Human resource management and the wellbeing of hotel employees during COVID-19. *International Journal of Hospitality Management, 93*, 102765. DOI: 10.1016/j.ijhm.2020.102765 PMID: 36919177

Ahlquist, J. (2017). Digital student leadership development. *New Directions for Student Leadership, 2017*(153), 47–62. DOI: 10.1002/yd.20229 PMID: 28199059

Ahmed, S., Ahmed, R., Ashrafi, D. M., Ahmed, E., & Annamalah, S. (2024). Building trust in cybernetic payment network: Insights from an emerging economy. *Journal of Open Innovation, 10*(3), 100331. Advance online publication. DOI: 10.1016/j.joitmc.2024.100331

Ahuchogu, M.Magnus Chukwuebuka Ahuchogu. (2025). AI and Bias in Recruitment: Ensuring Fairness in Algorithmic Hiring. *Journal of Informatics Education and Research, 5*(3). Advance online publication. DOI: 10.52783/jier.v5i3.3262

Akbar, M. A., Varias, V., Risa, T. D., Bhirawa, M. A., & Nugraha, R. (2025). Workplace stress in the era of digital transformation: A psychological approach to employee well-being. *RIGGS: Journal of Artificial Intelligence and Digital Business, 4*(3), 3496–3506. DOI: 10.31004/riggs.v4i3.2493

Akinsola, O. K., & Liang, W. (2025). *The Role of Corporate Governance in Addressing Legal Challenges in Global Supply Chains: Regulatory Compliance and Ethical Standards.*

Akinwalere, S., Chang, K., & Barbhuiya, S. (2025). Sustainability-Embedded Leadership for Successful Change Management. *Sustainability (Basel), 17*(17), 7973. DOI: 10.3390/su17177973

Alabed, A., Javornik, A., & Gregory-Smith, D. (2022). AI anthropomorphism and its effect on users' self-congruence and self–AI integration: A theoretical framework and research agenda. *Technological Forecasting and Social Change, 182*, 121786. DOI: 10.1016/j.techfore.2022.121786

Alam, S., & Khan, M. F. (2024). Enhancing AI-Human Collaborative Decision-Making in Industry 4.0 Management Practices. *IEEE Access : Practical Innovations, Open Solutions, 12*, 119433–119444. DOI: 10.1109/ACCESS.2024.3449415

Al, B. (2024). Uzaktan ve hibrit çalışma modellerinde liderliğin dönüşümü: Dijital liderlik ve sanal ekip yönetimi üzerine bibliyometrik bir analiz. *Sosyal Bilimler Metinleri, 2024*(2), 121–140. DOI: 10.56337/sbm.1561098

Albannai, N. A. A., & Raziq, M. M. (2025). Navigating ethical, human-centric leadership in AI-driven organizations: A thematic literature review. *Service Industries Journal*, •••, 1–28. DOI: 10.1080/02642069.2025.2534360

Alhussein, G., Ziogas, I., Saleem, S., & Hadjileontiadis, L. J. (2025). Speech emotion recognition in conversations using artificial intelligence: A systematic review and meta-analysis. *Artificial Intelligence Review, 58*(7), 198. DOI: 10.1007/s10462-025-11197-8

Allen, S., Murrell, A., & Pil, F. (2025). DEI backlash – Implications for organizational DEI alignment and employee belongingness. *Equality, Diversity and Inclusion*, •••, 1–29. DOI: 10.1108/EDI-02-2025-0147

Allen, T. D., Golden, T. D., & Shockley, K. M. (2015). How effective is telecommuting? Assessing the status of our scientific findings. *Psychological Science in the Public Interest : A Journal of the American Psychological Society, 16*(2), 40–68. DOI: 10.1177/1529100615593273 PMID: 26403188

Almutairi, M., Chiang, C., Bai, Y., & Gomez-Zara, D. (2025, June). tAIfa: Enhancing team effectiveness and cohesion with AI-generated automated feedback. In *Proceedings of the 4th Annual Symposium on Human-Computer Interaction for Work* (pp. 1–25). ACM. DOI: 10.1145/3729176.3729197

AlNuaimi, B. K., Singh, S. K., Ren, S., Budhwar, P., & Vorobyev, D. (2022). Mastering digital transformation: The nexus between leadership, agility, and digital strategy. *Journal of Business Research*, *145*, 636–648. DOI: 10.1016/j.jbusres.2022.03.038

Al-Rjoub, H., Zabian, A., & Qawasmeh, S. (2008). Electronic monitoring: The employees point of view. *Journal of Social Sciences (New York, N. Y.)*, *4*(3), 189–195. DOI: 10.3844/jssp.2008.189.195

Alsalman, F. A., & Chyad, S. A. (2025). Impact of Emotional Intelligence on Leadership and Team Dynamics in Agile Software Engineering Projects. *IEEE Access : Practical Innovations, Open Solutions*, *13*, 74217–74228. DOI: 10.1109/ACCESS.2025.3563424

Alshahrani, A., Griva, A., Dennehy, D., & Mäntymäki, M. (2025). The role of leadership and communication in AI assimilation: Case studies from Saudi Arabia's public sector organizations. Transforming Government: People. *Transforming Government*, *19*(4), 875–894. DOI: 10.1108/TG-06-2025-0187

Altenried, M. (2020). The platform as factory: Crowdwork and the hidden labour behind artificial intelligence. *Capital and Class*, *44*(2), 145–158. DOI: 10.1177/0309816819899410

Alwali, J., & Alwali, W. (2025). Linking AI-driven HRM and emotional intelligence to leadership effectiveness and employee performance. *Leadership and Organization Development Journal, 6*. Annapareddy, 1–21. .DOI: 10.1108/LODJ-05-2025-0358

Amabile, T. M., & Pratt, M. G. (2016). The dynamic componential model of creativity and innovation in organizations: Making progress, making meaning. *Research in Organizational Behavior*, *36*, 157–183. DOI: 10.1016/j.riob.2016.10.001

American Psychological Association. (n.d.). Employers need to focus on workplace burnout: Here's why. https://www.apa.org/topics/healthy-workplaces/workplace-burnout

Andrade, L. (2025). Key Caring Indicators (KCIs) and Key Fairness Indicators (KFIs): A Strategic Framework for IT Leadership. SSRN *Electronic Journal*. DOI: 10.2139/ssrn.5161753

Andrade, M. D., Martínez-Córcoles, M., Fialho, P., & Guimaraes, M. (2025). The effects of being under watch: The impact of electronic monitoring on remote workers' psychological safety. *Journal of Management & Organization*, •••, 1–18. DOI: 10.1017/jmo.2025.10039

Andreasson, L., & Henfridsson, O. (2009). Digital differentiation, software product lines, and the challenge of isomorphism in innovation: A case study.

Angelis, P., Hompe, E., Krause, K., Perez, N., Auchincloss, H., Lanuti, M., Schumacher, L., & Sachdeva, U. (2026). The implementation of a mobile application and web-based platform for peri-operative patient-tailored education and tracking of patient-reported outcomes after esophagectomy. *Diseases of the Esophagus : Official Journal of the International Society for Diseases of the Esophagus*, *39*(1), doaf132. Advance online publication. DOI: 10.1093/dote/doaf132 PMID: 41525277

Annapareddy, V. N., Singireddy, J., Preethish Nandan, B., Lakarasu, P., & Burugulla, J. K. R. (2025). Emotional intelligence in artificial agents: Leveraging deep multimodal big data for contextual social interaction and adaptive behavioral modelling. *Available at SSRN* 5241039. DOI: 10.2139/ssrn.5241039

Antonopoulou, H., Halkiopoulos, C., Barlou, O., & Beligiannis, G. N. (2021a). Transformational leadership and digital skills in higher education institutes: During the COVID-19 pandemic. *Emerging Science Journal*, *5*(1), 1–15. DOI: 10.28991/esj-2021-01252

Antonopoulou, H., Halkiopoulos, C., Barlou, O., & Beligiannis, G. N. (2021b). Associations between traditional and digital leadership in academic environment: During the COVID-19 pandemic. *Emerging Science Journal*, *5*(4), 405–428. DOI: 10.28991/esj-2021-01286

Appliview. (2025, June 30). How AI Can Help Identify and Address Employee Burnout. https://www.appliview.com/blog/how-ai-can-help-identify-and-address-employee-burnout/

Aravidou, K., Triantari, S., & Zervas, I. (2025). Leadership and Mediation Approaches for Social Cohesion in the Greek Public Sector. *Administrative Sciences*, *15*(7), 248. DOI: 10.3390/admsci15070248

Arboh, F., Zhu, X., Atingabili, S., Yeboah, E., & Drokow, E. K. (2025). From fear to empowerment: The impact of employees AI awareness on workplace well-being–a new insight from the JD–R model. *Journal of Health Organization and Management*. Advance online publication. DOI: 10.1108/JHOM-06-2024-0229 PMID: 39875341

Argyris, C., & Schön, D. A. (1996). *Organizational learning II: Theory, method, and practice*. Addison Wesley.

Arham, A. F., Norizan, N. S., Arham, A. F., Hasbullah, N. N., Malan, I. N. B., & Alwi, S. (2022, March). Digital leadership in education: A meta-analysis review. In *International Conference on Business and Technology* (pp. 849–857). Cham: Springer International Publishing.

Ariwala, P. (2025). AI governance: Building trust and compliance with reliable AI. *Maruti Techlabs*. https://marutitech.com/responsible-ai-governance/

Arrieta, A. B., Díaz-Rodríguez, N., Del Ser, J., Bennetot, A., Tabik, S., Barbado, A., Garcia, S., Gil-López, S., Molina, D., Benjamins, R., Chatila, R., & Herrera, F. (2020). Explainable artificial intelligence (XAI): Concepts, taxonomies, opportunities and challenges toward responsible AI. *Information Fusion*, *58*, 82–115. DOI: 10.1016/j.inffus.2019.12.012

Artsın, M., & Bozkurt, A. (2025). Charting new horizons: What agentic artificial intelligence (AI) promises in the educational landscape. In *EDULEARN25 Proceedings* (pp. 2019-2023). IATED.

Arunprasad, P., Dey, C., Jebli, F., Manimuthu, A., & El Hathat, Z. (2022). Exploring the remote work challenges in the era of COVID-19 pandemic: Review and application model. *Benchmarking*, *29*(10), 3333–3355. DOI: 10.1108/BIJ-07-2021-0421

Asemota, M. O., & Owoeye, G. (2025). Integrating human-centric AI into corporate learning: Balancing automation with empathy. *Development and Learning in Organizations*. Advance online publication. DOI: 10.1108/DLO-01-2025-0014

Asfahani, A. M. (2025). Navigating digital leadership: Unraveling the dynamics of remote work environments. *Tem Journal*, *14*(1), 823–835. DOI: 10.18421/TEM141-73

Ashkanasy, N. M., & Daus, C. S. (2002). Emotion in the workplace: The new challenge for managers. *The Academy of Management Perspectives*, *16*(1), 76–86. DOI: 10.5465/ame.2002.6640191

Ashkanasy, N. M., & Daus, C. S. (2005). Rumors of the death of emotional intelligence in organizational behavior are vastly exaggerated. *Journal of Organizational Behavior*, *26*(4), 441–452. DOI: 10.1002/job.320

Ashktorab, Z., Dugan, C., Johnson, J., Pan, Q., Zhang, W., Kumaravel, S., & Campbell, M. (2021). Effects of Communication Directionality and AI Agent Differences in Human-AI Interaction. *Proceedings of the 2021 CHI Conference on Human Factors in Computing Systems*, 1–15. DOI: 10.1145/3411764.3445256

Asıl, S. (2025). *Yapay zekâ etiği: Temel ilkeler, sorunlar ve disiplinlerarası yaklaşımlar. İnönü Üniversitesi İletişim Fakültesi Elektronik Dergisi (İNİF E-Dergi), 10*(1), 152–175.

Athanasiadou, C., & Theriou, G. (2021). Telework: Systematic literature review and future research agenda. *Heliyon, 7*(10), e08165. Advance online publication. DOI: 10.1016/j.heliyon.2021.e08165 PMID: 34703928

Avlani, A., & Charalampous, M. (2024). Exploring the significance of remote leadership competencies in the virtual workplace: A systematic literature review. *Authorea Preprints*.

Avolio, B. J., & Gardner, W. L. (2005). Authentic leadership development: Getting to the root of positive forms of leadership. *The Leadership Quarterly, 16*(3), 315–338. DOI: 10.1016/j.leaqua.2005.03.001

Avolio, B. J., Sosik, J. J., Kahai, S. S., & Baker, B. (2014). E-leadership: Re-examining transformations in leadership source and transmission. *The Leadership Quarterly, 25*(1), 105–131. DOI: 10.1016/j.leaqua.2013.11.003

Avolio, B. J., Walumbwa, F. O., & Weber, T. J. (2009). Leadership: Current theories, research, and future directions. *Annual Review of Psychology, 60*(1), 421–449. DOI: 10.1146/annurev.psych.60.110707.163621 PMID: 18651820

Awasthi, Y. (2025). Agentic AI Redefined: A New Paradigm in Artificial Intelligence.

Aydogan, S. (2025). Impact of AI-augmented digital leadership on remote team performance: An exploratory study of Turkish SMEs. *Access Journal, 6*(3), 615–633. DOI: 10.46656/access.2025.6.3(9)

Ayyagari, R., Grover, V., & Purvis, R. (2011). Technostress: Technological antecedents and implications. *Management Information Systems Quarterly, 35*(4), 831–858. https://doi-org.ezproxy.mdx.ac.uk/10.2307/41409963. DOI: 10.2307/41409963

Babu, J., Joseph, D., Kumar, R. M., Alexander, E., Sasi, R., & Joseph, J. (2025). Emotional AI and the rise of pseudo-intimacy: Are we trading authenticity for algorithmic affection? *Frontiers in Psychology, 16*, 1679324. DOI: 10.3389/fpsyg.2025.1679324 PMID: 41050799

Bachkirova, T., & Kemp, R. (2025). 'AI coaching': Democratising coaching service or offering an ersatz? *Coaching (Abingdon, UK), 18*(1), 27–45. DOI: 10.1080/17521882.2024.2368598

Bach, T. A., Khan, A., Hallock, H., Beltrão, G., & Sousa, S. (2024). A systematic literature review of user trust in AI-enabled systems: An HCI perspective. *International Journal of Human-Computer Interaction, 40*(5), 1251–1266. DOI: 10.1080/10447318.2022.2138826

Bader, V., & Kaiser, S. (2019). Algorithmic decision-making? The user interface and its role for human involvement in decisions supported by artificial intelligence. *Organization, 26*(5), 655–672. DOI: 10.1177/1350508419855714

Badrinarayanan, V. (2024). Trust building strategies for virtual leaders in the post pandemic era. *Project Leadership and Society*, *5*, 100126. DOI: 10.1016/j.plas.2024.100126

Bagai, R., & Mane, V. (2024). *Designing an AI-Powered Mentorship Platform for Professional Development: Opportunities and Challenges*. DOI: 10.48550/ARXIV.2407.20233

Bai, A., & Vahedian, M. (2023). *Beyond the screen: Safeguarding mental health in the digital workplace through organizational commitment and ethical environment.* arXiv preprint arXiv:2311.02422.

Baird, A., & Maruping, L. M. (2021). The next generation of research on IS use: A theoretical framework of delegation to and from agentic IS artifacts. *Management Information Systems Quarterly*, *45*(1), 315–341. DOI: 10.25300/MISQ/2021/15882

Balasubramaniam, N., Kauppinen, M., & Rannisto, A. (2023). *Transparency and explainability of AI systems: From ethical guidelines to requirements*. Elsevier.

Ballesteros, B. (2025, July 12). Case study: Effective governance in AI-powered organizations. *Tellix*. https://tellix.ai/case-study-effective-governance-in-ai-powered-organizations/

Ball, K. (2010). Workplace surveillance: An overview. *Labor History*, *51*(1), 87–106. DOI: 10.1080/00236561003654776

Ball, K. S., & Margulis, S. T. (2011). Electronic monitoring and surveillance in call centres: A framework for investigation. *New Technology, Work and Employment*, *26*(2), 113–126. DOI: 10.1111/j.1468-005X.2011.00263.x

Baltaci, A., & Balcı, A. (2017). Complexity leadership: A theorical perspective. *International Journal of Educational Leadership and Management*, *5*(1), 30–58. DOI: 10.17583/ijelm.2017.2435

Bandura, A. (1986). *Social Foundations of Thought and Action: A Social Cognitive Theory*. Prentice-Hall.

Banerjee, S., Singh, P. K., & Bajpai, J. (2018). A comparative study on decision-making capability between human and artificial intelligence. In Panigrahi, B. K., Hoda, M. N., Sharma, V., & Goel, S. (Eds.), *Nature Inspired Computing* (pp. 203–210). Springer., DOI: 10.1007/978-981-10-6747-1_23

Bankins, S., Ocampo, A. C., Marrone, M., Restubog, S. L. D., & Woo, S. E. (2024). A multilevel review of artificial intelligence in organisations: Implications for organisational behavior research and practice. *Journal of Organizational Behavior*, *45*(2), 159–182. DOI: 10.1002/job.2735

Bapayeva, S., Kassymzhanova, A., Chernikova, T., Almuratova, A., & Ermekbayeva, L. (2025). Psychological study of personal readiness for change and actual functional states of adolescents. *аз У Хабаршысы. Психология Ж не леуметтану Сериясы*, *92*(1), 4–26. DOI: 10.26577/JPsS202592101

Barac, M., Băban, A., & Dumitru, G. (2024). Wearable Technologies for Detecting Burnout and Well-being: Current State and Future Directions. *Sensors (Basel)*, *24*(2), 456. DOI: 10.3390/s24020456 PMID: 38257549

Bar-Gil, O., Ron, T., & Czerniak, O. (2024). AI for the people? Embedding AI ethics in HR and people analytics projects. *Technology in Society*, *77*, 102527. DOI: 10.1016/j.techsoc.2024.102527

Barnes, E., & Hutson, J. (2024). Navigating the complexities of AI: Interpretability and transparency [International journal].

Barney, J. (1991). Firm resources and sustained competitive advantage. *Journal of Management*, *17*(1), 99–120. DOI: 10.1177/014920639101700108

Barocas, S., Hardt, M., & Narayanan, A. (2023). *Fairness and machine learning: Limitations and opportunities*. MIT Press.

Barrett, L. F. (2006). Are emotions natural kinds? *Perspectives on Psychological Science : A Journal of the Association for Psychological Science*, *1*(1), 28–58. DOI: 10.1111/j.1745-6916.2006.00003.x

Barsade, S. G., & O'Neill, O. A. (2014). What's love got to do with it? A longitudinal study of the culture of companionate love and employee and client outcomes in a long-term care setting. *Administrative Science Quarterly*, *59*(4), 551–598. DOI: 10.1177/0001839214538636

Baruah, A., Shaikh, M., Kumar, R. M., Shaikh, I. A. K., Thomas, S. N., & Natrayan, L. (2024, April). Artificial Intelligence influence on leadership styles in human resource management for employee engagement. In *2024 Ninth International Conference on Science Technology Engineering and Mathematics (ICONSTEM)* (pp. 1–5). IEEE. DOI: 10.1109/ICONSTEM60960.2024.10568819

Bastola, A., Wang, H., Hembree, J., Yadav, P., Gong, Z., Dixon, E., . . . McNeese, N. (2023). *LLM-based smart reply (LSR): Enhancing collaborative performance with ChatGPT-mediated smart reply system.* arXiv preprint arXiv:2306.11980

Batarseh, F. A., & Freeman, L. (Eds.). (2022). *AI assurance: Towards trustworthy, explainable, safe, and ethical AI.* Academic Press.

Batool, A., Zowghi, D., & Bano, M. (2023). *Responsible AI governance: A systematic literature review.* arXiv preprint arXiv:2401.10896.

Batool, B. F. (2013). Emotional intelligence and effective leadership. *Journal of Business Studies Quarterly*, *4*(3).

Batson, C. D. (2011). *Altruism in humans.* Oxford University Press.

Baumgarten, S., & Bourgadel, C. (2024). Digitalisation, neo-Taylorism and translation in the 2020s. *Perspectives: Studies in Translatology*, *32*(3), 508–523. DOI: 10.1080/0907676X.2023.2285844

Becker, B. E., & Huselid, M. A. (2006). Strategic human resources management: Where do we go from here? *Journal of Management*, *32*(6), 898–925. DOI: 10.1177/0149206306293668

Behler, A. M. C., & Berry, D. R. (2022). Closing the empathy gap: A narrative review of the measurement and reduction of parochial empathy. *Social and Personality Psychology Compass*, *16*(9), e12701. DOI: 10.1111/spc3.12701

Belgrave, L. L., & Seide, K. (2019). Grounded Theory Methodology: Principles and Practices. In Liamputtong, P. (Ed.), *Handbook of Research Methods in Health Social Sciences*. Springer., DOI: 10.1007/978-981-10-5251-4_84

Bell, B. S., McAlpine, K. L., & Hill, N. S. (2023). Leading virtually. *Annual Review of Organizational Psychology and Organizational Behavior*, *10*(1), 339–362. DOI: 10.1146/annurev-orgpsych-120920-050115

Benbya, H., Pachidi, S., & Jarvenpaa, S. (2021). Special issue editorial: Artificial intelligence in organizations: Implications for information systems research. *Journal of the Association for Information Systems*, *22*(2), 10. DOI: 10.17705/1jais.00662

Benjamin, R. (2019). *Race after technology: Abolitionist tools for the new Jim Code*. Polity Press.

Berente, N., Gu, B., Recker, J., & Santhanam, R. (2021). Managing artificial intelligence. *Management Information Systems Quarterly*, *45*(3), 1433–1450. DOI: 10.25300/MISQ/2021/16274

Berlin Knowledge, E. S. M. T. (2021, July 19). Predicting burn-out risk in the digital era. https://esmt.berlin/knowledge/predicting-burn-out-risk-digital-era

Berlin, E. S. M. T. (2023, January 22). HR teams can (and should) use AI to predict employee burnout. https://esmt.berlin/knowledge/hr-teams-can-and-should-use-ai-predict-employee-burnout

Bernstein, E., Bunch, J., Canner, N., & Lee, M. (2018). Beyond the holacracy hype. *Harvard Business Review*, *96*(4), 38–49.

Bersin, J. (2021). *The big reset: What happens after the pandemic*. Deloitte Insights.

Bersin, J. (2022). *Irresistible: The seven secrets of the world's most enduring, employee-focused organizations*. Deloitte Press.

Bertino, E., Kundu, A., & Sura, Z. (2019). Data Transparency with Blockchain and AI Ethics. *ACM Journal of Data and Information Quality*, *11*(4), 1–8. DOI: 10.1145/3312750

BetterUp Labs. (2021). *The future of coaching: AI and human-centered leadership*. BetterUp.

Bhagat, D., Hanwate, A., Salunkhe, R. V., Jagyasi, T., Sardare, P., & Sahu, M. (2025). *Future perspectives on surveillance systems*. IGI Global., DOI: 10.4018/979-8-3693-6996-8.ch014

Bhatia, M., Khare, V., & Chande, P. K. (2025). *Decision Making with Exponential Technologies for Leaders*. Emerald Publishing Limited., DOI: 10.1108/978-1-83662-486-8

Bhatia, S., Mittal, V., & Sabharwal, S. (2024). *Building trust and transparency in AI*. IEEE.

Bianchi, I. (2024). *Human Rights and Algorithmic Accountability: Building Effective Governance Structures for Fair AI Systems*.

Bickmore, T., & Picard, R. W. (2005). Establishing and maintaining long-term human–computer relationships. *ACM Transactions on Computer-Human Interaction*, *12*(2), 293–327. DOI: 10.1145/1067860.1067867

Bilderback, S. (2025). Ethical blind spots in leadership: Addressing unconscious bias in post-COVID workforce management. *Journal of Ethics in Entrepreneurship and Technology*, *5*(1), 85–102. Advance online publication. DOI: 10.1108/JEET-01-2025-0002

Binns, R. (2018). Fairness in machine learning: Lessons from political philosophy. In *Conference on Fairness, Accountability and Transparency* (pp. 149–159). PMLR.

Birnbaum, D., & Somers, M. (2023). Past as prologue: Taylorism, the new scientific management and managing human capital. *The International Journal of Organizational Analysis*, *31*(6), 2610–2622. DOI: 10.1108/IJOA-01-2022-3106

Bizilj, S., Boštjančič, E., & Sočan, G. (2021). Perceived efficacy of virtual leadership in the crisis of the COVID-19 pandemic. *Changing Societies & Personalities*, *5*(3), 389–404. DOI: 10.15826/csp.2021.5.3.141

Blagoev, V., Shustova, E., & Protas, N. (2022). Work motivation of bank employees in case of implementing AI and robots in the bank activities: Comparative analysis of Russia and Kazakhstan. *Ikonomicheski Izsledvanii a*, *7*, 63–80.

Bloom, N., Liang, J., Roberts, J., & Ying, Z. J. (2015). Does working from home work? Evidence from a Chinese experiment. *The Quarterly Journal of Economics*, *130*(1), 165–218. DOI: 10.1093/qje/qju032

Boeri, T., Caiumi, A., & Paccagnella, M. (2020). Mitigating the work-safety trade-off. *ovid Economics, 2(8), 60-66.*

Bondarouk, T., & Ruël, H. (2009). Electronic human resource management: Challenges in the digital era. *International Journal of Human Resource Management*, *20*(3), 505–514. DOI: 10.1080/09585190802707235

Boris, T. (2025, August 11). AI-human leadership integration: Executive leadership in the AI Era. *LinkedIn*. https://www.linkedin.com/pulse/ai-human-leadership-integration-executive-ai-era-boris-thoenissen-hwqce/

Boulton, C. (2021). With Viva, Microsoft aims to augment the employee experience [Preprint]. *CIO (Framingham, Mass.)*.

Boyatzis, R. E. (2008). Competencies in the 21st century. *Journal of Management Development*, *27*(1), 5–12. DOI: 10.1108/02621710810840730

Boyatzis, R. E. (2018). The behavioral level of emotional intelligence and its measurement. *Frontiers in Psychology*, *9*, 1438. DOI: 10.3389/fpsyg.2018.01438 PMID: 30150958

Boyatzis, R. E., & McKee, A. (2005). *Resonant leadership: Renewing yourself and connecting with others through mindfulness, hope, and compassion*. Harvard Business School Press.

Bozkurt, A., & Sharma, R. C. (2024). Trust, credibility and transparency in human-AI interaction: Why we need explainable and trustworthy AI and why we need it now? https://files.eric.ed.gov/fulltext/EJ1459191.pdf

Bradberry, T., & Greaves, J. (2009). *Emotional Intelligence 2.0*. TalentSmart.

Bratianu, C., & Staneiu, R.-M. (2024). The Emergence of Neuroleadership in the Knowledge Economy. *Encyclopedia*, *4*(3), 1100–1116. DOI: 10.3390/encyclopedia4030071

Bravo-Duarte, F., Tordera, N., & Rodríguez, I. (2025). Overcoming virtual distance: A systematic review of leadership competencies for managing performance in telework. *Frontiers in Organizational Psychology*, *2*, 1499248. DOI: 10.3389/forgp.2024.1499248

Breaugh, J., Rackwitz, M., & Hammerschmid, G. (2023). Leadership and institutional design in collaborative government digitalisation: Evidence from Belgium, Denmark, Estonia, Germany, and the UK. *Government Information Quarterly*, *40*(2), 101788. DOI: 10.1016/j.giq.2022.101788

Brinson, N., Amini, B., Lemon, L., & Bawole, C. (2024). Electronic performance monitoring: The role of reactance, trust, and privacy concerns in predicting job satisfaction in the post-pandemic workplace. *Cyberpsychology (Brno)*, *18*(5), 10. Advance online publication. DOI: 10.5817/CP2024-5-10

Brock, J. K. U., & Von Wangenheim, F. (2019). Demystifying AI: What digital transformation leaders can teach you about realistic artificial intelligence. *California Management Review*, *61*(4), 110–134. DOI: 10.1177/1536504219865226

Brown, M. E., & Treviño, L. K. (2006). Ethical leadership: A review and future directions. *The Leadership Quarterly*, *17*(6), 595–616. DOI: 10.1016/j.leaqua.2006.10.004

Bruning, F., & Boak, G. (2025). Artificial intelligence coach bots: Coaches' perceptions of potential future impacts on professional coaching, a qualitative study. *Journal of Work-Applied Management*. Advance online publication. DOI: 10.1108/JWAM-12-2024-0178

Brunn, M., Billings, S., Birke, J., Brockmüller, S., Nielsen, M., Kilian, S., & Oelmann, Y. (2024). On the importance of diversity in ecological research. *Plants, People, Planet*, *6*(6), 1207–1214. DOI: 10.1002/ppp3.10553

Brynjolfsson, E., & McAfee, A. (2014). *The second machine age: Work, progress, and prosperity in a time of brilliant technologies*. W. W. Norton & Company.

Brynjolfsson, E., Mitchell, T., & Rock, D. (2018). What can machines learn and what does it mean for occupations and the economy. *AEA Papers and Proceedings. American Economic Association, 108*, 43–47. DOI: 10.1257/pandp.20181019

Bryson, J. J. (2018). Patiency is not a virtue: The design of intelligent systems and systems of ethics. *Ethics and Information Technology, 20*(1), 15–26. DOI: 10.1007/s10676-018-9448-6

Budhwar, P., Malik, A., De Silva, M. T. T., & Thevisuthan, P. (2022). Artificial intelligence - challenges and opportunities for international HRM: A review and research agenda. *International Journal of Human Resource Management, 33*(6), 1065–1097. DOI: 10.1080/09585192.2022.2035161

Bughin, J., Hazan, E., Lund, S., Dahlström, P., Wiesinger, A., & Subramaniam, A. (2018). Skill shift: Automation and the future of the workforce. *McKinsey Global Institute, 1*, 3–84.

Buolamwini, J., & Gebru, T. (2018). *Gender Shades: Intersectional accuracy disparities in commercial gender classification.* Proceedings of Machine Learning Research, 81, 77–91. https://proceedings.mlr.press/v81/buolamwini18a/buolamwini18a.pdf

Buolamwini, J., & Gebru, T. (2018). Gender shades: Intersectional accuracy disparities in commercial gender classification. *Proceedings of the 1st Conference on Fairness, Accountability and Transparency*, 77–91. DOI: 10.48550/arXiv.1801.00006

Bustos, O., Pomares-Quimbaya, A., & Stellian, R. (2025). Machine learning, stock market forecasting, and market efficiency: A comparative study. *International Journal of Data Science and Analytics, 20*(7), 6815–6839. DOI: 10.1007/s41060-025-00854-4

Caliskan, A., Bryson, J. J., & Narayanan, A. (2017). Semantics derived automatically from language corpora contain human-like biases. *Science, 356*(6334), 183–186. DOI: 10.1126/science.aal4230 PMID: 28408601

Calvano, M. (2024). Design and evaluation of high-quality symbiotic AI systems through a human-centered approach. In *Proceedings of the 28th International Conference on Evaluation and Assessment in Software Engineering* (pp. 488–493). ACM. https://doi.org/DOI: 10.1145/3661167.3661223

Calvo, R. A., & D'Mello, S. (2010). Affect detection: An interdisciplinary review of models, methods, and their applications. *IEEE Transactions on Affective Computing, 1*(1), 18–37. DOI: 10.1109/T-AFFC.2010.1

Calvo, R. A., & Peters, D. (2014). *Positive computing: Technology for wellbeing and human potential*. MIT Press. DOI: 10.7551/mitpress/9764.001.0001

CanGrade. (2025, August 19). Leveraging AI to Predict and Prevent Employee Burnout. https://www.cangrade.com/blog/talent-management/leveraging-ai-to-predict-and-prevent-employee-burnout/

Caniëls, M. C. (2023). How remote working increases the importance of positive leadership for employee vigor. *Frontiers in Psychology*, *14*, 1089557. DOI: 10.3389/fpsyg.2023.1089557 PMID: 36743246

Carayannis, E. G., Dumitrescu, R., Falkowski, T., & Zota, N.-R. (2024). Empowering SMEs—"Harnessing the potential of Gen AI for resilience and competitiveness.". *IEEE Transactions on Engineering Management*, *71*, 1–22. DOI: 10.1109/TEM.2024.3456820

Carmeli, A. (2003). The relationship between emotional intelligence and work attitudes, behavior and outcomes: An examination among senior managers. *Journal of Managerial Psychology*, *18*(8), 788–813. DOI: 10.1108/02683940310511881

Carrasco-Garrido, C., De-Pablos-Heredero, C., & Rodríguez-Sánchez, J. L. (2023). Exploring hybrid telework: A bibliometric analysis. *Heliyon*, *9*(12), e23119. DOI: 10.1016/j.heliyon.2023.e22472 PMID: 38076145

Carvajal, A., Sanchez, R., Bacay, R., Sanchez, A., Moldez, R., Llego, J., Bation, N., & Pangilinan, A. (2024). *The Reflective Leader's Handbook: Mapping the Path to Effective Leadership*.

Cascio, W. F., & Montealegre, R. (2016). How technology is changing work and organizations. *Annual Review of Organizational Psychology and Organizational Behavior*, *3*(1), 349–375. DOI: 10.1146/annurev-orgpsych-041015-062352

Cavallo, K., & Brienza, D. (2002). Emotional competence and leadership excellence at Johnson & Johnson: The emotional intelligence and leadership study. *Consortium for Research on Emotional Intelligence in Organizations*, *1*(12), 1–12.

Cavazotte, F., Moreno, V., & Hickmann, M. (2012). Effects of leader intelligence, personality and emotional intelligence on transformational leadership and managerial performance. *The Leadership Quarterly*, *23*(3), 443–455. DOI: 10.1016/j.leaqua.2011.10.003

Çelik, E., & Taşkıran, E. (2023). Dijital liderlik. In *Örgütsel Davranış* (s. 81–102).

Çeri, M., & Doğan, A. (2025). Yapay zekâ destekli insan kaynakları yönetimi: Çalışan deneyiminin dönüşümü. *İzmir Yönetim Dergisi*, *6*(1), 122–141.

Chakraborty, T., Sharada, V. S., & Sharma, J. (2024). Data-driven decisions for employee motivation: Strategies for implementing technology in performance reviews in a tech landscape. In Rajapakshe, W. (Ed.), *Employee performance management for improved workplace motivation* (pp. 311–338). IGI Global. DOI: 10.4018/979-8-3693-4387-6.ch013

Chang, T.-S. (2023). Evaluation of an artificial intelligence project in the software industry based on fuzzy analytic hierarchy process and complex adaptive systems. *Journal of Enterprise Information Management*, *36*(4), 879–905. DOI: 10.1108/JEIM-02-2022-0056

Charmaz, K. (2017). Special Invited Paper: Continuities, Contradictions, and Critical Inquiry in Grounded Theory: Continuities, Contradictions, and Critical Inquiry in Grounded Theory. *International Journal of Qualitative Methods, 16*(1). https://doi.org/ (Original work published 2017)DOI: 10.1177/1609406917719350

Charmaz, K., & Thornberg, R. (2020). The pursuit of quality in grounded theory. *Qualitative Research in Psychology*, *18*(3), 305–327. DOI: 10.1080/14780887.2020.1780357

Chen, F. (2022). Human-AI Cooperation in Education:Human in Loop and Teaching as leadership. *Journal of Educational Technology and Innovation*, *2*(1). Advance online publication. DOI: 10.61414/jeti.v2i1.34

Cheng, Z., Caliskan, A., Dinh, N. B. K., & Zhu, C. (2024). A systematic review of digital academic leadership in higher education. *International Journal of Higher Education, 13*(4), 38–50. DOI: 10.5430/ijhe.v13n4P38

Cherniss, C. (2001). *The business case for emotional intelligence*. Consortium for Research on Emotional Intelligence in Organizations.

Chiang, R. H. L., & Storey, V. C. (2012).. . *Management Information Systems Quarterly*, *36*(4), 1165–1188. DOI: 10.2307/41703503

Choi, E. (2022). A Paradigm Shift in Beauty Education in Response to the Digital Transformation Era -Based on Analysis of Trends in the Cosmetics and Beauty Industry-. *Journal of the Korean Society of Cosmetology*, *28*(4), 675–688. DOI: 10.52660/JKSC.2022.28.4.675

Choustoulakis, E., Nikoloudakis, D., & Pollalis, Y. (2025). *AI-Powered Solutions for Employee Retention within the HR Framework: Trends and Challenges*.

Chowdhury, S. A., Barsa, N. J., Fuad, M. N., Nath, A., Khan, S. R., & Aziz, F. (2025). HOW AI IS RESHAPING EMPLOYEE TRAINING AND DEVELOPMENT: INSIGHTS FROM HR PROFESSIONALS. SSRN *Electronic Journal*. DOI: 10.2139/ssrn.5220821

Chowdhury, S., Budhwar, P., Dey, P. K., Joel-Edgar, S., & Abadie, A. (2022). AI–employee collaboration and business performance: Integrating knowledge-based view, socio-technical systems and organisational socialisation framework. *Journal of Business Research, 144*, 31–49. DOI: 10.1016/j.jbusres.2022.01.069

Chromčáková, Tereza, I. K., & Kriesel, O.J. (2025). *AI disruption in the workplace: Navigating employee engagement in an age of automation.*

Citron, D. K., & Pasquale, F. (2014). The scored society: Due process for automated predictions. *Washington Law Review (Seattle, Wash.), 89*, 1–34.

Ciulla, J. B. (2004). *Ethics, the heart of leadership* (2nd ed.). Praeger. DOI: 10.5040/9798216967286

Clarke-Joell, C. (2025, February 28). The AI-human Power Play: Leading hybrid teams in the age of automation. *VKTR.com*. https://www.vktr.com/leadership/the-ai-human-power-play-leading-hybrid-teams-in-the-age-of-automation/

Cobo, M. J., López-Herrera, A. G., Herrera-Viedma, E., & Herrera, F. (2011). Science mapping software tools: Review, analysis, and cooperative study among tools. *Journal of the American Society for Information Science and Technology, 62*(7), 1382–1402. DOI: 10.1002/asi.21525

Coelho, S., Vendrell-Ferran, Í., & Stephan, A. (2023). Emotional abilities and art experience in autism spectrum disorder. *Phenomenology and the Cognitive Sciences*. Advance online publication. DOI: 10.1007/s11097-023-09917-y

Cooper, G. (2023). Examining science education in ChatGPT: An exploratory study of generative artificial intelligence. *Journal of Science Education and Technology, 32*(3), 444–452. DOI: 10.1007/s10956-023-10039-y

Corbin, J., & Strauss, A. (2015). Basics of Qualitative Research: Techniques and Procedures for Developing Grounded Theory. *Sage (Atlanta, Ga.).*

Coronado-Maldonado, I., & Benítez-Márquez, M.-D. (2023). Emotional intelligence, leadership, and work teams: A hybrid literature review. *Heliyon, 9*(10), e20356. DOI: 10.1016/j.heliyon.2023.e20356 PMID: 37790975

Côté, S. (2014). Emotional intelligence in organizations. *Annual Review of Organizational Psychology and Organizational Behavior, 1*(1), 459–488. DOI: 10.1146/annurev-orgpsych-031413-091233

Cowgill, B. (2019). *Bias and productivity in humans and algorithms* (Columbia Business School Research Paper No. 19-54)

Cozzini, S., & Luca, M. (2024). Living in Digital Ecosystems: Are We Aware of This? (pp. 113–132). DOI: 10.1007/978-3-031-76961-0_6

Crawford, K., & Calo, R. (2016). There is a blind spot in AI research. *Nature*, *538*(7625), 311–313. DOI: 10.1038/538311a PMID: 27762391

Creanga, A., Kramer, B., Wolfson, C., Mary, M., Stierman, E., Clifford, S., Ezennia, A., Rhule, J., Martin, N., Vance-Reed, M., Bruce, T., DiPietro, B., Burgess, A., Warren, N., Lawson, S., Meyerholz, S., & Bower, K. (2024). Centering Equity and Fostering Stakeholder Collaboration and Trust—Pillars of the Maternal Health Innovation Program in Maryland. *Health Equity*, *8*(1), 406–418. DOI: 10.1089/heq.2023.0127 PMID: 39011083

Culnan, M. J., & Armstrong, P. K. (1999). Information privacy concerns, procedural fairness, and impersonal trust: An empirical investigation. *Organization Science*, *10*(1), 104–115. DOI: 10.1287/orsc.10.1.104

D'Mello, S., & Kory, J. (2015). A review and meta-analysis of multimodal affect detection systems. *ACM Computing Surveys*, *47*(3), 1–36. DOI: 10.1145/2682899

Daft, R. L., & Lengel, R. H. (1986). Organizational information requirements, media richness and structural design. *Management Science*, *32*(5), 554–571. DOI: 10.1287/mnsc.32.5.554

Dai, L., Jiang, Y. H., Chen, Y., Guo, Z., Liu, T. Y., & Shao, X. (2024, November). Agent4EDU: Advancing AI for education with agentic workflows. In *Proceedings of the 2024 3rd International Conference on Artificial Intelligence and Education* (pp. 180-185). DOI: 10.1145/3722237.3722268

Dai, R., Thomas, M. K. E., & Rawolle, S. (2025). The roles of AI and educational leaders in AI-assisted administrative decision-making: A proposed framework for symbiotic collaboration. *Australian Educational Researcher*, *52*(2), 1471–1487. DOI: 10.1007/s13384-024-00771-8

Damasio, A. R. (1994). *Descartes' error: Emotion, reason, and the human brain*. Putnam.

Daniels, M. (2025). AI-Powered Game-Based Learning for Project Management Education. *European Conference on Games Based Learning, 19*, 209–216. DOI: 10.34190/ecgbl.19.1.4203

Danish, R., Aslam, N., Cheema, A., Hassan, U., & Pakistan. (2014). *THE IMPACT OF TRANSFORMATIONAL LEADERSHIP AND EMPLOYEE COMMITMENT ON ORGANIZATIONAL CITIZENSHIP BEHAVIOR*. *26*, 2451–2455.

Darshani, R. K. N. (2025). *THE ROLE OF FAMILY-FRIENDLY HR POLICIES IN REDUCING EMPLOYEE BURNOUT IN THE MODERN WORKPLACE.*

Dart, A. I. (2025, March 30). How can AI be Used to Detect Employee Burnout. https://www.dartai.com/blog/how-can-ai-detect-employee-burnout

Das Swain, V., Zhong, Q. J., Parekh, J. R., Jeon, Y., Zimmermann, R., Czerwinski, M. P., & Hernandez, J. (2025, April). AI on my shoulder: Supporting emotional labor in front-office roles with an LLM-based empathetic coworker. In *Proceedings of the 2025 CHI Conference on Human Factors in Computing Systems* (pp. 1–29). ACM DOI: 10.1145/3706598.3713705

Dash, R., McMurtrey, M., Rebman, C., & Kar, U. K. (2019). Application of artificial intelligence in automation of supply chain management. *Journal of Strategic Innovation and Sustainability, 14*(3), 43–53. DOI: 10.33423/jsis.v14i3.2105

Das, I. R., Talukder, M. B., & Kumar, S. (2024). Implication of Artificial Intelligence in Hospitality Marketing. In *Utilizing Smart Technology and AI in Hybrid Tourism and Hospitality* (pp. 291–310). IGI Global. DOI: 10.4018/979-8-3693-1978-9.ch014

Davenport, T. H., & Bean, R. (2023, November 15). AI ethics at Unilever: From policy to process. *MIT Sloan Management Review*. https://sloanreview.mit.edu/article/ai-ethics-at-unilever-from-policy-to-process/

Davenport, T. H., Guha, A., Grewal, D., & Bressgott, T. (2020). How artificial intelligence will change the future of marketing. *Journal of the Academy of Marketing Science, 48*(1), 24–42. DOI: 10.1007/s11747-019-00696-0

Davenport, T. H., Harris, J. G., & Morison, R. (2010). *Analytics at work: Smarter decisions, better results*. Harvard Business Press.

Davenport, T. H., Harris, J. G., & Shapiro, J. (2010). Competing on talent analytics. *Harvard Business Review, 88*(10), 52–58. PMID: 20929194

Davenport, T. H., & Miller, S. (2022). *Working with AI: Real stories of human–machine collaboration*. MIT Press. DOI: 10.7551/mitpress/14453.001.0001

Davenport, T. H., & Mittal, N. (2023). *All-in on AI: How smart companies win big with artificial intelligence*. Harvard Business Review Press.

Davenport, T. H., & Ronanki, R. (2018). Artificial intelligence for the real world. *Harvard Business Review, 96*(1), 108–116.

Davidson, J., Schnepp, J., Buttrick, H., & Gupta, A. (2025). A framework for ethical AI-HRM development and use. *AI and Ethics, 6*(1), 28. Advance online publication. DOI: 10.1007/s43681-025-00858-7

Davila-Gonzalez, S., & Martin, S. (2024). Human digital twin in Industry 5.0: A holistic approach to worker safety and well-being through advanced AI and emotional analytics. *Sensors (Basel)*, *24*(2), 655. DOI: 10.3390/s24020655 PMID: 38276347

Davis, E. B., Kimball, C. N., Aten, J. D., Andrews, B., Van Tongeren, D. R., Hook, J. N., Davis, D. E., Granqvist, P., & Park, C. L. (2019). Religious meaning making and attachment in a disaster context: A longitudinal qualitative study of flood survivors. *The Journal of Positive Psychology*, *14*(5), 659–671. DOI: 10.1080/17439760.2018.1519592

Davis, M. H. (1983). Measuring individual differences in empathy: Evidence for a multidimensional approach. *Journal of Personality and Social Psychology*, *44*(1), 113–126. DOI: 10.1037/0022-3514.44.1.113

Davis, M. H. (1994). *Empathy: A social psychological approach.* Westview Press.

Davis, S., Nolen, S., & Koretsky, M. (2024). Inclusive Excellence in Practice: Integrating Equitable, Consequential Learning and an Inclusive Climate in Higher Education Classrooms and Institutions. *Frontline Learning Research*, *12*(4), 22–54. DOI: 10.14786/flr.v12i4.1331

Day, D. V., Fleenor, J. W., Atwater, L. E., Sturm, R. E., & McKee, R. A. (2014). Advances in leader and leadership development: A review of 25 years of research and theory. *The Leadership Quarterly*, *25*(1), 63–82. DOI: 10.1016/j.leaqua.2013.11.004

De Cremer, D., & Narayanan, D. (2023). How AI tools can—And cannot—help organizations become more ethical. *Frontiers in Artificial Intelligence*, *6*, 1093712. DOI: 10.3389/frai.2023.1093712 PMID: 37426304

de Saint Laurent, C. (2018). In defence of machine learning: Debunking the myths of artificial intelligence. *Europe's Journal of Psychology*, *14*(4), 734–747. DOI: 10.5964/ejop.v14i4.1823 PMID: 30555582

Dearborn, K. (2002). Studies in Emotional Intelligence redefine our approach to leadership development. *Public Personnel Management*, *31*(4), 523–530. DOI: 10.1177/009102600203100408

Deci, E. L., & Ryan, R. M. (2000). The "what" and "why" of goal pursuits: Human needs and the self-determination of behavior. *Psychological Inquiry*, *11*(4), 227–268. DOI: 10.1207/S15327965PLI1104_01

Deckker, D., & Sumanasekara, S. (2024). Systematic Review on AI in Gender Bias Detection and Mitigation in Education and Workplaces. *International Journal of Research in Computing*, *3*(1), 1. DOI: 10.64701/ijrc/345/8905

Dellermann, D., Ebel, P., Söllner, M., & Leimeister, J. M. (2019). Hybrid intelligence. *Business & Information Systems Engineering, 61*(5), 637–643. DOI: 10.1007/s12599-019-00595-2

Demerouti, E., Bakker, A. B., Nachreiner, F., & Schaufeli, W. B. (2001). The job demands-resources model of burnout. *The Journal of Applied Psychology, 86*(3), 499–512. DOI: 10.1037/0021-9010.86.3.499 PMID: 11419809

Demerouti, E., Schaufeli, W. B., & Bakker, A. B. (2025). Revitalising burnout research. *Work and Stress, 39*(2), 135–153. DOI: 10.1080/02678373.2025.2473385

Demetriou, A., Golino, H., Spanoudis, G., Makris, N., & Greiff, S. (2021). The future of intelligence: The central meaning-making unit of intelligence in the mind, the brain, and artificial intelligence. *Intelligence, 87*, 101562. DOI: 10.1016/j.intell.2021.101562

Denzin, N. K., & Lincoln, Y. S. (2018). *The SAGE Handbook of Qualitative Research* (5th ed.). SAGE.

Derks, D., van Duin, D., Tims, M., & Bakker, A. B. (2015). Smartphone use and work–home interference. *Journal of Occupational Health Psychology, 20*(4), 411–420. DOI: 10.1037/a0039085

Dewangan, S., & Kumar, S. (2024). AI and Big Data Analytics Revolutionizing Industry 5.0: Unlocking the Power of Smart Manufacturing and Beyond. In Darwish, D. (Ed.), (pp. 398–410). Advances in Business Information Systems and Analytics. IGI Global., DOI: 10.4018/979-8-3693-0413-6.ch016

Dhawas, P., Bondade, A., Patil, S., Khandare, K. S., & Salunkhe, R. V. (2024 b). *Intelligent automation in marketing*. IGI Global., DOI: 10.4018/979-8-3693-3354-9.ch003

Dhawas, P., Ramteke, M. A., Thakur, A., Polshetwar, P. V., Salunkhe, R. V., & Bhagat, D. (2024 a). *Big data analysis techniques: Data preprocessing techniques, data mining techniques, machine learning algorithm, visualization*. IGI Global., DOI: 10.4018/979-8-3693-0413-6.ch007

Dhiman, S. K. (2023). *The Routledge Companion to Leadership and Change* (1st ed.). Routledge., DOI: 10.4324/9781003147305

Dierendonck, D., & Lam, H. (2022). Interventions to enhance eudaemonic psychological well-being: A meta-analytic review with Ryff's Scales of Psychological Well-being. *Applied Psychology. Health and Well-Being, 15*(2), 594–610. DOI: 10.1111/aphw.12398 PMID: 36073601

Dietvorst, B. J., & Bharti, S. (2020). People reject algorithms in uncertain decision domains because they have diminishing sensitivity to forecasting error. *Psychological Science*, *31*(10), 1302–1314. DOI: 10.1177/0956797620948841 PMID: 32916083

Dignum, V. (2019). *Responsible artificial intelligence: How to develop and use AI in a responsible way* (1st ed.). Springer., DOI: 10.1007/978-3-030-30371-6

Diller, S. J., & Passmore, J. (2023). Defining digital coaching: A qualitative inductive approach. *Frontiers in Psychology*, *14*, 1148243. DOI: 10.3389/fpsyg.2023.1148243 PMID: 37868604

Dimitriadi, Y. (2019). Who you're gonna call? The development of university digital leaders. a case study. *Mediaeval Studies*, *10*(19), 102–118.

Dingel, J. I., & Neiman, B. (2020). How many jobs can be done at home? *Journal of Public Economics*, *189*, 104235. Advance online publication. DOI: 10.1016/j.jpubeco.2020.104235 PMID: 32834177

Dirks, K. T., & Ferrin, D. L. (2002). Trust in leadership: Meta-analytic findings. *The Journal of Applied Psychology*, *87*(4), 611–628. DOI: 10.1037/0021-9010.87.4.611 PMID: 12184567

Dodgson, J. E. (2020). Quality in research: Asking the right question. *Journal of Human Lactation : Official Journal of International Lactation Consultant Association*, *36*(1), 105–108. DOI: 10.1177/0890334419890305 PMID: 31895604

Doshi-Velez, F., & Kim, B. (2017). Towards a rigorous science of interpretable machine learning (arXiv:1702.08608). https://arxiv.org/abs/1702.08608

Dredge, R., & Schreur, L. (2020). Social media use and offline interpersonal outcomes during youth: A systematic literature review. *Mass Communication & Society*, *23*(6), 885–911. DOI: 10.1080/15205436.2020.1810277

Duan, Y., Edwards, J. S., & Dwivedi, Y. K. (2019). Artificial intelligence for decision making in the era of Big Data – evolution, challenges and research agenda. *International Journal of Information Management*, *48*, 63–71. DOI: 10.1016/j.ijinfomgt.2019.01.021

Dweck, C. S. (2006). *Mindset: The new psychology of success*. Random House.

Dwivedi, D. (2025). Emotional intelligence and artificial intelligence integration strategies for leadership excellence. *Advances in Research*, *26*(1), 84–94. DOI: 10.9734/air/2025/v26i11235

Dwivedi, R., Dave, D., Naik, H., Singhal, S., Omer, R., Patel, P., Qian, B., Wen, Z., Shah, T., Morgan, G., & Ranjan, R. (2023). Explainable AI (XAI): Core ideas, techniques, and solutions. *ACM Computing Surveys*, *55*(9), 1–33. DOI: 10.1145/3561048

Dwivedi, Y. K., Hughes, L., Ismagilova, E., Aarts, G., Coombs, C., Crick, T., Duan, Y., Dwivedi, R., Edwards, J., Eirug, A., Galanos, V., Ilavarasan, P. V., Janssen, M., Jones, P., Kar, A. K., Kizgin, H., Kronemann, B., Lal, B., Lucini, B., & Williams, M. D. (2021). Artificial intelligence (AI): Multidisciplinary perspectives on emerging challenges, opportunities, and agenda for research, practice and policy. *International Journal of Information Management*, *57*, 101994. DOI: 10.1016/j.ijinfomgt.2019.08.002

Edgar, F., Zhang, J., Podgorodnichenko, N., Akmal, A., & Peng, K. (2025). Understanding employees' environmentally sustainable work behavior: The roles of self-transcendence values, innovative work attitudes and sustainable performance management. *International Journal of Productivity and Performance Management*, *75*(11), 1–28. DOI: 10.1108/IJPPM-11-2024-0783

Edmondson, A. (1999). Psychological safety and learning behavior in work teams. *Administrative Science Quarterly*, *44*(2), 350–383. DOI: 10.2307/2666999

Edmondson, A. (2018). *The fearless organization: Creating psychological safety in the workplace for learning, innovation, and growth*. Wiley.

Edmondson, A. C., & Lei, Z. (2014). Psychological safety: The history, renaissance, and future of an interpersonal construct. *Annual Review of Organizational Psychology and Organizational Behavior*, *1*(1), 23–43. DOI: 10.1146/annurev-orgpsych-031413-091305

Edwards, J., Nguyen, A., Lämsä, J., Sobocinski, M., Whitehead, R., Dang, B., Roberts, A., & Järvelä, S. (2025). Human- AI collaboration: Designing artificial agents to facilitate socially shared regulation among learners. *British Journal of Educational Technology*, *56*(2), 712–733. DOI: 10.1111/bjet.13534

Eggers, J. P., & Kaplan, S. (2013). Cognition and capabilities: A multi-level perspective. *The Academy of Management Annals*, *7*(1), 295–340. DOI: 10.5465/19416520.2013.769318

Ehlers, U. D. (2020). Digital leadership in higher education. *Journal of Higher Education Policy and Leadership Studies*, *1*(3), 6–14. DOI: 10.29252/johepal.1.3.6

Ekdahl, D., & Osler, L. (2023). Expressive avatars: Vitality in virtual worlds. *Philosophy & Technology*, *36*(2), 1–28. DOI: 10.1007/s13347-023-00628-5

El Maouch, M., & Jin, Z. (2024). Between meanings and senses-making spaces: Agency and ownership emergence formalization from cultural-historical activity theory position, for an AI-friendly model. *Integrative Psychological & Behavioral Science, 58*(1), 99–137. DOI: 10.1007/s12124-023-09770-3 PMID: 37193931

Elia, J. (2009). Transparency rights, technology, and trust. *Ethics and Information Technology, 11*(2), 145–153. DOI: 10.1007/s10676-009-9192-z

Endsley, M. R. (2023). Supporting human-AI teams: Transparency, explainability, and situation awareness. *Computers in Human Behavior, 140*, 107574. DOI: 10.1016/j.chb.2022.107574

Eng, K., & Kohsuwan, P. (2025). The Influence of DEI and Organizational Justice on Employee Engagement: A Comparative Study between Gen Y and Z. *HUMAN BEHAVIOR. Development and Society, 26*, 221–233. DOI: 10.62370/hbds.v26i2.278787

English, V. (2025). Comparing Traditional AI, Agentic AI and Agentic Rag for Dialogic Online Education. *Asian Journal of Education and Training, 11*(4), 198–210. DOI: 10.20448/edu.v11i4.7926

Eppler, M. J., & Mengis, J. (2004). The concept of information overload. *The Information Society, 20*(5), 325–344. DOI: 10.1080/01972240490507974

Eubanks, D. L., Palanski, M., Olabisi, J., Joinson, A., & Dove, J. (2016). Team dynamics in virtual, partially distributed teams: Optimal role fulfillment. *Computers in Human Behavior, 61*, 556–568. DOI: 10.1016/j.chb.2016.03.035

Eubanks, V. (2018). *Automating inequality: How high-tech tools profile, police, and punish the poor.* St. Martin's Press.

Falckenthal, B., Au-Yong-Oliveira, M., & Figueiredo, C. (2025). Intergenerational Tacit Knowledge Transfer: Leveraging AI. *Societies (Basel, Switzerland), 15*(8), 213. DOI: 10.3390/soc15080213

Fambrough, M. J., & Kaye Hart, R. (2008). Emotions in leadership development: A critique of emotional intelligence. *Advances in Developing Human Resources, 10*(5), 740–758. DOI: 10.1177/1523422308323542

Faraj, S., Pachidi, S., & Sayegh, K. (2018). Working and organizing in the age of the learning algorithm. *Information and Organization, 28*(1), 62–70. DOI: 10.1016/j.infoandorg.2018.02.005

Farzaan, M. A. M., Ghanem, M. C., El-Hajjar, A., & Ratnayake, D. N. (2024). AI-enabled system for efficient and effective cyber incident detection and response in cloud environments. *arXiv Preprint* arXiv:2404.05602.

Fast, N. J., & Schroeder, J. (2020). Power and decision making: New directions for research in the age of artificial intelligence. *Current Opinion in Psychology*, *33*, 172–176. DOI: 10.1016/j.copsyc.2019.07.039 PMID: 31473586

Fayard, A.-L., Weeks, J., & Khan, M. (2021). Designing the hybrid office. *Harvard Business Review*, 1–11.

Feddes, A. R., Mann, L., & Doosje, B. (2015). Increasing self-esteem and empathy to prevent violent radicalization: A longitudinal quantitative evaluation of a resilience training focused on adolescents with a dual identity. *Journal of Applied Social Psychology*, *45*(7), 400–411. DOI: 10.1111/jasp.12307

Feijóo-García, M., Holstrom, M., & Newell, B. (2024). Simulation-Based Learning and Argumentation to Promote Informed Design Decision-Making Processes within a First-Year Engineering Technology Course. *Sustainability (Basel)*, *16*(7), 2633. DOI: 10.3390/su16072633

Feintzeig, R. (2020, October 28). The AI coach will see you now. *The Wall Street Journal.*

Felber, J. (2024, October 8). The future of leadership: Balancing AI integration with human connection. *Forb.* https://www.forbes.com/councils/forbesbusinesscouncil/2024/10/08/the-future-of-leadership-balancing-ai-integration-with-human-connection/

Ferreira, C., Robertson, J., & Pitt, L. (2023). Business (un)usual: Critical skills for the next normal. *Thunderbird International Business Review*, *65*(1), 39–47. DOI: 10.1002/tie.22276

Fiegler-Rudol, J., Lau, K., Mroczek, A., & Kasperczyk, J. (2025). Exploring human–AI dynamics in enhancing workplace health and safety: A narrative review. *International Journal of Environmental Research and Public Health*, *22*(2), 199. Advance online publication. DOI: 10.3390/ijerph22020199 PMID: 40003424

Figueiredo, R., Soares, R., & de Matos Ferreira, J. J. (2020). Key strategic drivers for business digital transformation: systematic literature review. *Dynamic Strategic Thinking for Improved Competitiveness and Performance*, 137-153.

Fiol, C. M., & O'Connor, E. J. (2017). Unlearning established organizational routines. *Organization Studies*, *38*(5), 733–758. DOI: 10.1177/0170840616689369

Fitzpatrick, K. K., Darcy, A., & Vierhile, M. (2017). Delivering cognitive behavior therapy to young adults with symptoms of depression and anxiety using a fully automated conversational agent. *JMIR Mental Health*, *4*(2), e19. DOI: 10.2196/mental.7785 PMID: 28588005

Floridi, L., & Cowls, J. (2022). A unified framework of five principles for AI in society. In *Machine Learning and the City: Applications in Architecture and Urban Design* (pp. 535–545). Springer.

Floridi, L., & Cowls, J. (2019). A unified framework of five principles for AI in society. *Harvard Data Science Review, 1*(1), 1–15. DOI: 10.1162/99608f92.8cd550d1

Floridi, L., Cowls, J., Beltrametti, M., Chatila, R., Chazerand, P., Dignum, V., Luetge, C., Madelin, R., Pagallo, U., Rossi, F., Schafer, B., & Vayena, E. (2018). AI4People—An ethical framework for a good AI society: Opportunities, risks, principles, and recommendations. *Minds and Machines, 28*(4), 689–707. DOI: 10.1007/s11023-018-9482-5 PMID: 30930541

Forbes. (2025, July 1). How To Use AI Tools To Detect Burnout And Retain Talented Employees. https://www.forbes.com/sites/dianehamilton/2025/07/01/how-to-use-ai-tools-to-detect-burnout-and-retain-talented-employees/

Fragiadakis, G., Diou, C., Kousiouris, G., & Nikolaidou, M. (2024). *Evaluating Human-AI Collaboration: A Review and Methodological Framework* (Version 2). arXiv. DOI: 10.48550/ARXIV.2407.19098

Fragouli, E. (2025). Leading and managing pedagogical innovation in hybrid universities: A case study of faculty adaptation to digital work. *The Business & Management Review, 16*(3), 28–40. DOI: 10.24052/BMR/V16NU03/ART-03

Frankish, K., & Ramsey, W. M. (Eds.). (2014). *The Cambridge handbook of artificial intelligence*. Cambridge University Press. DOI: 10.1017/CBO9781139046855

Frey, C. B., & Osborne, M. A. (2017). The future of employment: How susceptible are jobs to computerisation? *Technological Forecasting and Social Change, 114*, 254–280. DOI: 10.1016/j.techfore.2016.08.019

Froese, F. J., Blay, T., Gibson, C. B., Shaffer, M. A., & Benitez, J. (2025). Global virtual work: A review, integrative framework, and future research opportunities. *Journal of International Business Studies, 56*(6), 1–29. DOI: 10.1057/s41267-025-00775-1

Gaikwad, H., & Bhabad, V. (2025). Title: Critical Review of the Role of Legendary Women in Organisational Development in India. *International Journal of Science & Technoledge, 16*(4), 8627. Advance online publication. DOI: 10.71097/IJSAT.v16.i4.8627

Galinsky, A. D., Maddux, W. W., Gilin, D., & White, J. B. (2008). Why it pays to get inside the head of your opponent. *Psychological Science, 19*(4), 378–384. DOI: 10.1111/j.1467-9280.2008.02096.x PMID: 18399891

Gallagher, S. (2008). Direct perception in the intersubjective context. *Consciousness and Cognition, 17*(2), 535–543. DOI: 10.1016/j.concog.2008.03.003

Gallagher, S. (2012). Empathy, simulation, and narrative. *Science in Context, 25*(3), 355–381. DOI: 10.1017/S0269889712000117

Gandía, J. A. G., Ancillo, A. D. L., & Del Val Núñez, M. T. (2025). Knowledge and artificial intelligence on employee behaviour advancing safe and respectful workplace. *Journal of Innovation & Knowledge, 10*(4), 100750. DOI: 10.1016/j.jik.2025.100750

Gandomi, A., & Haider, M. (2015). Beyond the hype: Big data concepts, methods, and analytics. *International Journal of Information Management, 35*(2), 137–144. DOI: 10.1016/j.ijinfomgt.2014.10.007

García-Madurga, M. Á., Gil-Lacruz, A. I., Saz-Gil, I., & Gil-Lacruz, M. (2024). The role of artificial intelligence in improving workplace well-being: A systematic review. *Businesses, 4*(3), 389–410. DOI: 10.3390/businesses4030024

Gardner, L., & Stough, C. (2002). Examining the relationship between leadership and emotional intelligence in senior level managers. *Leadership and Organization Development Journal, 23*(2), 68–78. DOI: 10.1108/01437730210419198

Garnov, A. (2023). ESG technologies and risks in Russia and the world. Modern methods of management. *Scientific Research and Development. Economics of the Firm, 12*(3), 4–8. DOI: 10.12737/2306-627X-2023-12-3-4-8

Gartner. (2024a). Gartner CEO survey finds growth is the top business priority for 2024, reaching highest level in 10 years. https://www.gartner.com/en/newsroom/press-releases/2024-05-22-gartner-ceo-survey-finds-growth-is-the-top-business-priority-for-2024--reaching-highest-level-in-10-years

Gartner. (2024b). Gartner survey finds 38% of HR leaders reported they are piloting, planning implementation, or have already implemented generative AI. https://www.gartner.com/en/newsroom/press-releases/2024-02-27-gartner-finds-38-percent-hr-leaders-piloting-generative-ai

Gaur, S. (2025). *Equity and Inclusion of Women in Top Indian Organisations: Imperatives for Leadership Towards a Responsible World* (pp. 181–219). DOI: 10.1007/978-981-96-0108-0_10

Gehman, J., Glaser, V. L., Eisenhardt, K. M., Gioia, D., Langley, A., & Corley, K. G. (2017). Finding Theory–Method Fit: A Comparison of Three Qualitative Approaches to Theory Building. *Journal of Management Inquiry, 27*(3), 284-300. https://doi.org/ (Original work published 2018)DOI: 10.1177/1056492617706029

Gelfand, M. J., Raver, J. L., Nishii, L., Leslie, L. M., Lun, J., Lim, B. C., Duan, L., Almaliach, A., Ang, S., Arnadottir, J., Aycan, Z., Boehnke, K., Boski, P., Cabecinhas, R., Chan, D., Chhokar, J., D'Amato, A., Subirats Ferrer, M., Fischlmayr, I. C., & Yamaguchi, S. (2011). Differences between tight and loose cultures. *Science*, *332*(6033), 1100–1104. DOI: 10.1126/science.1197754 PMID: 21617077

Genkova, P., Flynn, M., Morley, M., & Rašticová, M. (Eds.). (2025). *Handbook of Diversity Competence: European Perspectives*. Springer Nature Switzerland., DOI: 10.1007/978-3-031-69308-3

George, G., Kulkarni, M., & Varghese, B. (2025). AI in creating inclusive work environments for neurodiverse employees. *Advances in Autism*, *12*(1), 1–20. DOI: 10.1108/AIA-05-2025-0046

George, J. M. (2000). Emotions and leadership: The role of emotional intelligence. *Human Relations; Studies Towards the Integration of the Social Sciences*, *53*(8), 1027–1055. DOI: 10.1177/0018726700538001

Gerçek, M., & Özveren, C. G. (2023). Yapay zeka araçları İKY için nasıl değer yaratabilir? Çalışan duygu analizinin uygulama alanlarının incelenmesi. *Yönetim Bilimleri Dergisi*, *21*(50), 1048–1076. DOI: 10.35408/comuybd.1285706

Ghavifekr, S., & Pei, X. (2023). Leading global digitalization in higher education. In *Global Perspectives on the Internationalization of Higher Education* (pp. 1–15). IGI Global. DOI: 10.4018/978-1-6684-5929-4.ch001

Gherhes, C., Vorley, T., Vallance, P., & Brooks, C. (2022). The role of system-building agency in regional path creation: Insights from the emergence of artificial intelligence in Montreal. *Regional Studies*, *56*(4), 563–578. DOI: 10.1080/00343404.2021.1886273

Gibbons, S. (2025, December 2). Future leaders will win through human and AI collaboration. *Forb*. https://www.forbes.com/sites/serenitygibbons/2025/12/02/future-leaders-will-win-through-human-and-ai-collaboration/

Gifford, J. (2022). Remote working: Unprecedented increase and a developing research agenda. *Human Resource Development International*, *25*(1), 105–113. DOI: 10.1080/13678868.2022.2049108

Gill, M. J. (2014). The possibilities of phenomenology for organisational research. *Organizational Research Methods*, *17*(2), 118–137. DOI: 10.1177/1094428113518348

Gillpatrick, T. (2020). Innovation and the digital transformation of education. *The Journal of Limitless Education and Research*, *5*(3), 194–201. DOI: 10.29250/sead.797372

Gkinko, L., & Elbanna, A. (2023). Designing trust: The formation of employees' trust in conversational AI in the digital workplace. *Journal of Business Research, 158*, 113707. DOI: 10.1016/j.jbusres.2023.113707

Glikson, E., & Woolley, A. W. (2020). Human trust in artificial intelligence: Review of empirical research. *The Academy of Management Annals, 14*(2), 627–660. DOI: 10.5465/annals.2018.0057

Goffman, E. (1959). *The presentation of self in everyday life*. Anchor Books.

Göldi, A., Rietsche, R., & Ungar, L. (2025). Efficient Management of LLM-Based Coaching Agents' Reasoning While Maintaining Interaction Quality and Speed. *Proceedings of the 2025 CHI Conference on Human Factors in Computing Systems*, 1–18. DOI: 10.1145/3706598.3713606

Goleman, D. (1998). Working with] Working with emotional intelligenceemotional intelligence. Bantam.

Goleman, D. (1995). *Emotional intelligence*. Bantam Books.

Goleman, D. (1998). What makes a leader? *Harvard Business Review, 76*(6), 93–102. PMID: 10187249

Goleman, D. (1998). *Working with emotional intelligence*. Bantam Books.

Goleman, D., Boyatzis, R. E., & McKee, A. (2013). *Primal leadership: Unleashing the power of emotional intelligence* (2nd ed.). Harvard Business Review Press.

Gomez, C., Cho, S. M., Ke, S., Huang, C.-M., & Unberath, M. (2025). Human-AI collaboration is not very collaborative yet: A taxonomy of interaction patterns in AI-assisted decision making from a systematic review. *Frontiers of Computer Science, 6*, 1521066. DOI: 10.3389/fcomp.2024.1521066

González-Sala, F., Osca-Lluch, J., Tortosa Gil, F., & Peñaranda Ortega, M. (2017). Beneficios de las relaciones entre los miembros de los comités editoriales y las revistas científicas. El caso de las revistas iberoamericanas de psicología. *Revista Española de Documentación Científica, 40*(4), 189. DOI: 10.3989/redc.2017.4.1460

Goswami, M., Jain, S., Alam, T., Deifalla, A. F., Ragab, A. E., & Khargotra, R. (2023). Exploring the antecedents of AI adoption for effective HRM practices in the Indian pharmaceutical sector. *Frontiers in Pharmacology, 14*, 1215706. DOI: 10.3389/fphar.2023.1215706 PMID: 38034991

Govindaraju, M., & Kumar, P. (2025). Building and Leading High-Performing Product Teams in Fast-Paced and Innovative Environments. *International Journal of Research in Modern Engineering & Emerging Technology*, *13*(3), 389–401. DOI: 10.63345/ijrmeet.org.v13.i3.25

Grant, A. M. (2017). The third "generation" of workplace coaching. *Coaching (Abingdon, UK)*, *10*(1), 37–53. DOI: 10.1080/17521882.2016.1266005

Greenleaf, R. K. (2002). *Servant leadership: A journey into the nature of legitimate power and greatness* (L. C. Spears, Ed.; illustrated & annotated ed.). Paulist Press.

Greenwald, A. G., McGhee, D. E., & Schwartz, J. L. K. (1998). Measuring individual differences in implicit cognition: The Implicit Association Test. *Journal of Personality and Social Psychology*, *74*(6), 1464–1480. DOI: 10.1037/0022-3514.74.6.1464 PMID: 9654756

Greer, L. L., de Jong, B. A., Schouten, M. E., & Dannals, J. E. (2018). Why and when hierarchy impacts team effectiveness: A meta-analytic integration. *The Journal of Applied Psychology*, *103*(6), 591–613. DOI: 10.1037/apl0000291 PMID: 29369654

Gridach, M., Nanavati, J., Abidine, K. Z. E., Mendes, L., & Mack, C. (2025). Agentic ai for scientific discovery: A survey of progress, challenges, and future directions. *arXiv* preprint arXiv:2503.08979.

Grossman, S. (2023). *The Future of Burnout: AI's Role in Prevention*. Detection, and Recovery.

Groves, K. S., Pat McEnrue, M., & Shen, W. (2008). Developing and measuring the emotional intelligence of leaders. *Journal of Management Development*, *27*(2), 225–250. DOI: 10.1108/02621710810849353

Guan, S. S. A., Hain, S., Cabrera, J., & Rodarte, A. (2019). Social media use and empathy: A mini meta-analysis. *Social Networking*, *8*(4), 147–157. DOI: 10.4236/sn.2019.84010

Gundhus, H. O., Talberg, N., & Wathne, C. T. (2022). From discretion to standardization: Digitalization of the police organisation. *International Journal of Police Science & Management*, *24*(1), 27–41. DOI: 10.1177/14613557211036554

Gunning, D., Stefik, M., Choi, J., Miller, T., Stumpf, S., & Yang, G. Z. (2019). XAI—Explainable artificial intelligence. *Science Robotics*, *4*(37), eaay7120. Advance online publication. DOI: 10.1126/scirobotics.aay7120 PMID: 33137719

Günsel, A., & Yamen, M. (2020). Digital Taylorism as an answer to the requirements of the new era. In *Agile Business Leadership Methods for Industry 4.0* (pp. 103–119). Emerald Publishing., DOI: 10.1108/978-1-80043-380-920201007

Gupta, M. (2024). AI-powered conflict resolution: Transforming virtual team dynamics in real time. *Proceedings of the International Journal for Multidisciplinary Research*, *6*(6), 31182–31195. DOI: 10.36948/ijfmr.2024.v06i06.31182

Gupta, N., & Heggond, S. (2026). Agentic artificial intelligence-driven tutoring: A multi-agent cognitive architecture for personalized adaptive learning in Education. *International Journal of Applied Resilience and Sustainability*, *2*(2), 572–598. DOI: 10.70593/deepsci.0202022

Gurulakshmi, S., & Gayathri, R. (2024). The Human-AI Partnership: Elevating Leadership With Emotional Intelligence. In Sayed, Z. (Ed.), (pp. 255–284). Advances in Logistics, Operations, and Management Science. IGI Global., DOI: 10.4018/979-8-3693-7372-9.ch011

Gyton, G., & Jeffery, R. (2017). These are the experts deciding the future of HR… shouldn't you know who they are? *People Management*, 24.

Haefner, N., Wincent, J., Parida, V., & Gassmann, O. (2021). Artificial intelligence and innovation management: A review, framework, and research agenda. *Technological Forecasting and Social Change*, *162*, 120392. DOI: 10.1016/j.techfore.2020.120392

Hall, K. M. (2024). *Shaping Digital Well-being: Developing a Well-being Lens on the Socio-technical Systems Perspective in Information Systems Research* (Cumulative Doctoral Dissertation). University of Bayreuth, Germany.

Hambrick, D. C. (2007). Upper echelons theory: An update. *Academy of Management Review*, *32*(2), 334–343. DOI: 10.5465/amr.2007.24345254

Hammerschmidt, T., Stolz, K., & Posegga, O. (2025). Bridging the gap: Inequalities that divide those who can and cannot create sustainable outcomes with AI. *Behaviour & Information Technology*, •••, 1–30. DOI: 10.1080/0144929X.2025.2500451

Hamzah, N. H., Radzi, N. M., & Omar, I. M. (2025). Digital leadership competencies through a systematic literature review: Bridging educational development and organizational success. *International Journal of Medical Education*, *24*(7), 37–64.

Hancock, P. A., Billings, D. R., Schaefer, K. E., Chen, J. Y. C., de Visser, E. J., & Parasuraman, R. (2011). A meta-analysis of factors affecting trust in human–robot interaction. *Human Factors*, *53*(5), 517–527. DOI: 10.1177/0018720811417254 PMID: 22046724

Hanif, I. (2022). Predicting employee burnout rate using neural network. [PDF]. https://scholar.ui.ac.id/files/65849867/Predicting_Employee_Burnout....pdf

Hanisch, M., Goldsby, C. M., Fabian, N. E., & Oehmichen, J. (2023). Digital governance: A conceptual framework and research agenda. *Journal of Business Research, 162*, 113777. DOI: 10.1016/j.jbusres.2023.113777

Hannah, S. T., Jennings, P. L., & DeRue, D. S. (2020). Leader self-awareness: A critical driver of organizational effectiveness. *Organizational Dynamics, 49*(3), 100707. DOI: 10.1016/j.orgdyn.2019.100707

Hannah, S. T., Woolfolk, R. L., & Lord, R. G. (2009). Leader self-structure. *The Leadership Quarterly, 20*(1), 34–49. DOI: 10.1016/j.leaqua.2008.11.003

Hanna, M. G., Pantanowitz, L., Jackson, B., Palmer, O., Visweswaran, S., Pantanowitz, J., Deebajah, M., & Rashidi, H. H. (2025). Ethical and bias considerations in artificial intelligence/machine learning. *Modern Pathology, 38*(3), 100686. DOI: 10.1016/j.modpat.2024.100686 PMID: 39694331

Hansen, P. G., & Jespersen, A. M. (2013). Nudge and the manipulation of choice: A framework for the responsible use of the nudge approach to behaviour change in public policy. *European Journal of Risk Regulation, 4*(1), 3–28. DOI: 10.1017/S1867299X00002762

Harms, P. D., & Credé, M. (2010). Emotional intelligence and transformational and transactional leadership: A meta-analysis. *Journal of Leadership & Organizational Studies, 17*(1), 5–17. DOI: 10.1177/1548051809350894

Hart, K. L., & Perlis, R. H. (2021). Authorship inequality: A bibliometric study of the concentration of authorship among a diminishing number of individuals in high-impact medical journals, 2008-2019. *BMJ Open, 11*(1), e046002. DOI: 10.1136/bmjopen-2020-046002

Hartley, M. (2024). Enhancing employee engagement and retention: The critical role of psychological safety in the onboarding process. *Strategic HR Review, 24*(3), 100–105. Advance online publication. DOI: 10.1108/SHR-10-2024-0080

Harwell, D. (2019). Rights group files federal complaint against AI-hiring firm HireVue, citing "unfair and deceptive" practices. *The Washington Post.*

Hasan, A. (2022). Artificial intelligence (AI) in accounting and auditing: A literature review. *Open Journal of Business and Management, 10*(1), 440–465. DOI: 10.4236/ojbm.2022.101026

Hassan, S. (2025). *Measuring Diversity, Equity, and Inclusivity in an Organisation: Scale Development for DEI Index* (pp. 401–416). DOI: 10.4018/979-8-3693-6011-8.ch016

Hassan, S. C., & Kumar, S. (2024). Safe Green Hydrogen: Production and Storage as an Emerging Source of Energy for Sustainable Future. In Raboaca, M. S., Djohra, S., Moussaoui, O., Mihaltan, T. C., & Koussa, M. (Eds.), (pp. 143–153). Advances in Chemical and Materials Engineering. IGI Global., DOI: 10.4018/979-8-3693-1014-4.ch008

Hausknecht, J. P., Rodda, J., & Howard, M. J. (2009). Targeted employee retention: Performance based and job related differences in reported reasons for staying. *Human Resource Management*, *48*(2), 269–288. DOI: 10.1002/hrm.20279

Hayashi, A. (2005). Emotional intelligence and outdoor leadership. *Journal of Experiential Education*, *27*(3), 333–335. DOI: 10.1177/105382590502700320

Healthcare, H. C. L. (2024). How effective managers detect and defuse workplace burnout. https://hclhealthcare.in/guardians-of-wellbeing-how-effective-managers-detect-and-defuse-workplace-burnout/

Heavin, C., & Power, D. J. (2018). Challenges for digital transformation–towards a conceptual decision support guide for managers. *Journal of decision systems*, *27*(sup1), 38-45.

Heifetz, R. A., Grashow, A., & Linsky, M. (2009). *The practice of adaptive leadership: Tools and tactics for changing your organization and the world.* Harvard Business Press.

Helfat, C. E., Finkelstein, S., & Mitchell, W.. (2007). *Dynamic capabilities: Understanding strategic change in organizations*. Blackwell Publishing.

Helfat, C. E., & Peteraf, M. A. (2015). Managerial cognitive capabilities and the microfoundations of dynamic capabilities. *Strategic Management Journal*, *36*(6), 831–850. DOI: 10.1002/smj.2247

Helliwell, J. F., Layard, R., Sachs, J., De Neve, J. E., Aknin, L. B., & Wang, S. (2024). World happiness report: Origins, purpose, contents, impact and future. In *Encyclopedia of happiness, quality of life and subjective wellbeing* (p. 296). Edward Elgar Publishing. DOI: 10.4337/9781800889675.00048

Hemalatha, A.. (2021). Impact of artificial intelligence on recruitment and selection of information technology companies. In *2021 International Conference on Artificial Intelligence and Smart Systems (ICAIS)* (pp. 60–66). IEEE. https://doi.org/DOI: 10.1109/ICAIS50930.2021.9396036

Henderson, M. D. (2025). Agentic AI and the ethics of leadership maintenance: Rethinking responsibility in algorithmic organizations. *Leadership and Organization Development Journal*, •••, 1–15. DOI: 10.1108/LODJ-05-2025-0319

Heritage, J. (2018). The ubiquity of epistemics: A rebuttal to the "epistemics of epistemics" group. *Discourse Studies*, *20*(1), 14–56. DOI: 10.1177/1461445617734342

Herman, J. L. (1992). *Trauma and recovery*. Basic Books.

Hernaus, T., Černe, M., & Škerlavaj, M. (2021). The interplay between relational job design and cross-training in predicting employee job/task citizenship performance. *Human Resource Development Quarterly*, *32*(4), 625–646. DOI: 10.1002/hrdq.21427

Hickok, M., & Maslej, N. (2023). A policy primer and roadmap on AI worker surveillance and productivity scoring tools. *AI and Ethics*, *3*(3), 673–687. DOI: 10.1007/s43681-023-00275-8 PMID: 37360144

Higgs, M., & Aitken, P. (2003). An exploration of the relationship between emotional intelligence and leadership potential. *Journal of Managerial Psychology*, *18*(8), 814–823. DOI: 10.1108/02683940310511890

Higgs, M., & Dulewicz, V. (2002). *Making sense of emotional intelligence: Vol* (2nd ed.). National Foundation for Educational Research.

HireBee. (2025, March 20). 100 + AI in HR Statistics 2025 | Insights & Emerging Trends. https://hirebee.ai/blog/ai-in-hr-statistics/

Hmoud, B. (2021). Trust in artificial intelligence systems: A conceptual framework. *Journal of Enterprise Information Management*, *34*(5), 1452–1471. DOI: 10.1108/JEIM-03-2020-0092

Hmoud, B. I. F., & Várallyai, L. (2019). Will artificial intelligence take over human resources recruitment and selection? *Network Intelligence Studies*, *7*(13), 21–30.

Hoch, J. E., & Dulebohn, J. H. (2017). Team personality composition, emergent leadership and shared leadership in virtual teams: A theoretical framework. *Human Resource Management Review*, *27*(4), 678–693. DOI: 10.1016/j.hrmr.2016.12.012

Hochschild, A. R. (1983). *The managed heart: Commercialization of human feeling*. University of California Press.

Hofstede Insights. (2020). *Country scores*. https://www.hofstede-insights.com/product/compare-countries/

Hofstede, G. (1980). Culture's Consequences: International Differences in Work Related Values. *Sage (Atlanta, Ga.)*.

Holford, W. D. (2019). The future of human creative knowledge work within the digital economy. *Futures: The Journal of Policy. Futures, 105*, 143–154. DOI: 10.1016/j.futures.2018.10.002

Holter, S., & El-Assady, M. (2024). Deconstructing Human-AI Collaboration: Agency, Interaction, and Adaptation. *Computer Graphics Forum, 43*(3), e15107. DOI: 10.1111/cgf.15107

Homann, M. (2025, November 26). EU AI act: What companies need to know. EQS Group. https://www.eqs.com/compliance-blog/eu-ai-act/

Hossain, K. A. (2025). Problem of Toxic Leadership Instead of Modern Leadership at New Age in the 21st Century. *Open Journal of Leadership, 14*(04), 507–603. DOI: 10.4236/ojl.2025.144026

Hosseini Tabaghdehi, S. A., & Ayaz, Ö. (2025). *AI ethics in action*. Emerald.

Hosseini, S., & Seilani, H. (2025). The role of agentic AI in shaping a bright future: A systematic review. *Array (New York, N.Y.), 26*(1), 100399. DOI: 10.1016/j.array.2025.100399

Howe, L. (2025, October 8). Why AI empathy won't replace human leaders (yet). *Forb*. https://www.forbes.com/sites/laurenhowe/2025/10/08/why-ai-empathy-wont-replace-human-leaders-yet/

Howirtz, M., Milosavljevic, M., & Van den Bulck, H. (2023). The use of artificial intelligence by public service media: Between advantages and threats. In El Morr, C. (Ed.), *AI and society: Tensions and opportunities* (pp. 127–140). CRC Press.

Hrustek, L., Furjan, M. T., & Pihir, I. (2019, May). Influence of digital transformation drivers on business model creation. In *2019 42nd International Convention on Information and Communication Technology, Electronics and Microelectronics (MIPRO)* (pp. 1304-1308). IEEE. DOI: 10.23919/MIPRO.2019.8756666

Huang, E. J., Easterday, M., & Gerber, E. (2025). AI That Helps Us Help Each Other: A Proactive System for Scaffolding Mentor-Novice Collaboration in Entrepreneurship Coaching. *Proceedings of the ACM on Human-Computer Interaction, 9*(7), 1–30. DOI: 10.1145/3757549

Huang, G., Lo, W.-H., Liu, G., Luo, Y., & Jin, Y. (2025). Toward AI Standardization: A Triadic Human-AI Collaboration Framework for Multi-Level Autonomous Mobility. *2025 IEEE Conference on Artificial Intelligence (CAI)*, 1568–1577. DOI: 10.1109/CAI64502.2025.00292

Huang, K. (Ed.). (2025). *Agentic AI: Theories and Practices*. Springer Nature Switzerland., DOI: 10.1007/978-3-031-90026-6

Huang, M. H., & Rust, R. T. (2018). Artificial intelligence in service. *Journal of Service Research*, *21*(2), 155–172. DOI: 10.1177/1094670517752459

Huang, M. H., & Rust, R. T. (2021). Engaged to a robot? The role of AI in service. *Journal of Service Research*, *24*(1), 30–41. DOI: 10.1177/1094670520902266

Huang, Y.-T. (2024). How the Compensation Gap between Median Full-Time Non-Managerial Employees and Executives Affects Audit Quality: Evidence from the Big 4 Accounting Firms. *International Journal of Business and Economic Sciences Applied Research*, *17*(2), 26–36. DOI: 10.25103/ijbesar.172.03

Huda, Md. N., Talukder, M. B., & Kumar, S. (2024). Securing Healthcare AI: Applied Federal Learning. In P. Bhattacharya, H. Liu, P. K. Dutta, J. J. P. C. Rodrigues, & G. Sethi (Eds.), *Revolutionizing Healthcare 5.0: The Power of Generative AI* (Vol. 571, pp. 255–272). Springer Nature Switzerland. DOI: 10.1007/978-3-031-75771-6_17

Hughes, C.. (2019). *Managing Technology and Middle- and Low-Skilled Employees: Advances for Economic Regeneration* (1st ed.). Emerald Publishing., DOI: 10.1108/9781789730777

Humainism. (2025). Microsoft, Salesforce, Lenovo. DiploFoundation. *Among Eight Tech Firms Adopting UNESCO's AI Ethics Framework- Humainism*. https://humainism.ai/updates/microsoft-salesforce-lenovo-among-eight-tech-firms-adopting-unescos-ai-ethics-framework/

Hummel, D., & Maedche, A. (2019). How effective is nudging? A quantitative review on the effect sizes and limits of empirical nudging studies. *Journal of Behavioral and Experimental Economics*, *80*, 47–58. DOI: 10.1016/j.socec.2019.03.005

Hurst, A. (2021). Developing future-ready skills with peer coaching. In MacDonald, A. (Ed.), *The Future of Workplace Learning* (pp. 5–7). MIT Sloan Management Review.

Hussain, S., & Anis-Farahwahida, M. K. (2025). Reimagining Gender-Inclusive Leadership: A Conceptual Analysis of Digital HRM Practices and Structural Barriers. *International Journal of Research and Innovation in Social Science*, *9*, 2295–2304. DOI: 10.47772/IJRISS.2025.91100183

Hu, X., Gao, H., Agafari, T., Zhang, M. Q., & Cong, R. (2025). How and when artificial intelligence adoption promotes employee knowledge sharing? The role of paradoxical leadership and technophilia. *Frontiers in Psychology*, *16*, 1573587. DOI: 10.3389/fpsyg.2025.1573587 PMID: 40470012

Iaia, L., Fait, M., Munnia, A., Cavallo, F., & De Nuccio, E. (2024). The scientific approach to facilitate the human-machine interactions. The case of Carrozzeria Fratelli Basile. *Journal of Management History, 30*(2), 243–262. DOI: 10.1108/JMH-12-2022-0087

Iansiti, M., & Lakhani, K. R. (2020). *Competing in the age of AI.* Harvard Business School Press.

IBM Institute for Business Value. (2020). *The cognitive enterprise: Reinventing your company with AI.* IBM.

Info, C. L. (2025, February 28). Data privacy and AI governance: Challenges and solutions. *Cookie law info.* https://www.cookielawinfo.com/data-privacy-and-ai-governance/

Insightful. (2025). Spot Early Signs of Employee Burnout with Analytics Tools. https://www.insightful.io/blog/detect-early-signs-of-employee-burnout

Iorio, J., & Taylor, J. E. (2015). Precursors to engaged leaders in virtual project teams. *International Journal of Project Management, 33*(2), 395–405. DOI: 10.1016/j.ijproman.2014.06.007

Islam, M. A., Somu, S., & Aldaihani, F. M. F. (2026). The rise of agentic AI: Synthesis of current knowledge and future research agenda. *Global Business and Organizational Excellence, 45*(3), 402–416. DOI: 10.1002/joe.70019

Ivchyk, V. (2025). *Preparing management systems for AI integration.*

Ivchyk, V. (2024). Overcoming barriers to artificial intelligence adoption. *Three Seas Economic Journal, 5*(4), 14–20. DOI: 10.30525/2661-5150/2024-4-3

Jain, C., & Kanwar, M. J. (2024). *The AI-driven workplace: How automation is reshaping flexible work arrangements.*

Jain, R., Garg, N., & Khera, S. N. (2023a). Effective human–AI work design for collaborative decision-making. *Kybernetes, 52*(11), 5017–5040. DOI: 10.1108/K-04-2022-0548

James, C., Davis, K., Charmaraman, L., Konrath, S. H., Slovak, P., Weinstein, E., & Yarosh, L. (2017). Digital life and youth well-being, social connectedness, empathy, and narcissism. *Pediatrics, 140*(Suppl. 2), S71–S75. DOI: 10.1542/peds.2016-1758F

Jami, P. Y., Walker, D. I., & Mansouri, B. (2023). Interaction of empathy and culture: A review. *Current Psychology.* Advance online publication. DOI: 10.1007/s12144-023-04422-6

Jarrahi, M. H. (2018). Artificial intelligence and the future of work: Human-AI symbiosis in organizational decision making. *Business Horizons, 61*(4), 577–586. DOI: 10.1016/j.bushor.2018.03.007

Javed, B., Naqvi, S. M. M. R., Khan, A. K., Arjoon, S., & Tayyeb, H. H. (2019). Impact of inclusive leadership on innovative work behavior: The role of psychological safety. *Journal of Management & Organization, 25*(1), 117–136. DOI: 10.1017/jmo.2017.3

Jeffery, S. (2025). *The Low-Code AI Maturity Model: Leading Responsible AI Transformation with Microsoft Power Platform*. Apress. DOI: 10.1007/979-8-8688-1730-4

Jerab, D. (2025, January 10). *Effective leadership strategies for virtual and remote teams. SSRN.* https://doi.org/DOI: 10.2139/ssrn.5092307

Jesuthasan, R., Malcolm, B., & Cantrell, S. (2021). *Work without jobs.* MIT Press.

Jetha, A., Bakhtari, H., Rosella, L. C., Gignac, M. A. M., Biswas, A., Shahidi, F. V., Smith, B. T., Smith, M. J., Mustard, C., Khan, N., Arrandale, V. H., Loewen, P. J., Zuberi, D., Dennerlein, J. T., Bonaccio, S., Wu, N., Irvin, E., & Smith, P. M. (2023). Artificial intelligence and the work–health interface: A research agenda for a technologically transforming world of work. *American Journal of Industrial Medicine, 66*(10), 815–830. DOI: 10.1002/ajim.23517 PMID: 37525007

Jia, J., Ning, X., & Liu, W. (2025). The consequences and theoretical explanation of workplace AI on employees: A systematic literature review. *Journal of Digital Management, 1*(1), 14. DOI: 10.1007/s44362-025-00016-3

Jiang, J. A., Wade, K., Fiesler, C., & Brubaker, J. R. (2021). Supporting Serendipity: Opportunities and Challenges for Human-AI Collaboration in Qualitative Analysis. *Proceedings of the ACM on Human-Computer Interaction, 5*(CSCW1), 1–23. DOI: 10.1145/3449168

Jiang, J., Karran, A. J., Coursaris, C. K., Léger, P. M., & Beringer, J. (2023). A situation awareness perspective on human-AI interaction: Tensions and opportunities. *International Journal of Human-Computer Interaction, 39*(9), 1789–1806. DOI: 10.1080/10447318.2022.2093863

Jimerson, S. (2023). Strategies for Scientific Journals to Advance Diversity, Equity, Inclusion, Scholarship, Science, and Practice. *Medical Research Archives, 11*(9). Advance online publication. DOI: 10.18103/mra.v11i9.4434

Jobin, A., Ienca, M., & Vayena, E. (2019). The global landscape of AI ethics guidelines. *Nature Machine Intelligence, 1*(9), 389–399. DOI: 10.1038/s42256-019-0088-2

Johansson, H., & Scaramuzzino, G. (2019). The logics of digital advocacy: Between acts of political influence and presence. *New Media & Society, 21*(7), 1528–1545. DOI: 10.1177/1461444818822488

Jöhnk, J., Weißert, M., & Wyrtki, K. (2021). Ready or not, AI comes—An interview study of organizational AI readiness factors. *Business & Information Systems Engineering, 63*(1), 5–20. DOI: 10.1007/s12599-020-00676-7

Johnston, K. A., & Rosin, K. (2011, May). *Global virtual teams: How to manage them.* In *2011 International Conference on Computer and Management (CAMAN)* (pp. 1–4). IEEE. DOI: 10.1109/CAMAN.2011.5778849

Jones, R. J., Woods, S. A., & Guillaume, Y. R. F. (2016). The effectiveness of workplace coaching. *Journal of Occupational and Organizational Psychology, 89*(2), 249–277. DOI: 10.1111/joop.12119

Jooyoung Kim, H. J. (2025, November 19). Dynamics of generative AI responsiveness and empathy in enhancing work performance: Moderating effects of organizational culture. International Journal of Human–Computer Interaction. https://www.tandfonline.com/doi/full/10.1080/10447318.2025.2584727

Joshi, S. (2025a). *Review of artificial intelligence in management, leadership, decision-making and collaboration.*

Joshi, S. (2025b). *Artificial intelligence in leadership and management: Current trends and future directions.*

Joshi, S. (2025). *Comprehensive Review of Artificial Intelligence in Management, Leadership, Decision-Making and Collaboration. SSRN.* DOI: 10.2139/ssrn.5221744

Joshi, S. (2025). *Enhancing U.S. K-12 Competitiveness for the Agentic Generative AI Era: A Structured Framework for Educators and Policy Makers.* Social Sciences. DOI: 10.20944/preprints202510.0669.v1

Judkins, J. T., Hwang, Y., & Kim, S. (2025). Human-AI interaction: Augmenting decision-making for IT leader's project selection. *Information Development, 41*(3), 1009–1035. DOI: 10.1177/02666669241249744

K. G., A., & Joseph, J. (2025). The compassion illusion: Can artificial empathy ever be emotionally authentic? *Frontiers in Psychology, 16*, 1723149. DOI: 10.3389/fpsyg.2025.1723149 PMID: 41333308

Kahneman, D. (2011). *Thinking, fast and slow.* Farrar, Straus and Giroux.

Kahn, W. A. (1990). Psychological conditions of personal engagement and disengagement at work. *Academy of Management Journal, 33*(4), 692–724. DOI: 10.2307/256287

Kamalov, F., Calonge, D. S., Smail, L., Azizov, D., Thadani, D. R., Kwong, T., & Atif, A. (2025). Evolution of ai in education: Agentic workflows. *arXiv preprint arXiv:2504.20082.*

Kamsker, P. D., Janschitz, G., & Monitzer, S. (2020). Digital transformation and higher education: A survey on the digital competencies of learners to develop higher education teaching. *International Journal for Business Education, 160*(1), 2.

Kandasamy, U. C. (2024). *Ethical leadership in the age of AI: Challenges, opportunities and framework for ethical leadership* (arXiv:2410.18095). arXiv. https://arxiv.org/abs/2410.18095

Kane, G. C., Palmer, D., Phillips, A. N., Kiron, D., & Buckley, N. (2019). Accelerating digital innovation inside and out. *MIT Sloan Management Review, 60*(4), 1–8.

Kaplan, S. (2008). Framing contests: Strategy making under uncertainty. *Organization Science, 19*(5), 729–752. DOI: 10.1287/orsc.1070.0340

Karakose, T., Demirkol, M., Yirci, R., Polat, H., Ozdemir, T. Y., & Tülübaş, T. (2023). A Conversation with ChatGPT about Digital Leadership and Technology Integration: Comparative Analysis Based on Human–AI Collaboration. *Administrative Sciences, 13*(7), 157. DOI: 10.3390/admsci13070157

Karakose, T., & Tülübaş, T. (2023). Digital leadership and sustainable school improvement: A conceptual analysis and implications for future research. *Educational Process: International Journal, 12*(1), 7–18. DOI: 10.22521/edupij.2023.121.1

Karaman, F. (2024). Sivil havacılık sektöründe çevik ve dijital liderlik tarzlarının örgütsel çeviklik ve çalışan performansları ile ilişkisi. *JOEEP: Journal of Emerging Economies and Policy, 9*(2), 129–147.

Karami, M. (2025). AI driven HR analytics for workforce resilience and agility: A strategic framework for the digital era. *Strategic HR Review.* Advance online publication. DOI: 10.1108/SHR-11-2025-0119

Katta, B. (2025). Ethical AI in Data Engineering: Mitigating Bias in Data-Driven Decision-Making. *Journal of Information Systems Engineering & Management, 10*(61s), 239–250. DOI: 10.52783/jisem.v10i61s.13350

Kaushik, M., & Guleria, N. (2020). The impact of pandemic COVID-19 in workplace. *European Journal of Business and Management, 12*(15), 9–18. DOI: 10.7176/EJBM/12-15-02

Kayaalp, A., Page, K. J., & Gumus, O. (2021). Job satisfaction and transformational leadership as the antecedents of OCB role definitions: The moderating role of justice perceptions. *International Journal of Business Science and Applied Management, 16*(2), 89–101. DOI: 10.69864/ijbsam.16-2.149

Kellerman, B., & Seligman, M. E. P. (2023). *Tomorrow's leadership*. Oxford University Press.

Kellett, J. B., Humphrey, R. H., & Sleeth, R. G. (2002). Empathy and complex task performance: Two routes to leadership. *The Leadership Quarterly, 13*(5), 523–544. DOI: 10.1016/S1048-9843(02)00142-X

Kelley, S. (2022). Employee perceptions of the effective adoption of AI principles. *Journal of Business Ethics, 178*(4), 871–893. DOI: 10.1007/s10551-022-05051-y PMID: 35818389

Kellogg, K. C., Valentine, M. A., & Christin, A. (2020). Algorithms at work: The new contested terrain of control. *The Academy of Management Annals, 14*(1), 366–410. DOI: 10.5465/annals.2018.0174

Kerr, R., Garvin, J., Heaton, N., & Boyle, E. (2006). Emotional intelligence and leadership effectiveness. *Leadership and Organization Development Journal, 27*(4), 265–279. DOI: 10.1108/01437730610666028

Kessler, M. M. (1963). Bibliographic coupling between scientific papers. *American Documentation, 14*(1), 10–25. DOI: 10.1002/asi.5090140103

Khalid, S., Islam, A., & Ajmal, M. (2025). The end of human-only knowledge management: Agentic AI in education. *Journal of Management Science Research Review, 4*(4), 2024–2042.

Khammissa, R. A. G.. (2022). Burnout phenomenon: Neurophysiological factors, clinical features, and management. *Frontiers in Psychiatry, 13*, 947869. PMID: 36113033

Khan, M. A. (2024). *Examining the influence of organizational structure and leadership on innovation in hybrid work settings: The mediating role of organizational culture in enhancing team collaboration and innovation outcomes.*

Khanam, Z. (2026). Fairness, trust and commitment in pharmaceutical retailer-supplier coordination. *International Journal of Retail & Distribution Management, 54*(4), 411–425. Advance online publication. DOI: 10.1108/IJRDM-06-2024-0284

Khan, M., Khan, M. S., Arshad, M., Sulaiman, R., & Zhang, K. (2025). Fostering employee green behavior through inclusive leadership: Roles of sustainable HRM practices and commitment to organizational change. *Journal of Organizational Change Management, 38*(5), 983–1001. Advance online publication. DOI: 10.1108/JOCM-10-2024-0650

Kieser, A. (1994). Why organisation theory needs historical analyses—And how this should be performed. *Organization Science, 5*(4), 608–620. DOI: 10.1287/orsc.5.4.608

Kim, M., & Beehr, T. A. (2022). The role of organisation-based self-esteem and job resources in promoting employees' job crafting behaviors. *International Journal of Human Resource Management, 33*(19), 3822–3849. DOI: 10.1080/09585192.2021.1934711

Kinowska, H., & Sienkiewicz, Ł. J. (2023). Influence of algorithmic management practices on workplace well-being: Evidence from European organisations. *Information Technology & People, 36*(8), 21–42. DOI: 10.1108/ITP-02-2022-0079

Kiritchenko, S., Nejadgholi, I., & Fraser, K. C. (2021). Confronting abusive language online: A survey from the ethical and human rights perspective. *Journal of Artificial Intelligence Research, 71*, 431–478. DOI: 10.1613/jair.1.12590

Klein, M. (2020). Leadership characteristics in the era of digital transformation. *Business & Management Studies: An International Journal, 8*(1), 883–902. DOI: 10.15295/bmij.v8i1.1441

Kloepfer, S., & Carbon, C.-C. (2025). Leadership and trust in virtual teams. *Human Systems Management, 44*(5), 890–900. DOI: 10.1177/01672533251331488

Kniffin, K. M., Narayanan, J., Anseel, F., Antonakis, J., Ashford, S. P., Bakker, A. B., Bamberger, P., Bapuji, H., Bhave, D. P., Choi, V. K., Creary, S. J., Demerouti, E., Flynn, F. J., Gelfand, M. J., Greer, L. L., Johns, G., Kesebir, S., Klein, P. G., Lee, S. Y., & Vugt, M. (2021). COVID-19 and the workplace. *The American Psychologist, 76*(1), 63–77. DOI: 10.1037/amp0000716 PMID: 32772537

Kober, G. (2025, January 24). AI-first leadership: Embracing the future of work. *Harvard Business Impact.* https://www.harvardbusiness.org/insight/ai-first-leadership-embracing-the-future-of-work/

Kock, H., Mayfield, M., Mayfield, J., Sexton, S., & De La Garza, L. M. (2019). Empathetic leadership. *Journal of Leadership & Organizational Studies, 26*(2), 177–190. DOI: 10.1177/1548051818806290

Koen, J. (2022). *The artificial intelligence readiness prism: A multi-dimensional framework for assessing AI integration, ethics, and cultural alignment.*

Koivisto, M., & Grassini, S. (2024). Author correction: Best humans still outperform artificial intelligence in a creative divergent thinking task. *Scientific Reports, 14*(1), 4239. DOI: 10.1038/s41598-024-54745-y PMID: 38378767

Kolb, D. A. (1984). *Experiential learning: Experience as the source of learning and development*. Prentice Hall.

Kolbjørnsrud, V. (2024). Designing the Intelligent Organization: Six Principles for Human-AI Collaboration. *California Management Review*, *66*(2), 44–64. DOI: 10.1177/00081256231211020

Kolditz, T. A. (2007). *In extremis leadership*. Harvard Business School Press.

Kollmann, T., Kollmann, K., & Kollmann, N. (2023). Artificial leadership: Digital transformation as a leadership task between the chief digital officer and artificial intelligence. *International Journal of Business Science and Applied Management, 18*(1), 76–95. DOI: 10.69864/ijbsam.18-1.172

Konrath, S. H., Martingano, A. J., Davis, M., & Breithaupt, F. (2023). Empathy trends in American youth between 1979 and 2018: An update. *Social Psychological & Personality Science*. Advance online publication. DOI: 10.1177/19485506231218360

Konrath, S. H., O'Brien, E. H., & Hsing, C. (2011). Changes in dispositional empathy in American college students over time: A meta-analysis. *Personality and Social Psychology Review : An Official Journal of the Society for Personality and Social Psychology, Inc., 15*(2), 180–198. DOI: 10.1177/1088868310377395

Kordon, A. (2020, August). Applied artificial intelligence-based systems as competitive advantage. In *2020 IEEE 10th International Conference on Intelligent Systems (IS)* (pp. 6–18). IEEE. https://doi.org/DOI: 10.1109/IS48319.2020.9200097

Korinek, A., & Balwit, A. (2022). Aligned with whom? *Direct and social goals for AI systems* (No. w30017). National Bureau of Economic Research.

Kostopoulos, G., Gkamas, V., Rigou, M., & Kotsiantis, S. (2025). Agentic AI in education: State of the art and future directions. *IEEE Access : Practical Innovations, Open Solutions, 13*, 177467–177491. DOI: 10.1109/ACCESS.2025.3620473

Kotkar, R. V., & Potdar, S. M. (2024). Investigating the development and uses of natural language processing in educational settings. *IBMRD's. Journal of Management Research, 13*(1), 77–85. DOI: 10.17697/ibmrd/2024/v13i1/173526

Koubaa, A. (2026). Toward Self-Driving Universities: Can Universities Drive Themselves with Agentic AI? *arXiv preprint arXiv:2602.18461.*

Kozlowski, S. W. J., Mak, S., & Chao, G. T. (2015). Team-centric leadership. *The Leadership Quarterly, 27*(2), 289–299. DOI: 10.1016/j.leaqua.2015.02.002

Kranzberg, M. (1986). Technology and history: "Kranzberg's laws". *Technology and Culture, 27*(3), 544–560. DOI: 10.2307/3105385

Krauter, J. (2024). Bridging the Uncanny Valley: Improving AI Chatbots for Effective Leadership Mentoring. *Open Journal of Leadership, 13*(03), 342–384. DOI: 10.4236/ojl.2024.133021

Kreiner, G. E., Hollensbe, E. C., & Sheep, M. L. (2006). On the edge of identity: Boundary dynamics at the interface of individual and organizational identities. *Human Relations; Studies Towards the Integration of the Social Sciences, 59*(10), 1315–1341. DOI: 10.1177/0018726706071525

Krings, W., Nissen, A., & Seebacher, U. (2025). *Mastering Cultural Intelligence in the Era of CommTech and Predictive Communication Intelligence.*, DOI: 10.1007/978-3-031-90302-1_17

Krishnasamy, L., Dhanaraj, R. K., Pamucar, D., & Ouaissa, M. (Eds.). (2025). *Distributed Deep Learning and Explainable AI (XAI) in Industry 4.0* (Vol. 55). Springer Nature Switzerland., DOI: 10.1007/978-3-031-94637-0

Krueger, J. W. (2018). Direct social perception. In Newen, A., de Bruin, L., & Gallagher, S. (Eds.), *The Oxford handbook of 4E-cognition* (pp. 301–320). Oxford University Press. DOI: 10.1093/oxfordhb/9780198735410.013.15

Kruger, J., Epley, N., Parker, J., & Ng, Z.-W. (2005). Egocentrism over e-mail. *Journal of Personality and Social Psychology, 89*(6), 925–936. DOI: 10.1037/0022-3514.89.6.925 PMID: 16393025

Kucharska, W., & Bedford, D. A. D. (2020). Love your mistakes!—They help you adapt to change. How do knowledge, collaboration and learning cultures foster organisational intelligence? *Journal of Organizational Change Management, 33*(7), 1329–1354. DOI: 10.1108/JOCM-02-2020-0052

Kücking, F., Hübner, U., Przysucha, M., Hannemann, N., Kutza, J. O., Moelleken, M., Erfurt-Berge, C., Dissemond, J., Babitsch, B., & Busch, D. (2024). Automation bias in AI-decision support: Results from an empirical study. *Studies in Health Technology and Informatics, 317*, 298–304. DOI: 10.3233/SHTI240871 PMID: 39234734

Kufel, J., Bargieł-Łączek, K., Kocot, S., Koźlik, M., Bartnikowska, W., Janik, M., Czogalik, Ł., Dudek, P., Magiera, M., Lis, A., Paszkiewicz, I., Nawrat, Z., Cebula, M., & Gruszczyńska, K. (2023). What is machine learning, artificial neural networks and deep learning?—Examples of practical applications in medicine. *Diagnostics (Basel), 13*(15), 2582. DOI: 10.3390/diagnostics13152582 PMID: 37568945

Kuhn, T. S. (1970). *The Structure of Scientific Revolutions*. University of Chicago Press.

Kumar, M. (2023). The Impact of Economic Exclusion on the Constitutionally Guaranteed Entitlements of Economic Justice, Equality of Opportunity and Right to Live with Human Dignity of the Transgenders. *Journal of Law and Sustainable Development, 11*(11), e1748. DOI: 10.55908/sdgs.v11i11.1748

Kumar, N., & Shrivastava, A. (2025). The artificial intelligence (AI) revolution: Evolving business decision-making in the digital age. *Business Information Review, 02663821251364069*(3), 183–196. Advance online publication. DOI: 10.1177/02663821251364069

Kumar, S. (2014). Establishing linkages between emotional intelligence and transformational leadership. *Industrial Psychiatry Journal, 23*(1), 1–3. DOI: 10.4103/0972-6748.144934

Kumar, S. (2023). Impact of Digitalization in Higher Education and Smart Learning Techniques. In *Sustainable Development Goal Advancement Through Digital Innovation in the Service Sector* (pp. 198–207). IGI Global. DOI: 10.4018/979-8-3693-0650-5.ch013

Kumar, S. (2024). The Role of Digital Marketing on Customer Engagement in the Hospitality Industry. In Bansal, R., Ngah, A. H., Chakir, A., & Pruthi, N. (Eds.), (pp. 177–191). Advances in Business Information Systems and Analytics. IGI Global., DOI: 10.4018/979-8-3693-0815-8.ch010

Kumar, V., Kumar, S., Durana, P., Chaudhuri, R., Vrontis, D., & Chatterjee, S. (2025). Enhancing organizational readiness for generative AI integration: An empirical investigation. *The International Journal of Organizational Analysis*. Advance online publication. DOI: 10.1108/IJOA-03-2025-5310

Kunal, R. M., & Bansal, J. (2023). The Future of OpenAI Tools: Opportunities and Challenges for Human-AI Collaboration. *2023 2nd International Conference on Futuristic Technologies (INCOFT)*, 1–6. DOI: 10.1109/INCOFT60753.2023.10424990

Lai, K. W. (2011). Digital technology and the culture of teaching and learning in higher education. *Australasian Journal of Educational Technology*, *27*(8). Advance online publication. DOI: 10.14742/ajet.892

Laila, D., Izzatul, R., & Miftah, M. (2025). Transformasi digital di dunia pendidikan: Implementasi dan dampak teknologi pembelajaran. *Journal of Science and Technology: Alpha*, *1*(2), 37–41.

Lai, V., Carton, S., Bhatnagar, R., Liao, Q. V., Zhang, Y., & Tan, C. (2022). Human-AI Collaboration via Conditional Delegation: A Case Study of Content Moderation. *CHI Conference on Human Factors in Computing Systems*, 1–18. DOI: 10.1145/3491102.3501999

Lalande, S., Beselt, L., & Maniate, J. (2025). Evaluating the Impact of a Health Equity Continuing Professional Development Initiative: A Program Evaluation of the Critical Dialogues for Action Series. *The Journal of Continuing Education in the Health Professions*. Advance online publication. DOI: 10.1097/CEH.0000000000000629 PMID: 41427822

Lattice. (2023). How to Measure Burnout Across a Global Organisation. https://lattice.com/articles/how-to-measure-burnout-across-a-global-organisation

Lawani, I. (2025). Reframing AI: Strategic Leadership for Inclusive Growth and Innovation. *American Journal of Leadership and Governance*, *10*(1), 73–91. DOI: 10.47672/ajlg.2798

Law, T., & McCall, L. (2024). Artificial intelligence policymaking: An agenda for sociological research. *Socius: Sociological Research for a Dynamic World*, *10*, 1–13. DOI: 10.1177/23780231241261596

Leban, W., & Zulauf, C. (2004). Linking emotional intelligence abilities and transformational leadership styles. *Leadership and Organization Development Journal*, *25*(7), 554–564. DOI: 10.1108/01437730410561440

Lee, C.-C., Yeh, W.-C., Yu, Z., & Lin, X.-C. (2023). The relationships between leader emotional intelligence, transformational leadership, and transactional leadership and job performance: A mediator model of trust. *Heliyon*, *9*(8), e18007. DOI: 10.1016/j.heliyon.2023.e18007

Lee, J. D., & See, K. A. (2004). Trust in automation: Designing for appropriate reliance. *Human Factors*, *46*(1), 50–80. DOI: 10.1518/hfes.46.1.50.30392 PMID: 15151155

Lee, S. M., Thomer, A. K., & Lampe, C. (2022). The use of negative interface cues to change perceptions of online retributive harassment. *ACM on Human–Computer Interaction, 6*(CSCW2). *Proceedings of the ACM on Human-Computer Interaction, 334*(CSCW2), 1–23. DOI: 10.1145/3555226

Leonardi, P. M. (2014). Social media, knowledge sharing, and innovation: Toward a theory of communication visibility. *Information Systems Research, 25*(4), 796–816. DOI: 10.1287/isre.2014.0536

Li, N., Zhou, H., & Mikel-Hong, K. (2024). *Generative AI enhances team performance and reduces need for traditional teams* (arXiv:2405.17924). arXiv.

Lichtenthaler, U. (2020). Extremes of acceptance: Employee attitudes toward artificial intelligence. *The Journal of Business Strategy, 41*(5), 39–45. DOI: 10.1108/JBS-12-2018-0204

Licklider, J. C. R. (1960). Man-computer symbiosis. *IRE Transactions on Human Factors in Electronics, HFE-1*(1), 4–11. DOI: 10.1109/THFE2.1960.4503259

Liden, R. C., Wayne, S. J., Zhao, H., & Henderson, D. (2008). Servant leadership: Development of a multidimensional measure and multi-level assessment. *The Leadership Quarterly, 19*(2), 161–177. DOI: 10.1016/j.leaqua.2008.01.006

Lietz, C. A., Gerdes, K. E., Sun, F., Geiger, J. M., Wagaman, M. A., & Segal, E. A. (2011). The Empathy Assessment Index (EAI): A confirmatory factor analysis of a multidimensional model of empathy. *Journal of the Society for Social Work and Research, 2*(2), 104–124. DOI: 10.5243/jsswr.2011.6

Li, K., Sun, K. P., Ching, N. L., & Wu, M. (2025). *The Education 5.0 Imperative: Strategies to Thrive amid AI's Transformative Tide*. DOI: 10.5281/zenodo.17014956

LinkedIn. (2025, February 28). AI's New Frontier in HR: Predicting Burnout Before It Strikes! https://www.linkedin.com/pulse/ais-new-frontier-hr-predicting-burnout-before-strikes-michael-watson-nwibc

Li, S., & Wang, Y. (2024). A study on the positive and negative effects of different supervisor monitoring in remote workplaces. *Frontiers in Psychology, 15*, 1383207. DOI: 10.3389/fpsyg.2024.1383207 PMID: 38699578

Litvinova, Y., Mikalef, P., & Luo, X. (2024). Framework for human–XAI symbiosis: Extended self from the dual-process theory perspective. *Journal of Business Analytics, 7*(4), 224–255. DOI: 10.1080/2573234X.2024.2396366

Liu, C., Chuang, Y.-C., Qin, L., Ren, L., Chien, C.-W., & Tung, T.-H. (2025). Machine-learning-based model for analysing and accurately predicting factors related to burnout in healthcare workers. *BMJ Public Health*, *3*(2), 000777. https://pmc.ncbi.nlm.nih.gov/articles/PMC12414203/. DOI: 10.1186/s12889-025-21809-1 PMID: 40922936

Liu, H. Y. (2023). Digital Taylorism in China's e-commerce industry: A case study of internet professionals. *Economic and Industrial Democracy*, *44*(1), 262–279. DOI: 10.1177/0143831X211068887

Li, X., Zhou, Y., & Wang, L. (2024). The burnout prediction using wearable and artificial intelligence technologies: A review. *Journal of Medical Internet Research*, *26*, e54029.

London, M., & Smither, J. W. (2002). Feedback orientation. *Human Resource Management Review*, *12*(1), 81–100. DOI: 10.1016/S1053-4822(01)00043-2

Lone, M. A., & Lone, A. H. (2018). Does emotional intelligence predict leadership effectiveness? An exploration in non-Western context. *SA Journal of Human Resource Management*, *5*(1), 28–39. DOI: 10.1177/2322093718766806

Long, D., & Magerko, B. (2020). What is AI literacy? Competencies and design considerations. *Proceedings of the 2020 CHI Conference on Human Factors in Computing Systems*, 1–16. DOI: 10.1145/3313831.3376727

López, T., Riedler, T., Köhnen, H., & Fütterer, M. (2022). Digital value chain restructuring and labour process transformations in the fast-fashion sector: Evidence from the value chains of Zara & H\&M. *Global Networks*, *22*(4), 684–700. DOI: 10.1111/glob.12353

Lubbadeh, T. (2020). Emotional intelligence and leadership-the dark and bright sides. *Modern Management Review*, *25*(27), 39–50. DOI: 10.7862/rz.2020.mmr.5

Ma, S., Zhang, C., Wang, X., Ma, X., & Yin, M. (2024). *Beyond recommender: An exploratory study of the effects of different AI roles in AI-assisted decision making* (arXiv:2403.01791). arXiv.

Madanchian, M., & Taherdoost, H. (2025). Ethical theories, governance models, and strategic frameworks for responsible AI adoption and organizational success. *Frontiers in Artificial Intelligence*, *8*, 1619029. DOI: 10.3389/frai.2025.1619029 PMID: 40741285

Madanchian, M., & Taherdoost, H. (2025). *Tech-Driven Leadership: Strategies to Maximize Business Potential with Emerging Technologies* (1st ed.). Emerald Publishing Limited., DOI: 10.1108/978-1-83708-046-5

Madanchian, M., Taherdoost, H., Vincenti, M., & Mohamed, N. (2024). Transforming Leadership Practices through Artificial Intelligence. *Procedia Computer Science, 235*, 2101–2111. DOI: 10.1016/j.procs.2024.04.199

Maestre Vidal, J., & Sotelo Monge, M. A. (2020). Obfuscation of malicious behaviors for thwarting masquerade detection systems based on locality features. *Sensors (Basel), 20*(7), 2084. DOI: 10.3390/s20072084 PMID: 32272806

Mahat, S., & Devale, A. (2025).. . *Corporate Social Responsibility Innovation in Ethical Technology Leadership., 12*, 25–33.

Mahendra, R., & Sularto, R. B. (2024). Impact on Companies That Employ Underage Children. *International Journal of Social Science and Human Research, 7*(5). Advance online publication. DOI: 10.47191/ijsshr/v7-i05-66

Majumder, S., Salman, S., & Dey, N. (2026). AI in human resources: Efficiency, ethics, and emerging challenges. *AI and Ethics, 6*(59), 59. Advance online publication. DOI: 10.1007/s43681-025-00862-x

Makarius, E. E., Mukherjee, D., Fox, J. D., & Fox, A. K. (2020). Rising with the machines: A sociotechnical framework for bringing artificial intelligence into the organization. *Journal of Business Research, 120*, 262–273. DOI: 10.1016/j.jbusres.2020.07.045

Makridakis, S. (2017). The forthcoming artificial intelligence (AI) revolution: Its impact on society and firms. *Futures: The Journal of Policy. Futures, 90*, 46–60. DOI: 10.1016/j.futures.2017.03.006

Malik, A., De Silva, M. T. T., Budhwar, P., & Srikanth, N. R. (2021). Elevating talents' experience through innovative artificial intelligence-mediated knowledge sharing: Evidence from an IT-multinational enterprise. *Journal of International Management, 27*(4), 100871. DOI: 10.1016/j.intman.2021.100871

Malik, M., Raziq, M. M., Sarwar, N., & Tariq, A. (2025). Digital leadership, business model innovation and organizational change: Role of leader in steering digital transformation. *Benchmarking, 32*(5), 1632–1662. DOI: 10.1108/BIJ-04-2023-0283

Manaff, N. A., & Azahari, M. H. (2024). Digital technology's effect on teaching and learning. *International Journal of Research in Education Humanities and Commerce, 5*(02), 129–135. DOI: 10.37602/IJREHC.2024.5211

Manda, V. K., Christy, V., & Jitta, M. (2024). *Ethical AI and Decision-Making in Management Leadership.*, DOI: 10.4018/979-8-3693-4147-6.ch009

Mann, H. (2024). *Artificial Integrity: The paths to leading AI toward a human-centered future*. John Wiley & Sons.

Manoharan, G., Rao, C. V. G., Ashtikar, S. P., Kumar, S., & Nivedha, M. (2024). Voyage Virtuoso: Artificial Intelligence in Transforming Tourism. In Kumar, S., Talukder, M. B., & Pego, A. (Eds.), *Advances in Hospitality, Tourism, and the Services Industry* (pp. 79–97). IGI Global., DOI: 10.4018/979-8-3693-1978-9.ch004

Marathe, A., & Sen, A. (2021). Empathetic reflection: Reflecting with emotion. *Reflective Practice*, *22*(4), 566–574. DOI: 10.1080/14623943.2021.1927693

Margherita, A., & Bua, I. (2021). The role of human resource analytics in organizational resilience. *Journal of Business Research*, *131*, 573–586. DOI: 10.1016/j.jbusres.2021.03.033

Markus, H. R., & Kitayama, S. (1991). Culture and the self. *Psychological Review*, *98*(2), 224–253. DOI: 10.1037/0033-295X.98.2.224

Martingano, A. J., Konrath, S., Zarins, S., & Okaomee, A. A. (2022). Empathy, narcissism, alexithymia, and social media use. *Psychology of Popular Media*, *11*(4), 413–422. DOI: 10.1037/ppm0000419

Marvi, R., Foroudi, P., & AmirDadbar, N. (2025). Dynamics of user engagement: AI mastery goal and the paradox mindset in AI–employee collaboration. *International Journal of Information Management*, *83*, 102908. DOI: 10.1016/j.ijinfomgt.2025.102908

Maslach, C., & Jackson, S. E. (1981). The measurement of experienced burnout. *Journal of Organizational Behavior*, *2*(2), 99–113. DOI: 10.1002/job.4030020205

Maslach, C., & Leiter, M. P. (2016). *Burnout*. Wiley.

Maslach, C., Schaufeli, W. B., & Leiter, M. P. (1996). *Maslach Burnout Inventory manual*. Consulting Psychologists Press.

Matsumoto, D.. (2008). Mapping expressive differences. *Journal of Personality and Social Psychology*, *94*(6), 925–937. DOI: 10.1037/0022-3514.94.6.925 PMID: 18505309

Mayer, J., & Salovey, P. (1997). Emotional Emotional development and Emotional intelligence: Educational Implications. 3–34.

Mayer, C.-H. (2024). Leaders' views on leadership and skills development in the Fourth Industrial Revolution. *SA Journal of Industrial Psychology*, *50*. Advance online publication. DOI: 10.4102/sajip.v50i0.2172

Mayer, D. M., Aquino, K., Greenbaum, R. L., & Kuenzi, M. (2012). Who displays ethical leadership? *Academy of Management Journal, 55*(1), 151–171. DOI: 10.5465/amj.2008.0276

Mayer, J. D., Salovey, P., & Caruso, D. R. (2008). Emotional intelligence: New ability or eclectic traits? *The American Psychologist, 63*(6), 503–517. DOI: 10.1037/0003-066X.63.6.503 PMID: 18793038

Mayer, R. C., Davis, J. H., & Schoorman, F. D. (1995). An integrative model of organizational trust. *Academy of Management Review, 20*(3), 709–734. DOI: 10.2307/258792

Mayo Clinic. (2023). Job burnout: How to spot it and take action. https://www.mayoclinic.org/healthy-lifestyle/adult-health/in-depth/burnout/art-20046642

McAfee, A., & Brynjolfsson, E. (2017). *Machine, platform, crowd.* Norton.

McCarthy, J., Minsky, M. L., Rochester, N., & Shannon, C. E. (1955). A proposal for the Dartmouth Summer Research Project on artificial intelligence. *AI Magazine, 27*(4), 12.

McGrath, M. J., Duenser, A., Lacey, J., & Paris, C. (2024). *Collaborative human-AI trust (CHAI-T): A process framework for active management of trust in human-AI collaboration* (Version 1). arXiv. DOI: 10.48550/ARXIV.2404.01615

McKinsey & Company. (2025). *Seizing the agentic AI advantage: A CEO playbook to solve the gen AI paradox and unlock scalable impact with AI agents.*

McNabb, K. (2025, March 14). The acceleration of generative AI: How businesses are scaling for competitive advantage. Hackett. https://www.thehackettgroup.com/insights/the-acceleration-of-generative-ai-how-businesses-are-scaling-for-competitive-advantage/

Medlama, M., Vianney, L., Piring, R., Ilham, S., & Annamalah, S. (2025). The impact of artificial intelligence on leadership decision-making: Opportunities and challenges. *Communications on Applied Nonlinear Analysis, 32*(9s), 1878–1885. DOI: 10.52783/cana.v32.4359

Meijerink, J., & Bondarouk, T. (2023). The duality of algorithmic management: Toward a research agenda on HRM algorithms, autonomy and value creation. *Human Resource Management Review, 33*(1), 100876. DOI: 10.1016/j.hrmr.2021.100876

Meijerink, J., Bondarouk, T., & Lepak, D. P. (2021). Organizational boundaries and HRM in the digital age. *Human Resource Management Review, 31*(1), 100775. DOI: 10.1016/j.hrmr.2020.100775

Mellifont, D., Watharow, A., Daniels-Mayes, S., Smith-Merry, J., & O'Donovan, M.-A. (2024). *Ethical Inclusion and Participation of People with Disability in Research: Problematising Vulnerability* (pp. 71–90). DOI: 10.1108/S2398-601820240000011005

Meng, Q., Wu, T.-J., Duan, W., & Li, S. (2025). Effects of employee–artificial intelligence (AI) collaboration on counterproductive work behaviors (CWBs): Leader emotional support as a moderator. *Behavioral Sciences (Basel, Switzerland), 15*(5), 696. DOI: 10.3390/bs15050696 PMID: 40426473

Menteşe, S., & Menteşe, C. D. (2023). Dijitalleşen dünyada yöneticilerin değişen karar mekanizmaları. *Munzur Üniversitesi Sosyal Bilimler Dergisi, 12*(2), 153–173. DOI: 10.61337/tusbd.1362971

Mentzas, G., Lepenioti, K., Bousdekis, A., & Apostolou, D. (2021). Data-Driven Collaborative Human-AI Decision Making. In Dennehy, D., Griva, A., Pouloudi, N., Dwivedi, Y. K., Pappas, I., & Mäntymäki, M. (Eds.), *Responsible AI and Analytics for an Ethical and Inclusive Digitized Society* (Vol. 12896, pp. 120–131). Springer International Publishing., DOI: 10.1007/978-3-030-85447-8_11

Mezzenzana, F., & Peluso, D. (Eds.). (2023). *Conversations on empathy: Interdisciplinary perspectives on imagination and radical othering*. Routledge. DOI: 10.4324/9781003189978

Microsoft Research. (2022). *Viva insights technical documentation*. Microsoft.

Microsoft. (2021). *Microsoft Viva Insights: Measuring wellbeing and productivity*. Microsoft Corporation.

Microsoft. (2023, 15 November). *What can Copilot's earliest users teach us about generative AI at work?* Retrived from: https://www.microsoft.com/en-us/worklab/work-trend-index/copilots-earliest-users-teach-us-about-generative-ai-at-work/

Mihajlov, S., & Mihajlov, N. (2025). Adaptive Leadership in Complex Systems: Moving Beyond Bureaucratic Constraints. *Economic and Social Development in Bipolar and Multipolar Environment (Book of Proceedings)*, 126.

Mikalef, P., & Gupta, M. (2021). Artificial intelligence capability: Conceptualization, measurement calibration, and empirical study on its impact on organizational creativity and firm performance. *Information & Management, 58*(3), 103434. DOI: 10.1016/j.im.2021.103434

Mikalef, P., & Pateli, A. (2017). Information technology-enabled dynamic capabilities and their indirect effect on competitive performance: Findings from PLS-SEM and fsQCA. *Journal of Business Research, 70*, 1–16. DOI: 10.1016/j.jbusres.2016.09.004

Miller, E. (2025, February 16). AI governance in practice: Strategies for ethical implementation at scale. Magnimind Academy. https://magnimindacademy.com/blog/ai-governance-in-practice-strategies-for-ethical-implementation-at-scale/

Miller, T. (2019). Explanation in artificial intelligence: Insights from the social sciences. *Artificial Intelligence*, *267*, 1–38. DOI: 10.1016/j.artint.2018.07.007

Mills, S. (2022). Personalized nudging. *Behavioural Public Policy, 6*(1), 150–159. https://doi.org/. 2020.7DOI: 10.1017 /bpp

Misra, G., Singh, P., & Mishra, A. (2025). Personal and Social Dynamics of Marginalization and Demarginalization. *Personality and Social Psychology Review : An Official Journal of the Society for Personality and Social Psychology, Inc.*, *29*(4), 396–408. DOI: 10.1177/10888683251364487 PMID: 41017247

Mitsugi, N., Ijuin, K., Oshiyama, C., Hara, E., & Nishimura, T. (2025). An AI-mediated framework for recursive learning: Transforming individual experiences into organizational knowledge and autonomous engagement in elderly care. *Frontiers in Digital Health*, *7*, 1529072. DOI: 10.3389/fdgth.2025.1529072 PMID: 40678716

Mittelstadt, B. D., Allo, P., Taddeo, M., Wachter, S., & Floridi, L. (2016). The ethics of algorithms. *Big Data & Society*, *3*(2), 2053951716679679. Advance online publication. DOI: 10.1177/2053951716679679

Modise, J. (2023). Fostering Stronger Leadership in the South African Police Service. *Leveraging the Potential of Promotions.*, *8*, 25.

Mohamed, N. (2025). Artificial intelligence and machine learning in cybersecurity: A deep dive into state-of-the-art techniques and future paradigms. *Knowledge and Information Systems*, *67*(8), 1–87. DOI: 10.1007/s10115-025-02429-y

Mohammad Badruddoza Talukder. Firoj Kabir, K. M., & Das, I. R. (2023). Emerging Concepts of Artificial Intelligence in the Hotel Industry: A Conceptual Paper. *International Journal of Research Publication and Reviews, Vol 4, no*, pp 1765-1769. https://doi.org/https://doi.org/10.55248/gengpi.4.923.92451

Mohammad Badruddoza Talukder. Sanjeev Kumar, I. R. Das. (2024). Perspectives of Digital Marketing for the Restaurant Industry. In *Advancements in Socialized and Digital Media Communications* (p. 17). DOI: 10.4018/979-8-3693-0855-4.ch009

Mohammed, N. Y., Omar, H. A., & Aziz, A. A. (2022). Contributions of Leadership Styles to Digital Transformation-An Exploratory Study of the Opinions of a Sample of Administrative Leaders at the Northern Technical University. *Ingenierie des Systemes d'Information*, *27*(6), 865–873. DOI: 10.18280/isi.270602

Moka, H. R. (2025, March 24). How AI Can Predict and Prevent Workplace Burnout. https://www.mokahr.io/myblog/ai-predict-prevent-employee-burnout/

Molina, D. A., Kharlov, V., & Chen, J.-S. (2024). Towards Effective Human-AI Collaboration in Decision-Making: A Comprehensive Review and Conceptual Framework. *2024 Portland International Conference on Management of Engineering and Technology (PICMET)*, 1–6. DOI: 10.23919/PICMET64035.2024.10653303

Möllers, M., Berger, B., & Klein, S. (2024). Contrasting human-AI workplace relationship configurations. In Constantiou, I., Joshi, M. P., & Stelmaszak, M. (Eds.), *Research Handbook on Artificial Intelligence and Decision Making in Organizations* (pp. 282–303). Edward Elgar Publishing., DOI: 10.4337/9781803926216.00025

Mollica, R. F. (2006). *Healing invisible wounds*. Vanderbilt University Press.

Monica, N., & Anandan, C. (2023). *Correlation level of happiness and employee engagement. 04*, 460–463.

Monod, E., Mayer, A.-S., Straub, D., Joyce, E., & Qi, J. (2024). From worker empowerment to managerial control: The devolution of AI tools' intended positive implementation to their negative consequences. *Information and Organization, 34*(1), 100498. DOI: 10.1016/j.infoandorg.2023.100498

Montani, F., Courcy, F., Battistelli, A., & De Witte, H. (2021). Job insecurity and innovative work behaviour: A moderated mediation model of intrinsic motivation and trait mindfulness. *Stress and Health*. https://doi-org.ezproxy.mdx.ac.uk/10.1002/smi.3034

Moon, E. Y., Park, J., & Ka, Y. (2024). A latent profile analysis of protean career attitude and vocational identity status. [Preprint]. *Journal of Career Development, 51*(5), 527–543. Advance online publication. DOI: 10.1177/08948453241266801

Morin, S. (2024). Name Bias: Application Through the 4-Step Process Using Foundations of Critical Theory in Organizational Settings. *Business Ethics and Leadership, 8*, 163–171. DOI: 10.61093/bel.8(1).163-171.2024

Mortensen, M., & Haas, M. (2018). Rethinking teams. *Harvard Business Review, 96*(2), 74–81.

Mousavi, R., Hazarika, B., Chen, K., & Rienzo, T. (2022). The role of dissonance reduction and co-creation strategies in shaping smart service satisfaction – the case of Uber. *Behaviour & Information Technology, 41*(1), 51–71. DOI: 10.1080/0144929X.2020.1795258

Mseer, I., & Ali Samhan, A. A. (2025). Collaboration Between Humans and AI. In Alaali, M., Musleh Al-Sartawi, A. M. A., & Aydiner, A. S. (Eds.), *The Paradigm Shift from a Linear Economy to a Smart Circular Economy* (Vol. 586, pp. 1299–1308). Springer Nature Switzerland., DOI: 10.1007/978-3-031-87550-2_83

Muldoon, J., Deal, N. M., Smith, D., & Shivanapura Lakshmikanth, G. (2022). The past masters: The impact of the evolution of management thought on history. *Journal of Management History*, *29*(1), 10–28. Advance online publication. DOI: 10.1108/JMH-10-2021-0057

Müller, R., & Turner, R. (2010). Leadership competency profiles of successful project managers. *International Journal of Project Management*, *28*(5), 437–448. DOI: 10.1016/j.ijproman.2009.09.003

Mumford, M. D., Zaccaro, S. J., Harding, F. D., Jacobs, T. O., & Fleishman, E. A. (2007). Leadership skills for a changing world. *The Leadership Quarterly*, *11*(1), 11–35. DOI: 10.1016/S1048-9843(99)00041-7

Munyaka, I., Ashktorab, Z., Dugan, C., Johnson, J., & Pan, Q. (2023). Decision Making Strategies and Team Efficacy in Human-AI Teams. *Proceedings of the ACM on Human-Computer Interaction, 7*(CSCW1), 1–24. DOI: 10.1145/3579476

Muthusubramanian, M., Jangoan, S. & others. (2024). *Demystifying explainable AI*. IJ.

Myszak, J. M., & Filina-Dawidowicz, L. (2025a). Leaders' Competencies and Skills in the Era of Artificial Intelligence: A Scoping Review. *Applied Sciences (Basel, Switzerland), 15*(18), 10271. DOI: 10.3390/app151810271

Nabeel, M. (2024). AI-Enhanced Project Management Systems for Optimizing Resource Allocation and Risk Mitigation: Leveraging Big Data Analysis to Predict Project Outcomes and Improve Decision-Making Processes in Complex Projects. *Asian Journal of Multidisciplinary Research & Review*, *5*(5), 53–91. DOI: 10.55662/AJMRR.2024.5502

Nahar, K., Faruq, O., & Rayhan, Z. (2025). Technical analysis of AI-driven solutions for aligning HR policies with employee satisfaction. *Информатика. Экономика. Управление - Informatics. Economics. Management*, *4*(2), 3038–3048. DOI: 10.47813/2782-5280-2025-4-2-3038-3048

Naidu, T. (2025, November 18). Leadership in the age of AI: Balancing people, processes, and technology. https://www.ghodawat.com/leadership-in-the-age-of-ai-balancing-people-processes-and-technology/

Nalbantoğlu, C. B. (2023). Yapay zeka ve uygulamalarının örgüt kültürü üzerine etkisi. *İzlek Akademik Dergi, 7*(2), 1–10.

Nasaj, M., Badi, S., Murtagh, N., & Ding, L. (2025). Collective AI anxiety and team innovative behaviour: The role of coping strategies. *Construction Innovation*. Advance online publication. DOI: 10.1108/CI-08-2024-0222

Nembhard, I. M., & Edmondson, A. C. (2006). Making it safe. *Journal of Organizational Behavior*, *27*(7), 941–966. DOI: 10.1002/job.413

Nesbit, P. L. (2012). The role of self-reflection, emotional management of feedback, and self-regulation processes in self-directed leadership development. *Human Resource Development Review*, *11*(2), 203–226. DOI: 10.1177/1534484312439196

Neto, B. (2022). Labor process and future relevance of the critique of capital. *Critique (Glasgow)*, *50*(1), 155–166. DOI: 10.1080/03017605.2022.2050534

Newman, A., Donohue, R., & Eva, N. (2017). Psychological safety: A systematic review of the literature. *Human Resource Management Review*, *27*(3), 521–535. DOI: 10.1016/j.hrmr.2017.01.001

Newman, S. A., & Ford, R. C. (2021). Five steps to leading your team in the virtual COVID-19 workplace. *Organizational Dynamics*, *50*(1), 100802. DOI: 10.1016/j.orgdyn.2020.100802 PMID: 36536689

Nie, T., Tian, M., Cai, M., & Yan, Q. (2023). Job Autonomy and Work Meaning: Drivers of Employee Job-Crafting Behaviors in the VUCA Times. *Behavioral Sciences, 13*(6), 493. https://doi.org/, S., Berends, H., Faraj, S., & Huysman, M. (2020). Make way for the algorithms: Symbolic actions and change in a regime of knowing. *Organisation Science, 32*(1), 18–41.DOI: 10.3390/bs13060493Pachidi

Nikiforidis, K., Kyrtsoglou, A., Vafeiadis, T., & Kotsiopoulos, T. (2025). XAI in smart manufacturing. *ICT Express, 47.*

Niranjan, K., Narayana, K. S., & Rao, M. N. (2021, January). Role of artificial intelligence in logistics and supply chain. In *2021 International Conference on Computer Communication and Informatics (ICCCI)* (pp. 1–3). IEEE. DOI: 10.1109/ICCCI50826.2021.9402625

Noble, S. U. (2018). *Algorithms of oppression.* NYU Press. DOI: 10.18574/nyu/9781479833641.001.0001

Nora, M. (2025). Protecting human dignity and meaningful work in the age of AI: A social autonomy framework for ethical decision making in the workplace. https://scarab.bates.edu/cgi/viewcontent.cgi?article=1574&context=honorstheses

Nussbaum, M. C., & Capabilities, C. (2011). The human development approach. *Creating capabilities. Cambridge, MA: Belknap Press of Harvard*, 87.

Nyakora, P., & Monda, D. (2025). Developing AI Literacy as a Core Competency for Future Leaders. *International Journal of Research and Innovation in Social Science, IX*(XIV), 1723–1726. DOI: 10.47772/IJRISS.2025.914MG00129

O'Neil, C. (2016). *Weapons of math destruction.* Crown.

Obied, A. S. (2025). Digital leadership in the academic environment: A systematic literature review. *Social Sciences & Humanities Open, 11*, 101542. DOI: 10.1016/j.ssaho.2025.101542

OECD. (2021). *Measuring telework in the COVID-19 pandemic.* OECD Digital Economy Papers.

Ojando, E. S., Benito, M., & Prats, M. À. (2017). Students as digital leaders in the classroom. *Aloma: revista de psicologia, ciències de l'educació i de l'esport Blanquerna, 35*(1), 53-60.

Okoli, I., Appoh, M., & Alabi, O. (2024). Developing a Scalable and Inclusive Curriculum for Youth Leadership in Various American Communities. *Journal of Frontiers in Multidisciplinary Research, 5*(1), 197–204. DOI: 10.54660/.JFMR.2024.5.1.197-204

Olatunji, S., & Wills, F. (2025). *Cognitive Schemas Shaping Leadership Behavior in Algorithmic Contexts.*

Oliveira, P., Carvalho, J. M. S., & Faria, S. (2025). AI Integration in Organisational Workflows: A Case Study on Job Reconfiguration, Efficiency, and Workforce Adaptation. *Information (Basel), 16*(9), 764. DOI: 10.3390/info16090764

Omrani, N., Rejeb, N., Maalaoui, A., Dabić, M., & Kraus, S. (2022). Drivers of digital transformation in SMEs. *IEEE Transactions on Engineering Management, 71*, 5030–5043. DOI: 10.1109/TEM.2022.3215727

Omrani, N., Rivieccio, G., Fiore, U., Schiavone, F., & Agreda, S. G. (2022). To trust or not to trust? An assessment of trust in AI-based systems: Concerns, ethics and contexts. *Technological Forecasting and Social Change, 181*, 121763. Advance online publication. DOI: 10.1016/j.techfore.2022.121763

Onan, G. (2024). Digital transformation and digital leadership in higher education institutions: Insights from the literature. *Uluslararası Sosyal Bilgilerde Yeni Yaklaşımlar Dergisi, 8*(2), 198–213.

Onifade, A. Y., Ogeawuchi, J. C., Abayomi, A. A., Agboola, O. A., Dosumu, R. E., & George, O. O. (2022). A conceptual framework for integrating AI adoption metrics into B2B marketing decision systems. *International Journal of Management and Organizational Research, 1*(1), 237–248. DOI: 10.54660/IJMOR.2022.1.1.237-248

Onnis, L. L. (2016). What is a sustainable remote health workforce? People, practice and place. *Rural and Remote Health, 16*(3), 1–13. DOI: 10.22605/RRH3806

Ooi, R. W. G. (2025). *From Neurons to Organisations: Awakening Regenerative Leadership through Neuroplasticity, AI, and Integrative Consciousness*. Social Sciences. DOI: 10.20944/preprints202501.0743.v2

Orlikowski, W. J. (2007). Sociomaterial practices: Exploring technology at work. *Organization Studies, 28*(9), 1435–1448. DOI: 10.1177/0170840607081138

Osler, L., & Zahavi, D. (2022). Sociality and embodiment: Online communication during and after Covid-19. *Foundations of Science*. Advance online publication. DOI: 10.1007/s10699-022-09861-1

Oxford Gomez, M., Klare, D., Ceballos, N., Dailey, S., Kaiser, S., & Howard, K. (2022). Do you dare to compare? The key characteristics of social media users who frequently make online upward social comparisons. *International Journal of Human-Computer Interaction, 38*(10), 938–948. DOI: 10.1080/10447318.2021.1976510

Ozcelik, H., Langton, N., & Aldrich, H. (2008). Doing well and doing good: The relationship between leadership practices that facilitate a positive emotional climate and organizational performance. *Journal of Managerial Psychology, 23*(2), 186–203. DOI: 10.1108/02683940810850817

Pabuçcu, R., & İşcan, Ö. F. (2025). Yapay zekâ ve liderlik: Dönüştürücü liderlik tarzının çalışan tutumlarına etkisi. *Uluslararası Ekonomi, İşletme ve Politika Dergisi, 9*(1), 195–210. DOI: 10.29216/ueip.1607837

Palmer, B. R., Gignac, G., Ekermans, G., & Stough, C. (2008). A comprehensive framework for emotional intelligence. Emotional intelligence: Theoretical and cultural perspectives. 17–38.

Palmer, B., Walls, M., Burgess, Z., & Stough, C. (2001). Emotional intelligence and effective leadership. *Leadership and Organization Development Journal, 22*(1), 5–10. DOI: 10.1108/01437730110380174

Pandey, V. (2025). Leadership in the AI Era: Navigating and shaping the future of organizational guidance. *Available at* SSRN *5331975*. SSRN *Electronic Journal*. DOI: 10.2139/ssrn.5331975

Pang, B., & Lee, L. (2008). Opinion mining and sentiment analysis. *Foundations and Trends in Information Retrieval, 2*(1–2), 1–135. DOI: 10.1561/1500000011

Papagiannidis, E., Mikalef, P., Conboy, K., & Van de Wetering, R. (2023). Uncovering the dark side of AI-based decision-making: A case study in a B2B context. *Industrial Marketing Management, 115*, 253–265. DOI: 10.1016/j.indmarman.2023.10.003

Paramjeet. (2025, June 14). The empathy-AI nexus in leadership: Toward verified, human-centered decision systems. *LinkedIn*. https://www.linkedin.com/pulse/empathy-ai-nexus-leadership-toward-verified-decision-paramjeet--fe8hf/

Parasuraman, R., & Manzey, D. H. (2010). Complacency and bias in human use of automation: An attentional integration. *Human Factors, 52*(3), 381–410. DOI: 10.1177/0018720810376055 PMID: 21077562

Parasuraman, R., & Riley, V. (1997). Humans and automation. *Human Factors, 39*(2), 230–253. DOI: 10.1518/001872097778543886 PMID: 18689061

Parent-Rocheleau, X., & Parker, S. K. (2022). Algorithms as work designers: How algorithmic management influences the design of jobs. *Human Resource Management Review, 32*(3), 100838. DOI: 10.1016/j.hrmr.2021.100838

Parker, S. K., & Grote, G. (2022). Automation, algorithms, and beyond: Why work design matters more than ever in a digital world. *Applied Psychology = Psychologie Appliquée, 71*(4), 1171–1204. DOI: 10.1111/apps.12241

Park, J., Woo, S. E., & Kim, J. (2024). Attitudes towards artificial intelligence at work: Scale development and validation. *Journal of Occupational and Organizational Psychology, 97*(3), 920–951. DOI: 10.1111/joop.12502

Park, S., & Nan, X. (2025). Generative AI and misinformation: A scoping review of the role of generative AI in the generation, detection, mitigation, and impact of misinformation. *AI & Society, 41(2), 1501-1515.*

Paschen, J., Wilson, M., & Ferreira, J. J. (2020). Collaborative intelligence: How human and artificial intelligence create value along the B2B sales funnel. *Business Horizons, 63*(3), 403–414. DOI: 10.1016/j.bushor.2020.01.003

Pascoe, J. L., Lu, L., Moore, M. M., Blezek, D. J., Ovalle, A. E., Linderbaum, J. A., Callstrom, M. R., & Williamson, E. E. (2024). Strategic considerations for selecting artificial intelligence solutions for institutional integration: A single-center experience. *Mayo Clinic Proceedings. Digital Health, 2*(4), 665–676. DOI: 10.1016/j.mcpdig.2024.10.004 PMID: 40206525

Passmore, J., & Tee, D. (2023). Can chatbots like GPT-4 replace human coaches? Issues and dilemmas for the coaching profession, coaching clients and for organisations. *The Coaching Psychologist, 19*(1), 47–54. DOI: 10.53841/bpstcp.2023.19.1.47

Pastor, I. (2014). Leadership and emotional intelligence: The effect on performance and attitude. *Procedia Economics and Finance*, *15*, 985–992. DOI: 10.1016/S2212-5671(14)00658-3

Pati, A. K. (2025). Agentic AI: A comprehensive survey of technologies, applications, and societal implications. *IEEE Access : Practical Innovations, Open Solutions*, *13*, 151824–151837. DOI: 10.1109/ACCESS.2025.3585609

Patidar, N., Mishra, S., Jain, R., & Prajapati, D. (2024). Transparency in AI decision-making. *SSRN*.

Pei, J., Wang, H., Peng, Q., & Liu, S. (2024). Saving face: Leveraging artificial intelligence-based negative feedback to enhance employee job performance. *Human Resource Management*, *63*(5), 775–790. DOI: 10.1002/hrm.22226

Petrescu, G. M., tef, A. L., Cîmpan, I., Cri an, E. L., & Salan ă, I. I. (2023). Drivers Of Digital Transformation In Product Development, Business Modeling And Human Resources Management. *Annals of the University of Oradea, Economic Science Series, 32*(1).

Petriglieri, G., Ashford, S. J., & Wrzesniewski, A. (2019). Agony and ecstasy in the gig economy. *Administrative Science Quarterly*, *64*(1), 124–170. DOI: 10.1177/0001839218759646

Peukert, M. (2025). *Cultivate an AI Mindset: Identifying and Efficiently Leveraging the Opportunities and Challenges of Artificial Intelligence*. Springer Fachmedien Wiesbaden., DOI: 10.1007/978-3-658-49826-9

Picard, R. W. (1997). *Affective computing*. MIT Press. DOI: 10.7551/mitpress/1140.001.0001

Piszczek, M. M., & Berg, P. (2014). Expanding the boundaries of boundary theory: Regulative institutions and work–family role management. *Human Relations; Studies Towards the Integration of the Social Sciences*, *67*(12), 1491–1512. DOI: 10.1177/0018726714524241

Pollak, Z. (2021). Predicting customer lifetime values—Ecommerce use case. *arXiv Preprint*, arXiv:2102.05771.

Popovič, A., Hackney, R., Tassabehji, R., & Castelli, M. (2018). The impact of big data analytics on firms' high value business performance. *Information Systems Frontiers*, *20*(2), 209–222. DOI: 10.1007/s10796-016-9720-4

Porfírio, J. A., Carrilho, T., Felício, J. A., & Jardim, J. (2021). Leadership characteristics and digital transformation. *Journal of Business Research, 124*, 610–619. DOI: 10.1016/j.jbusres.2020.10.058

Posada, J., Newlands, G., & Miceli, M. (2023). Labor, automation, and human-machine communication. *The Sage handbook of human-machine communication*, 384-391.

Prabhu, M. (2022). *15 Qualities of an Ideal Leader According to Kautilya a.k.a. Chanakya*. Vedic Management Center.

Preston, S. D., & de Waal, F. B. M. (2002). The communication of emotions and the possibility of empathy in animals. In Post, S. G., Underwood, L. G., Schloss, J. P., & Hurlbut, W. B. (Eds.), *Altruism & altruistic love* (pp. 284–308). Oxford University Press. DOI: 10.1093/acprof:oso/9780195143584.003.0025

PricewaterhouseCoopers. (2024). AI Jobs Barometer. PwC. https://www.pwc.com/gx/en/issues/artificial-intelligence/ai-jobs-barometer.html

Priya, M., Radhakrishnan, G. V, & Arya, S., & G., S. (. (2025). The Role of Inclusive Leadership in Enhancing Employee Engagement. *Journal of Information Systems Engineering & Management, 10*, 1062–1074. DOI: 10.52783/jisem.v10i35s.6190

Provost, F., & Fawcett, T. (2013). *Data science for business: What you need to know about data mining and data-analytic thinking*. O'Reilly Media.

Purnomo, A. H., Fitriansyah, F., Adi, A. S., Hafsari, P., & Fitrianto, Y. (2023, December). Modular-Integration for Smart Governance Development Efficiency in Developing Countries. In MICEB: Mulawarman International Conference on Economics and Business (Vol. 6, No. 1, pp. 55-65).

Pyae, A. (2025). *The Human-AI Handshake Framework: A Bidirectional Approach to Human-AI Collaboration* (Version 1). arXiv. DOI: 10.48550/ARXIV.2502.01493

Qayyum, A., Khan, T., Majid, A., Hassan, S., & Jamil, R. (2025). AI-generated inclusive packaging: Bridging consumer well-being and branding outcomes. *International Journal of Retail & Distribution Management, 53*(10-11), 1009–1024. DOI: 10.1108/IJRDM-01-2025-0020

Qin, J., Nan, Y., Li, Z., & Meng, J. (2025). Effectiveness of communication competence in AI conversational agents for health: Systematic review and meta-analysis. *Journal of Medical Internet Research, 27*, e76296. DOI: 10.2196/76296 PMID: 41183242

Quaquebeke, N. V., & Gerpott, F. H. (2023). The now, new, and next of digital leadership: How artificial intelligence (AI) will take over and change leadership as we know it. *Journal of Leadership & Organizational Studies*, *30*(3), 265–275. DOI: 10.1177/15480518231181731

Raghavan, M., Barocas, S., Kleinberg, J., & Levy, K. (2020). Mitigating bias in algorithmic hiring: Evaluating claims and practices. *Proceedings of the 2020 ACM Conference on Fairness, Accountability, and Transparency (FAccT '20).* https://dl.acm.org/doi/10.1145/3351095.3372828

Raghavan, M., Barocas, S., Kleinberg, J., & Levy, K. (2020). Mitigating bias in algorithmic hiring: Evaluating claims and practices. In *Proceedings of the 2020 Conference on Fairness, Accountability, and Transparency* (pp. 469–481). DOI: 10.1145/3351095.3372828

Ragu-Nathan, T. S., Tarafdar, M., Ragu-Nathan, B. S., & Tu, Q. (2008). The consequences of technostress for end users in organizations. *Information Systems Research*, *19*(4), 417–433. DOI: 10.1287/isre.1070.0165

Rahsepar Meadi, M., Sillekens, T., Metselaar, S., Van Balkom, A., Bernstein, J., & Batelaan, N. (2025). Exploring the ethical challenges of conversational AI in mental health care: Scoping review. *JMIR Mental Health*, *12*, e60432. DOI: 10.2196/60432 PMID: 39983102

Rahwan, I., Cebrian, M., Obradovich, N., Bongard, J., Bonnefon, J.-F., Breazeal, C., Crandall, J. W., Christakis, N. A., Couzin, I. D., Jackson, M. O., Jennings, N. R., Kamar, E., Kloumann, I. M., Larochelle, H., Lazer, D., McElreath, R., Mislove, A., Parkes, D. C., Pentland, A. S., & Wellman, M. (2019). Machine behaviour. *Nature*, *568*(7753), 477–486. DOI: 10.1038/s41586-019-1138-y PMID: 31019318

Raisch, S., & Krakowski, S. (2021). Artificial intelligence and management: The automation–augmentation paradox. *Academy of Management Review*, *46*(1), 192–210. DOI: 10.5465/amr.2018.0072

Rana, R., Higgins, N., Stedman, T., March, S., Gucciardi, D. F., Barua, P. D., & Joshi, R. (2025). Passive AI Detection of Stress and Burnout Among Frontline Workers. *Nursing Reports*, *15*(11), 373. DOI: 10.3390/nursrep15110373 PMID: 41295797

Randriamiary, D. (2024). Reframing the role of leaders navigating the challenges and opportunities of tomorrow's workplace in the age of artificial intelligence. *Available at SSRN47160.* SSRN *Electronic Journal*. DOI: 10.2139/ssrn.4716033

Ransbotham, S., S., Khodabandeh, S., Kiron, D., Candelon, F., Chu, M., & LaFountain, B. (2020). Expanding AI's impact with organisational learning. *MIT Sloan Management Review*.

Ransbotham, S., Kiron, D., Gerbert, P., & Reeves, M. (2017). Reshaping business with artificial intelligence: Closing the gap between ambition and action. *MIT Sloan Management Review*, *59*(1).

Ransbotham, S., Kiron, D., Khodabandeh, S., Iyer, S., & Das, A. (2025). *The emerging agentic enterprise: How leaders must navigate a new age of AI*. MIT Sloan Management Review and Boston Consulting Group.

Rathor, A., & Sharma, M. (2025, April 22). AI and global data privacy laws: Compliance, challenges & trends. *Lawrbit*. https://www.lawrbit.com/global/ai-and-global-data-privacy-laws/

Rauffet, P. (2022). *Tools and methods for Human-Autonomy Teaming: Contributions to cognitive state monitoring and system adaptation* (Version 2). arXiv. DOI: 10.48550/ARXIV.2212.01435

Ravid, D. M., Tomczak, D. L., White, J. C., & Behrend, T. S. (2019). EPM 20/20: A review, framework, and research agenda for electronic performance monitoring. *Journal of Management*, *46*(1), 100–126. DOI: 10.1177/0149206319869435

Reed, P. (2023). Impact of social media use on executive function. *Computers in Human Behavior*, *141*, 107598. Advance online publication. DOI: 10.1016/j.chb.2022.107598

Rehman, J., Hawryszkiewycz, I., & Sohaib, O. Towards the Knowledge-Smart Professional Service Firms: How High-Performance Work Systems Support the Transformation. *J Knowl Econ* **14**, 3640–3670 (2023). https://doi.org/10.1007/s13132-022-00903-4Roulston, K. (2022). Qualitative interviewing and epistemics. *Qualitative Research*, *18*(3), 322–341. DOI: 10.1177/1468794117721738

Reilly, S. M. (2010). *The use of electronic surveillance and performance measures in the workplace: A qualitative investigation* (Doctoral dissertation, Durham University)

Reverberi, C., Rigon, T., Solari, A., Hassan, C., Cherubini, P., Antonelli, G., Awadie, H., Bernhofer, S., Carballal, S., Dinis-Ribeiro, M., Fernández-Clotett, A., Esparrach, G. F., Gralnek, I., Higasa, Y., Hirabayashi, T., Hirai, T., Iwatate, M., Kawano, M., Mader, M., & Cherubini, A. (2022). Experimental evidence of effective human–AI collaboration in medical decision-making. *Scientific Reports*, *12*(1), 14952. DOI: 10.1038/s41598-022-18751-2 PMID: 36056152

Reza, S. A., Rahman, M. K., Rahman, M. D., Sharmin, S., Mithu, M. F. H., Hasnain, K. N., . . . Kabir, R. (2025). Machine learning enabled early warning system for financial distress using real-time digital signals. *arXiv Preprint*, arXiv:2510.22287.

Rhodes, E. P. (2025). Measuring the human experience of AI in the workplace working paper (preprint version). Available at *SSRN, 54*.

Ridho, M. R., Lesmana, I., Safitri, H. D. A., Meirani, R. K., & Prestiadi, D. (2023, February). Digital leadership in the scope of education. In *International Conference on Educational Management and Technology (ICEMT 2022), Advances in Social Science, Education and Humanities Research (ASSEHR 727) pp* (pp. 52-61). DOI: 10.2991/978-2-494069-95-4_7

Rodzina, L., & Kristoffersen, S. (2013). Context-dependent car navigation as kind of human-machine collaborative interaction. *2013 International Conference on Collaboration Technologies and Systems (CTS)*, 253–259. DOI: 10.1109/CTS.2013.6567238

Rojas, C., Zuccarelli, E., Chin, A., Patekar, G., Esquivel, D., & Maes, P. (2022). Towards enhancing empathy through emotion augmented remote communication. In *CHI Conference on Human Factors in Computing Systems* (Paper 454, pp. 1–9). https://doi.org/DOI: 10.1145/3491101.3519797

Rosete, D., & Ciarrochi, J. (2005). Emotional intelligence and its relationship to workplace performance outcomes of leadership effectiveness. *Leadership and Organization Development Journal*, *26*(5), 388–399. DOI: 10.1108/01437730510607871

Roshanaei, M., Rezapour, R., & Seif El-Nasr, M. (2025). Talk, listen, connect: How humans and AI evaluate empathy in responses to emotionally charged narratives. *AI & Society*, 1–17.

Rubin, M., Arnon, H., Huppert, J. D., & Perry, A. (2024). Considering the role of human empathy in AI-driven therapy. *JMIR Mental Health*, *11*(1), e56529. Advance online publication. DOI: 10.2196/56529

Rudiyanto, T., Kunda, H., Dunn, A., Shenderovskiy, S., & Gibson, R. (2023). Ethical and legal concerns of artificial intelligence in the workplace: Examining current legislations in the United States. *Lex Publica*, *10*(1), 84–100. DOI: 10.58829/lp.10.1.2023.84-100

Russell, S., & Norvig, P. (2021). *Artificial intelligence: A modern approach* (4th ed.). Pearson.

Ryan, M. (2020). In AI we trust: Ethics, artificial intelligence, and reliability. *Science and Engineering Ethics*, *26*(5), 2749–2767. DOI: 10.1007/s11948-020-00228-y PMID: 32524425

Sacavém, A., de Bem Machado, A., dos Santos, J. R., Palma-Moreira, A., Belchior-Rocha, H., & Au-Yong-Oliveira, M. (2025). Leading in the digital age: The role of leadership in organizational digital transformation. *Administrative Sciences, 15*(2), 43. DOI: 10.3390/admsci15020043

Sadek, M., Calvo, R., & Mougenot, C. (2023). Designing value-sensitive AI: A critical review and recommendations for socio-technical design processes. *AI and Ethics, 4*(4), 949–967. DOI: 10.1007/s43681-023-00373-7

Sadri, G. (2012). Emotional intelligence and leadership development. *Public Personnel Management, 41*(3), 535–548. DOI: 10.1177/009102601204100308

Safdari Sharabiani, A. (2021). Genuine empathy with inanimate objects. *Phenomenology and the Cognitive Sciences, 20*(5), 831–846. DOI: 10.1007/s11097-020-09715-w

Şahin, G. (2025). *Examples of Innovative Science Education Practices in the Future Classrooms*. DOI: 10.58830/ozgur.pub1137.c4680

Saifudin, S., Januarti, I., & Laguador, J. (2025). Measuring the Role of Female Auditor Behavior: Evidence in Indonesia. *Journal of Accounting and Strategic Finance, 8*(2), 298–319. DOI: 10.33005/jasf.v8i2.614

Salaheldin, S., & Hussein, S. (2025). The determinants of AI adoption and its impact on employee engagement: Evidence from Egyptian organizations. *International Journal of Management and Applied Research, 12*(2), 45–67. DOI: 10.18646/2056.122.25-004

Salameh-Ayanian, M., Tamer, N., & Jabbour Al Maalouf, N. (2025). The Importance of Emotional Intelligence in Managers and Its Impact on Employee Performance Amid Turbulent Times. *Administrative Sciences, 15*(8), 300. DOI: 10.3390/admsci15080300

Salas, E., Driskell, J. E., & Hughes, S. (1996). The study of stress and human performance. *Human Factors, 38*(2), 186–198.

Salovey, P., & Mayer, J. D. (1990). Emotional intelligence. *Imagination, Cognition and Personality, 9*(3), 185–211. DOI: 10.2190/DUGG-P24E-52WK-6CDG

Salunkhe, R. V., Joshi, S. A., Mane, P. D., Irkhede, T., Deosarkar, K. S., & Nausheen, I. (2026). *AI-powered personalization in smart kitchens: Adaptive cooking systems for health, taste, and sustainability*. IGI Global., DOI: 10.4018/979-8-3373-4042-5.ch009

Salunkhe, R. V., Raut, C. A., Chimote, G., Sarwate, S., Kolte, R. R., Ingole, P. K., & Kuthe, A. (2026). *Scaling faculty AI literacy: Strategic models for institutional transformation and sustainable adoption*. IGI Global., DOI: 10.4018/979-8-3373-4129-3.ch012

Salunkhe, R. V., Sathe, T. R., Shete, R. M., Wagh, P., Kolte, R., & Raut, R. (2026). *Nanomaterials discovery using AI-based technology accelerators: Innovation through predictive modeling and intelligent experimentation*. IGI Global., DOI: 10.4018/979-8-3373-2883-6.ch005

Sanka, V. (2025). Ethical AI in big data: Challenges in bias, fairness, and transparency. *International Journal of Scientific Research in Science and Technology*, *12*(1), 731–737. DOI: 10.32628/IJSRST25121220

Sanni, B. (2025). *Leveraging Artificial Intelligence in Women's Leadership Training: Personalized Learning Paths for Skill Enhancement*.

Santos, S., Lucas, M., & Bem-Haja, P. (2022). Bridging the digital competence gap: Tell us what you need. In *International Conferences ICT, Society, and Human Beings* (pp. 104-111).

Santos, S., & Soliven, P. C. (2025). Gender Disparities in Accounting Education: Systematic Review using PRISMA. *International Journal of Advanced Multidisciplinary Research and Studies*, *5*(5), 734–739. DOI: 10.62225/2583049X.2025.5.5.4999

Sargsyan, L. (2025). Integrating agentic ai in higher education: Balancing opportunities, challenges, and ethical imperatives. *Foreign Languages in Higher Education*, *29*(1 (38)), 87–100. DOI: 10.46991/FLHE.2025.29.1.087

Schlaerth, A., Ensari, N., & Christian, J. (2013). A meta-analytical review of the relationship between emotional intelligence and leaders' constructive conflict management. Group Processes & Intergroup Relations. *Group Processes & Intergroup Relations*, *16*(1), 126–136. DOI: 10.1177/1368430212439907

Schmauder, C., Karpus, J., Moll, M., Bahrami, B., & Deroy, O. (2023). Algorithmic nudging: The need for an interdisciplinary oversight. *Topoi*, *42*(3), 799–807. DOI: 10.1007/s11245-023-09907-4

Schön, D. A. (1983). *The reflective practitioner*. Basic Books.

Schulz, A. W. (2017). The evolution of empathy. In Maibom, H. (Ed.), *The Routledge handbook of philosophy of empathy* (pp. 64–74). Routledge. DOI: 10.4324/9781315282015-7

Schwarzmüller, T., Brosi, P., Duman, D., & Welpe, I. M. (2018). How does the digital transformation affect organizations? Key themes of change in work design and leadership. *Management Review*, *29*(2), 114–138.

Searle, J. R. (1980). Minds, brains, and programs. *The Behavioral and Brain Sciences*, *3*(3), 417–457. DOI: 10.1017/S0140525X00005756

Sementelli, A. J. (2019). Faculty in Tamara-Land: Taylorism, ritual, and performance. *Administrative Theory & Praxis*, *41*(1), 21–34. DOI: 10.1080/10841806.2018.1512338

Sevinç, H. G. (2025). Yönetimin değişen paradigması: Yapay zekâ liderliği. *Liberal Düşünce Dergisi*, *118*(118), 89–116. DOI: 10.36484/liberal.1542213

Sewell, G., & Taskin, L. (2015). Out of sight, out of mind in a new world of work? Autonomy, control, and spatiotemporal scaling in telework. *Organization Studies*, *36*(11), 1507–1529. DOI: 10.1177/0170840615593587

Shahzad, M. U. (2024). Core competencies for digital leadership development: A perspective from the lens of paradox theory. *The Bottom Line (New York, N.Y.)*, *37*(4), 454–472. DOI: 10.1108/BL-10-2023-0278

Shamsi, M., Iakovleva, T., Olsen, E., & Bagozzi, R. P. (2021). Employees' work-related well-being during COVID-19 pandemic: An integrated perspective of technology acceptance model and JD-R theory. *International Journal of Environmental Research and Public Health*, *18*(22), 11888. DOI: 10.3390/ijerph182211888 PMID: 34831642

Shanafelt, T. D., & Noseworthy, J. H. (2017). Executive leadership and physician well-being. *Mayo Clinic Proceedings*, *92*(1), 129–146. DOI: 10.1016/j.mayocp.2016.10.004 PMID: 27871627

Shao, R. (2023, April). An empathetic AI for mental health intervention: Conceptualizing and examining artificial empathy. In *Proceedings of the 2nd Empathy-Centric Design Workshop* (pp. 1–6). DOI: 10.1145/3588967.3588971

Sharma, G. (2025, June 12). The human-AI partnership: Redefining leadership in strategy execution. *LinkedIn*. https://www.linkedin.com/pulse/human-ai-partnership-redefining-leadership-strategy-execution-sharma-nqfac/

Sharma, S., Mittal, P., Kumar, M., & Bhardwaj, V. (2025). The role of large language models in personalized learning: A systematic review of educational impact. *Discover Sustainability*, *6*(1), 243. DOI: 10.1007/s43621-025-01094-z

Shen, J., DiPaola, D., Ali, S., Sap, M., Park, H. W., & Breazeal, C. (2024). Empathy toward artificial intelligence versus human experiences and the role of transparency in mental health and social support chatbot design: Comparative study. *JMIR Mental Health*, *11*, e62679. DOI: 10.2196/62679 PMID: 39321450

Shen, L., Qiu, N., & Wang, Z. (2025). Psychological safety and trust as drivers of teachers' continued use of AI tools in classrooms. *Scientific Reports*, *15*(1), 31426. Advance online publication. DOI: 10.1038/s41598-025-13789-4 PMID: 40858670

Shenoy, A., & Sardana, A. (2020). Multilogue-net: A context-aware RNN for multi-modal emotion detection and sentiment analysis in conversation. *arXiv Preprint*, arXiv:2002.08267. DOI: 10.18653/v1/2020.challengehml-1.3

Shneiderman, B. (2022). Human-centered AI: Ensuring human control while increasing automation. In *Proceedings of the 5th Workshop on Human Factors in Hypertext* (pp. 1–2). ACM. https://doi.org/DOI: 10.1145/3538882.3542790

Shrestha, Y. R., Ben-Menahem, S. M., & von Krogh, G. (2019). Organizational decision-making structures in the age of artificial intelligence. *California Management Review*, *61*(4), 66–83. DOI: 10.1177/0008125619862257

Silva, A., & Coelho, N. (2022). The moderating role of organizational culture on the relationship between workers' attitudes towards telework and happiness. *Kybernetes*. Advance online publication. DOI: 10.1108/K-02-2022-0231

Singh, A., & Pandey, J. (2024). Artificial intelligence adoption in extended HR ecosystems: Enablers and barriers. An abductive case research. *Frontiers in Psychology*, *14*, 1339782. DOI: 10.3389/fpsyg.2023.1339782 PMID: 38327504

Singh, S. (2023). Leadership challenges and strategies in the era of AI transformation. In *2023 International Conference on Computational Science and Computational Intelligence (CSCI)* (pp. 119–124). https://doi.org/DOI: 10.1109/CSCI62032.2023.00025

Sinkovics, N. (2016). Enhancing the foundations for theorising through bibliometric mapping. *International Marketing Review*, *33*(3), 327–350. DOI: 10.1108/IMR-10-2014-0341

Siradjuddin, S., Jafar, A., Syariati, A., & Charatwattananich, M. (2025). The dynamics between technological support, work-life balance, and Islamic leaders' productivity in Indonesia. *International Journal of Management and Sustainability*, *14*(1), 286–297. DOI: 10.18488/11.v14i1.4140

Skrzypczyńska, K. (2020). Significance of emotional intelligence in leadership. *Journal of Positive Management*, *9*(4), 66. DOI: 10.12775/JPM.2018.155

Smith, H. (2025). *Transforming Traditional Norms: Education and Mentorship Strategies to Challenge Patriarchal Structures.*

Smith, A., & Jones, B. (2022). Predictive analytics in workplace well-being: From burnout detection to prevention strategies. *Journal of Behavioral Health, 11*(1), 34–50.

Smith, J. (2017). What is empathy for? *Synthese, 194*(3), 709–722. DOI: 10.1007/s11229-015-0771-8

Solove, D. J. (2008). *Understanding privacy.* Harvard University Press.

Somaratne, S., De Silva, D., & Athukorala, R. (2025). Mapping Human-AI Collaboration: A Skill Framework for the Effective Use of AI. *2025 3rd International Conference on Communication, Security, and Artificial Intelligence (ICCSAI)*, 1253–1261. DOI: 10.1109/ICCSAI64074.2025.11064159

Song, B., Soria Zurita, N. F., Nolte, H., Singh, H., Cagan, J., & McComb, C. (2021). Addressing challenges to problem complexity: Effectiveness of AI assistance during the design process. In *IDETC-CIE 2021: International Design Engineering Technical Conferences and Computers and Information in Engineering Conference.*

Song, B., Zhu, Q., & Luo, J. (2024). Human–AI collaboration by design. *Proceedings of the Design Society, 4*, 2247–2256. DOI: 10.1017/pds.2024.227

Souli, S. P., & Pierrakeas, C. (2025). Contemporary Trends in University Administration with the Integration of Digital/New Technologies. *Administrative Sciences, 15*(11), 437. DOI: 10.3390/admsci15110437

Souza, R. A., Tessarolo, G., Bosco, N., Santos, A., Kempner, A., Marques, T., da Costa-Silva, V., Diniz-Filho, J. A., & Souza, T. (2024). BIODIVERSITY (UN) KNOWLEDGE: A SYSTEMATIZATION OF GAPS, LIMITATIONS, DEFICITS, BIASES, AND NOISE. *Oecologia Australis, 28*(3), 159–177. DOI: 10.4257/oeco.2024.2803.01

Sposato, M. (2024). Leadership training and development in the age of artificial intelligence. *Development and Learning in Organizations, 38*(4), 4–7. DOI: 10.1108/DLO-12-2023-0256

Sposato, M., & Dittmar, E. C. (2025). The AI-powered future of digital transformation: Enhancing organizations and leadership development. *Journal of Work-Applied Management.* Advance online publication. DOI: 10.1108/JWAM-02-2025-0039

Sreelakshmy, R., Kumar, A. K., Titus, A., Hemajothi, S., Venkatesh, J., & Lavanya, A. (2023). Design and development of an AI-based intelligent door for home security system. In *2023 International Conference on Advances in Computing, Communication and Applied Informatics (ACCAI)* (pp. 1–8). IEEE. DOI: 10.1109/ACCAI58221.2023.10200307

Sriwilai, K., & Charoensukmongkol, P. (2016). Face it, don't Facebook it: Impacts of social media addiction on mindfulness, coping strategies and the consequence on emotional exhaustion. *Stress and Health : Journal of the International Society for the Investigation of Stress*, *32*(4), 427–434. DOI: 10.1002/smi.2637

Stajkovic, A. D., & Stajkovic, K. S. (2024). *Human Sustainability and Cognitive Overload at Work: The Psychological Cost of Working* (1st ed.). Routledge., DOI: 10.4324/9781003399087

Stanton, J. M., & Weiss, E. M. (2000). Electronic monitoring in their own words: An exploratory study of employees' experiences with new types of surveillance. *Computers in Human Behavior*, *16*(4), 423–440. DOI: 10.1016/S0747-5632(00)00018-2

Stein, S. J., Papadogiannis, P., Yip, J. A., & Sitarenios, G. (2009). Emotional intelligence of leaders: A profile of top executives. *Leadership and Organization Development Journal*, *30*(1), 87–101. DOI: 10.1108/01437730910927115

Stephan, A., Walter, S., & Wilutzky, W. (2014). Emotions beyond brain and body. *Philosophical Psychology*, *27*(1), 65–81. DOI: 10.1080/09515089.2013.828376

Stewart, J. M., Tittel, E., & Chapple, M. (2011). *CISSP: Certified information systems security professional study guide*. John Wiley & Sons.

Sułkowski, Ł., Dacko-Pikiewicz, Z., & Szczepańska-Woszczyna, K. (2024). *Philosophy and Leadership: An Evolution of Leadership from Ancient Times to the Digital Age* (1st ed.). Routledge., DOI: 10.4324/9781003490470

Sullivan, Y., & Wamba, S. F. (2024). Artificial intelligence and adaptive response to market changes: A strategy to enhance firm performance and innovation. *Journal of Business Research*, *174*, 114500. DOI: 10.1016/j.jbusres.2024.114500

Super, A. G. I. (2025, June 30). Future of Work: Top AI-Powered Workplace Analytics Trends to Watch in 2025. https://superagi.com/future-of-work-top-ai-powered-workplace-analytics-trends-to-watch-in-2025-and-how-to-stay-ahead-of-the-curve-with-employee-engagement-solutions/

Svenaeus, F. (2021). Empathy and togetherness online compared to IRL: A phenomenological account. *Journal of Phenomenological Psychology*, *52*(1), 78–95. DOI: 10.1163/15691624-12341384

Tah, E. N. (2024). Effects of artificial intelligence adoption on organizational success, productivity, and efficiency. https://comp.mga.edu/static/media/doctoralpapers/2024_Tah_0917113914.pdf

Talukder, M. B., Kumar, S., & Das, I. R. (2024). Implications of Blockchain Technology- Based Cryptocurrency in the cloud for the Hospitality Industry. In Darwish, D. (Ed.), (pp. 340–358). Advances in Computer and Electrical Engineering. IGI Global., DOI: 10.4018/979-8-3693-0900-1.ch018

Tannenbaum, S. I., & Wolfson, M. A. (2022). Informal (field-based) learning. *Annual Review of Organizational Psychology and Organizational Behavior*, *9*(1), 391–414. https://doi-org.ezproxy.mdx.ac.uk/10.1146/annurev-orgpsych-012420-083050. DOI: 10.1146/annurev-orgpsych-012420-083050

Tarafdar, M., Cooper, C. L., & Stich, J. F. (2017). The technostress trifecta: Techno eustress, techno distress, and design. *Information Systems Journal*, *29*(1), 6–42. DOI: 10.1111/isj.12169

Taylor, S. H., DiFranzo, D., Choi, Y. H., Sannon, S., & Bazarova, N. N. (2019). Accountability and empathy by design: Encouraging bystander intervention to cyberbullying on social media. *ACM on Human–Computer Interaction, 3*(CSCW). *Proceedings of the ACM on Human-Computer Interaction*, *118*(CSCW), 1–26. DOI: 10.1145/3359220

Teece, D. J., Pisano, G., & Shuen, A. (1998). Dynamic capabilities and strategic management. *Strategic Management Journal*, *18*(7), 509–533. DOI: 10.1002/(SICI)1097-0266(199708)18:7<509::AID-SMJ882>3.0.CO;2-Z

Teng, Z., Cai, Y., Gao, Y., Zhang, X., & Li, X. (2022). Factors affecting learners' adoption of an educational metaverse platform: An empirical study based on an extended UTAUT model. *Mobile Information Systems*, *2022*(1), 5479215. DOI: 10.1155/2022/5479215

Terblanche, N., & Cilliers, D. (2020). Factors that influence users' adoption of being coached by an artificial intelligence coach. *Philosophy of Coaching*, *5*(1), 61–70. DOI: 10.22316/poc/05.1.06

Terblanche, N., Molyn, J., De Haan, E., & Nilsson, V. O. (2022). Comparing artificial intelligence and human coaching goal attainment efficacy. *PLoS One*, *17*(6), e0270255. DOI: 10.1371/journal.pone.0270255 PMID: 35727801

Tewari, I., & Pant, M. (2020). Artificial intelligence reshaping human resource management: A review. In *2020 IEEE International Conference on Advent Trends in Multidisciplinary Research and Innovation (ICATMRI)* (pp. 1–4). IEEE. DOI: 10.1109/ICATMRI51801.2020.9398420

Thalpage, N. (2023). Unlocking the black box: XAI for trust and transparency. *Journal of Digital Art & Humanities*, *4*(1), 31–36. DOI: 10.33847/2712-8148.4.1_4

The Future of Jobs Report. 2023. (2023). *World Economic Forum*. https://www.weforum.org/publications/the-future-of-jobs-report-2023/

The Wellness Corner. (2025, July 23). Can AI Predict Mental Burnout Before It Happens? https://www.thewellnesscorner.com/blog/can-ai-detect-burnout-early

Theoharakis, V., Wapshott, R., & Cham, L. (2024). Work engagement and the impact of a social identity crafting approach to leadership: A case from Africa's air transport industry. [Preprint]. *Personnel Review*, *53*(7), 1729–1744. Advance online publication. DOI: 10.1108/PR-02-2023-0099

Tigre, F. B., Henriques, P. L., & Curado, C. (2025). The digital leadership emerging construct: A multi-method approach. *Management Review Quarterly*, *75*(1), 789–836. DOI: 10.1007/s11301-023-00395-9

Topol, E. (2019). *Deep medicine*. Basic Books.

Torre, F., Hägertz Engstam, L., & Teigland, R. (2025). *AI Leadership for Corporate Boards: Leading Responsible AI for Value Creation*. Springer Nature Switzerland., DOI: 10.1007/978-3-032-04087-9

Torres, I. (2024). Coaching to Leadership Trust Towards an Intrapreneurial Framework. *International Multidisciplinary Research Journal*. Advance online publication. DOI: 10.54476/ioer-imrj/687931

Trivedi, S. K., Vishnu, S., Singh, A., & Yadav, M. (2023). Research trends in sustainable E-payment systems: A study using topic modeling approach. *IEEE Transactions on Engineering Management*, *71*, 7511–7525. DOI: 10.1109/TEM.2023.3280216

Tsai, C.-H. (2024). The Relationship between Leadership Styles and Organizational Commitment – Exploring the Mediating Effect of Diversity, Equity, and Inclusion (DEI) Practices. *Global Journal of Human Resource Management*, *12*(6), 46–67. DOI: 10.37745/gjhrm.2013/vol12n64667

Tsang, E. W. K., & Zahra, S. A. (2008). Organizational unlearning. *Human Relations; Studies Towards the Integration of the Social Sciences*, *61*(10), 1435–1462. DOI: 10.1177/0018726708095710

Tuncer, S., & Ramirez, A. (2022). Exploring the Role of Trust During Human-AI Collaboration in Managerial Decision-Making Processes. In Chen, J. Y. C., Fragomeni, G., Degen, H., & Ntoa, S. (Eds.), *HCI International 2022 – Late Breaking Papers: Interacting with eXtended Reality and Artificial Intelligence* (Vol. 13518, pp. 541–557). Springer Nature Switzerland., DOI: 10.1007/978-3-031-21707-4_39

Turilli, M., & Floridi, L. (2009). The ethics of information transparency. *Ethics and Information Technology*, *11*(2), 105–112. DOI: 10.1007/s10676-009-9187-9

Tursunbayeva, A., Pagliari, C., Di Lauro, S., & Antonelli, G. (2022). The ethics of people analytics: Risks, opportunities and recommendations. *Personnel Review*, *51*(3), 900–921. DOI: 10.1108/PR-12-2019-0680

Tushar, P. N., Jaiswal, P., Shrivastava, P. C., Kumar, M., & Sundar, S. (2026). *Precision farming and smart irrigation systems for energy management.* In B. Soufiene (Ed.), *Enhancing autonomous and adaptive systems with AI and IoT* (pp. 251–288). IGI Global Scientific Publishing. DOI: 10.4018/979-8-3373-3146-1.ch009

Tushar, P. N., Shrivastava, P. C., Jaiswal, P., Singh, S., & Mishra, V. (2026). *Legal challenges in cloud computing.* In I. Oncioiu (Ed.), *Law and regulation of AI, blockchain, and digital rights* (pp. 63–102). IGI Global Scientific Publishing. DOI: 10.4018/979-8-3373-3186-7.ch003

Tushar, P. N., Shrivastava, P., Jaiswal, P., Mishra, S., & Yadav, A. (2026). *AI regulation in K–12 and higher education institutions.* In K. Carlson (Ed.), Ethical, legal, and pedagogical perspectives on AI in education. IGI Global. DOI: 10.4018/979-8-3373-3000-6

Tutar, H., & Güler, S. (2022). Digital leadership as a requirement for the new business ecosystem: a conceptual review. *Çankırı Karatekin Üniversitesi İktisadi ve İdari Bilimler Fakültesi Dergisi, 12*(3), 323-349.

Tversky, A., & Kahneman, D. (1974). Judgment under uncertainty: Heuristics and biases. *Science*, *185*(4157), 1124–1131. DOI: 10.1126/science.185.4157.1124 PMID: 17835457

Übellacker, T. (2025). *Making sense of AI limitations: How individual perceptions shape organizational readiness for AI adoption. arXiv preprint arXiv:2502.15870.*

Uddin, M. Z. (2025). *Trustworthy AI and explainability.* Springer. DOI: 10.1007/978-3-031-97359-8_4

Ueda, N., Kezar, A., Holcombe, E., Vigil, D., & Harper, J. (2024). Emotional Labor: Institutional Responsibility and Strategies to Offer Emotional Support for Leaders Engaging in Diversity, Equity, and Inclusion Work. *AERA Open*, *10*, 23328584241296092. Advance online publication. DOI: 10.1177/23328584241296092

Uğurlu, F. (2025). Yöneticilerin yapay zekaya yönelik algılarının liderlik stilleri üzerindeki etkileri. *Bucak İşletme Fakültesi Dergisi*, *8*(2), 117–127. DOI: 10.38057/bifd.1780438

Uhl-Bien, M. (2006). Relational leadership theory: Exploring the social processes of leadership and organizing. *The Leadership Quarterly*, *17*(6), 654–676. DOI: 10.1016/j.leaqua.2006.10.007

Uhl-Bien, M., & Arena, M. (2018). Leadership for organizational adaptability: A theoretical synthesis and integrative framework. *The Leadership Quarterly*, *29*(1), 89–104. DOI: 10.1016/j.leaqua.2017.12.009

Uncapher, M. R., & Wagner, A. D. (2018). Minds and brains of media multitaskers: Current findings and future directions. *Proceedings of the National Academy of Sciences of the United States of America*, *115*(40), 9889–9896. DOI: 10.1073/pnas.1611612115

Universal, A. I. (2025). AI-Driven Burnout Detection & Eco-Volunteering. https://www.universalai.in/wp-content/uploads/2025/01/AI-Driven-Burnout-Detection-Eco-Volunteering-Suhasini-Ghosh.pdf

Upadhyay, A. K., & Khandelwal, K. (2018). Applying artificial intelligence: Implications for recruitment. *Strategic HR Review*, *17*(5), 255–258. DOI: 10.1108/SHR-07-2018-0051

Urbani, R., Ferreira, C., & Lam, J. (2024). Managerial framework for evaluating AI chatbot integration: Bridging organizational readiness and technological challenges. *Business Horizons*, *67*(5), 595–606. DOI: 10.1016/j.bushor.2024.05.004

Usán Supervía, P., Salavera Bordás, C., Quílez Robres, A., Lozano Blasco, R., & Latorre Cosculluela, C. (2023). Empathy, self-esteem and satisfaction with life in adolescents. *Children and Youth Services Review*, *144*, 106755. Advance online publication. DOI: 10.1016/j.childyouth.2022.106755

Uzelac, A. (2010). Digital culture as a converging paradigm for technology and culture: Challenges for the culture sector

Vafeiadis, M., & Xiao, A. (2021). Fake news: How emotions, involvement, need for cognition and rebuttal evidence (story vs. informational) influence consumer reactions toward a targeted organization. *Public Relations Review*, *47*(4), 102088. DOI: 10.1016/j.pubrev.2021.102088

Van der Waa, J., Verdult, S., van den Bosch, K., van Diggelen, J., Haije, T., van der Stigchel, B., & Cocu, I. (2021). Moral decision making in human-agent teams: Human control and the role of explanations. *Frontiers in Robotics and AI*, *8*, 640647. DOI: 10.3389/frobt.2021.640647 PMID: 34124173

van Eck, N. J., & Waltman, L. (2010). Software survey: VOSviewer, a computer program for bibliometric mapping. *Scientometrics*, *84*(2), 523–538. DOI: 10.1007/s11192-009-0146-3

Van Rooy, D. (2024). Human–machine collaboration for enhanced decision-making in governance. *Data & Policy*, *6*, e60. DOI: 10.1017/dap.2024.72

Vanderheiden, E., Mayer, C.-H., & Barcelos, A. M. F. (Eds.). (2025). *Pedagogical Love in Adult Education: New Perspectives in Nurturing, Growth and Transformation*. Springer Nature Switzerland., DOI: 10.1007/978-3-031-82046-5

Vasconcelos Furtado, J.. (2024). *Influence factors of organisational citizenship behaviors in Latin American countries: A Brazilian case study*. Management Research. [Preprint], DOI: 10.1108/MRJIAM-07-2023-1439

Venkatesh, V., Thong, J. Y. L., Chan, F. K. Y., Hu, P. J. H., & Brown, S. A. (2022). Extending the digital well being concept: A research agenda. *Management Information Systems Quarterly*, *46*(1), 1–24. DOI: 10.25300/MISQ/2022/16320

Verduyn, P., Ybarra, O., Résibois, M., Jonides, J., & Kross, E. (2017). Do social network sites enhance or undermine subjective well-being? A critical review. *Social Issues and Policy Review*, *11*(1), 274–302. DOI: 10.1111/sipr.12033

Verma, S. (2023). The role of artificial intelligence in enhancing emotional intelligence for strategic decision-making: A study across academic institutions in Punjab. Educational Administration: Theory and Practice, 1436–1442. https://doi.org/DOI: 10.53555/kuey.v29i3.9605

Vial, G., Benitez, J., Schmitz, K., & Mathiassen, L. (2023). Digital transformation: A review and research agenda. *Information Systems Journal*, *33*(2), 341–377. DOI: 10.1111/isj.12391

Vial, G., Cameron, A. F., Giannelia, T., & Jiang, J. (2023). Managing artificial intelligence projects: Key insights from an AI consulting firm. *Information Systems Journal*, *33*(3), 669–691. DOI: 10.1111/isj.12420

Visave, J. (2025). *Transparency in AI for emergency management*. Springer.

Vivek, R., & Krupskyi, O. P. (2024). EI & AI in leadership and how it can affect future leaders. *European Journal of Management Issues*, *32*(3), 174–182. DOI: 10.15421/192415

Von Eschenbach, W. J. (2021). *Transparency and the black box problem: Why we do not trust AI*. Springer. 1.

Vossen, H. G. M., & Valkenburg, P. M. (2016). Do social media foster or curtail adolescents' empathy? A longitudinal study. *Computers in Human Behavior*, *63*, 118–124. DOI: 10.1016/j.chb.2016.05.040

Votto, A. M., Valecha, R., Najafirad, P., & Rao, H. R. (2021). Artificial intelligence in tactical human resource management: A systematic literature review. *International Journal of Information Management Data Insights*, *1*(2), 100047. DOI: 10.1016/j.jjimei.2021.100047

Vrontis, D., Christofi, M., Pereira, V., Tarba, S., Makrides, A., & Trichina, E. (2021). Artificial intelligence, robotics, advanced technologies and human resource management: A systematic review. *International Journal of Human Resource Management*, •••, 1–30.

Vygotsky, L. S. (1978). *Mind in society: The development of higher psychological processes*. Harvard University Press.

Waller, M. A., & Fawcett, S. E. (2013). Data science, predictive analytics, and big data: A revolution that will transform supply chain design and management. *Journal of Business Logistics*, *34*(2), 77–84. DOI: 10.1111/jbl.12010

Walliman, N. (2022). *Research Methods: The Basics* (3rd ed.). Routledge, Taylor & Francis Group.

Walter, S., & Stephan, A. (2023). Situated affectivity and mind shaping: Lessons from social psychology. *Emotion Review*, *15*(1), 3–16. DOI: 10.1177/17540739221112419

Walther, J. B. (2011). Theories of computer-mediated communication. *The Handbook of Interpersonal Communication*, 443–479.

Wang, C., Yao, J., & Gao, L. (2024). How do leaders' positive emotions improve employees' psychological safety in China? The moderating effect of leader-member exchange. *Heliyon*, *10*(3), e25481. DOI: 10.1016/j.heliyon.2024.e25481 PMID: 38352780

Wang, Y. (2021). Artificial intelligence in educational leadership: A symbiotic role of human-artificial intelligence decision-making. *Journal of Educational Administration, 59*(3), 256–270. DOI: 10.1108/JEA-10-2020-0216

Wang, Y., Leon, P. G., Acquisti, A., Cranor, L. F., Forget, A., & Sadeh, N. (2014). A field trial of privacy nudges for Facebook. In *Proceedings of the SIGCHI Conference on Human Factors in Computing Systems* (pp. 2367–2376). https://doi.org/ DOI: 10.1145/2556288.2557413

Watermeyer, R.. (2021). Pandemic digitalization. *British Journal of Educational Technology, 52*(4), 1418–1430. DOI: 10.1111/bjet.13177

Wati, I., Suprayo, T., Junaedi, I., & Cahyono, A. (2024). MATHEMATICAL THINKING PROCESS OF STUDENTS IN SOLVING CONTROVERSIAL MATHEMATICS PROBLEMS BASED ON DECISION-MAKING TYPES. *AKSIOMA: Jurnal Program Studi Pendidikan Matematika, 13*(4), 1313. DOI: 10.24127/ajpm.v13i4.9641

Weick, K. E. (1995). Sensemaking in organizations. *Sage (Atlanta, Ga.).*

Weick, K. E. (1995). *Sensemaking in organizations.* Sage Publications.

Weick, K. E., Sutcliffe, K. M., & Obstfeld, D. (2005). Organizing and the process of sensemaking. *Organization Science, 16*(4), 409–421. DOI: 10.1287/orsc.1050.0133

Weidmann, B., Xu, Y., & Deming, D. J. (2025). Measuring human leadership skills with artificially intelligent agents. *arXiv preprint arXiv:2508.02966.*

Weisz, E., & Cikara, M. (2021). Strategic regulation of empathy. *Trends in Cognitive Sciences, 25*(3), 213–227. DOI: 10.1016/j.tics.2020.12.002

Weisz, E., Ong, D. C., Carlson, R. W., & Zaki, J. (2021). Building empathy through motivation-based interventions. *Emotion (Washington, D.C.), 21*(5), 990–999. DOI: 10.1037/emo0000929

Wells, D. L., Moorman, R. H., & Werner, J. M. (2007). The impact of the perceived purpose of electronic performance monitoring on an array of attitudinal variables. *Human Resource Development Quarterly, 18*(1), 121–138. DOI: 10.1002/hrdq.1194

Wendt, D. W. (2025). *AI Strategy and Security: A Roadmap for Secure, Responsible, and Resilient AI Adoption.* Apress. DOI: 10.1007/979-8-8688-1733-5

Wen, Y., Wang, J., & Chen, X. (2025). Trust and AI weight: Human-AI collaboration in organizational management decision-making. *Frontiers in Organizational Psychology, 3*, 1419403. DOI: 10.3389/forgp.2025.1419403

West, C. P., Dyrbye, L. N., & Shanafelt, T. D. (2018). Physician burnout. *Lancet, 388*(10057), 2272–2281. DOI: 10.1016/S0140-6736(16)31279-X PMID: 27692469

Westerman, G., Bonnet, D., & McAfee, A. (2014). The nine elements of digital transformation. *MIT Sloan Management Review, 55*(3), 1–6.

Westin, A. F. (1967). *Privacy and freedom.* Atheneum.

Why there will be plenty of jobs in the future – even with AI. (2024). *World Economic Forum.* https://www.weforum.org/agenda/2024/02/artificial-intelligence-ai-jobs-future/

Wikipedia. (2023). Occupational burnout. https://en.wikipedia.org/wiki/Occupational_burnout

Wilmer, H. H., & Chein, J. M. (2016). Mobile technology habits: Patterns of association among device usage, intertemporal preference, impulse control, and reward sensitivity. *Psychonomic Bulletin & Review, 23*(5), 1607–1614. DOI: 10.3758/s13423-016-1011-z

Wilson, H. J., & Daugherty, P. R. (2018). *Human + machine: Reimagining work in the age of AI.*

Wilson, H. J., & Daugherty, P. R. (2018). *Human + machine: Reimagining work in the age of AI.* Harvard Business Review Press.

Wilton, A. R., Pereira, B. M., Myers, L., Sandhu, H., Chibalin, A., & Preece, D. (2024). The Burnout Prediction Using Wearable and ArtIficial Intelligence (BROWNIE) Study: Integrating Physiological, Psychological, and Workplace Data. *BMC Nursing, 23*(1), 45. https://pmc.ncbi.nlm.nih.gov/articles/PMC10863108/. DOI: 10.1186/s12912-024-01711-8 PMID: 38225570

Wolff, S. B., Pescosolido, A. T., & Druskat, V. U. (2002). Emotional intelligence as the basis of leadership emergence in self-managing teams. *The Leadership Quarterly, 13*(5), 505–522. DOI: 10.1016/S1048-9843(02)00141-8

Wong, C. A., Cummings, G. G., & Ducharme, L. (2013). The relationship between nursing leadership and patient outcomes. *Journal of Nursing Management, 21*(5), 709–724. DOI: 10.1111/jonm.12116 PMID: 23865924

Woodcock, J. (2022). Artificial intelligence at work: The problem of managerial control from call centers to transport platforms. *Frontiers in Artificial Intelligence, 5*, 888817. DOI: 10.3389/frai.2022.888817 PMID: 36092976

Wood, D., Bruner, J. S., & Ross, G. (1976). The role of tutoring in problem solving. *Journal of Child Psychology and Psychiatry, and Allied Disciplines, 17*(2), 89–100. DOI: 10.1111/j.1469-7610.1976.tb00381.x PMID: 932126

Wood, M. A., Bukowski, W. M., & Lis, E. (2016). The digital self: How social media serves as a setting that shapes youth's emotional experiences. *Adolescent Research Review, 1*(2), 163–173. DOI: 10.1007/s40894-015-0014-8

Woods, A., Zajac, S., Middleton, E., Cavanaugh, K., Hayes, W., Johnson, S., & Holladay, C. (2024). Doing the Work: The Role of Inclusive Leadership in Promoting Psychological Safety and Openness to Diversity Through Diversity, Equity, and Inclusion Practices. *Psychology of Leaders and Leadership, 27*(1), 115–142. DOI: 10.1037/mgr0000158

Wooldridge, M. (2021). *A brief history of artificial intelligence*. Flatiron Books.

Workday. (2022). *Employee experience and sentiment analytics*. Workday Inc.

World Economic Forum. (2020). *The future of jobs report 2020*. World Economic Forum.

World Health Organization. (2019). Burn-out an "occupational phenomenon": International Classification of Diseases. https://www.who.int/news/item/28-05-2019-burn-out-an-occupational-phenomenon-international-classification-of-diseases

Wu, T. J., Li, J. M., & Wu, Y. J. (2022). Employees' job insecurity perception and unsafe behaviours in human–machine collaboration. *Management Decision, 60*(9), 2409–2432. Advance online publication. DOI: 10.1108/MD-09-2021-1257

Wu, X., Liu, Q., Qu, H., & Wang, J. (2023). The effect of algorithmic management and workers' coping behavior: An exploratory qualitative research of Chinese food-delivery platform. *Tourism Management, 96*, 104716. DOI: 10.1016/j.tourman.2022.104716

Wu, Y. J., Antone, B., DeChurch, L., & Contractor, N. (2023). Information sharing in a hybrid workplace: Understanding the role of ease-of-use perceptions of communication technologies in advice-seeking relationship maintenance. *Journal of Computer-Mediated Communication, 28*(4), zmad025. DOI: 10.1093/jcmc/zmad025

Xu, G., Xue, M., & Zhao, J. (2023). The association between artificial intelligence awareness and employee depression: The mediating role of emotional exhaustion and the moderating role of perceived organisational support. *International Journal of Environmental Research and Public Health, 20*(6), 5147. DOI: 10.3390/ijerph20065147 PMID: 36982055

Yadav, M., & Rangnekar, S. (2016). Role clarity and organizational citizenship behaviour: Does tenure matter? A study on Indian power sector. *Global Business Review*, *17*(3, suppl), 207S–224S. DOI: 10.1177/0972150916631216

Yadav, M., Rangnekar, S., & Srivastava, A. P. (2019). Demographic variables as moderators between QWL and OCB. *Industrial and Commercial Training*, *51*(7/8), 396–408. DOI: 10.1108/ICT-04-2018-0040

Yadav, R., & Lata, P. (2019). Role of emotional intelligence in effective leadership. *International Journal on Leadership*, *7*(2), 27–32.

Yan, L. (2025). From passive tool to socio-cognitive teammate: A conceptual framework for agentic AI in human-AI collaborative learning. *arXiv preprint arXiv:2508.14825v1*.

Yen, R., Feng, L., Mehra, B., Pang, C. C., Hu, S., & Li, Z. (2023). StoryChat: Designing a narrative-based viewer participation tool for live streaming chatrooms. In *CHI Conference on Human Factors in Computing Systems* (Paper 795, pp. 1–18). https://doi.org/DOI: 10.1145/3544548.3580912

Yeşil, S. (2011). Sanal takımlar: Kritik başarı faktörleri üzerine derinlemesine bir bakış ve bir değerlendirme. *Journal of Graduate School of Social Sciences*, *15*(1).

Yıldız, F. Z. (2025). İnsan kaynakları yönetiminde yapay zeka: Uygulamalar ve gelecek yönelimleri üzerine kapsamlı bir çalışma. *Yönetim Bilimleri Dergisi*, *23*(57), 1569–1594. DOI: 10.35408/comuybd.1569970

Yılmaz, C. (2023). Uzaktan çalışma kabusu: İnsan kaynakları yöneticilerinin uzaktan çalışmada kullandıkları uzaktan denetim mekanizmaları. *Journal of Mehmet Akif Ersoy University Economics and Administrative Sciences Faculty*, *10*(3), 1956–1975.

Yin, J. J., & Hoang, K. (2025). AI-enabled knowledge renewal: The role of leaders' AI attitudes and unlearning in enhancing employees' creative performance. *Journal of Knowledge Management*. Advance online publication. DOI: 10.1108/JKM-02-2025-0209

Yogman, M., Garner, A., Hutchinson, J., Hirsh-Pasek, K., & Michnick Golinkoff, R. (2018). The power of play: A pediatric role in enhancing development in young children. *Pediatrics*, *142*(3), e20182058. DOI: 10.1542/peds.2018-2058

Yoo, Y., Henfridsson, O., & Lyytinen, K. (2012). The new organizing logic of digital innovation. *Information Systems Research*, *23*(4), 1398–1408. DOI: 10.1287/isre.1120.0426

Yost, A. B., Behrend, T. S., Howardson, G., Darrow, J. B., & Jensen, J. M. (2018). Reactance to electronic surveillance: A test of antecedents and outcomes. *Journal of Business and Psychology, 34*(1), 71–86. DOI: 10.1007/s10869-018-9532-2

Yozi, K., & Mbokota, S. (2024). Leadership for the future: Empowering virtual teams with emotional intelligence. *Journal of Leadership & Organizational Development, 43*(2), 189–204.

Yukl, G., & Gardner, W. (2020). *Leadership in organizations* (9th ed.). Pearson.

Yurdasever, E. (2024). İşletmelerde çalışanlara yönelik duygu analizinin uygulanması: Potansiyel faydalar ve zorluklar. *Ömer Halisdemir Üniversitesi İktisadi ve İdari Bilimler Fakültesi Dergisi, 17*(3), 462–488.

Zamir, N. A. (2025). THE ROLE OF LEADERSHIP IN SUPPORTING ARTIFICIAL INTELLIGENCE (AI) INTEGRATION IN ORGANIZATIONS.

Zárate-Torres, R., Rey-Sarmiento, C. F., Acosta-Prado, J. C., Gómez-Cruz, N. A., Rodríguez Castro, D. Y., & Camargo, J. (2025). Influence of leadership on human–artificial intelligence collaboration. *Behavioral Sciences (Basel, Switzerland), 15*(7), 873. DOI: 10.3390/bs15070873 PMID: 40723657

Zarins, S., & Konrath, S. (2017). Changes over time in compassion-related variables in the United States. In Seppälä, E. M., Simon-Thomas, E., Brown, S. L., Worline, M. C., Cameron, C. D., & Doty, J. R. (Eds.), *The Oxford handbook of compassion science* (pp. 331–352). Oxford University Press.

Zaslavskaia, V. (2024). *Intelligent Data Management for Small Business Enhancement.* KnE Social Sciences., DOI: 10.18502/kss.v9i32.17424

Zeb, A., Ahmad, S., & Saeed, G. (2018). Leadership effectiveness and organizational performance: Exploring gaps in the existing literature. *Business and Economic Review, 10*(01), 95–106. DOI: 10.22547/BER/10.1.4

Zeike, S., Bradbury, K., Lindert, L., & Pfaff, H. (2019). Digital leadership skills and associations with psychological well being. *International Journal of Environmental Research and Public Health, 16*(14), 2628. DOI: 10.3390/ijerph16142628 PMID: 31340579

Zervas, I., & Triantari, S. (2025). Trust and Ethical Influence in Organizational Nudging: Insights from Human Resource and Marketing Practice. *Journal of Theoretical and Applied Electronic Commerce Research, 20*(3), 176. DOI: 10.3390/jtaer20030176

Zhang, Q., Wang, F., Liao, G., & Li, M. (2025). How does AI trust foster innovative performance under paternalistic leadership? The roles of AI crafting and leader's AI opportunity perception. *Behavioral Sciences (Basel, Switzerland), 15*(8), 1064. DOI: 10.3390/bs15081064 PMID: 40867421

Zhang, S., Yu, J., Xu, X., Yin, C., Lu, Y., Yao, B., Tory, M., Padilla, L. M., Caterino, J., Zhang, P., & Wang, D. (2024). Rethinking Human-AI Collaboration in Complex Medical Decision Making: A Case Study in Sepsis Diagnosis. *Proceedings of the CHI Conference on Human Factors in Computing Systems*, 1–18. DOI: 10.1145/3613904.3642343

Zhang, X., Qian, J., Wang, B., & Chen, M. (2020). The role of reward omission in empowering leadership and employee outcomes: A moderated mediation model. *Human Resource Management Journal, 30*(2), 226–243. DOI: 10.1111/1748-8583.12260

Zhong, L. (2017). Indicators of digital leadership in the context of K-12 education. [JETDE]. *Journal of Educational Technology Development and Exchange, 10*(1), 3. DOI: 10.18785/jetde.1001.03

Zhou, L., Zhang, L., & Konz, N. (2022). Computer vision techniques in manufacturing. *IEEE Transactions on Systems, Man, and Cybernetics. Systems, 53*(1), 105–117. DOI: 10.1109/TSMC.2022.3166397

Zhou, M. X., Mark, G., Li, J., & Yang, H. (2019). Trusting virtual agents: The effect of personality. *ACM Transactions on Interactive Intelligent Systems, 9*(2–3), 1–36. DOI: 10.1145/3232077

Zimmerman, B. J. (2000). Attaining self-regulation. *Handbook of Self-Regulation*, 13–39.

Živković, S. (2022). Inspiring digital transformation: An integrative leadership competency framework. *Ekonomska Misao i Praksa, 31*(1), 237–254. DOI: 10.17818/EMIP/2022/1.11

Zuboff, S. (2019). *The age of surveillance capitalism*. PublicAffairs.

Zwane, N. C. (2025). An integrated framework for academic staff well-being: Positive and relational lenses. *SA Journal of Human Resource Management, 23*. Advance online publication. DOI: 10.4102/sajhrm.v23i0.3032

About the Contributors

Nitin Vihari Poluru is the senior lecturer in the Business School at Middlesex University Dubai. He holds an MBA and a Ph.D. in Human Resource Management. His research has earned publication in leading international journals of repute in Human Resource Management and Organizational Studies. He is a Chartered Member of the Chartered Institute of Personnel and Development (CIPD), UK. He is a Senior Fellow of the Higher Education Academy, UK. His teaching and research interests are Leadership, Human Resource Management, Corporate Sustainability Leadership, Organizational Behaviour, and Business Research Methods.

***

Tushar received his B.Tech in Electronics and Communication from U.P.T.U., Lucknow, in 2007, followed by an M.B.A. from Jiwaji University, Gwalior, in 2009. He later completed his M.E. in Communication Control and Networking from M.P.C.T., Gwalior, where he was honored as a Gold Medalist. He has completed his Ph.D. research work and is presently serving as an Assistant Professor at the United College of Engineering & Research, Prayagraj, bringing more than 17 years of academic experience. His key research interests include antenna and microwave communication, QCA design, artificial intelligence, machine learning, and deep learning.

Rituparna Basak, an Assistant Professor of Psychology at Muralidhar Girls' College, Kolkata, since 2016, earned her Ph.D. in Applied Psychology from the University of Calcutta. She received JRF and SRF fellowships from the Indian Statistical Institute, Kolkata. In addition to her role, she teaches as a guest faculty member at various institutions. Dr. Basak actively researches various organizational, psychological, social, and educational issues across diverse groups. She has presented numerous papers at national and international conferences and published extensively in reputed journals, contributing significantly to the field of psychology.

Rajashree K. C is a Biomedical Engineer with a Master's in Business Administration from Saveetha University, specializing in Hospital Management and Marketing, and holds a Ph.D. in Healthcare Management. An energetic and enthusiastic professor, she excels in academics and as a multitasker, organizing seminars, workshops, cultural programs, and other extra-curricular activities. She serves as the Coordinator of NSS Unit of Saveetha School of Management, leading them to achieve multiple accolades including the Best Club award. A prominent researcher with publications in Web of Science, Scopus, and UGC-listed journals, she actively enhances her expertise through conferences, workshops, MOOCs, and certifications, including Quality Coordination in Hospitals. Awarded the "Young Academician Award" and "Young Teacher Award," she is passionate about innovation, student skill development, and inspiring young minds through exemplary teaching and mentorship.

Tanusree Chakraborty is a Ph. D in Applied Psychology from Calcutta University, MA (Applied Psychology) with Specialization in Organizational Psychology, PGDHRM and MBA (HR), with 20 plus years of work experience. She has been associated with a number of B-Schools and Universities of repute in Kolkata, Madurai, Bangalore, and Chennai. Presently she is working with Administrative Staff College of India (ASCI), Hyderabad as a Faculty in the Centre for Management Studies. Having thoroughly good academic track record with university ranks, she is an Ex-research fellow of Indian Council of Medical Research. She has around 60 publications under her credit in reputed journals and books, among which Internet Research Journal, International Journal of Human Resource Management, International Journal of Productivity and Performance Management are great feathers in her cap. She has presented research papers in 80 plus international conferences of repute, where she has been awarded the Best Paper Award many times. She has conducted Management Development Programmes with the State Productivity Councils and National Productivity Councils. She has trained practicing managers of several Public and Private sector companies, in the areas of Behavioral Sciences and Human Resource Management. As a psychologist she has conducted Psychometric testing with 12,000 plus employees. As a trainer, she has trained 15,000 plus employees in her career. Companies where she has been a resource person include Indian Oil, BHEL, NHPC, NTPC, THDCIL, WBPDC, DVC, BPCL, DRDO, PFC, GAIL, ONGC, Exide Industries, NMDC, Power Grid Corp, Department of Science and Technology- GoI, National Institute of Communications Finance etc. Among the banks, she has associated herself as a trainer with State

Bank of India, Canara Bank, Central Bank of India, Punjab National Bank, Axis Bank, etc. She has published books with the IGI Global Publishers, titled Appreciative Inquiry Approaches to Organizational Transformation, with Taylor and Francis, CRC Press, Human Resource Management in a Post-Epidemic Global Environment-Roles, Strategies, and Implementations, Agile Leadership for Industry 4.0 and Interdisciplinary Approaches in Management Education, Digitalization in Higher Education, Gender Equality in Modern Perspectives etc. A few more books are in the advanced stages of forthcoming publication. She has been a panel member in admission and recruitment processes, GDPIs conducted in academic institutes and corporate. Besides, she has also been a regular faculty for management institutes of repute including ASCI, teaching MBA and PGDM, where she has been a passionate teacher supporting students in academics and other institution building activities. She has been an active member in clubs and committees of the institutes she has worked for. She has been a reviewer and editor of reputed books and journals, and Editor-in Chief of the ASCI PGDM Chronicle- A Bi-annual Newsletter.

Iva Rani Das is a dynamic individual, currently pursuing her MPhil in the Marketing Department of Dhaka University. Alongside her academic pursuits, she holds key positions as an Assistant Director at the Daffodil Institute of Technology and serves as Guest Faculty in the Business Faculty at the Asian Institute of Business and Technology. Her scholarly achievements extend beyond the classroom, with publications in esteemed national and international journals. Iva's dedication to education and research makes her a driving force in the fields of business and marketing.

Narayanage Jayantha Dewasiri, Ph.D., is a Chartered Manager at the Chartered Management Institute, UK. He conducts research at the Open University of Sri Lanka and the Sri Lanka Institute of Marketing. He is the founding Editor-in-Chief of the South Asian Journal of Marketing. His research interests are in corporate social responsibility, corporate governance, marketing and sales, management, and finance. He is working as the Head of Field Force at the HMD Global Inc., Sri Lanka. He also serves as a senior lecturer at University of Sabaragamuwa, Sri Lanka. He can be reached at dnjay@ou.ac.lk

Divya Dubey Lecturer, Jindal Institute of Behavioural Sciences (JIBS) O. P. Jindal Global University, Sonipat, India Email: ddishu67@gmail.com. Dr. Divya Dubey is a Lecturer at the Jindal Institute of Behavioural Sciences (JIBS), O. P. Jindal Global University, Sonipat, India. She holds a PhD in Forensic Psychology and is a licensed expert in Layered Voice Analysis (LVA 6.50), a forensic tool used for deception detection and behavioral risk assessment. She earned a Master's degree in Psychology with specialization in Industrial and Clinical Psychology from the University of Lucknow and a postgraduate diploma in Forensic Psychology from the National Forensic Sciences University (NFSU), Gujarat. She has undertaken advanced training in criminal profiling at The Forensic Criminology Institute, Alaska, USA, and holds a postgraduate diploma in Cyber Security from Amity University, Dubai. Dr. Dubey has professional experience working with incarcerated populations at Tihar Jail, New Delhi, where she was associated with the Mental Health Foundation (India) on the SAMARTHAN project, delivering Psychological First Aid and supporting correctional mental health interventions. She has previously served as adjunct faculty at Amity University, Dubai, Executive Director at A-to-Z Decisions Consultancy, and as a consultant with Spire Solutions, Dubai, providing specialized LVA training to Dubai Police and the Ministry of Defence, Abu Dhabi. Her research interests include adolescent delinquency, criminal propensity, emotional intelligence, and correctional and rehabilitation interventions.

Karan Gupta is a BBA Administration student at CHRIST (Deemed to be) University, Delhi NCR.

Sharad Gupta is a seasoned educator and corporate trainer with over two decades of experience in academia, research, and professional development. He is currently pursuing a Ph.D. focused on Blockchain-enabled Employee Life Cycle Frameworks at CHRIST (Deemed to be University), India. He holds an e-Diploma in CORe from Harvard Business School, along with advanced degrees in Education (M.Ed.), Commerce (M.Com.), and an MBA in Marketing and Finance. Dr. Gupta serves as an Assistant Professor at CHRIST (Deemed to be University), Pune Lavasa Campus, where he specializes in Human Resource Management, Leadership Development, and Corporate Strategy. He has held key administrative roles, including Convener of the Institution Innovation Council, fostering innovation and entrepreneurial growth. With international teaching experience in Malaysia and the Maldives, he has guided MBA, Ph.D., and Professional Doctorate students across culturally diverse environments. Dr. Gupta has co-authored several books, including Innovative Pedagogy: A Beginner's Guide to Modern Teaching Strategies and WealthWise: Lessons from India's Warren Buffett. His research contributions extend to journals and conferences, focusing on HR analytics, AI in education, and blockchain applications. Recognized for his expertise in instructional design, Dr. Gupta has developed e-learning modules, designed corporate training programs, and managed digital learning platforms during his tenure with leading organizations like Bajaj Housing Finance and ICICI Bank. He brings a unique blend of academic rigor and industry acumen, making impactful contributions to both fields. Dr. Gupta continues to innovate in education and research, bridging the gap between academic theories and real-world applications, and inspiring the next generation of learners and leaders.

Vibhuti Jain is Working as an Assistant Professor at Department of Management Studies, Graphic Era (Deemed to be University)

Pooja Jaiswal received her B.Sc. degree in Science from J.K. Institute of Applied Physics & Technology, University of Allahabad, in 2007. She earned her B.Tech and M.Tech degrees in Electronics and Communication from the same institute in 2010 and 2012, respectively. She has served as an Assistant Professor at the United College of Engineering & Research, Prayagraj, with over five years of academic experience. Her research interests include quantum computing, image processing, and deep learning applications. She is currently pursuing her Ph.D. at J.K. Institute of Applied Physics & Technology, University of Allahabad, India.

Babita Jha is an associate professor at CHRIST (Deemed to be) University, Delhi NCR. She has 18+ years of teaching experience.

Manish Kumar is presently working as Associate Professor in Department of Biochemistry, Faculty of Science, P. K. University, village-Thanra, Karera, Shivpuri (M.P.)- 473660, India. He did his B.Sc. (H) Biochemistry, M.Sc. Biochemistry from Bundelkhand University, Jhansi (U.P.) and M.Phil. Biochemistry from Singhania University, Jhunjhunu (Rajasthan). He did his doctoral degree Ph.D. Biochemistry from Sam Higginbottom University of Agriculture, Technology and Sciences, Prayagraj (U.P.). He received best thesis research award for Ph.D. Biochemistry from UPKAR's foundation, Lucknow as well as young scientist award in biochemistry field. He has Co-supervised 14 PG students and supervising 6 Ph.D. students. He has been published many research papers and review papers in national and international journals with good Impact Factor and NAAS rating. He has teaching experience more than 8 years and research experience more than 14 years.

Pardeep Kumar Assistant Professor, Department of Mathematics, Lovely Professional University, Phagwara, Punjab, India Dr. Pardeep Kumar holds a Ph.D. in Mathematics from Lovely Professional University (2021). His research expertise lies in Stochastic Processes, with a specialized focus on Markov Models, Engineering System Reliability, and Reliability Theory. He actively contributes to the modeling and reliability analysis of IoT-enabled and sensor-integrated systems for next-generation engineering applications. Dr. Kumar has a profound command of Stochastic Modelling, Reliability Testing, and advanced analytical methods for complex system behavior under uncertainty. His work emphasises practical implementations in smart technologies and cyber-physical systems. He has an exceptional academic track record, having qualified the prestigious CSIR-UGC NET twice, securing All India Ranks (AIR) of 15 and 32, respectively. To date, Dr. Kumar has published 26 high-quality research papers in reputed national and international journals, reflecting his continued contribution to the advancement of mathematical reliability and its engineering applications.

Sanjeev Kumar Is a Professor in Lovely Professional University Punjab India. He received Undergraduate in Hotel Management from Osmania University, Postgraduate in Tourism Management from Madurai Kamaraj University. He completed Doctor of Philosophy in Hospitality Management in 2019 from Amity University Jaipur India. His research areas lies in food Service Industry, his research focuses on Alcoholic beverages, Event management and Sustainable Management Practices, Metaverse, AI Machine Learning and Artificial Intelligence. He published more than 120 research papers, articles and chapters in Scopus Indexed, UGC Approved and peer reviewed Journals and books. Dr. Sanjeev Kumar participated and acted as resource person in various National and International conferences, seminars, session chair, research workshops and industry talks and his work has been widely cited. Dr. Sanjeev also edited more than 20 books with various International Publishers such as IGI Global, Cambridge Scholars, Emerald, CABI, Bentham Science, Taylor & Francis. Dr Sanjeev is an active researcher and has published numerous research articles in prestigious National and International journals and books.

Richa Kapoor Mehra is working as an Associate Professor of Philosophy and Area chair of Social Sciences and Humanities (SSH) at O.P Jindal Global University, India, she has earned her PhD in Philosophy from Jawaharlal Nehru University, Delhi. While pursuing PhD, she was recipient of Junior Research Fellowship from prestigious Indian Council of Philosophical Research (ICPR). She has completed Masters and bachelor's in philosophy from Miranda House, University of Delhi. She was awarded with Miranda House award and Delhi University rankers prize for scoring highest marks in bachelor's program. She has also worked at Miranda House, University of Delhi, Amity University, Noida, B.M.L Munjal University and IIIT Kalyani. Recently she has designed a course on Critical Thinking and Analysis for undergraduate business students at O.P Jindal Business School. Dr. Mehra has launched the department of philosophy at Amity University, Noida and hence designed various philosophy course for undergraduate students. She has been awarded with the Excellent Academician Award, in an International Conference organized by University of Sri Jayewardenepura, Sri Lanka. She has presented several research

Ali Najeeb is the Vice Rector and Chief Operating Officer (COO) of Villa College (VC), Maldives and CEO of Bristol Institute of Business Management (BIBM), Sri-Lanka. He is also an Adjunct Associate Professor at the School of Hospitality, Tourism and Events, Taylor's University, Malaysia. He holds a PhD in Management and HR strategy at the University of Wollongong, Australia, a Master's Degree in Human Resource Management at the University of Newcastle, Australia, and BA in Business Studies from the University of the South Pacific, Fiji. He is a Chartered Professional Member of Chartered Institute of Personnel and Development (CIPD) and a Certified Professional Member of Australian Human Resource Institute (AHRI). Besides his official roles, he also holds several advisory roles and membership in local and international NGOs and professional bodies. His research interests include higher education leadership, governance and management, industrial relations, employment law and labour issues in small island states,sustainability, artificial intelligence, migrant workers, HRM/ER in tourism and hospitality industry. He has published several research papers in refereed international journals, shared his experience in local and international panel discussions and presented his research work in international scholarly conferences. He is a recipient of the Emerald Literati Award for Excellence 2014 – the outstanding paper award. Dr Najeeb is a former school principal and worked as a Director of the Education and Development Centre in the Ministry of Education. He is also a former fulltime member of the Employment Tribunal, Maldives. Besides his administrative, teaching and research work, he is actively engaged in management and corporate consultancy and training.

P. Praveen Kumar holds an MCom, MBA, and PhD in Finance from Pondicherry University. He secured the University 1st Rank in his Under Graduation. His teaching interests include Financial Accounting, Financial Management, Mergers & Acquisitions, Security Analysis & Portfolio Management, and other finance-related courses. His research interests extend to multi-disciplinary areas.

Navya Puttaraju is a Human Resources professional with international experience across the Middle East, South Asia, and Africa. She holds a Master of Arts in Human Resource Management and Development from Middlesex University, Dubai and is an Associate member of the Chartered Institute of Personnel and Development (CIPD). She applies Lean Six Sigma principles as a certified practitioner to support structured process improvement and operational efficiency in HR service delivery. She also utilises Agile and Scrum methodologies as a Certified ScrumMaster® to enable iterative development and implementation of HR digitalisation initiatives. She is an International Coaching Federation (ICF)

Certified Coach, integrating coaching approaches into change management and organisational development practices.

SK Pooja is a very enthusiastic and determined PGDM student in the Administrative Staff College of India, specialising in Human Resources and Marketing. She is quite inclined towards People Management and has a goal of making a difference in the field with great strategies. She believes in the art of People Management and is curious and passionate about research into developing Innovative HR Solutions, Talent Acquisition, and Employee Engagement. She is an analytical person and is great with people; therefore, she would be one emerging professional who can bring change to tomorrow's HR shape.

Ramadevi Vitthal Salunkhe is an Assistant Professor in the Department of Artificial Intelligence at G. H. Raisoni College of Engineering, Nagpur, India, and a Research Scholar pursuing her Ph.D. in Computer Science and Engineering at VNIT, Nagpur. She holds an M.Tech and B.E. in Computer Science and Engineering and has over 11 years of experience spanning academia, central and state government institutions, and the IT industry. Her research focuses on artificial intelligence, machine learning, big data analytics, and intelligent automation. She has authored and co-authored books, several IGI Global book chapters, and presented at international conferences, including ICMCER 2024 (Thailand) and ARET 2025 (India). She also serves in academic leadership roles, mentors student projects, organizes technical events, and is a member of the International Association of Engineers (IAENG).

Smita Dattatray Salunkhe is an Assistant Professor at KES Society's Rajarambapu Institute of Technology (Autonomous), Rajaramnagar, Islampur, Maharashtra, India, affiliated with Shivaji University, Kolhapur. She holds expertise in her domain and is actively engaged in teaching, research, and academic development. Her research interests include emerging technologies and their applications, and she has contributed to academic publications and scholarly activities.

Gülizar Gülcan Şeremet completed his undergraduate education at Ankara University in Türkiye in 2014.She received his master's degrees in Healthcare Management from GaziUniversity. She received his doctora degrees in Healthcare Management from Ankara Hacı Bayram Veli University. She is currently a faculty member in the Department of Healthcare Management at Çankırı Karatekin University.

Mushtaq Ahmad Shah is a finance expert with a PhD in Infrastructure Finance. He teaches banking, finance and economics at Lovely Professional University in

India. Dr. Shah has over 8 years of experience teaching and researching at various institutions. He's written articles in academic journals and presented his work at conferences on banking, partnerships between public and private sectors, and behavioral finance.

Geetha Priya has Overall 20+ years of experience along with PMP certified project lead with experienced in all stages of the project lifecycle from inception through monitoring and closing to deliver projects that exceed expectations on time and within allocated budget. Responsible and accountable for the coordinated management and client for the projects directed towards business and other organizational benefits.Automation / AI projects have been successfully completed and benefited with cost savings. Several on-site transitions and transformation projects have been implemented from onsite to India. Rich exposure in Due Diligence, transition and transformation projects relates to Supplier chain, P2P, T&E, Vendor management, Treasury, Procurement & Telecom Billing industries. Expertise in the areas of Inventory Management (IM), Warehouse Management (WM), Sales and Distribution. Certified in Lean six sigma Green Belt, PMP and proven ability to streamline, increase productivity, improve internal/external customer relationships. Expertise in Digital automation projects and programs towards clients' products and projects.

Koushik Vedula is currently pursuing a Post Graduate Diploma in Management (PGDM) at the Administrative Staff College of India (ASCI). His academic interests are centered around Finance and Human Resources (HR), with a strong focus on the synergy between Technology and Finance. Koushik is particularly passionate about exploring how technological advancements can revolutionize financial management and decision-making processes. He has actively participated in various projects and competitions in the fields of finance and management, aiming to contribute to research at the intersection of technology, finance, and organizational behavior.

Bhumika Wadhwani is an undergraduate student pursuing a Bachelor of Business Administration in Business Analytics at CHRIST (Deemed to be University), Lavasa, India. Her academic and research interests lie in marketing, human behavior, content strategy, leadership, and emerging technologies. She is particularly interested in exploring how artificial intelligence and digital innovations influence consumer behavior, organizational dynamics, and leadership practices in modern work environments. Alongside her academic pursuits, she has gained practical experience in content development, research, and digital strategy through internships with social sector organizations, contributing to report writing, social media communication, and analytical projects. Her interdisciplinary approach combines business analytics with creativity and human-centered thinking. Bhumika aims to contribute to research and practice that bridges data-driven insights with strategic communication, leadership development, and evolving digital ecosystems.

Mohit Yadav is an Professor in the area of Human Resource Management at Jindal Global Business School (JGBS). He has a rich blend of work experience from both Academics as well as Industry. Prof. Mohit holds a Ph.D. from Department of Management Studies, Indian Institute of Technology Roorkee (IIT Roorkee) and has completed Master of Human Resource and Organizational Development (MHROD) from prestigious Delhi School of Economics, University of Delhi. He also holds a B.Com (Hons.) degree from University of Delhi and UGC-JRF scholarship. He has published various research papers and book chapters with reputed publishers like Springer, Sage, Emerald, Elsevier, Inderscience etc. and presented research papers in national and International conferences both in India and abroad. He has many best paper awards on his credit too. He is reviewer of various international journals like Computers in Human Behavior, Policing etc. His areas of interest are Organizational Behavior, HRM, Recruitment and Selection, Organizational Citizenship Behavior, Quality of work life and role.

Index

A

Adaptive Leadership 103, 137, 151, 193, 408, 410, 437, 450, 467
Affective Computing 336, 340, 341, 360, 364, 367, 373, 382, 383
Affective Empathy 367, 377, 378, 379
Agentic AI 1, 31, 33, 34, 35, 39, 40, 41, 42, 43, 44, 45, 46, 47, 48, 49, 50, 51, 52, 53, 54, 55, 56, 57, 58, 59, 60, 61, 62, 65, 66, 131, 132, 133, 134, 135, 136, 139, 140, 141, 142, 143, 144, 145, 146, 148, 150, 151, 152, 154, 155, 156, 158, 159, 160, 172, 173, 188, 191, 192, 194, 195, 196, 197, 201, 202, 203, 204, 205, 207, 208, 210, 212, 213, 216, 265, 266, 267, 268, 270, 271, 272, 273, 274, 275, 278, 279, 280, 281, 282, 284, 285, 286, 287, 288, 289, 333, 334, 336, 337, 338, 339, 340, 341, 342, 343, 344, 345, 347, 348, 349, 350, 351, 352, 353, 354, 355, 356, 357, 358, 367, 447, 448, 449, 453, 455, 456, 457, 460, 461, 462, 464, 465, 466, 467, 468, 469
AI-Driven Decision Support 30
AI Ethics 64, 73, 86, 88, 89, 92, 97, 98, 125, 194, 237, 319, 337, 406, 407, 408, 410
AI governance 18, 35, 56, 72, 73, 86, 89, 96, 98, 99, 117, 258, 260, 281, 315, 369
Algorithmic Management 8, 9, 23, 25, 29, 30, 142, 146, 149, 150, 156, 159
Augmented Intelligence 249, 259, 265, 267, 268, 271, 274, 275, 276, 283
Augmented Leadership 30, 37, 55, 56, 61, 62, 66, 104, 106, 111, 180, 184, 407, 408
Automation 11, 13, 19, 22, 24, 25, 32, 34, 39, 40, 41, 42, 43, 45, 50, 56, 57, 63, 64, 65, 66, 83, 84, 96, 97, 104, 106, 110, 114, 120, 121, 122, 132, 134, 136, 143, 147, 148, 151, 159, 179, 192, 196, 208, 274, 275, 278, 281, 288, 292, 295, 296, 297, 298, 300, 301, 302, 305, 306, 307, 308, 309, 310, 312, 313, 315, 320, 327, 328, 329, 335, 336, 345, 352, 364, 365, 368, 399, 400, 404, 405, 411, 453, 458

B

burnout prediction 253, 255, 258, 262, 263

C

Case study 97, 128, 130, 217, 232, 233, 234, 299, 324, 326, 327, 464, 465
Continuous Improvement 123, 310, 452
Cultural Dimensions 311, 316

D

Decision Governance 137, 143, 147, 148, 153, 154, 155
decision-making 1, 3, 6, 8, 9, 11, 13, 14, 15, 16, 23, 24, 28, 30, 32, 33, 34, 35, 37, 38, 40, 43, 48, 49, 52, 53, 54, 56, 58, 59, 60, 61, 62, 66, 73, 74, 76, 78, 85, 86, 87, 88, 89, 90, 91, 93, 99, 103, 104, 105, 107, 108, 109, 110, 111, 112, 113, 114, 115, 116, 117, 118, 120, 122, 125, 127, 128, 129, 130, 131, 132, 133, 134, 136, 138, 139, 140, 141, 142, 143, 144, 147, 151, 155, 156, 157, 164, 165, 167, 170, 172, 176, 178, 181, 184, 186, 190, 191, 193, 194, 195, 196, 201, 202, 205, 206, 207, 208, 209, 210, 211, 213, 219, 223, 225, 226, 227, 229, 230, 232, 235, 236, 241, 242, 243, 244, 246, 258, 266, 268, 269, 273, 274, 275, 276, 278, 280, 282, 283, 284, 287, 288, 296, 297, 299, 308, 310, 311, 319, 326, 328, 334, 335, 338, 342, 351, 355, 356, 367, 375, 384, 387, 399, 400, 403, 404, 406, 407, 408, 409, 411, 417, 432, 439, 448, 449, 451, 453, 455, 456, 462

Digital Leadership 4, 6, 16, 17, 23, 26, 127, 131, 132, 135, 136, 138, 140, 141, 142, 143, 145, 152, 155, 160, 193, 269, 303, 326, 447, 448, 449, 450, 451, 452, 455, 456, 459, 461, 462, 464, 465, 467, 468, 469
Digital Transformation 4, 23, 26, 132, 138, 140, 155, 156, 157, 160, 164, 192, 194, 217, 240, 281, 283, 286, 288, 290, 293, 296, 297, 299, 309, 311, 312, 334, 447, 448, 449, 450, 451, 452, 454, 455, 456, 464, 465, 466, 467, 468, 469
Digital Well-being 265, 266, 267, 268, 269, 271, 272, 273, 278, 280, 281, 283, 287, 288, 291
Diversity 2, 10, 32, 81, 93, 113, 118, 121, 123, 201, 202, 211, 215, 220, 221, 222, 223, 224, 225, 226, 229, 230, 232, 234, 237, 239, 240, 242, 245, 246, 381, 385, 399, 404, 405, 408, 438, 461

E

early warning systems 249, 256, 257
Emotion 12, 16, 27, 34, 58, 66, 71, 90, 168, 178, 198, 202, 206, 207, 209, 259, 325, 345, 346, 347, 355, 359, 360, 366, 367, 369, 374, 379, 385, 388, 390, 394, 396
Emotional Intelligence 8, 12, 20, 29, 32, 33, 35, 37, 38, 60, 61, 63, 65, 66, 72, 77, 81, 82, 83, 84, 85, 86, 90, 91, 96, 105, 107, 120, 126, 163, 167, 169, 170, 171, 172, 173, 174, 177, 183, 184, 185, 187, 190, 191, 192, 193, 194, 195, 196, 200, 203, 204, 205, 206, 207, 211, 212, 214, 217, 333, 334, 336, 337, 338, 339, 340, 341, 342, 344, 359, 360, 362, 364, 365, 366, 367, 374, 376, 390, 408, 413, 414, 415, 416, 417, 418, 419, 420, 421, 422, 423, 424, 425, 426, 427, 428, 431, 432, 433, 434, 435, 436, 437, 438, 439, 440, 441, 442, 443
Emotionally Intelligent Leadership 82, 377, 389
Emotional Quotient 420
Emotions 30, 34, 35, 36, 37, 38, 40, 66, 71, 80, 91, 123, 172, 209, 245, 295, 299, 301, 308, 338, 367, 372, 373, 374, 377, 381, 382, 383, 385, 386, 388, 389, 390, 392, 394, 395, 396, 413, 414, 415, 416, 417, 418, 419, 421, 423, 435, 439, 440
Empathetic Leadership 1, 14, 31, 32, 33, 34, 35, 36, 37, 38, 39, 41, 42, 43, 45, 46, 47, 49, 50, 52, 53, 54, 55, 56, 57, 58, 59, 61, 62, 66, 119, 120, 163, 184, 191, 193, 195, 197, 220, 234, 333, 335, 337, 339, 341, 344, 347, 353, 354, 356, 363, 367, 379
Empathy 1, 2, 3, 6, 9, 12, 14, 15, 26, 27, 30, 32, 33, 34, 35, 36, 37, 38, 39, 42, 43, 45, 47, 48, 49, 51, 52, 57, 59, 61, 62, 66, 69, 70, 71, 72, 73, 74, 79, 80, 81, 82, 83, 84, 85, 86, 87, 90, 91, 92, 93, 94, 96, 98, 99, 100, 105, 107, 108, 109, 122, 123, 164, 165, 167, 168, 169, 170, 171, 175, 176, 177, 180, 181, 188, 189, 191, 192, 193, 195, 197, 200, 201, 202, 204, 206, 207, 208, 212, 225, 227, 228, 234, 235, 236, 258, 265, 272, 277, 308, 333, 334, 335, 336, 337, 338, 339, 340, 341, 342, 343, 344, 345, 346, 347, 348, 349, 350, 351, 354, 355, 356, 357, 360, 367, 368, 369, 371, 372, 373, 374, 375, 376, 377, 378, 379, 380, 381, 382, 383, 384, 385, 386, 387, 388, 389, 390, 391, 392, 393, 394, 395, 396, 401, 408, 415, 419, 420, 422, 423, 436, 439, 441, 449, 451
Empathy Constraints in AI 30
Empathy Scaffolding 80, 333, 337, 339, 340, 348, 354, 355, 357, 367, 385, 386
Empathy scaffolds 70, 71, 73, 80, 81, 92, 94, 371, 373, 374, 382, 383, 384, 385, 386, 387, 389, 390
Employee Well-Being 14, 15, 33, 38, 40, 46, 48, 50, 53, 62, 73, 78, 79, 129, 151, 155, 253, 257, 266, 270, 288, 290, 302, 305, 312, 350, 380
Equitable Leadership 202, 219, 220, 227,

228, 234, 235, 236, 237, 238
Equity 53, 72, 89, 117, 121, 178, 201, 209, 214, 219, 220, 221, 222, 223, 224, 225, 226, 227, 229, 230, 231, 232, 233, 234, 236, 237, 238, 240, 241, 242, 243, 245, 246, 257, 350, 399, 447, 462
Ethical AI 18, 70, 85, 86, 104, 113, 123, 171, 189, 221, 240, 242, 243, 258, 299, 346, 369, 408, 462
Ethical AI Governance 258, 369
Ethical Decision-Making 37, 73, 90, 118, 176, 184, 195, 201, 206, 207, 208, 213, 342, 351, 384
Ethical Governance 51, 55, 66, 72, 74, 76, 88, 90, 92, 113, 118, 121, 173, 194, 195, 200, 202, 205, 208, 219, 235, 237, 258, 265, 268, 269, 273, 274, 276, 278, 279, 280, 286, 287, 288, 409, 451, 461, 462
Explainable AI 54, 67, 73, 74, 91, 99, 114, 119, 123, 187, 216, 259

F

fairness 17, 18, 26, 37, 38, 45, 52, 53, 54, 55, 56, 66, 67, 72, 74, 75, 76, 77, 79, 88, 92, 93, 94, 96, 107, 113, 114, 116, 121, 123, 146, 156, 164, 166, 167, 169, 171, 173, 174, 175, 177, 178, 179, 180, 183, 185, 189, 191, 192, 194, 200, 201, 202, 209, 214, 220, 221, 226, 227, 228, 232, 237, 239, 242, 257, 258, 276, 277, 279, 280, 286, 290, 292, 304, 315, 337, 350, 355, 360, 369, 374, 381, 388, 399, 400, 402, 403, 404, 406, 407, 408, 409, 411
Framework 5, 17, 19, 20, 21, 23, 26, 32, 35, 37, 46, 47, 48, 49, 50, 62, 64, 66, 67, 70, 71, 73, 77, 83, 84, 89, 94, 96, 98, 100, 111, 112, 125, 126, 128, 129, 131, 132, 137, 138, 139, 140, 141, 142, 143, 144, 145, 146, 147, 152, 153, 154, 155, 157, 158, 159, 160, 169, 171, 172, 173, 179, 185, 188, 189, 191, 195, 204, 205, 206, 207, 208, 209, 212, 214, 216, 218, 221, 222, 224, 233, 234, 240, 245, 265, 269, 270, 271, 272, 273, 278, 282, 283, 286, 287, 288, 291, 292, 296, 305, 307, 315, 317, 319, 324, 338, 340, 361, 367, 368, 385, 392, 400, 410, 419, 442, 451, 453, 466, 469

G

governance 14, 18, 28, 32, 34, 35, 42, 44, 45, 48, 51, 53, 54, 55, 56, 57, 58, 60, 61, 62, 66, 67, 70, 72, 73, 74, 75, 76, 82, 86, 87, 88, 89, 90, 92, 93, 94, 96, 97, 98, 99, 103, 104, 105, 106, 110, 112, 113, 114, 117, 118, 119, 120, 121, 122, 123, 133, 134, 136, 137, 138, 139, 140, 142, 143, 145, 146, 147, 148, 149, 150, 151, 152, 153, 154, 155, 156, 172, 173, 174, 179, 181, 184, 185, 186, 188, 189, 194, 195, 200, 201, 202, 203, 204, 205, 208, 209, 210, 211, 212, 219, 230, 234, 235, 236, 237, 239, 243, 249, 258, 260, 265, 266, 267, 268, 269, 270, 271, 273, 274, 275, 276, 278, 279, 280, 281, 286, 287, 288, 315, 317, 347, 353, 354, 357, 369, 376, 400, 403, 405, 406, 407, 408, 409, 448, 449, 451, 455, 456, 461, 462, 466

H

Higher Education 21, 128, 241, 395, 434, 447, 448, 449, 452, 453, 454, 457, 458, 459, 460, 461, 462, 464, 465, 466, 467, 468, 469
Human–AI Collaboration 8, 11, 27, 31, 35, 42, 43, 44, 45, 54, 67, 127, 129, 194, 197, 204, 206, 207, 208, 212, 368, 455, 462
Human–AI Interaction Competence 30
Human–AI partnership 213
Human-Centered AI 61, 170, 176, 260, 327
Human–Machine Collaboration 6, 13, 14, 28, 328, 360
Hybrid Workplaces 81, 198

I

Inclusion 10, 72, 73, 81, 123, 186, 202, 209, 219, 220, 221, 222, 223, 225, 226, 227, 229, 230, 233, 236, 237, 239, 241, 242, 243, 245, 246, 258, 335, 343, 346, 350, 381, 385, 387, 402, 404, 405, 407, 408
Inclusive Leadership 22, 34, 59, 201, 202, 205, 213, 220, 225, 226, 227, 228, 229, 230, 231, 232, 233, 234, 237, 242, 244, 246, 350
Individual Unlearning 268, 272, 273, 284, 285, 287, 288
interpretability 75, 76, 97, 118, 133, 134, 255, 400, 402, 409

J

Job Autonomy 310, 311, 325

L

Leadership 1, 2, 3, 4, 5, 6, 7, 8, 9, 10, 11, 12, 13, 14, 15, 16, 17, 18, 20, 21, 22, 23, 24, 26, 27, 28, 29, 30, 31, 32, 33, 34, 35, 36, 37, 38, 39, 40, 41, 42, 43, 44, 45, 46, 47, 48, 49, 50, 51, 52, 53, 54, 55, 56, 57, 58, 59, 60, 61, 62, 63, 64, 65, 66, 67, 69, 70, 71, 72, 73, 74, 75, 76, 77, 79, 80, 81, 82, 83, 84, 85, 86, 87, 88, 89, 90, 91, 92, 93, 94, 95, 96, 97, 98, 99, 100, 103, 104, 105, 106, 107, 108, 110, 111, 112, 113, 115, 116, 118, 119, 120, 121, 122, 123, 124, 125, 126, 127, 130, 131, 132, 133, 134, 135, 136, 137, 138, 139, 140, 141, 142, 143, 144, 145, 146, 147, 148, 149, 150, 151, 152, 153, 154, 155, 156, 157, 159, 160, 163, 164, 165, 166, 167, 168, 169, 170, 171, 172, 173, 174, 175, 176, 177, 178, 179, 180, 181, 182, 183, 184, 185, 186, 187, 188, 190, 191, 192, 193, 194, 195, 196, 197, 198, 199, 200, 201, 202, 203, 204, 205, 206, 207, 208, 209, 210, 211, 212, 213, 214, 215, 216, 217, 218, 219, 220, 221, 222, 224, 225, 226, 227, 228, 229, 230, 231, 232, 233, 234, 235, 236, 237, 238, 239, 240, 241, 242, 243, 244, 245, 246, 251, 266, 267, 269, 270, 272, 274, 276, 277, 278, 279, 281, 282, 284, 285, 286, 287, 288, 295, 303, 311, 316, 317, 319, 322, 323, 326, 327, 328, 333, 334, 335, 336, 337, 338, 339, 340, 341, 342, 343, 344, 345, 346, 347, 348, 349, 350, 351, 352, 353, 354, 355, 356, 357, 358, 359, 360, 361, 362, 363, 365, 366, 367, 368, 369, 371, 372, 373, 374, 375, 376, 377, 378, 379, 380, 381, 382, 383, 384, 385, 386, 387, 389, 390, 391, 399, 400, 401, 403, 404, 405, 406, 407, 408, 409, 410, 411, 413, 414, 415, 416, 417, 418, 419, 420, 421, 422, 423, 424, 425, 426, 427, 428, 431, 432, 433, 434, 435, 436, 437, 438, 439, 440, 441, 442, 443, 447, 448, 449, 450, 451, 452, 455, 456, 458, 459, 460, 461, 462, 463, 464, 465, 466, 467, 468, 469
Leadership Competency Framework 131, 132, 137, 138, 143, 144, 469
Leadership Development 3, 6, 14, 59, 60, 63, 70, 71, 73, 74, 80, 81, 91, 92, 94, 122, 137, 154, 155, 157, 186, 192, 193, 194, 195, 197, 198, 199, 200, 201, 202, 203, 204, 205, 206, 207, 208, 209, 210, 211, 212, 213, 217, 234, 237, 333, 335, 337, 339, 340, 344, 348, 349, 351, 352, 354, 355, 357, 360, 368, 369, 371, 372, 374, 381, 382, 384, 389, 390, 411, 413, 414, 415, 421, 424, 426, 434, 438, 440, 443, 462, 464, 469
leadership development ecosystems 203, 204, 208
Leadership Styles 6, 9, 17, 121, 205, 211, 245, 423, 437, 442, 467

M

machine learning 7, 17, 18, 20, 25, 26, 39, 63, 78, 104, 105, 106, 109, 116, 143, 146, 156, 188, 249, 252, 253, 255, 257, 259, 281, 296, 298, 302, 311, 321, 324, 328, 329, 341, 388, 410, 456

O

Organizational Citizenship Behaviour 239, 411
Organizational Culture 5, 9, 23, 27, 40, 46, 53, 60, 62, 72, 81, 82, 92, 93, 165, 182, 183, 188, 198, 211, 220, 222, 225
Organizational Ethics 184, 356
Organizational Outcomes 207, 219
Organizational readiness 58, 73, 74, 82, 99, 100

P

proactive intervention 258
Psychological safety 2, 8, 10, 16, 22, 25, 30, 49, 53, 54, 69, 70, 71, 72, 73, 74, 75, 77, 78, 79, 81, 83, 90, 92, 93, 100, 163, 167, 172, 176, 177, 178, 184, 185, 192, 195, 197, 202, 203, 204, 208, 209, 210, 212, 213, 223, 225, 226, 227, 229, 236, 242, 245, 246, 272, 281, 285, 287, 290, 335, 337, 338, 339, 343, 345, 346, 347, 349, 350, 354, 355, 357, 361, 366, 367, 371, 375, 381, 387, 389, 390

Q

Quotient 420

R

Reflective Leadership Development 198

S

Scaffolds 70, 71, 73, 80, 81, 92, 94, 371, 373, 374, 382, 383, 384, 385, 386, 387, 389, 390
Strategic Leadership 131, 135, 136, 138, 139, 142, 143, 145, 151, 155, 243, 452
Sustainable Empathy 382

T

Team Collaboration 23

U

unconscious bias 121, 202, 221, 224, 229, 232, 234, 239, 285, 401
University 1, 26, 29, 64, 103, 131, 163, 191, 219, 249, 265, 291, 295, 324, 333, 359, 362, 363, 364, 365, 371, 393, 394, 396, 397, 399, 413, 427, 437, 458, 459, 465, 467, 468, 469

V

Visibility Bias 1, 10, 30

W

wearable technology 253, 259
Workforce Resilience 265, 275, 282, 286, 287, 288, 292
workplace well-being 21, 23, 96, 251, 258, 263

www.ingramcontent.com/pod-product-compliance
Lightning Source LLC
LaVergne TN
LVHW061532290926
849162LV00004B/770